INDIAN AFFAIRS ANNUAL 2008

INDIAN AFFAIRS ANNUAL 2008
(In 9 Vols.)

Vol. 7

Chronology of Events
(30-11-2007 to 16-01-2008)

Shailendra Sengar

KALPAZ PUBLICATIONS

KALPAZ PUBLICATIONS
DELHI - 110052

Indian Affairs Annual 2008

Rs. 6300 (Set)

ISBN: 81-7835-693-7 (Set)
ISBN: 81-7835-700-3 (Vol. 7)

Published in 2008 in India by
Kalpaz Publications
C-30, Satyawati Nagar,
Delhi-110052
E-mail: kalpaz@hotmail.com
Phone : 9212729499

Laser Type Setting by: Quick Media, Delhi
Printed at : Singhal Print Media, Delhi

INDIAN AFFAIRS ANNUAL 2008

Chronology of Events

(30-11-2007 to 16-01-2008)

4770. (30-11-2007) NEW DELHI : The Union Minister of Shipping, Road Transport and Highways, Thiru T.R. Baalu has approved a sum of Rs. 688.02 lakh for road improvement projects in the state of Tamil Nadu. The approval has been made for the following works on National Highways of the State: o An amount of Rs. 361.91 lakh has been approved for Improvement of Riding Quality Programme (IRQP) from km 136/00 to 146/00 on NH-210 between Sanavalli and Mangalam in Ramnad district. This road is an important National Highway which connects Trichy and Ramanathapuram and runs through many important towns like Pudukkottai, Karaikudi, Devakottair and Devipattinam, Ramnad and Remeswaram an important pilgrim centre in Tamil Nadu. The road is badly damaged due to increasing traffic volume and seasonal rainfall. Hence, it is absolutely necessary to urgently repair this the stretch. o An amount of Rs. 322.76 lakh has been approved under Improvement of Riding Quality Programme (IRQP) between km 217 to km km 226/0 on NH-208 between T.Kunnathur and Pudupatti in Madurai district .The road is an important National Highway of interstate connectivity and connects two important tourism centres Coutrallam and Madurai. It starts from Kollam (Kerala State) and passes through Shengottah, Tenkasi, Sivagiri, Rajapalayam and terminates at Thirumangalam. Due to incessant rainfall, the riding surface of the stretches are badly damaged and causing much inconvenience to the fast moving vehicles. Hence, it is necessary to improve the riding quality of the road to allow free flow of traffic. An amount of Rs 3.35 lakh has been approved for feasibility study and preparation of the Detailed Project Report (DPR) for construction of bypass to Chockampatty town from km 119/2 to 121/2of NH 208 (Kollam-Theni Road) in Tirunelveli district.

4771. (30-11-2007) NEW DELHI : The performance of various schemes/ programmes for promoting and developing khadi and village industries (KVI) sector, being implemented by Khadi and Village Industries Commission (KVIC) throughout the country, including Bihar, is regularly monitored and reviewed by the Government from time to time. A State-level review of the KVI programme was conducted by KVIC on 10th and 11th April, 2007 at Patna, where various programme implementing agencies were called. 5 Bankers review meetings were conducted in Bihar during 2006-07 to take stock of the progress in the implementation of Rural Employment Generation Programme (REGP). This was stated by the Minister for Micro, Small & Medium Enterprises, Shri Mahabir Prasad in a written reply to a question in Rajya Sabha today.

4772. (30-11-2007) NEW DELHI : India has been unanimously elected the Chairman of the Executive Council of the General Assembly of United Nations World Tourism Organisation (UNWTO). In its 82nd meeting held on November 29, 2007, at Cartegena de Indias, Colombia, the Executive Council elected India as its Chairman for a period of one year. The Minister of Tourism and Culture Smt. Ambika Soni attended the meeting. The Council meets twice a year and is empowered to take all measures necessary in consultation with the Secretary General for the implementation of the decisions and the recommendations of the Assembly and to report to the Assembly. In addition, the Executive Council meets between sessions of the UN General Assembly and, in the absence of any contrary provisions in the statutes the Council, takes such administrative and technical decisions as may be necessary, within the functions and financial resources of the organization, and reports decisions which have been taken to the Assembly at its following session, for approval. The General Assembly of the UNWTO consists of more than 150 countries. The membership of the Executive Council is by process of election according to which 30 member are elected on a regional rotational basis for a period of four years.

4773. (30-11-2007) NEW DELHI : The Union Cabinet today gave its approval for placing the National Urban Housing and Habitat Policy, 2005 on the table of the House & general circulation to State Governments/ UTs and other stakeholders for implementation. The policy put into effect by various stakeholders, will promote sustained development of urban housing and settlements, with a focus on social housing for EWS/LIG.

4774. (30-11-2007) NEW DELHI : The Union Cabinet today gave its approval for tariff elimination / reduction on 555 products through a protocol of amendment of India-Singapore Comprehensive Economic Cooperation Agreement and also for offering to Singapore any subsequent improvement made at the time of ASEAN-India Free Trade Agreement (AIFTA) in terms of product coverage timeline, Rules of Origin (RoO) with appropriate amendments to India-Singapore CECA The tariff concessions would further enhance growth in bilateral trade with economic benefits to both countries. As Singapore is a member country of ASEAN, betterment made in the ASEAN-India FTA over CECA may be incorporated in CECA to maximize gains to both countries. The tariff elimination / reduction will commence from 1st December, 2007.

4775. (30-11-2007) NEW DELHI : The Union Cabinet today gave its approval for sale of 49% equity stake of Bharat Petroleum Corporation Limited (BPCL) in BSL to Shell or its affiliate for a consideration of Rs. 152.40 crores in cash. The proposed sale will enable BPCL to withdraw from a joint venture company which has a competing business interest *i.e.* production and sale of branded lubricants in India. This would enable BPCL to concentrate on building and promotion of its own brand of lubricants resulting in improved brand image, higher growth, efficiency and profits.

4776. (30-11-2007) NEW DELHI : The Union Cabinet today gave its approval for enhancing the capital of State Bank of India by subscribing to the Rights Issue of Equity shares of the State of India amounting to around Rs. 10, 000 crore (Rupees Ten Thousand Crore) against issue of SLR, Marketable Government Securities and create a Securities Redemption Fund for redeeming these Securities on the due date. The actual number of shares to be subscribed, the total amount subscribed, coupon rate and tenure of the securities, and other modalities will be worked out by the Government in consultation with the Bank, keeping in view the extant SEBI guidelines, market conditions and other relevant factors. It will enable the Government to receive likely around Rs. 1358 crore by way of dividend and taxes from the Bank during the years 2008-09, as against an expenditure of around Rs. 790 crore as interest to be paid to the Bank for proposed securities. However, in subsequent years, the Government is likely to receive higher amount of additional revenues (Rs. 1552 crore in the year 2009-10 and Rs. 1892 crore in the year 2010-11 and thereafter). The additional growth of the bank due to its increased capital base will also have multiplier effect on the overall performance of the bank, which will gain in terms of its position in the industry, ratings-both in international as well as domestic markets, and increased valuation of its stock, besides boost to the economy at large. The transaction will be completed within the current financial year and a Securities Redemption Fund will be created thereafter.

4777. (30-11-2007) NEW DELHI : The Union Cabinet today gave its approval for moving official amendments in the 'Maintenance and Welfare of Parents and Senior Citizens Bill, 2007' in Lok Sabha. The Bill will provide effective care and protection to the senior citizens and provide speedy and inexpensive legal framework to grant maintenance to them.

4778. (30-11-2007) NEW DELHI : The Union Cabinet today gave its approval for signing of Extradition Treaty between India and Egypt and for ratification thereof. The Treaty would provide a legal framework for seeking extradition of terrorists, economic offenders, and other criminals from and to the Arab Republic of Egypt.

4779. (30-11-2007) NEW DELHI : The Union Cabinet today gave its ex-post-facto approval to the Agreement signed on 17th September, 2007 between India and Serbia on exemption from visa requirement for the holders of Diplomatic and official passports for its implementation. The decision will promote the bilateral relations and visa-free entry, transit and stay for up to ninety days for Indian diplomatic and official passport holders in the territory of Serbia.

4780. (1-12-2007) NEW DELHI : A day-long workshop on National Road Safety Policy and National Road Transport Policy was organized here today to arrive at a broad consensus before these two policies are considered for adoption at the central level. The workshop was inaugurated by the Secretary Road Transport and Highways, Shri Brahm Datt. Secretaries/Commissioners in charge of the Transport, Managing Directors of State Transport Undertakings, senior police officers and other stake holders from various states and union territories, participated in the Workshop. Speaking on the occasion Shri Brahm Dutt said that a broad consensus on the two documents was necessary as the ultimate objectives envisaged in these two policies could only be achieved with the active support of all the states and other stake holders.

4781. (1-12-2007) NEW DELHI : We are pained at the choice of expression and vocabulary of Smt. Sonia Gandhi. In hurling political abuses she seems bent on outdoing her General Secretary B K Hariprasad. If it was an extempore speech, we would have given Smt. Sonia Gandhi benefit of doubt for poor understanding of Indian languages. However her expression were read out from written text and therefore the abuses were pre-planned. It hardly lies in the mouth of Congress President who gifted to this country Ottovio Quattrochi to refer to one of the country's most honest politician as "BAIMAAN". The terrorist in the past 5 years have succeeded elsewhere in the country but failed in Gujarat. The protector of the Gujarat people should be thanked across the country. The "MAUT KE SAUDAGAAR" are those who seek to protect "AFZAL GURU" from hanging and protecting the accused of the Godhara train fire incident through self serving committees comprising of former judges. It is the terrorist who are the "MERCHANTS OF DEATH" It is the UPA which is soft on terror. Let it not be forgotten that all terrorist attacks during UPA remain unresolved. Those who attacked Akshardham and Indian Parliament were either liquidated or convicted.

4782. (1-12-2007) NEW DELHI : British film maker and director, Michael Jaffer whose film 'Full Circle' is being screened at IFFI-2007 believes that Indian films have great entertainment value since they take the viewers into an altogether different world which provides a possibility to escape the real harsh world in which we all live. While speaking to media persons here today, Jaffer stated, 'I have grown up watching Indian films and I am inspired by the manner in which they entertain people.' He described his film "Full Circle" as a purely fictional effort to provide pure escapism and entertainment to the viewers. Commenting, on the influence of Hollywood movies on British cinema, Jaffer conceded that it was difficult to compete with the mighty Hollywood machine, but expressed the hope that the unique identity and culture symbolized by British cinema would be retained. Asked about his views on the future of Art Cinema, Jaffer opined that it was a cinema with greater depth and should therefore continue to exist, though he forecasted that such cinema would eventually be able to find more and more viewers through TV and DVD/VCD formats rather than through widespread theatre screenings. The director informed media persons of his keen desire to look for co-production opportunities all around the world including India and expressed openness to consider making a film in Hindi as well. 'Full Circle' is Michael Jaffer's first mainstream English film.

4783. (1-12-2007) NEW DELHI : A day-long workshop on National Road Safety Policy and National Road Transport Policy began here today at Vigyan Bhawan. The workshop was inaugurated by the Secretary Road Transport and Highways, Shri Brahm Datt. Keynote address on the occasion was delivered by Shri S Sundar a distinguished fellow of the Tata Energy Research Institute, (TERI) and Chairman of the Committee on Road Safety and Traffic Management Board. This Committee has recently submitted its report to the government. Shri Sundar pointed out that Road Safety scenario is increasingly becoming a major area of concern for the policy makers and stressed that various policy, structural and societal changes are needed to make the roads safe in the country. He was of the opinion that in order to improve the current worrisome scenario, road safety must be treated as a public health issue and dealt with accordingly. Shri Sundar stressed that we should evolve a structural preventive programme to deal with the alarming number of road accidents, just as we have a mechanism and organizational structure in place, to control the diseases like Malaria, AIDS and TB. Secretaries/Commissioners in charge of the Transport and Managinf Directors of State Transport Undertakings from various states and union territories, are participating in the day long Workshop.

4784. (1-12-2007) NEW DELHI: The government on Friday said it was in touch with Malaysia on the alleged harassment of people of Indian origin in that country and the observations by a Malaysian Minister against Tamil Nadu Chief Minister M. Karunanidhi. Making a *suo motu* statement in both Houses of Parliament, External Affairs Minister Pranab Mukherjee said India was in touch with the Malaysian authorities on the alleged harassment of the participants of a rally, organised by the Hindu Rights Action Force in Kuala Lumpur on November 25, and related matters. On the sidelines of the India-European Union Summit, Prime Minister Manmohan Singh too voiced concern over the issue. "This is a matter which concerns us. Whenever people of India run into difficulties, it is a source of concern," he told reporters when asked to comment on the matter. However, he refused to say anything more. In Parliament, Mr. Mukherjee said: "The government remains deeply solicitous for the welfare of people of Indian origin living abroad. There is a large community of people of Indian origin in Malaysia, who are citizens of that country. We have friendly relations with Malaysia and we are in touch with the authorities there on the related matter."

4785. (1-12-2007) NEW DELHI : The Bharatiya Janata Party (BJP) would commence the campaign on 2nd and 5th December for the second round of polls in the states of Gujarat and Himachal Pradesh respectively, with over 250 meetings, rallies and programmes. BJP National Vice President and In-Charge of its Central Election Management and Coordination Committee, Shri Mukhtar Abbas Naqvi, said that for the second-round fight for the 95 seats in Gujarat and 65 seats in Himachal, the Party would reach out to all corners of these states with its message of "nationalism". Shri Naqvi said that while the campaigning for the second-round of polls is planned with over 200 events, the campaign for the first-round of polls, that started on 27 November, is featuring about 135 meetings. He said that while on 2nd December, the Party's senior leader Shri Lal Krishna Advani would start the campaign from Pattan and Mehsana, Party President Shri Rajnath Singh would launch his electoral missles from the source of the Narmada at Sabarkantha and Sarkhej in Ahmedabad. The Party's former President Shri Venkiah Naidu would visit Kheda and Vadodara, and Shrimati Sushma Swaraj would provide the edge to the campaign in Godhra, Nadiad and Ahmedabad. Chief Minister Narendra Modi would address rallies in the south Gujarat locations of Ahwa, Dharampur, Surat, and Ankleshwar. Alongside the Party's senior leaders Dr. Murli Manohar Joshi, Arun Jaitley, Anant Kumar, Vinay Katiyar, Madhya Pradesh Chief Minister Shivraj Chauhan, Rajasthan Chief Minister Vasundhara Raje Scindhia, Bihar Deputy Chief Minister Shri Sushil Modi, Gopinath Munde, former Karnataka Chief Minister Yeddyurappa, former Jharkhand Chief Minister Arjun Munda, S S Ahluwalia, Kalraj Mishra, Navjot Singh Sidhu, Hema Malini, Shatrughan Sinha, over 40 national leaders and 30 local leaders would herald the campaign in each corner of Gujarat. Shri Naqvi further said that on similar lines, on 5th December, the Party is starting its campaign for the second-round polls of 65 seats with the slogan of "Bhrastachar Mukt-Vikas Yukt" Himachal. In Himachal, while Party senior leader Shri Lal Krishna Advani would kick-off the campaign from Kullu, Party President Shri Rajnath Singh would launch an aggressive campaign from Solan. Party senior leader Dr. Murli Manohar Joshi would hold meetings in Paonta Sahib in Sirmaur district. Former Party President Shri Venkiah Naidu would be in Hamirpur, and star campaigner Shrimati Sushma Swaraj would expose the corruption and misgovernance of the Congress government in Nurpur. Senior leaders Shri Shanta Kumar and Prem Kumar Dhumal would also address various meetings. In both Gujarat and Himachal, senior leaders would hold round-the-clock meetings to keep up the aggression and pace of the campaign. For instance, Party senior leader Shri Lal Krishna Advani would be spending 6 days in Guajrat and 4 days in Himachal. Party President Rajnath Singh would devote 7 days in Gujarat and 5 days in Himachal. Dr. Joshi would spend 4 days in Gujarat and 3 days in Himachal. Venkiah Naidu would be 4 days in Gujarat and 3 days in Himachal.

4786. (1-12-2007) NEW DELHI : Following is the text of the Prime Minister, Dr. Manmohan Singh's statement on India-Portugal Bilateral Summit here today: "Prime Minister Jose Socrates and I have just concluded very fruitful talks today. Our bilateral Summit meeting carried forward the momentum generated by the successful visit of the President of Portugal to India in January 2007. It was during Portugal's Presidency of the EU in 2000 that the Portuguese leadership proposed a Summit level meeting between India and the EU. The eighth India-EU Summit held yesterday, under the Portuguese Presidency, thus has an added significance for India-Portugal bilateral relations. We agreed that we should rekindle our historical links and build a strong, contemporary relationship that reflects the vast goodwill that our people have for each other and the immense potential for bilateral collaboration. We shared the view that the present level of bilateral trade at US$397 million is far below our potential. We agreed to make full use of the opportunities that are emerging from the rapid growth of India and the expansion of the European Union to actively enhance trade and investment, including by encouraging greater business-to-business interaction. Indian and Portuguese majors in the IT and pharmaceuticals sectors have recently entered each other's markets. We agreed to encourage more such investments. We also discussed avenues for trilateral cooperation especially with the Community of Portuguese Speaking Countries. We are already cooperating in the field of hydrocarbons in Angola. Science and technology is yet another promising area in which we can pool our resources. There has been exchange of scientists and we would like to build upon this. We have identified high technology areas such as information technology, biotechnology, bio-informatics and nano-technology as focus areas for joint collaboration. For this we will re-energize the existing inter-governmental mechanisms. Parliamentary exchanges between the two countries are an intrinsic element of our mutual desire to broad-base our relations. Our respective Parliaments have constituted Friendship Groups, and we both agreed that this initiative deserved our full support. We have also agreed to promote greater bilateral exchanges in the fields of sport, culture and tourism. We welcomed the signing of the Memorandum of Understanding between the All India Football Federation and the Portuguese Professional Football League. I am sure all football lovers in India will welcome this. There is also immense scope for working together in the area of restoration and conservation of our cultural heritage. Portugal has the third largest Indian origin community in Europe. I conveyed to Prime Minister Socrates our admiration for Portugal's tolerant and open society. The richness of Portuguese culture in Goa, Daman and Diu is well known to every Indian, and we celebrate this legacy. We also exchanged views on regional and international issues. We are grateful to Portugal for its most friendly understanding and support to India's candidature for permanent membership of an expanded UN Security Council. Based on our talks today I can say that we have a warm, trusted and reliable friend in Portugal, and specifically in Prime Minister Socrates. India looks forward to taking this important relationship forward in all areas."

4787. (2-12-2007) NEW DELHI : IFFI - 2007 has been a smooth affair but for minor irritants. This was the general view at the media interaction held by Chief secretary of Goa, Shri J. P. Singh and Director, DFF, Smt. Neelam Kapur held today with a view to apprise the media of their assessment and also to elicit media response on various issues related to the Festival. Shri J. P. Singh said that the whole effort has been to improve film culture in the State so that Goa attains recognition at the international level. He said, the joint effort of DFF and the Government of Goa greatly improved the content as well as infrastructure for IFFI - 2007. He said, Film Bazaar this year has been a tremendous success and hoped that National Film Development Corporation (NFDC) would further strengthen the role of Film Bazaar in future. The software used in the Festival this year has been a great leap forward and is likely to result in smoother operations in the coming years. The newly introduced system of ticketing was a great success and vastly facilitated the operations, he added. Smt. Neelam Kapur in her remarks, said that plans are already under discussion to bring about improvements during the next year. Steps for facilitation of delegate and media registration are being examined and would be put in place in due course. We need to work on improving the international participation in the Festival, she said. To the suggestion of raising prize money to invite larger international participation, Smt. Kapur said, it was among the measures being contemplated in this regard. She clarified that mainstream cinema was taken off from this year's Festival by the Film Federation of India and its affiliated bodies due to certain reservations/constraints on their part. Smt. Kapur felt that greater publicity is needed to ensure more entries in the Indian Panorama section so that the number of entries is larger and diversity of Indian cinema can be truly reflected. The publication of Festival daily news letter in Hindi will be looked into, the Director said. As suggested by the Union Minister of Information & Broadcasting and Parliamentary Affairs, Shri P. R. Dasmunsi a special screening of Hindi film 'Goal' will be done for the football lovers besides delegates at the Festival, tomorrow.

4788. (2-12-2007) NEW DELHI : The Defence Research Development Organisation (DRDO) carried out the first launch of a single stage interceptor missile against an electronic ballistic missile as target from Wheeler Island. The Endo-atmospheric interceptor intercepted the missile at 15 kilometres altitude exactly as designed for high supersonic speed. All the elements of ballistic missile defence (BMD) required for control and monitoring performed in a copybook fashion validating the design of the "Endo-atmospheric" layer of BMD system. High-tech instrumentation provided precise and accurate data regarding the performance of the interceptor missile. This has given confidence to the scientists to proceed with the next test that shall see adversary ballistic missile being intercepted by Endo-atmospheric" interceptor missile. The next test is expected to take place shortly.

4789. (2-12-2007) NEW DELHI : Noted film maker Budhadeb Dasgupta will be the Chief Guest at the closing ceremony of IFFI-2007. Film personality Kabir Bedi would compere the Event to be held at Kala Academy tomorrow. This was stated by Director, DFF, Smt. Neelam Kapur at the media interaction today. She informed the media that a total of 176 films from 46 countries were screened during the 11-day Festival. Of these, 14 were in Competition Section, 64 in Cinema of the World, 39 under the Retrospective/Homage Category and 59 were in various categories of the Indian cinema. The screening of Portugal-Spain movie 'Fados' directed by the Spanish legend Carlos Saura would bring curtains down on the 38th edition of IFFI. The closing ceremony will be attended by the Chief Minister of Goa, Shri Digambar Kamat and film personalities from India and abroad.

4790. (2-12-2007) NEW DELHI : The cement industry should explore alternate/ non-conventional sources of energy. With the ever-growing thrust on conservation of fossil fuel resources, Shri N.N. Prasad, Joint Secretary, Department of Industrial Policy & Promotion (DIPP), has emphasised that there is a need for integrating the alternate and renewable energy into the system. "I understand that the cement industry has already made a beginning in this direction. Some of the cement plants have tried waste derived fuels in the recent past. Government on its part, is giving special emphasis to generation of grid quality power from non-conventional and renewable energy sources, like hydropower, wind power, solar energy etc.", he further stated while delivering the valedictory address at the International Seminar on Cement & Building Materials, here on Friday (30th November) evening. The 4-day (27-30 November, 2007) Seminar was organised by the National Council for Cement and Building Materials (NCB). While presenting the National Awards for Energy Efficiency, Environmental Excellence and Quality Excellence in Indian Cement Industry for the years 2005-06 and 2006-07, Shri Prasad congratulated all the award winners and underlined the role of NCB in motivating the cement industry for competitive improvement. He further said, these success stories of such plants will generate larger interest amongst the industry and more and more number of plants would join the bandwagon of energy savers. Giving an overview of the Seminar, Shri M. Vasudeva, Director General of NCB said that the quality of cement and building materials produced in India meets international standards and benchmarks and can compete in international markets. He said the Seminar provided a comprehensive update on cement and construction technologies including related plant and machinery. More than 100 technical papers were presented under seventeen technical sessions including five special lectures during the past four days. In the special publication brought out on the occasion of the seminar, experts have drawn attention to various issues to achieve higher energy efficiency, environmental standards & productivity in cement manufacture, efficient transport of cement, design of energy efficient and disaster resistant buildings/structures and quality construction through advanced technologies as well as human resource development in the rapidly changing scenario. Utilisation of low-grade raw materials, optimization of mining operations using computer modelling are some of the areas discussed in the seminar. New techniques and strategies for conservation of natural resources have been highlighted in the discussions.

4791. (3-12-2007) PANJI : Curtains came down on the 38th International Film Festival of India today with the screening of Portugal-Spain film 'Fados', directed by Carlos Saura. Director Mr. Lin Chih Ju bagged the best film award with the Golden Peacock and a cash award of 10 lakhs for the Taiwanese film 'The Wall'. The film won the top award for a finely crafted film about dreams, hope, betrayal and love that depicts ordinary people coping in politically challenging times. The film is highly cinematic, affecting and makes the political personal. The filmmaker has created a complete world within the four wall of a simple house. The most promising director award went to Ms. Pongpat Wachirabunjong for her debut Thai film 'Khaw Hai Rak Johg Jaroen' (Me Myself) with the Silver Peacock and a cash award of Rs. 5 lakhs. The film about whether we have the freedom to choose our own life. It depicts a story of hope for a world without discrimination while recognizing the difficulties of coping with being different. The Special Jury Award has been shared by Mr. Golam Rabanny Biplab for story writing of the Bangladeshi film 'Swopnodanay' (on the wings of dreams) and the child artist (Miss) Julia Urbini for her performance in the Mexican film 'Mas Que A Nada En El Mundo' (more than anything in the world). Each winner was presented a Silver Peacock medal, a cash prize of Rs. 2,50,000 and a certificate. 'Swopnodanay' is 'a simple story of a poor man who has the chance to dream of another life but discovers the things he already has are more important than the dream. This classic story has been told simply without western influence and resonates a truth about life for millions of people around the world'. 'Mas Que A Nada En El Mundo' 'depicts the story of a child craving for her mother's love. The performance of the child actor is central to the film's success. Playing the child character, Julia Urbini gives an enchanting, nuanced performance that helps make this film special. The five-member jury was headed by the eminent film maker from Hungary Ms. Marta Mazaros, who has directed more than 60 films and has won awards in several Intl Film Festivals. Other members of the Jury are, Ms. Meltem Cumbul a leading actress from Turkey; Mr. Shaji N Karun, Cinematographer, Film Director and Script writer from Kerala; a noted Argentinian film director Mr. Pablo Cesar and Mr. Robert Sarkies, a young film maker from New Zealand. Chief Guest at the closing ceremony noted Bengali film maker Budhadeb Dasgupta said that this year's Festival had many innovations and good quality films were screened. Success of a film festival depends on films it offers and from this perspective IFFI - 2007 has been a success, he said. Shri Dasgupta felt that more film makers and directors from the international cinema should be invited at the Festival as that would raise the level of the Festival and provide much to learn for the new Indian film makers. Chief Minister of Goa, Shri Digambar Kamat in his remarks said that overall perception is that this edition of the Festival has been a success but Goa would continue to strive for further improving the Film Festival in the coming years.

4792. (3-12-2007) NEW DELHI : The President Smt. Pratibha Devisingh Patil gave away awards to 42 persons and institutions for their significant contribution towards the empowerment of persons with disabilities on the occasion of the International Day of Disabled Persons here today. The event was organized by the Ministry of Social Justice and Empowerment. The Union Minister for Social Justice and Empowerment, Smt. Meira Kumar, the MOS in the Ministry, Smt. Subbulakshmi Jagdeesan and Dr. Shakeel Ahmad, Minister of State for Communication and Information Technology were also present on the occasion. Speaking on the occasion the President said that persons with disabilities (PWDs) have a right to lead a life of dignity and self-respect.. This would be possible only if they get adequate opportunities to pursue their education and thereafter, get gainful employment and status in society. She said that there is a need to ensure that children with special needs get access to education at par with others. To ensure this, the President said that they should be provided with the right kind of teaching and learning environment, material in accessible format and barrier-free schools. Referring to the PWD Act, the President said that it provides for reservations in Government employment. She said that there is still a backlog in filling up of reserved position. As a major commitment, these must be got filled up in a time bound manner, the President emphasized. She said that the requirement of the day is that persons with disabilities are given vocational training so that they become employable in the private sector. She hoped that the private sector would take pro-active steps to provide opportunities to differently abled persons. This will also be an opportunity for employers to meet their social responsibility obligations, she said. Smt. Patil further said that we should lay special emphasis on the empowerment of women, children and the elderly with disabilities, to bring them into the mainstream of society and improve their quality of life. For many children, the presence of an impairment leads to lack of participation in activities that are part of a normal childhood. She said that women with disabilities are doubly disadvantaged on account of their gender as well as due to their disability and they become vulnerable to exploitation and atrocities. Elderly persons with disabilities, in the twilight of their lives, are likely to be neglected and exploited and therefore they need special consideration. The President said that special programmes should be worked out for them. In her address on the occasion, Smt. Meira Kumar stressed the government's resolve to ensure gainful employment for the persons with disability. The Minister informed that the Government had been taking measures to ensure that the statutory three percent reservation provided for persons with disabilities in identified posts is effectively implemented in the Government establishments and public sector undertakings. Referring to the latest reports from the DOPT, the Minister expressed satisfaction that in the years 2004 and 2005, the disabled persons filled nine percent and seven percent vacancies respectively which was higher than the statutorily prescribed three percent.

4793. (3-12-2007) NEW DELHI : The Lok Sabha has today passed the Rajiv Gandhi Institute of Petroleum Technology Bill 2007. The Bill is aimed at declaring the Institute as an "Institution of National Importance" and to provide for its incorporation and matters connected therewith. Earlier, on 29.11.2007, Rajya Sabha had passed this Bill. With this Parliamentary nod has been received for enactment of the Bill. The Rajiv Gandhi Institute of Petroleum Technology (RGIPT) is envisaged to serve as the fountainhead for the nurturing of world class technical human resources capable of serving as the leaders and innovators of tomorrow in the field of Petroleum Technology. The total estimated capital cost of the project is Rs.435 crore which would be met partially through budgetary support of Rs. 285 crore and Rs.150 crore from Oil Industry Development Board. The total estimated recurring expenditure of Rs. 260.58 crore would be met from the accrual of interest on Endowment Fund of Rs. 250.00 crore to be created with the contribution of Oil Public Sector Undertakings (PSUs), student fees, donations and other earnings of the Institute through Research & Development, consultancies, students' placement fees, etc. The Institute is envisaged to be self sufficient and self-reliant by the year 2015-16. It is important to note that Government had come out with the New Exploration Licensing Policy in 1999 and with the passage of time this policy has been made more and more attractive to foreign companies as well as Indian private and public sector companies. As on date, only 30% of the sedimentary basins in India has been explored and there is still a vast potential in terms of acreages that are to be explored. The Government is committed to increase the exploration coverage to an extent of 100% by the year 2015. In a recent study conducted by consultant Price Waterhouse Coopers for Petrofed, the gap between the availability and requirement of trained manpower in India is projected to be about 36000 by the year 2019 and the existing institutes may not be adequate to meet the increasing requirement of technical manpower in the petroleum sector. The proposed Rajiv Gandhi Institute of Petroleum Technology is expected to meet this shortfall to a significant extent. The Institute will commence its academic operations by admitting students from the academic year 2008-09. To start with, there will be two undergraduate courses namely B. Tech. in Petroleum Production & Reservoir and B. Tech. in Petroleum Refining and one MBA course on Petroleum Management. The institute will become fully operational in 2015-16. On its becoming fully operational the Institute would have 7 B. Tech, 6 Integrated Masters Degrees, 8 M.Tech/MBA and 12 PGD and Ph.D programmes.

4794. (3-12-2007) NEW DELHI : The recommendation of the Standing Committee on Defence to accord Deemed University status to the Armed Forces Medical College (AFMC), Pune has been considered by the Government. As per the University Grants Commission guidelines, according Deemed University status involves converting AFMC, Pune into a Society under the Societies Registration Act, 1860 or into a separate Trust under the Public Trust Act. After due consideration, therefore, the proposal has not been found acceptable by the government. This information was given by the Defence Minister Shri AK Antony in a written reply to Dr. KS Manoj in Lok Sabha today.

4795. (3-12-2007) NEW DELHI : Out of total 40 recommendations in part-I of Kelkar Committee report, 26 recommendations were accepted for implementation out of which 18 have been implemented so far. 8 recommendations were accepted for implementation with certain modifications out of which 6 have been implemented so far. Out of remaining 6 which were to be deliberated upon, further 2 have been implemented and 1 has been dropped after due deliberations. While in respect of part-II of the report, out of 19 recommendations, 4 recommendations have been implemented, further action is not required/envisaged in respect of 13 recommendations and one has been dropped after due deliberations. Since May 2001, when the Defence Industry sector was opened up for Indian private sector participation with FDI permissible upto 26%, 73 Letters of Intent/Industrial Licenses have been issued to private companies for manufacture of wide range of defence items. Of the above, a few projects have started implementation. The market for defence goods is user driven and is based on requirement projected by the services in their annual and long-term acquisition plan as a result of which full capacity utilization may not always be feasible.

4796. (3-12-2007) NEW DELHI : The Congress said that, for us the Gujarat elections are not a one issue election they are not a one person election. The Gujarat election is about the failure of the BJP on all fronts, on all issues, on all facets. And one made a reason for that is that the BJP is held hostage to the whims and caprices of one man in their own party—the present Chief Minister of Gujarat. They are captives to the dictatorship of their own one man. No one in the BJP can question it; no one in the BJP dares to correct him; no one can try to cure him, also because he is incurable. Even the former prime minister Shri Vajpayee had to remind him and request him with folded hands to follow raj dharma. So everybody else is a supplicant and in their own party one man is the dictator. This also shows the level of inner party democracy in the BJP, in Gujarat in particular. Leaders and party members of thirty years and forty years, fifty years standing are marginalized, sidelined, why because the BJP is captive to Modi and unfortunately for the nation and for Gujarat Modi is captive in turn, to one issue. And those who think that we are hesitant to raise it, for any reason political or otherwise, are sadly mistaken as our repeated raising proves. He deserves to be tried and convicted by Indian courts on his track record on human rights. Indeed he deserves to be tried and convicted by international courts of justice and we are certainly not hesitant to say it. And let me say that a person of his track record, merchants of death is not only an apposite phrase, it is a mild phrase. Indeed the continuance of Modi in India, in Gujarat, is an insult to the memory of Gandhiji, the great son of the same state. Also it is an insult to the memory of Gandhiji because the United Nation has declared October 2 as International nonviolence day. It is an insult to the very concept of nonviolence because the biggest practitioner of nonviolence came from that state and the biggest practitioner of the opposite of that creed also unfortunately rules that state today. To a question whether Gujarat is the single biggest issue, Shri Singhvi said, I started by saying we do not believe in single biggest issue. I am only responding to what you have heard in the last couple of days to clarify that those who think that human rights are issues to be ignored are sadly mistaken. But that does not mean the hierarchic issues in 123. For us many of these issues are important. Human Rights are of course violated with physical abuse which this government, the chief minister has done in ample measure. But Human Rights are no less violated when you find mal-governance and corruption which is in this booklet. We will take them in Gujarat, we will take them in Delhi whether it is electricity, whether it is the lack of any development in terms of concrete figures, all of them are important. To a question on the status of Shri Bhajan Lal and his son Shri Kuldeep Bishnoi forming a new party, Shri Singhvi said, that anybody who has the slightest knowledge of Indian political history knows the status, outcome and sad plight of those who leave, negate or rebel against the mother party which has given them everything to which they owe their political status. And in fact such people choose to ignore the lessons of that history then they are definitely condemned to repeat it. Naturally we have taken note of the remarks, the completely false and insulting remarks, made in particular by a suspended member of the party. A person who by those remarks, has obviously compounded the felony since he is already under suspension. But unlike others who are used to knee-jerk outbursts, the Congress Party functions institutionally through a constituted disciplinary action committee which will no doubt take appropriate action. To a question on Israel lunching a rocket whether it is under US pressure, Shri Singhvi said, I do not know about the facts of the case you are mentioning I can only say that government of India and India never functions under any pressure. That much I can categorically deny.

4797. (3-12-2007) NEW DELHI : The Union Cabinet has approved the amendments proposed by the Ministry to the Armed Forces Tribunal Bill, 2005. A notice for moving the amendments has also been referred to the Rajya Sabha Secretariat. The salient features of the Armed Forces Tribunal Bill, 2005 includes the provisions for the adjudication or trial by the Armed Forces Tribunal of disputes and complaints with respect to commission, appointments, enrolment and conditions of service in respect of persons subject to the Army Act, 1950, the Navy Act, 1957 and the Air Force Act, 1950 and also to provide for appeals arising out of orders, findings or sentences of courts-martial held under the said Acts and for matters connected therewith or incidental thereto. The Bill amongst others contains provisions for establishment of the Tribunal and Benches thereof; eligibility criteria for appointment of Chairperson and Members; jurisdiction, powers and authority of the Tribunal; and provisions relating to procedure and appeal etc. The Tribunal will consist of a Chairperson and such number of Judicial and Administrative Members as determined by the Central Government. A total number of approximately 169 and 9,755 cases filed by the Armed Forces personnel are pending in the Supreme Court and various High Courts, respectively. A provision exists in the Bill to transfer cases pending before any court including a High Court to the Tribunal. It is expected that the setting up of the Tribunal will result in speedy and less expensive dispensation of justice to the Defence Services personnel. This information was given by the Defence Minister Shri AK Antony in a written reply to Shri Milind Deora in Lok Sabha today.

4798. (3-12-2007) NEW DELHI : The Army came to know of some pilferage of special rations meant for soldiers in Siachen. Based on this information, the Jammu and Kashmir police carried out raids and recovered certain items of special rations and stores from Chumathang, Tangtse, Hunder/Khalsar/Sasoma and Nubra (Panamik). Eleven First Information Reports (FIRs) have been lodged with the police and 31 civilians have been arrested. Two Courts of Inquiry were ordered to investigate into the matter. Based on the first Court of Inquiry for Chumathang, the Army Commander has directed administrative action against three officers and two Junior Commissioned Officers. The second Court of Inquiry is in an advanced stage. This information was given by the Defence Minister Shri AK Antony in a written reply to Shri Raghuveer Singh Koshal in Lok Sabha today.

4799. (3-12-2007) NEW DELHI : The objective of Sainik Schools is to create an opportunity in each state to contribute to the Officers pool in the armed forces and to bring public school education within the reach of the common man. There has been a constant improvement in the academic standards of Sainik Schools. However, the infrastructure standards and general facilities of these schools have been facing a decline. With a view to maintain the academic standards in Sainik Schools, an elaborate programme of in-service training to the teachers and competition oriented training for the cadets is being implemented with the assistance of experts from the Services and professional educational institutions/bodies. The Ministry of Defence also provides training grants to the schools with a view to upgrade training infrastructure and skills. Sainik Schools are established on receipt of a specific request from a State Government agreeing to provide land along with funds for the creation and maintenance of basic infrastructure, equipment and facilities besides scholarships for the cadets of the state. There are 22 Sainik Schools functioning in the country. The Ministry of Defence has accorded 'in principle' approval for the establishment of new Sainik Schools at Chingchip (Mizoram), Ravangla (Sikkim) & Ambikapur (Chhattisgarh). This information was given by the Defence Minister Shri AK Antony in a written reply to Shri Raghunath Jha in Lok Sabha today.

4800. (3-12-2007) NEW DELHI : The summary of recommendations of J.C. Pant Committee, constituted in December, 2001 to review the management structure and operating mechanism of Kendriya Vidyaiaya Sangathan (KVS), is annexed. KVS has already implemented several of these recommendations in various forms. This information was given by the Minister of State for Human Resource Development, Shri M.A.A. Fami in a written reply in Rajya Sabha today.

4801. (3-12-2007) NEW DELHI : Following is the text of the keynote address of the Vice President of India Mohd. Hamid Ansari at the launch of the "International National Trusts Organization" at a function organised by Indian National Trusts for Art and Cultural Heritage (INTACH) here today: "Ladies and Gentlemen, this is an international gathering of a different kind and I feel privileged to be here with you today at the formal launch of the International National Trusts Organization. It is a rare sight to see such a congregation of conservation specialists in Delhi, sharing their experiences, debating and developing collective strategies to promote international cooperation in heritage management and conservation. The need for international cooperation in heritage management has been recognized much before today's period of globalization. The 'Convention Concerning The Protection of the World Cultural and Natural Heritage' adopted in 1972 by the General Conference of the UNESCO had clearly spelt out that the cultural and natural heritage of countries needs to be preserved as "part of the world heritage of the mankind as a whole" and that "it is incumbent on the international community as a whole to participate in the protection" of this heritage to complement, and not in lieu of, the efforts of the concerned State. The Convention had also noted that the cultural and natural heritage is " increasingly threatened with destruction not only by the traditional causes of decay, but also by changing social and economic conditions".

4802. (3-12-2007) NEW DELHI : Government has launched a Scheme for setting up of Terminal Market Complexes under National Horticulture Mission which would establish forward linkages through wholesalers, distribution centres, retail cash and carry stores, processing units and exporters. This will, besides helping in developing better market linkages for the farmers, increasing farm income and bringing efficiency in the supply chain, indirectly help in increasing the export of fresh fruits, vegetables and flowers. The State Governments of Andhra Pradesh, Bihar, Madhya Pradesh, Maharashtra, Orissa, Punjab, Rajasthan and Union Territory of Chandigarh have identified land at suitable locations for setting up of terminal markets. The State Governments of Bihar, Madhya Pradesh, Punjab and Union Territory of Chandigarh have issued notices inviting Expression of Interest from the entrepreneurs. The modern infrastructure facilities for grading, storage and cold storage, as envisaged in the terminal market projects, would help in boosting the prospects of export of fruits, vegetables and flowers from the country but no quantification of expected increase in exports has been done under the Scheme. The amount likely to be spent on the project would be known only on finalization of bids on case-to-case basis. This information was given by Shri Kanti Lal Bhuria, Minister of State for Agriculture in written reply to a question in the Lok Sabha today.

4803. (3-12-2007) NEW DELHI : The National Bamboo Mission of Department of Agriculture & Cooperation has been implemented in 25 States in the country with an objective to promote the growth of the bamboo sector through area based regionally differentiated strategies and to increase the coverage of area under bamboo in potential areas, etc. So far, an amount of Rs.98.93 crore has been released to various States and as per their initial reports, an area of 21234 ha. has been brought under bamboo plantation, 5217 ha. Existing stock improved, 220 Nurseries established, 1199 farmers/entrepreneurs trained. Besides, State-level workshops/demonstration, etc. were conducted. The partnership has been useful in setting up nurseries, raising bamboo plantations and training of farmers/ entrepreneurs in bamboo cultivation. This information was given by Shri Kanti Lal Bhuria, Minister of State for Agriculture in written reply to a question in the Lok Sabha today.

4804. (3-12-2007) NEW DELHI : The Government has introduced interest subvention scheme for providing crop loans upto Rs. 3 lakh per borrower at 7% rate of interest per annum. The policy came into force with effect from Kharif 2006-07. To implement the scheme, Government also provided interest subvention @ 2% p.a. to Public Sector Banks, Regional Rural Banks (RRBs) and Cooperative Banks on their own involvement of funds in the crop loan disbursement. The interest subvention scheme has been continued for the year 2007-08 also with a budgetary provision of Rs. 1677 crore. The scheme is under implementation in the entire country. All the farmers availing crop loans upto a principal amount of Rs. 3 lakh are eligible beneficiaries under the scheme. This information was given by Shri Kanti Lal Bhuria, Minister of State for Agriculture in written reply to a question in the Lok Sabha today.

4805. (3-12-2007) NEW DELHI : Government has decided to corporatise the Delhi Milk Scheme to provide more autonomy in its operation and management, flexibility in financial matters having regards to the consumers and the organization's interest to make it more efficient and viable. Expression of Interest (EOI) from reputed professional agencies to prepare feasibility report and Memorandum of Understanding (MOU)/Articles of Association (AOA) and other related job have been invited in the matter. This information was given by Shri Kanti Lal Bhuria, Minister of State for Agriculture in written reply to a question in the Lok Sabha today.

4806. (3-12-2007) NEW DELHI : Some complaints had been received from various States about supply of poor quality of foodgrains under Public Distribution System (PDS) by Food Corporation of India (FCI). During 2005-06, complaints had been received from Andhra Pradesh, Kerala, Karnataka and Bihar about supply of inferior quality rice by FCI. During 2006-07, complaint had been received from Rajasthan regarding supply of inferior quality wheat by FCI for PDS. Similarly, in 2007-08, complaints have been received from Maharashtra & Tamil Nadu about poor quality foodgrains being supplied in PDS. The Government had issued instructions to FCI that only good quality foodgrains conforming to Prevention of Food Adulteration Act (PFA) standards should be distributed through PDS. Besides, the following steps are being taken to ensure the supply of good quality foodgrains for PDS:- (i) Adequate opportunities are provided to the officials of the State Governments/UT Administrations to inspect the stocks prior to lifting from the Food Corporation of India (FCI) godowns. (ii) Instructions have been issued to all the State Governments/UT Administrations that an officer not below the rank of Inspector should be deputed to check the quality of foodgrains before lifting from the FCI godowns. (iii) The samples of foodgrains are to be jointly drawn and sealed by the officers of the State Governments/UT Administrations and the FCI from the stocks for display at the counters of Fair Price Shops (FPSs) for the benefit of consumers. (iv) Instructions have been issued to all State Governments that all the stocks available with the State Government Agencies & Fair Price Shops should be regularly inspected for their quality and only those stocks of wheat should be distributed, which meet the required quality specifications. This information was given by Dr. Akhilesh Prasad Singh, Minister of State for Consumer Affairs, Food and Public Distribution and Agriculture in reply to a question in Lok Sabha today.

4807. (3-12-2007) NEW DELHI : The Government is implementing the following Schemes which provide foodgrains for homeless people: 1. Antodaya Anna Yojna (AAY) was launched in December, 2000 for the poorest of the poor families, from amongst BPL families covered under TPDS in the States and Union Territories. These families are issued foodgrains at highly subsidized rate of Rs. 2/-per kg. for wheat and Rs. 3/-per kg. for rice. The States/UTs are required to bear the distribution cost, and make available foodgrains to the beneficiaries at the price fixed by Government as above. The scale of issue is 35 kg per family per month with effect from 1st April, 2002. 2. 5% of BPL allocation to Hostels/Welfare Institutions: With a view to meet requirement of Hostels / Welfare Institutions *viz.* N.G.Os / Charitable Institutions which help shelter less/ homeless poor and other categories not covered under TPDS or under any other Welfare Scheme, an additional allocation of foodgrains (rice and wheat) equal to 5% of the BPL allocation of each State/UT is made to States/UTs at BPL rates. This Scheme was introduced during 2002-03. 3. Annapurna Scheme: For indigent senior citizens of 65 years of age or above who though eligible for old age pension under the National Old Age Pension Scheme (NOAPS) but are not getting the pension, are covered and 10 kgs. foodgrains per person per month are supplied free of cost under this scheme. Implementation of the Scheme is done by States/UTs. Improvement of implementation of AAY is being attempted as part of 9-Point Action Plan for strengthening of TPDS. Implementation of the other two welfare schemes is periodically reviewed by the Government with State Governments/ UTs Governments. While evaluation of AAY along with TPDS was covered in the study done by ORG MARG, for the other two schemes no specific evaluation studies have been taken up. The ORG MARG report mentioned that more than 90% of AAY families were dependent on ration shops for foodgrains, foodgrains earmarked for AAY were intact and sold as per prescribed issue prices, and 85% AAY households lifted rice under the scheme. This information was given by Dr. Akhilesh Prasad Singh, Minister of State for Consumer Affairs, Food and Public Distribution and Agriculture in reply to a question in Lok Sabha today.

4808. (3-12-2007) NEW DELHI : The Vice President of India Mohd. Hamid Ansari presented the awards for 'Dr. Mahbub Ul Haq Memorial SAARC Inter-

School Debate Competition' at a function here today. The topic of the Debate was the 'Global warming and climate change'. He presented the winner trophy to the team of Pakistan and the runner of trophy to the team of India. The Best speaker (For) award was presented to Mr. Prerak Pradhan of Nepal and the Best speaker (Against) award was presented to Mohd. Aeeal Hasan of Maldives. The function was jointly organized by United Nations Development Programme (UNDP) and Rajiv Gandhi Institute for Contemporary Studies. Addressing on the occasion, the Vice President said that the debate was named after a person who was a man of great vision and was concerned with the security for all. Expressing his concerns on the deteriorating environmental conditions he said that we are confronted with the problems of extraordinary dimensions. All these problems are due to our own doing. He cautioned that the nature has acute sense of balance and if we disturb the balance, humankind will have to face the consequences. Congratulating the winners of the debate, the Vice President said that today the awareness among the masses about these important issues is inadequate and he hoped that these winners will spread the right message.

4809. (3-12-2007) NEW DELHI : The ground water is used mainly for agricultural and domestic purposes and it is also used for industrial and commercial purposes. The studies conducted by Central Ground Water Board (CGWB) reveal that the water tables are dipping due to cumulative effect of domestic, agricultural and industrial use, including withdrawals of ground water by soft drinks and bottled drinking purposes. The Central Ground Water Authority (CGWA) has been constituted for the purpose of regulation and control of ground water management. The Authority has been vested with powers to invoke penal provisions, as may be necessary under the law. This information was given by the Minister of State for Water Resources, Shri Jai Prakash Narayan Yadav in response to a question by Shri Naveen Jindal in the Lok Sabha today.

4810. (3-12-2007) NEW DELHI : The average annual precipitation over the country is 1170 millimetre (mm). However, there is large spatial and temporal variation in the rainfall. The rainfall varies from about 100 mm in Western Rajasthan to over 10,000 mm in Cherapunji (Meghalaya). About 75% of the rainfall occurs during the monsoon period (June to October) and that too from a few spells of intense rainfall. As a result, there is considerable variation in the availability of water. There are instances of over-exploitation of the water resources, mostly ground water, in specific regions leading to lowering of ground water table and that of over irrigation in certain areas causing drainage congestion & water logging. The availability, demand and supply of water is not worked out Plan-wise. This information was given by the Minister of State for Water Resources, Shri Jai Prakash Narayan Yadav in response to a question by Shri G. Karunakara Reddy in the Lok Sabha today.

4811. (3-12-2007) NEW DELHI : The average annual water availability in the country has been assessed as 1869 billion cubic metre (BCM). It is estimated that owing to topographic, hydrological and other constraints, the utilizable water is 1123 BCM. The National Commission for Integrated Water Resources Development Plan in its report has made an assessment for water requirement for various sectors. As per the report, 629 BCM of water is being utilized for diverse purposes including irrigation for which 524 BCM of water is being utilized. The estimated total water requirements for the years 2010, 2025 and 2050 are 710 BCM, 843 BCM and 1180 BCM and that for irrigation are 557 BCM, 611 BCM and 807 BCM respectively. The availability of water in the country as a whole is considered adequate to meet the present level of demand of water for irrigation. This information was given by the Minister of State for Water Resources, Shri Jai Prakash Narayan Yadav in response to a question by Shri Braja Kishore Tripathy in the Lok Sabha today.

4812. (3-12-2007) NEW DELHI : The census of Minor Irrigation projects was undertaken with reference year 1986-87. Minor Irrigation projects in the States are undertaken by various Departments and Organizations under different developmental schemes. A good number of projects are commissioned by the cultivators themselves with their own resources. In order to have a sound data base of Minor Irrigation projects in the country, first Minor Irrigation Census was organized by Ministry of Water Resources in collaboration with States/UTs with reference year 1986-87. In the Minor Irrigation Census, information is collected for 5 types of Minor Irrigation projects namely Dug wells, Shallow tube wells, Deep Tube wells, Surface flow and Surface lift schemes. The items on which information is collected are location of the project, ownership, source of finance, physical characteristics of the project, utilization status, reasons for under utilization, water lifting and water distribution devices used, culturable command area, irrigation potential created and irrigation potential utilized during reference period. The report of the first census was released in 1993. The report contains state-wise and district wise tables on number of schemes according to various characteristics. After the first census, two more censuses of Minor Irrigation projects have been organized by the Ministry. The Second MI Census with reference year 1993-94 was completed and the Report was published in March 2001. The 3rd MI Census with reference year 2000-01 was launched in the year 2000 in 33 States/UTs. All India Report for the census was released in November 2005. The results of the 2nd and 3rd census are available on Ministry of Water Resources' website: www.mowr.gov.in. The 4th MI Census with reference year 2006-07 has been launched in all States/UTs in the country. Currently the States/UTs are in the process of training/data collection. This information was given by the Minister of State for Water Resources, Shri Jai Prakash Narayan Yadav in response to a question by Shri Mahavir Bhagora in the Lok Sabha today.

4813. (3-12-2007) NEW DELHI : Subernarekha Barrage project (West Bengal) envisages construction of a barrage across Subernarekha river downstream of Chandil dam and Galudih barrage near Bhosraghat to irrigate 1,14,198 ha annually in the Midnapur district of West Bengal through a left bank canal and its distribution system covering a culturable command area of 96,860 ha as approved by the Planning Commission in 1995. The project was taken up for construction in the year 1995-96 at an estimated cost of Rs. 215.61 crore (1987 price level). As per the existing guidelines on AIBP, the irrigation projects benefiting drought prone/tribal/flood prone areas are eligible for up to 90% grant of the project cost included in AIBP depending on the extent of irrigation benefits provided by the project to such area that has been proposed in AIBP. The extent to which, the Suberna Rekha project could receive funding under AIBP could be decided on receipt of proposal from State Government of West Bengal as per guidelines of the AIBP in force. Irrigation being a state subject, the planning, execution, funding as well as priority of execution of such projects is within the purview of the concerned State Government. This information was given by the Minister of State for Water Resources, Shri Jai Prakash Narayan Yadav in response to a question by Shri Prabodh Panda in the Lok Sabha today.

4814. (3-12-2007) NEW DELHI : The Prime Minister Dr. Manmohan Singh inaugurated the 12th International Conference of National Trusts under the aegis of INTACH here today. Inaugurating the conference Dr. Manmohan Singh said, "We have been conscious of the need to preserve, protect and promote our cultural heritage, here in India. But we cannot be satisfied with the status quo. We have not always succeeded in doing what we ought to do. Our cultural properties have been exposed to various threats - natural and manmade - over the centuries. Conquerors, explorers, colonizers, vandals and thieves have added their bit to the vagaries of nature and the passage of time". Urging the civil society organizations and citizens to actively participate in the protection and preservation of our heritage and monuments, the Prime Minister said we should look beyond the Government. The Prime Minister urged the participants to sent a message around the world that nobody had the right to destroy what humanity inherited from the past. Earlier, welcoming the delegates the Minister for Tourism and Culture Smt. Ambika Soni said that the task of promoting culture cannot be in a water tight insular condition - it has to be of fundamental benefit to all mankind in general and of the region in particular. It has to be, not only an integrated response to our common historical evolution, but carry with it also the story of our region, It has to be an extension of the great cultural and civilisational ethos of our sub-continent as of the many regions that constitute our globe. Smt. Soni said, that if we do not know where we come from, it is difficult to know where we are going. Heritage provides this valuable knowledge of the past which helps us in preparing a road map for the future. It is our root and our identity. It is a precious economic and cultural asset. Stating that heritage does not belong to any community or nation Smt. Soni said "Like environment, we believe heritage belongs not to any one community or a particular nation but to the entire humanity. Therefore, the primary objective of promoting and preserving cultural heritage for the benefit of the present as well as the future generations needs to be carried forward jointly in active collaboration with not only all sections of society within a nation-state but the international community as a whole". The Minister reminded the participants of the cardinal responsibility to preserve heritage and said, "As global citizens it is our bounden duty to safeguard our heritage both tangible and intangible, so that the best of our history, culture and civilization is not only enjoyed by us, but can be passed on to our children and our grandchildren in a form that instills in them a pride on who they are". She further stated, "If we can undertake this task with sensitivity, transparency and dedication with the application of knowledge, science and technology in a collaborative manner among communities societies and nations; we will not only be able to preserve our precious heritage but also help in bringing closer cooperation among diverse people".

4815. (3-12-2007) NEW DELHI : Air Marshal KM Sundara AVSM VSM takes over as Air Officer-in-charge Maintenance at Air Headquarters, New Delhi, responsible for Maintenance Management of all Weapon Systems and Equipment of IAF, on 03 Dec 07. Air Marshal Rama Sundara is an Electrical Engineering graduate from MC Hassan, Karnataka. He holds a Masters Degree in Defence Studies from the prestigious "Defence Services Staff College". Wellington. He has undergone the Senior International Defence Management Course at the Naval Post Graduate School, Monterery, USA besides being trained abroad on the MiG-23 & Mig-29 fighter aircraft systems. He is a fellow of Institution of Engineers and Institution of Electrical & Tele Communication Engineers and active member of the Aeronautical Society of India. The Air Marshal has a rich and varied experience in various facets of the maintenance organization in the IAF ranging from fighter aircraft to the ground based communication systems. He was involved in induction of MiG-23 and MiG-29 aircraft into Indian Air Force and setting up of the MiG-29 overhaul facilities. He has worked as the Chief Engineering Officer at Air Force Station Kalaikonda besides commanding Air Force Station Sulur. As the Assistant Chief of Air Staff (Systems), he was responsible for the maintenance of a varied range of Radars, Communications, Armament, Guided weapons, Avionics Modification and System development in his previous appointment as Senior Maintenance Staff Officer at Headquarters Maintenance Command, the Air Marshal was overseeing the indigenisation and modernization of all assets of IAF. He took keen interest in undertaking the extension of Airframe/Aeroengine which were otherwise meant to be disposed off without any effective utilization. He was actively involved with PSUs, DRDO Academic Institutions and Civil Agencies for industry-service interaction and evolving better maintenance service support. For his distinguished service, Air Marshal Rama Sundara was conferred the Vishisht Seva Medal in 1994 and Ati Vishisht Seva Medal in year 2006 by the President of India. The Air Marshal is an avid sportsman, his speciality being the Adventure sports. He has undergone a Skydiving course and likes to relax with a sedate game of gold. Born in year 1950, Air Marshal Rama Sundara is married to Nalini, who hold Masters Degree in Physics and trained Teacher.

4816. (3-12-2007) NEW DELHI : The Appointments Committee of the Cabinet has approved the following appointments/extension: Smt. Veena Sreeram Rao, IAS (KN:72), presently Director General, CAPART (Ministry of Rural Development) as Secretary, Ministry of Development of North Eastern Region. Shri U.K. Varma, IAS (MP:76), presently in the cadre, as Additional Secretary, Ministry of Information and Broadcasting. Extension of tenure of Shri P.P. Mathur, IAS(MP:72), Additional Secretary and Financial Adviser in the Department of Agriculture and Cooperation (Ministry of Agriculture) up to 31st March, 2008.

4817. (3-12-2007) NEW DELHI : The number of pensioners as on 31.03.2007 is 26,53,181 and the amount accumulated in Pension Fund is Rs. 80,776.22 crores, at face value (provisional). Last valuation *i.e.* 8th Valuation was completed on 31.03.2004. This information was given by the Minister of State for Labour and Employment Shri Oscar Fernandes (Independent Charge) in a written reply in the Lok Sabha today.

4818. (3-12-2007) NEW DELHI : The reports received from the State Governments indicate that there are some cases of children working in the hybrid cotton fields where children were found to be mostly working with their parents. As per the Child Labour (Prohibition & Regulation) Act, 1986, employment of children is presently not prohibited in cotton fields. However, the State Governments have taken steps to ensure that children do not work on processes involving handling of pesticides in the hybrid cotton fields. Government is regularly monitoring the enforcement of Child Labour (Prohibition & Regulation) Act, 1986 by the States. In order to step up enforcement of the Child Labour (Prohibition & Regulation) Act, a fortnight long nationwide 'Enforcement Drive against Child Labour' was launched by the Government on 14th November 2007. During this period, the State Governments had been specifically directed to conduct inspections/raids and also launch awareness campaign against child labour. This information was given by the Minister of State for Labour and Employment Shri Oscar Fernandes (Independent Charge) in a written reply in the Lok Sabha today.

4819. (3-12-2007) NEW DELHI : Reliable estimates of labour force in the country are obtained through quinquennial labour force survey conducted by National Sample Survey Organisation. The last such quinquennial survey, for which results are available, was conducted during 2004-05 according to which the annual rate of growth of employment has been 2.95% as against 2.97% growth in labour force during 1999-2000 and 2004-05. The employment in the unorganised sector has increased to 432.66 million in 2004-05 from 369.0 million in 1999-2000 whereas employment in the organised sector has declined to 26.44 million in 2004-05 from 27.96 million in 1999-2000. The approach paper to 11th Five Year Plan envisages creation of 70 million job opportunities (65 million in non agricultural sector). It also provides a framework to restructure policies to achieve a new vision based on faster, more broadbased and inclusive growth. It aims at making employment generation an integral part of the growth process and devise strategies to accelerate not only growth of employment but also wages of the poorly paid. It also suggests that the 11th Plan should aim at raising the rate of growth of Industrial sector to 10% and manufacturing growth to 12% per annum and also place a special emphasis on infrastructure and skill formation. This information was given by the Minister of State for Labour and Employment Shri Oscar Fernandes (Independent Charge) in a written reply in the Lok Sabha today.

4820. (3-12-2007) NEW DELHI : According to the last two quinquennial surveys conducted by National Sample Survey Organisation, on usual status basis, the employment opportunities have increased by 62.1 million during the period 1999-2000 to 2004-2005. Keeping in view incidence of unemployment, both in urban and rural areas, Government has been implementing various employment generation and poverty alleviation programmes/schemes. Some of these are: Sampoorna Grameen Rozgar Yojana (SGRY); Swarnjayanti Gram Swarozgar Yojana (SGSY); Rural Employment Generation Programme (REGP); Prime Minister's Rozgar Yojana (PMRY) and Swarna Jayanti Shahari Rozgar Yojana (SJSRY). Besides, recognizing the serious problem of unemployment, the National Rural Employment Guarantee Act (NREGA) was enacted on 7.9.2005. NREGA provides for the enhancement of livelihood security of the households in rural areas of the country by providing at least one hundred days of guaranteed wage employment in every financial year to every household whose adult members volunteer to do unskilled manual work. It was implemented in 200 identified districts in the country in its first phase with effect from 2.2.06 and has been extended to 130 more districts in the second phase w.e.f 1.4.2007. However, the Government has now decided to extend the National Rural Employment Guarantee Act (NREGA) to the rural areas of all the remaining districts in the country including the Union Territories with effect from 1.4.2008. During the current financial year, a total number of 2.11 Crore households have been provided employment up to October, 2007. This information was given by the Minister of State for Labour and Employment Shri Oscar Fernandes (Independent Charge) in a written reply in the Lok Sabha today.

4821. (3-12-2007) NEW DELHI : The Reports of ILO has revealed that there has been a decline in poverty and increase in productivity in South Asian Region during the last decade. As per the ILO Report (Key Indicators of the Labour Market) share of working poor (1 US $ a day) in the total employment for South Asia has come down from 56.6 percent in 1996 to 33.5 percent in the year 2006. As per the Report, the annual percentage change in Labour productivity in South Asia was 2.3 percent in 1996, which further increased to 5.8 percent in the year 2006. In case of India, the annual growth rate of Labour Productivity (defined as value added per person employed) during 1980 to 2005 was 3.7 percent. Poverty ratio, in India, which was 36 percent in 1993-94, has come down to 27.5 percent in 2004-05 (Uniform Recall Period bases). This information was given by the Minister of State for Labour and Employment Shri Oscar Fernandes (Independent Charge) in a written reply in the Lok Sabha today.

4822. (3-12-2007) NEW DELHI : Direct tax collections continued to record a growth of over 40 percent for the first eight months of the current fiscal. Net tax collections stood at Rs.1,45,053 crore, up from Rs.1,00,135 crore during the same period last fiscal, registering a growth of 44.86 percent and achieving over 54 percent of budgeted direct tax target of Rs.2,67,490 crore. Corporate Tax registered a growth of 46.62 percent at Rs.86,526 crore, up from Rs.59,015 crore during the previous fiscal, while Personal Income Tax (including FBT, STT and BCTT) grew by 42.48 percent at Rs.58,303 crore, up from Rs.40,920 crore. Growth in Securities Transaction Tax (STT) was 78.93 percent (Rs.4,924 crore against Rs.2,752 crore) and Fringe Benefit Tax (FBT) was 16.76 percent (Rs.3,064 crore against Rs.2,624 crore). Banking Cash Transaction Tax (BCTT) grew by 14.34 percent (Rs.359 crore against Rs.314 crore). Corporate tax growth was highest in the North-Eastern region (Guwahati) at 255.64 percent, followed by Mumbai (103.17 percent), Kerala (76.45 percent), Eastern Uttar Pradesh (71.22 percent) and Bihar & Jharkhand (51.98 percent). Personal income tax growth was highest in Madhya Pradesh & Chhattisgarh region at 157.67 percent, followed by Gujarat (68.83 percent), Andhra Pradesh (56.62 percent), North Western region, *i.e.* Punjab, Haryana, Himachal Pradesh and Jammu & Kashmir (53.22. percent) and Maharashtra (47.24 percent). Tax deduction / collection at source increased by over 50 percent, while self-assessment tax (paid voluntarily before submission of earlier year's tax return) increased by over 73 percent, indicating continued improvement in tax administration and tax compliance levels.

4823. (3-12-2007) NEW DELHI : India's exports during October, 2007 were valued at US $ 13302.71 million which was 35.65% higher than the level of US $ 9806.69 million during October, 2006. In rupee terms, exports touched Rs.52560.85 crore, which was 17.88% higher than the value of exports during October, 2006. Cumulative value of exports for the period April-October, 2007 was US $ 85583.30 million (Rs.347793.90 Crore) as against US $ 70792.52 million (Rs.324863.93 Crore) registering a growth of 20.89% in Dollar terms and 7.06% in Rupee terms during the same period last year. India's imports during October, 2007 were valued at US $ 20785.29 million representing an increase of 24.27 % over the level of imports valued at US $ 16725.65 million in October, 2006. In Rupee terms, imports increased by 7.99%. Cumulative value of imports for the period April-October, 2007 was US $ 129989.72 million (Rs.528546.44 Crore) as against US $ 103735.88 million (Rs.475862.57 Crore) registering a growth of 25.31% in Dollar terms and 11.07% in Rupee terms during the same period last year. Oil imports during October, 2007 were valued at US $ 6126.22 million which was 14.59% higher than oil imports valued at US $ 5346.14 million in the corresponding period last year. Oil imports during April-October, 2007 were valued at US $ 37525.44 million which was 9.25% higher than the oil imports of US $ 34349.77 million in the corresponding period last year. Non-oil imports during October, 2007 were estimated at US $ 14659.07 million which was 28.82% higher than growth of non oil imports of US $ 11379.52 million in October, 2006.

Non-oil imports during April-October, 2007 were valued at US $ 92464.28 million which was 33.26% higher than the level of such imports valued at US $ 69386.11 million in April-October, 2006. The trade deficit for April-October, 2007 was estimated at US $ 44406.42 million which was higher than the deficit at US $ 32943.35 million during April-October, 2006.

4824. (3-12-2007) NEW DELHI : The target for textile exports for the current year has been fixed at US$ 25.06 billion keeping in view the growth that had taken place in this sector after the termination of Multi Fibre Arrangement (MFA). This was stated by Shri E.V.K.S. Elangovan, Minister of State for Textiles while addressing the meeting of the Parliamentary Consultative Committee of the Ministry of Textiles, here today. He said that with the termination of MFA in December 2004, exports of textiles and clothing had taken a giant leap in 2005-2006. He said the exports had reached US$ 17.5 billion in 2005-06 an increase of about 25% over the previous financial year. However, the Minister said this momentum could not be maintained in 2006-07 and exports of textiles and clothings still managed to reach US$18.73 billion thereby registering a growth of about 7 % over the financial year 2005-06. During the meeting the Minister informed the members that as per textiles industry, the 14% appreciation in value of Indian rupee vis-a-vis the US$ since October 2006 has not only had an adverse impact on the textile exports but also led to considerable loss of jobs in the textiles sector. The worst hit apparel exports segments constitutes about 50% of textile exports and 95% of the apparel manufacturers are in the micro, small and medium enterprises sector and operate on slim margins, he added. Giving the latest foreign trade statistics for the first quarter of the current year, the Minister said that it indicates a decline of 14% in textiles exports in dollar terms and 22% in rupee terms compared to the first quarter of the previous year. He said that the total textile exports in this period have been US$ 4.01 billion compared to US$ 4.6 billion last year. On the imports front, the Minister stated that total textiles imports were of the order of Rs.12857 crore. 51% of this was on account of import of yarn and fabrics and 44% was of import of raw material. Imports have increased by little over 6% since 2005-06. However, the import of textiles as a percentage of total imports has been going down steadily and comprises only 1.49% of the total imports for 2006-07, the Minister added. With a view to strengthen the textiles industry, the Minister informed the members that the Government has taken several measures since July, 2007 which include increase in Duty Entitlement Pass Book and Duty Drawbacks rates, exemption from services tax on select services, reduction in interest rates of pre-shipment and post-shipment credit and faster clearance of arrears of terminal excise duties and Central Sales Tax. In addition to it, the Ministry of Textiles has decided to continue Technology Upgradation Fund Scheme (TUFS) and Scheme for Integrated Textile Parks (SIPP) to equip the Textiles industry with latest technology and world class infrastructure as a part of medium term strategy. The Minister also informed the Members that on 29th November this year, the Finance Minister has announced a fresh additional relief package for exporters by way of tax exemption on more services from the ambit of service tax and 2% additional subvention in pre-shipment and post-shipment credit for certain export sectors along with reduction in the import duty on number of man made fibres and their intermediates. Apart from the Relief Packages provided for arresting the decline in textile exports, the Minister stated that the Government is also providing financial assistance to the Councils for Market Development and Market Assistance. He said that the Councils are also participating in Fairs and Exhibitions with a view to enhance our profile in the established markets and also to tap potential markets in countries. Participating in the discussion, the Members expressed concern over the decline in textile exports which may lead to the loss of employment opportunities. They appreciated the various steps taken by the Ministry to ameliorate the difficulties of the textile manufacturers and exporters. The Meeting was attended, among others, by S/Shri Mahesh Kumar Kanodia, Mohan Rawale and Abdul Rashid Shaheen, Members of Parliament from Lok Sabha.

4825. (3-12-2007) NEW DELHI : The Government is providing financial support under Market Development Assistance (MDA) and Market Access Initiative (MAI) Schemes for participation in Buyer/Seller Meets, Trade Fairs and Exhibitions through Export Promotion Councils, for providing greater exposure to global markets. This information was given by the Minister of State for Textiles, Shri E.V.K.S. Elangovan, in the Lok Sabha today, in a written reply to a question by Shri Abu Ayes Mondal. However, it is not possible to quantify the generation of foreign exchange through such exhibitions/fairs. The details of activities undertaken by the Councils have been included in the Annual Reports of the Councils, which have been laid in both the Houses of Parliament. The Minister further informed that the participants in the Exhibitions/ Fairs, are eligible to receive financial assistance from the Marketing Development Assistance funds provided by the Government to meet part of their expenses.

4826. (3-12-2007) NEW DELHI : As per data generated by the DGCIS, India's textiles and clothing exports during 2006-07 were of the value of US$ 18729.93 million, as against exports valued at US$ 17520.07 million during the year 2005-06, registering a growth of 6.91%. DGCIS's latest provisional foreign trade's statistics indicate that India's exports in the first quarter of this financial year registered a decline of 14% in US$ terms compared to the corresponding period of the preceding financial year. This information was given by the Minister of State for Textiles, Shri E.V.K.S. Elangovan, in the Lok Sabha today, in a written reply to a question by Shri Harisinh Chavda and Shrimati Sangeeta Kumari Singh Deo. The Minister further informed that the textiles industry is attributing this decline mainly to the appreciation of Indian Rupee vis-a-vis US Dollar. Government has announced following steps to strengthen and support the textiles industry: (i) DEPB rates were enhanced by 3% for 9 sectors including textiles (also handlooms), RMGs and handicrafts. For other items, DEPB rates were enhanced by 2%. (ii) ECGC premium reduced by 10%. (iii) Amount of Rs.600 crore released for clearing arrears of CST reimbursement and terminal excise duty. (iv) Duty drawback rates enhanced by 10-40% of the existing rates. (v) Subvention on credit rate allowed upto 2%. (vi) Refund of service tax paid by exporters on services linked to export of goods. (vii) The Technology Upgradation Fund Scheme (TUFS) has been made operational from 1-4-1999 to facilitate the modernisation and upgradation of the sector. The TUFS has been extended beyond 31.3.2007 and has been modified in consultation with the industry and approval of the Competent Authority w.e.f. 1st November 2007. The Scheme is now in operation. For the speedy modernisation of the textiles processing sector, Government has introduced, w.e.f 20.4.2005, a credit linked capital subsidy scheme @10% under TUFS, in addition to the existing 5% interest reimbursement. (viii) The fiscal duty structure has been generally rationalised to achieve growth and maximum value addition within the country. Except for mandatory excise duty on man-made filament yarns and man-made staple fibres, the whole value addition chain has been given the option of excise exemption. (ix) The import of specified textiles and garment machinery has been allowed at a concessional rate of customs duty to encourage investment and to make our textiles product competitive in the global market. The cost of machinery has also been reduced through fiscal policy measures. (x) The Duty-free import of 21 items of trimmings and embellishment items is allowed to garment exporters. This can be upto 3% of their actual export performance during the previous year. (xi) In 2004-05 Budget, the entire textile sector, except for man-made fibre and filament yarn was provided optional exemption from excise duty. In 2005-06 Budget, Central Value-added Tax (CENVAT) on Polyester Filament Yarn has been reduced from 24% to 16%. These modifications in fiscal levies aim at attracting more investments for modernization of textile sector. (xii) To facilitate import of state of the art machinery to make our products internationally competitive in post quota regime, in 2005-06 Budget, the customs duty on textile machinery has been brought down to 10% except 23 machinery appearing in List 49 which attracts Basic Customs Duty (BCD) of 15%.

4827. (3-12-2007) NEW DELHI : The Minister of State for Textiles, Shri E.V.K.S. Elangovan, informed the Lok Sabha today, in a written reply to a question by Shri Subhash Maharia that the Government has taken a number of measures for enabling the textiles industry, including the knitwear industry, to achieve the export targets. These include extension of the Technology Upgradation Fund Scheme for modernization of machinery and acquiring state of the art technology and the Scheme for Integrated Textile Parks for equipping the industry with world class infrastructure. The Working Group on Textiles and Jute industry has recommended an outlay of Rs.3000 crores for the Scheme for Integrated Textile Parks during Eleventh Five Year Plan. An outlay of Rs.450 crore has been provided for the Scheme for Integrated Textile Parks during 2007-08. The Minister further informed that in addition, the Government has extended a package of concessions to the textiles sector which include enhancement in duty drawback rates and DEPB rates. Government is also providing funds to the sector under Market Development Assistance Scheme and Market Access Initiative Scheme, whereby funds have been provided to the knitwear sector for promotional activities and for reimbursement to exporters for participation in trade fairs and exhibitions abroad.

4828. (3-12-2007) NEW DELHI : The Ministry of Social Justice and Empowerment is implementing a scheme of Post Matric Scholarships for Scheduled Castes for studies in India. Under the scheme there is also provision for providing scholarships for Commercial Pilot License Course (CPL). The number of awards for Commercial Pilot License Course was 20 per annum. Keeping in view the acute shortage of trained pilots in the fast growing aviation sector in the country and demand from the Scheduled Caste applicants for Commercial Pilot License Course, the Government of India has decided to enhance the awards from 20 to 50 from the current financial year onwards.

4829. (3-12-2007) NEW DELHI : The Government has sponsored a project on "National Biomass Resource Atlas" to the Indian Institute of Science, Bangalore available in the country, excluding biomass plantation. Further, a potential of 5,000 MW of surplus power generation through optimum bagasse based cogeneration has been estimated in the existing sugar mills of the country, with a crushing capacity of 2,500 Tonnes Cane Crushed per Day (TCD). A cumulative capacity of 1,140 MW including bagasse cogeneration, was installed for generation of power from biomass, till March, 2007. A target for addition of 1,700 MW capacity, consisting of 500 MW of biomass power projects and 1,200 MW of bagasse cogeneration projects has been proposed during XIth plan period *i.e.* upto 2012. This information was given by the Minister of State in the Ministry of New and Renewable Sources, Sh Vilas Muttemwar in a written reply to a question in the Rajya Sabha today.

4830. (3-12-2007) NEW DELHI : The Government is encouraging promotion of biomass based off-grid small power projects for meeting unmet demand of electricity in electrified / un-electrified villages in the country under various programmes viz Village Energy Security Programme (VESP), Remote Village Electrification Programme (RVEP) and Biomass Gasifier programme. Biomass based systems / devices are encouraged for meeting inter-alia electricity needs under VESP. The RVEP aims to provide basic facilities of lighting / electricity in those remote, un-electrified census villages and remote un-electrified hamlets of electrified census villages, where grid connectivity is either not feasible or not cost effective, through various renewable energy sources, including biomass. Under RVEP, support has been provided for electrification of 47 villages / hamlets using biomass gasifier systems in the country including 10 villages / hamlets in Orissa. A total of 78 test projects have been taken up under VESP for implementation in 11 states including 12 test projects in Orissa. So far, 608 small hydro power projects (upto 25 MW station capacity) with an aggregate capacity of 2015 MW have been set up in the country. The annual estimated generation from these projects is 4028 million units per year. A target of adding 1400 MW from small hydro power has been planned during the 11th Five Year Plan. This information was given by the Minister of State in the Ministry of New and Renewable Sources, Sh Vilas Muttemwar in a written reply to a question in the Rajya Sabha today.

4831. (3-12-2007) NEW DELHI : 39 sites which could be considered suitable for wind power development have been identified in the East Coast. Wind surveys have been conducted in costal areas including East Coast under the Wind Resource Assessment programme of the Ministry 216 potential sites in 13 States/Union Territories have been identified as otential sites for setting up of wind power projects including 32 sites in the State of Andhra Pradesh. A wind power potential of about 8200 MW has been estimated in the State of Andhra Pradesh. The Government promotes setting up of commercial wind power projects in the country, by providing fiscal incentives such as concessional import duty on certain components of wind electricity generator, excise duty exemption, ten years tax holiday on income generated from wind power projects, benefit of accelerated depreciation and loan from Indian Renewable Energy Development Agency (IREDA). Technical support including detailed wind resource assessment to identify further potential sites is provided by the Centre for Wind Energy Technology (C-WET). This apart, preferential tariff is being provided for wind power in most of the potential States. Wind power projects are mostly set up as commercial projects with private investments in potential states. A wind power installed capacity of 7660 MW has been achieved in the country. It includes demonstration wind farm projects of 71 MW supported by the Ministry with the objective to open up potential areas for commercial development of wind power. Central Financial Assistance (CFA) is provided for setting up demonstration projects in those states, where commercial activity has not yet been initiated. The Ministry, Wind turbine manufacturers, Wind Power Associations, O&M providers, State Nodal Agencies etc. participate in various exhibitions to highlight the benefit and create awareness about wind energy. This information was given by the Minister of State in the Ministry of New and Renewable Sources, Sh Vilas Muttemwar in a written reply to a question in the Rajya Sabha today.

4832. (3-12-2007) NEW DELHI : The Ministry of New and Renewable Energy will extend all help, support and cooperation if such SEZs are for manufacture of renewable energy equipment. Maharashtra, Tamil Nadu, Karnataka, Madhya Pradesh and Chhattisgarh have evinced interest to facilitate setting up of such SEZs in those States. In addition, Indian Renewable Energy Development Agency (IREDA), a non-banking financial company under the administrative control of this Ministry, is envisaging formation of a Special Purpose Vehicle company for setting up, maintaining and managing a SEZ for production of renewable energy equipment. IREDA is in the process of discussing the issue with State Governments and private sector parties. This information was given by the Minister of State in the Ministry of New and Renewable Sources, Sh Vilas Muttemwar in a written reply to a question in the Rajya Sabha today.

4833. (3-12-2007) NEW DELHI : Under the Electricity Act 2003, National Electricity Policy 2005 and Tariff Policy 2006 it is obligatory upon State Electricity Regulatory Commissions to fix certain percentage for purchase of power from renewable energy sources in the area of a distribution licensee and to fix preferential tariffs for the same. Replying a question whether Government is considering to make any comprehensive policy for compulsory use of renewable energy resources through biomass, hydropower, wind, solar and municipal waste in the country, particularly for commercial establishments, as well as Government establishment, Minister of State in the Ministry of New and Renewable Sources, Sh Vilas Muttemwarstated this in a in a written reply in the Rajya Sabha today. It was further stated that grid-interactive renewable power installed capacity in the country has reached 11,063 MW as on 31.10.2007. The Government has been providing several concessions in the form of fiscal and financial incentives to encourage the use of renewable energy sources. These include capital/interest subsidy, accelerated depreciation, nil/concessional excise and customs duties. Further, as applicable to all new infrastructure projects, profits earned from sale of renewable power are exempt from Income Tax for any 10 years out of the first 15 years of project's operation. This apart, preferential tariff for grid interactive renewable power is being given in most potential States. Publicity and awareness on the use of renewable energy systems / devices is also created through print, postal and electronic media and special events like the Rajiv Gandhi Akshay Urja Diwas are being organised. District-level Advisory Committees have been constituted in the states to facilitate effective coordination of renewable energy schemes / programmes.

4834. (3-12-2007) NEW DELHI : Rajya Sabha, The Government of India has given top priority for promotion and use of bio-fuels, which includes bio-diesel and bio-ethanol. Considering the importance of promotion and use of bio-fuels for transportation, stationary and other applications, the Government of India has issued a Notification in July, 2006 giving specific responsibilities to various Union Ministries and Departments. The Government emphasise use of non-edible oils such as Jatropha curcas, Pongmia pinnata oils, etc. for production of bio-diesel and use of forest & non-forest wastelands for plantation of non-edible oil seed bearing plants. The Ministry of New & Renewable Energy has sponsored Research and Development projects on bio-fuels to some leading R&D Institutions. Process parameters for production of bio-diesel from JatroPha curcas (Ratanjot) and Pongamia pinnata (Karanja) have been optimized; field trials on diesel car have been carried out with different levels of blend of bio-diesel produced from Jatropha and Pongamia with diesel. The vehicle response has been found to be comparable with diesel vehicles. A 200 litre capacity per batch bio-diesel reactor has been designed, fabricated and developed. The MNRE has prepared a Draft National

Policy on Bio-fuels, which is under consideration of Govt. of India. The Ministry of Rural Development (MoRD) has provided financial support to nine States in 2005-06 for raising of about 18 crore seedlings of Jatropha and Pongamia and to 18 States in 2006-07 for raising of another about 18 crore seedlings of these plants. The proposal of the MoRD for establishment of the National Mission on Bio-diesel and launch of its demonstration phase (Phase-I) is under consideration of Government of India. Department of Bio-Technology has initiated a Micro-mission programme on production and demonstration of superior quality planting material of Jatropha based on oil content of 30-35% and seed yield of 3-5 tonnes per hectare. They have raised 22.48 lakh plants under nursery at different places and have initiated R&D projects for improvement of oil quality and seed yield and identification of superior varieties. The Ministry of Agriculture through National Oil Seeds and Vegetable Oils Development (NOVOD) Board is promoting Jatropha and Pongamia under the Scheme of Integrated Development of Tree borne oil seeds. The NOVOD Board has undertaken model plantation of Jatropha in about 10,000 hectare area and Karanja in about 1400 hectare area for producing parent material for undertaking large scale plantation. NOVOD Board have identified elite planting material of Jatropha and pongamia under their R&D programme and have preserved the germ plasm. Besides, NOVOD Board has sanctioned model plantation of Jatropha in 1445 hectare and Karanja in 55 hectare during 2007-08. Indian Council of Agricultural Research (ICAR), under All India Coordinated Research Project (AICRP) on agro-forestry, have initiated efforts in respect of Jatropha for collection of germ plasm, evaluation trials for growth, seed yield and oil content, hybridization, reproductive biology, agri-silvicultural trials, molecular characterization, biochemical activities and farmers training. ICAR has identified a Jatropha variety for commercial cultivation. Presently, the activities initiated on research & development for development of superior quality planting materials and bio-diesel production technologies, testing of diesel engines using bio-diesel and their demonstration have been initiated. This information was given by the Minister of State in the Ministry of New and Renewable Sources, Sh Vilas Muttemwar in a written reply to a question in the Rajya Sabha today.

4835. (3-12-2007) NEW DELHI : The Government is committed to extend 90 per cent subsidy under the Remote Village Electrification programme to all remote villages including those in the State of West Bengal A request from West Bengal to declare hills of Darjeeling as a special category area was received by the government, but it has not been approved. This information was given by the Minister of State in the Ministry of New and Renewable Sources, Sh Vilas Muttemwar in a written reply to a question in the Rajya Sabha today.

4836. (3-12-2007) NEW DELHI : A wind power capacity of 3700 MW has already been installed in the State of Tamil Nadu upto September, 2007 in locations lying mostly in Palghat, Shengottah, and Aralvoimozhi passes. About 300 MW capacity Wind Power Projects is likely to be added in the State upto

March, 2008. Total quantum of electricity likely to be generated is about 26 Billion Units from these projects. New Wind Power Projects have been planned in Theni Circle of Theni District in Tamil Nadu. This information was given by the Minister of State in the Ministry of New and Renewable Sources, Sh Vilas Muttemwar in a written reply to a question in the Rajya Sabha today.

4837. (3-12-2007) NEW DELHI : The Planning Commission estimates poverty at national and state level from the large sample surveys on Household Consumer Expenditure conducted by the National Sample Survey Organisation (NSSO). The estimates of poverty, at all India level, for 'Scheduled Tribes' (STs), 'Scheduled Castes' (SCs) and 'All' Population show that the decrease in population of STs below poverty line in rural areas has been slower over the period as compared to SCs and for 'All' population whereas decline in poverty among urban population of STs has been faster than 'All' population. Further, higher poverty ratios are observed among SCs in urban areas as compared to STs. This was stated by the Minister for Tribal Affairs, Shri P.R. Kyndiah in a reply to a question by Smt. Brinda Karat in Rajya Sabha today. He further added that a National Tribal Policy has already been formulated which among other stipulate raising the standard of living of STs as one of its objectives. This Ministry is implementing several schemes preferentially targeted to tribals living below poverty line. Under the scheme, Special Central Assistance to Tribal Sub Plan (SCA to TSP), which is a special area programme and covers the tribal population living below the poverty line, funds are provided by this Ministry to the TSP states as an additive to the State Plan, to fill up critical gaps especially in family based income generating activities and the infrastructure incidental thereto. The objective of the scheme is to boost the demand-based income generating programme meant for raising the economic and social status of tribals. National Scheduled Tribes Finance Development Corporation (NSTFDC) provides concessional financial assistance to Scheduled Tribes having annual family income upto double the poverty line income limit for undertaking self-employment ventures/ activities. Besides, the Ministry of Rural Development is also implementing poverty alleviation programmes such as Sampoorna Grameen Rozagar Yojana (SGRY) to provide wage employment and Sawarnjayanti Gram Swarozgaar Yojana (SGSY) to provide self-employment to the rural poor. A Rural Housing Programme under the name Indira Awas Yojana (IAY) is also being implemented throughout the country to provide shelter to the rural people living Below the Poverty Line (BPL). All these programmes have special provisions for the tribal population.

4838. (3-12-2007) NEW DELHI : The Ministry releases grants to the States for construction of Ashram School in Tribal Sub Plan (TSP) Areas, boys and girls hostels and Post Matric Scholarship is a continuous process. The grant-in-aid is released only if the proposals are complete in all respects including availability of land free of cost, confirmation about availability of matching share in the State budget, Utilization Certificate for grants released in previous years and physical progress reports in respect of proposals sanctioned in previous years and the availability of funds. This was stated by the Minister for Tribal Affairs, Shri P.R. Kyndiah in a reply to a question by Shri M.A.M. Ramswamy in Rajya Sabha today.

4839. (3-12-2007) NEW DELHI : Concepts of waste management have already been incorporated in the school curriculum prepared by National Council of Educational Research and Training (NCERT). Class XII Geography textbook deals with 'Environmental Pollution' and 'Urban Waste Disposal'. Similarly, textbooks for Classes VI, VII, X and XI contain Chapters on the subjects such as 'Garbage in Garbage out', ' Managing the Garbage We Produce', etc. This information was given by the Minister of State for Human Resource Development, Shri M.A.A. Fatmi in a written reply to a question by Shri Vijay J. Darda in Rajya Sabha today.

4840. (3-12-2007) NEW DELHI : Prime Minister, Dr. Manmohan Singh in his address delivered to the Nation on the occasion of the 60th Independence Day had, inter-alia, announced the setting up of eight new Indian Institutes of Technology (IITs) in the country during the Eleventh Five Year Plan. The Central Government have received requests from various State Governments including Governments of Uttar Pradesh & Orissa to set up new IITs in their States. Based on the recommendation of the Scientific Advisory Council to the Prime Minister, under the Chairmanship of Prof. C.N.R. Rao, the Government have already decided to establish three new IITs, one each in Bihar in the East, Rajasthan in the West and Andhra Pradesh in the South, during the 11th Plan period. Decision on the location of the remaining Institutes has not yet been taken. This information was given by the Minister of State for Human Resource Development, Smt. D. Purandeswari in written replies in Rajya Sabha today.

4841. (3-12-2007) NEW DELHI : Madhya Pradesh is already having various centrally funded technical educational institutions *viz.* Maulana Azad National Institute of Technology (MANIT), Bhopal; Atal Bihari Vajpayee Indian Institute of Information Technology and Management (ABV-IITM), Gwalior; Pt. Dwarka Prasad Mishra Indian Institute of Information Technology Design and Manufacturing (PDPM-IITDM), Jabalpur and Indian Institute of Management (IIM) at Indore. Further, Indian Institute of Science Education and Research (IISER) has been approved to be established in Bhopal. Planning Commission has given its 'in-principle' approval for setting up a School of Planning and Architecture in Bhopal. At present there is no proposal to upgrade Atal Bihari Vajpayee Indian Institute of Information Technology & Management, Gwalior (ABVIIITMG) as an IIT. This information was given by the Minister of State for Human Resource Development, Smt. D. Purandeswari in a written reply to a question by Smt. Maya Singh in Rajya Sabha today.

4842. (3-12-2007) NEW DELHI : Subject to the finalisation of the 11th Five Year Plan, it is proposed to provide one Central University in each of the 16 States which do not have a Central University so far, namely Bihar, Chhattisgarh, Goa Gujarat, Haryana, Himachal Pradesh, Jammu and Kashmir, Jharkhand, Karnataka, Kerala, Madhya Pradesh, Orissa, Punjab, Rajasthan, Tamil Nadu and Uttarakhand during the 11th Plan period. This information was given by the Minister of State for Human Resource Development, Smt. D. Purandeswari in a written reply to a question by Shri Uday Pratap Singh in Rajya Sabha today.

4843. (3-12-2007) NEW DELHI : The Prime Minister, Dr. Manmohan Singh addressed the 12th National Conference of National Trust organization and the Indian National Trust for Art and Cultural Heritage here today. Speaking at the occasion the Prime Minister said that we need civil society organizations and citizens to actively participate in the protection and preservation of our heritage and monuments. The Prime Minister sought active involvement of scientists, archaeologists, anthropologists, city planners and local governments in the preservation of our ancient heritage. Following is the text of the PM's Address at the occasion: "I am delighted that the International National Trusts Organization and the Indian National Trust for Art and Cultural Heritage have joined together to organise this important conference here in New Delhi. We in India are honoured to host this important meeting. Delhi after all is a particularly apt venue for such a conference, given its long and magnificent history and the wealth of its living heritage. With its 5000 years of history, Delhi, or the many Delhi's that make today's Delhi, represents a fusion of faiths, a fusion of cultures and a fusion of civilizations. Like India itself, Delhi lives in many centuries at the same time. The old and the new co-exist and inter-mingle. We have been conscious of the need to preserve, protect and promote our cultural heritage, here in India. But we cannot be satisfied with the status quo. We have not always succeeded in doing what we ought to do. Our cultural properties have been exposed to various threats - natural and manmade - over the centuries. Conquerors, explorers, colonizers, vandals and thieves have added their bit to the vagaries of nature and the passage of time. It is in recognition of this record and the need to protect and preserve what is left, that our Constitution enjoined on us the responsibility to take measures for the preservation and conservation of our heritage. We have over the years built up a legal framework and created institutional arrangements, through the Archaeological Survey of India (ASI) and the provincial Archaeological Departments. We need to look beyond the government. We need civil society organizations and citizens to actively participate in the protection and preservation of our heritage and monuments. I compliment the Indian National Trusts for Art and Cultural Heritage (INTACH) and particularly Shri Mishraji for all the good work they have done so far and wish them greater success and greater sense of fulfilment in their work in years to come. The main theme of this conference is "Heritage and Development". There is a very clear and positive correlation between the preservation of heritage and the level of development of a society. We do see that developed countries have been able to generate the resources required for protection and preservation of monuments. However, one must not draw a simplistic correlation between the two. To assume that all we need to do is more resources to do more for our heritage would be wrong and a simplistic vision. Resources are undoubtedly required. But what is more important is the mindset - a value system and a culture - that respects the past and wishes to learn from it. Unless we respect our inheritance, unless we are prepared to learn from it, we will not invest in its preservation. In developing countries like ours, a great part of public policy attention is focused on the immediate challenge of survival and development. Public opinion is often focused on issues of livelihood and security, and there is little attention paid to larger issues of culture and preservation. One must not get trapped into this binary choice between development and conservation of heritage. The two must go together. We need, therefore, strategies and policies that facilitate such a "walking on two legs".

4844. (3-12-2007) NEW DELHI : Following is the text of the President, Smt. Pratibha Devising Patil's address at the presentation of the National Awards for the empowerment of persons with disabilities and release of a postal stamp here today: I am delighted to participate in the presentation ceremony of the National Awards for the Empowerment of Persons with Disabilities, which is taking place on the occasion of the International Day of Disabled Persons. Today, we are honouring those who have made outstanding contributions for the welfare and rehabilitation of persons with disabilities. Their work is noble as it is motivated by the sensitivity of one human being towards another and at the same time, it seeks the inclusion of differently abled persons into the mainstream of society. India is committed to the full empowerment of persons with disability. It has a national policy framework and is implementing it with the support of civil society groups. India is also engaged in global efforts to seek equal opportunities for the disabled. India participated in the drafting of the UN Convention on the Rights of Persons with Disabilities; signed it on the day it was opened for signature on 30th March 2007 and was among the first seven countries to ratify the Convention on 1st October 2007. The Convention is a significant development as it recognizes disabled persons as "right-holders" rather than those who deserve sympathy and charity. Under the Convention on the Rights of Persons with Disabilities a number of obligations have been accepted by India to provide facilities, options and opportunities to persons with disabilities to live their lives with dignity. The definition of concepts like communication, specially for persons with visual and hearing disabilities, in the Convention have introduced an element of sensitivity while addressing issues like communication with reference to persons with disabilities. We fully recognize that differently abled persons are equal partners in the economic progress of the country. India, therefore, has become the first to join the Global Partnership for Disabilities and Development launched by the World Bank. India has been progressive in recognizing the rights of persons with disabilities. Legislation enacted in the last decade and half has done much to bring the issues of persons with disabilities to the forefront of discourse and planning.

The Persons with Disability Act of 1995 and the National Policy for Persons with Disabilities of 2006 are important policy frameworks. I understand that the Government is in the process of updating legislation in consultation with stakeholders throughout the country. The new obligations in the UN Convention should be taken into account while amending the Act. Persons with disabilities have a right to lead a life of dignity and self-respect, this is not a favour given to them. This can be possible only if they get adequate opportunities to pursue their education and thereafter, get gainful employment and status in society. The goal of inclusive and universal education is being pursued under the Sarva Shiksha Abhiyan. I strongly support this approach. However, there is a need to ensure that children with special needs get access to education at par with others. This means, we have to provide the right kind of teaching-learning environment, material in accessible format and barrier-free schools. Further, teachers in these schools should also be trained to provide education to children with disabilities. I have heard that in Maharashtra the state government is going to provided insurance cover to 35000 disabled students, which will include expenses for their medicines. Some other schemes for the benefit of the disabled are also being drawn up. I feel such schemes should also be implemented in other states and the Union Government should also help.

4845. (4-12-2007) NEW DELHI : In exercise of the powers conferred by clause (1) of article 217 of the Constitution of India, the President is pleased to appoint (i) Shri Justice A.C. Arumuga Perumal Adityan, (ii) Shri Justice P. Murgesen, (iii) Shri Justice Sabapath Tamilvanan and (iv) Shri Justice M. Jeyapaul, Additional Judges of the Madres High Court, as Permanent Judges of the Madras High Court, in that order of seniority, with effect from the dates they assume charge of their respective offices.

4846. (4-12-2007) NEW DELHI : In exercise of the powers conferred by clause (1) of article 224 of the Constitution of India, the President is pleased to appoint Shri Padoor Natuviledom Ravindran, to be an Additional Judge of the Kerala High Court, for a period of two years with effect from the date he assumes charge of his office.

4847. (4-12-2007) NEW DELHI : The target of employment set under Rural Employment Generation Programme (REGP) during 2006-07 was fully achieved. This was stated by Shri Mahabir Prasad, Union Minister for Micro, Small and Medium Enterprises in a written reply to a question in Lok Sabha today. The Khadi and Village Industries Commission (KVIC) conducts regular review of the implementation of the programme, in order to take stock of the implementation of the scheme, in the States and Union Territories. Separate review meetings of various regions were organized by KVIC in addition to reviewing the progress in each State/UT by calling its field officers on a regular basis. To meet the demand and also to absorb unspent balances in the field offices, targets were revised on the basis of actual project cost so that the funds availed in the field can be properly utilized. An estimated 4,771 projects are pending with various banks for sanctioning which involve about Rs. 64.62 crore of margin money. The State and Divisional offices of KVIC regularly pursue the matter with the banks in order to expedite the sanction of the projects. KVIC has also taken initiative for organizing State level review meetings on a regular basis, jointly with State Khadi and Village Industries Boards and Lead District Managers of project financing branches of banks. Such reviews are held regularly in each quarter so that the implementation of the programme is expedited. Such meetings will also take up issues such as achieving the stipulated target by each State/UT, etc. In addition to above steps, KVIC has also constituted local Committees, in each State for short listing the project proposals, promoting training and assisting/guiding the entrepreneurs in the preparation of projects and forwarding them to the banks for consideration.

4848. (4-12-2007) NEW DELHI : The eligible loan limit under the Credit Guarantee Fund Scheme for Micro and Small Enterprises has been raised from Rs.25 lakh to Rs.50 lakh with effect from 2 July 2007. All new and existing micro and small enterprises in the manufacturing and service sector (excluding retail trade) are eligible for coverage under the Scheme. This was stated by Shri Mahabir Prasad, Minister for Micro, Small and Medium Enterprises in a written reply to a question in Lok Sabha today.

4849. (4-12-2007) NEW DELHI : The Minister for Tourism and Culture Smt. Ambika Soni has said that there are 3667 monuments protected by Archaeological Survey of India (ASI). The Statewise position is at Annexure - I. Besides, there are 3573 monuments protected by State Governments. The State wise position is at Annexure - II. There are a large number of monuments which are neither under the control of Archaeological Survey of India nor under State Governments. In a written reply in the Rajya Sabha today she said, there is no database which gives details of unprotected monuments. The National Mission on Monuments and Antiquities has been launched to prepare a national database of the archaeological remains, sites, antiquities and monuments of the country. The Central Government may declare any ancient monument or archaeological site and remains as protected under the Ancient Monuments, and Archaeological Sites and Remains Act, 1958 keeping in view the importance of the site.

4850. (4-12-2007) NEW DELHI : The Union Rural Development Minister, Dr. Raghuvansh Prasad Singh has assured the NGOs and agencies engaged in the poverty eradication programmes in India of full support in their efforts. Addressing a three day conference on " What it takes to eradicate poverty' jointly organised by the Poor Areas Civil Society (PACS) programme by Development Alternatives in partnership with Department for International Development, UK (DFID) and Price Waterhouse Coopers (PWC) here today Dr.Singh stressed the need to cater the person at the bottom of our society, more specifically the rural BPL family members. Poverty can not be eradicated without getting rid of unemployment problem. This can be achieved by providing either a permanent job or mean of regular as well as sustainable income, he added. Giving details of the Swarna Jayanti Gram Swarozgar Yojana (SGSY), an ambitious employment generation schemes launched by his ministry Dr. Singh informed the formation of nearly 26 lakh Self Help Groups (SHGs) so far under the scheme. The minister called for the proper marketing logistic help to the rural artisan in proper packaging and branding of their products. Civil Society must come forward in helping neaely 5.5 crore BPL rural poor, especially the rural women engaged in Self employment activities under the SHGs to get financial help from banls, financial institutions and have their bank accounts open extending all possible help so as to become able to earn with dignity The three day Conference is being organised to analyse policies, institutional financing, direct action and other instruments that have, or have not, helped improve the lives of the poor, the marginalized and the excluded before its conclusion. Over 1000 participants and panchayat heads from remote villages covered under the programme are participating in this conference. PACS programme is conceptualized and supported by the UK Government's Department for International Development (DFID. Its Project details and results with a reach of over 13 lakh rural households in the 108 poorest districts of the country and the objective of empowering the poor in the most backward and poorest districts of India the programme has helped the poor realize their entitlements in an effective and sustainable manner.

4851. (4-12-2007) NEW DELHI : The Minister for Tourism and Culture Smt. Ambika Soni has said that there are instances of scribing and graffiti on walls in some monuments due to lack of awareness and ignorance of the value of our cultural heritage among the general public. In a written reply in the Rajya Sabha today she said, periodic awareness programmes are organized at the monuments from time to time by involving public as well as students. The watch and ward staff have been asked to be vigilant in order to detect such acts of vandalism and the supervisory staff instructed to undertake regular inspections. In addition the regular watch and ward staff, private security personnel, State police guards and CISF have also been provided for the safety and security of selected monuments. Media Campaign for raising the awareness has also been launched. Besides the above, penalty clauses exist in the Ancient Monuments and Archaeological Sites and Remains Act, 1958 in which such acts are punishable by imprisonment of 3 months or with a fine of Rs.5000/- or both.

4852. (4-12-2007) NEW DELHI : The Government today launched a comprehensive scheme for prevention of trafficking and rescue & rehabilitation of trafficked women and children. The scheme 'Ujjawala' will have specific components for reintegration and repatriation of the victims including cross border victims. Launching the scheme here today, Smt. Renuka Chowdhury, Minister for Women and Child Development said that her Ministry has adopted a multi-pronged approach, which has legislation, policy and programmatic interventions to combat trafficking in a holistic manner. Rehabilitation and reintegration of the victims is ultimate objective of the proposed scheme besides prevention of trafficking. Under the scheme, some innovative inputs like mobilization of adolescent groups through formation of Bal and Balika Sangha, community vigilance groups and sensitization of police. Immediate relief that include food and shelter and trauma care/counseling will also be provided to the rescued victims, she said. Underlining the importance of public participation to check trafficking, the Minister said that the proposed scheme will be implemented through NGO and initially about 50 projects will be taken up benefiting over 2500 victims directly. She said that one of the difficult tasks is repatriation of cross-border victims. The scheme would provide inputs for safe repatriation of such victims with shelter facilities at the borders. Corporate sectors are also being involved for skill training, capacity building, job placement and income generating activities for rescued victims, the Minister added. Referring proposed amendments to the Immoral Traffic Prevention Act, Smt. Renuka Chowdhury said that the act is being amended to target the traffickers and to withdraw those provisions, which re-victimize the victims of trafficking. She express the hope that 'Ujjawala' would go a long way in tackling the problem of trafficking, a heinous crime.

4853. (4-12-2007) NEW DELHI : Central Water Commission (CWC) under Ministry of Water Resources is monitoring storage position of 81 important reservoirs spread all over the country, of which as many as 36 reservoirs have significant hydro-power benefits with installed capacity of more than 60 MW each. The combined live storage in these 81 reservoirs at the beginning of monsoon *i.e.* 1st June, 2007 was 25 per cent of their designed capacity and stood at 69 per cent of the designed capacity as on 29th November 2007. The present storage is 90 per cent of the last year's storage and 115 per cent of last 10 years average storage during the same period. Out of these 81 reservoirs there are presently 10 reservoirs where this year's storage is 80 per cent or less than the average of previous 10 years and in the remaining 71 reservoirs the storage is more than 80 per cent of the average of previous 10 years. In order to derive the best possible benefits from the available water, Central Water Commission is keeping in touch with the Department of Agriculture and Cooperation and providing information of the weekly storage position to the Crop Weather Watch Group for evolving suitable crop strategies and also apprising the situation to various Departments and Ministries involved in Water Resources Planning. Basinwise storage position as on 29th November 2007 is as follows: The storage position in ten basins namely Ganga, Narmada, Mahi, Sabarmati, Krishna, Godavari, Tapi, Kutch. Cauvery & Neighbouring East flowing Rivers and West Flowing rivers of South is better than average of previous 10 years. Indus is flowing close to normal and Mahanadi & Neighbouring East Flowing Rivers is deficient. Out of 36 reservoirs with significant hydro potential, 8 reservoirs have storage build up less than the average of last 10 years capacity.

4854. (4-12-2007) NEW DELHI : Three proposals seeking prior approval of the Central Government for grant of prospecting licence(PL) for iron ore in favour of M/s. JSW Steel Ltd., M/s. Essar Steel Ltd. and M/s. Tata Steel Ltd. have been received from the State Government of Jharkhand since 01.01.2006 till date. The State Government has sent comparative chart of merits in respect of eligible applicants for PL in the proposals pertaining to M/s. JSW Steel Ltd. and M/s. Tata Steel Ltd. As per the information given by the State Government, M/s. Essar Steel Ltd. is the sole applicant for PL on the recommended area. The State Government has recommended grant of PL in favour of all the three companies on the ground that these companies have proposed to set up value-addition industries in the State. Till date the Government of India has conveyed prior approval for grant of PL for iron ore in favour of M/s. JSW Steel Ltd. This information was given by Dr. T. Subbarami Reddy, Minister of State for Mines in a written reply to a question in the Parliament today.

4855. (4-12-2007) NEW DELHI : The Self Help Groups (SHGs)-Bank Linkage Programme has emerged as the major Micro Finance programme in the country, which is being implemented by Commercial Banks, Regional Rural Banks and Cooperative Banks. As on March 31, 2007, 29.24 lakh SHGs have been linked to banks involving a total credit flow of Rs. 18,040 crore (cumulative figure since 1992). Similarly, under Swarnjayanti Gram Swarozgar Yojana (SGSY), 43551 SHGs were disbursed loan amounting to Rs.26,150.74 lakh, which is 64% of the total loan disbursed under the scheme, during the year 2006-07. The Nationalised Banks have a predominant share in the lending under this scheme. Banks have been advised that micro credit should form an integral part of the bank's corporate credit plan and should be reviewed at the highest level on a quarterly basis. They have also been advised to focus on relatively less banked areas, engage in capacity building and empowerment of the groups to the desired extent and adhere to then-system and practices and lending policies with a view to ensure better transparency and people friendly practices. The Government of India has introduced the Micro Financial Sector (Development and Regulation) Bill, 2007 on 20th March 2007 in the Lok Sabha, which envisages a formal statutory framework for the promotion, development and regulation of the micro finance sector. This information was given by Shri Pawan Kumar Bansal, Minister of State for Finance in reply to a question raised by Shri Shahid Siddiqui in the Rajya Sabha today.

4856. (4-12-2007) NEW DELHI : At present, 29 foreign banks have their branch operations in India. Five foreign banks have expressed their desire to open their maiden branch presence in India. Foreign banks operating in India are required to lend to the priority sector to the extent of 32% of their Adjusted Net Bank Credit (ANBC) or credit equivalent amount of Off-Balance Sheet Exposure, whichever is higher, which also includes 10% lending for small enterprises and 12% for export credit. However, no target has been stipulated for foreign banks for providing loans to farmers and scheduled-castes and scheduled-tribes. Though no stipulation has been made for foreign banks to open their branches in rural areas, as per the Branch Authorisation Policy issued by RBI, banks are encouraged to open branches in rural and under-banked areas. Further, while considering applications for opening branches, RBI gives weightage to the nature and scope of banking facilities provided by banks to common persons, particularly in rural and under-banked areas. This information was given by Shri Pawan Kumar Bansal, Minister of State for Finance in reply to a question raised by Shri Motilal Vora and Shri Satyavrat Chaturvedi in the Rajya Sabha today.

4857. (4-12-2007) NEW DELHI : The Minister of Petroleum and Natural Gas Shri Murli Deora in a written reply in the Rajya Sabha today informed the House that Public Sector Undertakings, Oil and Natural Gas Corporation Limited(ONGC) and Oil India Limited (OIL) employ the latest technology for pursuing their E&P objectives. These technologies are being inducted through work association/ contractual services or through outright purchase. In last 5 years, oil Public Sector Undertakings (PSUs) have added more reserves than the oil & gas production in corresponding years. "ONGC has made two gas discoveries during 2006-07 in Mahanadi offshore as a result of exploratory efforts" Shri Deora added. Referring to the estimated Hydrocarbon resources are about 28 billion tones, he informed that out of this, about 8.8 billion tones of in-place reserves have been established. During XI plan period, 80% of Indian sedimentary basinal area will be under exploration including deepwater and frontier areas also. Centre for High Technology (CHT), a registered society under Ministry of Petroleum & Natural Gas, has signed an agreement with Shell Global Solutions International B.V.(Shell GSI) of the Netherlands for an "Integrated Business Improvement" for four Indian refineries at Mathura (IOCL), Chennai (CPCL), Vizag (HPCL) and Kochi (BPCL). As our economy is growing at a rate of about 9% of Gross Domestic Products (GDP), Shri Deora informed that demand for petroleum products is likely to increase from 119.8 MMT in 2006-07 to 131.767 MMT in 2011-12. At present, there is 70% import dependence for petroleum products. In 2006-07, crude oil processing was about 141.463 Million Metric Tonnes (MMT), which is 11.4% higher than 126.986 MMT in 2005-06.

4858. (4-12-2007) NEW DELHI : Negotiations between India and Japan are going on for putting in place a bilateral currency swap arrangement to take care of short term liquidity needs during a balance of payment crisis. The proposed swap arrangement is essentially a bilateral agreement between India and Japan to exchange a maximum amount US $ 3 billion for respective domestic currency to meet temporary Balance of Payment (BOP) problems, by either country, for an initial period of 90 days at a specified interest rate payable on dollar amounts received and thereafter through renewals, up to a maximum period of 630 days. The proposal of Ministry of Railways namely "Dedicated Multi-modal High Axle Load Freight Corridor with computerized train control system on Delhi-Mumbai and Delhi-Howrah routes" has been posed to Government of Japan seeking

Official Development Assistance (ODA). However, the final decision regarding the sources of funding for this project, including Japanese assistance is under consideration of Ministry of Railways. This information was given by Shri Pawan Kumar Bansal, Minister of State for Finance in reply to a question raised by Shri B.J. Panda and Ms. Pramila Bohidar in the Rajya Sabha today.

4859. (4-12-2007) NEW DELHI : Government has so far awarded 14 exploration blocks (one onland and thirteen offshore blocks) in Mahanadi basin in and around Orissa. Oil India Limited (OIL) is presently carrying out hydrocarbon exploration works in the onland block (MN-ONN-2000/1), awarded under second round of New Exploration Licensing Policy (NELP-II). OIL is the operator in this block with a participating interest of 40% while other public sector undertakings (PSUs), Indian Oil Corporation Ltd. (IOC), GAIL (India) Ltd. and Oil and Natural Gas Corporation Ltd. (ONGC) are partners in this block with a 20% participating interest each. OIL has already completed the first phase of work and carried out acquisition, processing and interpretation (API) of 463.68 Ground Line Kilometres (GLK) of 2D seismic data against the commitment of 200 GLK of 2D seismic. The block is now in the second phase of the exploration period and OIL is planning to drill one well in Mahanadi onland basin in the district of Cuttack. In addition, Oil & Natural Gas Corporation Limited (ONGC) and Reliance Industries Limited (RIL) are carrying out hydrocarbon exploration in 13 blocks in offshore areas of Mahanadi basin. Minimum Work Programme commitment in first phase of exploration is 65,390 km of 2D seismic, 12,900 sq.km. of 3D seismic and 12 exploratory wells. ONGC has made two gas discoveries in Mahanadi offshore as a result of exploratory efforts. The above information was given by the Minister of Petroleum and Natural Gas Shri Murli Deora in a written reply in the Rajya Sabha today.

4860. (4-12-2007) NEW DELHI : The Minister of Petroleum and Natural Gas Shri Murli Deora informed the House in a written reply in the Rajya Sabha today that as passing on the entire impact of the steep increase in the global oil prices to the consumers would have resulted in hardship to the common man, the retail selling prices of petrol, diesel, PDS Kerosene and domestic LPG have not been increased in tandem with the international oil prices. He stressed that Government continues to provide subsidy support to PDS kerosene and domestic LPG. The Global prices of crude oil and petroleum products since 2004, have remained high and volatile. The price of crude oil and petroleum products in the international market fluctuates on daily basis. Shri Deora further said that the Government has adopted a principle of equitable burden sharing between the Government and the oil PSUs to protect the interest of vulnerable sections of society. In this context, Government had issued oil bonds to the extent of Rs. 11,500 crore and Rs. 24,121 crore during the years 2005-06 and 2006-07 respectively to Public Sector Oil Marketing Companies (OMCs) as part of compensation for the under-recoveries incurred by them. For the year 2007-08, Government has approved the issuance of oil bonds to the tune of 42.7% of total under-recoveries. The upstream oil companies have also contributed Rs. 14,000 crore and Rs. 20,507 crore during the years 2005-06 and 2006-07 respectively and Rs. 8,788 crore during the period Apr-Sep'07, by offering discounts on crude oil and petroleum products. The prices of sensitive petroleum products are fixed by the OMCs in consultation with the Government. He emphasized that the Government is closely monitoring international oil prices and will continue to protect interest of consumers.

4861. (4-12-2007) NEW DELHI : ONGC Videsh Ltd. (OVL) and its partner IPR Energy Red Sea Inc. have made a significant new oilfield discovery in its first Exploration well North Ramadan-I drilled in the North Ramadan Concession, Gulf of Suez, Egypt. The discovery was made in April 2007 and well was tested at naturally flowing rate of 2979 barrels of oil per day. As per provisions in Production Sharing Contract, CONTRACTOR (ONGC Videsh Ltd. and IPR Energy Red Sea Inc.) have the right and the obligation to freely export and otherwise dispose of the entitled Crude Oil. However, the priority shall be given to meet the requirements of the Arab Republic of Egypt (A.R.E.) market. Each country has model collaboration agreement for oil sharing and agreements are generally based on such model agreements. Though, the efforts are being made to have right on its share of equity oil, however, in case of some countries where such rights are not available, the agreements are entered on the basis of commercial considerations. The above information was given by the Minister of Petroleum and Natural Gas Shri Murli Deora in a written reply in the Rajya Sabha today.

4862. (4-12-2007) NEW DELHI : State Governments are the owners of the dams and as such the responsibility of dam safety rests with them. The role of Central Government is confined to giving advisory services with regard to safety and rehabilitation of such dams. As per the Dam Safety Procedures laid down by the Standing Committee of Dams in India, all large dams (irrespective of their age) are required to be inspected twice a year during the pre- and post-monsoon periods. These inspections are to be carried out by the Dam Safety Organizations of respective States / owners of dams and the consolidated information is to be submitted in the form of Annual Reports to Dam Safety Monitoring Directorate, Central Water Commission. An all Party Delegation of Government of Kerala met the Prime Minister on 31.8.2006 and gave a memorandum, wherein, they have requested Government of India for immediate intervention in the matter so as to persuade Tamil Nadu to come forward for an amicable settlement of the issue. They have also raised the issues of Government of Tamil Nadu's non-cooperation in the joint inspection of the seepage management, instrumentation of the Mulla Periyar Dam and not allowing Kerala Officers to access the basic data for evaluating the safety of the dam. Meanwhile, the Supreme Court passed an order on 25.9.2006 on the suit filed by Government of Tamil Nadu praying for Declaration of Kerala Irrigation and Water Conservation (Amendment) Act 2006 passed by Kerala Legislature as unconstitutional, stating "the two State Governments independently or with the intervention of the Union of India may try to sort out, if possible, the dispute". The Union Minister (WR) convened an inter-State meeting of the Chief Ministers of States of Tamil Nadu & Kerala on Mullaperiyar dam issue on 29.11.2006 at New Delhi. The Union Minister (WR) further discussed matter with the Ministers (WR/PW) from the States of Tamil Nadu & Kerala on 18.12.2006. The States of Tamil Nadu and Kerala reiterated their respective stand in the meetings and no consensus could be reached regarding a solution acceptable to both States. This information was given by the Minister of State for Water Resources, Shri Jai Prakash Narayan Yadav in response to a question by Shri A. Vijayaraghavan in the Rajya Sabha today.

4863. (4-12-2007) NEW DELHI : There are 99 dams in the country (as per the National Register of Large Dams 2002) which have become more than 100 years old. It cannot be said that the time limit of utility of most of them has expired, as they are still being utilized for the purpose for which they were built. Any properly engineered and maintained dam has no limit of life with regard to its safety. As per the records available in Central Water Commission, no dam has been reported weak. Maintenance of the dams is the responsibility of the State Governments/dams owners. At national level, a Dam Safety Organisation (DSO) was established in Central Water Commission in May 1979 to develop guidelines for Safety Inspection of Dams, Check Lists, Formats for Data Book and Periodical Inspection of dams and other dam safety literature which have been provided to all the States for guidance of the field engineers. A draft Legislation on Dam Safety has also been prepared and circulated to all the States for adoption. This information was given by the Minister of State for Water Resources, Shri Jai Prakash Narayan Yadav in response to a question by Shri Amir Alam Khan in the Rajya Sabha today.

4864. (4-12-2007) NEW DELHI : As per information received from the Ministry of Environment & Forests, water cess is levied and collected by the State Pollution Control Boards for prevention and control of water pollution. Differential rates of cess are collected depending upon the use of water, the rate being higher where pollution load is expected to be more, which results in higher cost of pollution abatement and varies from 2 paise per 1000 litres for domestic purposes to 30 paise per 1000 litres for industrial purposes. The Ministry of Water Resources has no proposal for imposing a higher rate of cess on ground water on bottled water units, commensurating with their profit margin. This information was given by the Minister of State for Water Resources, Shri Jai Prakash Narayan Yadav in response to a question by Shri B.K. Hariprasad in the Rajya Sabha today.

4865. (4-12-2007) NEW DELHI : There are polluted stretches of various rivers in India, with the Ministry of Environment & Forests providing assistance to various State Governments for implementation of pollution abatement works under the National River Conservation Plan. Government of Punjab have informed that due to urbanization and industrialization, pollution is increasing in the rivers passing through the State. In respect of Yamuna river, in seven rounds of observations made by the Central Pollution Control Board in June-Dec. 2006, the water quality at Palla was meeting the desired criteria of Dissolved Oxygen (DO); Biochemical Oxygen Demand (BOD) in three rounds and did not meet the criteria in respect of Total Coliform. Water quality did not meet any of these criteria in Yamuna at Agra Canal (Madanpur Khadar), Agra Canal (Okhla) and Okhla after confluence with Shahdara drain and Nizamuddin Bridge. As per Government of NCT of Delhi, the water quality of river Yamuna is meeting the criteria with respect to DO and BOD at Palla and, after confluence of Najafgarh Drain, it does not meet the criteria of DO, BOD and Coliform. Upper Yamuna River Board have informed that Delhi Jal Board have reported from time to time that high concentration of ammonia in Yamuna waters has been found at Wazirabad due to releases of untreated effluents from Haryana. However, as per the Government of Haryana, pollution in river Yamuna is well within the norms when it enters Delhi State and joint sampling is done by the State and Central Pollution Control Boards on monthly basis and the results are within limits. In respect of river Ghaggar, its waters are polluted by effluents discharged from factories located in the various States en route. In respect of silting in rivers, Government of Punjab have informed rivers Sutlej, Beas and Ravi of Punjab have been tamed by construction of dams with the result that free flow of water and accompanying silt in these rivers is minimal. Ghaggar is a seasonal river having flash floods and brings a lot of sand/silt. However, as the sand is being mined, there is hardly any increase in the net silt load. As per Government of Haryana, there is no trend of silt increase in rivers Ghaggar and Yamuna and silt is also removed from river bed through different quarries. Upper Yamuna River Board have informed that as a result of pollution, the water carrying capacity of the river is not affected. Silting in rivers is a natural phenomena, the magnitude of which varies from year to year. In view of mining/ quarrying of sand/ silt, the Governments of Punjab and Haryana have indicated that there is no substantial/ adverse effect on the carrying capacity of the rivers. As per Government of Haryana, it is neither practical nor necessary to artificially increase the carrying capacity of the rivers. As per Government of Punjab, there is no necessity at present for framing any policy in this matter. This information was given by the Minister of State for Water Resources, Shri Jai Prakash Narayan Yadav in response to a question by Shri Ajay Singh Chautala in the Rajya Sabha today.

4866. (4-12-2007) NEW DELHI : The Artificial Recharge of Ground Water Advisory Council under the Ministry of Water Resources in its 2nd meeting held on 12th September, 2007 at New Delhi discussed the steps to be taken for studying the impact of climate change on India's hydrological cycle, besides other issues. Steps taken by the Ministry of Water Resources for rain water harvesting and water conservation include:- (i) Dissemination of information on rain water harvesting and ground water recharge to all stakeholders. (ii) Conducting of mass awareness and training programmes on rain water harvesting. (iii) Institution of National

Water Award and Bhoomijal Samvardhan Puraskar in the Ministry of Water Resources for NGOs/Gram Panchayats/Urban Local Bodies. This information was given by the Minister of State for Water Resources, Shri Jai Prakash Narayan Yadav in response to a question by Prof. Alka Balram Kshatriya and Smt. Shobhana Bhartia in the Rajya Sabha today.

4867. (4-12-2007) NEW DELHI : There are no specific recommendation of Planning Commission regarding division of responsibility in handling water by various Ministries resulting in mulplicity and dilution of authority/accountability. However, in the Tenth Plan Document, the need for proper coordination was duly emphasized and a suggestion was made for single administrative Ministry for water and to begin with, setting up of a National Water Resources Programme Coordination Committee under the chairmanship of Member, Planning Commission was indicated. The Standing Committee on Water Resources in its observation had desired the Ministry of Water Resources to urge the Planning Commission to take urgent steps in this regard. The Planning Commission has since reviewed the position. Keeping in view the responsibilities already vested with the Ministry of Water Resources and inter-Ministerial coordination machineries already in position, the Planning Commission is of the view that the existing administrative arrangements in regard to the water sector need not be disturbed for the present.

4868. (4-12-2007) NEW DELHI : Ministry of Environment & Forests has informed that there are news reports based on studies carried out in Brazil which inter-alia includes assessment of emission of Methane from reservoirs of India. The Ministry of Environment & Forests has also informed that this study is without any Indian experimental data and no scientific study, as on date, has been brought out pertaining to Methane emission from the reservoirs of Indian Dams. However, measures in respect of removal of vegetation *i.e.* trees etc. from the reservoir area with a view to reduce the emission of Methane from reservoir constitute part of the planning process. This information was given by the Minister of State for Water Resources, Shri Jai Prakash Narayan Yadav in response to a question by Smt. Hema Malini in the Rajya Sabha today.

4869. (4-12-2007) NEW DELHI : The Bhakra Beas Management Board (BBMB), constituted under the Punjab Reorganisation Act, 1966 (Act) was envisaged, inter alia as per Section 79(1)(c) of the Act, for the administration, maintenance and operation of the irrigation headworks of Rupur (Ropar), Harike and Ferozepur. Government of Punjab has not transferred the said headworks to BBMB. The issue of transfer of control of the said headworks by Punjab to BBMB was discussed in Inter-State meetings involving States of Punjab, Haryana and Rajasthan. However, no agreement was arrived. The matter is now sub judice. Hon'ble High Court of Rajasthan in a judgement dated 02.05.05 in a Civil Writ Petition directed BBMB to take over control of the above head works from Punjab within 30 days. The State of Punjab filed a Special Leave Petition against the judgement and Hon'ble

Supreme Court stayed the operation of the order of the Hon'ble High Court of Rajasthan. The matter is now before the Hon'ble Supreme Court and is dependant on its orders. This information was given by the Minister of State for Water Resources, Shri Jai Prakash Narayan Yadav in response to a question by Shri Lalit Kishore Chaturvedi in the Rajya Sabha today.

4870. (4-12-2007) NEW DELHI : "National Policy on Flood Control" has not been formulated. However, the issues related to flood management are duly addressed in the National Water Policy, 2002. Activities related to flood management are implemented by the respective State Governments from their own resources. The State-wise allocation for the year 2007-08 for activities under plan schemes is given below, Government of India provides technical support through studies and maintaining a network of flood forecasting stations. Assistance is also provided for flood management works in critical reaches including bank erosion activities under central schemes. States also receive financial assistance under Calamity Relief Fund (CRF) and National Contingency Calamity Fund (NCCF).

4871. (4-12-2007) NEW DELHI : As per proposals received from the State Governments/UT Administrations, an additional 1,66,96,676 children are likely to be covered in 3479 Educationally Backward Blocks (EBBs) in 2007-08 under the Mid-Day Meal Scheme after its extension to the upper primary stage. The additional amount allocated and released to States/UTs towards extension of Mid Day Meal Scheme to upper primary classes in 3479 EBBs for 2007-08 is at Annexure-1. Funds are allocated to States/UTs on the basis of the State proposals approved by the Mid Day Meal Programme Approval Board (MDM-PAB) every year. Enrolment in primary schools (classes I - V) has steadily increased from 107.1 million in 1995-96, the year in which Mid Day Meal Scheme was introduced, to 130.8 million in 2004-05. Similarly, drop out rate (Primary) is also decreased from 42.07 in 1995-96 to 29.00 in 2004-05. State wise details of enrolment and drop out rate (primary) for the years 1995-96 and 2004-05 are at Annexure-2. This progress is due to Mid Day Meal Scheme in combination with various interventions provided under different schemes of the Central and State Governments for universalization of Elementary Education. This information was given by the Minister of State for Human Resource Development, Shri M.A. A. Fatmi in a written reply in Lok Sabha today.

4872. (4-12-2007) NEW DELHI : A sum of Rs.7324 Crores was provided in the Union Budget 2007-08 for the Mid Day Meal Scheme, representing 37% increase over the budget provision for 2006-07. Funds are released on the basis of the State proposals approved by the Mid Day Meal Programme Approval Board (MDM-PAB) every year. A statement indicating the State wise release of funds as on 29.11.2007 under different components of the programme for primary (Classes I -V) and upper primary (Classes VI-VIII) is annexed. In addition, the cost of food grains is reimbursed to FCI and Transportation costs are reimbursed based on claims preferred by the State Governments/UT Administrations. This information was given by the Minister of State for Human Resource Development, Shri M.A. A. Fatmi in a written reply in Lok Sabha today.

4873. (4-12-2007) NEW DELHI : The mineral production from mining and quarrying sector in September 2007 marginally decreased by 0.81% as compare to that of the preceding month. However, the mineral sector has shown a positive growth of 5.26% during the current financial year *i.e.* April-September 2007 as compare to that of the previous year. The mineral production in September 2007 was also higher by 5.99% as compare to that of the corresponding month of previous year. The total value of mineral production (excluding atomic & minor minerals) in the country during September 2007 was Rs. 6683 crore. The contribution of coal was the highest at Rs. 2537 crore (38%). Next in the order of importance were: petroleum (crude) Rs. 1556 crore, iron ore Rs. 1091 crore, natural gas (utilized) Rs. 754 crore, lignite Rs. 198 crore and limestone Rs. 164 crore. These six minerals together contributed about 94% of the total value of mineral production in September 2007. Production level of important minerals in September 2007 were: coal 314 lakh tones, lignite 24 lakh tones, natural gas (utilized) 2609 million cu.m., petroleum (crude) 28 lakh tonnes, bauxite 1318 thousand tonnes, chromite 356 thousand tones, copper conc. 21 thousand tones, gold 248 kg., iron ore 140 lakh tonnes, lead conc. 9 thousand tones, manganese ore 168 thousand tones, zinc conc. 92 thousand tones, apatite & phosphorite 155 thousand tones, dolomite 322 thousand tones, limestone 140 lakh tones and magnesite 19 thousand tones. A nominal production of diamond was also reported in the current month. In September 2007 the output of bauxite increased 12.97%, iron ore 12.20%, apatite & phosphorite 8.12%, zinc conc. 3.30% and magnesite 3.29 percent. The production of copper conc. maintained the level of previous month and that of natural gas (utilized) decreased marginally. Whereas the production of limestone decreased 1.18%, coal 1.47%, lignite 1.71%, petroleum (crude) 2.85%, manganese ore 3.37%, chromite 4.11%, gold 5.34%, lead conc. 8.81% and dolomite 9.64 percent. Ministry of Mine, Government of India New Delhi, December 4, 2007/Agrahayana 13, 1929

4874. (4-12-2007) NEW DELHI : Chitranjan Locomotive Works (CLW) produced 97 electric locomotives against the target of 94 electronic locomotives and Diesel Locomotive Works (DLW) produced 137 diesel locomotives against the target of 127 diesel locomotives during first seven months of the fiscal 2007-08 (April-October 2007). Rail Coach Factory (RCF) produced 783 coaches against the target of 778 coaches where as Integral Coach Factory (ICF) produced 668 coaches against the target of 682 coaches during the same period. Rail Wheel Factory (RWF) produced 73755 wheels and 22336 axles against the target of 73072 wheels and 22335 axles during April-October 2007. During the month of October 2007, CLW, DLW, ICF, RCF and RWF have produced 18 electric locomotives, 19 diesel locomotive, 118 coaches, 136 coaches, 11083 wheels and 2001 axles respectively against the target of 18 electric locomotives, 18 diesel locomotive, 130 coaches,

133 coaches, 10400 wheels and 2000 axels. Except ICF, all other units have exceeded or attain the target. The punctuality percentage of mail/express trains was 92.8 per cent in Broad Gauge and 99.5 per cent in Metre Gauge during the month of October 2007 compared to 92.4 per cent and 99.3 per cent respectively during the same period last year. Railways have realized an amount of Rs. 21 crore approximately during the month of October 2007 through ticket checking.

4875. (4-12-2007) NEW DELHI : Following is the text of the keynote address by Dr. Anbumani Ramadoss, Union Minister for Health & Family Welfare, today at the New Delhi International Ministerial Conference on Avian and Pandemic Influenza: "Welcome to incredible India and welcome to this almost incredible conference. This conference is momentous. It has woven so many of us together into a world that is truly united in the fight against Avian and Pandemic Influenza. When India hosted the Asia Conference on Avian Influenza in June last year I had one apprehension. Were we being over zealous by engaging with Avian and Pandemic Influenza so frequently? One year down the line, our concern now is whether we all our doing enough to keep the pandemic at bay.The global threat of Avian & Pandemic Influenza continues. Over 61 countries have experienced outbreaks of Avian Influenza since 2003. To date, millions of birds have been culled, and the economic cost to the affected countries has been colossal. It is likely that the virus infections among domestic poultry have become endemic in some parts of the world. While the number of people infected appears small, the case fatality rate is very high with over 61% deaths. We will hear about these facts in greater detail as we progress with the Conference. But, the question we need to ask upfront is whether as a global community we are really doing enough? We could all draw solace from the UN System & World Bank Progress Report on the Global State of Influenza Pandemic Readiness and Capacity to Control Highly Pathogenic Avian Influenza released a few days ago. The report confirms improvement in country responses to Avian Influenza. The report, however, also underscores the need for greater effort in coordination of pandemic planning between countries. This conference is a manifestation of that much-needed 'greater effort'. We are indeed encouraged that more than 600 delegates from 105 countries and 20 international and inter governmental organizations have congregated here. We are immensely pleased to have with us seventy ministers from the public health and animal health sectors. In a world that is so intrinsically connected, avian & pandemic influenza can only be controlled if all countries work towards this agenda. Any country that lags in its efforts could become the weak link that negates the consolidated efforts of the rest of the world. We acknowledge that the capacities to respond to the threat of a pandemic would vary from country to country, given the wide range of cultural, economic and political differences. But we must stand together and move forward as one, in our commitment and resolve to fight this virus. We can collectively achieve this by setting agreed-to milestones and work towards realizing them with sincerity and transparency. For example, most countries have prepared their plans for responding to an outbreak of Avian and Pandemic

Influenza. India has clearly defined Action Plans for both animal and human health. We could agree that all of us will test these plans through mock drills or other similar mechanisms periodically. Similarly, we all agree that we need to build capacity for a sustained response to the pandemic. We now need to work towards actualizing this capacity. In other words, it is now necessary for each country to develop its own road map towards creating such a capacity with clearly defined milestones to measure success and an action plan for doing so. Before the conclusion of this conference, India would share with all of you, its vision of such a road map. I am sure that you would find it to be a simple yet effective tool in creating national and global capacity to resist and fight the threat of an avian influenza pandemic. This vision for the road map is based, amongst other things, on India's experience in successfully containing the outbreaks in 2006 and 2007. I take pride in informing you that during the avian influenza outbreaks in poultry, India maintained absolute transparency in sharing information promptly. We did not quibble over issues of pathogenocity of the virus nor about the fact that in 2007 the disease was confined and localized to a small farm of less than 150 birds in the north eastern part of the country. The containment measures mounted by the Government of India in the affected areas were greater than those known to be followed internationally. For instance, given the nature of the outbreak and the involvement of backyard poultry, India took a bold decision to cull birds across a radius of 10 kms. in the 2006 outbreak. We were, therefore, able to revert to the avian influenza free status within three to five months. Prompt and reasonable compensation has been the hallmark of our containment operations. Our National Action Plan for Preparedness, Control & Containment of Avian Influenza, establishes the framework for the compensation mechanism. The Plan recognizes that the programme of culling of affected birds will succeed only if a system of adequately compensating the poultry farmers is put in place and activated immediately after the outbreak of Avian Influenza is confirmed. The plan emphasizes that any expenditure incurred on compensation is more than justified by way of bringing about effective control of the disease. In addition compensation is paid for feed and feed materials destroyed in operations. The Government of India paid more than US $19, 47,619 as compensation for poultry and feed / feed material in 2006. More than US $2, 23,810 have been paid for birds culled in the 2007 outbreak.

4876. (4-12-2007) NEW DELHI : Shri Kamal Nath, Union Minister of Commerce and Industry, has stated that there is a vast scope and enormous potential to increase the bilateral trade and investment relations between India and Canada, especially in the field of environment technology. While welcoming Mr. Gordon Campbell, Premier, Province of British Columbia, Canada, last evening along with trade delegation and senior representatives from educational institutes and life science companies, the Commerce & Industry Minister informed that a Bilateral Investment Promotion and Protection Agreement is under negotiation between the two countries. Elaborating the purpose of his visit, Mr. Gordon Campbell informed that this visit was to develop trade and investment relationships and to discuss business opportunities apart from sharing expertise in urban infrastructure projects. During the discussions with Shri Kamal Nath, he informed that the British Columbia Province has innovative and skilled workforce, rich natural resources and is an excellent gateway location between North America and Asia to provide the foundation for almost unlimited economic opportunities. Shri Kamal Nath also emphasised that India's main strength is in the field of talent and enterprise, scientific manpower and skilled workforce. British Columbia occupies a million square kilometres, and is larger than California, Oregon and Washington states combined or combined area of France and Germany. British Columbia is a world leader in environmental technologies with approximately 1300 companies active across the province generating revenues of $ 1.9 billion and employing about 18,000 people and is home to 15 research centres of excellence and other clean technology research institutes. The bilateral trade in goods, between India and Canada, reached almost a record US $ 2 billion during 2006-07. India's exports to Canada include textiles & clothing, jewellery, diamonds and chemicals as well as variety of manufactured items. Canada's exports to India are dominated by pulp & paper, newsprint, metals and agricultural products. India is the 33rd largest source of foreign direct investment (FDI) in Canada and FDI in Canada by Indian software companies has increased rapidly. Top sectors attracting FDI inflows (from January 2000 to July 2007) from Canada are services sector (47.69%); chemicals - other than fertilizers (7.66%); computer software & hardware (6.44%); metallurgical industries (6.32%); and trading (6.13%).

4877. (4-12-2007) NEW DELHI : A Three-day International Conference on Avian and Pandemic Influenza is being held here from today. The inaugural plenary session was attended by representatives from over 100 countries. Director Generals of international organizations like WHO, FAO, World Bank OIE etc. participated in today's inaugural function. Shri Sharad Pawar, Minister of Agriculture, Dr. Anbumani Ramadoss, Minister of Health and Family Welfare, Dr. Margaret Chan, DG, WHO, Mr. Jacques Diouf, DG, FAO, Dr. Bernard Wallat, DG, OIE also participated in today's function. Dr. Anbumani Ramadoss, Minister of Health and Family Welfare delivered the keynote address. The Conference has 12 Sessions on various subjects pertaining to Avian and Pandemic Influenza. A Road Map prepared by India will be presented to the Conference on the last day *i.e.* December 6, 2007. Dr. Manmohan Singh, Prime Minister of India will address the Delegates on December 5, 2007.

4878. (4-12-2007) NEW DELHI : National Curriculum Framework-2005 (NCF-2005) was brought out by NCERT through a wide-ranging process of discussions and deliberations. The document was approved by Central Advisory Board of Education (CABE) in September, 2005. In accordance with NCF-2005, NCERT has developed new syllabi for all the stages of school education and initiated the process of textbook development in a phase-wise manner. Presently, the textbooks for classes I, II, III, IV, VI, VII, IX, X, XI and XII are available and textbooks for classes V and VIII will be made available from the academic session 2008-09. Further, considering the prevailing diversity and federal character of our nation, serious engagement of all States and UTs in translating the NCF ideas into reality is a major concern. In this context, with the financial and academic support of NCERT, States/UTs are engaged in the task of revising their syllabi and textbooks. This information was given by the Minister of State for Human Resource Development, Smt. D. Purandeswari in a written reply in Lok Sabha today.

4879. (4-12-2007) NEW DELHI : As per information compiled by Registrar General of India (Ministry of Home Affairs), from 2001 Census, there are 264 languages in India which are spoken by less than 10,000 people each. The future of these languages is threatened due to limited number of speakers. The Ministry of Human Resource Development has, therefore, initiated steps to formulate a new scheme for Preservation and Development o Languages not covered by 8th Schedule (Bharat Bhasha Vikas Yojana). The scheme is based on the recommendations of Working Group on Languages and Book Promotion under XIth Plan set up by Planning Commission. This information was given by the Minister of State for Human Resource Development, Smt. D. Purandeswari in a written reply in Lok Sabha today.

4880. (4-12-2007) NEW DELHI : The 53rd meeting of the Central Advisory Board of Education (CABE) in which political leaders and experts participated, held on 14-15 July 2005, discussed the draft Central Legislation to translate into action the 86th Constitutional Amendment aimed at making education a Fundamental Right for all children in the 6-14 years age group. Gender-wise, stage-wise and State-wise dropout rates for the year 2004-05 are annexed. Sarva Shiksha Abhiyan (SSA) is being implemented in partnership with the State and Union Territories to provide for universalisation of elementary education in the country in a time bound manner. To decrease the incidence of dropout, SSA provides, inter alia, for opening of new schools, strengthening of school infrastructure, appointment of additional teachers, interventions for enrolment of out of school children, promotion of girls education, inclusive education for children with special needs, training of teachers, supply of free textbooks for girls, SC & ST students and interventions for promoting community participation. As per a Scholarship scheme introduced by Central Board of Secondary Education (CBSE) from the academic session 2006-07, a girl studying in school affiliated to CBSE who is the only child of her parents and who secures 60% or more marks in class X examination for the year 2006 onwards is given scholarship of Rs. 500 per month for studying in classes XI and XII in a CBSE affiliated school which charges tuition fee of not more than Rs. 1000 per month during the academic year 2005-06. This information was given by the Minister of State for Human Resource Development, Smt. D. Purandeswari in a written reply to a question by Shri Rayapati Sambasiva Rao and others in Lok Sabha today.

4881. (4-12-2007) NEW DELHI : India is presently engaged in negotiations for a broad based Trade and Investment Agreement (TIA) only with the European Union (EU) among the western countries. The negotiations commenced on 28.6.2007 and both sides have so far discussed textual proposals. Trade and investment agreements are aimed at promoting bilateral trade by removing barriers to trade in goods and services and allowing market access through investment. This information was given by Dr. Ashwani Kumar, Minister of State for Industry, in a written reply in the Lok Sabha today.

4882. (5-12-2007) NEW DELHI : Shri Sushilkumar Shinde, Union Minister of Power issued a Statement on 5th December 2007 responding to the UP Chief Minister's Statement that electricity is the Central Government's responsibility and not of the State Government. Shri Shinde clarified that in our Constitution, Electricity is in the Concurrent List of Subjects. In fact, it is the main responsibility of the State Government to distribute and generate electricity. The Central Government's role is supplementary in nature. Shri Shinde said, "I think the Chief Minister needs to appreciate this Constitutional provision." In the last two Five Year Plans, UP has added only 536 MW of new capacity, whereas they should have added more than 3,000 MW keeping in view their requirement. Presently, UP has the peaking shortage of about 23% which is 2,500 MW. The Plant Load Factor that is the efficiency of the State's thermal power plants has declined to 56% against the national average of 77%. If UP were to run its power plants as per the national average of PLF, it could have generated additional power of 1,000 MW cutting its present shortage by 40%. Uttar Pradesh's State distribution network has very high aggregate technical and commercial losses averaging 45%. UP is the most indisciplined State with regard to grid discipline, regularly overdrawing power and putting the entire national grid at risk. The State has overdrawn 1800 Million Units between April and October 2007. Apart from overdrawing, the State has failed to pay Rs. 700 crores of overdrawal charges. This is the only State in India to have overdrawn and failed to pay to such an extent. The State has been issued a Show Cause Notice by the Central Electricity Regulatory Commission in this regard. Despite all this, the Central Government has been doing its utmost to alleviate the power situation for the people of Uttar Pradesh. The State receives the highest allocation from Central Generating Stations in India. The Central Generating Stations give about 4,800 MW of electricity to Uttar Pradesh. Under the Rajiv Gandhi Grameen Vidyutikaran Yojana, Uttar Pradesh has been sanctioned Rs. 2100 crores which is one-third of the entire amount sanctioned in the country. Similarly, in APDRP, the State has been sanctioned projects worth Rs. 1090 crores.

4883. (5-12-2007) NEW DELHI : The number of retired defence civilian pensioners is assessed to be 5, 08,537 as on 01.04.2007, including family pensioners. While Defence Civilian pensioners of the three Services receive their pension from Defence Pensions Budget (Demand No.21), some other pensioners, such as those from the Defence Accounts Department and the Coast Guard Organisation are paid pension out of the Civil Pension Budget (Demand No.39). Canteen facilities have not been extended to retired defence civilian pensioners because there is no provision. This information was given by the Defence Minister Shri AK Antony in a written reply to Smt. Viplove Thakur in Rajya Sabha today.

4884. (5-12-2007) NEW DELHI : The Government of Karnataka has requested to open the Bidar and Karwar Defence airports to civilian use. Government of India has already conveyed 'in principle' approval to the proposal in respect of Bidar airfield. However, no offer has been made for provision of additional land by the Government of Karnataka for Bidar airfield. For Karwar airport, the State Government has proposed to acquire and transfer additional land. However, at present, there is no runway at Karwar. The Naval air station is planned to be constructed only during subsequent phases of the project at Karwar. This information was given by the Defence Minister Shri AK Antony in a written reply to Shri Janardhana Poojary in Rajya Sabha today.

4885. (5-12-2007) NEW DELHI : The Government has been encouraging the Defence Public Sector Enterprises (PSEs) for exports. Defence Shipyards are utilising their capacities currently for orders placed on them by Indian Navy & Coast Guard. This leaves them with little spare capacity. Despite this Mazagon Dock Limited (MDL) has recently won an export order of Rs.340 crores of commercial vessels. This information was given by Minister of State for Defence Production Rao Inderjit Singh in a written reply to Shri Santosh Bagrodia in Rajya Sabha today.

4886. (5-12-2007) NEW DELHI : Audit has observed, vide C & AG's Report No. 19 of 2007 (Defence Services), which has been laid on the Table of the House on 24th August, 2007, that there was formation of cartel amongst suppliers who quoted identical rates in 117 cases at 11 Ordnance Factories. C & AG's report mentioned that order worth Rs.472.60 crore were placed during 2001-06 to such cartel. Before completion of the procurement contracts, the reasonableness of the price is assessed co-relating with the input material prices prevailing in the market, wholesale price index, last paid rate etc. Measure to break cartel formation are reviewed and fine-tuned on regular basis. The existing written guidelines to eliminate cartel formation were formulated by a committee in consultation with CVC in July 2007. The tender conditions are per the guidelines were modified by incorporating appropriate clauses. This information was given by Minister of State for Defence Production Rao Inderjit Singh in a written reply to Shri Mohammed Amin and Shri Prasanta Chatterjee in Rajya Sabha today.

4887. (5-12-2007) NEW DELHI : The sanctioned strength of Personnel Below Officer Rank (PBOR) including sepoys in the Army and those actually in place (as on 30th September, 2007) is 11,01,090 and 11,20,077 respectively. There is, therefore, no shortage of PBORs in the Army. However, there is a shortage of 11,371 officers in the Army which is mainly in the ranks of Lieutenant Colonel

& below. Several measures have been taken by the Government to enhance recruitment in the Army. All officers including those in Short Service Commission (SSC) have been made eligible to hold substantive rank of Captain, Major and Lieutenant Colonel and equivalents after 2, 6 and 13 years of reckonable service respectively. The term of SSC officers has been extended to 14 years. This has made the Army an attractive career option. Besides Army has undertaken sustained image projection publicity campaign to create awareness among the youth. Awareness campaigns, participation in career fairs and exhibitions, advertisements in print and electronic media are also some of the other measures in this direction. This information was given by the Defence Minister Shri AK Antony in a written reply to Shri Varinder Singh Bajwa in Rajya Sabha today.

4888. (5-12-2007) NEW DELHI : The Ministry of Environment and Forests is implementing the National Afforestation Programme (NAP) Scheme through a two-tier setup of Forest Development Agency (FDA) at forest division level and Joint Forest Management Committees (JFMCs) at village level. During the last three years (2004-05 to 2006-07), funds amounting to Rs. 773.87 crores were released under the NAP Scheme, including for maintenance of plantations raised during the Ninth Five Year Plan. The target for tree planting under the Item 16-B of Twenty Point Programme - 1986: "Area Covered (Under Plantation) - Public and Forest Lands" was fixed as 18.70 lakh hectares during 2006-07, against which the achievement was 16.56 lakh hectares. The State and Union Territory-wise targets and achievements, as per the Progress Report published by Ministry of Statistics and Programme Implementation, are given in the annexure. Some States and Union Territories could not achieve the targets for various reasons, including timely availability of funds and seedlings, and lands identified for tree planting.

4889. (5-12-2007) NEW DELHI : The area of tropical dry forests is 35.6% of the total forest cover of the country. This information provided by Forest Survey of India, Dehradun, It is a fact that forest fires, grazing, weed, infestation by pests and diseases and encroachments do adversely affect the sustainable forest management. Under the Centrally Sponsored Integrated Forest Protection Scheme, financial assistance is being provided to States/UTs to take up effective measures for protection and management of existing forests. In addition, various State/UTs Governments also take up protection measures under the respective schemes of the State/UT plan. This information was given by the Minister of State in the Ministry of Environment and Forests, Sh S.Regupathy in a written reply to a question in the Lok Sabha today.

4890. (5-12-2007) NEW DELHI : The Government of Maharashtra had submitted a number of proposals on conservation of lakes to this Ministry, for consideration under the National Lake Conservation Plan (NLCP). Out of these, 5 proposals for conservation of 13 lakes have already been approved at a total estimated cost of Rs.24.25 crore.. The remaining proposals on examination in this Ministry were found either technically deficient or not falling within the mandate of NLCP. The State Government has been asked to scrutinize the remaining proposals at their level, keeping the NLCP guidelines in view and also to explore the possibilities of inclusion of some of these lakes in the State Conservation Plan through the state budget available for this purpose. The proposals for new lakes are considered under NLCP subject to their admissibility as per guidelines, prioritization, pollution status and availability of funds under the Plan. This information was given by the Minister of State in the Ministry of Environment and Forests, Sh Namo Narain Meena in a written reply to a question in the Lok Sabha today.

4891. (5-12-2007) NEW DELHI : Environmental degradation is caused by rapid growth of population, industrial pollution, unplanned urbanization and unsustainable production and consumption patterns. Area under forest and tree cover, quality of water resources, air quality, etc.; are some of the parameters for perceiving the level of environmental degradation. The State of Forest Report 2003 reveals that the forest cover in the country is 678,333 km2 and constitutes 20.64 per cent of its geographic area. A comparison with the forest cover assessment of 2001 reveals an overall increase of 2,795 km2 or 0.41 per cent in forest cover of the country. The Central Pollution Control Board (CPCB) is monitoring air quality at 339 locations under the National Air Quality Monitoring Programme (NAMP). The monitored data reveals that the level of sulphur dioxide (SO2) and nitrogen dioxide (NO2) are within the prescribed air quality standards in residential areas of most of the cities. However, the levels of respirable suspended particulate matter (RSPM) exceed the prescribed norms. The Biochemical Oxygen Demand is considered as the pollution indicator for any river in the country. Out of total riverine length of approximately 45,000 kms in our country, CPCB study indicates that 14% of riverine length is severely polluted with biochemical oxygen demand (BOD) more than 6 mg/litre, 19% is moderately polluted with BOD 3-6 mg/litre, whereas rest of the riverine length of 67% is relatively clean with BOD less than 3 mg/litre. In order to improve the water quality of the rivers, the Ministry is implementing the National River Conservation Plan by providing assistance to the State Governments. The existing legal framework and policies, such as Air (Prevention & Control) Act 1980 & 1988, Water (Prevention & Control) Act 1974, Wildlife (Protection) Act 1972, and National Environmental Policy 2006, and various programmes of the Government address the concerns regarding environmental degradation. This information was given by the Minister of State in the Ministry of Environment and Forests, Sh Namo Narain Meena. in a written reply to a question in the Lok Sabha today.

4892. (5-12-2007) NEW DELHI : 191 countries have signed Vienna Convention for the protection of the ozone layer and the Montreal Protocol on substances that deplete the ozone layer. India became a Party to the Vienna Convention for the protection of ozone layer on 19th June, 1991 and the Montreal Protocol on substances that deplete the ozone layer on 17th September, 1992. A detailed

Country Programme for phaseout of Ozone Depleting Substances (ODSs) was prepared in 1993. The regulatory and fiscal measures have been ta ken to ensure phase out of ODSs as per the schedule specified in the Montreal Protocol with financial and technical support received from the Multilateral Fund (MLF). Similarly, developing countries are also phasing out ODSs as per the Protocol. Developed countries have phased out production and consumption of Chlorofluorocarbons (CFCs), Carbontetrachloride (CTC) and Halons on 1.1.1996 and will phase out Hydrochlorofluorocarbon (HCFC) by 2030. This information was given by the Minister of State in the Ministry of Environment and Forests, Sh Namo Narain Meena in a written reply to a question in the Lok Sabha today.

4893. (5-12-2007) NEW DELHI : 299 candidates have been qualified on the basis of the results of the Written Examination held by the Union Public Service Commission in April, 2007 and the Interviews held by the Services Selection Board of the Ministry of Defence for admission to the Army, Navy and Air Force wings of National Defence Academy for the 119th Course and Naval Academy 10+2 (Executive Branch) for the 39th Course commencing from January, 2008. There are some common candidates in the three lists for Army, Navy, Air Force and Naval Academy. The total number of such candidates in the three lists is 154. The number of vacancies as intimated by the Government is 335 (195 for Army, 39 for Navy, 66 for Air Force and 35 for Naval Academy 10+2 (Executive Branch). The results of Medical Examination have not been taken into account in preparing these lists. The candidature of all the candidates is provisional, subject to their submitting the requisite certificates in support of date of birth and educational qualifications etc. claimed by them, direct to the Additional Directorate General of Recruiting, Adjutant General's Branch, Integrated Headquarters, Ministry of Defence (Army), West Block No.III, Wing-I, R.K. Puram, New Delhi-110066 wherever this has not already been done and NOT to UPSC. In case, there is any change of address, the candidates are advised to promptly intimate direct to the Army Headquarters at the address given above. These results will also be available on the UPSC website at http://www.upsc.gov.in. However, marks of the candidates will be available on the website after 30 days from the date of declaration of final results. For any further information, the candidates may contact the Facilitation Counter of the Commission near 'C' Gate of UPSC premises either in person or on Telephone Nos. 23385271, 23381125, 23098543 between 1000 hrs. to 1700 hrs. on any working day.

4894. (5-12-2007) NEW DELHI : A case of tiger poaching has come to light during January, 2007 in the Kishanpur Sanctuary, adjoining Dudhwa National Park. However, only some decomposed carcass of the poached animal was found at the site. Further, it has been reported that a tiger skin has also been seized in the nearby South Kheri Division during transit this year. Steps taken by Government of India for conservation of tiger are includes legal administrative financial steps and international co-operations. This information was given by the Minister of

State in the Ministry of Environment and Forests, Sh S.Regupathy. in a written reply to a question in the Rajya Sabha today.

4895. (5-12-2007) NEW DELHI : The congress said here today that Modi has asked questions of the people of Gujarat. Let us ask those questions also of the people of Gujarat in the same tone and tenor as Modi. We also like to ask what should the people of Gujarat do with the chief minister who has no regard for the law? What should the people of Gujarat do with the chief minister who, because he assumes some one to be guilty, decides to liquidate him without trial, without due process of law, without court proceeding. What indeed should the people of Gujarat do with the chief minister who is a law unto himself, who obeys no law, regards no law and is a lawless dictator. The answer to our question, if we were to give the same answer as Modi has given, would be to physically liquidate such a chief minister. But we don't give that kind of answer or because we don't believe in that kind of politics or life. What we say and what the people of Gujarat say that such a chief minister should be constitutionally liquidated. He should be ejected and evicted form his Chief Ministerial post which he does not deserve to hold for one more day. This is the first time in the history of independent India, I can say without challenge, the first time in global political history that a sitting constitutional authority like a chief minister admits to clod-blooded murder. It is the first time anywhere that a constitutional authority like the chief minister owns up or claims a license to kill, to liquidate. I would like to ask you is the phrase 'merchant of death' appropriate? Is it too mild. Is this not Mr. Death himself speaking? This is a clear admission of guilt. We know the term encounter. Very often an encounter happens and may not be pre-planned, may not be deliberate. Here what you have is a pre-planned, deliberately designed cold-blooded murder. The chief minister of the state has given permanent standing orders to kill. Kill whom? Those whom he, not the courts, considers to be good or bad depending on his own perception. So here is a chief minister who is a judge, a jury, a prosecutor, a persecutor, all rolled into one. And what kind of party is this BJP? They are not objecting to him, they dare not question him, indeed they must justify him. They must bend over backwards to justify these notions, these thought processes in a democracy. We believe that what Mr. Modi has clearly, unequivocally admitted from a public forum justifies and deserves to be taken immediate suo motto cognizance by a court of law. We believe that such court of law should convict him for cold-blooded murder. Perhaps the people of Gujarat and the people of this country must wait for the next admission by Mr. Modi. Perhaps the next admission will be about causing the disappearance of Kausarbi, the wife of the person whom he admits to kill. We believe that this has a great intent, a specific intent behind it. Therefore we also believe that the Election Commission must immediately take suo motto note of this because it is intended to affect the ongoing electoral process in that state. And, of course, we also believe that this person has committed clear and gross contempt of court because he has several cases on the Sohrabuddin issue pending up to the Apex Court, I repeat, the Apex Court. And finally, we believe that this admission clearly belies the intent of the chief minister of Gujarat, of the state of Gujarat under his chief ministership to suppress and destroy evidence. Therefore we call upon all the courts seized with the Sohrabuddin issue or with other similar matters to expedite and conclude their trials. To a question that if your Party comes to power will your Party take action, Shri Singhvi said, first, we have already, in the earlier incidents in Gujarat, taken firm concrete action and the several Supreme Court proceedings which have gone earlier have been totally supported by the Congress. Second, there can be no two views or doubts that formally also, if and when we come to power, we have no doubt, that we will take appropriate action. To a question as to why there should be suo motto action and whether the Congress will approach the Election Commission, Shri Singhvi said, what makes you think we are not going to do it. Suo motto and complaining are not mutually exclusive categories. The Commission is entitled to take action even as I speak or even when the report comes. We will make a complaint tomorrow, we will make a complaint the day after. We have to draft a complaint and that does not stop the Commission and courts from taking suo motto action. We reserve the right to go to the Election Commission and we shall go to the Election Commission. The court and the Election Commission can take strong suo motto action both on the Representation of Peoples Act, on the Moral Court of Conduct and in respect of contempt where the Kasurbi and Sohrabuddin cases are pending. To a question as to how the Congress views the walk-out of your supporting party on the nuke deal, Shri Singhvi said, we had a very long debate on a particular issue and people may have walked out. First of all it is wrong to suppose that the walk-out is on a commonality or an agreement of issues between the two parties you mentioned, that will be very wrong. There was at least a 7-hour debate yesterday which was a very constructive debate which should not be ignored. There were individual issues in the debate which a particular party may not have liked and agreed with, you ought to ask them this question as to why they walked out. There is no question of Congress Party, there is a UPA government in this country and the UPA comprises India's largest ever coalition after Independence and each and every member of the UPA is rock solid behind us, you are ignoring all members of the UPA and no member of the UPA has shown the slightest opposition to the deal.

4896. (5-12-2007) NEW DELHI : Though no allocation with particular reference to Snow Leopard has been made by the Planning Commission, but the umbrella scheme of 'Development of National Parks & Sanctuaries' covers the conservation of Snow Leopard. Snow Leopard is an important flagship species of the mountainous region and is found mainly in the high altitude mountains of Jammu & Kashmir, Himachal Pradesh, Uttarakhand, Sikkim and Arunachal Pradesh. Both State and Central Government have been involved in developing strategies and action plan for protection and conservation of Snow Leopard. This information was given by the Minister of State in the Ministry of Environment and Forests, Sh S.Regupathy in a written reply to a question in the Lok Sabha today.

4897. (5-12-2007) NEW DELHI : The Minister for Steel, Chemicals and Fertilisers Shri Ram Vilas Paswan has said, the government will soon come out with new investment policies in respect of both nitrogen and phosphate sectors. It will be benchmarked to international standards and will encourage healthy competition and efficiency both in production and distribution. Shri Paswan was delivering the opening address at the Fertiliser Association of India's Annual Seminar on 'Holistic Approach to Agriculture and Fertilisers' here today. He said, the government is actively considering various options for an investment policy, which will be attractive to investors. He said, gas availability in the country is projected to improve from 2008 - 09 onwards and urged the industry to take advantage of this opportunity to add indigenous capacities. Shri Paswan said, the decision of the government to revive the closed units of the Hindustan Fertiliser Corporation and Fertiliser Corporation of India provides a unique opportunity for the industry to set up brown field projects utilizing the already existing infrastructure. The Minister said, the government is working out the modalities for encouraging fortified fertilizers to add vital micro nutrients to the soil. He said, the government is considering the inclusion of sulphur as a subsidized nutrient in the subsidy regime since there is sulphur deficiency in many regions of the country. Expressing concern over the indigenous Fertiliser industry's reluctance to import DAP during the current year, the Minister said, while the government has made sincere efforts to address the problems of the fertilisers industry, the industry has not reciprocated as far as DAP imports are concerned. Shri Paswan said, the government has however not allowed these problems to affect overall availability of fertilisers in the country in the interest of the farmers. The unprecedented increase in the international prices of fertilisers and fertiliser inputs, Shri Paswan said, cannot be justified solely by the increase in cost of production. He said, the price increase is having significant impact on government subsidies, which is becoming unsustainable. He urged the international suppliers to keep their long term relationship with India in perspective. The Minister said, the need of the hour is an immediate correction in these price trends. He called upon the industry to increase awareness of farmers through extension services saying the efforts of the government should be synergised by the industry to provide best solution to the farmers.

4898. (5-12-2007) NEW DELHI : The Government provides medial care and health investigation facilities to Indian zoos and wild life wings of various sate governments in the country. Central Zoo Authority provides funds for creation and improvement of veterinary facilities including disease diagnostic facilities across the country in recognized public sector Zoos and Veterinary departments / institutes, *viz.* at Bhubaneswar (Orissa), Anand (Gujarat), Bareilly (Uttar Pradesh), Guwahati (Assam), Jammu (Jammu and Kashmir), Kolkata (West Bengal) and Chennai (Tamil Nadu). The Central Zoo Authority has provided financial assistance to the Tamil Nadu Veterinary & Animal Sciences University, Chennai to the tune of Rs. 1, 19,693/- during the financial year 2006-07 for strengthening the diagnostic facilities. In addition, the Central Zoo Authority has also established a National Referral Centre at the Indian Veterinary Research Institute, Bareilly for providing super specialty services and diagnostic facilities to all Indian Zoos. The above facilities are adequate to meet the current requirements. This information was given by the Minister of State in the Ministry of Environment and Forests, Sh S.Regupathy in a written reply to a question in the Lok Sabha today.

4899. (5-12-2007) NEW DELHI : The Ministry of Environment and Forest have, so far, received 57 proposals for conversion of forest villages into revenue villages including 19 proposals from the State of Chhattisgarh. Of these 57 proposals, 15 proposals have been accorded approval under the Forest (conservation) Act, 1980, while 5 proposals were closed and 1 was rejected. 18 proposals were returned to the State Government as they were not coming under the purview of the Forest (conservation) Act. At present one proposal is at an advance stage of consideration in the Ministry and 17 proposals are lying with the concerned State Governments for furnishing additional information. This information was given by the Minister of State in the Ministry of Environment and Forests, Sh S.Regupathy in a written reply to a question in the Lok Sabha today.

4900. (5-12-2007) NEW DELHI : The Ministry of Rural Development through State Governments and Union Territory Administrations implements a number of Centrally Sponsored Schemes for poverty alleviation, employment generation, creation of rural infrastructure and providing basic amenities for people living in rural areas of the country. The Swarnjayanti Gram Swarojgar Yojana (SGSY) provides self employment, while the Sampoorna Gramin Rozgar Yojana (SGRY) aims at providing additional wage employment in rural areas thereby providing food security and improved nutrition, and creation of durable community assets and infrastructure. The National Rural Employment Guarantee Scheme (NREGS) presently implemented in 330 districts and will be extended in all the districts of the country w.e.f. 1.4.2008 aims to provide 100 days guaranteed employment to each household who is willing to take manual work. The Indira Awaas Yojana (IAY) provides shelter to the shelterless. Other Rural Development Progrmames such as Pradhan Mantri Gram Sadak Yojana (PMGSY) for rural connectivity, Accelerated Rural Water Supply Programme (ARWSP) and Total Sanitation Campaign (TSC) aim at development of rural infrastructure and rural amenities. Integrated Wastelands Development Programme (IWDP), Drought Prone Areas Programme (DPAP) and Desert Development Programme (DDP) are area development programmes which are implemented on watershed basis. The schemes of Computerization of Land Records (CLR) and Strengthening of Revenue Administration and Updating Land Records (SRA & ULR) are also implemented. Allocation (Budget Estimates) under various rural development schemes of the Ministry was Rs. 15998.40 crore, Rs. 24480.00 crore and 31443.62 crore during 2004-05, 2005-06 and 2006-07 respectively. During the same period, the actual releases were Rs. 18166.83 crore, Rs. 27488.83 crore and Rs. 30981.94 crore. Central funds released and utilized out of total available funds (opening balance, central releases, state releases and misc. receipts) under major schemes of the Ministry *viz.* SGRY, National Food for Works Programme (NFFWP), NREGS, SGSY, IAY, PMGSY, IWDP, DPAP, DDP, CLR, SRA & ULR, ARWSP and TSC during the last three years (*i.e.* 2004-05, 2005-06 and 2006-07) are given in the Annexure. The Ministry of Rural Development regularly evaluates the schemes implemented in the States/UTs through independent Research Organizations located in various parts of the country through Concurrent Evaluation, Impact Assessment Studies to assess the impact of the scheme and the shortcomings in the implementation at grass root level. The findings of these studies are brought to the notice of the State Government for remedial actions. The Ministry has also developed a comprehensive system of Monitoring the implementation and impact of the programmes including utilization of funds through Periodical Progress Reports, Performance Review Committee, Area Officer's Scheme, Vigilance and Monitoring Committee at the State/District Level with greater involvement of members of Parliament, National Level Monitors to monitor quality of work, adherence to implementation of schemes as per programme guidelines. Besides, the State have been advised to adopt a five- pronged strategy consisting of (i) creation of awareness about the schemes, (ii) transparency, (iii) People's Partnership, (iv) social audit through Gram Sabha and (v) strict vigilance and monitoring. This information was given by Union Minister for Rural Development Dr. Raghuvansh Prasad Singh in a statement in the Rajya Sabha Today.

4901. (5-12-2007) NEW DELHI : Government has decided to extend NREGS to all the remaining rural districts in the country, including the Union Territories with effect from 1.4.2008. A notification to this effect was issued on 28.9.2007. A sum of Rs. 159.44 crore have been released to the Phase III districts (except districts of Himachal Pradesh and Gujarat) for making preparatory arrangements like IEC, printing and procurement of statutory documents, training of officials and non-officials and preparation of perspective plans. NREGA is demand driven and not an allocation based programme. A National Employment Guarantee Fund has been established for providing funds to the States for implementation of the Act. For the current financial year, a budget provision of Rs.12,000 crores was made for implementation of the Act. Provisions are made in the budget for implementation of the Act on the basis of funds utilized by the States and also on the basis of demand for work in the previous year. Moreover, Adult members of any rural household may apply for employment under the Act subject to an over-all ceiling of 100 days of employment in a financial year per household. Therefore, no targets can be fixed for providing employment under the Act. Suggestions/requests had been received from various States for coverage of selected districts under NREGA. However, Government has decided to extend NREGA to all the remaining rural districts in the country including Union Territories with effect from 1.4.2008. This information was disclosed by the Union Minister for

Rural Development Dr. Raghuvansh Prasad Singh in reply to a written question in Rajya Sabha today.

4902. (5-12-2007) NEW DELHI : Shri Buddhadeb Saha from Burdwan, West Bengal has got the 1st Prize in the National level Photographic Competition for amateur photographers organized by the Ministry of Tribal Affairs in collaboration with the Photo Division, Ministry of Information & Broadcasting, New Delhi for his photograph "Eternity". 2nd Prize & 3rd Prize have been bagged by Shri Sailesh Nigam of Rewa, Madhya Pradesh and Shri Pranabendu Samajpati of Kolkata respectively for their photographs "Sound of Heart" and "World Cup II". The Jury did not find any entry suitable for the special talent award for the Best Tribal Photographer. The Photo Division conducted the photo competition for the Ministry of Tribal Welfares on the theme Joyful Tribals. A total of 1949 photographs were received from the 322 photographers from 23 States including the states of north east like Assam, Meghalaya, Nagaland and Sikkim and also the other states like Andhra Pradesh, Chattisgarh, Goa, Gujarat, Haryana, Himachal Pradesh, Jharkhand, Karnataka, Kerala, Madhya Pradesh, Maharashtra, New Delhi, Orissa, Punjab, Rajasthan, Tamil Nadu, Uttarakhand, Uttar Pradesh and West Bengal. The Jury comprising eminent photographer Michael Shylla from Meghalayla, Debatosh Sengupta, Director, Photo Division, and Gautam Budha Mukherjee, Secretary, Tribal Affairs screened the entries. Other 10 commendation awards and another hundred and eleven photographs for the exhibition. Commendation awards winners are S/Shri Kailash Soni from Indore, Dinesh Parmar from Vadodara, Somenath Mukherjee from Birbhum, WB, Kushlav and Subendu Dubey of Indore, Sashikant Vishnu Patil of Navi Mumbai and Amit Kumar Dan and Jayanta Roy from Kolkata. An exhibition of award winning as well as selected photographs got underway at Rabindra Bhawan, Copernicus Marg, New Delhi today.

4903. (5-12-2007) NEW DELHI : 52 proposals for production of documentaries on River Valley Development were received in North Eastern States during the last five years. Of these 50 were received by Doordarshan Kendra, Guwahati and two by the Programme Production Centre, Guwahati. Doordarshan Kendra, Guwahati approved 15 proposals. The evaluation committee turned down the rest 36 proposals, as they were not found suitable for production. Both the proposals received by Programme Production Centre, Guwahati were approved. The above information was given by the Minister of Information & Broadcasting and Parliamentary Affairs Shri P.R. Dasmunsi in a written reply in the Rajya Sabha today.

4904. (5-12-2007) NEW DELHI : The Union Minister of Shipping, Road Transport and Highways, Thiru T.R. Baalu has approved a sum of Rs. 2199.22 lakh for road improvement works in the state of Karnataka. The approval has been given for Improvement of Riding Quality from km 237.00 to km. 264 of NH-48 (Shiradi Ghat of western Ghats) Bangalore-Mangalore section in Karnataka. The Stretch is deteriorated due to the heavy flow of traffic and needs immediate improvement.

4905. (5-12-2007) NEW DELHI : The National Floor Level Minimum Wage has been revised from Rs. 66/- to Rs. 80/- per day with effect from 01.09.2007. The revision of National Floor Level Minimum Wages by the Government is a non-statutory measure. Thus the State/Union Territory Governments have been requested to revise the minimum wages upwards so as to ensure that in none of the scheduled employments, the minimum wages are less than the national floor level minimum wage of Rs. 80/- per day. Until the Central Government specifies the wage rate for workers in respect of different areas under Section 6 (1) of the National Rural Employment Guarantee (NREG) Act, 2005, the minimum wages fixed for agricultural workers by the State Governments/Union Territories under Section 3 of the Minimum Wages Act, 1948 shall be considered as the wage rate applicable to that area in view of the provision under Section 6 (2) of the NREG Act, 2005. This information was given by the Minister of State for Labour and Employment Shri Oscar Fernandes (Independent Charge) in a written reply in the Rajya Sabha today.

4906. (5-12-2007) NEW DELHI : A comprehensive proposal to eliminate child labour from the country in the 11th Plan has been submitted to the Planning Commission. It includes a convergent approach to tackle the problem of child labour alongwith a number of additional components like residential schools, etc. The Government is implementing National Child Labour Project (NCLP) Scheme for rehabilitating the child labour withdrawn from work in 250 districts of the country. Under the NCLP Scheme, children withdrawn from work are put in Special Schools where they are provided education, nutrition, vocational training, stipend and regular health checkup. The objective of the Scheme is to withdraw children from work and mainstream them into the formal system of education. Government is also making efforts to economically empower the families of these children by covering them under other poverty alleviation & income generation schemes of the Government. For the 11th Plan, Government has proposed expansion of the NCLP Scheme to 600 districts and has also proposed some additional features in the Scheme, such as residential schools in big cities for migrant child labour, vocational training for adolescents, etc. Government has formed a Core Group headed by Secretary (Labour & Employment) with representatives from other concerned Central Government Ministries, *viz.* Ministry of Women & Child Development, Human Resource Development, Rural Development, Social Justice and Empowerment and Urban Housing & Poverty Alleviation for convergence with the Schemes of these Ministries for educational rehabilitation of child labour and the economic upliftment of their families. This information was given by the Minister of State for Labour and Employment Shri Oscar Fernandes (Independent Charge) in a written reply in the Rajya Sabha today.

4907. (5-12-2007) NEW DELHI : The Central Board of Trustees, Employees' Provident Fund in which central trade unions are represented, in its 178th meeting has resolved not to exercise the option of investing 5% of the Employees' Provident

Fund monies in equities. This information was given by the Minister of State for Labour and Employment Shri Oscar Fernandes (Independent Charge) in a written reply in the Rajya Sabha today.

4908. (5-12-2007) NEW DELHI : In order to rehabilitate the released bonded labour, the Government is implementing a Centrally Sponsored Scheme for Rehabilitation of Bonded Labour since May 1978. The Scheme provides for rehabilitation assistance of Rs. 20,000 per bonded labour, which is equally shared by the Centre and State Government on 50:50 basis. During the last five years, 6123 bonded labourers have been identified and rehabilitated. With a view to rehabilitating children withdrawn from notified occupations and processes, the Government is implementing National Child Labour Project (NCLP) Scheme in 250 districts across 20 States of the country. During the last five years, a total of 3,41,290 children have been mainstreamed into the formal system of education. The Non Governmental Organizations are being associated to run the special schools in those districts, which are not covered under NCLP scheme for rehabilitation of child labour. This information was given by the Minister of State for Labour and Employment Shri Oscar Fernandes (Independent Charge) in a written reply in the Rajya Sabha today.

4909. (5-12-2007) NEW DELHI : Agriculture, Industry & Services sectors are the main constituents of the GDP. Skill training in these sectors is being provided by various Ministries / Departments and also by private training providers. It is presumed that production and productivity increase on employing skilled workforce. It has now become imperative to use skilled workforce due to rapid technological advancement and changing global manufacturing practices. DGE&T under Ministry of Labour & Employment has taken following initiatives during 2004-05 to 2006-07 for upgradation of Government Industrial Training Institutes in the country: (i) Upgradation of one hundred Govt. Industrial Training Institutes (ITIs) with domestic funding at a cost of Rs. 160 crore. (ii) Upgradation of 400 Govt. ITIs with World Bank assistance at a cost of Rs. 1581 crore. This information was given by the Minister of State for Labour and Employment Shri Oscar Fernandes (Independent Charge) in a written reply in the Rajya Sabha today.

4910. (5-12-2007) NEW DELHI : At present 965 employment exchanges are functioning in the country to cater to around 1028 million population as per census 2001. .Reliable estimates of employment and unemployment are obtained through quinquennial labour force surveys conducted by National Sample Survey Organisation. Last such survey conducted pertains to 2004-05. State-wise percentage of workers in the population on usual status basis during 1999-2000 & 2004-05 is given in the Annex. This information was given by the Minister of State for Labour and Employment Shri Oscar Fernandes (Independent Charge) in a written reply in the Rajya Sabha today.

4911. (5-12-2007) NEW DELHI : The findings of National Family Health Survey-III pertains to men and women of the age group 15-49. The Survey was conducted in the year 2005-06. According to this survey, 55% of employed women are paid in cash and an additional 12% get combination of Cash and in-kind. Thus, 67% of employed women in the age group 15 to 49 earn cash. Around 22% of women are not paid at all, while 11% are paid in - kind only. In case of employed men, 91% of employed men earn cash. Around 6% of employed men in the age group of 15-49 do not get paid at all where as around 3% get paid in kind only. The Equal Remuneration Act provides for payment of equal remuneration to men and women for the same work or work of a similar nature without any discrimination. This Act is implemented by the respective State Governments for the areas under their jurisdiction and monitored by the Central Government. The State Governments are also addressed from time to time to ensure strict compliance of the provisions of the Act. For the areas under the Central Government, the Act is implemented by the office of Chief Labour Commissioner (Central). This information was given by the Minister of State for Labour and Employment Shri Oscar Fernandes (Independent Charge) in a written reply in the Rajya Sabha today.

4912. (5-12-2007) NEW DELHI : The Government of Maharashtra has sent a proposal to the Union Government for advising the authorities of Mumbai Port Trust to jointly work with Maharashtra Government for preparing development plan of Eastern Coastal part of Mumbai. It has been decided to set up a Standing Committee under the Chairmanship of Chief Secretary, Maharashtra with Chairman, Mumbai Port Trust and other stockholders as members to sort out various issues of Mumbai Port vis-a-vis development of Mumbai City. This information was given by the Minister of Shipping, Road Transport and Highways, Thiru T.R. Baalu in a written reply in the Lok Sabha today.

4913. (5-12-2007) NEW DELHI : The Sethusamudram Ship Channel Project is an Indian Project and is located within the Indian side of the International Maritime Boundary Line. Certain issues have been raised by the Government of Sri Lanka, particularly on the environmental implications of the project. Consistent with the cordial and friendly relations between the two countries, the Government of India's endeavour is to address the genuine concerns of the Government of Sri Lanka through mutual discussions for which a mechanism has been put in place. This information was given by the Minister of Shipping, Road Transport and Highways, Thiru T.R. Baalu in a written reply in the Lok Sabha today.

4914. (5-12-2007) NEW DELHI : The Government has approved the project 'Deepening and Widening of Mumbai Harbour Channel and JN Port Channel' at an estimated cost of Rs.800 crores. The project is expected to be completed within a period of 27 months from the date of issue of work order. On completion of the project, the Port will be able to accommodate container vessels requiring a draught up to 14 metres of 6000 Twenty feet Equivalent Units (TEUs) capacity.

This information was given by the Minister of Shipping, Road Transport and Highways, Thiru T.R. Baalu in a written reply in the Lok Sabha today.

4915. (5-12-2007) NEW DELHI : Presently, the inter-island connectivity in the Union Territory of Lakshadweep is maintained with 2x100 passenger vessels. The 5 vessels operating in the island-mainland sector are also being utilized for inter-island connectivity during the voyage. During monsoon period from May to September all fair-weather and inter-island vessels are withdrawn from service and hence the inter-island passengers mainly depend on the two all-weather vessels. Due to non-availability of any other transport, helicopter service connecting Capital island, Kavaratti with all inhabited islands is also put into operation during the monsoon period. During fair-weather season all the vessels operate and accordingly, the movement of passengers in the inter-island sector do not suffer much. Keeping in view the long term shipping requirement in Lakshadweep sector, 6 passenger vessels of different sizes under 15 Years Perspective Plan and 4 passenger inter-island high speed vessels under PMGSY Scheme have been recommended for acquisition. Out of these, 3x150 and 1x15 passenger vessels have been delivered this year. The construction of the 3x50 passenger vessels has been completed and the delivery is expected in December, 2007. Contracts have been signed for construction of 2x250 passenger-cum-100 M.T. cargo vessel with M/s. Colombo Dockyard Limited and as per the contract the vessels are to be delivered by 2nd January, 2010 and 2nd July, 2010 respectively. One more 400 passenger vessel is also being considered for acquisition by the Government. As regards Andaman and Nicobar islands, presently, there are 5 vessels plying in inter-island sector. The frequency to the southern group of islands has increased from an average of 3 times a month in the past to 6 - 9 times a month at present. The foreshore sector is serviced by 16 vessels and the frequency has increased as compared to the past. Government is aware of the need for augmentation of the fleet size to meet the requirement of increased passenger traffic flow on this sector. 4 new vessels are under construction at various shipyards out of which two vessels are at advanced stage of construction and likely to be inducted sometime in 2008. In addition, acquisition of 4 vessels in the inter-island sector and 3 vessels in the foreshore sector has been recommended recently to meet the increased traffic flow. This information was given by the Minister of Shipping, Road Transport and Highways, Thiru T.R. Baalu in a written reply in the Lok Sabha today.

4916. (5-12-2007) NEW DELHI : The Shipping Corporation of India (SCI) has planned to acquire 62 vessels during the Eleventh Five Year Plan (2007-2012) to replace its existing ageing fleet and to augment the fleet of SCI. The Government has already approved the proposals of SCI for acquisition of 18 vessels of various categories during 2007-08. This information was given by the Minister of Shipping, Road Transport and Highways, Thiru T.R. Baalu in a written reply in the Lok Sabha today.

4917. (5-12-2007) NEW DELHI : As per information provided by the Government of J&K the proposed pollution free transport system between Kharnabal and Khadinyar on river Jhelum mainly comprises of navigational lock and gated structure for augmenting draft in the river during October to February (Winter months) when required draft (1.22 metres) for navigation is not available. Construction (on the navigation lock) started in 1984. Pakistan objected to the project alleging that storage is prohibited in river Jhelum. This resulted in suspension of work since 1987 when Government of India went for Government level dialogue instead of Commissioner level talks. Issue continues to be unresolved despite several rounds of Secretary level talks held since 1998 as part of composite dialogue. Periodic discussions are being held by Ministry of Water Resources (Indus Wing) with the State Government officials in this regard. So far as other rivers in the State, rivers flowing in Jammu province have a steep gradient and are not suitable for navigation. In Kashmir valley, for practical purposes, the development of water transport is confined to certain stretches of river Jhelum and various lakes. This information was given by the Minister of Shipping, Road Transport and Highways, Thiru T.R. Baalu in a written reply in the Lok Sabha today.

4918. (5-12-2007) NEW DELHI : There is a proposal to set up specialized state-of-the-art vehicle inspection and maintenance centres in all the States/Union Territories. However, the proposal is at nascent stage and the details have not been finalised. This information was given by the Minister of State for Shipping, Road Transport and Highways, Shri K.H. Muniyappa in a written reply in the Lok Sabha today.

4919. (5-12-2007) NEW DELHI : The Control of National Highways (Land and Traffic) Act, 2002 provides for the establishment of National Highway Administrations for implementation of the provisions of the Act. Accordingly, the constitution of 192 National Highway Administrations has been notified. The Act also provides for establishment of Tribunals for the redressal of the grievances arising out of the orders or action taken by the Highway Administrations. The constitution of 8 National Highway Tribunals has also been notified. The work relating to the preparation of Land Registers has been taken up by the Highways Administrations, but the desired level of success could not be achieved due to bottlenecks in retrieving the original updated land records from the local revenue authorities in the State/UTs. This information was given by the Minister of State for Shipping, Road Transport and Highways, Shri K.H. Muniyappa in a written reply in the Lok Sabha today.

4920. (5-12-2007) NEW DELHI : The Carriage by Road Act, 2007 has been notified in the Gazette of India on 1.10.07 which would replace the Carriers Act, 1865. The Act has 22 Sections covering various aspects such as mandatory registration of common carriers, liability aspects of common carrier, requirement of goods forwarding notes and goods receipts, scope for an agreement between the consignor and the common carrier for transportation of the consignment at a higher risk rate in return for higher liability, empowering common carrier to dispose of the consignment to recover its dues in the event of failure of the consignee to take the delivery of the consignment, requirement of insurance for transportation of hazardous/dangerous goods, force majeure provision to exonerate common carrier from his liabilities under certain circumstances, penalty for violating the provisions of the Act etc. A working group under the chairmanship of Shri S.K. Dash, Joint Secretary (Transport), Department of Road Transport & Highways has been constituted on 15.11.07 for the purpose of framing of rules under the Carriage by Road Act, 2007. The working group has been asked to submit its report within a period of 6 months. Keeping in view the procedural requirements involved in the framing of rules under the Act, it is not possible to envisage a specific date for enforcement of the Act at this stage. This information was given by the Minister of State for Shipping, Road Transport and Highways, Shri K.H. Muniyappa in a written reply in the Lok Sabha today.

4921. (5-12-2007) NEW DELHI : With a view to inducting information technology in Road Transport Sector through issuance of Driving Licence and Registration Certificate in Smart Card mode, the Government has already developed a software and made it available to all States/U.Ts. free of cost. Computerisation of the offices of R.T.Os in the country is an essential pre-requisite for this purpose. There is, however, no proposal to introduce zonal permit/uniform registration series for transport vehicles across the country. This information was given by the Minister of State for Shipping, Road Transport and Highways, Shri K.H. Muniyappa in a written reply in the Lok Sabha today.

4922. (5-12-2007) NEW DELHI : The Screening Committee in the Ministry of Coal will consider the applications received for allocation of 23 non-power coal blocks. The Government has decided to allocate Rampia (geological reserves of 275.24 million tonnes) and Dipside of Rampia (geological reserves of 360 million tonnes) coal blocks, located in the State of Orissa to the following six companies for generation of power: i) M/s Sterlite Energy Ltd. ii) M/s GMR Energy Ltd iii) M/s Lanco Group Ltd. iv) M/s Navbharat Power Pvt. Ltd. v) M/s Mittal Steel India Ltd vi) M/s Reliance Energy Ltd. This information was given by Dr. Dasari Narayana Rao, Minister of State for Coal in the Parliament today.

4923. (5-12-2007) NEW DELHI : The total number of patent filings by residents in India per million population was 3.40 in 2004-05 as compared to the world average of 250.72 worked out on the basis of the world population (6377.6 million) as per data given in the State of World Population 2004: United Nations Population Fund Report and the number of patents filed worldwide during 2004 (15,99,000) as per data given in World Intellectual Property Organisation (WIPO) Patent Report: Statistics on Worldwide Patent Activity, 2006 Edition. The number of patents in force in India in 2004 was 6,406, while it was 1,82,385 in China. The world average of patents in force in 2004 was 846.71 worked out on the basis of the world population (6377.6 million) as per data given in the State of World Population 2004: United Nations Population Fund Report and the number of patents in force worldwide during 2004 (5.4 million) as per data given in World Intellectual Property Organisation (WIPO) Patent Report: Statistics on Worldwide Patent Activity, 2006 Edition. There were a total of about 5.6 million patents in force worldwide in 2005 as per World Intellectual Property Organisation (WIPO) Patent Report: Statistics on Worldwide Patent Activity, 2007 Edition. However, this number includes patents obtained in different countries for the same invention also. Therefore, it will not be feasible to draw a conclusion on the proportion of patents in force in India vis-a-vis those in force worldwide. However, the number of Patents in India in force was 6857 in 2005.

4924. (5-12-2007) NEW DELHI : The High Level Committee on Manufacturing (HLCM) under the Chairmanship of the Prime Minister, while considering the Action Plan of the Ministry of Textiles for the growth of textile industry, inter alia, decided that the Ministry of Finance, in consultation with the Ministry of Textiles and the National Manufacturing Competitiveness Council (NMCC), would expeditiously consider the fiscal proposals required for the textiles sector. This information was given by the Minister of State for Textiles, Shri E.V.K.S. Elangovan, in the Rajya Sabha today, in a written reply to a question by Smt. Mohsina Kidwai. Consequently, the Government announced a set of measures in July, 2007 to provide relief to exporters by way of accelerated reimbursement of dues to exporters, reduction in the interest rate on pre-shipment and post-shipment credit and revision in drawback rates and Duty Entitlement Pass Book (DEPB) rates. In addition, the Government has also notified exemption of certain service tax in respect of exporters, the Minister added. The Minister further informed that a meeting was recently taken by the NMCC with the officials of Ministry of Finance, Ministry of Commerce & Industry and Ministry of Textiles, where representatives from Textiles industry associations were also present, on issues relating to restoring competitiveness in the Textiles & Garment Sector. Finance Minister also took a meeting with the Textile industry along with the officials of the Ministry of Textiles, the NMCC and the Ministry of Finance. The Government has announced a relief package in November, 2007, which reduces basic Customs Duty on certain items relating to textiles sector. Refund of service tax paid by exporters on taxable services linked to exports has been further extended. A support package for providing relief to export sectors, like Textiles, which have low import intensity, was also announced through additional subvention of 2% in pre-shipment and post-shipment credit to the textiles including Ready Made Garments and carpets but excluding man-made fibre. The Minister also informed that some new initiatives taken by the Government for the growth of textile sector, inter alia, include creation of Investment Regions to consolidate the phenomenon of agglomeration, visible in textiles to further reduce transaction costs and enhance competitiveness; launching of Manpower Development Scheme - known as the "Neighbourhood Apparel & Textile Training Institutes for Job Assurance (NATIJA)" - for establishing a network of employment-linked training facilities to meet the projected demand of 4 million trained workers over the next 5 years; and to revitalize handloom cooperatives on the pattern of agricultural cooperatives. Necessary action in this regard has since been initiated in consultation with the Planning Commission, Ministry of Finance, etc.

4925. (5-12-2007) NEW DELHI : The Prime Minister, Dr. Manmohan Singh has said that India is committed to share the experience of control and containment of the outbreak of influenza in poultry. He was speaking at a three-day International Ministerial Conference on Avian and Pandemic Influenza, here today. The PM said that focused governmental intervention must go hand-in-hand with community empowerment in addressing such health care challenges. It is important to include all stakeholders in the communication outreach. In the specific case of avian influenza, such communication should cover the entire production, marketing and commercial chain of poultry production. He said Avian Influenza, like all pandemics, is a global threat and we must all work together to find a global solution. Each Government will have to act locally, but think globally while dealing with the problem. He said we should guard against institutional fatigue in dealing with such pandemics and never lower our guard. He said our Road Map for 2008 would be shared at the Conference. While recognizing the need for a long-term vision to control and eliminate Avian Influenza and the threat of human pandemic, the necessity of taking urgent action now and in the present must also be seen. Through our Road Map 2008 we endeavour to suggest action points, which are deliverable and achievable in the next one year. India commits itself to adhere to the roadmap, he added. He hoped that the Conference will find it a useful reference for future programmes. In his welcome address, Shri Sharad Pawar, Minister of Agriculture and Consumer Affairs, Food and Public Distribution said that controlling Avian Influenza remains an enormous challenge particularly for the administration and the veterinary and medical communities. It has spread to new countries, continents and eco-systems. Therefore, he said, we collectively need to assess the current situation; the effectiveness of the strategies applied and revisit our policies. Minister for Health & Family Welfare, Dr. Anbumani Ramadoss in his speech said that the persistent though unpredictable threat to animal and human health is enhanced by the apprehension that a second strain of avian influenza, previous considered of little human risk, does indeed pose a real danger. We will need to continue to enhance and strengthen such global cooperation, he added.

4926. (5-12-2007) NEW DELHI : Government of India is implementing the National e-Governance Plan (NeGP) with the vision to make all Government services accessible to the common man in his locality, through common services delivery outlets - Twenty-seven (27) Central, State and Integrated Mission Mode

Projects (MMPs) have been identified under the NeGP to ensure availability of e-Government services. This was stated by Shri A.Raja, Minister of Communications and Information Technology last evening. Shri Raja was addressing the Parliamentary Consultative Committee attached to his Ministry. Subject of the discussion at the meeting was Common Service Centres and State Wide Area Networks (SWANs). Three pillars of NeGP for delivering services at doorstep of the citizen are: State Wide Area Networks (SWAN) for Connectivity ;National Data Bank/State Data Centres (SDC) for secure, data storage and Common Services Centres (CSC) as the primary physical front-end, Shri Raja said. The SWAN Scheme was approved in March 2005 with an overall outlay of Rs. 3334 crores to be spent in five years. The Scheme would establish Wide Area Networks in 29 States and 6 Union Territories across the country from the State Headquarter to the Block Level. This would provide a minimum connectivity of 2 Mbps from the State to the District, subdivision and Block level. This would be an extremely reliable, broadband secure connection and would function as the Government intranet. Implementation of the Scheme is in full swing with proposals of 28 States and UTs having been approved with the balance to be approved shortly, by the designated Empowered Committee. The State of Goa and the UTs of Andaman & Nicobar are not inclined to adopt the Scheme. Once implemented, the SWANs would go a long way in providing a network for G2G functions and for delivering G2C services, particularly in delivering the various services planned under the Mission Mode Projects of the NeGP, the members were informed. The Aim of the CSC Scheme is to establish 100,000 rural kiosks across the country with an equitable geographical spread - one CSC for every six census villages, through a Public Private Partnership. All CSCs would be broadband, internet-enabled, primarily through wireless connectivity and would provide for a mix of Government and private services at the doorstep of the citizen. The CSC is the delivery infrastructure for Government Services and in a sense would be the front end for the NeGP. The Scheme was approved in September 2006 at an estimated cost of Rs. 5742 crores over a four year period. Out of this cost, the Government is estimated to bear an expenditure of Rs. 1649 crores, with the balance coming from the private sector. The Government is not providing any upfront capital subsidy for the Scheme. The CSC infrastructure is to be set up by private entities at their own cost with the government only providing financial support (viability gap funding) for running these centres for a four year period, once the CSCs are established. The actual quantum of financial support to the private entities would be determined through a competitive process. The Scheme is currently under implementation and proposals of 26 States and UTs have been sanctioned till date.

4927. (6-12-2007) NEW DELHI : The Cabinet Committee on Economic Affairs today gave its approval for Construction of Ring Roads/Bypasses (including improvement of NH links in city), Grade Separated Intersections, Flyovers, Elevated roads, tunnels, Road Over Bridges, Underpasses and Service Roads at a cost of Rs.16,680 crore (Rs. 6,302 crore from Government + Rs.10,378 crore from

Private Sector), on BOT (Toll) basis. Out of Rs.16,680 crore of NHDP Phase - VII, Rs.10,500 crore will be spent on constructions for 700 km of ring roads and bypasses. The remaining amount of Rs.6,180 crore on stand alone Grade Separated Intersections, Road Over Bridges, Elevated Roads, Tunnel, Underpasses and Service Roads. Construction of ring roads, bypasses, grade separators, flyovers, Elevated roads, tunnels, Road Over Bridges, Underpasses, service roads, etc. will improve traffic safety and improve faster movement of vehicles with improved riding quality and time. This will lead to reduction in vehicle operating cost and significant reduction in fuel consumption for the vehicles resulting in energy conservation. The works of stand alone ring roads & bypasses are likely to be awarded by March, 2011 and is likely to be completed by December, 2014.

4928. (6-12-2007) NEW DELHI : On the question whether Government proposes to introduce reservation in jobs for minorities on the basis of caste/religion, the Union Minister of Minority Affairs Shri A.R. Antulay today informed the Lok Sabha that there is no such plan at present. Shri Antulay was replying to a written information in the Lok Sabha today.

4929. (6-12-2007) NEW DELHI : BJP condemns persecution of Hindus and PIOs in Malaysia ; demand government action in the matter The Bharatiya Janata Party strongly condemns the Malaysian government's policy of subjecting the country's Hindu community in particular, and People of Indian Origin (PIOs) in general, to discrimination, injustice and persecution. The BJP urges the UPA government to take up this matter with the Malaysian government at the highest level and with the seriousness it deserves. The Government of India should demand an immediate reversal of this anti-Hindu and anti-PIO policy, which runs counter to the obligation of all nations in the world to protect well-established and universally recognized human rights of all human beings, especially those belonging to minority communities. Shri P. Waytha Moorthy, Chairman of the Hindu Rights Action Force (HINDRAF) in Malaysia, today called on Shri L.K. Advani, Leader of the Opposition (Lok Sabha), Shri Jaswant Singh, Leader of the Opposition (Rajya Sabha) and other senior leaders of the BJP, and apprised them of the plight of the "forgotten", "marginalized" and "persecuted" Hindu community in his country. Some of the specific details given by him were as follows. 1. About 10,000 Hindu temples have been demolished in Malaysia since its independence fifty years ago. Most of these existed from the British colonial days and were as old as 150 years. "Hindus are stripped of their dignity and self-respect by this act" by the vindictive manner in which their temples have been razed to the ground. 2. There has been a steady attempt to "Islamise" Malaysia's multi-faith population (in which Muslims constitute 55%). The Shariah Court's rulings are being made binding on non-Muslims, especially in matters of inter-faith marriages and the religious identity of children. 3. Nearly 70% of the PIO population in Malaysia, which has been living in that country for over 200 years, remain manual labourers, living on daily wages. This underclass remains oppressed and suppressed, with the government making no special budgetary provision for their economic and educational advancement. 4. The number of Tamil, Telugu and Malayalam schools has dwindled drastically, even though the population has increased manifold. The government's neglect of the educational needs of the Indian community is deliberate, since the authorities want to cut off the PIOs' cultural and spiritual heritage. Shri Waytha Moorthy, who is a leading lawyer, also shared information about the Mayasian government's repressive crackdown of the peaceful, legitimate and democratic protests by the Hindus. He underscored the fact that the Hindus in Malaysia have always been loyal, law-abiding and peaceful citizens. Three lawyers involved in taking up the cases of HINDRAF and its supporters have been charged with sedition for speaking the truth. Thirty-one participants in the recent massive protest rally organized by HINDRAF have been falsely charged with murder under a law that denies them bail. "All this is being done to instill fear among the Hindus, so that they will not come out again to protest," Shri Moorthy said. The BJP believes that India has a moral obligation to take up the case of injustice and persecution of Malaysian Hindus and PIOs with the authorities in Kuala Lumpur. The UPA government cannot shirk from this responsibility either out of its commitment to anti-Hindu pseudo-secularism or under the pretext that this is an internal matter of Malaysia. Mr. Lee Kuan Yew meets Shri L.K. Advani; Shares concern over the condition of PIOs in Malaysia Singapore's elder statesman and former Prime Minister, Mr. Lee Kuan Yew, who now holds the position Minister Mentor, today called on Shri L.K. Advani at his residence. The two leaders had discussions on wide-ranging issues, in which the persecution of PIOs in Malaysia also figured. Mr. Lee Kuan Yew not only fully shared Shri Advaniji's appraisal of, and concerns over, the situation, but also said, "Discrimination on religious grounds in Malaysia affects not merely the Hindus. All the non-Muslim communities in Malaysia - Buddhists, Taoists and Christians - are getting worried."

4930. (6-12-2007) NEW DELHI : On a question whether Government has recently formulated any action plan for the development of muslim artisans, The Union Minister of Minority Affairs Shri A.R. Antulay today informed the Lok Sabha that an inter-ministerial group has been constituted to plan the implementation of a comprehensive programme for skill and entrepreneurship development among Muslims. The terms of reference, inter-alia, includes adopting a cluster approach for addressing the need for skill and entrepreneurship development that will benefit the largely self-employed Muslim population. Shri Antulay was replying to a written question in the Lok Sabha today

4931. (6-12-2007) NEW DELHI : The Union Minister of Minority Affairs Shri A.R. Antulay has informed the Lok Sabha that Government has approved to increase the authorized share capital of the National Minorities Development and Finance Corporation (NMDFC) from Rs. 650 crores to Rs.750 crore. NMDFC would utilize the funds for increasing its coverage under its various schemes *viz.*

Term-loan, micro-finance, education loans etc. The minister was replying to a written answer in the Lok Sabha today.

4932. (6-12-2007) NEW DELHI : The Union Minister for Rural Development, Dr. Raghuvansh Prasad Singh has called upon the Members of the Consultative Committee attached to his Ministry and to all members of the Parliament to help in successful implementation of Indira Gandhi National Old Age Pension Scheme (IGNOAPS) launched by the Prime Minister of India on 19th Nov., 2007. He informed the Members of the Consultative Committee that the State Governments have been asked to identify additional beneficiaries by using the BPL list of 2002 for rural areas and the corresponding list in urban areas. He informed the Members that 15 States have responded so far indicating the number of additional beneficiaries at 33,23 lakhs. However, after receiving information from all the States it is estimated that it will double the coverage from 87 lakh now to about 157 lakh. Dr. Singh was addressing the Members of the Consultative Committee attached to his Ministry in New Delhi yesterday. He also informed the Members that the States were requested to launch the programme at the State and District level and a number of States have done so. The new scheme is a very significant improvement over the old National Old Age Pension Scheme (NOAPS), the Members informed the Minister in the meeting. The Members raised the issue of increasing the BPL families and the need of revised criteria for identifying BPL families so that the benefit of the scheme goes to the poorest of the poor people. The Minister informed the Member that the Planning commission has set up a Group of Experts to reexamine the criteria of BPL families with a view to extend its coverage to more and more deserving people. He said that we have to work hard to get the new Old Age Pension Scheme implemented so that poorest of the poor person gets benefit of the scheme. He requested the Members of the Consultative Committee to oversee the implementation in their respective districts.

4933. (6-12-2007) NEW DELHI : A delegation led by Dr. Milan Petrovic, State Secretary in the Ministry of Agriculture and Water Management of Republic of Serbia called on the Union Minister of State for Agriculture, Shri Kanti Lal Bhuria here today. The Minister thanked the delegation for participating in the three-day International Ministerial Conference on Avian and Pandemic Influenza currently being held in New Delhi. Shri Bhuria said that both the countries shared a very cordial and friendly relationship at political, agricultural, commercial and educational level. He pointed out that both the countries have been supporting each other in the various international and multilateral fora. Shri Bhuria said that both the countries have great potential of bilateral cooperation in the field of agriculture. He also pointed out that an MOU which was finalized following the visit of experts from ICAR, has now been approved by the Government of Serbia. He conveyed Government of India's appreciation for this initiative of Serbia.

4934. (6-12-2007) NEW DELHI : A visiting delegation led by Mr. Olifant Mfa, Assistant Minister of Agriculture, Government of Botswana called on the Union

Minister of State for Agriculture, Shri Kanti Lal Bhuria here today. During the meeting, Shri Bhuria expressed the hope that the visit of Botwana delegation will prove useful for both the countries. He appreciated the achievements of Botswana in the field of Agriculture and economy. Shri Kanti Lal Bhuria said that the Memorandum of Understanding between the two countries on agriculture and allied sectors is being given the final shape. The main areas of cooperation as identified in the proposed MOU are: agricultural research; agricultural machinery; livestock; crops and horticulture including vegetables. He said that once this MOU is signed, it will pave the way for strong bilateral cooperation. Shri Kanti Lal Bhuria pointed out that India has great potential to export agricultural machines to Botswana such as small agricultural tractors, power tillers, seed cum fertilizer drills, threshers/multicrop threshers, crop reapers, straw reapers, combine harvesters, crop processing and value addition equipments etc., and allied equipment for cultivation of agricultural crops. He also thanked the delegation for participating in the three-day International Ministerial Conference on Avian and Pandemic Influenza currently being held in New Delhi. The Botswana delegation also evinced keen interest in bilateral coopeation. The Agriculture Minister of Botswana invited Shri Bhuria to visit Botswana.

4935. (6-12-2007) NEW DELHI : Disabled persons are provided reservation to the extent of 3 per cent against direct recruitment quota in the posts identified suitable for them in Group 'C' and Group 'D' categories as per the guidelines of Department of Personnel & Training (which is the nodal department for the purpose). Some of the concessions provided for them are age relaxation upto 10 years; exemption from the payment of application and examination fees; exempted from typing qualification for appointment on clerical posts if they are found otherwise qualified and are certified as being unable to type by the Medical Board; also a pass in matriculation is accepted in their cases (instead of insisting on minimum 50 per cent marks as in the case of other general candidates) provided other prescribed conditions are satisfied. This information was given by the Minister of State for Railways Shri R.Velu in written reply to a question in the Lok Sabha today.

4936. (6-12-2007) NEW DELHI : Indian Railways are now employing new generation electric locomotive which have a regenerative feature to generate electric power during braking by using three phase propulsion technology to convert kinetic energy as electric power during braking. Forty such locomotives are part of the fleet of Northern Railway, and work in prestigious Rajdhani / Shatabdi express and other important Mail/Express trains. The energy generated during braking by these locomotives was about 2 million kilowatt hours during October 2007. This information was given by the Minister of State for Railways Shri R.Velu in written reply to a question in the Lok Sabha today.

4937. (6-12-2007) NEW DELHI : The Minister for Tourism and Culture Smt. Ambika Soni has said that a new Mobile Exhibition Train - 'Azadi Express' has been flagged of on 28.9.07 from Delhi. The mobile exhibition on train will enable large number of people to visit the exhibition at their doorstep, touch their imagination and revive memories of the historic events, personalities and of the sacrifices made by a large number of freedom fighters known and unknown for attaining the freedom. The exhibition also shows the achievements of independent India in various fields. In a written reply in the Lok Sabha today she said, the total duration of the exhibition is approximately for 9 months and the total expenditure is Rs.9.27 crore (approximately). Directorate of Advertising and Visual Publicity, Ministry of I&B is the implementing agency for the Project. Ministry of Railways has also provided the special coaches and also made arrangements for running and maintenance at concessional charges.

4938. (6-12-2007) NEW DELHI : Shri Murli Deora, Minister of Petroleum & Natural Gas informed the Lok Sabha in a written reply today that the current projected annual under recoveries on petrol, diesel, PDS kerosene and domestic LPG are estimated to exceed Rs. 69,700 crore. Out of these under recoveries, he said about Rs. 33,600 crore are on account of domestic LPG and PDS kerosene. As much as 42.7% of total under recoveries will be met by the Government through oil bonds while About 1/3rd of under recoveries will be met by PSU upstream companies. "The balance will be absorbed by the PSU oil marketing companies" Shri Deora added. The Minister pointed out that the Government has also extended the PDS kerosene and Domestic LPG subsidy Scheme, 2002 and Foreign Subsidy (for far flung area) Scheme 2002 for a period of 3 more years from 1.4.2007 to 31.3.2010. The rate of subsidy admissible under the schemes through the Budget would be the same as applicable for the year 2006-07, *i.e.*, Re.0.82/litre for PDS kerosene and Rs.22.58/cylinder for domestic LPG. Shri Deora further mentioned that PDS kerosene is supplied at Rs. 9.09/litre (at Delhi) as against Rs. 24.39/litre (based on April-November 2007 international oil prices). Similarly, domestic LPG (at Delhi) is retailed at Rs. 294.75/cylinder against its international equivalent price of Rs. 487.95/cylinder for April-November 2007. The resulting under recoveries are being shouldered by the Government and the oil PSUs. International oil prices have increased to record levels and are above $86/bbl currently. He emphasized that to protect the common man, domestic retail prices of PDS kerosene and domestic LPG have not been increased over last three years.

4939. (6-12-2007) NEW DELHI : The Minister of Petroleum & Natural Gas Shri Murli Deora has said that the Government can review the royalty rates from time to time and shall not fix the royalty rate in respect of any mineral oil so as to exceed 20% of sale price of the mineral oil at the oilfields or the oil well-head as the case may be. Giving a written reply in the Lok Sabha today Shri Deora said that royalty rates are governed by the Oilfields (Regulation and Development) Act, 1948. He further told the House that after dismantling Administered Price Mechanism w.e.f. 1.4.2002, royalty rate regime was modified in consultation with stakeholders vide notification dated 16th December 2004 as follows: (i) Royalty on crude oil production from areas awarded on nomination basis to National Oil Companies (NOCs), exploration blocks awarded to Private/Joint Venture contractors prior to New Exploration Licensing Policy (NELP) and onland discovered fields awarded to Private/Joint venture contractors: (a) Onland areas@ 20% of Well Head Price. (b) Shallow water offshore areas (upto 400 metres water depth) @10% of Well Head Price. (c) Deep water offshore areas (>400 metres water depth) @ 5% of well head price during first 7 years after commercial production and normal rates as applicable to Shallow water areas (upto 400 metres water depth) during other periods. (d) Heavier Crude Oils of 25 API and less: 2.5% lesser than the applicable rates as above. (ii) Royalty on crude oil production from offshore discovered fields awarded to Private/Joint venture contractors is at the rates as specified in respective Production Sharing Contracts (PSCs). (iii) Royalty on crude oil and natural gas production from areas under Production Sharing regime is determined in accordance with the provisions of respective Production Sharing Contracts. Under New Exploration Licensing Policy (NELP), royalty on crude oil in onland areas is 12.5% of well head price and 10% in offshore areas. Royalty on natural gas is 10% of well head price. (iv) Royalty on natural gas production is 10% of the value of the natural gas obtained at well head. Shri Deora pointed out that the royalty received on crude oil and natural gas production from onland areas is paid to State Government exchequer from the date of oil and gas production. Royalty received from offshore areas is paid to the Central Government.

4940. (6-12-2007) NEW DELHI : The gap between the demand and supply of coal in the terminal year 2011-12 of the Eleventh Plan is projected to be 51.10 million tonnes as against the actual gap of 33.64 million tonnes in the terminal year 2006-07 of the Tenth Plan. During the period 2006-07 the actual production of coal was 430.86 million tonnes as against the projected demand of 474.18 million tonnes and actual coal off take of 464.5 million tonnes. As per the estimates of Geological Survey of India as on 1.4.2007, the geological coal resources of the country stand at 257.38 billion tonnes of which 99 billion Tonnes of reserves fall in proved category. This information was given by Shri Dasari Narayana Rao, Minister of State for Coal in the Parliament today.

4941. (6-12-2007) NEW DELHI : The Government has received representation from Road Safety Forum, Andhra Pradesh regarding uniform system of Driving Licence in the country. They have suggested for some common guidelines for the Drivers' Test, authorising proven NGOs to test the drivers and issue drivers' licences and issuing driving licences at the national level. Chapter-II of the Motor Vehicles Act, 1988 and Chapter-II of the Central Motor Vehicles Rules, 1989 prescribe a body of rules for testing and examination prior to grant of driving licences. These rules also prescribe procedure for granting the licences, validity in terms of various classes of vehicles and the time period and are applicable uniformly throughout the country. Further, Section 28 of the Motor Vehicles Act,

1988 empowers the State Governments for appointment of the licensing authorities and determining their jurisdiction, functions etc. There is no proposal to have a national system of giving driving licences as the same is the responsibility of the State Governments in terms of Motor Vehicles Act, 1988. Central Government has also no machinery to implement the provisions of Motor Vehicles Act, 1988 by itself. This information was given by the Minister of State for Shipping, Road Transport and Highways, Shri K.H. Muniyappa in a written reply in the Rajya Sabha today.

4942. (6-12-2007) NEW DELHI : The Government has received a representation from the Road Safety Forum against encouraging super-speed racing formula one car racing and other such events in India. The Road Safety Forum in their representation has stated that Formula 1 racing will increase high-speed driving in India, aggravating road accidents. They have cautioned that high-speed driving will have disastrous consequence on all the drivers in this country and, therefore, the country cannot afford such frivolities. Hence the Government should ban advertisements which encourage products relating to high-speed driving. The safety of road users is primarily the responsibility of the concerned State Government. However, this department has taken several steps to improve road safety for the road users which are as under: i) Road safety is the integral part of road design at the planning stage for National Highways/Expressways. ii) Various steps to enhance road safety such as road furniture, road markings/road signs, introduction of Highway Traffic Management System using Intelligent Transport System, enhancement of discipline among contractors during construction, road safety audit on selected stretches, have been undertaken by National Highways Authority of India (NHAI). iii) Refresher training to Heavy Motor Vehicle drivers in the unorganized sector. iv) Involvement of NGOs for road safety activities by Department of Road Transport and Highways and NHAI. v) Setting up of Model Driving Training School in the country by Department of Road Transport and Highways. vi) Publicity campaign on road safety awareness through audio-visual-print media by Department of Road Transport and Highways. vii) Institution of National Award for voluntary organizations/individual for outstanding work in the field of road safety by Department of Road Transport and Highways. viii) Tightening of safety standards of vehicles. ix) Provision of cranes and ambulances to various State Governments/NGOs under National Highway Accident Relief Service Scheme. National Highways Authority of India also provides ambulances at a distance of 50 Km. on each of its completed highways under its Operation & Maintenance contracts. xi) Widening and improvements of National Highways from 2 lanes to 4 lanes and 4 lanes to 6 lanes etc. This information was given by the Minister of State for Shipping, Road Transport and Highways, Shri K.H. Muniyappa in a written reply in the Rajya Sabha today.

4943. (6-12-2007) NEW DELHI : The World Road Statistics, 2006, which provides the data for the year 2003 in respect of India, indicates that the number of persons killed per lakh of population in India is 8.08. As per the preliminary tentative data, covering the majority of States and Union Territories, the number of deaths due to road accident is estimated at more than a lakh (1,01,439) during the year 2006 as compared to the figure of 94,968 deaths for the year 2005. The safety of road users is primarily the responsibility of the concerned State Government. However, this department has taken several steps to improve road safety for the road users which are as under: i) Road safety is the integral part of road design at the planning stage for National Highways/Expressways. ii) Various steps to enhance road safety such as road furniture, road markings/road signs, introduction of Highway Traffic Management System using Intelligent Transport System, enhancement of discipline among contractors during construction, road safety audit on selected stretches, have been undertaken by National Highways Authority of India (NHAI). iii) Refresher training to Heavy Motor Vehicle drivers in the unorganized sector. iv) Involvement of NGOs for road safety activities by Department of Road Transport and Highways and NHAI. v) Setting up of Model Driving Training School in the country by Department of Road Transport and Highways. vi) Publicity campaign on road safety awareness through audio-visual-print media by Department of Road Transport and Highways. vii) Institution of National Award for voluntary organizations/individual for outstanding work in the field of road safety by Department of Road Transport and Highways. viii) Tightening of safety standards of vehicles. ix) Provision of cranes and ambulances to various State Governments/NGOs under National Highway Accident Relief Service Scheme. National Highways Authority of India also provides ambulances at a distance of 50 Km. on each of its completed highways under its Operation & Maintenance contracts. x) Widening and improvements of National Highways from 2 lanes to 4 lanes and 4 lanes to 6 lanes etc. This information was given by the Minister of State for Shipping, Road Transport and Highways, Shri K.H. Muniyappa in a written reply in the Rajya Sabha today.

4944. (6-12-2007) NEW DELHI : The Government as a part of the comprehensive development of National Highways has approved construction of 1000 km of expressways under National Highways Development Project (NHDP), Phase-VI at a cost of Rs.16680 crores on Build, Operate and Transfer (BOT) basis. The section of Vadodara-Mumbai (400 km) has already been identified and the other 600 km would be identified out of the potential corridors of Delhi-Chandigarh (249 kms), Bangalore-Chennai (334 kms), Delhi-Jaipur (261 kms), Delhi-Meerut (66 kms), Kolkata-Dhanbad (277 kms) and Delhi-Agra (200 kms). In addition, construction of 134 km of eastern peripheral expressway around Delhi has been approved by the Central Government. This information was given by the Minister of State for Shipping, Road Transport and Highways, Shri K.H. Muniyappa in a written reply in the Rajya Sabha today.

4945. (6-12-2007) NEW DELHI : The personnel of Mercantile Marine Departments (MMDs) being Central Government employees are covered under the Central Government rules regarding voluntary retirement and no separate Voluntary Retirement Scheme is required for them. Inspite of shortage of surveyors, MMDs have been making best efforts for efficient functioning. The policy formulated by the Government is followed uniformly by all MMDs. Their performance is regularly monitored through periodical performance report. As and when complaints are received, they are examined as per procedure and appropriate action is initiated as warranted. The Government has framed rules for conduct of various surveys that are required for certification of ships. The MMD Surveyors follow certification procedure uniformly irrespective of the size of the company. The fees charged for smaller vessel or for smaller inspections are generally less than those for bigger ships and inspections so as to ensure that there is no undue financial burden on small entrepreneurs. This information was given by the Minister of Shipping, Road Transport and Highways, Thiru T.R. Baalu in a written reply in the Rajya Sabha today.

4946. (6-12-2007) NEW DELHI : The Government is in the process of finalising a new Model Concession Agreement (MCA) for Private Sector Projects in the Major Ports which will replace the existing Model License Agreement. The new MCA is expected to strengthen the framework for an open and transparent environment for the development and operation of port facilities by private investors and enhance their bankability. This information was given by the Minister of Shipping, Road Transport and Highways, Thiru T.R. Baalu in a written reply in the Rajya Sabha today.

4947. (6-12-2007) NEW DELHI : As per the estimates of the Indian National Shipowners' Association, there is a shortfall of about 834 officers in Indian Flag vessels as of June, 2007. However, there is no shortage of ratings for manning the Indian ships. Overall global shortage of maritime personnel and higher salary offered to Indian maritime personnel in foreign vessels are the seasons for the shortage of manpower. A proposal for hiring foreign crew to meet the shortage of officers is under consideration. The Government has initiated following measures to increase availability of manpower: (i) Expanding the facilities for marine education and training by allowing private colleges to be opened. (ii) Ensuring quality training at the maritime institutes as per international standards and introducing several new courses for pre and post sea training. (iii) Action has been initiated for induction of retired naval officers into the merchant navy. (iv) Introduction of tonnage tax obligation on shipping companies to give onboard training to cadets. (v) Permitting two years age relaxation and fee concession to encourage girl candidates to join maritime sector. (vi) The training and examination systems have been reviewed to minimize the avoidable delays for obtaining certificate of competency. This information was given by the Minister of Shipping, Road Transport and Highways, Thiru T.R. Baalu in a written reply in the Rajya Sabha today.

4948. (6-12-2007) NEW DELHI : Maintaining price stability has always been a priority for the Government. As there was pressure on prices of some of the essential commodities from the second half of 2006-07, a series of measures were undertaken to contain inflation. These included fiscal measures and administrative measures by the Central Government; direct measures to augment domestic availability of essential commodities by importing these through the PSUs besides monetary measures initiated by the Reserve Bank of India. The rate of inflation has significantly moderated in recent months. The headline inflation measured in terms of the Wholesale Price Index (WPI) declined to 3.0 per cent in October 2007. Inflation measured in terms of Consumer Price Indices also declined in September and October 2007.

4949. (6-12-2007) NEW DELHI : Kuwait Petroleum Corporation (KPC), the National Oil Company of Kuwait is keen to participate in setting up grass root projects in India in the oil and gas sector. This was conveyed by Mr. Saad A. Al Shuwaib in a meeting with the Minister of Petroleum & Natural Gas Shri Murli Deora here today. Mr. Saad said that KPC is exploring opportunities in the refinery and petrochemical activities. He informed the Minister that Kuwait is committed to India for further developing present business relationship into partnerships. Speaking on the occasion, Shri Deora stressed that this was one of the best times for foreign companies to invest in Indian oil and gas sector projects as in most of the hydrocarbon activities 100% foreign direct investment is allowed including in refineries, upstream activities etc. He pointed out that three grass root projects are being implemented by Indian national oil companies at Paradip (Orissa) by IOC, Bina (M.P.) by BPCL and Bhatinda (Punjab) by HPCL. The Bina and Bhatinda projects are being implemented as joint venture projects with Oman Oil Company and global steel major, Mittal Investments, respectively. Further, there are other projects/plans for setting up refinery - petrochemical complexes by IOCL at Panipat. ONGC at Mangalore, Kakinada, HPCL at Vishakhapatnam, etc. Assuring fullest support of Indian Government, the Minister underlined that joint venture projects between KPC and Indian Oil PSUs would be tremendously beneficial. The Indian side explained that promoting refinery projects in India is very competitive as capital cost in India is low and project consultancy by PSU technology company Engineers India Ltd. is of high quality and at competitive cost. Indian side also suggested that Kuwaiti company could also join Indian Public Sector Oil Companies in bidding for upcoming offer of exploration blocks under NELP-VII. The two sides re-iterated their time tested and long-standing friendly relations. Kuwait is a major crude oil supplier to India and supplied about 11 million metric tones during 2006-07.

4950. (6-12-2007) NEW DELHI : A postage stamp to commemorate 125 years of the Daly College, Indore will be released at Indore on December 8, 2007. The Daly College was founded in 1882. However, the story started in 1869 when General Sir, Henry Daly was appointed Agent to the Governor General in Central

India. Those days, the Indore Residency School which was hitherto running in the building of the East of the Indore Residency Post Office. This in 1867 was to be called the Indore Residency College with Mr. Aberigh-Macay, as the Principal. Henry Daly retired in 1881, and it was decided to develop the separate classes for the princes into a full-fledged school and name it "The Daly College" with an independent building. The building was constructed by the Military Works Department. On 14th November, 1885, it was inaugurated by Viceroy Lord Dufferin. The Daly College is affiliated to the Central Board of Secondary Education, New Delhi and trains students to appear for the All India Secondary and Senior Secondary School Certificate Examinations under the 10+2 scheme. The Daly College has produced eminent persons who made a mark in different walks of life.

4951. (6-12-2007) NEW DELHI : The Initial spectrum is allotted to the service providers in accordance with the relevant provisions of their respective Service License Agreements. There are no upfront charges for spectrum and spectrum usage charges only are levied (on revenue share basis). The amount of Rs. 1651.57 crore is charged as one time entry fee fro the telecom service license for all service areas in the country. This information was given by Dr. Shakeel Ahmad, Minister of State for Communications and Information Technology in the Rajya Sabha today in a written reply to a question by Shri Rajeev Chandrasekhar.

4952. (6-12-2007) NEW DELHI : A day long high-level event "The Future in our Hands: Addressing the Leadership Challenge of Climate Change" was convened on 24 September 2007 by the United Nations Secretary-General. The Indian delegation was led by Sh. P. Chidambaram, Hon'ble Finance Minister who informed the world leaders that India's per capita consumption of energy and emission of CO2 are amongst the lowest in the world. He also highlighted the efforts being made by India supportive of sustainable and clean development. It was also mentioned that Climate Change should be dealt based on the principle of common but differentiated responsibilities, and requirement of any action has to be commensurate to the respective capabilities. It was also emphasized that the only forum where the issue of climate change can be decided upon is the United Nations Framework Convention on Climate Change (UNFCCC). A need was also felt to strengthen the Clean Development Mechanism of Kyoto Protocol. The world leaders also hoped that intense negotiations would be held in the Conference of Parties to UNFCCC, at Bali, Indonesia, for a post 2012 agreement. India is engaged in the International Climate Change Regime, including the UNFCCC and its Kyoto Protocol, as also various partnerships with other countries under the UNFCCC. India has been pressing hard that as per the requirements of Kyoto Protocol the Annex-I developed countries should take deeper and longer commitments for the second phase of Kyoto Protocol. Further, India is actively participating in the Climate Change dialogue and at the Adhoc Working Group discussions coordinated by the UNFCCC Secretariat. In these negotiations, India has been pressing that 'Adaptation Fund' under the Kyoto Protocol should be operationalised at the earliest. While India does not have any Green House Gases abatement commitments under the Kyoto Protocol, nevertheless a range of policies and programmes help mitigate climate change. Besides, India spends every year over 2 per cent of the GDP in development measures with strong adaptation content. The Government has also set up "Expert Committee on Impacts of Climate Change" to study the impacts of anthropogenic climate change on India, and to identify the measures that we may have to take in the future. Further, a 'Council on Climate Change', chaired by Prime Minister, has also been set up. The focus of the Council is to evolve a coordinated response to issues relating to climate change at the national level and provide oversight for formulation of action plans in the area of assessment, adaptation and mitigation of climate change. This information was given by the Minister of State in the Ministry of Environment and Forests, Sh Namo Narain Meena in a written reply to a question in the Rajya Sabha today.

4953. (6-12-2007) NEW DELHI : Scientific surveys and independent studies are conducted on river Ganga from time to time by various agencies, independent institutions, researchers, environmentalists etc. The Central Pollution Control Board (CPCB) conducted a comprehensive survey on pollution of Ganga basin in 1984 on the basis of which the Government launched the Ganga Action Plan in 1985. Recession of glaciers of Himalayan region is part of a worldwide phenomenon and can not be prevented on a large scale in view of the nature of Indian Himalayan glaciers being debris covered, the economic feasibility, the scale of operation and the likelihood of pollution. Due to enhanced melting of ice, consequent upon faster recession, the run-off of the Himalayan Rivers may increase marginally. Pollution abatement measures like interception and diversion works to capture the raw sewage flowing into the rivers for treatment, installation of Sewage Treatment Plants, creation of low cost sanitation facilities, Electric/improved wood crematoria, River Front Development etc. are implemented under Ganga Action Plan in the polluted stretches identified by CPCB. So far a sewage treatment capacity of 1747 mld has been created under both the phases of Ganga Action Plan which includes the capacity for its tributaries. With the pollution abatement works completed so far under GAP Phase - I & II, the water quality of the river Ganga has shown improvement at major locations over its pre-GAP quality. At present the Centrally Sponsored Scheme of National River Conservation Plan covers 164 towns along polluted stretches of 35 identified rivers spread over 20 States in the country for abatement of pollution. This information was given by the Minister of State in the Ministry of Environment and Forests, Sh Namo Narain Meena in a written reply to a question in the Rajya Sabha today.

4954. (6-12-2007) NEW DELHI : Conservation of rivers is a dynamic activity with the ever increasing pollution load due to increase in population. Review of the strategies of conservation policy and identification of additional towns and rivers is a continuous process. Water being a State subject, it is the responsibility of State Governments to create proper sewerage infrastructure to prevent pollution from entering the rivers. Central Government only supplements the efforts of the State Governments by providing one time grant for capital works for identified polluted stretches of rivers. The National River Conservation Plan (NRCP) presently covers pollution abatement works in the polluted stretches of 35 rivers spread over 164 towns in 20 states in the country at an approved cost of Rs.4793 crore. Ganga and Yamuna are among the major rivers covered under this Plan. A total of 667 schemes for abatement of pollution in rivers Ganga & Yamuna have been completed so far resulting in creation of 1704 mld (million litres per day) of sewage treatment capacity at an expenditure of Rs. 1431 crores. With the pollution abatement works completed in both the phases under Ganga Action Plan so far, the water quality of the river Ganga has shown improvement at major locations over its pre-GAP quality. In respect of river Yamuna, the quality of river water has not shown the desired improvement owing to the large gap between the demand and the availability of sewage treatment capacity particularly in Delhi, and the lack of availability of fresh water for ensuring minimum flow in the river. The Report for the year ended March 2000 of the Comptroller and Auditor General of India (No.5A of 2000) on a review of the Ganga Action Plan from the 1993 to 2000, contained observations pertaining to delay in execution of works, discontinuation of Water Quality Monitoring, poor Operation and Maintenance (O&M) of assets created under the Plan in the states among others. Besides meeting the statutory obligation of providing Action Taken Report to the observations, the Government has taken remedial measures to improve the performance. These measures include strengthening of monitoring of the implementation of works, resumption of water quality monitoring through independent agencies, and requirement of submission of a detailed O&M Plan by the State Governments before sanction of projects. This information was given by the Minister of State in the Ministry of Environment and Forests, Sh Namo Narain Meena in a written reply to a question in the Rajya Sabha today.

4955. (6-12-2007) NEW DELHI : The pollution margins (limits) for various categories of industries are notified under Environment (Protection) Act, 1986. The limits have also been prescribed by the State Pollution Control Boards (SPCBs) / Pollution Control Committees (PCCs) under the Water (Prevention and Control of Pollution) Act, 1974 and the Air (Prevention and Control of Pollution) Act, 1981 while granting consent to industrial units to establish / operate. The pollution margins (limits) are applicable to all the specified categories of industries based on types of industries and its location. There is no mandatory provision under the environmental legislations, such as, Environment (Protection) Act, 1986, Water (Prevention and Control of Pollution) Act, 1974 and the Air (Prevention and Control of Pollution) Act, 1981, for an industry to reveal its carbon foot print (carbon emission) details. This information was given by the Minister of State in the Ministry of Environment and Forests, Sh Namo Narain Meena in a written reply to a question in the Rajya Sabha today.

4956. (6-12-2007) NEW DELHI : The State Government of Rajasthan has submitted proposals for 'Rejuvenation of Nakki lake in Mount Abu' and 'Conservation and Sustainable Management of Pushkar Sarovar in Ajmer' for their consideration under the National Lake Conservation Plan. The proposal for 'Rejuvenation of Nakki Lake in Mount Abu', has been examined by the designated committee of the Ministry and accorded conditional approval. The decision has been communicated to the State Government. The proposal for 'Conservation and Sustainable Management of Pushkar Sarovar in Ajmer' has also been examined in the Ministry and found deficient in terms of certain administrative inputs. The Government of Rajasthan has been informed accordingly. This information was given by the Minister of State in the Ministry of Environment and Forests, Sh Namo Narain Meena in a written reply to a question in the Rajya Sabha today.

4957. (6-12-2007) NEW DELHI : On 17.10.2007, Government has taken a decision on the recommendations dated 28.8.2007 of Telecom Regulatory Authority of India (TRAI) on Review of license terms & conditions and capping of number of access providers". TRAI has made the said recommendation after following a consultation process with the stakeholders including Cellular Operators Association of India (COAI). COAI and others have challenged the Government decision on these recommendations in Telecom Disputes Settlement and Appellate Tribunal (TDSAT) and the matter is sub-judice. This information was given by Dr.Shakeel Ahmad, Minister of State for Communications and Information Technology in the Rajya Sabha today in a written reply to a question by Shri Ravi Shankar Prasad and Shri Ram Jethmalani.

4958. (6-12-2007) NEW DELHI : The number of Post Offices functioning in rental buildings in the year 2006-07 was 383 for which rent of rupees 24.75 lacs has been paid during the year 2006-07. The construction of new departmental buildings on the existing vacant plots is a continuous process and buildings are constructed in phased manner subject to the availability of adequate funds and priority. This information was given by Dr. Shakeel Ahmad, Minister of State for Communications and Information Technology, in the Rajya Sabha today in a written reply to a question by Shri Ajay Maroo.

4959. (6-12-2007) NEW DELHI : Two wind energy projects covering an area of 340.46 hectares were accorded approval under the Forest (Conservation) Act, 1980 during the year 2005-06 by the Central Government in Dhule district of Maharashtra, in which no displacement of people was involved. In projects where displacement of people is involved, the resettlement is done as per the Central Government and the concerned State Governments' Relief and Rehabilitation Policy. In case of displacement of people belonging to the Scheduled Tribes, the views of Ministry of Tribal Affairs are also taken into consideration. This information was given by the Minister of State in the Ministry of Environment and Forests, Shri S. Regupathy in a written reply to a question in the Rajya Sabha today.

4960. (6-12-2007) NEW DELHI : As per National Association of Software and Service Companies, the larger companies have reported relatively higher growth rates compared to smaller companes in Financial Year 2007. There could be several reasons for this, which include: their ability to bid for larger deals (which smaller companies are often not qualified to bid for. As per Software Technology Parks of India, the growth of big companies is higher based on their export performance in the recent years. The reasons for higher growth rate of big companies include: Brand Value, diversified expertise, capability to serve client across the globe in different geography. On the other hand small companies in the IT industry are addressing only niche markets/expertise, and are able to serve only to particular geography, which also result in limited growth. As per the Electronics and Computer Software Export Promotion Council, the turnover of companies in general is taken as criteria for the categorization. This information was given by Dr. Shakeel Ahmad, Minister of State for Communications and Information Technology, in the Rajya Sabha today in a written reply to a question by Dr.Murli Manohar Joshi and Shri Raj Mohinder Singh Majitha.

4961. (6-12-2007) NEW DELHI : Several projects on multidisciplinary aspects of Climate Change have been completed and funded by the Government of India, Global Environment Facility (GEF) and also under bilateral cooperation. India has received an indicative allocation of US$ 74.9 millions to fund climate change projects (2006-2010) in the country through GEF, which is the multilateral financial mechanism. Government of India has already set up an Expert Committee under the Chairmanship of Principal Scientific Adviser to Government of India on impacts of Climate Change to identify the impacts of anthropogenic Climate Change on India and to identify the measures that we may have to take in the future in relation to addressing vulnerability to anthropogenic Climate Change impacts. The composition of the Expert Committee includes eminent scientists and representatives of various Ministries and Departments concerned. This information was given by the Minister of State in the Ministry of Environment and Forests, Sh Namo Narain Meena in a written reply to a question in the Rajya Sabha today.

4962. (6-12-2007) NEW DELHI : The First River Action Plan *i.e.* the Ganga Action Plan was taken up by the Ministry of Environment & Forests in 1985. Since then its scope has increased to cover all the major rivers of the country in stages and the programme was renamed as National River Conservation Plan (NRCP) in 1995. At present the Centrally Sponsored Scheme of NRCP covers 164 towns along polluted stretches of 35 identified rivers spread over 20 States in the country at an approved cost of Rs.4793 crore. The major rivers covered under the Plan include Ganga, Yamuna, Gomti, Damodar & Mahananda besides the rivers Satluj, Krishna, Cauveri and Godavari. The pollution abatement works undertaken under

NRCP include interception and diversion works to capture the raw sewage flowing into the rivers for treatment, installation of Sewage Treatment Plants, creation of low cost sanitation facilities, Electric/improved wood crematoria, River Front Development etc. This information was given by the Minister of State in the Ministry of Environment and Forests, Sh Namo Narain Meena in a written reply to a question in the Rajya Sabha today.

4963. (6-12-2007) NEW DELHI : To reduce environmental pressure on ecosystems such as riversheds, mangroves, coastal zones, forests and grasslands the Government has enacted acts such as Environment (Protection) Act, 1986, Forest (Conservation) Act, 1980, Wildlife (Protection) Act 1972 and issued notifications under these to regulate activities in ecologically fragile areas such as Coastal Zones, Management of Hazardous Substances, established a procedure for according environment and forest clearance which inter alia provides for examination of use of resources such as land, water and energy, constituted authority to regulate Ground Water use. The present Water (Prevention and Control of Pollution) Act, 1974, and Air (Prevention and Control of Pollution) Act, 1981 provides adequate powers to the competent authorities to prevent and control the pollution and mitigate the same and if necessary take punitive actions. In addition Water (Prevention and Control of Pollution) Act, 1979, provides for collection of 'water cess' for water abstracted. This information was given by the Minister of State in the Ministry of Environment and Forests, Sh Namo Narain Meena in a written reply to a question in the Rajya Sabha today.

4964. (6-12-2007) NEW DELHI : The National River Conservation Plan (NRCP), a Centrally sponsored Scheme administered by the Ministry of Environment & Forests presently covers pollution abatement works in 35 rivers spread over 164 towns in 20 States of the country. The State Governments play a pivotal role in the pollution abatement/control measures. The pollution abatement works under NRCP are implemented through Implementing Agencies nominated by the State Governments for the purpose. Water being a State subject, it is the responsibility of State Governments to create proper sewerage infrastructure to prevent pollution from entering the rivers. Central Government only supplements the efforts of the State Governments by providing one time grant for capital works for identified polluted stretches of rivers. River Conservation Programme is a mammoth task and needs cooperation of all stakeholders like State Governments, Local Bodies, public at large etc. The State Governments/ Local Bodies are encouraged to fulfil their responsibilities towards Operation & Maintenance (O&M) of assets created under by generating additional revenue through innovative measures like levying of user charges, sale of sludge and through institutional mechanism under Public-Private Partnership (PPP) models to augment resources. Besides the above, cooperation of NGOs, schools, private sector and general public are also tapped in the Public Participation & Awareness campaigns for conservation of rivers. This information was given by the Minister of State in the Ministry of Environment and Forests, Sh Namo Narain Meena in a written reply to a question in the Rajya Sabha today.

4965. (6-12-2007) NEW DELHI : During the 12th World Lake Conference (Taal 2007), organized under the aegis of International Lake Environment Committee (ILEC) Foundation and hosted by the Ministry of Environment & Forests, Government of India, at Jaipur (Rajasthan) from 28th October to 2nd November, 2007, a Jaipur Declaration was adopted at the valedictory session of the Conference. The declaration recognized the importance of lakes & wetlands for the goods & services they provide and expressed concern over the deteriorating state of these water bodies globally. It called upon the governments and international organizations to take measures for development of water quality standards, appropriate research methodologies, guidelines, treatment technologies etc. in respect of lakes & wetlands and promote their restoration & management through various measures. It also emphasized the need for strong institutional & financial mechanism for regional and international cooperation in the area of lakes & wetlands management. This information was given by the Minister of State in the Ministry of Environment and Forests, Sh Namo Narain Meena in a written reply to a question in the Rajya Sabha today.

4966. (6-12-2007) NEW DELHI : The 180th meeting of the Central Board of Trustees (EPF) was convened here today to consider agenda placed before the Board for consideration. The Draft Annual Report on the work and activities of the Employees' Provident Fund Organization (EPFO) for the year 2006-07 was adopted by the Board after detailed deliberations. Apart from this, the Board also adopted the Consolidated Annual Accounts for the year 2005-06. The revised estimates for 2007-08 and Budget Estimates for the year 2008-09 were also approved by the Board. The Board Meeting was chaired by Shri Oscar Fernandes, the Minister of Labour and Employment. The meeting was attended by the representatives of Employees, Employers and the Central and State Governments.

4967. (6-12-2007) NEW DELHI : Broadcasting Engineering Consultancy India Ltd. (BECIL), a department under the Ministry of Information and Broadcasting has earned a profit of Rs.7.92 crores lakhs in the year 2006-07 as against Rs.2.27 crores in the previous year. This increase by around 3.5 times is matched by a three fold increase in the business turn over during the year which short up to Rs.98.67 crores as against Rs. 31.52 crores in the previous year. The major activities, which contributed towards this impressive performance included the successful implementation of common transmission infrastructure (CTI) to private broadcasters during FM Phase II, wherein the company created CTI for 245 FM channels in 87 cities using for Prasar Bharati infrastructure spread over the entire country, execution of orders for setting up studios for a large number of FM Phase II broadcasters and commissioning of Lok Sabha TV channel and multi-media studio for Rashtrapati Bhawan. The company also took up the consultancy and system integration or establishment of interim transmission set ups in the city of Delhi, Mumbai, Calcutta, Chennai, Jaipur, Hyderabad and Bangalore for various FM broadcasters and providing transmission power to broadcasting organisations. In FM radio sector, the company has orders worth Rs.183 crores for bringing up CTI in 87 cities. The company has also submitted a proposal of Rs.97.72 crores to the Ministry of External Affairs for re-enforcement of radio coverage in Afghanistan involving medium wave, short wave hp transmissions alongwith studio centres.

4968. (6-12-2007) NEW DELHI : Indian Defence scientists today successfully carried out the second launch of a Single Stage Interceptor Missile against an incoming ballistic missile target of enemy represented by a modified Prithvi Missile at the Wheeler Island near Bay of Bengal, close to the Dhamra coast in Orissa. The endo-atmospheric Interceptor intercepted the missile at 15 Km altitude exactly as designed at high supersonic speed at 11 this morning. All the elements of Ballistic Missile Defence System such as Long Range Tracking Radar, Multi-function Fire Control Radar, Mission Control Centre, Launch Control Centre, Mobile Launcher, Mobile and Multi Layer Communication System, Data Links to Interceptor participated in the mission. The Interceptor and all the Elements performed in a copybook fashion validating the design of the Endo-Atmospheric layer of the BMD system. The Defence Minister Shri AK Antony has congratulated the DRDO team led by Dr. V. K. Saraswat for this significant accomplishment.

4969. (6-12-2007) NEW DELHI : In September 2000, the member States in the United Nations unanimously adopted the Millennium Declaration in the meeting of the General Assembly. The Millennium Development Goals commit the international community to an expanded vision of development, one that vigorously promotes human development as the key to sustaining social and economic progress in all countries, and recognizes the importance of creating a global partnership for development. The goals have been commonly accepted as a framework for measuring development progress. Following consultations among international agencies, including the World Bank, and the specialized agencies of the United Nations, the General Assembly recognized the Millennium Development Goals as part of the road-map for implementing the Millennium Declaration.

4970. (6-12-2007) NEW DELHI : External Affairs Minister, Shri Pranab Mukherjee informed the Rajya Sabha today in written reply to a question that the agreement between India and the US on the cooperation in civil uses of nuclear energy could result in substantial additional power generating capacity. The Integrated Energy Policy, 2006 sets a target for the year 2020 of 20,000 MW of nuclear power generation. This could double with international cooperation. Regarding the position of financial gains that the country would have from the nuclear agreement, the Minister said that it is critical that India's current GDP growth rate of 8-10% per annum is maintained in order to achieve the objective of eradication of poverty.

For this, it is necessary to explore and exploit all sources of energy. The additionality of nuclear energy will help to achieve India's energy targets and contribute to growth in vital sectors of India's economy including industry and agriculture.

4971. (6-12-2007) NEW DELHI : The Government has decided to introduce e-passports, also known as bio-metric passports, initially for diplomats and officials as a pilot project by the middle of 2008. Based on the experience gained from this pilot project, it is proposed to start issuance of e-passports in the ordinary category. Incorporation of bio-metrics in the passports will make them more secure against forgeries and will also further strengthen prevention of issue of multiple passports. The Government had entrusted the National Institute of Smart Government (NISG), Hyderabad, with the task of undertaking a time-bound study on the passport issuance system, including its IT aspects with the objective to deliver passport related services to the citizens in a timely, transparent, more accessible, reliable manner. NISG has submitted its report which has been accepted by the Government and it has been decided to launch "Passport Seva Project". The project is expected to result in the issue of passports within 3 days and in cases which require police verification, within 3 days after the completion of the verification process. Tatkal passports are expected to be issued the same day. The above information was given by Minister of State in the Ministry of External Affairs, Shri E. Ahamed in written reply to a question in Rajya Sabha today.

4972. (6-12-2007) NEW DELHI : In exercise of the powers conferred by Section 3 of the Essential Commodities Act 1955 (10 of 1955) the Central Government issued the Rice (Stock Declaration by Companies or Firms or Individuals) Order 2007 vide notification, dated 27.11.2007. The order requires submission of return by a Company or Firm or Individuals who purchases paddy (in terms of rice) or rice in excess of 10,000 Metric tonnes (MT) (total purchase made throughout the country) during the Kharif Marketing Season 2007-08 (October, 2007- September, 2008) to Secretary, Department of Food of the State from where maximum quantity has been purchased, in such Form and at such intervals as may be specified by the Central Government. In case of purchase of paddy (in terms of rice) or rice exceeds 25,000 Metric tonnes (total purchases made throughout the country), the return in the Form at intervals specified therein shall be furnished to the Under Secretary (Policy-III), Department of Food and Public Distribution, Room No. 292, Krishi Bhawan, New Delhi-110001 (Fax No. 011-23782213, e-mail: uspy34.fpd@nic.in). The concerned State Governments with which the returns are filed by any Company or Firm or individual declaring purchase of paddy (in terms of rice) or rice in excess of 10,000 MT shall submit a consolidated monthly report to the Under Secretary (Py-III), Department of Food and Public Distribution by the 10th of every month.

4973. (6-12-2007) NEW DELHI : The Minister for Civil Aviation, Shri Praful Patel has announced today that the list of dignitaries who are exempted from pre-embarkation security checks at Civil Airports has been extended to include the Deputy Chairman of Planning Commission, holders of Bharat Ratna Decoration, the Chief Election Commissioner, the Comptroller and Auditor General of India, the Attorney General of India and the Chiefs of Defence Staff, holding the rank of full General or equivalent. It may be recalled that the Bureau of Civil Aviation Security (BCAS) has a list of VVIPs/VIPs who are exempt from pre-embarkation security checks at all Civil Airports in the country. They include the President, the Vice President, the Prime Minister, former Presidents, former Vice Presidents, Speaker of the Lok Sabha, Chief Justice of India, Judges of Supreme Court, Leaders of Opposition in Lok Sabha and Rajya Sabha, Union Minister of Cabinet rank, Deputy Chairman of Rajya Sabha, Deputy Speaker of Lok Sabha, all Governors of States, Chief Ministers of States, Ministers of State of the Union Council of Ministers, Chief Justices of the High Courts, Lt. Governors of Union Territories, Chief Ministers of UTs, Deputy Chief Ministers of State, Deputy Chief Ministers of UTs, Ambassadors of foreign countries, Charge-D' Affairs and High Commissioners and their spouses, the Cabinet Secretary and others. The BCAS will now amend the list as per the directions of Ministry of Civil Aviation.

4974. (6-12-2007) NEW DELHI : The Union Finance Minister in his Budget Speech for 2007-08 announced in the Parliament the setting up of a Revolving Fund with a corpus Rs. 100 crore to accelerate the process of project preparation. To fulfil the commitment, Department of Economic Affairs has notified the Guidelines for India Infrastructure Project Development Fund Scheme to provide financial support for quality project development activities to the States and the Central Ministries through 'India Infrastructure Project Development Fund (IIPDF)' Scheme. Public Private Partnerships (PPPs) are being encouraged by Government of India as the preferred mode for execution and operation of infrastructure projects. Several initiatives have been taken by the Central Government to promote PPPs. These include streamlining and standardising the process of appraisal and approval of PPP projects in the Central sector through setting up of the PPP Appraisal Committee (PPPAC); providing Viability Gap Funding (VGF) to projects under the Scheme for Financial Support to PPPs in Infrastructure; setting up India Infrastructure Finance Company Ltd (IIFCL) as a Special Purpose Vehicle (SPV) to meet the long term financing requirements of potential investors; and facilitating dissemination of information on PPPs as well as capacity building of officers of Central Ministries and State Governments to develop, appraise and execute PPP projects. The overall response to PPP as the preferred mode for the implementation of infrastructure is encouraging. Project development has been identified as a critical area of attention to enable creation of a shelf of bankable Public Private Partnership projects that can be bid out. Accordingly, the Department of Economic Affairs (DEA) has embarked on a technical assistance programme, which provides the selected State Governments with in-house consultants to manage the process for project development. Fourteen states have indicated their requirement to avail of this technical assistance programme. The IIPDF Scheme aims to put in place a mechanism to fund potential Public Private Partnership projects' project development expenses including cost of engaging consultants and transaction advisor, thus increasing the quality and quantity of successful PPPs and allowing informed decision making by the Government based on good quality feasibility reports. The IIPDF Scheme will assist projects that closely support the best practices in PPP project identification and preparation.

4975. (6-12-2007) NEW DELHI : The Government is committed to provide one-third representation to women in State Assemblies and the Parliament and it is working for a broad consensus on the matter, this was stated by the Prime Minister, Dr. Manmohan Singh while inaugurating the 2nd East Asia Gender Equality Ministerial meeting here today. He said that participation of a critical mass of women in politics at the highest level would bring about a revolutionary change and in ensuring good governance. Recalling the contribution of late Shri Rajiv Gandhi for introducing one-third reservation for women in local bodies, the PM said that mobilization of large numbers of women in public life through Panchayats has brought about a significant shift in public policy and in social attitudes towards women. Calling for a mass movement for gender equality, Prime Minister said that it is a fundamental necessity for promoting social economic development. "Women's empowerment unleashes a potential that has remained suppressed for centuries. It enables society to tap into the huge reservoir of talent in one half of the human race", he added. Highlighting India's initiative to achieve gender equality, Smt. Renuka Chowdhury, Minister for Women and Child Development said that number of initiatives had been taken to improve the status of women and empower her politically, educationally, economically and legally. An inter-Ministerial committee has been constituted to look into the aspect of legal equality for women in all spheres and specially to remove discriminatory legislations and to enact new legislations for this purpose. Smt. Chowdhury said that the Bills for Protection of Women from Sexual Harassment at workplace, Unorganised Sector Workers' Social Security Bill and Amendment in the Maternity Benefit Act are on anvil. Underlining the importance of economic empowerment of women, the Minister said unless women, who constitute half the population are able to gain from the benefit of economic liberalization, development would continue to be lopsided. Referring the gender budgeting introduced by the Government to ensure committed funds for women related schemes, she said that her Ministry is taking up auditing of this budgeting to see that women get full benefit of the great initiative. Stressing on the holistic empowerment of women, she said that social, economic and political aspects impacting their lives must converge effectively. Despite all efforts to improve the status of women, the gender imbalances still continue. Such imbalance begin with the declining sex ratio, illiteracy and inadequate health care between girls and boys and culminates in the high rate of maternal mortality because of early marriages and poor health. Differentials in educational status and economic empowerment are heavily biased against women, the Minister added. Referring to common challenge before the South Asian countries, Smt.

Chowdhury said "we are still beset with the challenges of high maternal mortality, increasing proportion of gender-based violence, limited protection that exists for women, low representation of women in decision making etc." Hence, in the coming years, South Asian countries have to reduce disparities across regions and communities by ensuring equal access to basic physical infrastructure as well as health and education services to all. She expressed the hope deliberations during the meeting will lead to a declaration or guidelines to overcome these challenges. 2-days' meeting is being attended by Ministerial level delegations from Australia, Brunei Darussalam, Cambodia, China, Indonesia, Japan, Korea, Lao, People's Democratic Republic, Malaysia, Mynmar, New Zealand, Phillipines, Singapore, Thailand, Vietnam and representatives from international organizations including UNIFEM, UNICEF, UNFPA, UNDP, UNESCAP and UNODC. Thematic issues for the deliberations are - women in decision-making, violence against women and home based workers.

4976. (6-12-2007) NEW DELHI : Several new legislative and administrative measures taken by the Government have brought fiscal stability which improved tax revenues and tightened expenditure. This was stated by the Finance Minister, Shri P. Chidambaram while addressing the Meeting of the Parliamentary Consultative Committee attached to his Ministry, here today. He said that FRBM Act was passed as soon as the UPA Government came into power and then the Department of Revenue was energised to improve tax buoyancy. Shri Chidambaram said that the tax buoyancy is basically the result of good performance of Indian economy and the new initiatives taken by the Central Board of Direct Taxes (CBDT) and Central Board of Excise and Customs (CBEC). Speaking about Direct Taxes, Shri Chidambaram said that the TDS administration, refund bankers, tax return prepares scheme, large tax payers unit, E-filing of taxes and business process reengineering are some of the important initiatives which have brought an unprecedented growth of tax collections. He said that attitude of people to pay taxes has now been changing. The personal income tax grew by 42.5% and corporation tax by 46.6% during April-November 2007 over the corresponding period of last fiscal. The overall direct tax collection growth rate is 44.9% during this period, he added. Shri Chidambaram said that the number of taxpayers in the country has been increasing. While the number of assesses increased from 301.78 lakhs in 2003-04 to 319.26 lakhs in 2006-07, the number of assesses filing return of income increased from 234.25 lakhs to 275.44 lakhs during this period. The number of PANs as on 31st October, 2007 is 5,74,74,806 and around 8 to 9 lakhs PANs are being allotted every year. PANs de-duplication has been completed in respect of more than 95% cases. Shri Chidambaram said that pilot project of State Bank of India acting as a Refund Banker has been extended to select charges of four more cities *viz.*, Mumbai, Kolkata, Chennai and Bangalore apart from existing cities at Delhi and Patna. On indirect taxes, the Finance Minister said that customs duty rates are being decreased continuously, while the excise duty rates have decreased. He said that the concept of GST-Central and States should come into effect from

1st April, 2010 which would avoid the multiplicity of different kinds of taxes. The various initiatives taken by CBEC like risk management system for customs, automatic clearance of courier consignment, automation of central excise and service tax, e-payment, large tax payer units, streamlining of customs procedures are some of the major initiatives which contributed buoyancy in collection of indirect taxes. He said, during April-October, 2007, customs duty increased by 17.4%, central excise by 7.6% and service tax by 36.3% over the corresponding period of 2006-2007. Overall collections of indirect taxes grew by 15% during this period. The meeting was attended by S/Sh. K.V. Thangka Balu, M. Sreenivasulu Reddy, P.C. Thomas and Dr. C. Krishnan from Lok Sabha and S/Shri Rajkumar Dhoot, Bimal Jalan, S.M. Laljan Basha, and B.J. Panda from Rajya Sabha who gave several valuable suggestions. Ministers of State for Finance, Shri S.S. Palanimanickam and Shri Pawan Kumar Bansal apart from senior officers of the Finance Ministry also attended the meeting.

4977. (6-12-2007) NEW DELHI : Two cities namely Amritsar and Ludhiana are covered under Urban Infrastructure Governance (UIG) component of Jawaharlal Nehru National Urban Renewal Mission (JNNURM). So far, Government of Punjab have submitted 5 Detailed Project Reports (DPRs) out of which 2 projects have been sanctioned and 3 DPRs are under appraisal by technical appraisal agency. A sum of Rs.4110.38 lakh has been released for the projects approved under UIG in the last three years. Cities which are not covered under UIG component are covered under Urban Infrastructure Development Scheme for Small and Medium Towns (UIDSSMT) another Scheme of the Ministry. Under UIDSSMT no proposal for release of funds has been received from State Government of Punjab so far. This information was given by Shri Ajay Maken, Minister of State in the Ministry of Urban Development in the Rajya Sabha today in a written reply to a question by Shri Naresh Gujral.

4978. (6-12-2007) NEW DELHI : Maintenance of land records is a State subject. However, states and cities which have accessed funds under Jawaharlal Nehru National Urban Renewal Mission (JNNURM) have agreed to introduce Property Title Certification system within the Mission period of 7 years in respect of identified cities under the Mission. Proposal regarding introduction of such a system is to be submitted by respective State Governments. TheMission Directorate under JNNURM has not so far received any proposal under which any State has indicated that it would guarantee land title. This information was given by Shri Ajay Maken, Minister of State in the Ministry of Urban Development in the Rajya Sabha today in a written reply to a question by Shri Ramdas Agarwal and Shri Dara Singh.

4979. (6-12-2007) NEW DELHI : New Delhi Municipal Council (NDMC) has reported that monkey menace is rampant in many localities of the NDMC area. However, no case of biting and damaging of property by the monkeys has been reported in the NDMC area in recent months. NDMC has reported that 611 monkeys have been trapped during the period from March to November, 2007 utilizing the cages and the services of the specialist monkey catchers. The captured monkeys are released in the forest area in Asola - Bhatti Wild Life Sanctuary. As the problem is of local nature, appropriate steps are within the jurisdiction of local bodies/State Government. This information was given by Shri Ajay Maken, Minister of State in the Ministry of Urban Development in the Rajya Sabha today in a written reply to a question by Shri Vijay J.Darda.

4980. (6-12-2007) NEW DELHI : The work of residential apartments has been started and targeted to be completed by March, 2010. The work of practice Venue will commence in February/March, 2008 and is likely to be completed by May, 2010. The tendering process of temporary overlay will commence in June, 2009 and the work on ground will be commenced in January, 2010 and is expected to be completed by May, 2010. This information was given by Shri Ajay Maken, Minister of State in the Ministry of Urban Development in the Rajya Sabha today in a written reply to a question by Shrimati Prema Cariappa.

4981. (6-12-2007) NEW DELHI : The Government has asked all airlines to clarify as to what are the charged tax components and provide confirmation whether all the taxes shown by them in their tickets/website are deposited with the Government. The airlines have also been asked to submit the record of the taxes deposited with the Government at the earliest. In a letter dated 4th December 2007 the Director General of Civil Aviation has said that perusal of the fare shown on the airlines website has revealed that the airfares have two components - the basic fare and the taxes. It is not clarified as to whether components like Passenger Service Fee and Fuel Surcharge are included in the basic fare or have been clubbed under the heading of "taxes". The letter states that a "Tax" is defined to be a fee levied by Government on a product, income or activity and such amounts are to be deposited with the Government and a record is required to be maintained for the same. In view of the ambiguity in the airfares, the DGCA has sought a clarification from the airlines.

4982. (6-12-2007) NEW DELHI : A Technical Group on Estimation of Urban Housing Shortage was constituted by the Central Government. The Group estimated a housing shortage of 24.71 million dwelling units at the end of the Tenth Five Year Plan. The Technical Group has estimated the total Housing shortage during the entire 11th Five Year Plan as 26.53 million dwelling units. This information was given by the Minister of State for Housing & Urban Poverty Alleviation, Kumari Selja in the Rajya Sabha today, in a written reply to a question by Smt. Supriya Sule. The Government has launched the Jawaharlal Nehru National Urban Renewal Mission (JNNURM) to assist cities and towns in taking up housing and infrastructural facilities for the urban poor in 63 cities in the country under the Basic Services to the Urban Poor (BSUP) Programme. Other cities/towns are covered under Integrated Housing and Slum Development Programme (IHSDP). Both BSUP and IHSDP are under implementation since December, 2005. On completion of the Mission period of seven year, it is expected that all urban poor will be able to have access to a basic level of urban services. Provision of basic services to urban poor including security of tenure at affordable prices, improved housing, water supply, sanitation and ensuring delivery of other already existing universal services of the government for education, health and social security is a mandatory reform under BSUP & IHSDP schemes. Public Private Partnership is also a recognized optional reform under these schemes. Apart from schemes of BSUP & IHSDP under JNNURM, an amount of Rs.30 crores has been allocated in the budget for 2007-08 for an interest subsidy scheme for provision of housing to the Economically Weaker Sections (EWS)/Low Income Group (LIG) of the society.

4983. (6-12-2007) NEW DELHI : The Prime Minister, Dr. Manmohan Singh, inaugurated the 2nd East Asia Gender Equality Ministerial Meeting here today. Addressing the Conference, the Prime Minister reiterated that true and meaningful gender equality will be achieved by educating women, providing gainful employment opportunities and ensuring their sufficient representation in legislative bodies. Gender equality is a fundamental necessity for promoting social and economic development, Dr. Singh added. The Prime Minister used the occasion to reaffirm the Government's commitment to providing representation to women in the State Assemblies and the Central Parliament.

4984. (6-12-2007) NEW DELHI : A three-day International Ministerial Conference on Avian and Pandemic Influenza concluded here today. The Conference was attended by Representatives from 111 countries. Representatives from 29 International Organizations also participated which included Director Generals of International Organisations like WHO, FAO, World Bank, OIE, etc. The Prime Minister of India, Dr. Manmohan Singh addressed the delegates on the second day of the Conference *i.e.* 5th December, 2007. Minister for Agriculture, Government of India, Shri Sharad Pawar and Minister for Health & Family Welfare, Government of India, Dr. Anbumani Ramadoss were among those who addressed the Conference. The Conference had 12 Sessions on various subjects pertaining to Avian and Pandemic Influenza. The Conference was jointly organized by the Ministry of Health & Family Welfare and Department of Animal Husbandry (Ministry of Agriculture), Government of India. "A Vision and Road Map" was released by Government of India at the conclusion of the three-day Conference and handed over to World Bank and UN System Influenza Coordinator.

4985. (7-12-2007) NEW DELHI : Union Minister for Rural Development Dr. Raghuvansh Prasad Singh has called for ensuring the availability of safe drinking water in rural areas of the country. Addressing a two-day long National Rural Workshop on Water supply and Sanitation in Rural India here today

Dr. Singh stressed the importance of development of suitable technologies for addressing drinking water supply, safe and potable drinking water to all habitations of the country, sustainable sanitation options for achieving total sanitation by 2012, well before timelines of the Millennium Development Goal. Referring to the presence of Arsenic and Fluoride contents in the ground water of Bihar, West Bengal and Assam and Fluoride and Iron contents in Gujarat, Andhra Pradesh as well as salinity of water in the coastal areas of the country the Minister stressed for the training of local villagers in testing the water quality and equipping them with newly developed test kits. In order to ensure the availability of safe drinking water the department of Drinking Water Supply is already running a Quality Servillance Programme under the Bharat Nirman for which a budget of Rs.200 crore has been earmarked to provide test kits in village panchayats and open district level test laboratory and state level Referral laboratories in different states, the minister added. He also informed of the Data Management work done by the Department of Drinking Water Supply in doing the survey of available water sources every year instead of the existing norm of five year. On Total Sanitation Programme (TSC) the minister informed of the construction of nearly one crore toilets every year and hoped every rural school, aanganwadi centre will have proper toilets by March, 2008. He also called for the recycling of the solid/liquid waste products under solid/liquid waste management in the rural areas so as to into manure that the target will be achieved during the next four years.. Dr. Singh expressed the hope of attaining the millennium development goals by the year 2012 positively. The workshop has participation from representatives from various Ministries and Departments of Government of India lie Ministry of Rural Development, Ministry of Health & Family Welfare, Ministry of Science & Technology, CSIR, Central Ground Water Board, Central Water Commission etc. The participants included Senior Officials of 25 State Governments and institutions like the Bhabha Atomic Research Centre, Council for Scientific and Industrial Research (CSIR), National environmental an Engineering Resarch Institute (NEERI) - Nagpur, Indian Institute of Chemical Technology, National Geo Physical Research Institute, Central Glass & Ceramic Research Institute, National Metallurgical Laboratory, Central Salt & Marine Chemicals Research Institute, Industrial Toxicology Research Centre and Institute of Minerals and Materials Technology. Representatives from NGOs and academia like Centre for Science & Environment, SCOPE, Centre for Water Resources Development & Management, Indian Institute of Science, Dr. Poonuraj, Gandhigram Rural Institute, Dindigul-Deemed University and scientists from Indian Institute of Technology-New Delhi/are also participating in the workshop

4986. (7-12-2007) NEW DELHI : Government of India have announced the sale (re-issue) of "7.99 per cent Government Stock, 2017 for a notified amount of Rs. 5,000 crore (nominal) through a priced based auction using multiple price method. Government of India have also announced the sale (re-issue) of "8.33 per cent Government Stock, 2036" for a notified amount of Rs. 2,000 crore (nominal) through a price based auction using multiple price method. The auctions will be conducted by the Reserve Bank of India, Mumbai Office, Fort, Mumbai on December 14, 2007 (Friday). Up to 5% of the notified amount of the sale of both the stocks will be allotted to eligible individuals and Institutions as per the Scheme for Non-Competitive Bidding Facility in the Auction of Government Securities. Bids in the prescribed form obtainable from the Regional Director, Reserve Bank of India, Mumbai Office (Public Debt Office), Fort, Mumbai-400 001 and RBI website www.rbi.org.in should be submitted to that Office on December 14, 2007. The NDS members should submit competitive as well as non-competitive bids in electronic format using Primary Market Operation (PMO) module of NDS. All bids should be submitted by 12.30 P.M. The result of the auctions will be announced on December 14, 2007 and payment by successful bidders will be during banking hours on December 17, 2007 (Monday). Both the Stocks will be eligible for "When Issued" trading in accordance with the guidelines on 'When Issued transactions in Central Government Securities' issued by the Reserve Bank of India.

4987. (7-12-2007) NEW DELHI : The outstanding balances of 5.73 per cent Government Stock, 2008 and 4.69 per cent Government Stock 2008 are repayable at par on January 2, 2008 and no interest will accrue thereon from the said date. In the event of a holiday being declared on January 2, 2008 by any State Government under the Negotiable Instruments Act, 1881, the Loan will be repaid by the paying offices in that State on the previous working day. To facilitate repayment of the Loan on the due date, holders may tender the securities, duly discharged, at the Public Debt Offices, Treasuries/Sub-Treasuries and branches of State Bank of India and its Associate Banks (at which they are enfaced/registered for payment of interest) 20 days in advance of the due date for repayment. Full details of the procedure for receiving the discharge value may be obtained from any of the aforesaid paying offices.

4988. (7-12-2007) NEW DELHI : Government of India have announced the issue of '8.30 per cent Fertilizer Companies' Government of India Special Bonds, 2023' for Rs.3,890 crore (nominal). The first tranche of the Special Bonds are being issued at par to 22 Fertilizer Companies as compensation towards fertilizer subsidy during the current financial year on December 7, 2007 (Friday). The investment in the Special Bonds by the banks will not be reckoned as an eligible investment in Government securities by banks and insurance companies for their statutory requirements. However, such investment by the insurance companies will be eligible to be reckoned as investment under "other Approved Securities" category as defined under Insurance Regulatory and Development Authority (Investment) Regulations, 2000. Further, the investment by the Provident Funds, Gratuity Funds, Superannuation Funds, etc. in the Special Bonds will be treated as an eligible investment under the administrative order of the Ministry of Finance. The Special Bonds will be transferable and eligible for market ready forward transactions

(Repo). The bonds, however, will not be an eligible underlying security for ready forward transactions (Repo/Reverse Repo) with the Reserve Bank of India.

4989. (7-12-2007) NEW DELHI : Government attaches great importance to promoting small savings. Small savings schemes are safe and secure avenues for keeping the savings of citizens, especially in semi-urban and rural areas. It is also important that the interest rates applicable to small savings schemes should be comparable to the interest rates that are available on other savings instruments of comparable maturity. Among the small savings schemes, the Five Year Post Office Time Deposit Account and the Senior Citizens Savings Scheme have proved to be popular. The Post Office Monthly Income Account (POMIA) Scheme is also popular. There has been a demand from different sections of the people for restoring the element of bonus on POMIA. There has also been a demand that the Five Year Post Office Time Deposit Account and the Senior Citizens Savings Scheme should enjoy the same tax treatment as is applicable to five year bank deposits. Government has examined these requests in consultation with the State Governments. Last month, Government invited the Finance Ministers of State Governments to send their responses to certain specific proposals. These responses have since been received and have been examined carefully. Government is happy to announce the following decisions:- (i) the benefit of Section 80C of the Income Tax Act, 1961 will be extended to investments under: (a) Five Year Post Office Time Deposit Account; (b) Senior Citizens Savings Scheme. The benefit of the deduction shall be available in respect of investments made under these schemes with effect from 1.4.2007 (*i.e.*. Financial Year 2007-08) (ii) The bonus at the rate of 5 per cent will be payable on the deposits made under Post Office Monthly Income Account (POMIA) Scheme upon maturity of the deposit. This benefit will be available on investments made under POMIA in respect of new accounts opened under the Scheme on or after 8th December 2007. Together with bonus, the effective yield will be 8.9 per cent as against 8.3 per cent presently available under the Scheme. The return of 8.9 per cent compares very favourably with the return on bank deposits or Government securities of comparable maturity.

4990. (7-12-2007) NEW DELHI : Armed Forces Flag Day was observed today throughout the country. The day is observed to remember the sacrifices made by our gallant servicemen in defending the integrity of our motherland and salute the martyrs, honour the brave and express solidarity and support towards welfare of widows, children, disabled and sick ex-servicemen. On the occasion the Director General Resettlement (DGR) Maj Gen SG Chatterji went around pinning Armed Forces Flag on the President Smt Pratibha Patil, Vice President Mohammad Hamid Ansari, Defence Minister Shri AK Antony and the Service Chiefs. Similar functions were held throughout the country through students in schools, NCC cadets and Govt officials. The mobilized funds are utilized for giving grants to various welfare institutions like Paraplegic Rehabilitation Centre, Cheshire Homes, St. Dunstan's After Care Organisation for Blind, construction of War Memorial hostels, financial assistance towards marriage, medical and education grants and relief to ex-servicemen towards penury besides hosts of other welfare measure.

4991. (7-12-2007) NEW DELHI : The Union Public Service Commission (UPSC) has declared the result of the written part of the National Defence Academy & Naval Academy Examination (II), 2007, held in August, 2007. Candidates who have qualified the written part will be called for interview by the Service Selection Board of the Ministry of Defence for admission to Army, Navy and Air Force Wings of the National Defence Academy for the 120th Course and Naval Academy for the 40th Course, 10+2 (Executive Branch) commencing from July, 2008. The candidature of all the qualified candidates is provisional. In accordance with the conditions of their admission to the examination, they have required to submit Original Certificates of Age and Educational Qualification direct to the "Additional Directorate General of Recruiting, Adjutant General's Branch, Integrated Headquarters, Ministry of Defence (Army), West Block-III, Wing-1, R.K. Puram, New Delhi-66." The candidates must not send the original certificates to the UPSC. For any further information, the candidates may contact the Facilitation Counter of the Commission UPSC either in person or on Telephone Nos. 23385271, 23381125, 23098543 between 1000 hrs. to 1700 hrs. on any working day.

4992. (7-12-2007) NEW DELHI : Ms. Rosanne Wowchuk, Deputy Premier of Manitoba and Minister of Agriculture, Canada called on Shri Kanti Lal Bhuria, Minister of State for Agriculture, Food & PD here today. During the meeting the Minister said that both the sides, Canada, moreso Manitoba and India, are keen to forge closer cooperation in agriculture and allied sector. Referring to his recent visit in Rome in connection with the FAO conference, Shri Bhuria recalled his fruitful discussions with Mr. Gerry Ritz, Canadian Minister of Agriculture and Agri-food on the sidelines of the conference. Shri Bhuria said that Government of India is deeply interested in promoting Indo-Canadian bilateral relations. He further said that India is especially keen to enhance capabilities in the area of grain handling and storage, in which Canada excels. He said the Government of India is keen to extend cooperation in projects pertaining to agriculture, food processing and rural development, information exchange and collaboration in research and development of terminal markets. The Minister said that India is looking forward to the Memorandum of Understanding with Canada for cooperation in the areas of mutual interest, which is being worked out between the two countries.

4993. (7-12-2007) NEW DELHI : The Minister of Petroleum & Natural Gas Shri Murli Deora has assured Uttarakhand Chief Minister Maj. Gen.(Retd) B.C. Khanduri to undertake immediate review of the complaints regarding LPG shortages/backlog in certain areas of Uttarakhand. He said that his Ministry would ensure speedy clearance of any backlog/arrears in supply of domestic LPG caused due to various factors. In a meeting held here today Shri Deora asked senior officers of the Ministry to review the LPG supply position in Uttarakhand on an urgent basis as any shortage would cause hardships due to the inclement weather during winter.

Regarding the request of Uttarakhand Government for enhancing kerosene allocation Shri Deora pointed out that the allocation of kerosene for distribution through PDS network has not been revised since 2004 even though the number of LPG connections have increased significantly. He urged the Chief Minister to extend his support for the proposal of his Ministry for launching 'smart card scheme' as a pilot project in a district of the State to ensure supply to the intended/targeted beneficiaries. Shri Khanduri said that he would examine the issue immediately onhis return to the State capital. The Chief Minister assured to extend his fullest cooperation towards Petroleum Ministry's drive to eliminate diversion of subsidized products for unintended use.

4994. (7-12-2007) NEW DELHI : The Winter Session, 2007 of Parliament which commenced on November 15, 2007 concluded today. The Session provided 17 sittings of both the Houses of Parliament spread over a period of 23 days. Addressing the media Shri Priya Ranjan Dasmunsi, Minister of Parliamentary Affairs and I&B, said that during this brief session, 12 legislations and three Appropriation Bills were passed. 13 news bills were introduced in Lok Sabha and one in Rajya Sabha. Shri Dasmunsi said, it was a successful session wherein besides legislative business, four short during discussions were hold in Lok Sabha under Rule 193 and three short duration discussions were held in Rajya Sabha under Rule 176. Besides, 7 calling attention and one half an hour discussion were discussed in Lok Sabha. The Minister said, Lok Sabha lost 19 hours (18.6%) of its time due to disruptions, of which 17 hours were compensated with late sittings. Similarly the loss of 18 hours (22.5%) in Rajya Sabha was compensated with late sittings of 26 hours.

4995. (7-12-2007) NEW DELHI : The Indian Air Force would be showing the flying skills, marks manship of its pilots and its fire power capability at Pokhran air ground range on 08 Dec 07. The display would be witnessed by Hon'ble Raksha Mantri Shri AK Antony and Defence Secretary Shri Vijay Singh. The Chief of Air Staff, Air Chief Marshal Fali Major would also be present. The fire power demonstration would display IAF's preparedness and ability to deliver the lethal punch. During the display Su-30, MiG-27, Mirage 2000, MiG-21 (Bisons, Type 96), attack helicopters and armed helicopters would be displaying their ground attack capabilities. A unique feature of the display would be demonstration of carpet-bombing capability of the transport work horse AN-32. It is expected that over 50 fighters, transports, helicopters and UAVs would be taking part in the display. The ground attack capability would see realistic targets depicting radar installation, fuel installations, rail yards etc. of enemy being destroyed. The Su-30 aircraft would also be displaying its air defence capability in form of combat air patrol. After witnessing the display of IAF's fire power capability Shri AK Antony would be visiting AF Station Jaisalmer and interacting with air warriors and families. He would also pay homage at 'Vijay Stamb', a memorial raised in memory of those who laid their lives in battle of Longewala.

4996. (7-12-2007) NEW DELHI : Central Power Research Institute (CPRI), Bangalore is engaged in conducting testing of samples of all kinds of electro-mechanical and Electronic Energy Meters covering single phase and three phase meters including Low Tension and High Tension Trivector Meters as per National and International Standards. The tests are being carried out at the facilities available at CPRI, Bangalore and CPRI, Bhopal. CPRI is also carrying out the Third Party Inspection, Field evaluation of Energy Meters (Onsite testing of Energy Meters at consumer premises) as per the requirement of distribution companies, Electricity Regulatory Commissions and other Government agencies. The approximate number of type tested set of meters covering both single phase and three phase at CPRI, Bangalore and Bhopal is 275 since the last three years. Out of these, approximately 136 numbers did not comply with standards. In addition to this, CPRI, Bangalore & Bhopal have tested Energy Meters of different types for Acceptance, Routine, Temper test and selected test as per customer requirements. Approximately 238 meters out of 3282 samples have not complied with the requirements of Standards/ Client requirement. CPRI is also carrying out testing of Electronic Energy Meters at different customer locations under the aegis of Public Grievances Cell, Department of Power, Government of NCT of Delhi since 28.05.2007. Earlier in 2005-06, CPRI conducted testing of Electronic Energy Meters at various consumer premises as per requests received from M/s. Bombay Suburban Electric Supply (BSES), M/s. New Delhi Power Limited (NDPL) and Delhi Electricity Regulatory Commission (DERC). CPRI have tested a total of 555 meters upto 21.11.2007 in Delhi. Out of the meters tested, 7 have been found faulty. CPRI carries out tests according to relevant standards of testing which prescribe the minimum number of hours/days that a meter should undergo a test. These may vary for different types of meters and tests from 45 minutes to 40 days. This information was given by the Union Power Minister Shri Sushilkumar Shinde in the Lok sabha today.

4997. (7-12-2007) NEW DELHI : The Home Minister Shri Shivraj Patil has called upon young police officers to do their best to control crimes and help innocent people. He was addressing a group of Indian Police Service probationers who called on him here this morning. The group included 18 women officers. The Home Minister warned that the times to come would be challenging, as criminals have been making use of the latest technologies and new concepts. Police officers will have to continue to outwit them by upgrading their skills. Shri Patil said that police officers should be strong in their minds, while dealing with them, kind in their hearts to understand them and wise in the actions they take. The Home Minister said that police officers must strive to produce the best possible results in the given conditions. He reminded young officers that by ensuring peace and security, they can greatly contribute to the development of the nation. The Home Minister said that the Centre has been impressing upon the States to strengthen their police forces and provide more funds for policing. The Government has also been stressing the need to beef up the intelligence machinery both at the centre as well as in the states, because timely and actionable intelligence is the key to fight terrorism. On the Naxal situation, he said that less than 3% of the police stations in the country are affected by the Naxal violence and the government is trying to tackle the challenge in a holistic manner by addressing both security and development issues. Those present on the occasion included the Minister of State for Home, Shri Sriprakash Jaiswal and the Union Home Secretary, Shri Madhukar Gupta.

4998. (7-12-2007) NEW DELHI : The Union Minister of State in the Ministry of Rural Development. Shri Chandra Sekhar Sahu has informed the Lok Sabha today that Pradhan Mantri Gram Sadak Yojana (PMGSY) is a 100% Centrally Sponsored Scheme with the objective of providing connectivity by way of all-weather road to all unconnected habitations with a population of 500 persons and above in plain areas, and population of 250 persons an above in case of Hill, Desert and Tribal areas. As per the latest estimates, about 1.79 lakh unconnected habitations are eligible to be covered under PMGSY. Upto the end of the Tenth Five Year Plan 37,487 habitations have been provided connectivity under the scheme. Since inception of PMGSY, State Governments were required to submit the project proposals upto Phase-VII. A list, indicating the States which have either not submitted the project proposals upto Phase-VII or the States who have submitted their project proposals but not yet cleared, is annexed. Steps have been taken to accelerate the pace of implementation of the programme through enhanced allocation of funds, augmentation of contracting capacity, through modifications in Standard Bidding Document, provision of interest free advance to the contractors for procurement of plant and machinery, training of field staff including contractor's personnel, continuous and regular monitoring of the programme etc. States have been advised to increase the number of programme implementing units, wherever necessary and also ensure timely completion of the process of tendering and award of projects. The Minister was replying to a question in this regard.

4999. (7-12-2007) NEW DELHI : The Union Minister of State in the Ministry of Rural Development Shri Chandra Sekhar Sahu today informed the Lok Sabha that the Registrar General of India have estimated housing shortage of 148.25 lakh houses as per 2001 Population Census. The Ministry of Rural Development is implementing a number of schemes for poverty alleviation, employment generation and basic amenities like shelter to the homeless living Below Poverty Line (BPL) families, rural connectivity, safe drinking water and sanitation etc. in rural areas of the country. State-wise Central funds allocated under Indira Awaas Yojana (IAY) during last 3 years *viz.* 2004-05, 2005-06 and 2006-07 and housing shortage are given in the Annexure. The Ministry of Rural Development has developed a comprehensive system of monitoring the implementation of the Programmes including utilization of funds, through Periodical Progress Reports, Performance Review Committee meetings, Area Officer's Scheme. National Level Monitors, District Level Monitoring and Vigilance and Monitoring Committees at the State/

District Level. Besides, the States have been advised to adopt a five-pronged strategy consisting of (i) creation of awareness, (ii) transparency, (iii) people's participation, (iv) accountability/social audit and (v) strict vigilance and monitoring at all levels. These measures are to help in maximum utilization of funds under the rural development schemes and to improve the living condition of poor in rural areas. Shri Sahu was replying to a question related with the details of the landless/homeless farmers in the country as on date and the programmes to ameliorate their condition.

5000. (7-12-2007) NEW DELHI : As per reports appearing in the Lokmat Samachar dated August 29, 2007, Maharashtra Police at Thane, has raided premises of certain Companies acting as Auto Finance Companies, allegedly for duping the people of large sums of money. On the reported action taken by the Maharashtra State Police, relevant follow up legal action, including recovery, if any, of the amounts in question, would need to be taken by the Maharashtra Police in the relevant court of law. Activities of leasing and finance companies are regulated by the Reserve Bank of India. Such regulation is in addition to criminal liability as may arise from violation of any provisions of Indian Penal Code. As at present, there is no decision to bring any changes in the existing rules and regulations on the subject. This was stated by the Minister of Corporate Affairs, Shri Prem Chand Gupta in written reply to a question in the Lok Sabha today.

5001. (7-12-2007) NEW DELHI : Members of Parliament belonging to various political parties today lauded the role of Armed Forces Medical Services (AFMS) in health care both at home and abroad. Taking part in the discussions at the meeting of the Parliamentary Consultative Committee attached to the Ministry of Defence here, they recalled the stellar role played by AFMS during the earthquakes in Lattur, Bhuj and Jammu & Kashmir, Tsunami in the coastal areas and in Andaman & Nicobar Islands and of late in southern Kerala during the outbreak of Chikungunya. The Members appreciated the quality of education being provided by the Armed Forces Medical College in Pune to produce some of the best health care specialists over the years. Addressing the meeting, the Defence Minister Shri AK Antony said AFMS is a classic model of inter-service integration wherein all the three Services are jointly committed to the task of providing comprehensive health care services to its clientele. The training is carried out as per the joint requirement of the three Services and inter-service transfers and postings are carried to meet the specific needs of specialists and medical officers in various establishments of three Services. Shri Antony said this is one Service which is constantly under observation from all quarters since they deal with precious human lives. They have not only to perform at all times but also the qualities of services rendered by them have to be above average. It is a matter of pride that the Armed Forces Medical Services have responded upto the expectations wherever called upon to do so whether it be during Low Intensify Conflicts or Counter Insurgency operations or open combat or else during the provisioning of humanitarian aid.

Inspite of their constraints which are now being addressed, AFMS continue to perform creditably each and every time. Taking part in the discussions, the members suggested that all vacant posts at various hospitals of AFMS should be filled expeditiously. They were also of the view that the career prospects of the staff of AFMS should be made more attractive. Some members felt that AFMS should also address "Stress Factor" of Jawans. Earlier at the outset the Defence Minister congratulated the Defence Scientists for achieving a major milestone yesterday, when they carried out endo-atmospheric interceptor missile test successfully at Wheeler Island in Bay of Bengal off the coast of Orissa. He also described December 06 as a Red Letter Day as the Parliament passed the Armed Forces Tribunal Bill. Shri Antony said it had taken long years' of painstaking efforts to get legislative approval for this Bill which will go a long way in providing speedy justice to thousands of In and Ex-service personnel. Members who attended the meeting were Shri Naveen Jindal, Shri Shankhlal Majhi Shri Suresh Kalmadi, Shri MA Kharabela Swain and Shri PR Rajan. The Defence Secretary Shri Vijay Singh, Secretary Defence Research and Development Shri M Natrajan, Secretary Defence Finance Mrs. NK Narang and various senior civil and military officials also attended the meeting.

5002. (7-12-2007) NEW DELHI : The National Urban Housing & Habitat Policy 2007 seeks to promote various types of public-private partnerships for realizing the goal of " Affordable Housing For All' with special emphasis on the urban poor. This was stated by Kumari Selja the Minister of State for Housing & Urban Poverty Alleviation, while briefing the media persons, after tabling the Policy in both houses of the Parliament here today. The Minister said that the new Policy has been formulated keeping in view the changing socio-economic parameters of the urban area and growing requirement of shelter and related infrastructure. Giving further details, the Minister further said that this Policy intends to promote sustainable development of habitat in the country with a view to ensuring equitable supply of land, shelter and services at affordable prices to all sections of society. Given the magnitude of the housing shortage and budgetary constraints of both the Central and State Governments, the National Urban Housing and Habitat Policy, 2007 focuses the spotlight on multiple stockholders namely, the Private Sector, the Cooperative Sector, the Industrial Sector for labour housing and the Services/ Institutional Sector for employee housing. In this manner, the Policy will seek to promote various types of public-private partnerships for realizing the goal of "Affordable Housing for All". Elaborating the procedure followed for formulating the new Policy, the Minister stated that the formulation of the National Housing Policy is an ongoing process which started in 1986. Last time policy was revised in 1998. Since then there have been major changes in Habitat and Human Settlement issues. Particularly, the urban housing sector has been facing emerging challenges with regard to availability of affordable shelter, growth of slums, and gaps in provision of basic services to the urban poor. The urban housing shortage has been estimated at about 24.7 million units at the end of the 10th Five Year

Plan (2006-07). 99% of the shortage pertains to Economically Weaker Sections (EWS) and Low Income Groups (LIG) categories. The Minister said that all these aspects were considered in a Conference of Housing Ministers' of State and Union Territories in November, 2004 and it was decided to update the National Housing and Habitat Policy with emphasis on urban housing and improved habitat. A Task Force was constituted in January, 2005 and a National Urban Housing and Habitat Policy was drafted. This was circulated amongst various stake holders. Based on wide ranging inputs received, the National Urban Housing and Habitat Policy, 2007 has been finalised and laid in the Parliament today.

5003. (7-12-2007) NEW DELHI : The Government in October, 2005 has approved the expansion plan of Visakhapatnam Steel Plant (VSP) at an estimated cost of Rs. 8692 crores (base June 2005 prices) for increasing its liquid steel capacity from 3 million tonnes to 6.3 million tonnes per annum by the year 2009. While considering the proposal for expansion, an assessment has been made in respect of the international market, export trends and internal consumption vis-a-vis the projected rate of return on the investment. Assessment of returns on the investment for Expansion Phase-1 has already been made in the Project Report. The entire capital cost of the expansion plan will be met by the VSP from internal resources and extra budgetary resources at an incremental debt-equity ratio of 1:1. This information was given by the Minister of State for Steel Dr. Akhilesh Das in a written reply in the Rajya Sabha today. The Minister denied that Visakhapatnam Steel Plant is dependent on continued demand only from China.

5004. (7-12-2007) NEW DELHI : The draft final report of the study on Traffic & Transport Policies and strategies in Urban Areas has been submitted by M/s Wilbur Smith Associates Pvt. Ltd. The draft final report has been reviewed in the meeting of the Advisory Committee on 23.11.2007 and certain modifications have been suggested for incorporation in the final report. This information was given by Shri Ajay Makan, Minister of State in the Ministry of Urban Development in the Lok Sabha today in a written reply to a question by Shri Manjunath Kunnur.

5005. (7-12-2007) NEW DELHI : The Delhi Development Authority (DDA) has reported that in Master Plan of Delhi-2021 (MPD 2021), it has been estimated to accommodate 230 lakhs of projected population by 2021 for which the additional requirement of urban extension would be 20,000 to 22,000 ha. of urbanisable land within development time-frame of 15-16 years. The MPD 2021 recommends a three-pronged strategy to accommodate the projected population of 230 lakhs by 2021 namely: To encourage the population to deflect in the NCR towns; To increase the population holding capacity of the area within existing urban limits through redevelopment; and Extension of the present urban limits to the extent necessary. This information was given by Shri S.Jaipal Reddy, Minister of Urban Development in the Lok Sabha today in a written reply to a question by Shri G.M.Siddeswara.

5006. (7-12-2007) NEW DELHI : Urban Transport including roads, highways/ expressways/MRTS/metro is one of the sectors admissible under Urban Infrastructure Governance Component of Jawaharlal Nehru National Urban Renewal Mission. Ministry of Urban Development has formulated National Urban Transport Policy which, among other things, seeks to ensure safety of pedestrians and cyclists. This information was given by Shri Ajay Maken, Minister of State in the Ministry of Urban Development in the Lok Sabha today in a written reply to a question by Shri K.C.Pallani Shamy.

5007. (7-12-2007) NEW DELHI : Delhi Metro Rail Corporation (DMRC) Ltd. has reported that the average earnings per day of DMRC in Delhi during the current financial year are Rs. 67.63 lakh. DMRC has fulfilled all its loan repayment commitments till date aggregating to Rs. 268.72 crore. Efforts are being made by DMRC to substitute some items of sophisticated equipment like automatic fare control system, signaling and telecommunication under the overall programme of indigenization. Drinking water, toilet facilities, etc. have been provided at stations for the welfare of the commuters. Recently, feeder buses have been introduced to carry passengers to and from Metro stations. This information was given by Shri Ajay Maken, Minister of State in the Ministry of Urban Development in the Lok Sabha today in a written reply to a question by Shri Rewati Raman Singh.

5008. (7-12-2007) NEW DELHI : Based on National Sample Survey 61st Round data, the Planning Commission has brought out the figures of number of people living below poverty line in the urban areas. The Planning Commission has used two methods - Uniform Recall Period method and Mixed Recall Period method. According to Uniform Recall Period method, the estimated number of urban resident below poverty line is 8.08 million. According to Mixed Recall Period method, the estimate is 6.82 million in 2004-05. The Government has launched Jawaharlal Nehru National Urban Renewal Mission (JNNURM) to address the issues of provision of Housing and other civic facilities for the urban poor in 63 cities in the country under the Basic Services to the Urban Poor (BSUP) Programme. Other cities/towns are covered under Integrated Housing and Slum Development Programme (IHSDP). Both BSUP and IHSDP are under implementation since December 3, 2005. The Mission period is 2005-2012. This information was given by the Minister of State for Housing & Urban Poverty Alleviation, Kumari Selja in the Lok Sabha today, in a written reply to a question by Shri Hansraj G. Ahir.

5009. (7-12-2007) NEW DELHI : The Ministry of New and Renewable Energy supports Research, Design and Development activities in various areas of Renewable Energy including solar energy in the country. More than 550 projects in the aforesaid technology areas have been financially supported. During the 10th Five Year Plan period an expenditure of Rs. 72,65 crore has been incurred on Research and Development in the area of New and Renewable Energy which includes Rs. 13.15 crore on solar energy. An amount of Rs. 1500 crore has been proposed for Research, Design and Development in New and Renewable Energy for the 11th Five Year Plan. Guidelines for supporting and accelerating these activities leading to eventual manufacture and deployment of various Renewable Energy Systems including solar energy have been put in place. In addition, during the 11th Plan Period various types of fiscal and financial incentives have been proposed to provide promotion for various solar energy systems and devices in the country.

5010. (7-12-2007) NEW DELHI : A target for addition of 1,700 MW capacity, consisting of 500 MW of biomass power projects and 1,200 MW of bagasse cogeneration projects has been proposed during XIth plan period *i.e.* upto 2012. A cumulative biomass power potential of about 18,000 MWe from the surplus agro residues have been estimated in the country. This has been stated in the National Biomass Resource Atlas prepared by Indian Institute of Science, Bangalore, under a project sponsored by the Ministry,. The States of Andhra Pradesh, Assam, Bihar, Chhattisgarh, Gujarat, Haryana, Himachal Pradesh, Karnataka, Kerala, Madhya Pradesh, Maharashtra, Orissa, Punjab, Rajasthan, Tamil Nadu, Uttar Pradesh and West Bengal are having potential for setting up biomass based power projects of 100 MW or above. The biomass power potential in the identified districts of the above States ranges from 10 MW to 100 MW. Sugar mills having crushing capacity of 2500 Tonnes of cane crushed per day in the States of Maharashtra, Uttar Pradesh, Tamil Nadu, Karnataka, Andhra Pradesh, Bihar, Gujarat, Punjab and Haryana have an estimated potential of about 5000 MW surplus power generation through optimum bagasse based cogeneration. The Government is providing incentives for setting up of power generation projects based on biomass and bagasse cogeneration in the form of capital subsidy and fiscal incentives such as accelerated depreciation, relief from taxes and duties, term loans from Indian Renewable Energy Development Agency (IREDA). This apart, policies have been introduced in potential states for wheeling, banking and buy-back of electricity generated from commercial biomass power and bagasse cogeneration projects. This information was given by the Minister of State in the Ministry of New and Renewable Energy Shri Vilas Muttemwar in a written reply to question in the Lok Sabha today.

5011. (7-12-2007) NEW DELHI : The Ministry of New and Renewable Energy has agreed to Mini Tidal Power Project in Durgaduani, Sunderbans Islands, West Bengal, in principle. The formal sanction would be issued after the approval for investment is obtained. This project will have 3.65 MW capacity. The West Bengal Renewable Energy Development Agency (WBREDA) earlier submitted a Detailed Project Report (DPR) in 2001 for setting up this project. On advice after examination by an Expert Group, WBREDA obtained required statutory clearances and also revised the cost estimates before resubmission to the Ministry in June,2006. The revised cost estimates were Rs.40.15 crores. WBREDA entered into an MOU with the National Hydroelectric Power Corporation Limited (NHPC), Faridabad for updation and upgradation of this DPR and its execution. The updated DPR prepared by NHPC has been received in the Ministry in November, 2007 and is under examination. As per this DPR, the project capacity has been raised to 3.75 MW with cost projections of Rs.53.98 crores and project completion period of 33 months from the date of sanction. The Ministry has already agreed to it in principle. This information was given by the Minister of State in the Ministry of New and Renewable Energy Shri Vilas Muttemwar in a written reply to question in the Lok Sabha today.

5012. (7-12-2007) NEW DELHI : An Expert Committee constituted by the Planning Commission has prepared an Integrated Energy Policy Report (IEPR) covering all sources of energy including renewable energy sources. This report has highlighted the need to maximally develop domestic supply options and diversify energy sources. It has also projected that renewables may account for 5 to 6 per cent of India's energy mix by 2031-32 and has observed that the distributed nature of renewables can provide many socio-economic benefits for the country, specially in remote and rural areas. The recommendations of the IEPR are yet to be accepted by the Government. This information was given by the Minister of State in the Ministry of New and Renewable Energy Shri Vilas Muttemwar in a written reply to question in the Lok Sabha today.

5013. (7-12-2007) NEW DELHI : Pursuant to a decision taken on April 12, 2007, the Government has initiated the process of examining the feasibility of revival of the closed fertiliser units of HFC and FCI, (including Durgapur, Talcher, Barauni and Ramagundam) subject to the confirmed availability of gas. Specifically, Rashtriya Chemicals & Fertilisers (RCF) has shown interest in the Durgapur and Tacher Units; National Fertilisers Ltd. (NFL) has shown interest in Barauni and Ramagundam Units; and Krishak Bharati Cooperative Ltd. (KRIBHCO) has shown interest in the Gorakhpur Unit. The revival process of the closed units is in the stage of examination and preparation of techno-ecnomic feasibility reports. Therefore, at this stage, it is not feasible to indicate a definite time schedule for finalisation of tender or for commencement of construction work. In reply to another question the Minister said, Government has recently granted authorisation to GAIL for laying Jagdishpur-Haldia pipeline. In terms of the authorisation issued, the pipeline must be commissioned within 36 months from the date of the start of the project. Further, the fertiliser companies willing to revive the closed units in this sector are already in discussion with GAIL for firm commitment/ agreement for connectivity and gas availability. No agreement has been finalized yet. This information was given by the Minister of State for Chemicals & Fertilisers Shri B.K. Handique in a written reply in the Rajya Sabha today.

5014. (7-12-2007) NEW DELHI : The 74 bulk drugs specified in the First Schedule of the Drugs (Prices Control) Order, 1995 (DPCO,95) and the formulations based thereon are under price control and their prices are fixed/revised by the National Pharmaceutical Pricing Authority (NPPA) in accordance with the provisions of the DPCO, 95. These bulk drugs have been kept under price control on the basis of criteria mentioned in "Modification in Drug Policy, 1986", announced in September, 1994. Prices of non-Scheduled formulations are fixed by the manufacturers themselves keeping in view the various factors like cost of production, marketing/selling expenses, R&D expenses, trade commission, market competition, product innovation, product quality etc. The Government takes corrective measures where the public interest is found to be adversely affected. The Government has delegated powers to the National Pharmaceutical Pricing Authority (NPPA) for fixation of prices of non-Scheduled formulations under Para 10(b) of Drugs (Prices Control) Order, 1995 (DPCO, 1995). Further, Government has also reduced the permissible price increase limit in 12 calendar months from 20 per cent to 10 per cent for more effective check on price increases. The monitoring of prices of non-Scheduled formulations is currently on the basis of data from ORG-IMS. Based on in-house data-based analysis by NPPA of ORG IMS data for the period December, 1994 to July, 2007, it has been observed that the prices of 15 top medicines of 15 top bulk drugs which went out of price control consequent to the promulgation of DPCO'95, have gone up by 9.65% annually. This information was given by the Minister of State for Chemicals & Fertilisers Shri B.K. Handique in a written reply in the Rajya Sabha today.

5015. (7-12-2007) NEW DELHI : The Government is reviewing the laws concerning or impacting women which include Indecent Representation of Women (Prohibition) Act, 1986, Immpral Traffic (Prevention) Act, 1956, The Protection of Women Against Sexual Harassment at Workplace Bill, 2007 and Dowry Prohibition Act, 1961. This was stated by Smt. Renuka Chowdhury, Minister for Women and Child Development in a reply to a question by Shri Adhalrao Patil Shivajirao and Shri Anandrao V. Adsul in Lok Sabha today. She further added that crimes and violence against children are being addressed by legislations like Indian Penal Code, Criminal procedure Code, Child Labour Act and Juvenile Justice Act. These Acts are being reviewed from time to time to make these more effective and stringent. Ministry of Women sand Child Development is administratively concerned with Juvenile Justice (JJ) Act. Recently Rules under JJ Act have been notified with the approval of the Ministry of Law.

5016. (7-12-2007) NEW DELHI : The Ministry of Tribal Affairs has taken appraisal of the scheme of 'Grant-in-aid to Voluntary Organizations working for Welfare of Scheduled Tribes", through Expenditure Finance Committee as per established procedure. This was stated by the Minister of Tribal Affairs, Shri P.R. Kyndiah in a reply to a question by Shri Subhash Sureshchandra deshmukh in Lok Sabha today. He further added that the revised guidelines on the basis of the appraisal aim at enhancing the reach of welfare schemes of Government and fill the gaps in service deficient tribal areas, in sectors such as education, health, drinking water, agro-horticultural productivity, social security etc. through the efforts of voluntary organization, he added.

5017. (7-12-2007) NEW DELHI : The President of India, Smt. Pratibha Devisingh Patil released briefing kits for legislators at Rashtrapati Bhavan today, on the National Rural Mission, Age at Marriage and Sex Selection. The Indian Association of Parliamentarians on Population and Development (IAPPD) has brought out these kits. The Union Minister for Health and Family Welfare, Dr. Anbumani Ramdoss and some Members of Parliament and members of State Legislatures were present. These kits help legislators orient themselves about issues on population and development. Speaking to the legislators, the President urged them to not only highlight health related issues in legislatures, but also to put forth solutions. Smt. Patil said she was closely associated with the IAPPD, which she described as useful and active organisation. The President said she has closely studied the 'ASHA' scheme of the Union Ministry for Health and Family Welfare and referred to a scheme started by a private doctor in Purandar Taluka of Pune District of Maharashtra in which, women villagers from different communities who have studied till middle school are given training in the local language, for providing basic medical help to villagers. Trained doctors are always available to these women on walky-talkies in case they need advice in serious cases for which even trained doctors can also be sent to attend to the patient. In addition to providing this basic medical help, these women as a value addition, also work on social issues such as urging mothers to send their children to school. As a result school drop out rates have gone down and women have become more vocal at local panchayat meetings on issues affecting them such as wife beating etc. The overall effect has been an improvement in the social atmosphere and resolution of village problems. The President said, "This is what India needs." Smt. Patil urged the legislators present, to study this scheme and also suggested that the Union Health and Family Welfare Ministry could think of ways in which this scheme could be fitted into 'ASHA'. She observed that while as the Governor of Rajasthan, she had discussed the matter with the State Government and the scheme had been started as a pilot project in a few districts.

5018. (8-12-2007) NEW DELHI : The Ministry of Environment & Forests has taken a number of steps for conservation & protection of medical plants which will be implemented in nine states. The United Nations Development Programme (UNDP) Project entitled 'National Programme on Promoting Conservation of Medical Plants & Traditional Knowledge for Enhancing Health & Livelihood Security' has been operationalised. It will be implemented in nine states, namely Karnataka, Kerala, Tamil Nadu, Maharashtra, Andhra Pradesh, Rajasthan, Orissa, west Bengal and Madhya Pradesh. The project is being coordinated by Foundation for Revitalization of Local Health Traditions (FRLHT), Bangalore. The Government is supporting a Centre of Excellence on 'Medical Plants & Traditional Knowledge' at FRLHT, Bangalore. The National Afforestation Programme (NAP) Scheme is under implementation which includes models such as 'Mixed Plantation of Trees having Minor Forest Produce Medical Values' that relates to promotion of medical plants through afforestation and regeneration. Conservation and protecting medical plants through enforcement of the Indian Forest Act, 1927; Wildlife (protection) Act, 1972; Forest (Conservation) Act, 1980; Environment (Protection) Act, 1986; Biological Diversity Act, 2002 and the rules under these Acts promotes conservation of Medical Plants. Under the NAP scheme, during the last 3 years (2004-05 to 2006-07), a total sum of Rs. 7773.87 crores was released to ongoing Forest Development agencies in different States, for afforestation activities including promotion of medical plants among other things.

5019. (8-12-2007) NEW DELHI : Showcasing flying skills and pinpoint marksmanship, Indian Air Force (IAF) air warriors pounded and blasted away an array of assorted targets with impunity that included mock enemy radar sites, troops, ammunition dumps, convoys, petrol, oil and lubricant (POL) dumps with rockets, laser-guided bombs, missiles and front guns at the fire power demonstration (FPD) held at the air-to-ground weapons firing range at Pokhran, near Jaisalmer, today. A similar demonstration was last held at the same venue on March 14, 2004. Defence Minister Shri AK Antony witnessed an hour-long live demonstration of IAF's preparedness and ability to deliver the lethal punch that is capable of crippling any potential adversary. Among other senior officials present included the IAF Chief, Air Chief Marshal FH Major, Air Marshal KD Singh, Air Officer Commanding-in-Chief, South Western Air Command and Defence Secretary Shri Vijay Singh. Also witnessing the event were service personnel from other IAF Commands and various training establishments. Nearly 50 IAF aircraft participated in the event that were flown from airfields as diverse as Jodhpur, Jaisalmer, Barmer, Bikaner, Agra and Gwalior. They included the Su-30 MKI, Mirage-2000, Mig-27 upgrade, Mig-27 ML, Mig-21 Bisons, Mig-21 (Type-96) in the fighter class; Mi-35 helicopter gunship and Mi-17 IV helicopter and the AN-32 medium-lift tactical transport aircraft. In addition, an 'unmanned aerial vehicle' (UAV) maintained a constant vigil of the proceedings transmitting real-time imagery and information of the 'tactical battle area' (TBA) enabling correct operational decisions to be taken by the commander. The sprawling range in the arid Rajasthan desert is home to IAF's largest air-to-ground weapons firing facility where flying squadrons train in delivery of heavy armament. IAF pilots invariably hone their armament delivery skills at the Pokhran range that incidentally is also minutes flying-time from Longewala, the famed location near the western Indian border where IAF pilots stopped on tracks a regiment of Pakistani T-59 tanks on December 5-6, 1971 with their devastating air-to-ground firing exploits from the Hunter aircraft that continue to inspire generations of IAF pilots even today. The FPD was conducted in three phases. The first phase showcased the general capability and attributes of fighter aircraft. The second phase included 'counter-air operations' against airfield installations by fighter aircraft in their endeavour to suppress the enemy's air defence capability. The third phase included 'counter surface force operations' including 'battlefield interdiction' and 'battlefield air strike'.

5020. (8-12-2007) NEW DELHI : The Ministry of New and Renewable Energy stands committed to facilitate and promote all efforts to establish dedicated Special

Economic Zones for production of equipment involved in the renewable energy generation sector by domestic as well as foreign investors. Maharashtra, Tamil Nadu, Karnataka, Madhya Pradesh and Chhattisgarh have evinced interest to facilitate setting up of SEZs for renewable energy sector. Discussions with the interested State Governments and Investors are ongoing, with active participation of IREDA.

5021. (10-12-2007) NEW DELHI : Few would think that there is anything connecting 16 year old Ashok and 60 year old Keshar Bibi in two distant villages of Rajasthan. The Red Ribbon Express is bringing together people from different generations, social strata and mindsets towards creating a social movement against HIV by dissemination of prevention messages and adoption of healthy and safe behaviours. "I will now go and motivate the women in my village to opt for hospital deliveries," said an enthused Keshar Bibi who attended one of the performances at Kothputli village. Ashok at the same time is keen on gathering more information about safer sexual practices to disseminate the information among his peers in the village. Close to 50,000 people have been directly reached out already by the Red Ribbon Express Campaign in its ten day sojourn. Migrant workers, youth, women, Panchayati Raj representatives, district level officials have been touched by HIV prevention messages. During its passage the campaign has completed a tour of four districts of Rajasthan, including far flung villages that have been difficult to reach with HIV information. The year long campaign was launched from Delhi by UPA Chairperson, Smt. Sonia Gandhi in commemoration of World AIDS Day on December 1. While the train made halts at four stations in Rajasthan - Alwar, Jaipur, Sawai Madhopur and Kota- getting an overwhelming response, the bus has covered 27 block panchayats and the villages within these blocks. Alongside, folk artists of the Song and Drama Division have conducted 50 performances taking messages to far flung villages. The cycle caravan, which travels with the train, has visited more than 200 villages holding nukkad shows aimed at dissemination of HIV messages and adoption of healthy lifestyles. Nearly 2,000 representatives from government departments in Rajasthan, Panchayati Raj members, police, members of the self help groups, non governmental organizations, opinion leaders and youth have been sensitized and trained to create ground support and local participation in the national HIV response. It is expected that these people will take the leadership to carry the HIV messages into the communities. The Express will commence its journey in Madhya Pradesh from December 11, 2007. It will cover 11 stations in 10 districts of Madhya Pradesh in three phases. In its first phase, it will cover Guna, Nagda, Ratlam, Ujjain, Indore, Bhopal and Itarasi districts, before proceeding to Nagpur in Maharashtra.

5022. (10-12-2007) NEW DELHI : Shri M.S. Srinivasan, Secretary, Ministry of Petroleum & Natural Gas has emphasized the importance of safety in the operations undertaken in the vital sectors like oil and gas. Inaugurating a three-day Conference on Safety Competencies in Petroleum Refining, Petrochemicals and Gas Processing, here today, he called upon the corporate undertakings to take no chances on the safety front and follow safety practices in a chain from the top management to the bottom levels in the organizations. Referring to the serious implications of accidents in oil and gas sector, Shri Srinivasan pointed out that more than 100 products are produced from crude oil and so also natural gas which are life and blood for economic development. Similarly, technology is life and blood of the hydrocarbon industry. The rapid evolution of technological applications, in oil and gas sector in terms of products and processes, needs to be carefully handled so that operations remain safe as even a small incident in complex scientific operations could lead to entire plants coming to a halt. Petroleum Secretary also called for increased on-site training of the manpower so that possibilities of accident led disruptions and losses are avoided. In his key note address on the occasion CMD, Engineers India Ltd. (CIL) Mr. Mukesh Rohtagi elaborated the need for building competencies both in terms of technology as also trained human resources to avoid accidents. He pointed out that mostly it is human error which causes accidents due to the mistakes like wrong anticipation etc. He called upon Oil Industry Safety Directorate (OISD) to run various courses particularly short term as well as on-site for building competencies in this regard. The programme of 3-day Conference organized by OISD on "Safety Competencies in Refining, Petrochemicals and Gas Processing" been designed to facilitate the participants to understand the global competencies and emerging challenges in the changing and accelerating world on the latest trends to achieve excellence in safety. This event is providing a platform to professionals, practicing engineers, managers and HSE personnel from refineries & gas processing plants, process licensors, design consultants from all over world to come together in the interactive sessions in the areas of process technologies, plant reliability, safety, environment and occupational health. Successful operation of Oil & Gas Industry requires quite a high reliability of plant & machineries, operational efficiency and safety. Competencies are required right from stage of design & Engineering, during execution, maintenance, inspection & operation of the facility.

5023. (10-12-2007) NEW DELHI : The Prime Minister Dr. Manmohan Singh will inaugurate the "India Telecom 2007- Digital Divide to Digital Opportunities" in the capital on Wednesday, December 12, 2007. The Conference is being organized jointly by the Department of Telecommunications and FICCI. The Curtain Raiser Ceremony for the Conference was flagged off with the Signing of Tripartite MoUs for the first two Telecom Centres of Excellence being set up in the Public Private Partnership (PPP) mode on October 16, 2007. With the support and encouragement of the Government, the first two TCoEs are being set up by IIM, Ahmedabad in association with Idea Cellular Ltd on 'Telecom Policy, Governance, Regulation and Management especially marketing and Customer Care' and by IIT, Kharagpur in association with Vodafone Essar on 'Next Generation

Telecom Networks and Network Technology'. This year "India Telecom 2007-Digital Divide to Digital Opportunities" is being organized from December 12 to 15, 2007 at Pragati Maidan, New Delhi in association with Federation of Indian Chambers of Commerce and Industry with active support of Cellular Operators Association of India, Telecom Equipment Manufacturers Association and Association of Unified Telecom Service Providers of India. The objective of the India Telecom 2007 exhibition cum conference is to discuss new growth drivers that are revolutionizing the telecom sector in India and around the world and assess challenges and opportunities associated with new technologies and growth frontiers. It would also focus on showcasing the huge potential that India holds in the Telecom sector for inviting investments in telecom equipment manufacturing. The conference will bring together a galaxy of national and international visionaries, operators, equipment manufacturers and experts representing top institutions, cutting edge technology companies and major investors along with existing and upcoming communications infrastructure companies for interation with the high-level policy makers. The India Telecom series of exhibition will be held every year.

5024. (10-12-2007) NEW DELHI : The Prime Minister Dr. Manmohan Singh released an Autobiography of Dr. K.K. Birla here today. Speaking on the occasion he said that we are on the threshold of new era of industrial development. He pointed out that the past century has seen many waves of industrialisation saying that the last began after 1991. Recalling the contribution of Dr. KK Birla to the industrial development along with freedom struggle and development of education, Dr. Singh expressed hope that peers like Dr. KK Birla will remains active and guide the country though the new phase. He acknowledged that the experience and knowledge of Dr. Birla will be of great value to younger generations of our business leaders.

5025. (10-12-2007) NEW DELHI : The Prime Minister, Dr. Manmohan Singh addressed the Passing Out Parade of the Platinum Jubilee Course of the Indian Military Academy in Dehradun today. He said that the Government is fully committed to the technological modernization of our Armed Forces. Addressing the Parade, Dr. Singh said that we will not shy away from investing whatever is required in the training and equipment of our armed forces. While Government will find the resources required, the leadership of our armed forces must focus attention on improving efficiency of expenditure and, to use a common phrase, continually improve the "bang to buck" ratio. The Prime Minister said that our Government will make sincere efforts to ensure that the service conditions of our armed forces are such as to continue to attract the best and brightest among our young men and young women to opt for a career in our armed forces. Institutions like the IMA and other institutions of our armed forces, must develop the intellectual and organisational framework for such jointness in thinking and in action, he added.

5026. (10-12-2007) NEW DELHI : The Union Public Service Commission (UPSC) has declared the final results of the Combined Defence Services Examination (I)-2007 conducted by UPSC and interviews held by Service Selection Board of the Ministry of Defence for admission to the 124th Course of Indian Military Academy, Dehradun; Naval Academy, Goa and Air Force Station, Begumpet, Hyderabad (Pre-Flying) Training Course *i.e.* (183rd F(P) Course). There are some common candidates in various courses/wings. The number of vacancies, as intimated by the Government is 250 for Indian Military Academy [including 32 vacancies reserved for NCC 'C' Certificate (Army Wing) holders], 30 for Naval Academy, Goa - Course [including 6 reserved for NCC 'C' Certificate (Naval Wing) holders] and 52 for Air Force Academy. The result of Medical examination have not been taken into account in preparing these lists. UPSC have a Facilitation Counter near Examination Hall Building in its Campus.

5027. (10-12-2007) NEW DELHI : A Gazette Notification has been issued by the Government on the 7th December, 2007, notifying the scheme for extending financial assistance to sugar undertakings with a view to improve their liquidity position. This will in turn enable them to clear cane price arrears of 2006-07 and 2007-08 sugar seasons related to statutory minimum price.

5028. (10-12-2007) NEW DELHI : The President of India said here that I am indeed happy to participate in the Human Rights Day function organized by the National Human Rights Commission of India, commemorating the adoption of the Universal Declaration of Human Rights by the United Nations in 1948. Every year, more and more people, the world over are gathering to demonstrate their support for the fundamental principles of human rights particularly in democratic states. Human rights and democracy are closely intertwined. The defence of democracy itself means the defence of individual and collective human rights. In democratic societies, fundamental human rights and freedoms are put under the guarantee of law and therefore, their protection becomes an obligation for those who are entrusted with the task of their protection. Today is also a solemn occasion to seriously introspect about the status of human rights as also the mechanisms and their effectiveness in the implementation of basic fundamental rights, which are inclusive of human dignity, right to food, healthcare, education, shelter and such other things. Human rights have a direct relationship with human development and therefore, the universality of human rights demands an equitable global order. To achieve this end, the importance of "Right to Development" cannot be over emphasized as a basic human right for all people across the globe. This entails a greater space for development issues on the global agenda, a greater focus on the needs of the developing countries and a greater voice for developing countries in international institutions like the United Nations, the World Bank and the International Monetary Fund. India has been progressive in recognizing the rights of persons with disabilities. Legislation enacted in the last decade and half has done much to bring the issues of persons with disabilities to the forefront of discourse and planning. The Persons with Disability Act of 1995 and the National Policy for Persons with Disabilities of 2006 are important policy frameworks. I understand that the Government is in the process of updating legislation in consultation with stakeholders throughout the country. The new obligations in the UN Convention should be taken into account while amending the Act. Human dignity is the backbone of human rights. The Constitution of India proclaims "the dignity of the individual" as a core value in its Preamble. Therefore, it is important that the development process in the country is equitable and that there is a wider spread of the fruits of development. Opportunities for growth for all sections of society in particular for the disadvantaged and vulnerable are important. Disparities should be removed to ensure that needs of everyone are met. Appropriate strategies should be developed to achieve this result. It is only when the potential of all human beings is fully realized that we can talk of true human development.

5029. (11-12-2007) NEW DELHI : The Vice President of India Mohd. Hamid Ansari released the book titled "'The State of Indian Democracy' edited by Mr. Sumit Ganguly, Mr. Larry Diamond and Mr. Marc F. Plattner at a function organized by Centre for Policy Research" here today. The newest volume in the acclaimed Journal of Democracy series examines the state of India's democracy. Addressing on the occasion, the Vice President said that India has proven itself capable of preserving democracy and with the economic reforms it has now begun to achieve notable improvements in economic growth that promise to upgrade the living standards of its citizens, strengthen its institutions and make it an increasingly prominent player on the world stage. India is becoming even more important subject for scholars of comparative democracy. He expressed his concern on the question of corruption in public life. Complementing the contributors of the book, the Vice President said that the book gives a clear and insight view of Indian Democracy. The essays in the nineteenth Journal of Democracy book titled 'The State of India's Democracy' focus on India's economy, society and politics providing illuminating insights into the past accomplishments and continuing challenges of Indian democracy. Contributors :Rajat Ganguly, M.V. Rajeev Gowda, Christophe Jaffrelot, Niraja Gopal, Jayal Jenkins, Sunila S. Kale, Pratap Mehta, Subrata K. Mitra, Aseema Sinha, E. Sridharan, Praveen Swami, Arvind Verma and Steven I. Wilkinson.

5030. (11-12-2007) NEW DELHI : Shri Vilas Muttemwar, Hon'ble Minister for New and Renewable Energy, said that there is lack of knowledge and information about Renewable energy and its various sources. Releasing a book titled 'Multiple Choice Questions on Renewable Energy' today, he said that this publication is coming at a vary appropriate time when a number of programmes have been taken by the Ministry to create awareness about renewable energy. Congratulating its Author, Dr. Arun K.Tripathi, the Minister said that this is a remarkable work. The Ministry has started Quiz Programmes for School Children all over India on visual channels. Shri V. Subramanian, Secretary, MNRE, said we had to frame Questions and Answers and give them for Quiz Programmes. At the same time we received a number of questions from School Children. Shri Subramanian added that this was the point, when we felt a need of knowledge bank on this subject. Courses in Engineering Colleges will also have detailed subjects on Renewable Energy and its uses. This book contains over 1500 multiple choice questions covering various sectors of Renewable Energy, including solar, wind, biomass, biogas, biofuels, hydro, energy form wastes, hydrogen, geothermal, ocean, tidal and waves. This book has three levels of questions, ranging from school to graduate levels. A comprehensive overview of renewable energy development in India has also been presented. This book is useful for the academicians, students pursuing engineering or agriculture related courses, aspirants of various competitive exams, professionals and the stakeholders in the Renewable Energy sector. It can also be used for quiz Programmes organized in schools, universities, engineering institutions and on Television. This book has been written by Dr. Arun K Tripathi, Director Ministry of New and Renewable Energy and has been published by TERI Press, New Delhi.

5031. (11-12-2007) NEW DELHI : Under the provisions of the Drugs (Prices Control) Order 1995, the National Pharmaceuticals Pricing Authority (NPPA), notifies the prices of scheduled bulk drugs and formulations. These bulk drugs and formulations have been defined under Para 2(a) and Para 2(h) respectively of DPCO, 1995. The manufacturing/marketing companies are required to obtain the prescribed statutory approvals in respect of bulk drugs and formulations under the provisions of DPCO 1995 and also obtain the prescribed statutory approvals under the Drug and Cosmetics Act, 1940 as well. It is reiterated that DPCO'1995 and the Drug and Cosmetics Act, 1940 are independent of each other. The DPCO' 1995 primarily relates to price(s) of scheduled bulk drugs and related formulations. Accordingly, prices fixed/notified under DPCO'1995 have to be mandatorily implemented by the manufacturing/marketing companies. The prices fixed and notified under the DPCO'1995 do not grant or provide any exemption or immunity whatsoever from compliance of the provisions of the Drugs & Cosmetics Act, 1940 and/or the provisions of DPCO, 1995.

5032. (11-12-2007) NEW DELHI : Shri Kamal Nath, Union Minister of Commerce and Industry, has said that the promotion of Small & Medium Enterprises (SMEs) are crucial to India's growth and for addressing issues of poverty and unemployment. While addressing the TIE Entrepreneurial Summit 2007, here today, he stressed that the entrepreneurship is critical for increasing competitiveness as new services, products, processes and innovations increase efficiency, thereby improving the competitive strength of the economy as a whole. Shri Kamal Nath said: "We are extremely fortunate in India that people here have an abundance of entrepreneurial spirit. India has been relatively successful in creating a policy environment that takes advantage of this intangible, yet vital, asset. Entrepreneurs have emerged as the engine of economic and social development throughout the world- by generating employment, growth and international competitiveness". Elaborating on the role played by the entrepreneurs, Shri Kamal Nath observed that Industry has been one of the major drivers of the growth of the Indian economy. The last four years have witnessed impressive rates of industrial growth averaging around 10%. In 2006-07, the industrial growth was quite impressive at 11.5%, while the rate of growth of manufacturing was even higher at 12.5%. This has resulted in FDI inflows to India growing at a fast rate. Compared to US$5.5 billion in 2005-06, FDI inflows reached US $15.5 billion during 2006-07 which corresponds to an increase of 185%, he further added. Earlier while addressing the CEOs at the breakfast session "Doing Business in India", the Minister said that for the past three years, India has been clocking an 8% plus growth. In 2006-07, this rate of growth was 9.4%. The 11th Five-year plan has set up a target of 9% growth. Savings, which are about 30% of GDP are estimated to grow to 35%. Similarly, gross capital formation is likely to touch 37.5%. It is expected that the private sector will be predominant in capital formation. Shri Kamal Nath informed the entrepreneurs that the business climate of India can be judged from the fact that it is considered to be amongst the three top investment destinations. Continuous reforms in investment policies have resulted in India practicing one of the most liberal policy regime. Almost all sectors are thrown open to FDI with no requirement of prior approvals. For the past three years, we have been lowering our tax structures. Though, we have made important strides, there are still some development challenges. We need to take the benefit of globalization and reforms to the poorest of the poor. We need to work more on governance infrastructure, business climate, skill development, environment and equality of growth.

5033. (11-12-2007) NEW DELHI : The Pension Fund Regulatory and Development Authority (PFRDA) has been elected as a member of the Executive Committee of the International Organization of Pension Supervisors (IOPS). This has enabled PFRDA to closely interact with other pension regulators on issues pertaining to best practices in the development and supervision of the pension sector. A communication to this effect has been received by PFRDA from IOPS, the Annual General Meeting of which was held in Beijing in China on 14th November 2007. IOPS is an independent body representing international entities involved in the supervision and regulation of private pension arrangements. IOPS has 60 members representing more than 40 countries having different types of pension and regulatory systems. The main objective of the IOPS is to improve the quality and effectiveness of pension supervision and work closely with other international organizations involved in pension supervision and policy development.

5034. (11-12-2007) NEW DELHI : In what could be described as a growing importance of the Southern Air Command (SAC) with headquarters located at Thiruvananthapuram, the Indian Air Force (IAF) held a week-long multi-role exercise named 'DAKSHIN PRAHAR' that concluded yesterday. The entire exercise, conducted in two phases at Thiruvananthapuram and Hyderabad, was envisioned at SAC. A very significant and contemporary concept of 'Flexi Airspace' was the foundation of this exercise. The IAF and the Airport Authority of India (AAI) jointly shared the airspace by means of close coordination so that a smooth flow of traffic was maintained without causing disruption to scheduled flights. This was the first time that coordination of civil-military traffic for simultaneous air activity took place at such large scale. During the exercise, state of the art aircraft such as Mirage-2000 that took off from Thiruvananthapuram and Dundigal, Su-30s from some forward bases in Gujarat and Northwestern Rajasthan and Jaguars from Arakkonam, simulated friendly and hostile forces over long aerial ranges covering the length and breadth of the country using Air to Air Refuelling facilities and off-base operations. Operational tactics were formulated to cater to contemporary threat scenario involving Beyond Visual Range (BVR) weaponry, state of the art avionics laden combat aircraft and far reaching Air Defence Weapons. Other aircraft that took part in the associated logistical support were the mammoth IL-76, the workhorse AN-32 and ubiquitous Mi-8 helicopters. Unmanned Air Vehicles (UAVs) were also used in the exercise. An important aspect of integration during this exercise was the role of Indian Navy and Coast Guard in pooling in its resources and infrastructure at various places like Vizag, Goa, Mangalore, Arakkonam and Kochi to smoothen the process of 'Inter-operability' that led to better conduct of joint operations. Navy and Coast Guard provided search and rescue ships right up to Lakshadweep & Minicoy area. Airfields and support services were thrown open to use by the Airport Authority of India that regulated the incessant airline traffic across the southern skies. Indian Army facilitated communication networking and troops for exercise apart from utilising Air Defence Artillery guarding a high value target against air raids. Air Force troops also took part in this action with their MANPADS (Man Portable Air Defence Systems). In addition to this, a satellite was manoeuvred to cover the specified targets on ground and send high resolution imagery for analysis before and after the attack. It was supplemented by the UAV that took photographs and sent it to SAC Ops Room. DAKSHIN PRAHAR thus proved to be the trail blazer as an 'Integrated Civil-Military' operational exercise that has now operationalised the so far militarily dormant southern peninsular airspace. The synergetic effort of tri-service cooperation with integration of AAI vindicated the theory of achieving grand success of pursuing a common objective through teamwork and combined effort. With the success of DAKSHIN PRAHAR, a new chapter of joint civil-military sharing of airspace, airfields, radars and professional expertise has begun.

5035. (11-12-2007) NEW DELHI : Shri Kamal Nath, Union Minister of Commerce and Industry, has stressed on the vitality of technological upgradation for Indian project exporters for competing in the international markets. Distributing the annual Export Awards of the Project Exports Promotion Council of India (PEPC) here today, Shri Kamal Nath underlined the efforts of the developed countries who are increasingly upgrading their technology, project management skills and equipment. Informing that he is fully aware of the Project Exports industry, the Minister stated that a review for considering the proposals to simplify procedures and also follow up issues relating to taxes for moving towards conducive policies for consistent growth in project exports is underway. Representatives from the Project exports industry and senior officials from the Ministry of Commerce and Industry were also present at the function. Shri Kamal Nath expressed satisfaction over the fact that project exports are increasing and the value of project exports from India has touched Rs.11381 crore during 2006-07 while its growth over the previous year was more than 87% in dollar terms. In order to further accelerate exports growth, he said, we should look out for product diversification and newer markets. More efforts are needed to explore emerging opportunities in the African, Caribbean and CIS regions. Shri Kamal Nath stated that Indian project exporters have serviced an impressive array of clientele in diverse fields of operation. PEPC, set-up by the Ministry of Commerce and Industry, Government of India in 1984 (as Overseas Construction Council of India), is an apex coordinating agency and in line with the Foreign Trade Policy of the Government of India, not only undertakes the necessary export promotion initiatives but also provides necessary technical information, guidance and support to Indian construction and engineering contractors/builders and consultants - in public or private sector - to set up overseas projects in any service module : Construction/Turnkey/Process and Engineering Consultancy Services etc. Project EPC also provides the necessary technical and market information, guidance and export promotion facilitation to the traders/manufacturers of Project Construction Items.

5036. (11-12-2007) NEW DELHI : Shimoga District in Karnataka has become the first district in the country to be declared 'Open Defecation Free District'. It has achieved this status under Total Sanitation Campaign, way ahead of the dead line in 2009. Hemavathi of Emmehatti village in Bhadravathi Taluk in Shimoga district is the mother of three children, two of them school going girls. Coming from a poor family they never considered that an alternative to the general practice of open defecation was available. As long as they can remember everybody they knew have been defecating in the open on the road adjacent to the village pond. But this practice was discarded when the message of Total Sanitation Campaign (TSC) percolated down to their village. With the help of Government grants and their own savings the family has erected a toilet with dry areca and coconut leaves as sidewalls and tarpaulin cover as roof. Emmehatti Gram Panchayat is one of the 39 GPs in Bhadravati Taluk where all the households now have individual toilets. The village with a population of nearly 3000 has constructed 246 toilets since the TSC was launched two years ago. The villagers feel that the toilets help not only the women but also the sick and disabled in the house. Changing the age old practice of defecation in the open is a complex issue related to habits, myths, ignorance, socio-economics, technicalities, space etc. The Total Sanitation Campaign in Shimoga has laid more emphasis on creating awareness about the need for good sanitation facilities at the grass roots. Slogans like 'One Temple for each village; One toilet for each house', 'Toilet is important to protect ones honour' have been successful in driving home the point about the importance of toilets in everyday life, thus managing to convert the mindset of the people thereby radically transforming old habits. Community participation and social responsibilities have also been the two major factors responsible for the tremendous success of the Campaign.

5037. (11-12-2007) NEW DELHI : In a significant move which will bring about socio-economic development of the backward areas of Bastar region predominantly inhabited by tribal population in Chhattisgarh state and further the industrial progress and mining activities in the region, Indian Railways have taken a momentous step to expand the reach of its network in this backward area meeting the long pending demand of the local populace. In a shining example of Public-Public Partnership, Ministry of Railways, Steel Authority of India Limited (SAIL), National Minerals Development Corporation (NMDC) and State Government of Chhattisgarh have come together to construct a 235 kilometer new broad gauge railway line from DalliRajhara to Jagdalpur via Rowghat in Chhattisgarh. A Memorandum of Understanding (MOU) in this regard was signed today among these four agencies in the presence of the Union Minister of Railways Shri Lalu Prasad, Union Minister of Chemical & Fertilizers and Steel Shri Ram Vilas Paswan, Chief Minister of Chhattisgarh, Dr. Raman Singh and Minister of State for Railways Shri R.Velu. The signatories to the agreement included Shri K.C. Jena, Chairman Railway Board; Shri Shivraj Singh, Chief Secretary, Government of Chhattisgarh; Shri S.K. Roongta, Chairman, SAIL; and Shri Rana Som, Chairman and MD, NMDC. Senior officials of Ministry of Railways, Ministry of Chemical & Fertilizers, SAIL and NMDC were among those present on the occasion. Speaking on the occasion, the Union Railway Minister Shri Lalu Prasad said that this new railway line is an important project which will help to accelerate economic development in the country. Shri Lalu Prasad said that the railway line will pass through iron ore rich regions of Beladila and Rowghat, which will lead to the increase in the steel production in the country. The Minister pointed out that the new line will also facilitate the bulk transportation of forest products, in addition to transportation of ores and minerals. The new line will provide lot of employment opportunities to tribal and backward classes people and will lead to development of backward areas of Bastar, Narayanpur in Chhattisgarh, the Railway Minister added. Referring to the earlier MOU signed in 1998, Shri Lalu Prasad said that the project could not take off during the last decade due to some reasons. The Minister informed that the issue was resolved in a special meeting convened by his Ministry last month involving all the concerned agencies which paved the way for today's revised Memorandum of Understanding. In his address, Dr. Raman Singh, Chief Minister of Chhattisgarh said that the new railway connectivity could be termed as the life line of the backward Bastar region. He said that it will also work as a bridge between North and South. Referring to the beautiful, highly dense and unique forests of the region, Dr. Raman Singh said that the new railway line will also be important from the tourism point of view. Dr. Singh said that the new line will substantially add to the earnings of the Railways also. In his address, Shri Ram Vilas Paswan, Union Minister for Chemical & Fertilizers said that this new railway line will meet the long pending demand of the local people. He also pointed out that today's MOU symbolizes best example of Public-Public partnership. He said that it is appreciating that Railway Ministry is continuing the concept of developing backward areas in the country. He said that the Public sector in the country is performing with efficiency and called upon them to spend a certain percentage of their profit to meet what is known as Corporate Social Responsibility.

5038. (11-12-2007) NEW DELHI : The ambit of the National Awards for E-Governance has been expanded with the introduction of two new award categories from this year. In addition to the six categories in which awards were presented last year, this year (2007-08), it has been decided to award exemplary work in a 'focus sector' which shall be selected every year. Agriculture has been selected as the focus sector for 2007-08. The other category introduced this year is for a 'Special Award' for significant work done in areas not specifically covered by other categories, taking the total award categories from six to eight. These awards are presented every year by the Department of Administrative Reforms and Public Grievances (DAR&PG) jointly with the Department of Information Technology, Government of India, seeking to recognize and promote excellence in implementation of E-governance initiatives. For the year 2007-08 a total of 24 awards will be presented, Golden, Silver and Bronze icon in each of the following categories: (i) Excellence in Government Process Re-engineering; (ii) Exemplary Horizontal Transfer of ICT-based Best Practice; (iii) Outstanding Performance in Citizen-Centric Service Delivery; (iv) Innovative Technology Usage in E-governance; (v) Exemplary Usage of ICT by PSUs; (vi) Best Government Website; (vii) Special Award for significant work done in areas not specifically covered by other categories *e.g.* Knowledge Management, Project Management, Information Security etc. and (viii) Specific Sectoral award - Agriculture (Focus Sector for the current year).

5039. (11-12-2007) NEW DELHI : Inaugurating the New Office of the National Board of Examinations (NBE) in New Delhi today, the Union Minister for Health & Family Welfare, Dr. Anbumani Ramadoss emphasized that more attention will be given to those areas of postgraduate medical education, which take care of the future needs in the country. These areas may be emergency medical and surgical needs of rural population, public health, maternal and child health, control of infectious diseases, family medicine, etc. He complimented the National Board for providing opportunities to medical aspirants in postgraduate medical education in different broad and super specialities as well as different Postdoctoral Fellowship Programmes in various sub-specialities in the country. Besides, the Minister of State for Health & Family Welfare, Smt. Panabaka Lakshmi, the President and Executive Director of NBE and the other members of the Governing Body of NBE were also present at the function. The following is the summary of the Health Minister's speech: I am happy to learn that the NBE has taken special measures to increase the expertise for the medical graduates in the Family Medicine discipline. The Family Physician is likely to be more successful in providing comprehensive services to our communities, specially in rural areas. Moreover to practice holistic medicine, as is the case with general practice, the physician should also understand the social, cultural and economic conditions of the family. The Family physicians, thus, can also play a crucial role in strengthening the healthcare delivery system in the country. The linkages of NBE with several accredited institutions/ hospitals should be further strengthened. The Board should ensure that the specialists services through the accredited private hospitals are also provided in the neglected areas/regions of the country as well as to the poor population on subsidized basis. Special Incentives may be given to such hospitals. Another area where the NBE can focus in future is to make a uniform and standardized postgraduate medical education and examinations all over the country. There is a need to evolve and develop new student friendly examination methodologies, which test the competency and skills of students more objectively. Modern information technologies like internet, interactive CDs, teleconferencing etc. can play a useful role in improving the quality of postgraduate medical education in our country as well, specially when our country is one of the world leader in software computer technologies. Our country is so diverse geographically and demographically that there are a wide range of health problems. The Government health infrastructure and facilities in the rural areas are not adequate in several States, where the private and corporate hospitals can also play an important role by providing some technical medical facilities to governmental institutions. The public and private health institutions must network and be complement to each other in selected health related issues. I hope the NBE accredited institutions in the private sector will take a lead in this area. I congratulate all the Officers & staff members of National Board of Examination and hope with the facilities available in the new building they would be able to operate more efficiently.

5040. (11-12-2007) NEW DELHI : The growth of Budget Accommodation in the country has been the priority of the Ministry of Tourism, Govt. of India. In order to encourage and stimulate such hotels rooms; interest subsidy has been paid to hotels since last two decades. The interest subsidy is paid @ 3% of the interest paid by the hotel on the loan taken from the designated financial Institutions. The subsidy was higher @ 5% for identified tourist circuits and destinations. A new scheme in the form of capital subsidy to one, two, three star and Heritage category (heritage hotels are those built in buildings constructed prior to 1950) of hotels has been administered during the Tenth Five Year plan. Under this scheme incentive/ subsidy was given @ 10% of the loan taken subject to a maximum of Rs. 25 lakh for one star, Rs. 50 lakh for a two star and Rs. 75 lakh for three star and Heritage category of hotels. In order to make the scheme more investor friendly, under the direction of Minister of Tourism and Culture Smt. Ambika Soni, a fresh scheme with the focus on the rooms created has been prepared which will be offered to the entrepreneurs.

5041. (11-12-2007) NEW DELHI : Shri Kamal Nath, Union Minister of Commerce and Industry, has expressed satisfaction over the outcome of the signing of Agreement on S&T cooperation between India and Austria on 30th November, 2007 as a follow up to the deliberations in the Joint Economic Cooperation (JEC) held in New Delhi further to the Agreement on Infrastructure Cooperation in the health sector that was signed earlier. The Indian side is very active on drafting Memorandum of Undertaking for Cooperation in all the areas of Agricultural Sector for proposing the same to Austrian side as agreed to in the JEC on 11th April, 2007, Shri Kamal Nath informed during the bilateral discussion with Mr. Martin Bartenstein, Austrian Federal Minister for Commerce and Labour, here today. Senior officials from both the countries including Presidents of CII and FICCI were also present on the occasion. Commending the Austrian support to the proposed India-EU broad based Bilateral Trade and Investment Agreement, Shri Kamal Nath hoped that both India and EU both stand to gain significantly by entering into this bilateral Agreement in view of strong complementarities between the economies on the two sides which would create a positive environment for this Agreement. Providing details of the liberal foreign direct investment (FDI) regime in sectors like core-infrastructure, manufacturing and energy etc., where except for a small list of activities, FDI upto 100% is permitted in all sectors without the requirement of prior government approval, Shri Kamal Nath informed that India is ranked among the most attractive destination for investment. This is borne out by the huge FDI in the past few years that touched almost US $ 16 billion in the last financial year. The tax reforms in India would further impress the Austrian companies as value-added tax has already been introduced in India about 2 years back, while the goods and services tax is likely to be introduced by 2010, the Minister informed. Outlining the huge advantages, which India offers in terms of large number of young people in India that could take care of shortage of working hands in the developed countries, the Minister stated that the huge skilled human resource base in India could be combined with Austrian technology and investment to create mutually beneficial situation. Shri Kamal Nath expressed happiness that the Austria-India Business Interest Group set up in Vienna and Indo-Austria Business Economic Forum set up in India are playing an important role in creating awareness about opportunities on both the sides. The Road Show organised to supplement these efforts held in Austria with a focus on automotive, transport, energy and infrastructure sectors was a great success, he informed. Shri Kamal Nath called on the need to encourage the strong SME sector in Austria with 85% of the companies having less than 100 employees for establishing business relations with the SME sector in India to provide a strong foundation for economic relationship. The bilateral trade between India and Austria is showing a consistent growth. During 2005-2006, bilateral trade was of the order of US $ 476 Million and touched US $ 588 Million during 2006-07. Major export items to Austria include drugs, pharmaceuticals & fine chemicals, machinery & instruments, cotton yarn, fabrics etc. and footwear leather & leather goods. The major imports from Austria are machinery except electrical & electronics, transport equipments, iron & steel, organic chemicals etc. The main areas of bilateral cooperation could be tourism, waste management & recycling, rail transport, telecommunications, energy production & distribution and aviation.

5042. (12-12-2007) NEW DELHI : The Prime Minister Dr. Manmohan Singh addressed the IPS probationers here today. Following is the text of his remarks on the occasion: "I am very happy to have this opportunity to meet you. I have still memories of my visit to your academy fresh in my mind and last year when I went to Hyderabad I did get a glimpse of the type of training that you receive, the arduous work that you put in. I am confident that in you we have men and women who can rise to the occasion in the service of our nation in the chosen field that you are now entering. Ours is a country, which is undergoing rapid transformation. Removal of mass poverty through sustained social and economic growth is the prime concern of our polity so that within a reasonable period of time we can soften the harsh edges of extreme poverty. Development however is never a smooth process. There are some people who gain in the process of development, there are some who loose and the task of heading viable polity is to contain the tensions that arise in processes of social and economic change bring about some disruptive features which are inherent in the processes of modernization and although we all seek rapid economic development, development cannot take place in political and social vacuum. Law and order is the primary base on which civilized societies can function. If there is no stable law and order enforcement, the elementary functions of any market economy that is enforcement of contracts cannot take place. And therefore, great importance attaches to how our internal security organizations function, the dedication, the commitment, their knowledge with which they tackle the task for law and order enforcement is of the greatest concern to the success of this vast gigantic country moving ahead fast enough on the road to rapid social and economic development. And I am very happy to note that more and more women are now joining the police services. We have to understand the problems of disadvantaged sections of our communities be they dalits, be they scheduled tribes, be they women because we cannot have peace and security if large segments of our population are untouched by processes of change or our law enforcement agencies do not have adequate grip over what troubles these disadvantaged sections of our society and that is where I feel that in particular fields that you are dealing with, it is very important that our intelligence setup must be among the very best. Information technologies, communication technologies to the extent that they can be used, there must be optimum use. And I would also like to say that we are now in an age where knowledge is advancing at a very rapid pace. So we cannot assume that what you have learnt today will stand you in good strength through out your life. I think in the fast changing world where knowledge is increasing at a phenomenal pace, constant learning and relearning is the road to success. Therefore, I would like you to imbibe in your career that life is one long process of learning and relearning. This is what I would say I have learnt in my life. As I get old I find there are limits to what I can imbibe afresh but at your age when you are beginning your careers I think you must have a zest for knowledge and that should be a strong motivating factor for all our national services and more so the police services. And I was saying that processes of development are never free of tensions. Some segment of society gains and some segments of society loose and there are always tensions. Therefore, I think the sociology of development, the economics of development, the political management and the processes of governance which we must handle with tact and care. These are also areas which you both in your capacity as police officers and also as concerned citizens must pay attention to every day.

5043. (12-12-2007) NEW DELHI : Developing countries must equip themselves to develop capacities to become climate resilient. For this, technology solutions and financial resources are required at an accelerated rate to cope with and adapt to the inevitability of increased global warming in the coming decades. This was stated today by Union Minister for Science and Technnology and Earth Sciences, Shri Kapil sibal who is leading the Indian delegation at the 13th Conference of Parties of the United Nations Framework Convention on Climate Change, Bali.

5044. (12-12-2007) NEW DELHI : We have the fullest respect for the highest court and will duly reply to the notice. We believe that Shri Narendra Modi's speech at Mangrol was a political response to the earlier speech by Smt. Sonia Gandhi. He was essentially urging strong steps to combat terrorism. This is a legitimate political debate. We will like to have parameters for such a political debate in place. There ought not to have a judicial review of a political debate between Smt. Sonia Gandhi and Shri Narendra Modi on this issue of terrorism. There is no question of Shri Narendra Modi ever justifying fake encounters.

5045. (12-12-2007) NEW DELHI : In the run up to the National Energy Conservation Day, a hundred and five students from across the country participated in the National Painting Competition today expressing inspiring ideas on energy conservation and energy efficiency. The paintings drawn by children reflected their interest in the energy conservation activities and their concern about energy crises and climate change, and have effectively conveyed inspiring ideas in their impressive paintings. The vibrant designs, the confident depiction of the topic and remarkable composition seen in these paintings reflects clear understanding of the subject themes in the minds of these young children. The interest in energy conservation that has been generated in the children and their parents as a result of this Painting Competition suggests that it is meeting its original objectiveness of enhancing awareness in this area. The Hon'ble President of India, Smt. Pratibha Devisingh Patil will present the prizes to winning students. Winners will be awarded with cash prizes : First prize of Rs. 1,00,000, Second prize (4 nos.) of Rs. 50,000 each and Third prize (8 nos.) of Rs. 25,000 each on National Energy Conservation Day function to be held in Delhi on December 14, 2007. The Ministry of Power and Bureau of Energy Efficiency launched the National Awareness Campaign in order to promote energy conservation in the country. Painting competition for students at the school, State and at National level has been included as one of the activities of the campaign, which would not only make the children aware about the need for conserving energy, but at the same time would also educate and involve their parents as well in this cause. The competition aims to motivate children towards thinking about energy conservation, and offers them a chance to explore their creativity. This year, the themes were electricity savings, climate change and green transport. Across the country, 24,385 schools and 5.25 lakh students of 4th and 5th Standard participated in the school level painting competition. This participation was about 35% higher than that in the previous year. Chhattisgarh recorded the highest number of participation with more than one lakh students participating in the school level competition. A committee of experts in each State capital examined the entries forwarded by the school Principals, and selected up to 50 best paintings. The selected students were invited to participate in the State/UT level painting competition which was held in all the state capitals.

5046. (12-12-2007) NEW DELHI : Reports have appeared in some sections of the media that a new Airport is being built at Amravati in Maharashtra for the convenience of the President, ignoring the interests of the farmers of the Vidarbha region. The reports are factually incorrect and misleading. The proposed new Airport is one of the various initiatives of the Govt. of Maharashtra for the development of Vidarbha region and not aimed at the convenience of the President. The President is very much concerned about the farmers' issues in the country particularly of the Vidarbha region of Maharashtra from where farmers' suicides were reported. The President has already advised the Central Government for an early solution of matters related to debt relief of farmers. The President always insists on giving top priority to the progress and welfare of farmers.

5047. (12-12-2007) NEW DELHI : In the run up to the National Energy Conservation Day, a hundred and five students from across the country participated in the National Painting Competition today expressing inspiring ideas on energy conservation and energy efficiency. The paintings drawn by children reflected their interest in the energy conservation activities and their concern about energy crises and climate change, and have effectively conveyed inspiring ideas in their impressive paintings. The vibrant designs, the confident depiction of the topic and remarkable composition seen in these paintings reflects clear understanding of the subject themes in the minds of these young children. The interest in energy conservation that has been generated in the children and their parents as a result of this Painting Competition suggests that it is meeting its original objectiveness of enhancing awareness in this area. The Hon'ble President of India, Smt. Pratibha Devisingh Patil will present the prizes to winning students. Winners will be awarded with cash prizes : First prize of Rs. 1,00,000, Second prize (4 nos.) of Rs. 50,000 each and Third prize (8 nos.) of Rs. 25,000 each on National Energy Conservation Day function to be held in Delhi on December 14, 2007. The Ministry of Power and Bureau of Energy Efficiency launched the National Awareness Campaign in order to promote energy conservation in the country. Painting competition for students at the school, State and at National level has been included as one of the activities of the campaign, which would not only make the children aware about the need for conserving energy, but at the same time would also educate and involve their parents as well in this cause. The competition aims to motivate children towards thinking about energy conservation, and offers them a chance to explore their creativity. This year, the themes were electricity savings, climate change and green transport. Across the country, 24,385 schools and 5.25 lakh students of 4th and 5th Standard participated in the school level painting competition. This participation was about 35% higher than that in the previous year. Chhattisgarh recorded the highest number of participation with more than one lakh students participating in the school level competition. A committee of experts in each State capital examined the entries forwarded by the school Principals, and selected up to 50 best paintings. The selected students were invited to participate in the State/UT level painting competition which was held in all the state capitals.

5048. (12-12-2007) NEW DELHI : Four envoys presented their credentials to the President of India, Smt. Pratibha Devisingh Patil at a ceremony at Rashtrapati Bhavan here today. The Envoys who presented their credentials were: - His Excellency Mr. Mark Sofer, the Ambassador of Israel, His Excellency Mr. Juan Alfredo Pinto Saavedra, the Ambassador of Colombia, His Excellency Mr. Bob H. Hiensch, the Ambassador of the Netherlands and His Excellency Mr. Hideaki Domichi, the Ambassador of Japan. The President, during her interaction with the Heads of Missions, stated that India was committed to promoting peace and prosperity in the world and building friendly relations with all countries. The President emphasised the importance of people-to-people contacts for enhancing understanding of each others cultures and generating goodwill. Smt. Patil said areas of mutual cooperation should be identified and economic ties increased. The credential presentation ceremony was attended by the senior members of the diplomatic missions, senior officials of the Ministry of External Affairs and of the Rashtrapati Bhavan.

5049. (12-12-2007) NEW DELHI : Ministry of Health, Department of AYUSH organized a National campaign on Ksharsutra technique of Ayurveda for the treatment of Fistula-in-Ano and piles in New Delhi in August 2007. The scientific presentation and research data made available at the campaign convinced the participants, specially the allopathic doctors to adopt Ksharsutra as a better management technique for Fistula-in-Ano. One of the major recommendations of the national campaign was to organize state level campaigns on Ksharsutra so that Ksharsutra centres are established in district hospitals, community hospitals and medical college's hospitals. Task Forces have been constituted both at the National and State level to implement the programme in the States. This initiative of Department of AYUSH is picking up very well and the first state level campaign was launched in Chattisgarh on 22nd November, 2007 at Raipur. The campaign-cum-workshop of Ksharsutra inaugurated by Chief Minister and was attended by Health Minister, Health Services officers and 35 allopathic doctors/surgeons and 120 Ayurvedic doctors and opinion makers. As a follow up action Chattisgarh has decided to set up Ksharsutra clinic in the existing district hospitals. The training programme for the trainers will soon be organized in the faculty of Ayurveda, BHU, Varanasi. State Medical College, Raipur and Ayurvedic College, Raipur have been identified as the State training centres of Ksharsutra for Chattisgarh State. Other States have also fixed up dates for their State campaigns on similar lines. Himachal Pradesh is organizing State Ksharsutra campaign on 10-11 December, 2007 at Palampur, Andhra Pradesh on 12-13 December 2007 at Hyderabad, Kerala State on 19-20 December, 2007 at Thiruvananthapuram, Jammu & Kashmir on 26-27 December, 2007 at Jammu and Government of Uttrakhand will organize State campaign-cum-workshop on Ksharsutra on 29-30 December, 2007 at Dehradun. A standardized training module in this regard has been prepared which will be implemented in the 15 regional Ksharsutra training-cum-treatment centres in the country. For sustainable research and development on the Ksharsutra technique, a National Resource Centre - a Centre of Excellence on Ksharsutra will be established in the faculty of Ayurveda, Institute of Medical Sciences, BHU, Varanasi.

5050. (12-12-2007) NEW DELHI : Inaugurating the Indian Red Cross Society - State Secretaries Meeting on "Promotion of Voluntary Blood Donation through Indian Red Cross" today, the Union Minister for Health & Family Welfare, Dr. Anbumani Ramadoss said that voluntary non-remunerated blood donors who give blood regularly are the lowest risk donors because they are motivated solely by altruism and have no reason to conceal any information about their state of health and life style that may make them unsuitable as blood donors. Representatives of State Red Cross Societies, NACO, WHO and International Federation of Red Cross (IFRC) were present at the function.

5051. (12-12-2007) NEW DELHI : Congress said here today that as we are all aware yesterday the first phase of polling in Gujarat was over and from our own internal feedback and study of the pattern of voting that we received from the Party it is absolutely clear that Shri Narender Modi's government will be decisively voted out and that the Indian National Congress will form the next government in Gujarat and we expect that in the next phase the same trend and pattern will be followed and after the 23rd of December the people of Gujarat will get a truly secular government, a government which is not divisive and will work for inclusive economic and social growth of the people of Gujarat and perhaps it is as a result of the clear indication of the pattern of voting and of the current atmosphere prevailing in Gujarat that even Shri Atal Behari Vajpayee wrote an appeal to the people of Himachal Pradesh hoping to influence the vote in Himachal that's going to follow but did not very ostentatiously make the same appeal to the people of Gujarat because perhaps he knew very well that as far as the election in Gujarat is concerned Shri Advani's assertions and the assertions of Narender Modi are totally wrong and Shri Modi's government and the BJP will be voted into oblivion. To a question on Shri Modi being served a contempt notice, Smt. Jayanthi said, on the one hand there is a contempt notice from the highest Court in the land and on the other hand there is a notice from the Election Commission of India. Earlier also we are aware of the strictures that have been passed by various courts against Shri Narender Modi and his government. The Indian National Congress has all along said that this is a man who rules the state of Gujarat in a fascist manner, who does not respect law, who does not respect the Constitution, who does not respect any constitutional authority and who came into government on the previous occasion on the dead bodies of Godhra after sponsoring state sponsored carnage and rioting. Here is a man who does not respect rule of law or even the common rules and the common practices of decency. Even his own party colleagues are unable to work because of his fascist and authoritarian tendencies. All this the Congress Party has repeatedly said and today he stands in a position where a contempt notice has been issued to him by the Supreme Court for his blatant, unconstitutional public declaration on the Sohrabuddin issue. Certainly the law of the land will take its course and we hope that the honourable Supreme Court will deal suitably with him for the offences he has committed. Certainly the people of Gujarat will give him a fitting reply by sending him into the oblivion of political exile. To a question about Shri Vajpayee appealing to the people of Himachal and not to the people of Gujarat did you mean that he does not support Shri Narender Modi, Smt. Jayanthi said, yes, that is what I inferred. I do not know about the internal matters of the BJP but I think that it is very clear that Shri Vajpayee himself does not believe that Shri Modi will win in Gujarat nor does he support Modi. To a question that does Shri Vajpayee have a better political acumen than Shri Advani, Smt Jayanthi said, I do not wish to compare the political acumen. I am just pointing out that it's very ostentatious, possibly because we understand that the government of Gujarat has lost to the BJP.

5052. (12-12-2007) NEW DELHI : The Prime Minister Dr. Manmohan Singh has said that the key to the growth of Telecom has been liberalization, reforms and competition. The Prime Minister was speaking at the India Telecom-2007 Conference which he inaugurated here today. The Prime Minister also released a Report on Indian Telecom. The Prime Minister said that three years ago, a target of 250 million telephone subscribers by 2007 was considered too ambitious. "You have proved the critics wrong and have reached the milestone well in time. I congratulate the industry for this phenomenal expansion and growth. Today, as my colleague A Raja mentioned around eight million new telephone subscribers are being added in India every month. This is mostly in the mobile telephone segment. Mobile telephony has been growing at an annual rate of over 90 per cent since 2003". The Prime Minister said that we need to make use of this precious and limited resource in an optimal manner. All technological options must be explored to maximize its utilization. The policy regime for make spectrum available should be fair, transparent, equitable and forward looking. It should not create entry barriers to newcomers or barriers to the continued growth of the important sector. At the same time, the revenue potential to the government must not be lost sight of, he added. Shri A.Raja, Minister of Communications and Information Technology, in his address said that in the past three and a half years alone, we have commitments of about US$ 2 billion investment in IT and Telecom sector by 2010. In the telecom manufacturing itself there has been commitment of more than US $ 2 billion and we expect fresh commitment of about US $ 2 billion in next one year. These investments will contribute significantly to the employment and GDP growth, he added. Dr.Shakeel Ahmad, Minister of State for Communications and Information Technology, delivered a vote of thanks.

5053. (12-12-2007) NEW DELHI : Shri A. Raja, Minister of Communications and Information Technology, has said that to be a world leader and to reach masses we have to use state of the art technology especially in wireless domain. The Minister was speaking at a ceremony of signing MoUs for Centres of Excellence at the India Telecom 2007, here today. While we have adopted all the leading communication technologies in the world, we also need to see an Indian face of technologies such as E-commerce, Tele working, E-governance, E-health and E-education etc. that affect day to day life of common man. This is a must to enable embracing of technologies by the masses. This will also bridge the digital divide and will lead to harnessing of full potential of our telecom growth. While the growth of telecom sector is very satisfactory, it is essential to foster development of Telecom R&D facilities in India. We, as a country, have special requirements especially for rural and remote areas and indigenous R&D would be able to address those requirements effectively, Shri Raja added. Shri Raja lauded the concept of cluster of Centres of Excellence across the country is a timely move for inculcating the best practices, nurturing innovations and acting as incubator for R&D efforts. This is one of the most important Public Private partnership initiatives in the Indian Telecom sector. It also has a unique concept of Coordination Center to facilitate collaborative research and sharing of research findings. MoUs for 2 COEs have already been signed in October, 2007. Five MoUs for COEs have been signed by the IIT Delhi with Airtel, IIT Kanpur with BSNL, IIT Mumbai with Tata Teleservices, IISc Bangalore with Aircel and the Government of India. The India Telecom 2007- Digital Divide to Digital Opportunities" Conference is being organized jointly by the Department of Telecommunications and FICCI. The objective of the India Telecom 2007 exhibition cum conference is to discuss new growth drivers that are revolutionizing the telecom sector in India and around the world and assess challenges and opportunities associated with new technologies and growth frontiers. It would also focus on showcasing the huge potential that

India holds in the Telecom sector for inviting investments in telecom equipment manufacturing. The conference will bring together a galaxy of national and international visionaries, operators, equipment manufacturers and experts representing top institutions, cutting edge technology companies and major investors along with existing and upcoming communications infrastructure companies for interaction with the high-level policy makers. The India Telecom series of exhibition will be held every year.

5054. (12-12-2007) NEW DELHI : The Prime Minister, Dr. Manmohan Singh, inaugurated India Telecom-2007 here today. Addressing the conference, Dr. Manmohan Singh said that growth in the telecom sector is a critical component of our infrastructure plans. Drawing attention towards the large rural-urban divide in connectivity, the Prime Minister said that telecom connectivity has the potential to play a transformational role in our rural areas. Dr. Singh expressed concern about capabilities in telecom R&D and manufacturing and stressed that the policy regime for making spectrum available should be fair, transparent, equitable and forward looking. Referring to spectrum availability, the Prime Minister said "I have asked the Group of Ministers tasked with this to expeditiously conclude its deliberations and suggest a roadmap regarding availability and timing".

5055. (12-12-2007) NEW DELHI : Shri Kamal Nath, Union Minister of Commerce and Industry, has called for improving the road connectivity of the four hubs / regions proposed to be developed in the Delhi-Mumbai Industrial Corridor (DMIC) Project. In his communication to the Chief Minister of Madhya Pradesh on 10th December 2007, Shri Kamal Nath has requested for initiating / undertaking the following action for improving the road connectivity of the four industrial regions (Pithampur-Dhar-Mhow; Neemuch-Nayagaon; Shajapur-Dewas and Ratlan-Nagda) under the DMIC Project: i) The State Highway (SH-31) between Nagda (on National Highway-79) and Gujri (on National Highway-3) be four laned for providing the Pithampur-Dhar-Mhow Mega Industrial Region better connectivity with NH-79 and NH-59. ii) Widening and strengthening of the Dewas-Ujjain-Badnawar stretch of State Highway (SH-18) to improve the connectivity of the Shajapur-Dewas Industrial Region to ensure improved linkage between National Highway-3 and National Highway-79, passing through Ratlam. iii) Strengthening of State Highway-41 between Sarangapur-Akodia-Shujalpur-Ashta-Kannod for improving the road connectivity between National Highway-86 and National Highway-59A for serving both the Shajapur-Dewas Industrial Region as well as the Indore-Pithampur-Mhow belt. iv) For converting the Jhabua-Thandla Road-Ratlam Road into a four laned State Highway to help the growth of the Ratlam-Nagda Mega Industrial Region. v) To facilitate the growth of the Ratlam-Nagda region, Ratlam-Sailana road link for improvement/augmentation; and vi) Jaora-Sailana-Banswara (Rajasthan) road be converted into a two / four lane State Highway. Besides the above six road links, Shri Kamal Nath has suggested for improving the connectivity of Indore with Mumbai, the financial capital of the country. "I suggest that between Indore and Nashik, the road link be similarly converted into an expressway with the Government of Madhya Pradesh taking the responsibility of developing it between Indore and Shirpur on the Maharashtra-Madhya Pradesh border and for the remaining portion upto Nashik being so developed", the letter says. As regards National Highways, Shri Kamal Nath has written to the Minister for Shipping, Transport and Highways, Shri T.R. Baalu, explaining that the government has already accorded its in-principle approval to the development of the DMIC project, which passes through six states including Madhya Pradesh. Shri Kamal Nath has urged Shri Baalu to improve the transport connectivity in the above four industrial regions of Madhya Pradesh by four laning the Dewas-Sehore-Bhopal stretch of NH 86 extension and the road connecting Jaora on NH 79 with Maksi and passing through Mehidpur on SH 27 and Tararia being converted into an extension of the NH network.

5056. (12-12-2007) NEW DELHI : The Union Minister of State (Independent Charge) for Labour & Employment Shri Oscar Fernandes will chair the 42nd session of Standing Labour Committee (SLC) here tomorrow. The meeting will review the Action Taken Report on the conclusions/recommendations of the 41st Session of the Indian Labour Conference, the apex tripartite body at National level, besides finalizing the items to be included in the Agenda for the next Indian Labour Conference to be held later. The tripartite meeting will be attended by senior representatives of Central Trade Union Organisations, Central Organizations of Employers and Labour Ministers and senior officers from State Governments and UT administration and the representatives from Central Ministries/Departments of the Government of India. Prior to the meeting of SLC, Shri Oscar Fernandes will also chair a meeting of the Labour Ministers of States to share his concern on some of the important issues like skill development and employment of youth, increasing the coverage of establishments under the purview of EPF & MP Act, 1952, rationalization of network of dispensaries and hospitals under ESIC Schemes, implementation of Rastriya Swasthya Bima Yojna (RSBY), recently announced by the Government and the nationwide drive on enforcement of the provisions of Child Labour (Prohibition & Regulation) Act launched recently by the Government of India. Among the issues in the agenda to be discussed in the SLC meeting include Issues concerning contractualisation of labour, role of social partners in appropriate skill development for employability, corporate social responsibility and the problems and issues concerning Migrant Labour (Domestic and Abroad).

5057. (12-12-2007) NEW DELHI : Denudation of forests or deforestation is very important from climate change perspective as this constitutes about 20% of the total global emissions. Global emission due to deforestation can be addressed in two principal ways- first by reducing rate of deforestation, and second by intensification of conservation efforts. India has a very strong policy framework as regards conservation of forests. The Reducing Emissions from Deforestation in Developing Countries (REDD) mechanism proposes mobilization of resources particularly by the developed countries to provide incentives for these efforts in the developing countries. Shri Kapil Sibal, Union Minister for Science and Technology and Earth Sciences, and Shri Namo Narain Meena, Minister of State for Environment met Mr. Rachmat Witoelar, Indonesian Environment Minister and President of CoP/MoP, UNFCCC and shared the concerns of Parties on REDD matters being deliberated upon in CoP at Bali. They emphasised the importance of forest conservation especially in the Asia- Pacific region and Africa, besides other parts of the world. The Leaders agreed that sustainable management of forests leading to conservation and enhancement of forest carbon stocks needed to be an important part of the proposed REDD mechanism. Indian delegation under the guidance of Shri Kapil Sibal successfully negotiated the Conclusion on REDD agenda item taking due note of the Indian interest in conservation and development of forests which is vital for sustaining the livelihoods of more than 200 million forest dependent people. Besides India, many countries like China, Pakistan, Brazil, Bhutan, Indonesia, Papua New Guinea, Costa Rica and Thailand supported the proposal for moving ahead with the concept of conservation, and increase in forest cover under the REDD. Indian contribution in reaching a positive conclusion of the long pending REDD agenda from last two years was much appreciated by all parties.

5058. (13-12-2007) NEW DELHI : In exercise of the powers conferred by clause (1) of article 217 of the Constitution of India, the President is pleased to appoint (i) Shri Justice Desaraju Apparao. (ii) Shri Justice Gandhi Bhavani Prasad and (iii) Shri Justice Gurram Venkata Seethapathy, Additional Judges of the Andhra Pradesh High Court as Judges of that High Court, in the same order of seniority, with effect from the dates they assume charge of their respective offices.

5059. (13-12-2007) NEW DELHI : The Minister of Petroleum and Natural Gas Shri Murli Deora has clarified reports by certain news agencies in internet today that Smt. Vimla Devi, w/o Late ASI Shri Nanak Chand who was killed in the 2001 terrorist attack complained at the function held to pay tribute to the martyrs that she was yet to get land for a petrol pump which was allotted to her as part of compensation following the killing of her husband. In a statement here today Shri Murli Deora has said, "It is ascertained that the person's name is Smt. Ganga Devi and not Smt. Vimla Devi. My Ministry has given top-most priority in providing relief to the families of victims of terrorist attack on Parliament as per the policy. Out of nine cases, three Retail Outlets(ROs) were commissioned in the year 2003. One RO was commissioned in 2006 and four have been commissioned in 2007. The RO allotted to Smt. Ganga Devi, w/o Late Shri Nanak Chand was commissioned on 25.1.07. The RO is functioning smoothly without any problems. The monthly sales in this RO is 40kl of petrol and 150kl of diesel and the allottee has not approached BPCL officials with any problem so far. I have personally reviewed the progress in commissioning the ROs from time to time and have also taken up the matter with the Chief Ministers of States for allotment of land for setting up the ROs. After much efforts, we have been able to provide relief to the families of terrorist victims. In doing so, we have also accommodated their requests for choice of location which in some cases has resulted in extending the date of commissioning of the R.O".

5060. (13-12-2007) NEW DELHI : Shri Vishwanathan Anand and Ms. Dola Banerjee have done the country proud by winning the World Chess Championship 2007 and World Cup title in the Recurve Women's Division respectively. In appreciation of their outstanding achievements, the Ministry of Youth Affairs and Sports has sanctioned a cash award of Rs.10 lakh each to both the players. Shri Vishwanathan Anand won the World Chess Championship, 2007 held in Mexico City from September 12, 2007 to September 30, 2007. Ms. Dola Banerjee won the World Cup title in the Recurve Women's Division held in Dubai on 24th November 2007. Ms. Banerjee beat the Korean, Choi Eun Young, in a very tight and exciting match.

5061. (13-12-2007) NEW DELHI : The Home Minister, Shri Shivraj Patil has condemned today's blast in the Rajdhani Express in Assam. The following is the text of his statement. "I am deeply anguished to learn about the blast in the Rajdhani Express in Assam this morning. I convey my sympathies to those killed and pray for speedy recovery of those injured in the incident. People of our country understand the designs of terrorists and will not be cowed down by such incidents. The State Governments and Railways will take necessary steps to provide protection to passengers and see that such incidents do not recur. Necessary assistance in this respect will be extended to them".

5062. (13-12-2007) NEW DELHI : The Cabinet Committee on Economic Affairs today gave its approval for implementation of "Marketing Support and Services Scheme" comprising components of (i) Domestic Marketing, (ii) International Marketing and (iii) Publicity during the 11th Plan (2007-2012) with a budget provisions of Rs.316.81 crore to also meet outstanding / committed liabilities under the old scheme of Marketing Support and Services including erstwhile Export Promotion Scheme implemented in the 10th Plan period relating to proposals sanctioned during that period amount to Rs26.32 crore approximately. With the assistance under the scheme, Handicrafts artisans will get enhanced opportunities for access to Domestic as well as International high end markets and various marketing channels. This will enable the artisan to (i) achieve full time employment, (ii) get better returns on their products, besides creating new opportunities for productive employment in rural areas. The scheme will be implemented for a period of 5 years beginning 2007-08, and up to 2011-12.

5063. (13-12-2007) NEW DELHI : The Cabinet Committee on Economic Affairs today gave its approval for establishment of an integrated network of Trauma Centres along the Golden Quadrilateral, North-South and East-West Corridors of the National Highways by upgrading the trauma care facilities in 140 identified State Government Hospitals - 20 to Level I Trauma Centres; 40 to Level II Trauma Centre and 80 to Level III Trauma Centre at a total cost of Rs.732.75 crore during the XIth Five Year Plan period. Setting up of the integrated network of Trauma Centres along the Golden Quadrilateral, North-South and East West Corridors will ensure that each accident victim on these corridors is able to get competent medical assistance within the shortest possible time thereby saving precious lives.

5064. (13-12-2007) NEW DELHI : The Cabinet Committee on Economic Affairs today gave its approval for development of Harbour Wall Berths (18-22 at Indira Dock), at an estimated cost of Rs.353 crore, by Mumbai Port Trust through its internal resources. The Project consists of Construction of 10 m X 882 m RCC platform on piles, Deepening of Berth Pocket and Navigational Channel, Strengthening of the existing berths and providing 6 numbers 30 T Electrical Level Luffing (ELL) Wharf Cranes and other cargo handling equipments. The Project is scheduled to be completed by February 2010. After the completion of the project the Mumbai Port will be able to handle larger, deeper and wider vessels. The Harbour Wall Berths will be able to handle General Cargo and Bulk Cargo vessels of 35000 / 40000 DWT with 11.5-12 M draft. The capacity of the Harbour Wall Berths after development would be 8 Million Tonnes Per Annum.

5065. (13-12-2007) NEW DELHI : The Cabinet Committee on Economic Affairs today gave its approval for implementation of the modernization of observation and forecast facilities of India Meteorological Department (IMD) to improve the weather forecasting services in India Phase - I at an estimated cost of Rs.920.00 crore in two years. This would help the IMD for establishment of end-to-end forecasting system with demonstrative hardware at an estimated cost of Rs.208 crore as a part of Phase - I. The modernization of IMD Phase-I would help in: (i) developing capability to manage, maintain and fulfil its mandate on a sustainable basis. (ii) Dissemination of forecast products at district level, particularly for use by the farming community and for better planning, disaster management and agro advisories. (iii) Getting more tailor made applications for different sectors like civil aviation, tourism, agriculture, power generation and hydrological purposes etc. which will generate additional revenue (iv) More accurate monitoring and warnings for severe weather events like thunderstorms, dust storms, heavy rainfall, Gale winds, hail heat waves and cold waves etc. (v) Improving the monitoring of tropical cyclones and better prediction of their movement and rainfall.

5066. (13-12-2007) NEW DELHI : The Union Cabinet today gave its approval for the following :- (i) for appointing two Public Sector Mutual Funds, namely, UTI MF and SBI MF, for investment of Post Office Life Insurance Fund (POLIF) and Rural Post Office Life Insurance Fund (RPOLIF) in relaxation of provisions of General Financial Rules. (ii) Constitution of the Investment Board as the apex body for the purpose of laying down the policy guidelines and investment strategy, which will set the frame work for the day to day decisions on investment. (iii) Sanction for creation of Posts as follows: One post of CIO of the level of Addl. Secretary. Four posts of the level of Director/JAG Eleven posts for secretarial support The above decision would help in managing POLIF & RPOLIF proffessionally in line with other Life Insurance Companies.

5067. (13-12-2007) NEW DELHI : The Union Cabinet today gave its approval for further pursuing the Gram Nyayalayas Bill, 2007 in Parliament and to move Official Amendments in Rajya Sabha. This Legislation would reduce considerable number of pending cases in subordinate judiciary. This would establish a system of judiciary which will be less expensive, free from protracted procedural wrangles, quick and available at the grass-roots level, accessible to the common man and render justice to him as enshrined in article 39A of the Constitution.

5068. (13-12-2007) NEW DELHI : The Union Cabinet toady gave its approval for involving an expenditure of Rs.746.79 crores for up-gradation/construction of road from Zaranj to Delaram in Afghanistan and execution of the project by Border Roads Organisation. The construction of the road from Delaram to Zaranj would help Afghanistan to provide communication facility in remote part of the country. It will demonstrate Government of India's commitment to the rebuilding of Afghanistan. Additionally, it would give India improved access into Afghanistan and Central Asia. This would also open an alternate route for Afghanistan to an Iranian seaport. India's presence in general would further strengthen our interests in Afghanistan.

5069. (13-12-2007) NEW DELHI : The Union Cabinet today gave its ex post facto approval for setting up of "Sardar Vallabhbhai Patel Institute of Textiles Management" (SVPITM), Coimbatore with a Plan support of Rs.29.00 crore during the 11th Five Year Plan. The Institute would be a centre of excellence in the field of textiles management and research studies. This decision would enable the Institute to have infrastructural facilities, *viz.* Purchase of land, Administrative Block, Hostels, Canteen, Computer Labs, Computers and Software & Teaching aids at a cost of Rs.18.00 crores.

5070. (13-12-2007) NEW DELHI : The Union Cabinet today gave its approval for introduction of the following : (i) Hospital Patient Care Allowance for categories of Group C&D (non Ministerial) employees working in Railway General Hospitals (those with 30 beds or more) and Super speciality railway hospitals (those with 10beds or more) And (ii) Patient Care Allowance for the Group C&D (non-Ministerial) Railway employees working in Railway Health Units/Clinics, Railway General Hospitals having less than 30 beds, and Super-Speciality Railway Hospitals having less than 10 beds subject to the following conditions :- (a) Hospital Patient Care Allowance shall be admissible at the rate of Rs.700 p.m. & Rs.695/- p.m. in respect of the identified Group C&D (non-Ministerial) categories of Railway employees, respectively. Patient Care Allowance shall be admissible at the rate of Rs. 690/- p.m. in respect of the identified Group C & D (non Ministerial) categories of Railway employees. (b) Night Duty Allowance and Risk Allowance, if admissible to the categories of staff identified for grant of Hospital Patient Care Allowance/Patient Care Allowance would cease to the admissible from the date of introduction of Hospital Patient Care Allowance on the Railways. (c) The orders in this regard would have prospective effect *i.e.* the 1st of the month in which orders are issued by the Ministry of Railways. With this decision the demand for introduction of this allowance on the Railways demanded by the Staff side would be met.

5071. (13-12-2007) NEW DELHI : The Union Cabinet today gave its approval for the extension of coverage of Ex-Servicemen Contributory Health Schme (ECHS) to the following two categories which are not at present convered under the scheme:- (i) Uniformed Coast Guard Pensioners; (ii) Retired personnel Defence Security Corps (DSC) who left the Army service pre-maturely without earning any pension but joined DSC later and are in receipt of pension by virtue of their service in DSC. This decision will benefit the Uniformed Coast Guard Pensioners and retired Defence Security Corps personnel, who are in receipt of pension by virtue of their service in DSC in getting medical care after retirement which is not available to them as of now.

5072. (13-12-2007) NEW DELHI : The Union Cabinet today gave its approval for the extension of the National Commission for Safai Karamcharis w.e.from 01.01.08 to 31st March 2009 with a Chairman, one lady Member and three other Members. The Cabinet also approved the continuation of the existing 32 posts in the Secretariat of National Commission for Safai Karamacharis w.e.from 1.1.08 till 31st March, 2009. This will facilitate the socio-economic development of Safai Karamcharis.

5073. (13-12-2007) NEW DELHI : The Union Cabinet today gave its approval for the signing of the Agreement on behalf of the Government of India with the Government of the Republic of Senegal for the Avoidance of Double Taxation and the Prevention of Fiscal Evasion with respect to taxes on income. This Agreement, when it enters into force, will stimulate the flow of investment, technology and services from India to Senegal and vice versa. It will provide tax stability to the residents of India and Senegal and facilitate mutual economic cooperation.

5074. (13-12-2007) NEW DELHI : Union Minister for Science and Technology and Earth Sciences, Shri Kapil Sibal, leading the Indian Delegation at the 13th Conference of Parties of the United Nations Framework Convention on Climate Change in Bali, practically set the Agenda Tone for the Round Table (RT) discussions on Technology Transfer in the context of climate change and global warming. The appeal of the Minister to create a GEM (Global Enterprise for Mitigation Technologies) drew maximum attention and acclaim. He said, technology is a mixed blessing - while it is often the source of our problems, it also holds the promise of enduring solutions. In our move towards a low-carbon economy, technology has a vital role to play, and therefore it is quite right that mitigation technologies engage significantly the attention of policy-makers and scientists. Shri Sibal said that India believes that the three major elements: appropriate funding modalities and approaches; a facilitative IPR environment and enhancing the absorptive capacity within developing countries. The G-77+China have already put forward a proposal for the creation of a new multilateral technology cooperation fund that would finance the development, deployment, diffusion and transfer of technologies for both mitigation and adaptation to developing countries. Shri Sibal emphasized its centrality for future action. Observing that one of the main barriers to technology adoption lies in the poor absorptive capacities of developing countries, the Minister said that technology diffusion cannot be forced through the harmonization of standards. Standards and norms must reflect the development levels of where they are being deployed. Shri Sibal concluded that the global challenge to combat global warming needs a global response. Much like the Human Genome project, the global community might consider a Human GEM project: a Global Enterprise for Mitigation technologies. Other panelists in the Round Table were Maxwell Jumah, Deputy Minister from Ghana, Andy Karsner from Us Department of Energy, Stigson,- President of the World Business Council for Sustainable Development and representative of the GEF. Shri. Sibal's speech also triggered a number of interventions from the floor as well. However the US, even while acknowledging the collaborative R & D with India in mitigation observed that legal and commercial frameworks within developing countries are the main constraints for diffusion of technologies. The IPR of advanced technologies lie in the private sector and the companies perforce look for compensation for investments in research. The officiating Chairman of the Round Table even while agreeing with the rationale of protection of IPR's referred to Shri Sibal's speech. A facilitative IPR regime, the Minister had argued, that balances rewards for innovators with the common good of humankind is the need of the hour. This may be done through a system of regulated royalties to innovators for deployment in developing countries. Such an approach has been adopted successfully in the case of pharmaceutical technologies for the benefit of HIV/AIDS victims in developing countries. If there was a moral imperative to adopt such an approach in the case of pharmaceuticals the moral case of a similar approach for saving our planet is even more compelling.

5075. (13-12-2007) NEW DELHI : The Reserve Bank of India has constituted a Working Group on the rehabilitation of sick micro & small industries under the Chairmanship of CMD, Punjab National Bank. This information was given by Shri Mahabir Prasad, Minister for Micro, Small & Medium Enterprises (MSME) while chairing the Third Meeting of the National Board of Micro, Small & Medium Enterprises here today. The Minister said Secretary, MSME had written to more than 40 MSME organisations to let the Government know about at least 100 such sick units, which became sick primarily because of credit related problems. Outlining the performance of National Small Industries Corporation (NSIC), the Minister said, during the last three years NSIC took certain steps to help the micro & small entrepreneurs in a big way. For this, a number of new schemes were launched like distribution of steel, copper etc. providing financial assistance in collaboration with banks, providing export credit insurance with the help of ECGC, helping new entrepreneurs through incubators, implementing Performance and Credit Rating Scheme, signing of MoUs with small scale entrepreneurs' organisations etc. As a result of which NSIC made profit in the last two years. Shri Prasad further informed that NSIC gave dividend to the Government during 2006-07. The second meeting of the National Board of Micro, Small & Medium Enterprises was held in New Delhi on 18th September, 2007 under the chairmanship of the Minister of Micro, Small & Medium Enterprises, Shri Mahabir Prasad. The main topic of the agenda for the Second Meeting was related to consideration of a draft Procurement Preference Policy for Micro and Small Enterprises. Representatives of MSME Associations and Trade Unions, from all over the country and senior officials of various ministries from the central as well as the state governments participated in the daylong deliberations.

5076. (13-12-2007) NEW DELHI : Responding to the immense devastation caused by the fury of cyclone 'Sidr' in Bangladesh, the Indian Navy has been carrying out transhipment of food supplies to Bangladesh. Relief operations in the form of air transhipment of essential supplies were first undertaken in the immediate aftermath of the cyclone. The magnitude of disaster required us to respond further and 5000 tonnes of rice, amongst other aid is being shipped by four Indian Naval ships from the Eastern Naval Command based at Visakhapatnam. The unique qualities of flexibility and versatility enable Indian Naval ships to be at the forefront of any humanitarian assistance and disaster relief operations. It would be remembered that during the devastating Tsunami-of December 2004, the Indian Navy had launched simultaneous operations to bring succour to not only the affected in our country but also those in Sri Lanka, Indonesia and Maldives. Naval ships again in July 2006 responding to humanitarian urgency in war-torn Lebanon undertook the onerous task of evacuating 2280 personnel. During the ongoing operation, four Amphibious ships of Indian Navy namely INS Gharial, Mahish, Cheetah and Kumbhir have been actively involved in making shuttle service between Visakhapatnam and Chittagong. These are Amphibious ships and specifically designed for landing troops, equipment, ashore during actual operations.

5077. (13-12-2007) NEW DELHI : The 42nd Session of the Standing Labour Committee (SLC) which concluded here today has decided that in the next session the Indian Labour Conference, all issues connected with contracualisation of Labour and issues related to Migrant workers would be discussed. It also decided that the Role of Social Partners in appropriate Skill Development for employability would also be on the agenda of the Indian Labour Conference to be held later. The SLC meeting also reviewed the Action Taken Report of the conclusions arrived at the 41st Session of the Indian Labour Conference held earlier. Presiding over the Meeting, the Minister of Labour, Shri Oscar Fernandes called upon the corporate India to be a partner in making a more humane and just society and said that the country needs a new partnership for Inclusive Growth and the industry must be pro-active in offering employment to the less privileged, at all levels of the job ladder. Emphasizing that the employer and employee have to work together in tandem to achieve the common objective of prosperity, he said that the industry must consider investing in people and their skills. The State Labour Ministers, the representatives of Central Trade Unions, representative of employers, and delegates from State Governments and Central Ministries/Departments attended the 42nd session of the Standing Labour Committee. The Minister said that we must end forever the debate whether the country's march to progress has benefited India and not 'Bharat'. Emphasizing that India is Bharat, he said that the Government is committed to work with industry for the transformation of country's economic and social landscape. He said that Employment generation is an important pillar of any strategy of inclusive growth. While our Government will continue to create a friendly atmosphere for the growth of manufacturing, at the same time, leaders of industry must also facilitate employment creation in their industries, he said. In a modern, democratic society, business must assume wider social responsibility, the Minister added. Referring to the Contract Labour (Regulation and Abolition) Act, 1970, the Minister said that while trade unions have demanded that the Act should be amended to provide for automatic absorption of contract Labour, the employers' organizations are vehemently opposed to it on the grounds that such a step would lead to capital-intensive measures like mechanisation, automation, etc. and would result in fall in employment. He said that we have received requests from both Workers' and Employers' Organizations for further discussion on contractualisation of Labour. Highlighting the importance of social dialogue amongst tripartite constituents in shaping and influencing the Labour policy in the country during the past six decades, Shri Fernandes said that the industrial relations are nothing more or nothing less than human relations and hence the need for bipartite and tripartite dialogue to ensure inclusive growth to provide a human face to development. He reiterated the Government's firm commitment towards strengthening the spirit of social dialogue through collective wisdom to protect the interests of Labour and capital.

5078. (13-12-2007) NEW DELHI : The Minister of Labour, Shri Oscar Fernandes has called upon the corporate India to be a partner in making a more humane and just society. Presiding over the 42nd Meeting of the Standing Labour Committee (SLC) here today, Shri Fernandes said that the country needs a new partnership for Inclusive Growth and the industry must be pro-active in offering employment to the less privileged, at all levels of the job ladder and it must consider investing in people and their skills and offer scholarships to promising young people. He said that the employer and employee have to work together in tandem to achieve the common objective of prosperity. The Standing Labour Committee Session is being attended by the State Labour Ministers, the representatives of Central Trade Unions, representative of employers, and delegates from State Governments and Central Ministries/Departments Speaking on the occasion, the Minister said that we must end forever the debate whether the country's march of progress has benefited India and not 'Bharat'. Emphasizing that India is Bharat, he said that the Government is committed to work with industry for the transformation of country's economic and social landscape. He said that the Government does not believe in an adversarial relationship with industry but in a genuine partnership and social responsibility has to be an integrated process implemented by Government and corporate in close association. He said that Employment generation is an important pillar of any strategy of inclusive growth. While our Government will continue to create an environment friendly atmosphere for the growth of manufacturing, leaders of industry must also facilitate employment creation in their industries, he said. In a modern, democratic society, business must assume wider social responsibility, the Minister added. Referring to the Contract Labour (Regulation and Abolition) Act, 1970, the Minister said that while trade unions have demanded that the Act should be amended to provide for automatic absorption of contract Labour, the employers' organizations are vehemently opposed to it on the grounds that such a step would lead to capital-intensive measures like mechanisation, automation, etc. and would result in fall in employment. He said that we have received requests from both Workers' and Employers' Organizations for further discussion on contractualisation of Labour. Shri Fernandes said that the interests of Labour and Capital are identical, for on their well being depends the prosperity of the industry. He said that we have always believed in collective wisdom and cooperation of all stakeholders in the nation building and this Government has always given utmost importance to social dialogue amongst all the social partners. Referring to the spirit of tripartism, Shri Fernandes said that the government, workers and employers have developed a sense of responsibility and responsiveness towards one another, exhibited respect to the views of one another and agreed to work in mutual interest. Over the years, he said, the recommendations of the Tripartite Conferences/Committees have shaped and influenced Labour policy in all its aspects and the recent amendment in the Payment of Bonus Act was as a result of the deliberations of the last Indian Labour Congress as also the announcement of various welfare schemes *viz.*, Aam Aadmi Bima Yojna, Old Age Pension Scheme and Health Insurance Scheme which are clear examples of fruitful outcome of effective and frank social dialogue amongst social partners.

5079. (13-12-2007) NEW DELHI : The Minister of Petroleum and Natural Gas Shri Murli Deora informed the Parliamentary Consultative Committee attached to his Ministry that the cumulative production of Coal Bed Methane (CBM) gas till 31.10.2007 was 4.7 Million Standard Cubic Metre (MMSCM). Chairing the meeting held here last evening, Shri Deora said that commercial production and sale of CBM gas has commenced w.e.f. 14.7.2007 from the block Raniganj South in West Bengal operated by Great Eastern Energy Corporation Limited. He also added that by 2015, entire area of Indian sedimentary basins is likely to be under exploration with a target of covering 80% during XI Plan. At present, after concluding six rounds of New Exploration Licensing Policy (NELP), 162 production sharing contracts have been signed and area under exploration has increased four times *i.e.* to 44% of Indian sedimentary basins. Before implementing the NELP, 11% of Indian sedimentary basin area was under exploration. As the development of Exploration and Production sector has been significantly boosted through NELP, Government is today launching the Seventh Round of global bidding for exploration blocks under NELP (NELP-VII). Shri Deora informed the members that GAIL will be the Government nominee under Production Sharing Contracts (PSCs) for the entire PSC period to receive the gas produced from Panna-Mukta and Tapti (PMT) fields at PSC price and terms. It has also been decided that the PMT Joint Venture will commence supplies of all uncontracted/surplus quantities to GAIL immediately. This would help in ensuring greater availability of natural gas to the fertilizer and power sectors. The Minister further elaborated measures taken by the Government to insulate consumers & common men from the impact of the volatile international oil prices. As a result of the unprecedented rise in international oil prices, the annualized under-recoveries of the Public Sector Oil Marketing Companies (OMCs) are expected to be about Rs.69,700 crore during 2007-08. He said, "As passing on the entire impact of the steep increase in the oil prices to the consumers would have resulted in hardship to the common man, the retail selling prices of sensitive petroleum products namely petrol, diesel, PDS Kerosene and domestic LPG have not been increased in tandem with the international oil prices". He added that the Government is closely monitoring the prices of petrol, diesel, PDS kerosene and domestic LPG. Referring to the Parliament (both Houses) passing the Rajiv Gandhi Institute of Petroleum Technology Bill 2007 recently, Shri Deora informed that the Institute will commence its activities by admitting students from the academic year 2008-2009. To start with, there will be two undergraduate courses namely B. Tech in Petroleum Production & Reservoir and B. Tech. in Petroleum Refining and one MBA course on Petroleum Management. The Institute will become fully operational in a few years.

5080. (13-12-2007) NEW DELHI : The Prime Minister, Dr. Manmohan Singh, interacted with the Haj Goodwill Delegation here today. Following is the text of the remarks of the Prime Minister on the occasion: "I am very happy to be present here to convey to you my greetings and very best wishes for a very very successful Haj pilgrimage. In Islam, performance of Haj is considered a rare privilege and blessed are those who have this opportunity. So I congratulate you for undertaking this sacred pilgrimage and my prayer and the prayer of all people of India is that all those pilgrims who will go for the performance of Haj will pray for the peace, amity and prevalence of harmony in our country. The message of Islam is the message of peace and brotherhood. The fact as Pranab Mukherjee has mentioned we have 150 million Muslims. Islam is a part of our civilisational heritage and therefore this message of peace, harmony, amity must go forth from this land and you are the real ambassadors. Each one of you is the ambassador of our country. So, when you are in the sacred soil of Saudi Arabia, please convey the people of India's, the Government of India's greetings to all the high dignitaries of the Royal Kingdom. We are very grateful to His Majesty, King Abdullah who it was our privilege to welcome last year on our Republic Day. He has always taken a very deep interest in promoting brotherly relations between our two countries and I request you to convey to all the high dignitaries that you meet, right from His Majesty, our greetings and best wishes. When you are in Saudi Arabia, please look at the arrangements that are being made for the comfort of our pilgrims. Whatever efforts were required, we made. We have Antulay Ji, Ahmed Saheb, Pranab Mukherjee Saheb, they have taken great pains to ensure that our pilgrims are looked after well. But, if there are any deficiencies, you can point that out and the officials on the spot will be available to set matters right. So with these words, I once again congratulate you for undertaking this sacred pilgrimage. May the purpose for which you are performing this sacred pilgrimage be successful and I on behalf of people of India once again give you my warm greetings."

5081. (13-12-2007) NEW DELHI : The Tourism and Culture Minister Smt. Ambika Soni has said that creation of Tourism Infrastructure at World Heritage Sites is a priority for her Ministry and efforts are being made to have better coordination with various Central Ministries such as Civil Aviation, Railways, Surface Transport and Urban Development and respective State Governments to execute these projects expeditiously. Addressing the meeting of the Consultative Committee Meeting of the Parliament attached to the Ministry of Tourism and Culture at Agra today, she said, creation of infrastructure for promotion of tourism and conservation of heritage is always taken up in the larger national perspective keeping in mind the importance of the place and tourist traffic. Smt. Soni said the Tourism Ministry has sent a presentation to the Prime Minister on the areas where better coordination is required among various Central Ministries for promotion of tourism and betterment of related infrastructure in the Country. She said despite budgetary constraints and increasing land cost in the country, Tourism Ministry is making all efforts to create additional rooms for budget tourists. The Minister said the Government would like to have better hotel facilities in public-private private partnership in the country particularly at the major pilgrimage sites of all religions in the country. Smt. Ambika Soni urged the members of the committee to identify tourism projects in their areas which are environment friendly. Responding to the suggestions of the members to strengthen the monitoring system of the tourism projects and conservation of monuments, she said local MPs will be invited during her or senior official's visit to the tourist projects for their suggestion and concerns, if any. The Minister said, it is important that the people should be sensitized about the preservation and conservation of heritage sites and monuments and to the needs of guests from foreign countries. Members attending the meeting stressed the need to have better road and air connectivity, development of civic amenities and infrastructure and proper monitoring of funds released to complete different tourism related projects in the country. Those who attended the meeting include Ch.Lal Singh, Sh. B.S. Dangawas, Parasnath Yadav, Prasanna Acharya, Nakul Das Rai, V.K.Thummar, Shripad Yasso Naik and Sunil Khan (all Lok Sabha) and Dr. Chandan Mitra, Shri Tarini Kanta Roy and Shri Amir Alam Khan (All from Rajya Sabha). The Union Tourism Secretary Shri S. Banerjee and Union Culture Secretary Shri Abhijit Sengupta also attended the meeting.

5082. (13-12-2007) NEW DELHI : Defence related activities such as joint exercises, high-level visits, transfer of technology and activities relating to co-development and co-production will be discussed at the 10th Meeting of the Indo-French High Committee on Defence Cooperation to be held here on December 17-18, 2007. The meeting will be co-chaired by the Defence Secretary Shri Vijay Singh and representative of French Minister of Defence Mr. Thierry Borja de Mozota. Under this High Committee, there are three sub-committees. The Sub Committee on Military Cooperation has representatives from the headquarters of Integrated Defence Services and the three Services. The second Sub Committee deals with strategic issues and the third one is on Defence Industry Procurement and Research & Technology. The Sub Committee on Military Cooperation will role out plan for service to service activities for the forth coming year while the Sub Committee on Strategic Issues will discuss matters relating to regional issues. The Sub Committee on Defence Industry Procurement and Research & Technology will discuss the Transfer of Technology, joint development and production. It may be recalled that a bilateral MoU on supply of defence equipment was signed with France in January 1982 in the context of the sale of Mirage Aircraft, aimed at the uninterrupted supply of defence equipment, services and related technology from France to India. A Defence Cooperation Working Group set up under the MoU met regularly until 1995. Later, as a result of initiative of the Former President Jacques Chirac during his visit to India in 1998, a Government to Government agreement was reached and cooperation in the field of Defence was revitalized following which the Indo-French High Committee on Defence Cooperation meetings are conducted every year alternatively in India and France. The 9th Meeting of this Committee was held on November 09-10, 2006 in Paris.

5083. (14-12-2007) NEW DELHI : Addressing the Indo-US Healthcare Summit today the Union Minister for Health & Family Welfare, Dr. Anbumani Ramadoss said that he was happy that the NRIs, specially physicians in the recent times are concerned about the improvement in the health care delivery in India. Dr. P.C.K. Nayar, President, MCI, Dr. Ajay Kumar, President, IMA, Dr. Hemant Patel, President, American Association of Physicians of Indian Origin (AAPI), Dr. Narendra R. Kumar, Coordinator, Indo-US Healthcare Summit, were present at the function.

5084. (14-12-2007) NEW DELHI : The Minister of Railways, Shri Lalu Prasad has announced an ex-gratia of Rs. 5,00,000/- (Five lakh) to families of each of the dead in bus-train collision in Moga district in Punjab today. He also announced an ex-gratia of Rs. 50,000/- each for grievously injured and Rs. 15,000/- each for those who suffered simple injuries in the collision. This morning at around at 8.20 a.m. a mini bus dashed with train no. 4629 Ludhiana-Ferozepur Sutlej Express at a manned level crossing Gate No. 50-B between Jagraon-Ajitwal stations of Ferozepur Division. Sixteen persons were killed in this unfortunate incident and other thirteen who received injuries have been shifted to the hospitals. No causality or injury has been reported to any train passenger. An inquiry has been ordered and would be conducted by the Commissioner of Railway Safety.

5085. (14-12-2007) NEW DELHI : Shri Kamal Nath, Union Minister of Commerce and Industry, Government of India, has called on the new generation of Indian entrepreneurs to go global and look for synergies and integrations arising out of developments in the international trade and business environment. Speaking to a select gathering of invitees including senior media critics and journalists at the global launch of his book titled, " India's Century: The Age of Entrepreneurship in the World's Biggest Democracy" in London today, Shri Kamal Nath explained that the book's central theme was India's emergence, from the backwaters of global economy to its frontline, generating aspirations for the future based on the recent outstanding achievements. The function was also attended by some of the Cabinet Ministers of the British Government, CEOs of a large number of UK-based MNCs, and a large section of Indian diaspora in London, Pointing to the current uncertainties in the global economy, Shri Kamal Nath, the Indian Trade Minister, urged the Indian entrepreneurs to stay globally competitive as this was possibly the only way to carry business forward. Not only was the lifespan of new and emerging technologies considerably changing - with what was new today becoming outdated tomorrow - but consumer preferences and consumption patterns were also living to shorter durations. In the changing milieu, it was imperative, the Minister observed, that the Indian entrepreneurs not only came up with globally competitive technological improvements in their product profiles but ensured globally competitive business practices to be perpetually alive to new opportunities for growth and partnerships. The book explores .the entrepreneurial spirit that, in combination with economic liberalism, had given the Indian economy momentum and placed it on the fast track. The book, published by McGraw-Hill of New York, is a first hand account of Shri Kamal Nath's ideas, initiatives and his successfully taking the Indian businesses onto the global platform whilst also offering a roadmap for the Indian entrepreneurs to benefit from emergent trade opportunities. The book explores and narrates India's journey of transformation into a global economy. It thereafter relates India's economic engagement with the leading nations of the world and how it could be profitable for stakeholders in the coming years. Shri Kamal Nath is India's public face in the World Trade Organisation (WTO) and amongst the acknowledged leaders of developing nations in global trade negotiations. He has held in the past responsibilities for the Ministries of Textiles and Environment and Forests, and served as a General Secretary of the Congress Party.

5086. (14-12-2007) NEW DELHI : Renewable Energy is energy derived from resources that are regenerative or for all practical purposes non-depleting beside environmentally benign. By these qualities, renewable energy sources are fundamentally different from fossil fuels. Mankind's traditional uses of wind, water, and solar energy are widespread in developed and developing countries; but the mass production of energy using renewable energy sources has become more commonplace recently, reflecting the major threats of climate change, depletion of fossil fuels, and the environmental, social and political risks of fossil fuels. Consequently, many countries promote renewable energies through tax incentives and subsidies. The role of new and renewable energy has been assuming increasing significance in recent times with the growing concern for the country's energy security. During the last two and half decades there had been a vigorous pursuit of activities relating to the development, trial and induction of a variety of renewable energy technologies for use in different sectors. The Ministry of New and Renewable Energy has been facilitating the implementation of broad-spectrum programmes covering more or less the entire range of new and renewable energy. These programmes broadly seek to supplement conventional fossil-fuel-based power through harnessing wind, small hydro and bio power; reach renewable energy to remote rural areas for lighting, cooking and motive power; use renewable energy in urban, industrial and commercial applications; and develop alternate fuels and applications for stationary, portable and transport uses apart from supporting research, design and development of new and renewable energy technologies, products and services. Commercialization of the renewable energy technologies started in 1993. The States were pursued to offer suitable sites and announce policies for private sector participation. Grid interactive renewable power projects are essentially private investment driven and almost all the renewable power capacity addition is coming through this route. Eventually, since renewable power would need to compete with conventional electricity, the challenge is to align it in terms of reliability, quality and cost. Accordingly, the focus is towards reducing the capital cost of projects and increasing their capacity factors, with the eventual aim of reducing the unit cost of renewable power generation.

5087. (14-12-2007) NEW DELHI : BJP spokesman said here that the first phase of polling for election the new legislative assembly of Gujarat is over. The turnout of voters has been fairly high. I appeal to the voters in the second phase to make it even higher, because it is the duty of every citizen to vote in an election. I am confident that the people will give a renewed and decisive mandate to the BJP under the leadership of Shri Narendra Modi. I am equally confident that the people of Himachal Pradesh will give a resounding victory to the BJP under the leadership of Prof. Premkumar Dhumal. Thus, the country's political scene is all set to be radically transformed in the last week of 2007. Thereafter, in 2008, the Congress-led UPA government will in all probability have to count its remaining time in office on the fingers of the hand.

5088. (14-12-2007) NEW DELHI : The President of India said here that I am happy to participate in the celebrations of the National Energy Conservation Day. I congratulate all those who have been awarded for their outstanding contributions to energy conservation. Your efforts are important to us and I hope that you will continue to excel. Today is an important occasion to reaffirm our commitment to sustainable development and inclusive growth by using our precious energy resources effectively and efficiently. Each one of us present here is fully aware and committed to bringing about a greater efficiency in the use of energy resources in all our activities-be it at home, at work, in our offices, on the road and in agriculture or in industry. I believe that each one of us also has the responsibility to help spread the message about the efficient use of energy and its conservation to each and every citizen of the country. Each individual can be a motivator for energy efficiency and such like-minded individuals can join forces to launch a national energy efficiency movement. Energy plays a key role in achieving the goals of sustainable development and poverty eradication. We are faced with the formidable task of meeting the increasing demand for energy. The effort would be three pronged - to enhance supply, use resources available in an optimal and economical manner and on the demand side look at ways to save energy. Technological advances can contribute in large measure to this process. Energy efficient equipment should be manufactured both for industrial and domestic use. Similarly, the process of manufacturing should be such that it cuts down on energy consumption at every stage. We would also have to ensure that there is better distribution of electricity as there are a large number of instances of power loss in transmission and there are also cases of power theft. All these issues need to be addressed. We must educate our people that energy is a resource that needs to be used judiciously. There are multiple requirements for energy and all citizens have a duty not to waste this precious resource. Increasing access to energy and enhanced energy efficiency is important for our development. Our own policies for sustainable development are by way of promotion of energy efficiency, increasing the share of renewable energy and changing the fuel mix. Fossil fuels will continue to play a dominant role in the energy mix in decades to come but the development and use of advanced and cleaner fossil fuel technologies should be increased. The sharp increase in energy prices has resulted in a renewed focus on energy diversification and efficiency. Promoting increased research and development in the field of various energy technologies in particularly renewable energy and advanced energy technologies can help in augmenting sustained and secure supply of energy. Even though India's per-capita emission of green house gases is much less than those of developed countries, in this age of climate change, as citizens of the globe, all of us need to make efforts towards energy conservation. Efficient use of energy is itself a mechanism for reducing global warming. I would call on all individuals, businesses, corporate organizations, Government offices and others to look at their energy consumption patterns and cut out wasteful expenditure of energy. Over the past few years several energy efficient gadgets have been introduced that curtail electricity consumption. Continuous R&D efforts should be made for making available machinery, vehicles and gadgets that have lower energy intensity. I strongly urge all large public and private buildings in the country to find scope for energy savings in their premises and to implement measures to achieve these savings. The energy savings movement in buildings needs to grow exponentially. Regular energy audits are very useful in monitoring progress made in this regard. Energy thus saved could be made available for those who do not have access to it or have a greater requirement for energy.

5089. (14-12-2007) NEW DELHI : Aritra Sahoo of Sutahata Sarboday Prathamik Vidyalaya, Sutahata, Purba Medinipore, West Bengal was given the first prize for her expression on energy conservation/energy efficiency. The President of India, Smt. Pratibha Devisingh Patil gave away the prizes here today to the winners of the National Painting Competition organized by the Ministry of Power and Bureau of Energy Efficiency for creating awareness regarding energy conservation activities.

5090. (14-12-2007) NEW DELHI : The Defence Minister Shri A K Antony will be leaving New Delhi on Sunday for a three-day official visit to Vietnam. He will be accompanied by a high-level delegation including Additional Secretary in the Ministry of Defence Shri P K Rastogi, Vice Chief of Army Staff Lt. Gen. M L Naidu, Air Marshal V R Iyer and Vice Admiral D K Dewan. During his stay in the capital Hanoi, Shri Antony will hold meetings with his Vietnamese counterpart Mr. Phung Quang Thanh. He will also make courtesy call on the President Mr. Nguyen Minh Triet and the legendry leader Gen. Vo Nguyen Giap. The Defence Minister will also visit various defence installations in Ho Chi Minh city besides holding discussions with the Indian Chamber of Business. Over the years Indo-Vietnamese Defence cooperation has grown steadily through visits by military delegations, ship visits from India and training of Vietnamese Defence personnel in India. The relationships got a boost in 1994 with the signing of the Protocol on Defence cooperation. It reached a high point in July 2007 when the two countries agreed on 'Strategic Partnership' during the visit of the Vietnamese Prime Minister to India. Vietnam has now become a member of the UN Security Council for a period of two years. Last month the 3rd India Vietnam Security Dialogue was held in New Delhi and a number of decisions were taken by both sides to provide further impetus to their relationships. The decisions include exchange of visits for better appreciation of requirements and problems, greater cooperation in the field of training of Service personnel - particularly involving junior level officers, security dialogue at least once a year, sharing of expertise on issues of common concern such as maritime security, border management and counter insurgency, conduct of training for Vietnamese officers in the field of UN

Painting Competition and stressed the need to inculcate in the future citizens the importance of energy conservation. The Union Minister of Power, Shri Sushilkumar Shinde indicated that the present shortages of 15,000 to 16,000 MW may be overcome by practicing energy conservation and efficiency. He informed that the Chief Ministers' conference on Power in May 2007 resolved to undertake Demand Side Measures. Ministry of Power has initiated schemes for lighting, building and agricultural sector. The lighting programme, the Bachat Lamp Yojana, is likely to be announced shortly and would provide the CFLs at the cost of incandescent bulbs by using the CDM revenues. Shri Shinde added that energy conservation efforts need to be translated into a mass movement so as to be inculcated in daily lives. It needs to be imbibed and practised by all citizens and must become a way of their lives. Secretary, Ministry of Power, Shri Anil Razdan in his welcome speech, stressed the need to lifestyle change based approach to energy conservation and efficiency. He said that the need for awareness and education is a very important strategy to convey the message of energy conservation and energy modesty to the public at large. Shri Razdan added that there is a need to reassess lifestyle and recognize that in adopting the energy efficient option, neither comfort nor cost is compromised.

5099. (14-12-2007) NEW DELHI : At the initiative of the Ministry of Tribal Affairs, the National Scheduled Tribes Finance and Development Corporation (NSTFDC) has convened a meeting of State Governments and its channellising agencies on 17 th December, 07 to address issues related to its financial assistance programme for the benefit of tribals groups which will include expansion the coverage of the programme and making delivery system more effective. NSTFDC, an undertaking of the Ministry of Tribal Affairs, provides financial assistance for the schemes and projects meant for the economic development of Scheduled Tribes through channellising agencies appointed by the States. During the one-day conference, issues like identifying more income generating activities for term loan to tribals, bridge loan to meet the gaps in funding requirements of tribal projects and financial assistance for tribal self-help groups will be deliberated upon. Assistance for skill development and entrepreneurial training for tribals groups will also be taken up during the meet. The Ministry of Tribal Affairs has signed a MOU with NSTFDC through which the Corporation is being encouraged to cover more and more tribal families and activities for financial assistance. Besides improving the living standards of STs through the activities of NSTFDC, the Ministry is also implementing various schemes for tribal development. The meeting will also provide an opportunity to review the implementation of these schemes with State Governments. The Shri P. R. Kyndiah, Minister for Tribal Affairs will inaugurate the meeting and Shri G.B. Mukherji, Secretary, Tribal Affairs will chair it. Secretaries of Tribal Welfare Departments from the State Governments and representatives of channellising and senior officials from concerned departments will attend the meeting.

5100. (14-12-2007) NEW DELHI : Inaugurating the National Conference on Tuberculosis and Chest Diseases today, the Union Minister for Health & Family Welfare, Dr. Anbumani Ramadoss said that India has the highest number of Tuberculosis (TB) cases in the world and significant progress has been made in controlling as well as treatment of the disease, since the beginning of the Revised National Tuberculosis Control Programme (RNTCP) in 1997. The RNTCP has now completed over nine years of its implementation. The treatment success of new infectious TB cases under the RNTCP has consistently exceeded the global benchmark of 85%. He added that the whole world is looking towards India to learn about such a successful and rapid expansion of TB control programme in the form of DOTS. Besides Dr. R.K. Srivastava, DGHS, Government of India, President and members of Tuberculosis Association of India (TAI) were also present at the meeting.

5101. (14-12-2007) NEW DELHI : The Vice President of India Mohd. Hamid Ansari released the book titled "Jhansi Mein Kranti (1857-86)" authored by Shri Vir Singh Parmar at a function here today. The function was organized by Shashwat Shiksha Shodh Sansthan, Raksa, Jhansi. Addressing on the occasion the Vice President said that we all should impart the learnings of freedom movement to the next generation and this process should continue. Complementing the author he said that he deserves appreciation from all for imparting his valuable knowledge regarding freedom movement especially of "Jhansi Kranti". He further said that the people should not forget how the freedom was achieved. A number of dignitaries were present on the occasion.

5102. (15-12-2007) NEW DELHI : India Telecom - 2008 will be held from December 11 to December 13, 2008. This was announced by Dr. Shakeel Ahmad, Minister of State for Communication and Information Technology here today. The Minister was speaking at the valedictory session of the India Telecom - 2007, which concluded here today. The Minister expressed satisfaction that the Conference had scaled up on a much larger scale and has been a bigger success compared to last year. The Conference was inaugurated by the Prime Minister Dr. Manmohan Singh on December 12, 2006. The Conference had five different sessions chaired by eminent persons. Session I was on 'Accelerating the Growth of Broadband' chaired by Mr. Michael Murphy, CTO-APAC, Nokia Siemens Networks. Session II was on 'Delivery of Cost Effective Voice & Data Services in Rural India'. Session III, on 'Investments in Indian Telecom Sector' was chaired by Smt. Manju Madhavan, Member (Finance), Department of Telecommunications. Session IV was devoted to 'Growth of Value Added Services (VAS)' segment and Session V was on 'Enabling Regulatory Framework for achieving the Desired Goals'. There was an Open House session today.

5103. (15-12-2007) NEW DELHI : The Prime Minister, Dr. Manmohan Singh, has inaugurated the Golden Jubilee year of the Institute of Economic Growth here today. Addressing on the occasion the Prime Minister expressed concerned about imbalances persist in our growth process, he said that the rural-urban divide and inter-regional divide are the areas of concern. While the performance of Indian economy has certainly improved in recent years. The Prime Minister said that the government has initiated several policies aimed at bridging the rural-urban divide but the task is Himalayan and there is much that State governments will have to do in this regard. The Prime Minister lauded the role of the Institute of Economic Growth, which has emerged as an important link between the ivory towers of the academic world and the real world of policy making and the institute has an impressive record of research in demography, agriculture, environment, industrial development, technology policy and project evaluation. Dr. Manmohan Singh also said that we need massive investments in social and economic infrastructure and need policies that will make public investment more productive and encourage private investment. We must pay more systematic attention to issues related to energy security. We need a strategy for "agriculture and industry", for "rural and urban", for "town and country" to use the language of Classical Political Economy, the Prime Minister added. On the occasion, the Prime Minister has also released two books "IEG at Fifty : Recollections, Retrospect and Prospect" and "Growth, Equity, Environment and Population". Chairman of the PM's Economic Advisory Council Prof. C. Rangrajan, Chairman Indian Council of Social Science Research Prof. Andre Beteille and Chairman, Board of Governors, Institute of Economic Growth Dr. C.G. Hanumantha Rao were also present on the occasion.

5104. (16-12-2007) NEW DELHI : The Vice President of India, Mohd. Hamid Ansari gave away the trophy to the Red Cavalry for winning the Amity Polo Club Tournament here today. The final of the tournament was played between the Red Cavalry and the Black Cavalry. On the occasion, the Equestrian displayed was performed by the 61 Cavalry. The tournament was organised to support under-privileged girl children.

5105. (16-12-2007) NEW DELHI : The Defence Minister Shri AK Antony arrived in Hanoi this evening on a three-day official visit to Vietnam. He was accorded a warm welcome by the Indian Ambassador to Vietnam, Mr. Lal Thla Muana, the Director General of External Relations of Vietnamese Ministry of Defence, Maj Gen Pham Thanh Lan and other senior Vietnamese officials at the Noi Bai Airport. Responding to the warm welcome from the Vietnamese side, Shri Antony said his visit will ' lead to greater mutually beneficial relationship' between the Armed Forces of the two countries. Shri Antony's visit to Vietnam is part of India's 'Look East Policy' and the two sides are expected to take up a number of issues to deepen their defence cooperation which has been gathering momentum after the signing of the 'strategic partnership' agreement last July. Vietnamese economy is on an upswing now with an annual GDP growth of over eight percent for the last two years. Since 1986, Vietnam has embarked upon a policy of Doi Moi (economic renovation) to introduce market economy. In a liberal investment climate, investors from all over the world are evincing ever-growing interest in Vietnam. Accompanied by a high level delegation consisting of senior officials of MoD and the Services, Shri Antony will be holding talks with his Vietnamese counterpart Gen Phung Quang Thanh Monday morning. He will also make courtesy calls on the Legendary leader Gen Vo Nguyen Giap and the Prime Minister of Vietnam, Mr. Nguyen Tan Dung.

5106. (17-12-2007) NEW DELHI/GANDHINAGAR: The curtains have come down on a heated campaign in Gujarat which saw Chief Minister Narendra Modi being served notice by the Election Commission and a contempt notice by the Supreme Court. Congress president Sonia Gandhi was also given a show cause notice by the Commission, as was her party colleague, general secretary Digvijay Singh. BJP deputy leader in the Lok Sabha V.K. Malhotra was also served notice by the Election Commission. Asked by journalists in New Delhi whether any decision on these notices would be taken before the counting of votes started on December 23, Central Election Commissioner spokesperson J.P. Prakash declined to comment. Mr. Prakash said a presiding officer in Sankheda was removed for dereliction of duty and an election agent was booked under the Representation of the People Act for canvassing within 200 metres of a polling station. Over 5,000 poll observers were posted inside polling stations in key areas and 6,000 video cameras were deployed to record the voting process in sensitive constituencies, Mr. Prakash said. Gujarat Congress legal cell convener Krishnakant Vakhariya filed a complaint with the Election Commission demanding action against Mr. Modi for addressing his party workers on the compound of a polling station in Ranip locality under the Sarkhej Assembly constituency in Ahmedabad where he had cast his vote. Claiming that Mr. Modi not only violated the model code of conduct by giving a speech asking the voters to vote for the BJP, he also committed a criminal offence by going along with police commandos to various polling stations across the city. The Congress also lodged complaints about some BJP candidates, including Education Minister Anandiben Patel, having used hired vehicles to ferry voters. Similar complaints were also lodged in Sarkhej, Kalupur and some other constituencies in Ahmedabad. The urban constituencies of Ahmedabad district showed a comparative poorer turnout at 59 to 61 per cent. The district-wise voting pattern in other districts were: Gandhinagar 59 to 62 per cent; Banaskantha 65 to 66 per cent; Kaira 63 to 65 per cent; Sabarkantha 61 to 63 per cent; Patan 63 to 65 per cent; Vadodara 63 to 65 per cent; Mehsana 65 to 66 per cent; and Anand 62 to 63 per cent.

5107. (17-12-2007) NEW DELHI : The 1st Meeting of the newly reconstituted National Council for Vocational Training (NCVT) was held under the chairpersonship of the Minister of Labour & Employment Shri Oscar Fernandes here today. The Council decided to increase the reservation for women candidates seeking admission under Craftsmen Training Scheme from 25 per cent to 30 per cent. The Council felt that the promotion of women should be given greater priority aiming to ensure their equal participation in social and economic process. Therefore, it was decided that 30 per cent of seats in all ITIs and ITCs in all courses may be reserved for women candidates and that these seats could be filled based on the general reservation policy of each of the states. It was pointed out in the meeting that some States have got more than 30% reservation for women. In such cases it was decided that they may continue with their policy and need not bring it down. The NCVT also decided to approve DGE&T proposal to set up adequate number of ITIs in un-serviced blocks of the country and train the youth belonging to SC/ST, backward classes and minority communities in these ITIs, particularly, with reference to traditional skills which these communities possess in good measure. The Ministry's proposal for inclusion of new trades under Craftsmen Training Scheme (CTS) for all occupations was also approved by the Council. The proposal said that there is a need to increase the number of trades from 110 to encompass all sectors of the economy. In the latest revision of National Classification of Occupations about 2900 trades have been listed. An effort, therefore, should be made to develop course curricula in a phased manner for all the occupations/trades in the country which require skilled workforce. \ The Council also decided setting up of a Career Counselling-cum-Placement Cell in every ITI/ITC. The proposal put before the Council envisages that State Governments/private bodies should provide appropriate infrastructure for the functioning of these Placement Cells and Principals of ITI/ITCs should monitor the performance of these centres on these basis.

5108. (17-12-2007) NEW DELHI : The development of tourism as an industry is being given emphasis by most countries of the world. Tourism has been playing its due role in India and has made a record growth. A recent study by the National Council for Applied Economic Research (NCAER) has revealed that tourism's contribution towards GDP is 5.9 per cent and towards employment (both direct and indirect) 8.78 per cent. There is an imperative need to promote tourism in a big way. India's success could attract more and more tourists for ecotourism, religious tourism, historical tourism, medical tourism etc. Every single State has some unique characteristics, which could interest tourists in one way or the other. The 'Incredible India' campaign has been quite successful and driven the growth of tourism in the country. It captures the underlying spirit of the country, its culture, tradition and spirituality. As a result tourist arrivals have increased dramatically. During the Tenth Plan period, tourist arrivals grew by a phenomenal 78 per cent while foreign exchange earnings increased by around 120 per cent. According to the Tourism Ministry, a whopping 420 million domestic tourists were recorded in 2006. The opening up of air transport and emergence of low-cost carriers has greatly helped boost up tourist arrivals to this country. A study conducted by FICCI on development perspective of eco and rural tourism revealed that it had the highest employment and investment ratio. Every additional investment of Rs 10 crore has the potential to generate 47.5 jobs. Further, every direct job created in tourism leads to a creation of 77 jobs in other related sectors of the industry, the study stated. Besides the multiplier effect of tourism generates high revenue-capital ratio in the Indian context. Indirect employment generated in the form of revival of traditional arts and crafts, development of communication, hotels etc. Another study by McKinsey has revealed that medical tourism could generate as much as Rs 100 billion of revenue for India by 2012. The success of medical tourism will build bigger capacities and draw more investment for the health sector. Attracting foreign tourists has become a priority and there are expectations of reaching the 10 million mark by the end of the 11th Plan period. There is presently one lakh approved quality accommodation which should be increased to two lakh by 2011, according to report by a working group on tourism for the Eleventh Plan. According to Subhash Goyal, President of the Indian Association of Tour Operators, "if we implement the suggestions by the Ministry of Tourism, it will not be difficult to attract 10 million (foreign) tourists".

5109. (17-12-2007) NEW DELHI : The Vice President of India Mohd. Hamid Ansari released the two volumes of the "The Oxford India Anthology of Modern Urdu Literature" edited by 'Ms. Mehr Afshan Farooqi' at a function here today. These volumes survey the field of Urdu Literature from the mid 19th to late 20th century and cover up the period of 100 years of literary production with about 90 authors and over 130 selections. These include major genres like poetry, drama and fiction as well as essays, autobiography and letters. Addressing on the occasion, the Vice President said that Ms. Farooqi has done a favour to all by publishing such a valuable book because such a book on Urdu literature was badly needed. This is a new way to entice people and a great service to the language as well as the readers.. A good and distinctive literature could be created through an open interaction of ideas and a free translation of classic text. Congratulating the editor of these volumes, the Vice President said that the focus of selection in these volumes is on literary excellence. He hoped that these volumes would enlighten the general readers as well as the students and scholars of Urdu literature. A number of literary personalities and dignitaries were present on the occasion.

5110. (17-12-2007) NEW DELHI : Prof. Saifuddin Soz, the Union Minister of Water Resources reviewed the problems and plans pertaining to the speedy implementation of various schemes taken up under the Accelerated Irrigation Benefit Programme (AIBP), flood management and anti erosion etc., with a high level delegation of Jammu and Kashmir Government led by Mr. Dilawar Mir, the Minister for Irrigation, Public Health and Engineering Department, here today. The State delegation apprised Prof. Soz of progress of various schemes and period when they were likely to be completed. Prof. Soz urged the State authorities for speedy implementation of works taken-up under the AIBP and other Centrally sponsored schemes so that early benefits could percolate to the people especially for far-flung areas. The Minister also impressed upon the officers and engineers of the Ministry of Water Resources to coordinate with the State authorities in order to ensure that all bottlenecks were removed and the projects completed on schedule. The meeting among other things also reviewed the implementation of various flood management and anti erosion schemes, spill-over works of the 10th Five Year Plan and major projects to be taken up under the 11th Five Year Plan. The Minister assured that the Centre would be extending adequate assistance, both financial and technical, for early execution of these schemes. The States authorities, on their part, should properly identify the priorities and give special attention to the remote and backward areas.

5111. (17-12-2007) NEW DELHI : The Defence Minister Shri AK Antony today drove down to the modest residence of Gen Vo Nguyen Giap in Hanoi today to call on the Vietnamese legendary figure who was instrumental in defeating three of five Permanent Members of the UN Security Council- France, US and China. He was the longest serving Defence Minister of Vietnam who faced most of the incursions and invasions on the Vietnamese territory as head of the military. He served from 1945 to 1979. Gen Giap went to the same school in Hue in Central Vietnam as Ho Chi Minh and late Prime Minister Pham Van Dong. Now in his nineties, Gen Giap appears frail but showed no signs of memory loss as he recounted vividly fond remembrances of his two visits to India when he went to New Delhi, Kolkata, Mumbai and the Andaman & Nicobar islands. Gen Giap recalled the contributions of Jawahar Lal Nehru and Ho Chi Minh to provide a solid foundation to Indo-Vietnamese relations. He also recalled the contributions India has made to Vietnam during the war periods, for the unification as also for its reconstruction. "Therefore, I feel like meeting old friends", he told Shri Antony. Gen Giap appreciated the giant strides made by India in science & technology, especially, in IT and expressed the hope that ' the Indian advantage' will also be extended to the people of Vietnam. He requested Shri Antony to convey his best wishes to the Prime Minister Dr. Manmohan Singh. Shri Antony said it was a really ' happy and exciting day' for him as during his younger days he had read about the heroism of Gen Giap and that he was meeting him in person today. He said, Gen Giaps heroic acts were indeed lessons in warfare. Gen Giap presented a copy of his memoir " People's War, People's Army" to Shri Antony.

5112. (17-12-2007) NEW DELHI : Shri Arjun Singh, Minister of Human Resource Development has said if India has to assume leadership and realise its dream of becoming a super power in the near future, we have to ensure that the abundant talent available in the form of human resource is efficiently honed and tapped. The Minister's speech was read out by Prof. B. Mungekar, Member, Planning Commission, as he could not make it to be present in the Conference. The Minister, further, said that in the 11th Five Year Plan, it is aimed to achieve a figure of 15 per cent enrolment rate. In this direction some policy initiatives have already been announced. In his speech, the Minister has further elaborated that there is a wide discrepancy in the capacity between the States with over 70 per cent of the capacity in degree level engineering education being available in the four States of Tamil Nadu, Andhra Pradesh, Karnataka and Maharashtra. This regional imbalance has to be minimized so that people from all parts of the country have a fairly equal access to quality education. 'Public-Private Partnership, in this regard, may also be desirable. While we do so, we must ensure that opportunities of quality technical education is provided to all, equitably' he added. \ 'Government is making all efforts possible to take the quality of the technical education to the next higher level and on par with the highest international standards. This is evident from the fact that India has been admitted as a provisional member of the Washington Accord, which would enable our technical programmes to be recognized as accredited as per the global standards', the Minister added. Prof. B. Mungekar delivered the keynote address. He said that the knowledge economy is one of the several ingredients for achieving 11th Five Year Plan target of 9 percent growth of GDP. This can be done by making education affordable to larger population of India and not by bypassing the poor or ignoring the backward regions of the country, not even backward regions of the developed States in India. Shri Mungekar reiterated Government's commitment to the education sector to the tune of 19.8 per cent of the total plan allocation but he said that education should be thoroughly restructured to the last decimal point. Pro. Mungekar narrated that our educational system is suffering from many impediments like lack of employability of the graduates, subject imbalance, lack of expansion, lack of faculty development, lack of networking of institutions, lack of regular upgradation of curriculum and lack of faculty exchange programme. But, he said, in order to make a breakthrough, educational institutions should be allowed to generate surpluses and the apex institutions should reinvent themselves by galvanizing reforms from within. 'we are still suffering from monopolistic mindset. This should be thoroughly discarded, he added.

5113. (17-12-2007) NEW DELHI : The Tourism Minister of Sri Lanka Mr. Milinda Moragoda today called on the Tourism & Culture Minister, Smt. Ambika Soni. During their 40 minutes meeting here both the Leaders discussed ways to promote and strengthen bilateral relations in the tourism sector. The visiting dignitary said that India is their largest market and his country is focusing on MICE Tourism and having success in it with the cooperation of Indian Companies. He said his country also wants promotion of some Buddhist centres in South India by India for Sri Lankan Tourists. The Sri Lankan Minister said he is also looking for investment from Indian Hotel chains in Sri Lanka for the construction and promotion of budget hotels. The Tourism & Culture Minister, Smt. Ambika Soni stressing the importance of historical and cultural ties between the two countries said the Joint Working Group constituted in 2004 for the purpose can discuss and workout the modalities of the promotion of tourism related projects between the two countries. Smt. Soni suggested the meeting of the JWG should be convened soon as a follow up of today's meeting. She said Sri Lanka can participate more and more in travel fairs/ marts to promote tourism related activities between the two countries. The Minister said India is promoting Buddhist Circuit Tourism in a big way and spots related to Buddhism are being developed not only in U.P. and Bihar but also in Orissa, Andhra Pradesh and North East. Both the Leaders agreed to convene the meeting of the Joint Working Group between the two countries at a convenient date to accelerate the pace of cooperation in tourism sector. In 2006 according to provisional estimates, 1,54,813 tourists arrived from Sri Lanka to India and the outbound tourist traffic from India to Sri Lanka in 2005 was 1,13323. Buddhist sites in India are the most attraction sites by the travelers from Sri Lanka.

5114. (17-12-2007) NEW DELHI : The Tourism and Culture Minister Smt. Ambika Soni has said that at a time when the entire world is talking about the climate change and conservation of natural resources, it is important to formulate comprehensive guidelines for adventure tourism. Inaugurating the 6th Annual Convention of the Adventure Tour Operators Association of India (ATOAI) here today the Minister said she also agrees that the existing national ecotourism policy needs to be revived in the light of the ongoing international debate on climate change. She said she has often come across complaints that by-diversity is being erodded further on account of adventure, world life and ecotourism. There was a genuine concern that adventure tourists are not only pollulting the place but have little regard for conserving the existing natural resources. The Minister cautioned the ATOAI that if they wish expand the scope of adventure toruism, they need to be careful and how they pursue it. Smt. Soni said responsible tourism in any form will not only help to preserve the natural resources but would enable generate revenue for the bettermend of the place and the local communities. On this Occasion the Minister also released a special 30 Second Television Commercial on Adventure Tourism and the Report on Incredible India campaign during 2007. The prime focus of this convention is to create widespread awareness about the multi-dimensional face of the Indian tourism sector. It seeks to promote India as one of the most exciting Adventure Tourism destinations in the world and intends focusing on the innumerable adventure and ecotourism opportunities in the country.

5115. (17-12-2007) NEW DELHI : Minister for Tribal Affairs, Shri P. R. Kyndiah has called for strengthening the lending system for tribals to increase the pace of developmental activities in their areas. Expressing concern over the huge gap in the living conditions of the people living in tribal areas, he said that in urban areas people are being chased by financial institutions extending loans for various purposes irrespective of the need of a person while in tribal areas situation is in total contrast where people are not getting assistance from financial institutions even for their survival. In this situation it is the duty of Government agencies like National Scheduled Tribes Finance and Development Corporation (NSTFDC) to strengthen its network for providing loans to the Scheduled Tribe people for development activities. Shri Kyndiah was addressing the conference of States' Tribal Development Departments and channelising agencies of NSTFDC. Underlining the importance of skill development and capacity building, Shri Kyndiah said financial institutions should not only provide loan through single window but also provide training to develop new skills so that tribals and can utilize the money and improve their traditional activities to become a small entrepreneur in his own world, he said. Referring 'Adivasi Mahila Sashaktikaran Yojana' of NSTFDC for providing concessional financial assistance for tribal women to enable them to undertake income generating activities, the Minister asked NSTFDCto expand the reach of the scheme. He also urged the State run financial institutes to consider self-help groups of tribal community as there is a tendency of tribals to involve in activities as part of a clan or whole community, rather than as an individual. Shri Kyndiah said that marketing support for our tribal farmers is another area which could be explored for providing financial support. Plantation like coffee and tea and horticulture would go a long way to help us reach the unreached tribals, he stressed. The meeting was convened by the National Scheduled Tribes Finance and Development Corporation (NSTFDC) at the initiative of the Ministry of Tribal Affairs,) to address issues related to its financial assistance programme for the benefit of tribals groups which include expansion the coverage of the programme and making delivery system more effective. NSTFDC, an undertaking of the Ministry of Tribal Affairs, provides financial assistance for the schemes and projects meant for the economic development of Scheduled Tribes through channellising agencies appointed by the States. During the conference, issues like identifying more income generating activities for term loan to tribals, bridge loan to meet the gaps in funding requirements of tribal projects and financial assistance for tribal self-help groups were deliberated upon. Assistance for skill development and entrepreneurial training for tribals groups was also discussed during the meet.

5116. (17-12-2007) NEW DELHI : The Prime Minister, Dr. Manmohan Singh, has congratulated Narain Karthikeyan for winning the Feature Race in A1GP. Applauding Karthikeyan's victory, the Prime Minister said he is a true representative of India's young spirit and he has set an example for the entire motorsports fraternity of India to follow.

5117. (17-12-2007) NEW DELHI : India and Vietnam have agreed on a slew of measures to further expand their relations in defence cooperation and 'take it to a new height'. The Defence Minister Shri AK Antony who is on a three day visit to Vietnam, announced at the meeting with his counterpart General Phung Quang Thanh in Hanoi today that New Delhi will transfer 5000 naval spares belonging to Petya class of ship to Vietnam to make many of the ageing ships operational. He also announced the deputation of a four member team to impart training on UN Peace Keeping Operations in the first half of next year. The two sides also agreed to set up a Joint Working Group to facilitate the signing of MOU on defence cooperation. Shri Antony said the measures taken today 'will open a new chapter in defence cooperation between the two countries that will take the strategic partnership ahead'. Shri Antony highlighted the traditionally close and cordial relations between India and Vietnam, the foundations for which were laid by Jawaharlal Nehru and President Ho Chi Minh in their very first meeting in Hanoi 50 years ago.. He said the commonality of views of the two countries in many areas are a reflection of their shared strategic interests. Shri Antony congratulated Vietnam on being elected as non-permanent member of UN Security Council for a period of two years and said New Delhi attaches tremendous importance to the Strategic Partnership forged between the two Prime Ministers in July this year. Gen Phung Quang Thanh in his remarks put forward various proposals including training of Vietnamese Defence Personnel, enhancing the exchanges of delegations, expanding training cooperation and cooperation between the defence industries of the two countries. He also suggested increase in the frequency of goodwill visits by naval ships, application of information technology in defence and e- technology and technical support to Vietnamese navy. The Vietnamese Defence Minister expressed gratitude to India for providing training to armed forces officers in various areas and said 'they are bringing back valuable knowledge and skills to their work areas'. So far, a total of 49 officers have attended various Army and Navy Courses and 64 officers have attended English language courses. Earlier, on his arrival at the Ministry of Defence Headquarters, Shri Antony inspected an inter-services guard of honour.

5118. (17-12-2007) NEW DELHI : The Home Minister, Shri Shivraj Patil has condemned yesterday's blast near Imphal in Manipur. The following is the text of his statement: " I strongly condemn the bomb blast which took place near Imphal in Manipur on 16th December, 2007. I convey my sympathies to the kins of those killed and pray for speedy recovery of those injured in the incident. Such desperate acts by anti-national elements will not help them in any manner and will only isolate them further. I am confident that the State Government will take all steps to avoid recurrence of such incidents and bring the culprits to book."

5119. (17-12-2007) NEW DELHI : The Indian Pharmacopoeia (IP) 2007 produced in fulfilment of the requirements in the Drugs and Cosmetics Rules, 1945 lays down the standards of drugs produced and/or marketed in India and thus contributes in the control of the quality of the medicinal products. The standards of this pharmacopoeia are authoritative, legally enforceable and intended to help in the inspection and licensing of manufacturing and distribution of drugs and pharmaceuticals. The Pharmacopoeia 2007 has been prepared in accordance with the principles and designed plan decided by the Scientific Body of the Indian Pharmacopoeia Commission. In addition to the past practices of requesting for comments, the contents of revised appendices and monographs have been publicized on the website of the Indian Pharmacopoeia Commission, for collecting comments widely from various institutions and organizations. All the feedback and inputs have been reviewed by the relevant Expert Committee to ensure the feasibility and practicability of the standards and methods revised in this edition of the Pharmacopoeia, as well as the principle of "openness, justice and fairness" has been kept in mind during compiling and editing. The Indian Pharmacopoeia 2007 has been published in three volumes. The Pharmacopoeial standards included in this publication adhere to the concept of harmonization with those used internationally, also keeping in view technological status for manufactures and analysis of different sectors of the industry, without compromising with the quality of the products. It is hoped that this publication would be able to fulfil the Mission of the Indian Pharmacopoeia Commission to promote public health both in India and other countries using drugs manufactured in India. It would also play a vital role in initiating new prospective for improving the quality of medicines and accelerate development of Pharma Sector in India.

5120. (17-12-2007) NEW DELHI : The Congress said here that we want to put before you that Himachal, which goes to the polls shortly, is going to see a sweep, a huge victory for the Congress Party which is going to come back to power, it is going to repeat the good governance which it has given for the last few years and we want to highlight before you that on the one hand there are speeches and lectures, attempts to mislead, to talk in the air without any reference to facts. That is the BJP in Himachal. On the other hand there are hard, cold facts and I would like to give you an illustrative example of some of those facts, they are clear unequivocal. The good governance which has been shown by the incumbent government in Himachal, the previous government left that state with a debt of over 15 hundred crore rupees. In a political sense they kind of willed it to the successor government, a huge debt burden. The Dhumal government (the previous government) retrenched 35 thousand workers as you all know, is not a very large state, and government employment is a major source of employment, Shri Shanta Kumar and Shri Dhumal constantly and continuously bickered, divided and fought. Shri Dhumal's government was plagued by serious corruption charges, the Computer and Auditor General has given a report indicting him. As against that you have cold, hard undeniable facts of good governance during the Congress regime. There are facts which show that this government has made genuine, sincere attempts to do significantly at least a portion of what they have promised. There is, for example, the Balupati-Bilaspur railway line which has been talked about but it is only the Central government which has sanctioned for Himachal that amount of roughly Rs. 2200 crore for a big project like that. The augmentation of power supply by over 6500 megawatts, has been done by implementing, operationalising and sanctioning additional projects. The tax holiday schemes, to attract investment in that state, have yielded an investment flow over 3000 crores for a small state. That involves additional employment of roughly 40 lakh people. The Rajiv Gandhi Grameen Vidhutikaran Yojana has been a great success which has covered 30000 households and care has been taken for at least 50 per cent of them are and fall below the poverty line. The National Rural Employment Guarantee Scheme has been extended to a few states where it is so, to every district of Himachal, including the hilly districts. There has been an additional sanction for the long-standing demand of the Rohtang tunnel where avalanches are a big issue there involving 1355 crore rupees. There are several other similar projects which includes nutritional programmes for women and children aggregating just under 4 lakh women and over 13 lakh children. Education has been a success story in Himachal, it was one of the first states to pass a unique law which made it compulsory for parents to send children to school. There has been reduction in stamp duty, there has been a great boost to agriculturists by reducing the market fee by half from 2 to 1 per cent. The basic point is the same and the basic point is that there is a vast difference, this noticeable chasm between merely talking in the air but based on the facts and figures on the one hand and that's the BJP for you in Himachal versus concrete hard work to show for its governance by the Congress Party in Himachal. Therefore we have absolutely no doubt that we shall be back with another dose of good and even better governance for the next term in Himachal. To a question what happens to Gujarat, Shri Singhvi said' Let's wait till next Sunday. Gujarat has been discussed every day and if you have not heard let me repeat it we are going to win hands down in Gujarat but if I speak of Himachal does not mean nothing will happen in Gujarat. To a question that the exit polls are saying something else, Shri Singhvi said, more than us, the institution which you represent, should have learnt not to rely on exit polls or opinion polls. You should have learnt that it is an exercise of hazard and peril for those of you who have done so, you should have learnt that there are results with a 100 per cent difference. For example in UP a short while a go, about the tallies, in Madhya Pradesh some years ago and those examples can be duplicated, so I do not believe in embarking on hazardous, perilous exercises as you might, I believe much more on our inner sources, on our Party sources, on our cadres, on our workers and their reports and they are all unanimous, that we are heading towards a well deserved, big, significant, clear unequivocal victories in both Himachal and Gujarat. To a question whether the Congress Party has issued a legal notice to the investigators in the Bofors case, Shri Singhvi said, yes, the person concerned, according to us, has exhibited a shoot and scoot policy, every few months with gaps of 8 or 9 months, the person concerned, a Swedish gentleman, shoots of some remarks about the Bofors episode, the first time he did so was 18 years after the Bofors incident, thereafter he does it periodically.

5121. (17-12-2007) NEW DELHI : Shri Vinod Rai has been appointed as the Comptroller and Auditor-General of India with effect from the date he assumes charge of his office. Shri Vinod Rai, belongs to Indian Administrative Service of Kerala Cadre-72 Batch and is presently working as Secretary, Deptt. of Financial Services, Ministry of Finance, Government of India.

5122. (18-12-2007) NEW DELHI : In recognition of the efforts made by the Government of India in modernising its intellectual property systems as well as infusing transparency and openness in the system, the 170 plus Member States of the World Intellectual Property Organization (WIPO), in the recently concluded General Assemblies of WIPO, endorsed India's recognition as an International Searching Authority (ISA) and an International Preliminary Examining Authority (IPEA). "The recognition of India as an ISA/IPEA puts India in a coveted league of only 15 nations and organization which are currently recognized at a global level by ISA/APEA", Shri Kamal Nath, Union Minister of Commerce and Industry, informed in a press briefing here today. He further said that it is a recognition of our efforts to recognise the intellectual property system as well as lay down benchmark for future milestones that we need to achieve. The status of ISA and IPEA would be beneficial for India in several ways. Apart from the international recognition that our IP system would get, it would also generate revenues in the form of fees that would be provided to us for functioning as an ISA/IPEA. Being the only English speaking nation in the Asian region to be recognized as an ISA/IPEA would mean that several international applications received by WIPO under the Patents Cooperation Treaty would be sent to the Indian Patent Offices for search and preliminary examination purposes. E-filing facilities for patents and trade marks applications was launched in July this year. In the last 3 years, several important milestones have been achieved in the field of Intellectual Property rights in India. The Patent Act was amended in 2005 in order to meet our international obligations. A Rs.153 crore modernization programme for augmenting the infrastructure and human resources in Intellectual Property Office, creation of awareness regarding IPRs and introducing IT enabled efficient systems was completed on 31 March 2007. During the briefing, Shri Kamal Nath also informed that India has retained the Second place in A.T. Kearney's 2007 Foreign Direct Investment Confidence Index, a position it has held since displacing the US in 2005. "India continues to attract investors in the high value-added services industries like financial services and informed technology. India is the 2nd most preferred location for investors in Asia and USA. However, for European investors, India has claimed the top slot, displacing China", he further informed.

5123. (18-12-2007) NEW DELHI : The Vice President of India Mohd. Hamid Ansari has emphasized that the whole matter of Minorities Rights need to be pursued in an activist approach. Addressing a function to mark the 'National Minorities Rights Day' organized by the National Commission for Minorities (NCM) here today, he said it is question of national interest that the minorities be given a helping hand. Shri Ansari said on this day 1992 the United Nations promulgated the declaration on the rights of persons belonging to national or ethnic, religious or linguistic minorities and that's why this day is being celebrated as the Minorities Rights Day. He also conferred this year's 'National Minorities Rights Award' to senior journalist Shri Javed Anand for his significant contribution in promoting communal harmony between different communities in the country. In his address the Chairperson of NCM, Mohd. Shafi Qureshi, reiterated the need to address the fears and susceptibilities of minority groups whether religious or linguistic through legal and constitutal safeguards of their rights. We as a nation should uphold the virtues of Constitutionalism and the rule of law otherwise, it is an invitation to disaster. Instead of widening the cleavages in the society, our efforts should be directed towards bridging the communal divide, he added.

5124. (18-12-2007) NEW DELHI : The 10th India-France High Committee on Defence Cooperation (HCC) meeting concluded in New Delhi today. The Defence Secretary Shri Vijay Singh and Mr. Thierry Borja de Mozota, Ministerial Representative of the French Defence Minister, headed the respective delegations at the two-day talks held in an atmosphere of frankness and mutual understanding. Three sub-committees also met on the sidelines of the HCC. The Sub-Committee on Military Cooperation charted a plan for service to service cooperation activities during the forthcoming year while the Sub-Committee on Strategic Issues discussed matters of mutual strategic interests. The Sub- Committee on Defence Industry Procurement and Research & Technology discussed matters of Transfer of Technology, joint development, production and research. The minutes of the three Sub-Committees were ratified in the HCC meeting.

5125. (18-12-2007) NEW DELHI : Welcoming the distinguished and august gathering of Vice-Chancellors of Technical / affiliating Universities, Directors of IITs, IIMs, NITs, IIITs, NITTTRs and other premier institutes along with Chairpersons of All India Boards (AIBs), Members of the Executive Committee of the AICTE and Principal Secretaries / Education Secretaries / DTEs of various States/UTs, Prof.R.A.Yadav, acting Chairman, AICTE described the conference as a modest beginning in the direction of initiating dialogue and building consensus. Critical issues regarding technical education were deliberated and a number of suggestions and recommendations were proposed.

5126. (18-12-2007) NEW DELHI : Shri Arjun Singh, Minister of Human Resource Development has honoured Teachers, Vice-Principals, Principals and students of Navodaya Vidyalayas for academic excellence today. While distributing Novodaya National Awards 2007, he said, "it is the occasion to celebrate the academic excellence that Navodaya Vidyalaya is providing to make India leader of the world". He further added "we are all proud of the fact that Navodaya Vidyalaya wherever presents, symbolises the best of the institutions, irrespective of caste, creed and religion. And the credit goes to teachers, their dedication and also to the students and their efforts directed to the excellence". He also announced the beginning of Navodaya National Integration Meet 2007. To create an awareness among students and teachers on the subject of Education for Peace, Navodaya Vidyalaya Samiti has organised the Meet this year with the focus on Education for Peace through the Arts from December 18-20, 2007, Bal Bhavan, New Delhi. Based on the theme Peace, it is an expression of desire to create "A Culture of Peace". Almost 500 students and teachers from all over India are participating in the event. Students have joined together from the far Southern areas such as

Pathanamthitta, Kerala, Bagalkot & Dharwad, Karnataka, from the remote W. Garo Hills, Meghalaya, the distant South Sikkim and from the beautiful Bishnupur, Manipur. Some have come from the hills of Ranchi in Jharkhand and from the rocky & barren hilltops of Gaya from Bihar, from Mau, Uttar Pradesh, and from the hills of Uttarkashi, Uttarakhand. Students have also come from Sagar, Madhya Pradesh, and from Koraput, Orissa, as also from the place of peace Wardha, Maharashtra. There are also children from Srinagar and Chandigarh, from the desert turned green regions of Rajasthan Banswada, & Jafferpurkalan the Vidyalaya which is closest to Delhi.

5127. (18-12-2007) NEW DELHI : The 141st meeting of the Employees State Insurance (ESI) Corporation has approved a fresh amnesty scheme for withdrawal of cases against the defaulting employers and employees apart from approving the Annual Report of the organization. The meeting was chaired by Shri Oscar Fernandes, the Union Minister of Labour & Employment and Chairman ESIC here today. The approved amnesty scheme will come in force from 1st January 2008 and will remain effective till the year end *i.e.* 31st December 2008. The Amnesty scheme envisages that the prosecution cases filed in the 1st Class Judicial Magistrate Courts for non-payment of contribution would be considered for withdrawal subject to payment of contribution due and statutory interest. The quantum of relief in damages leviable/levied to the extent of 75 per cent as specified under Regulation 31-C would be provided to the employers and the damages leviable/levied to the extent of 25 per cent only would be claimed from the employers. The employers will have to give an undertaking to the effect that they would be regular in compliance in future and there would not be default on their part. In order to minimize the need of inspections, introduction of a self-certification system has been approved by the ESI meeting. Presently, the employers are required to submit a six monthly return in respect of employees engaged by them and the contribution paid in respect of such employees. The ESI meeting has now approved that the employers employing upto 40 employees who are regular in compliance, will not be required to get the return certified by a Chartered Accountant and shall only submit a Self-Certificate. The ESI Corporation also enhanced the Permanent Disablement Benefit and Dependents' Benefit Rates to compensate the erosion in its real value to inflation. The meeting also approved the review of the 'Rajiv Gandhi Shramik Kalyan Yojana' and resolved that the condition of 50 per cent disability under non-employment injury cases be reduced to 40 per cent disability so that more Insured Persons (IPs) could be covered under the scheme. It also approved the creation of a Sub-Regional Office of International Social Security Association (ISSA) at ESIC Headquarters in New Delhi. The ESI Corporation is an affiliate Member of the ISSA which comprises of more than 365 Institutions and bodies in over 155 countries and promotes corporation at international level in the area of social security. Speaking on the occasion, Shri Oscar Fernandes said that the ESI Scheme is now catering to social security needs of more than one crore insured persons and their family members; a landmark which has been achieved by the Corporation this year. He however added that in relation to the number of working class of our country, it is still a relatively small percentage of the organized sector and, therefore, we should endeavour to achieve larger goals in this regard. The Minister said that there is a lot of scope for improvement and our objective should be that we should serve the employees in the best possible manner. He emphasized that the safety measures for the workers should be enhanced to prevent accidents at work place. The Minister said that the Corporation has spent a sizeable amount of Rs.1,054.52 crores on the medical and cash benefits of insured persons and their family members. The achievement of the Corporation for the year 2006-07 also includes - enhancement in the wage ceiling of coverage of employees under the ESI Act from Rs.7500/- to Rs.10,000/- p.m. w.e.f. 1.10.2006; inclusion of 10 more slabs of daily standard benefits rates from Rs.150/- to Rs.195/-; the increase in revenue collection which was Rs.2,453.48 crores; and enhancement in the ceiling of reimbursing medical care from Rs.900/- to Rs.1,000/- per IP family unit per annum. Similarly, rate of funeral expenses of deceased insured person has also been increased from Rs.2,500/- to Rs.3,000/-.

5128. (18-12-2007) CUTTACK: CPI(M) general secretary Prakash Karat said here on Monday that the party would oppose any decision of the Congress-led government that would harm the interests of the poor, workers, Adivasis, government employees and small traders. Speaking at the open session of the party's State conference here, Mr. Karat said the Left parties were providing crucial outside support to the UPA government; at the same time, they were playing an important role in opposing the 'anti-poor' moves of the Centre. "All the 61 MPs of the Left Front in Parliament will ensure that the Central Government does not take any decision that would jeopardise the integrity and sovereignty of the country," he added. On the nuclear deal and military collaboration with the U.S., Mr. Karat said the U.S. wanted India to be its junior partner. "But we would not allow this to happen and ensure that India does not become a strategic ally of the U.S." Criticising the Centre's economic policies, Mr. Karat said the claim of 9 per cent Gross Domestic Product growth rate had nothing to do with a majority of the people as the bulk of the wealth was now concentrated in a handful of people. "Five persons of the country now have combined net assets of Rs. 4,12,000 crore while the poor have become poorer due to the pro-rich policies adopted by the Congress-led government." Agriculture, price rise, unemployment, the public distribution system and national security were very close to the CPI(M) and the party could not compromise on any of these issues. Mr. Karat was critical of the BJP for pursuing communal politics and said the Left would continue their struggle to see that it did not come to power at the Centre again. He criticised the ruling Biju Janata Dal in Orissa for adopting a 'faulty' mines policy. Janardan Pati, who was re-elected State CPI(M) chief, said the party would emerge as a major force in Orissa in the next three years.

5129. (18-12-2007) NEW DELHI : The Prime Minister chaired a meeting of the Trade and Industry Council, here today. The meeting discussed the current economic situation and issues of concern to Indian industry. All the participants underlined the various positive trends in the economy and drew attention to positive expectations about the future of Indian economy both at home and abroad. The meeting discussed at length global economic trends and whether the concern regarding a global slow down would affect the growth process in India. Participants also gave their views on the domestic price situation, drawing attention to global trends in fuel and food prices. They expressed concern with persisting infrastructural and policy constraints on growth. The participants universally emphasized the need to expand educational and skill development opportunities in India to address the growing shortage of a variety of skilled and qualified persons. All participants emphasized the need for a major reform and expansion of Indian education. They sought a policy framework for attracting more private investment in education and to facilitate greater public-private partnership in education. Thanking the leaders of Indian Industry for their participation in the meeting, the Prime Minister said the Government was committed to doing whatever is necessary to ensure that the Indian economy continues to grow at 9 per cent, even in the face of a possible global slow down. The Prime Minister said, "Our policy must be tuned to sustain 9 per cent growth even if world growth slows down and global food and fuel prices continue to remain under pressure. India should have the ambition and the courage to sustain the current acceleration of growth no matter what happens globally. Our domestic economy can sustain such a growth process but we will need to pursue policies that can sustain growth. While India must remain alert to trends in the global economy, we must also recognize that the world is looking at India as a new engine of growth. If our economy continues to grow despite a global slow down, we will be able to lift millions of our people from poverty and generate employment for our youth". The Prime Minister drew attention to the 11th Plan strategy of giving special attention to education. He said that expenditure on education is being increased from 7 per cent of total plan outlay in the 10th Plan to 19 per cent in the 11th Plan. He invited Indian industry to come forward with new ideas on how Indian education can be expanded, modernized and made to address the challenge of the future. "We must not become slaves of the past. We need creative thinking and fresh thinking to address the challenges we face in education" the PM said. The meeting was attended by Union Finance Minister, Union Commerce and Industry Minister, Deputy Chairman Planning Commission, Chairman National Manufacturing Competitiveness Council, Chairman Economic Advisory Council to PM and Members of the Prime Minister's Trade and Industry Council including Mr. Ratan Tata, Mr. Keshub Mahindra, Mr. Mukesh Ambani, Mr. R.P. Goenka, Mr. Jemshed Godrej, Mr. N.R. Narayanamurthy, Mr. Rahul Bajaj, Dr. Anji Reddy, Mr. Sunil Mittal, Mr. Sunil Munjal and Mr.Deepak Parekh.

5130. (18-12-2007) NEW DELHI : On the eve of the 54th meeting of the National Development Council in Delhi tomorrow being called to approve the 11th Five Year Plan for the period 2008 to 2013, BJP National President Shri Rajnath Singh charged the central government of trying to sow the seeds of discord, disharmony and disintegration by seeking to incorporate the aspect of communal budgeting through moves to reserve 15% funds for the minorities. In a press statement Shri Rajnath Singh said that it is indeed unfortunate that under the Congress led UPA government, a critical vision document that sets the tone and direction for national growth and development for the next five years, is now being treated as a tool of political appeasement. By seeking to incorporate aspects of communal budgeting into the Five Year Plan, the BJP President said that such a move would give a fillip to competitive communal demands for budgetary allocations and in the process the holistic approach to national development would become a casualty. Shri Rajnath Singh said that the BJP has always been of the view that every segment of society must become equitable partners and beneficiaries of national growth and prosperity irrespective of religion, caste, creed or class. However, a communal approach to budgetary allocation would only accentuate the competitive and communal politics of appeasement. He charged the Congress led UPA government for adopting such a short sighted approach to national development for the sake of votes. Shri Rajnath Singh said such undue haste in implementing suggestions for adopting a communal approach to national budgeting was also not desirable in light of questions being raised about the validity of certain inputs and data behind the Sacchar Committee Report which in itself is also against the very spirit of the Constitution. He charged the Congress led UPA government of adopting this approach to cover up its own dismal failure on all fronts of governance and achieving national priorities. The BJP President said that if at tomorrow's meeting of the NDC, any overt or covert move is taken up to incorporate communal budgeting in the process of national planning in general and the 11th Five Year Plan in particular, then all BJP ruled states would firmly oppose it.

5131. (18-12-2007) NEW DELHI : India has once again proved that it can protect its own and developing countries' interest at international fora. It all happened at the Indonesian holiday resort, Bali, where about 190 countries from across the globe entered into a roadmap to take action to reduce greenhouse emissions in the atmosphere forcing climate change. In this UN conference on climate change India achieved a tough deal. It forcefully argued and defended against imposition of binding targets on developing countries and made the rich, industrialised nations to provide fund and support transfer of clean technology to poor and developing countries. Timely initiative by India at the fort-night long meet ensured that the developed countries cannot simply put the onus on the poor nations. Accordingly a decision was taken at the extended session where leaders have decided to adhere to new set of principles, that will, over the next two years, help the countries decide a post 2012 deal. By next two years, the deal will be drawn making it clear what is expected from each country. Under the United Nations Treaty called the UN framework on climate change, there is an existing deal called the Kyoto Protocol. It demands that the 36 big emitters, mostly industrialised nations, reduce their emissions by a fixed percentage by 2012. Bali conference was to discuss what happens after 2012. The Kyoto protocol expires in 2012. At present only the rich nations, responsible for more than 70 percent of emissions, are expected to cut carbon emissions. But they demanded that after 2012, even the developing countries also start some kind of emission cuts. This means a complete u- turn of the existing treaty. India and other similarly placed countries contend that such a step will pose a hurdle for economic growth. India argued that the rich countries who are the worst polluters should take responsibility. This argument has been taken care of and a roadmap for the future course of action finalised. An Indian delegate at the end of the conference said, "fourteen days of negotiations, running deep into mid-night on several occasions, finally brought us to the showdown. So, the rich nations should support a fund and clean technologies to make the not so rich to cut emissions. This will help these countries not to sacrifice their economic growth which is vital". The Science and Technology Minister Shri Kapil Sibal said, "it was a hard fought win, but we have secured India's position in the two year negotiations that delegates have agreed at Bali and which will be completed by 2009". Explaining the 90 minute high drama on the last day of the meeting, an Indian official said that a critical resolution demanding that the rich work on transferring clean technologies and fund such mechanisms for the sake of developing world was left out at the discussions and instead an American resolution demanding commitments from the developing world got floated. At this point India intervened to put forth its position and the European Union supported it besides the developing nations. Finally it was agreed that such countries would undertake climate change mitigation along with rich nations passing on technologies and funding that would help them to pursue economic growth and also cut emissions. Environmentalist who heads the Nobel Prize winning inter governmental panel on climate change, Mr.R.K.Pachauri said, "the future is going to be a low-carbon society and those who accept the fact are going to be the winners and those who don't will be left behind. The Indian industry will be the vanguard of this change. There is a need to bring about a technology revolution in India in the sectors like transport, power and building. India needs to make judicious use of water, electricity and build more rural infrastructure".

5132. (18-12-2007) NEW DELHI : A meeting was taken by Secretary (A&C) on 18th December, 2007 to review wheat crop prospects in the ongoing Rabi season. Principal Secretaries (Agriculture)/ Directors of Agriculture of 8 major wheat growing States- Uttar Pradesh, Madhya Pradesh, Punjab, Haryana, Bihar,

Rajasthan, Gujarat and Maharashtra participated. On the basis of the presentation made by the States, it was revealed that the wheat crop prospects looked satisfactory in terms of area coverage and the likely production. As compared to the normal wheat area of about 26 million ha, the coverage during 2007-08 is expected to touch 27.5 million ha. This would be marginally less (about 0.5 million) than the all time record of 2006-07 of 28.04 million ha. Crop area is lost due to moisture stress and initial higher temperature in Madhya Pradesh (Gwalior, Rewa and Sagar Divisions), Uttar Pradesh (Bundelkhand region) and rainfed areas of Rajasthan. The States of Punjab, Haryana, Gujarat and Bihar have reported to cover together about 2 lakh ha more area under wheat during 2007-08 as compared to 2006-07. The farmers especially of Punjab and Haryana have responded favourably to increased Minimum Support Price of Wheat with higher coverage under the crop. State Governments were of the opinion that the prevailing favourable climatic conditions and the interventions of National Food Security Mission especially inducing substantial higher consumption of quality seeds and nutrients would result in higher productivity and production. They were confident that if the current weather conditions continue favourably as required by the wheat crop, there would be no problem in achieving the production target of 75.5 million tones fixed by the Government of India.

5133. (18-12-2007) NEW DELHI : The Minister of Tourism and Culture has said that with the ongoing tourism boom in the country, sufficient trained manpower is required to meet the growing demands in hotel and travel related agencies. Interacting with a group of students of Tourism and Hospitality Management from Acharya Nagarjuna University, Andhra Pradesh here today she said the sector has immense potential to provide employment as more than two lakhs trained people will be required in the next three years by 2010. She said tourism has become a high profile sector with 400 million domestic tourists and about 5 million foreign tourists in the country. Calling upon the students to utilize the potential of employment generation in the tourism sector, Smt. Soni said they should not look for the Govt. jobs only but also create opportunities for themselves to become entrepreneurs. She said there are many schemes to provide financial subsidies and incentives in the tourism sector and if someone is talented there is no dearth of opportunities for them in the tourism sector. Lauding the Andhra Pradesh Govt. for creating world class infrastructure in the state, the Minister said such initiatives will bring more business to the state and youth can really look forward for employment opportunities in the changed scenario of development.

5134. (18-12-2007) NEW DELHI : The Indian Pharmacopoeia (IP) 2007 was released by the Union Minister for Health & Family Welfare, Dr. Anbumani Ramadoss today. Besides the Minister of State for Health & Family Welfare, Smt. Panabaka Lakshmi and Dr. Nitya Anand, Chairman, Scientific Body, Indian Pharmacopoeia Commission (IPC), the other members of the IPC were also present at the occasion. Speaking on the occasion, the Minister said that the Indian Pharmacopoeia is published in fulfilment of the requirements in accordance with the Drugs and Cosmetic Rules, 1945 for the standards of drugs manufactured and marketed in India. The standards given in this pharmacopoeia are authoritative, legally enforceable and intended to help in the inspection and licensing of manufacturing and distribution of drugs and pharmaceuticals. The Minister said that the recently formed Indian Pharmacopoeia Commission (IPC) under the Ministry of Health and Welfare, Government of India, has been able to complete the cumbersome task of Indian Pharmacopoeia 2007 with the untiring efforts of the expert members of the Scientific Body, CIPL staff and various other professionals and organizations. After independence, the Indian Pharmacopoeia 2007 is the 5th edition subsequent to Indian Pharmacopoeia 1996 and its Addenda 2000, 2002, 2005 and the Veterinary Products Supplement in 2002. As there had been rapid changes in the standards of drug and pharmaceuticals all over the world and to keep pace with the regulatory requirements, and in the wake of formation of Indian Pharmacopoeia Commission it was desired by one and all stakeholders to bring the new edition of the Indian Pharmacopoeia at the earliest. The Scientific Body of the IPC under the Chairmanship of Dr. Nitya Anand has done this job marvellously. He further said that the pharmacopoeial standards included in IP 2007 have been encouraged to adhere to the concept of harmonization with those used internationally as well as the technological status for manufacture and analysis of drugs and pharmaceuticals in different section of the industry without compromising with the quality of products. The publication has been considerably revised and improved by introducing advanced technology and experimental methods widely adopted in India and abroad. Appreciating the efforts made by the members of the IPC in bringing out the publication well in time, the Minister said IP 2007 drug standards will come into effect from 1st April 2007.

5135. (18-12-2007) NEW DELHI : Speaking at the inauguration of the buildings of Homoeopathic Pharmacopoeia Laboratory (HPL) and Pharmacopoeial Laboratory for Indian Medicine (PLIM) and PLIM's workshop on WHO Guidelines for GMP of Ayurveda, Siddha and Unani (ASU) Drugs and laying of Foundation Stone of PLIM Guest House at PLIM Campus today, the Union Minister for Health & Family Welfare, Dr. Anbumani Ramadoss said that the huge potential of our traditional systems is proven and hence there is no question why we cannot produce world class natural medicines. The Minister of State for Health & Family Welfare, Smt. Panabaka Lakshmi, Secretary (AYUSH), Smt. Anita Das, Dr. Salim Habayab, WHO Representative to India, Dr. D.R. Lohar, Director, PLIM and other officials from the Ministry and PLIM were present at the function.

5136. (18-12-2007) NEW DELHI : Shri Sontosh Mohan Dev, Minister for Heavy Industries & Public Enterprises released a book titled "Empowering Public Sector Enterprises in India" here today. The book has been brought out by the Department of Public Enterprises, and is the outcome of the proceedings of Chief Executives'

Conference on Public Sector Enterprises held on 8th March, 2007 in New Delhi. The book contains the inaugural address of the Hon'ble Prime Minister and dwells on various critical issues before the public sector enterprises, such as, competition, diversification, autonomy and corporate governance. Among other things, the book discusses the challenges before the CPSEs during the 11th Plan period. The book also contains the "Report of the Adhoc Group of Experts on Empowerment of Central Public Sector Enterprises" and addresses specific areas of issues of ownership by the Government, audit of Government companies, Constitutional issues etc. Releasing the book, the Minister said that full managerial and commercial autonomy to profit making PSEs had been achieved to a large extent. Major PSEs, particularly the Navratnas are global players. Shri Dev however observed, although some PSEs transformed themselves into sound commercial enterprises capable of competing with the best in the world, getting listed on the stock exchanges and enhancing professionalism of the Board of Directors would have to be their primary tasks. Dr. R.C. Panda, Secretary, Ministry Heavy Industries & Public Enterprises also spoke on this occasion.

5137. (18-12-2007) NEW DELHI : The Railways have generated Rs. 29416.42 crore of revenue earnings from freight traffic during the first eight months (*i.e.* April-November 2007) of the current financial year 2007-08 as compared to Rs. 26502.79 crore during the corresponding period last year, registering an increase of 10.99 per cent. Railways carried 501.38 million tonnes of freight traffic during April-November 2007 as compared to 464.39 million tonnes carried during the corresponding period last year, reflecting an increase of 7.97 per cent. The Net Tonne Kilo Metres (NTKM) went up from 304871 million during the months of April-November 2006 to 321460 million during April-November 2007, with an increase of 5.44 per cent. The earnings from freight traffic during the month of November 2007 was Rs. 3992.83 crore, compared to Rs. 3607.85 crore during the corresponding period last year showing an increase of 10.67 per cent. Railways carried 65.67 million tonnes of freight traffic during the month of November 2007 as compared to 61.06 million tonnes of freight traffic during the corresponding period last year, registering an increase of 7.55 per cent. The Net Tonne Kilo Metres (NTKM) went up from 39670 million during the month of November 2006 to 42093 million during November 2007, showing an increase of 6.11 per cent. Of the total earnings during the month of November 2007, Rs. 1515.15 crore came from transportation of 28.35 million tonnes of coal, followed by Rs. 629.86 crore from 11.78 million tonnes of iron ore, Rs. 331.27 crore from 6.49 million tonnes of cement, Rs. 245.05 crore from 2.89 million tonnes of petroleum oil and lubricant (POL), Rs. 244.58 crore from 2.51 million tonnes of foodgrains, Rs. 241.67 crore from 2.16 million tonnes of iron & finished steel, Rs. 231.11 crore from 3.40 million tonnes of fertilizers, Rs. 69.37 crore from 0.91 million tonnes of raw material for steel plants except iron ore and Rs. 484.77 crore from 7.18 million tonnes of other goods.

5138. (18-12-2007) NEW DELHI : Minister of State for Food Processing Industries, Shri Subodh Kant Sahai said that during the 11th Plan the ministry would launch a revamped comprehensive scheme for creating integrated cold chain infrastructure at different levels - farm level primary processing centres-cum-cold chain, collection/aggregation centres and strategic distribution center. Shri Sahai was addressing two days conference on winning intelligent supply chains organized by Indian Chambers of Commerce and Industry (FICCI). Shri Sahai further said that government will extend a grant of 10 crore for cold chain integration in the country along with subsidies to encourage private players to invest in the cold chain infrastructure. He said organized retail backed by efficient supply chain has the potential of raising the rate of growth of the food processing sector from 13 per cent to 20 per cent in the next three to five years. The Minister said the foreign investment norms in the retain sector could be eased if a study commissioned by it found that a large organized industry would not hurt stand alone small retailers. Addressing on the occasion the minister said that India would open up its 330 billion retain market after being convinced that the Kirana Stores would not be effected by the players. Shri Sahai further said that government also planned to establish 30 mega food parks across the country. These parks would seek to provide a mechanism to bring together farmers, processors and retailers, thus linking agriculture production to the market.

5139. (18-12-2007) NEW DELHI : The year 2007 witnessed several initiatives by the Ministry of Housing & Urban Poverty Alleviation such as unveiling of new National Urban Housing & Habitat Policy, restructuring the Scheme of Swarna Jayanti Shahari Rozgar Yojana (SJSRY), Skills Training for Employment and Promotion amongst the Urban Poor (STEPUP), Interest Subsidy Scheme of Housing for the Urban Poor, Integrated Low Cost Sanitation Scheme and Urban Statistics for HR and Assessments (USHA). The Ministry has also progressed well in the implementation of Jawaharlal Nehru National Urban Renewal Mission (JNNRUM). Kumari Selja, Minister of State (Independent Charge) for Housing & Urban Poverty Alleviation has said while giving a overview of the performance of the Ministry that considering the urban poverty issues becoming critical, the Ministry enhanced its budget for urban poverty alleviation by 40% during 2006-07. A major restructuring to the existing Swarna Jayanti Shahari Rozgar Yojana (SJSRY) has been worked out and will soon be in place. The focus is on the self-employment and development of micro-enterprise by the poor with focus on women, SCs/STs and minorities. The globalising urban economies are increasingly being faced with acute shortage of skills accordingly the Ministry has developed a scheme called Skills Training for Employment and Promotion amongst the Urban Poor (STEPUP). The scheme will form part of National Skill Development Mission, she added. Keeping in view the changing trends of urbanisation, Government has approved National Urban Housing & Habitat Policy, 2007 to replace the existing National Housing and Habitat Policy, 1998. With the goal of "Affordable Housing for All", the policy seeks to initiate various measures like public-private participation in land assembly, foreign direct investment, timely formulation and review of Master Plans and Zonal Plans, fiscal incentives for housing sector, strengthening modern technological advances to ensure low cost housing, simplification of various statues, increase in cooperation among Central Government, State Government and Urban Local Bodies, etc. It is expected that the new Policy will give rise to fresh initiatives to tackle the urban housing shortage. The Jawaharlal Nehru National Urban Renewal Mission (JNNRUM) was launched in December 2005 to cope with the problem of shortage in housing and infrastructure services in a mission mode for 63 select cities under Basic Services to Urban Poor (BSUP). For remaining cities, a scheme namely Integrated Housing and Slum Development Programme (IHSDP) has also been implemented under JNNRUM. So far, under the BSUP, the projects from 51 Mission Cities of 26 States have been approved with a total project cost of Rs 12900.45 Crore with a Central share of Rs. 6445.90 Crore covering 6,27,040 dwelling units and other basic civic amenities to the urban poor. Under the IHSDP, the projects from 18 states have been approved with a total project cost of Rs. 2102.64 Crore with a Central share of Rs. 2102.64 Crore covering 2,06,235 dwelling units and other basic civic amenities. The Ministry of Housing and Poverty Alleviation is also introducing a new scheme for providing interest subsidy on housing on EWS/LIG. The scheme encourages poor sections to avail of loan facilities through Commercial Banks/ HUDCO for the purposes of construction of houses and avail subsidy in interest payment. During the year 2007-08, Rs. 30 Crore has been allocated in the budget of the Ministry for the purpose.

5140. (18-12-2007) NEW DELHI : Shri Kamal Nath, Union Minister of Commerce and Industry, has called on the entrepreneurs in the sports goods export industry to focus on brand building, as this is an area which is an important ingredient in the value of the product. Shri Kamal Nath urged the industry to achieve maximum mileage from the Commonwealth Games in 2010 and work hard for cultivating global standards. He was speaking at the Export Awards function organised by the Sports Goods Export Promotion Council (SGEPC), here today. Shri Anil Mukhim, Chairman, SGEPC and senior officials from the Ministry and the Council were present on the occasion. While congratulating the award winners, the Minister hoped that the industry would conduct a SWOT analysis on the potential of this sector and draw a roadmap to evolve growth strategies for the future. "The major strengths of our industry are its people - the dynamic entrepreneurs and the skilled labour force at relatively cheaper costs. The skilled force was born out of India's age-old nurtured and mastered skills in the areas of metal processing, leather crafts, wood crafts and a host of other activities directly connected with the growth of this sector", he said. Observing that the global competitive environment has undergone a sea change and today business happens at the speed of thought, Shri Kamal Nath stated that the highway of this sector has been full of milestone but perhaps the future holds promises to be more exciting than the past. "The government on its part intends to ensure full support for the facilitation of further growth and development of this sector. The infrastructure development is likely to get more focus and this coupled with incentives and promotional schemes will provide the impetus to the exporting community to finally arrive on the world stage", the Minister further stated.

5141. (18-12-2007) NEW DELHI : Hanoi has welcomed the outcome of the talks between the Defence Ministers of India and Vietnam held here yesterday. The Vietnamese Prime Minister Mr. Nguyen Tan Dung complimented the Defence Minister Shri AK Antony, when the latter called on him last evening, for announcing a series of measures to consolidate and expand defence cooperation between the two countries to take it to newer heights. Mr. Dung said the strategic partnership between India and Vietnam 'will further speed up peace, stability and prosperous development in the region and the world'. Describing his ongoing visit as a continuation of the dialogue that Mr. Dung had with the Prime Minister Dr. Man Mohan Singh in New Delhi last July, Shri Antony said the two countries are in the process of setting up a Joint Working Group for drawing up a comprehensive MoU on Defence Cooperation.

5142. (18-12-2007) NEW DELHI : The Defence Minister Shri AK Antony laid a wreath at the Ho Chi Minh Mausoleum at Ba Dinh Square before winding up his two day stay in the Vietnamese capital Hanoi this morning. The embalmed body of Ho Chi Minh lies in state at this historic location where he had declared independence from French rule on 2 Sep 1945. After his death in 1969, the site was chosen for his mausoleum. Shri Antony spent about an hour at the Presidential Palace complex adjacent to the mausoleum. The majestic Presidential Palace was built by the French in the beginning of the twentieth century. However, when the iconic leader Ho Chi Minh became the President in 1954, he considered it to be too opulent to live in it. Instead, he decided to reside in an austere cottage in the same complex for the rest of his life. The Presidential Palace was used only for special official functions especially when he had to receive world leaders and statesmen, a tradition which is being followed even now. It was here that Ho Chi Minh had received Jawaharlal Nehru when the latter visited Hanoi in 1954. Shri Antony was 'deeply touched' by the simple living of Ho Chi Minh as he arote in the visitors' book ' I pay my respect to the leader whose life and times inspires generations of people across the world'. Shri Antony has since reached Ho Chi Minh city on the second leg of his visit to Vietnam.

5143. (18-12-2007) NEW DELHI : Direct tax collections continued to record a growth of over 40 percent for the period 1st April to 15th December 2007. According to provisional data, net tax collections stood at Rs.1,64,407 crore, up from Rs.1,15,377 crore during the same period last fiscal, registering a growth of 42.50 percent and achieving over 61 percent of budgeted direct tax target of Rs.2,67,490 crore. Corporate Tax registered a growth of 42.37 percent at Rs.98,391 crore, up from Rs.69110 crore during the previous fiscal, while Personal Income

Tax (including FBT, STT and BCTT) grew by 42.83 percent at Rs.65,774 crore, up from Rs.46,051 crore. Growth in Securities Transaction Tax (STT) was 74.36 percent (Rs.5,895 crore against Rs.3,381 crore) and Fringe Benefit Tax (FBT) was 16.10 percent (Rs.3,313 crore against Rs.2,854 crore). Banking Cash Transaction Tax (BCTT) grew by 17.04 percent (Rs.376 crore against Rs.322 crore). Overall direct tax growth was highest in the Mumbai region at 68.43 percent; followed by Pune region at 58.68 percent, North Western region (Chandigarh) at 47.98 percent, Andhra Pradesh (Hyderabad) at 43.82 percent and eastern Uttar Pradesh (Lucknow) at 39.79 percent. Corporate tax growth was highest in the North-Eastern region (Guwahati) at 244.18 percent;, followed by Kerala (Kochi) at 83.32 percent, Mumbai at 80.92 percent, eastern Uttar Pradesh (Lucknow) at 71.22 percent and Pune region at 56.24 percent. Personal income tax growth was highest in Madhya Pradesh & Chhattisgarh region (Bhopal) at 160.95 percent; followed by Nagpur region at 97.10 percent, Pune region at 60.39 percent, Andhra Pradesh region (Hyderabad) at 54.79 percent and Tamil Nadu region (Chennai) at 50.90 percent.

5144. (18-12-2007) NEW DELHI : Smt. D. Purandeswari, Minister of State, Human Resource Development has said that the phenomenon of privatization has led to the emergence of market economy. In the field of education too, there have emerged various compulsions in the public provision of education, which have given rise to the growth of private educational institutions in the last two decades. It is however imperative that a regulatory framework is put in place so that there is no commercialization of education and also there is effective prevention of racketeering and exploitation in this regard. She Was speaking in the valedintory founction of the Conference as chief guest here today. 'Subject to this, we should have no inhibition to allow private players to function in the country with a reasonable degree of autonomy and freedom for providing quality education. We need to draw up proper regulatory guidelines for the private sector, to ensure the quality of higher education. It is, therefore important that we develop effective regulatory framework for the private universities, particularly in terms of their admission, fees, teaching-learning process and governance. We must ensure that in the name of regulating the private institutions, we desist from making any attempt for controlling them. All we should do is to remove the bureaucratic shackles which lead to the undermining to the initiative and independence of private players', she added. Shri R.P. Agrawal, Secretary, Higher Education said that we should allow foreign Educational Institutions in India for collaboration as per AICTE guidelines but, these Institutions or Institutes cannot give degree in India as only UGC has authorized the Institutes or Institutions empowered by Parliament or by state legislatures to do so. Secondly, these foreign institutions should have some standing and they should not be 'fly by night' operators. Thirdly, if an Indian educational institute is twinning with some foreign educational institute, then, in case of some visa problem for students of the Indian Institute, then, the Indian institute should have some back up in the form of collaboration etc. with other Indian reputed institution or with other Indian University etc. Prof. Sukhadeo Thorat, Chairman UGC was the guest of honour in the valedictory function he said that in order to meet the requirements of industry and economy for the 11th Plan, the minimum target should be increasing the general enrolment ratio from 10 to 15 in the higher education. He also stressed the focus should be on expansion, quality & excellence, equity and relevance. He also added that better teachers, more Phds/M.Phil programmes are needed alongwith the application of best practices in governance in the institutions in India and abroad. Prof. R.A. Yadav, acting Chairman, AICTE welcomed the guest in the Valedictory Function and Prof. K. Narayana Rao, Member Secretary, AICTE proposed the vote of thanks. In this Valedictory function Vice Chancellors of Technical Universities/Deemed Universities, Directors of premier technical education institutes (including IITs, NITs, IIMs, IIITs and NITTTRs), eminent persons from academia and industry and Secretaries and Directors of Technical Education and other dignitaries were present.

5145. (19-12-2007) NEW DELHI : The Central Government has introduced an optional compounded levy scheme in respect of Pan Masala and Pan Masala containing tobacco, popularly known as Gutkha. This scheme has been introduced under Rule 15 of the Central Excise Rules, 2002. This scheme provides for payment of duty on the basis of number of packing machines installed in the factory premises of a manufacturer of these goods. The notification no. 38/2007 C.E dated 19.12.2007 has provided for an option for payment of Rs. twelve lakh as duty per month per packing machine per line for Gutkha pouches of RSP upto Rs. 1.50. Similarly, the duty per machine per line per month for Pan Masala pouches carrying RSP upto Rs. 1.50 has been fixed at Rs. ten lakh. Different duty slabs have been provided for pouches priced upto Rs. 6. In case of multiple track/ line packing machine, the rate of duty would be multiplied accordingly. A manufacturer opting for this scheme has to file an application giving details of the packing machine installed in the factory to the jurisdictional Assistant/Deputy Commissioner of Central Excise. Once this option is exercised by a manufacturer, it will remain effective for the entire financial year. Any addition or removal of packing machines can be made only under the physical supervision of the officer authorised for this purpose. In case a manufacturer opts for this scheme, there will normally be no inspection or search of his premises in a routine manner. Detailed instructions have also been issued to the field formations highlighting the salient features of this scheme. Taking note of the rampant evasion prevalent in this sector, the Chairman, Central Board of Excise and Customs had recently issued instructions to the field formations for verification of the packing machines present in the factory, the number of such machines working, and for sealing of non-working machines. This scheme is the part of the strategy of the indirect tax administration to encourage voluntary tax compliance, at the same time provides a sharp and uncompromising response to non-compliance.

5146. (19-12-2007) NEW DELHI : The President of India, Smt. Pratibha Devisingh Patil marked her birthday today by spending time with the destitute and mentally challenged persons in Delhi. Smt. Patil visited the Nirmal Hriday Home for the Dying Destitutes and met the persons staying there. The President spoke to a number of destitute persons and enquired about their well-being as well as spoke to the Sisters working there about their experiences and praised them for their selfless work. She also distributed blankets, sweaters and sweets to the persons at the Nirmal Hriday. The President said while leaving the Home that she has never celebrated her birthday but has instead worked and marked the day by spending time with those in need of care. She said that even as the Governor of Rajasthan she had spent this day with the destitute, the poor, the mentally challenged and those suffering from leprosy. The President later went to the Asha Kiran Home for the Mentally Challenged. There, she presented two TV sets and individually gave away sweets to the mentally challenged persons. Speaking on the occasion, the President said helping the poor and the needy are a way of service to God. Birthdays are occasions when an individual can reflect on what he can do for society. The President added that on such days kindness should flow from the heart of the person to help others. She commended the work of the staff of Asha Kiran. The Chief Minister of Delhi, Smt. Sheila Dixit and the Delhi Health Minister, Shri Yoganand Shastri were also present. Earlier in the day, the Prime Minister, Dr. Manmohan Singh and Smt. Gursharan Kaur, the Vice-President, Shri Mohammad Hamid Ansari and his wife, the Governor of Madhya Pradesh, Dr. Balram Jakhar, the Lt. Governor of Delhi, Shri Tejender Khanna and other dignitaries greeted the President. Smt. Patil also planted a sapling of Jamoon in the Nakshatra Garden in the Rashtrapati Bhavan premises.

5147. (19-12-2007) NEW DELHI : Shri Jairam Ramesh, Minister of State for Commerce, while speaking at the Foundation Day Lecture function at the National institute of Rural Development (NIRD) on theme of "Regional Growth in India: Disparities or Despairities" stated that transfers of resources from the Centre to States is an important component of the strategy to reduce inter-state disparities. The Minister stated that infrastructure holds the key for improving the economic prospects of the laggard States and added that, "Like inclusive growth, PPP has also become a mantra of sorts, seen as a panacea for our infrastructure needs. To my mind, PPP means private funds for public projects and not public funds for private projects as many private sector companies seem to think. There may well be niches where private resources can be mobilised but I can see no alternative to the public provision of infrastructure in the poorer and backward States. To expect that PPP will have any takers in the Northeast, for instance, is the height of folly. There is simply no other option but for the central government to take on the primary responsibility for building this infrastructure. But we need new models for government involvement. The public sector can take on the role of a venture capitalist, establish the infrastructure, trigger the economic activity and then exit. Government agencies will also need to be given the flexibility to enter into alliances with private companies for construction and management".

5148. (19-12-2007) NEW DELHI : In accordance with the Memorandum of Understanding on exchange and cooperation in the field of defence, signed between India and China in 2006, the first Sino Indian Joint Training Exercise "Hand in Hand 2007" will commence in Kunming, tomorrow. Based on the theme of counter terrorism, the exercise will be conducted from 20th to 25th Dec 07. One Armed Reconnaissance company of the PLA and an equivalent strength of Indian Troops will participate in the exercise which will include establishment of a joint command post, joint battle decision making and conduct of anti terrorism drills. The joint training exercise between the armies of the two countries is reflective of the growing relations between India and China in the field of defence. Earlier this year two ships of the Indian Navy made a port call at Qingdao and participated in a joint exercise with the PLA Navy. The countries also held their first ever Annual Defence Dialogue in China in Nov this year. The Indian contingent which arrived in Kunming China this afternoon (19 Dec 07) is being led by Brig DS Dadwal. Before departure of the contingent from Guwahati this morning, the contingent commander stated "this is an historic occasion and a very significant one. This is for the first time that troops of the Indian Army will be participating in a joint exercise with troops of the Peoples Liberation Army of China". A ceremonial welcome was accorded to the Indian Contingent on its arrival at Kunming Airport. The contingent was received by Senior Colonel Tian, Senior Colonel Zhang, Senior Colonel Wu Hiao Yi and more than 40 officers of PLA with a ceremonial band in attendance. A strong contingent of Chinese Media was also present on the occasion.

5149. (19-12-2007) NEW DELHI : The representatives of the Association of Part Time Correspondents (PTCs) of All India Radio/Doordarshan (Prasar Bharati) called on the Minister of Information & Broadcasting and Parliamentary Affairs, Shri P. R. Dasmunsi here today. The PTCs in their meeting requested the Minister to look into a number of issues that required his urgent attention including upgrading the efficiency and pay packets of the PTCs. The Minister has assured the representatives of PTCs that he would look into the matter and ensured that there would be a rise in their pay packets. He also assured them their concerns would be discussed at the meeting of Group of Ministers, which is likely to take place on the 3rd January, 2008.

5150. (19-12-2007) NEW DELHI : The Congress and Communist parties have both mastered the art of propagating deceit, lies and total lies. It is indeed ironical that both parties are constantly falsely accusing the BJP for crimes, which are actually clearly identified with their own parties. This can perfectly be described as "Ulta Chor, Kotwal Ko Datey". The recent statements of Congress President Smt. Sonia Gandhi and CPM leader Sh. Sitaram Yechury clearly confirm our charge. The BJP condemns both leaders for levelling baseless charges against the party. In a reported reply to the Election Commission on a notice for violation of Code of Conduct, Smt. Gandhi has once again accused the BJP and Sh. Narendra Modi as "Merchants of Fear and Death". The fifth flip-flop on, for whom this term was used, connotes utter confusion in the Congress camp. First, the Congress said that she did not utter this phrase at all. Then Congress explained that it was meant for police and not for Mr. Modi. Then they came up with yet another explanation that it was meant for Mr. Modi only. Later they clarified that it was for the system and not for Mr. Modi. Now, they have finally replied that it was meant for both the system as well as Mr. Modi! The party, which is responsible for the worst communal carnage of Sikhs in 1984, the brutal killings and forced sterilisation during the 1975 emergency period, thousands of deaths of minorities in Bhagalpur riots, tacit understanding with Maoists in various states for electoral gains, and hundreds of fake encounters in Punjab certainly has no moral right to talk about and accuse others of human right violations. A CBI report that the CPM cadres are harassing and beating up witnesses of Nandigram violence, is yet another testimony of the total state complicity in suppressing the truth that needs to be unearthed. The BJP demands that the CBI enquiry requires full protection to be provided to the victims of Nandigram. This needs to be done by removing the local police from the area and put the area under the complete control of central forces till the enquiry is over. Unless such a step is initiated, the truth will never surface. The graves of victims, which have been unearthed is in itself a reason enough for such a tough action. Despite such a terrible track record, the CPM leader Sh. Sitaram Yechury has the audacity to falsely accuse the BJP for hobnobbing with and protecting Maoists! It must be remembered that it is the CPM, which brokered peace between the Maoists and Government in Nepal. The CPM also stands completely exposed when they surrendered to the Muslim fundamentalists in the case of Taslima similar to the Congress submission before these forces in Shahbano case.

5151. (19-12-2007) NEW DELHI : In the Birth Centenary year of Shahid-e-Azam Bhagat Singh, Publications Division has brought out a set of two books Bhagat Singh: The Eternal Rebel in English and Bhagat Singh: Dastavejon Ke Aaine Mein in Hindi. These books were released by Hon'ble Minister for Information & Broadcasting and Parliamentary Affairs, Shri P. R. Dasmunsi here today. In his address he reminded that along with Bhagat Singh there were many other freedom fighters who laid down their lives for the nation. He said that the Government is planning several events in the coming year to pay tributes to them. Author of Bhagat Singh: The Eternal Rebel Shri Malvinder Jit Singh Waraich is a well known writer. His book is an intimate account of an enthusiastic chronicler of the revolutionary movement in India, which traces Bhagat Singh's family background and the nationalistic and revolutionary atmosphere of that time that led him to pursue his fight against the British rule and also against all forms of exploitation. Bhagat Singh: Dastavejon Ke Aaine Mein is written by Shri Chaman

Lal who is a scholar with special aptitude for freedom movement of the country. The book divided in four parts contains rare government documents related to Bhagat Singh, his letters, articles and photographs. Talking about the book he said that the day was also being observed as the 80th martyrdom anniversary of four brave sons of the motherland - Pandit Ram Prasad Bismil, Ashfaq Ullah Khan, Thakur Roshan Singh and Rajendra Lahiri, who played heroic roles in India's struggle of freedom and smilingly embraced the gallows. Their names will ever keep on inspiring the nation. Former Member of Parliament and renowned journalist, Shri Kuldeep Nayar was the Guest of Honour in the function. He recalled an incident when Bhagat Singh had said that the struggle does not end with independence and it would go on till there is no slavery and poverty in the world. He called for change for the people at grass root level. Addl. DG, Publications Division, Smt. Veena Jain in her welcome address paid rich tributes to Bhagat Singh..

5152. (19-12-2007) NEW DELHI : A meeting with the Chief Ministers to discuss the internal security situation will be held here tomorrow under the chairmanship of the Prime Minister, Dr. Manmohan Singh. Apart from the situation in Jammu & Kashmir and North Eastern States, Naxalite violence and terrorism in the hinterland will be the main focus of the meeting. Among the measures to effectively deal with the threats to internal security, augmentation and modernization of state police forces, training of police personnel, strengthening of the intelligence apparatus, investigation of terrorism-related cases, security in mega cities, border management, bilateral and international cooperation, etc., will figure in the day-long meeting. The meeting will be attended, among others, by the Union Home Minister, Shri Shivraj Patil. The last meeting with Chief Ministers on internal security issues was held on 5th September last year.

5153. (19-12-2007) NEW DELHI : Following is the text of intervention of Finance Minister Shri P. Chidambaram at the National Development Council meeting held here today: "While the National Development Council has met a few times since the UPA Government assumed office in May 2004, I believe this is the most important meeting. We are gathered here to consider and approve the draft of the Eleventh Five Year Plan for the period 2007-2012 - a period during which we hope we can consolidate the gains made in the last four years and place India, irreversibly, on the path of faster and more inclusive growth. Let me compliment the States on their achievement in fiscal consolidation. 26 States have so far enacted the Fiscal Responsibility Legislation. Consolidated gross fiscal deficit of the States is budgeted to be 2.4 per cent of GDP in 2007-08, which is below the desired level of 3 per cent of GDP. Notwithstanding the variations across the States, the consolidated revenue balances is budgeted to show a surplus of 0.4 per cent of GDP in 2007-08. Achievement of the targets set under the fiscal responsibility legislations has not only consolidated the fiscal health of the States, it has also improved the credibility of their budgetary operations. I would, however, like to caution that the States should not become complacent. They must continue to make efforts to mobilise resources and improve the efficiency of their expenditure. The Gross Budgetary Support (GBS) of the Central Government for the Eleventh Plan is estimated at Rs 14,21,711 crore (at 2006-07 prices). This is an unprecedented increase of 114.8 per cent over the GBS for the Tenth Plan. Nearly one-half of this budgetary support is earmarked for the priority sectors of education, health, rural development, agriculture and irrigation - priorities which, I believe, are shared by State Governments and to which State Governments also ought to make substantial allocations in their State plans. I would like to emphasise that the primary responsibility in these crucial sectors lies with the States. The Centre is ready and willing to help, and we are indeed doing so by increasing Budgetary support to State Plans from Rs.1,75,021 crore to Rs.3,24,851 crore (at 2006-07 prices). With that help, States must forge ahead in delivering education, health and other services in a more efficient and determined manner. A grave challenge that faces us ¯ as well as and many countries of the world ¯ is the availability of food and the rise in food prices. Many observers have pointed out that the era of cheap food prices is over. In the changed context, the relevance of an efficient public distribution system cannot be over emphasised. We need a PDS for the poor, but unless it is efficient, procures adequate quantities of food grains and delivers food to the poor, the PDS could become an albatross around our neck and an opportunity for rent seekers to enrich themselves. The first concern is procurement of adequate quantities of wheat and paddy/rice. Producing States must cooperate with the Central Government and its agencies. Some wheat producing and some rice producing States have contributed meagre or nearly zero quantities to the Central pool; yet they draw from the Central pool for their PDS. How is this fair to the States which bear a disproportionate share of the burden of procurement? How is this fair to the Central Government which is expected to maintain buffer stocks and put adequate quantities into the PDS system? I earnestly appeal to the wheat and paddy producing States to procure and contribute their fair share of food grains to the Central pool. The next concern is the deeply flawed distribution system. The most recent evaluation study on the Targeted Public Distribution System (TPDS) by the Programme Evaluation Organisation has found, inter alia, that taking into account all the inefficiencies of PDS, Government of India spends Rs. 3.65 to transfer Re 1 to the poor. About 58 per cent of subsidised grains do not reach the target group, of which a little over 36 per cent is siphoned off the supply chain. I ask you, respectfully, do not the poor of India deserve a better PDS? How can we sit back and watch helplessly the poor being robbed of their meagre entitlements? I urge Hon'ble Chief Ministers to collectively resolve today to help the Central Government set right both sides of the PDS - procurement and distribution - because a well functioning PDS is critical to maintaining price stability of food articles.

5154. (19-12-2007) NEW DELHI : The long-standing deadlock on the issue of bilateral traffic rights between India and Hong Kong was broken with the two sides arriving at an agreement after prolonged discussions held at New Delhi on 17-18 December, 2007. The Indian delegation was led by Shri R.K. Singh, Joint Secretary in the Ministry of Civil Aviation while the Hong Kong delegation was led by Mr. Esmond Lee, Deputy Secretary, Transport and Housing Bureau, Hong Kong. As per the new agreement, 27 new services for each side will be possible on the Indian Hong Kong route. While the Indian side can operate these 27 services from any point in India, the Hong Kong carriers can operate 10 services to Delhi, 6 services to Mumbai and 11 services altogether to Bangalore, Chennai and Calcutta. Chennai was added as a new point of call during these talks for the Hong Kong side. An agreement was also reached on the exercise of fifth freedom beyond traffic rights. Out of the 27 services, the carriers of India will be able to operate 14 services to West Coast North America including the cities of Los Angeles, San Francisco and Vancouver. Reciprocally, the Hong Kong carrier can exercise beyond fifth freedom rights through India on 14 services to Europe excluding UK. The two sides also entered into a liberalized code share agreement which will enable the airlines of the two sides to code share through their respective territories to any beyond point either with each other carriers or with a third country carrier. Indian carriers are already looking at serving New Zealand through code share over Hong Kong with Air New Zealand. With this agreement, there will be greater competition on the India Hong Kong route and the direct services between India and Hong Kong are set to increase. This will be in the overall interest of the travelling people and growth of trade and tourism.

5155. (19-12-2007) NEW DELHI : The Prime Minister, Dr. Manmohan Singh, chaired the 54th National Development Council meeting here today. Speaking on the occasion, the Prime Minister said that it is possible that with the correct set of policies and dedicated effort by both the Central and State governments, we will not only be able to maintain the momentum of high growth into the near future but may be able to raise it to 10% per annum. Dr. Singh said that we need to redouble our efforts to maintain the domestic drivers of growth and ensure that policy facilitates even faster growth. The Prime Minister reiterated that bridging the rural-urban divide is absolutely essential if we have to mitigate impoverishment. Drawing attention to the Equity Concerns, Dr. Manmohan Singh stated that the XI Plan focuses on the revival of agriculture, rural development and on a strong effort in promoting programmes that deliver essential services to the common man and also provide livelihood support. The Prime Minister emphasized that the outlays on agriculture, health and rural development have also tripled and taken together with education, these sectors account for more than half of the Central GBS as compared to less than 1/3rd in the X Plan. This structural shift was the hallmark of the XI plan, he added. The emphasis must be on ensuring that these programmes deliver what they promise. "We must work purposefully to realise the socio-economic transformation the Plan seeks to achieve", the Prime Minister said.

5156. (19-12-2007) NEW DELHI : Dr. Shakeel Ahmed said that I would like to draw your attention to Nagaland where the chief minister lost the vote of confidence on the 13th by 31-23 votes and despite the Congress Party's and opposition parties' demand and the ultimatum given, the Nagaland chief minister and the government should immediately step down fell on deaf years. The Congress Party demands that the chief minister and the government be dismissed immediately. To a question that in any case elections in Nagaland are to be held after two months, Dr. Ahmed said, that whenever elections will be held the present situation demands that the present government has no right to continue in office. They have clearly lost on the floor of the House and that too with a margin of at least 8 votes and to continue in office proves that they are politically characterless and it is the duty of their allies also not to support such a chief minister who has lost the no-confidence motion and hence the Congress Party's demand for the immediate dismissal of the government. To a question that this report is no doubt controversial and that according to the Speaker the chief minister has won the no-confidence motion, could you give the figure, Dr. Ahmed said, 31 voted against while only 23 were in the chief minister's favour and on this basis we are appealing to the Centre to dismiss the government of Nagaland immediately. To a question that you have refused to move the court in this regard against the order of the Speaker who said that they have won the vote of confidence and moving the court would mean that the legal process is on, Dr. Ahmed said, observers were there and the Central government should act immediately on the report of the Governor and if things still do not move in the proper direction then options are always open. To a question as to what is the Congress Party's stand on the issue of Gujars' demand on being given SC status and being a sensitive issue what would the Centre's stand be, Dr. Ahmed said, it no doubt is a sensitive issue and we are aware of the fact but according to press reports, a committee was set up by the state government and on what basis, it is better that the question be posed to the state government and the chief minister but if the state recommends suggestions to the Centre, the Centre will consider those suggestions. To a question as to what the BJP had to say in its press conference on the Gujar issue, Dr. Ahmed said, what the BJP said or what the chief minister said we are not aware of that but when the report comes to the Centre only then we will be in a position to give a reply.

5157. (19-12-2007) NEW DELHI : Reaching quality health care to every household is a daunting challenge in a country of over a billion people living in thousands of hamlets, villages, towns and cities. The National Rural Health Mission (NRHM) is a serious effort to address this challenge. Launched in April 2005 by the Hon'ble Prime Minister, the Mission has made significant progress, especially after the approval of the detailed Framework for Implementation of NRHM by the Union Cabinet in July 2006. In partnership with States and through state led innovations, NRHM is rapidly expanding accessible, affordable and accountable quality care for every household in the country. More than 5,30,000 ASHAs and Link Workers are connecting households to health facilities. The presence of community volunteers on this unprecedented scale has resulted in people's growing pressure on utilization of services from the public sector health system. States across the country are reporting significantly higher utilization of outpatient services, diagnostic facilities, institutional deliveries and inpatient care. Large scale demand side financing under the Janani Suraksha Yojana (JSY) has brought poor households to public sector health facilities on a scale never witnessed before. Over 50 lakh women have been covered under JSY so far since its introduction in 2005. While in some regions government health facilities have geared up by utilizing flexible finances under NRHM to cope with the increased workload, in many other regions there is a long way to go before health facilities fully gear themselves to meet the growing need of people's health care. Poor households have voted with their feet by coming to the public system as never before. The challenge of NRHM now is to provide quality health care to the growing number of households whose faith in the government system has been restored. NRHM cannot afford to let down poor households who have come to the public system with so much hope and aspiration. There is a sense of urgency in improving the facilities for quality health care.

5158. (19-12-2007) NEW DELHI : On the basis of complaint received regarding death of two children in plastic factories in Gujarat, National Commission for Protection of Child Rights (NCPCR) has asked the Gujarat Government to submit a detailed report about the matter. The Commission for Protection of Child Rights, has received a complaint regarding death of two children : Dinesh Dhirubhai aged of 10 years, on 29.11.2007 while working in a plastic factory, called 'Dhanabhai No Delo' in Kumbharwada Circle (near Naurang Plastic Factory) and also another child of about 16 years who died on 30.11.2007 due to a fatal accident in a plastic factory in the same Kumbharwada Circle in Gujarat. Accordingly, the Commission has written to the Secretary to Government of Gujarat (Department of Labour & Employment) on 11.12.2007 for submitting a detailed report within 21 days on the facts and circumstances of both the cases, including the following issues: (i) Whether reporting to the local police and post mortem have been conducted in both the cases. If so, copy of such reports may also be sent. (ii) Whether the work place, where the accident took place, is a factory within the definition of Factories Act, 1948 and also whether it falls within the purview of State Shops and Establishments Act. If so, whether all statutory safety requirements were prevalent in the said factories at the time of accidents. (iii) Whether the plastic factories in question involve occupation/processes, which are prohibited under the Child Labour (Prohibition and Regulation) Act, 1986. If so, how could the child : Dinesh Dhirubhai who is about 10 years of age, be engaged in such factory despite prohibition. (iv) Whether both the cases have been duly investigating under all applicable labour laws and appropriate penalties and necessary actions have been taken by the Department of Labour, Government of Gujarat. If so, what are the specific violations and the penalties imposed for the same. (v) Whether any compensation/ex-gratia has been paid to the families of the deceased.

5159. (20-12-2007) NEW DELHI : In a significant 120 page order delivered by Shri M.M.K. Sardana, Member on behalf of the Full Bench of the Commission consisting of Mr. Justice O.P. Dwivedi, Chairman, Shri M.M.K. Sardana and Shri D.C. Gupta, Members indicted entire cement industry in the private sector and its association *i.e.* Cement Manufacturers' Association of India, for indulging in cartel arrangements during the period February, 1990 - April, 1990. The public sector cement companies escaped the indictment as the provisions of the MRTP Act were not applicable to the Govt. companies at the relevant point of time *i.e.* 1990. Commission came to a conclusion that the cement industry in the private sector and its industry association except the three companies, who were not in operation during the relevant period, have been indulging in restrictive trade practices and had been acting in concert in fixing the retail prices of their produce drawing the mischief of Section 33 (1) (d) of the MRTP Act. The enquiry was instituted on an application made by the DG (I&R) of the MRTP Commission who had, inter alia, alleged that the respondents were indulging in cartelization by fixing the retail prices of cement in concert. Accordingly, the Commission ordered the respondents not to indulge in any agreement, directly or indirectly, through the instrumentality of CMA or otherwise in fixing the prices of their produce in concert or in follow up of a concert. The respondents were given eight weeks' time to file the affidavit of compliance from the date of pronouncement of the order *i.e.* 20th December, 2007. Monopolies & Restrictive Trade Practices Commission New Delhi.

5160. (20-12-2007) NEW DELHI : The Director General of Civil Aviation (DGCA) has today issued a show cause notice to Jet Airways and Kingfisher Airlines asking them as to why action should not be initiated against them under paragraph 15 of Schedule XI to the Aircraft Rules, 1937, for not furnishing the details of the charged tax components in their domestic airline tickets, as this was in violation of the conditions for operations annexed to the Permit to operate Scheduled Air Transport Services. It may be recalled that the Government had on 4th December 2007 asked all airlines to clarify as to what charged tax components in their tickets were. They had also been asked to provide confirmation whether all the taxes shown by them in their tickets/website had been deposited with the Government. The Airlines had been asked to submit the record of the taxes thus deposited. In a letter dated 4th December 2007 the Director General of Civil Aviation had said that perusal of the fare shown on the airlines website had revealed that the airfares had two components - the basic fare and the taxes. However, it was not clarified as to whether components like Passenger Service Fee and Fuel Surcharge were included in the basic fare or had been clubbed under the heading of "taxes". The letter stated that a "Tax" was defined to be a fee levied by Government on a product, income or activity and such amounts were to be deposited with the Government and a record was required to be maintained for the same. In view of the ambiguity in the airfares, the DGCA had sought a clarification from the airlines. In a letter dated 11 December 2007 a Reminder had been sent by the DGCA to all airlines advising them to furnish their reply latest by 19th December 2007, failing which it would be assumed that the airlines had nothing to say in the matter, and action as deemed fit, would be taken under the Aircraft Rules 1937. Since the airlines had not replied to the DGCA today, a show cause notice was issued to the airlines. The reply of the airlines have to reach the office of the DGCA by 4 January, 2008, failing which action as deemed fit would be taken against them.

5161. (20-12-2007) NEW DELHI : Following is the text of the Prime Minister's closing remarks at the Chief Minister's Conference on Internal Security: "We have come to the end of a long and rewarding discussion. My colleague, the Union Home Minister has summed up the proceedings in a detailed manner. The purposes of Conferences such as this one is two-fold. One purpose is to go into the details of specific problems pertaining to each state, to promote knowledge and information sharing between states so that we can learn from each other and to develop common approaches to tackling shared problems. The other and probably the more important - purpose, is to generate the necessary political consensus among the top leadership of the Centre and the States so that we stand united in our efforts to enforcing the rule of law, fighting terrorism and naxalism and maintaining public order. Conferences of this nature serve to send a strong massage that the political leadership of the country can rise above our political and party affiliations when it comes to facing national challenges, particularly those concerning internal security. We are all duty bound to uphold the values in our Constitution and to provide a safe and secure environment for our citizens. This is an essential obligation and I am reassured after hearing all of you today that we take this obligation in full seriousness. The opinions expressed in this room today have been varied and reflect the local realities in this vast country. I am happy that there is general agreement on the approach to tackling the problem of naxalism. Chief Ministers of states affected by this problem have been unanimous in their resolve to fight this menace. A wide range of alternative strategies have been suggested. All of them are of value and I am confident that the Home Ministry will discuss these ideas further with each of you. I believe that given the unique nature of this problem, it is time to have a dedicated force just to tackle naxalism. Affected states must set up Special Task Forces on the Andhra Pradesh pattern and the Centre will provide assistance for this purpose. I would also urge the Home Ministry to also consider establishing a dedicated trained force at the Centre either as part of an existing force or as a separate one. Such a trained, dedicated force would go a long way in assisting States tackle naxalite groups. Naxalite groups feed on the perceived lack of development. Correcting this requires a lot of effort. It requires motivated government personnel to work in affected areas, improved road and rail connectivity and better delivery of basic services. I will ask the Cabinet Secretary to chair a Task Force to promote coordinated efforts across a range of development and security activities so that we can tackle the naxal problem in a comprehensive manner. Terrorism continues to be a major concern. It is incumbent on all of us to be ever alert to this persistent threat which cannot the easily wished away. Facing this problem will require patience, alertness, constant vigil, coordination between agencies, cooperation of common citizens and most importantly, high level intelligence gathering capabilities. Each state must enhance its ability to counter terror threats and if this involves incurring costs, we will help them. Every possible step must be taken to free our citizens from the shadow of terror. Very often, terrorist acts are designed to promote communal discord. It is important that all of us should be alert to this danger. I draw satisfaction from the fact that the Indian people have not allowed terrorist acts to disturb communal harmony. However, we must remain ever alert and deal firmly with these elements who seek to fan communal tensions and strife. Our strategies for internal security must also make effective provisions to curb and control violence against scheduled castes and weaker sections of society. We have discussed a large number of other security concerns, including those arising out of ethnic tensions and some forms of militancy. There is no single cause for any of these concerns and there is no unique solution. Some areas such as hill states have unique connectivity problems. The North East has problems related to ethnic diversity and poor connectivity. Some areas suffer from lack of development. In others, it is not development but disaffection among some groups which is a cause for concern. We need to address these concerns collectively. Yesterday, in the National Development council, I announced the setting up of a Task Force to study the specific problems of Hill states, including those in the North East. Hopefully, this will lead to an improvement in the economic and security situation in these states. Many states have emphasized the need for better trained security forces. I am happy that the Home Ministry will consider setting up a specialized training facility for training police trainers from across the country. This facility will be a mother institution for improving the training capabilities of state police forces. This would be a step forward. Many other suggestions have been made, I believe that the Home Ministry will take on board all your views and work with you to identify common approaches to tackling internal security problems. In conclusion, I thank you all once again for participating in this conference. I believe that we are all firm in our resolve to fighting all extremist and terrorist activities and to providing our citizens a safe and secure environment. With this, I bring this conference to a conclusion."

5162. (20-12-2007) NEW DELHI : A conference of the General Managers of the Indian Railways was held at Rail Bhawan today to discuss the progress of various railway activities. In his message to the General Managers, the Hon'ble Minister for Railways, Shri Lalu Prasad, expressed confidence that the targets for the year would not only be achieved but would also be bettered handsomely. He expressed hope that Indian Railways would soon achieve the 800 Million Tonne mark in freight loading and would then embark on the mission of loading 900 Million Tonne in 2008-09. The Minister also exhorted the General Managers to focus their attention more closely on ways and means of increasing railways revenues, timely completion of projects, improvements in passenger amenities and safety in railway working. The Hon'ble Minister of State for Railways, Shri Naran Bhai J. Rathwa addressed the General Manager's and complimented the Railway Organistion for keeping social obligations too in mind while striving for an ever high revenue generation. Chairman, Railway Board, Shri K.C.Jena and other members of the Railway Board were also present in the conference apart from the General Managers from sixteen Zonal railways and senior officers of the Ministry of Railways.

5163. (20-12-2007) NEW DELHI : The Ministry of Finance, Department of Economic Affairs and the German Government Bank, KfW signed two Loan Agreements for effectuating financial assistance from Germany amounting to Euro 190 millions on 20th December, 2007. The first agreement is for providing soft loan of Euro 140 million for the purpose of revamping the rural co-operatives in India through the project 'Reform of the Rural Cooperative Credit Structure Project' which will be implemented by NABARD. Government of Germany had committed the funds in separate tranches during the Indo-German Annual Negotiations held in 2005 and 2006 respectively. The funding is to be used for financing the cooperative credit structure reforms in the country, which is also being co-financed by the ADB. The project is being implemented by NABARD. In addition, Loan and Financing Agreement for ninth tranche of German assistance amounting to Euro 50 million for Pulse Polio Immunization Programme of the Health Ministry was also signed. Government of Germany has been extending support to Pulse Polio Immunization Programme since 1997 and have so far extended assistance of Euro 106.86 million in eight tranches which have largely been utilized. In addition, Germans have already committed Euro 31 million and Euro 14.08 million as financial support to Pulse Polio Immunization Programme in tenth and eleventh tranches respectively. The Agreements were signed by Shri Kumar Sanjay Krishna, Joint Secretary, Department of Economic Affairs on behalf of Government of India and Mr. Uwe Ohls, Senior Vice President for Asia, KfW on behalf of KfW.

5164. (20-12-2007) NEW DELHI : An abortive clandestine attempt has been made recently to dislodge the coalition government in Nagaland usurping all democratic norms and principles. Defections and resignations are being mustered by the local Congress leadership on the behest of the UPA Government at the centre. Even after burning their fingers in Bihar and Jharkhand and the resultant harsh indictment by the Highest Court, it seems that the Congress stands undeterred in indulging in the usual Government toppling game. The DAN Government which has successfully completed its term, where the Assembly elections are scheduled in February, 2008, choosing to destabilize it on the eve of elections reflects nothing less then a sinister design to take over and misuse the official machinery for purported electoral gains. The contemptuous ganging up of Congressmen defying the floor test where the majority has been proven and thereafter rushing to Delhi is clearly a proof of their insatiable desire to grab power. The policy of the UPA government has already put the entire North East in virtual political and social turmoil including noted Chinese intrusions in Arunachal Pradesh, spate of ULFA killings in Assam, rampant infiltration on the borders, strained ceasefire dialogues in Nagaland and now striking the roots of democracy by attempting to dislodge the Rio led DAN Government. The BJP which is a part of the coalition government in Nagaland would leave no stone unturned to oppose any such unconstitutional attempt by the UPA Government to impose President's rule. Even the people of Nagaland who have been watching all these developments are set to give a befitting reply to the battered Congress in the ensuing election.

5165. (20-12-2007) NEW DELHI : Air Force Jubilee Institute, Subroto Park, celebrated its 22nd Annual Sports Day on 20th December 2007. The Chief Guest, Air Marshal JN Burma AVSM VSM, air Officer-In - Charge Administration lauded the work of the school in the field of Sports & co-curricular activities and its special contribution in mainstreaming the mentally handicapped with the normal students. It was attended by a number of Air Force Personnel, parents and other dignitaries representing a cross- section of the society. Mrs. Shipra Sarcar, Principal presented the Schools' Sports Annual report in which achievements in sports & co-curricular, by the students were lauded. Chien Sharma and Sachika Ingale were declared best student of the year in sports jointly. Mrs. Padma Burma, wife of Air Officer-In-Charge Administration distributed the prizes and trophies to all meritorious students.

5166. (20-12-2007) NEW DELHI : The Government of India and Government of Singapore have signed a Protocol to amend the India-Singapore Comprehensive Economic Cooperation Agreement (CECA) to expand the tariff liberalization package within the Trade in Goods Chapter here today. To enhance bilateral trade and to strengthen economic relations in various fields, the Comprehensive Economic Cooperation Agreement (CECA) between India and Singapore was signed on 29th June, 2005 by the Prime Minister Dr. Manmohan Singh and H.E. Mr. Lee Hsien Loong, Prime Minister of Singapore and came into effect from 1-8-2005. The Bilateral trade has shown tremendous growth since then with India's exports to Singapore during 2005-06 and 2006-07 at US$ 5.4 billion and US$ 6.02 billion registering a growth of 35.61% and 10.98% respectively and Singapore's export to India during 2005-06 and 2006-07 at US$ 3.4 billion and US$ 5.5 billion registering a growth of 26.49% and 63.10% respectively. India had a positive trade balance of US$ 551 million against Singapore in 2006-07. Singapore had recently made a request for tariff elimination/reduction for certain products. The Government of India has now decided to agree to eliminate/reduce tariff on 539 products (at 8-digit HS code) as an additional concession within the existing India-Singapore CECA. Of the 539 tariff lines, tariff elimination is to be achieved in 5 equal cuts between 15th January 2008 and 1st December 2011 for 307 items. These 307 items comprise mainly of articles of base metal, machinery and mechanical appliances, chemicals and textile and textile articles. For another 97 products, tariff elimination is to be achieved in 9 equal cuts between 15th January 2008 and 1st December 2015. These 97 items comprise mainly of machinery and mechanical appliances, plastic and rubber articles and textile and textile articles. For 135 products, tariff reduction to 5% is to be achieved in 9 equal cuts between 15th January 2008 and 1st December 2015. These items comprise mainly of chemicals, plastic and rubber articles and machinery and mechanical appliances. Under the existing Trade in Goods Agreement, about 83% value of India's imports from Singapore are covered under products for which tariff is being eliminated or reduced. After the proposed additional tariff concessions, this coverage would go up to about 93%. It has also been decided to extend, under India-Singapore CECA, additional concessions that India may offer under ASEAN-India FTA in Goods in terms of product coverage, time-line, Rules of Origin, with appropriate amendments to India- Singapore CECA.

5167. (20-12-2007) NEW DELHI : India's ace driver Narain Karthikeyan who recently won the A1 GP event in China met the Tourism and Culture Minister Smt. Ambika Soni in her office at Transport Bhawan here today. Karthikeyan came to meet Minister wearing Incredible India T-shirt and the same logo was displayed on his racing car at the China event. He said that the logo inspired him during the race and in future also he will get inspiration from this logo. Smt. Soni lauding the success of Karthikeyan said he has made all Indians proud though his achievements. She wished Mr. Karthikeyan success in all his future endeavors. Secretary Tourism Shri S. Banerjee and other senior officials of the Tourism Ministry were also present on the occasion.

5168. (20-12-2007) NEW DELHI : Indian space programme witnessed several major accomplishments and scaled newer heights in mastering space technology during the year. It is significant to note that the remarkable successes were the result of well-orchestrated programmes undertaken by the department aimed at achieving total self-reliance in this cutting edge technology solely through indigenous efforts and utilizing the expertise available within the organization. Some of the recent, important developments, were the successful orbiting and recovery of a space capsule from the Indian soil using our own launch vehicle, launching of the state of the art remote sensing satellite Cartosat-2 with better than one meter resolution, launching of a satellite exclusively for an European customer under a commercial contract, successful ground testing of indigenously developed cryogenic upper stage and fabrication and installation of a large antenna for providing tracking and command support for deep space missions in general and Chandrayaan-I, India's first un-manned lunar mission in particular. Launch Vehicle Programmes: The launching of Polar Satellite Launch Vehicle (PSLV-C7) on January 10, 2007 carrying our own 680 kg remote sensing satellite Cartosat-2, 56 kg LAPAN-TUBSAT satellite from Indonesia, 6 kg Pehuensat from Argentina and 550 kg Space capsule Recovery Experiment (SRE) aimed at establishing

India's capability to orbit and bring back to earth successfully heralded a new era in the launch vehicle and satellite technology development in the country. PSLV-C7 also demonstrated our capability to launch multiple payloads into different orbits precisely. Space capsule Recovery Experiment carried two experiments to conduct studies in micro gravity was launched into 485 km by 639 km orbit. SRE comprises aero thermal structure, spacecraft platform, deceleration and floatation system besides the micro gravity payloads. After successfully accomplishing the mission the SRE was reoriented and de-orbited to splash down at the designated location in the Indian Ocean region on January 22, 2007. The precise splash down established India's capability to launch and control accurately to bring back a space capsule. The demonstration of SRE experiment has given confidence to undertake more complex manned missions into low earth orbit. Closely following this was the launch of PSLV-C8 on April 23, 2007 carrying an Italian satellite AGILE into a low earth orbit. Considering the mission requirements PSLV-C8 was launched in core alone configuration which also proved the versatility of PSLV as the vehicle. Geosynchronous Satellite Launch Vehicle (GSLV-F04) was launched successfully on September 2, 2007 carrying INSAT-4CR into the desired orbit. The launch of GSLV-F04 was significant as the previous flight GSLV-D3 had failed to accomplish the mission owing to a fabrication anomaly. The detailed failure analysis carried out established that the design of GSLV is robust and certain strict quality control measures needs to be enforced during fabrication and inspection. The successful launch of GSLV-F04 reinforced ISRO's ability to look at failures critically and draw lessons. The recent successful ground testing of the Cryogenic Upper Stage to be used in place of Russian cryogenic stages in GSLV was the crowning glory for ISRO. The cryogenic upper stage was tested for the full flight duration of 12 minutes and the test results fully met all the specified parameters. The development of cryogenic engines involves mastering materials technology, operating rotary pumps and turbines which run at 42,000 rpm at cryogenic temperatures. The successful testing has resulted in total self-reliance in launch vehicle technology.

5169. (20-12-2007) NEW DELHI : It has been reported in the press that some banks were deducting tax from pension of disabled ex-servicemen in violation of Government instructions. RBI was requested to have the matter investigated and remedial action taken. After examination, RBI discovered that in one specific instance, due to oversight, the pensioner's disability pension was wrongly taken into account while calculating Income Tax. RBI has issued instructions to all agency banks to strictly adhere to the provisions of para 88.3 of Defence Pension Payment Instructions 2005, regarding exemption of Income Tax of the disability pension of the pensioners of Armed Forces. Banks have been advised to issue suitable instructions to all their pension disbursing branches that Income Tax should not be deducted from the disability pension paid to the pensioners of the Armed Forces.

5170. (20-12-2007) NEW DELHI : The Bharat Heavy Electricals Ltd. would take over M/s Bharat Heavy Plate & Vessels Ltd. (BHPV), Vishakhapatanam as a subsidiary and initially invest Rs. 275 crore as CAPEX apart from investing Rs. 34 crore as equity in the company. The Department of Heavy Industry, had inter alia, proposed that Government may waive/write off loans and interests to BHPV amounting to Rs. 414.95 crore and to settle all outstanding liabilities of BHPV amounting to Rs. 263.97 crore. The Government approved "in principle" the take over of BHPV by BHEL. The Union Cabinet on 26th November, 2007 approved the financial restructuring and strengthening package of BHPV with the direction that the valuation of BHPV be carried out prudently on the basis of established principles. As a follow up to the Government decision, a study has been commissioned by SBI Caps for valuation of BHPV as an on-going concern.

5171. (20-12-2007) NEW DELHI : One of the major issues of concern for the promotion and development of the micro and small enterprises has been the delayed payments from the buyers. To address this issue, the erstwhile "The Interest on Delayed Payments to Small Scale and Ancillary Industrial Undertakings Act, 1993" as amended in 1998 was further strengthened and subsumed in the Micro, Small & Medium Enterprises Development (MSMED) Act, 2006, which has since been implemented from 2nd October 2006. Two of the effective measures provided under the provisions of said Act are - (i) "Requirement to specify unpaid amount with interest in the annual statement of accounts" (under Section 22) and (ii) "Interest not to be allowed as deduction from income" under Income-Tax Act, 1961 (under Section 23). The Government has accordingly notified necessary Instructions vide CBDT Instruction No.12/2006 on 14 December 2006 and Ministry of Corporate Affairs Notification No: G.S.R.719 (E) dated 16 November 2007, so that the provisions of the MSMED Act, 2006 providing measures to check delayed payments to micro and small enterprises (MSEs) are implemented in letter and spirit. The measure would go in a long way to minimize the problem being faced by MSEs in respect of delayed payments.

5172. (20-12-2007) NEW DELHI : The Ministry of Food Processing Industries concerned with a number of food processing sectors such as grain processing, meat processing, poultry & egg processing, milk products, fish processing, fruit and vegetable processing, consumer food industries. Over the last few years there has been a positive growth in ready to serve beverages, fruit juices and pulps, dehydrated and frozen fruits and vegetable products, tomato products, pickles, processed mushrooms and curried vegetables. From the year 1998-99, all ministries/ departments of the Government are required to spend at least 10% of the plan outlay in the Northeast including Sikkim. The North Eastern Region comprising of the States of Arunachal Pradesh, Assam, Manipur, Meghalaya, Mizoram, Nagaland, Tripura and Sikkim by virtue of its diverse agro-climatic conditions, variety of types and abundant rainfall, offers a wide range of agro-horticulture produce of premium quality. Ministry of Food Processing Industries extends financial assistance for Technology Upgradation/Modernization/Establishment of food processing units in the form of grant-in-aid @ 25% of the cost of plant and machinery and technical civil works subject to maximum of Rs. 50 lakh in general areas or 33.33% subject to a maximum of Rs. 75 lakh in difficult areas such as Jammu & Kashmir, Himachal Pradesh, Uttarakhand, Sikkim and North Eastern States, Andaman & Nicobar Island, Lakshadweep and ITDP Areas. Under the Mini Mission IV of Technology Mission for Integrated Development of Horticulture in North Eastern States including Sikkim, J & K, Uttarakhand and Himachal Pradesh, assistance at still higher rates *i.e.* @ 50% upto Rs. 4 crore for promotion of new units and upto Rs. 1 crore for Upgradation/modernization of existing units is available for processing of horticulture produce. Ministry of Food Processing Industries does not set up Food Processing Industries on its own. A revamped Scheme for Infrastructure Development will be implemented under which, it will give financial assistance in the form of grant for setting up of Mega Food Parks, cold chain infrastructure, value added centres and packaging centres preferably in the Public private Partnership (PPP) Model. The Mega Food Park Scheme will provide backward and forward linkages as well as reliable and sustainable supply chain. The cluster based demand driven approach will provide linkages from farm to market with linkages from local to regional level through Primary Processing Centre, Collection Centres, Strategic Distribution Centre-cum-Cold Chain at critical locations-having controlled Atmosphere storage and distribution centres where large quantities can be stored and supplied to distribution centres for fresh sale and to processing industries for processing. In addition, the Ministry will be providing assistance in the form of grant to private sector/public sector organizations through scheme for setting up of Food Testing Labs, Implementation of Quality Systems such as HACCP, ISO 9000, GHP and GMP, Promotion of Research and Development, Capacity building and Human Resource Development and other promotional activities.

5173. (20-12-2007) NEW DELHI : To enable the Press Information Bureau to serve media in Maharashtra and Goa better, the Principal Director General, (Media & Communications), Ms. Deepak Sandhu, launched today the new website of PIB, Mumbai - www.pibmumbai.gov.in. The website, developed and maintained by the National Informatics Centre, NIC, will aim to give authentic news about programmes and policies of Government of India and its organizations, in a format tailor- made for media in Maharashtra and Goa. Speaking on the occasion, Ms. Sandhu said, PIB had been adopting all modern means of communication to reach its users. She invited the Government of India organisations in Maharahstra to make the best use of the platform provided by the Mumbai website. pibmumbai.gov.in is a bilingual web-site in Marathi and English, which includes, news, features, backgrounders and important Government publications. Another important feature of the website is the 'Press Events' column, which shall display all important functions, press conferences and other events of media interest, that take place in Mumbai. The website distributes print quality photographs of major news events, which can be downloaded for media use. A comprehensive media and communication directory is also being constructed covering the entire Maharashtra and Goa region. The regional website of PIB Mumbai has been developed following a demand for distribution of news in e-format, by a large number of publications and media houses, as expressed during a media survey conducted earlier this year. For the benefit of very small publications, distribution of PIB releases in paper format will continue.

5174. (20-12-2007) NEW DELHI : Shri Kamal Nath, Union Minister of Commerce and Industry, has stated that good governance will contribute to an even higher rate of economic growth. The process of economic liberalisation and globalisation are intrinsically linked with good governance and the good economic governance will go a long way in building the necessary social capital needed for promoting growth, he said. He was speaking at the 102nd Annual Session of the PHD Chamber of Commerce and Industry, here today. He further said that the Indian economy has achieved a robust growth of 9% plus and this makes us one of the fastest growing economies in the world. "We are increasingly recognised as a global economic power. India of 2007 is more confident, more enterprising and more competitive. There are, however, a number of issues which the governance of this country has to address and address quickly", the Minister said. Shri Kamal Nath stated that the guiding force behind the concept of good governance is people's active participation, and added that the other indicators are: decentralization & deconcentration; accountability & transparency; full access to justice; elimination of all forms of discrimination; maintenance and fostering of peace; and adequate budgetary provision for social priority areas. Outlining the future challenges, Shri Kamal Nath stated that the foremost issue is 'inclusive growth' and ensuring that benefits of growth trickles down to all sections of society particularly the marginalized. Poverty, unemployment, low growth rate in agriculture sector, provision for safe drinking water and sanitation, education, housing and health care facilities for all are other vital challenges that have to be tackled urgently. Drawing global parallels, the Minister said that it has become more relevant to examine the relation between institutional capacities for effective economic governance at the national level and poverty elimination. "By studying the governance and poverty experiences of some newly industrialised, developing and transitional economies, findings and proposals should be applicable to their equivalents elsewhere. Let me cite the example of South East Asia. The per capita income of East Asian countries which were only marginally better off than the Sub Saharan Africa in 1960 became 5 times theirs by the year 1995. Good Governance in East Asian countries was identified as the prime factor responsible for their superior performance and, since then the link between economic development and governance is being increasingly realized", Shri Kamal Nath emphasised.

5175. (20-12-2007) NEW DELHI : The Ministry of Health & Family Welfare is receiving grants from the Global Fund Foundation, Switzerland to fight AIDS,

Tuberculosis and Malaria in the country. A meeting to review the current status, issues and challenges in implementing the Global Fund projects was held today under the Chairmanship of the Union Minister for Health & Family Welfare, Dr. Anbumandi Ramadoss in which Shri Rajat Gupta, Chair of the Board of Global Fund for AIDS, TB and Malaria (GFATM) and Prof. Michel Kazatchkine, Executive Director of the Fund, who are currently on a visit to India, also participated. Senior officials of the Ministry concerned with the implementation of the global fund projects made presentations and explained in detailed the implementation status of the Global Fund projects at the ground level. The representatives from the Global Fund appreciated the efforts made by the Indian Government in implementing the Global Fund projects and promised more fund allocation. They also signed with the Indian authorities a Multi-Million Dollar Global Fund grant to fight AIDS in India.

5176. (20-12-2007) NEW DELHI : Recognising that consumer awareness and education programme play a pivotal role in protecting consumers, "Jago Grahak Jago" campaign by the Government of India shall be intensified in the coming months. Shri Yashwant Bhave, Secretary, Department of Consumer Affairs gave these comments during a function to celebrate the National Consumer Day in the capital today. He said that enactment of Consumer Protection Act on 24 December, 1986 has proved to be a milestone in consumer movement and on this day, all stakeholders should take a pledge to protect the interest of consumers. Shri Bhave exuded confidence that an aware and enlightened consumer shall play a crucial role in enabling the transition to a knowledge base society. He highlighted that a 3-tier structure comprising of legal framework, Standards and consumer redressal is paramount for protecting the interest of consumer. Giving a small example regarding purchase of gold, Shri Bhave observed that about 18 to 39% samples of gold were found to be of lower Caratage which roughly translates into an annual lose of 7500 crores to consumers. To protect the interest of the consumers, the Government has started the hallmarking scheme and shall be expanding it further in the coming months. Shri Bhave also highlighted that other issues concerning the interest of the consumers such as MRP, Labelling, Standardisation etc. were being taken up by the Department through its consumer awareness publicity campaign. He also praised the efficacy of consumer forums and pointed out that out of 28 lakh complaints received by the consumer fora till now, more than 25 lakh cases have been disposed off. Delivering the keynote address, Shri S. Joe Bhatia, President and CEO, of American National Standards Institute (ANSI) emphasized the importance of framing standards to protect consumer interest. Citing the example of the concerns raised regarding toy safety in America, Shri Bhatia said that ANSI is playing the role of a facilitator for the industry to adopt voluntary standards so that consumers can get products with well-defined quality standards. He pointed out that the industry should come forward and adopt voluntary standards which are quick to respond and flexible. In his concluding address, Justice J.R. Kapoor, President, State Consumer Fora, Delhi described the Consumer Protection Act as a magnificent and one of the finest pieces of legislation ever enacted by any Government world wide. He remarked that if used effectively, Consumer Protection Act can drive all the unscrupulous traders out of business. Highlighting some of the recent judgments of consumer courts relating to penalty on airlines for delay in the flight, penalty on a bank for using strong arm tactics for loan recovery etc. Justice Kapoor asked the consumers to become aware of their rights and take pro-active steps in seeking redressal. Earlier in her welcome address, Smt. Alka Sirohi, Addl. Secretary, in the Department of Consumer Affairs highlighted the various measures being taken by the Government for protecting consumers. She said that the computerization of consumer forum network is being undertaken and soon consumers will have the facility of online registration of complaints. She also pointed out that amendment to Consumer Protection Act to ensure disposal of cases in a specific timeframe is being envisaged. On the occasion, Monographs on various issues concerning 'Consumer Protection' were also released. The monographs in Hindi have been brought out jointly by Indian Institute of Public Administration and the Department of Consumer Affairs, Government of India.

5177. (20-12-2007) NEW DELHI : The Vice President of India Mohd. Hamid Ansari has greeted the people of our country on the auspicious occasion of Id-ul-Zuha. In his greetings, the Vice President said that this festival celebrates the spirit of sacrifice that God requires of man. The joy of sharing and charity associated with this festival provides succour to the poor and unites us all in common brotherhood. The Vice President calls upon the people to celebrate this festival with compassion and serve the cause of humanity.

5178. (20-12-2007) NEW DELHI : The expansion and modernization of Ports remained amongst the top priority areas of the Government during the year 2007. Several developmental projects got underway at the major ports during the year. The year also witnessed significant growth in traffic and capacity at ports and also the growth in Indian Tonnage. During the year, the Perspective Plans have been prepared for 12 Major Ports alongwith a consolidated National Development Plan.

5179. (20-12-2007) NEW DELHI : The Government's approval for construction of Ring Roads/Bypasses etc. around the major cities across the country, upgradation of National Highways under NHDP Phase III A and III B, awarding of 18 contracts by NHAI under NHDP Phase III, IV and VI and approval of modified SARDP-NE programme for widening of NHs in NE States marked the major activities of the Department of Road Transport and Highways during the year 2007. The Department of Road Transport notified the rules for accreditation of bus body builders, Government approved the amendments in the Motor Vehicle Act and Sunder Committee recommended the creation of a dedication body on road safety and traffic management during the year.

5180. (20-12-2007) NEW DELHI : The President of India, Smt. Pratibha Devisingh Patil will stay at Rashtrapati Nilayam at Secunderabad and attend various official programmes from December 21, 2007 to January 6, 2008. The President will visit Puducherry on December 21st, where she will attend the inaugural function of the 34th Jawahar Lal Nehru National Science Exhibition for Children-2007. On December 22nd, the President will visit the Sri Aurobindo Ashram, Auroville, the Ashram school and the Painting Exhibition. The President will be on an official tour to the Andaman & Nicobar Islands from December 26th to 28th where she will be visiting the rehabilitation work sites in the Tsunami affected areas and interacting with the islanders. At Hyderabad, the President will attend various programmes organised by the State Government and the Ministry of Defence including visit to the Defence Research Establishments and the Air Force Training Institute.

5181. (20-12-2007) NEW DELHI : The President of India, Smt. Pratibha Devisingh Patil today greeted fellow citizens on the occasion of Idu'l Zuha, which is being celebrated tomorrow. In her message the President has said, "On the occasion of Idu'l Zuha, I extend my greetings and good wishes to all my fellow countrymen. Let us on this day remind ourselves of the spirit of service and sacrifice associated with this festival and motivate ourselves to work towards progress and prosperity of the nation".

5182. (20-12-2007) NEW DELHI : The introduction of the Unorganized Sector Workers Social Security Bill, 2007, the launching of the 'Rashtriya Swasthya Bima Yojana' (RSBY), major programme for upgradation of ITIs and ITCs, the Revised Integrated Housing Scheme (RIHS) 2007-08 for beedi workers etc., expansion of the National Child Labour Project (NCLP) Scheme to cover 250 districts with an additional $40 million Indo-US joint project on Child Labour in 21 districts, the initiation of concept of the national floor level minimum wage and its revision from Rs.66/- per day to Rs.80/- per day, constitution of two Wage Boards one for Working Journalists and another for Non-Journalist Newspaper Employees, action to provide the skills for youth with lesser educational qualification through the Skill Development Initiative Scheme in areas/clusters which have significant population of Muslims marked the activities and achievements of the Ministry of Labour and Employment during the year 2007.

5183. (20-12-2007) NEW DELHI : The General Council of Sangeet Natak Akademi, the National Academy of Music, Dance and Drama at its meeting held on 18 December 2007 elected Dr. S.K. Saxena, eminent scholar and professor of aesthetics, as Sangeet Natak Akademi Ratna (Akademi Fellow). The honour of Akademi Ratna is restricted to 30 living personalities at any given point of time. The General Council of the Akademi also selected 33 eminent persons for the Sangeet Natak Akademi Puraskar (Akademi Awards) for the year 2007. In the field of Music, eight eminent artists namely Vidyadhar Vyas and Govardhan Mishra for Hindustani Vocal Music, Nandan Mehta, Hindustani Instrumental (Tabla), Ramoo Prasad Shastri, Hindustani Instrumental (Violin), B. Krishnamoorthy, Carnatic Vocal Music, Vidya Sankar, Carnatic Instrumental (Veena), S.R.D. Vaidyanathan, Carnatic Instrumental (Nagaswaram) and Khayyam (Mohammad Zahoor Hashimi) for Creative & Experimental Music have been selected. Eight eminent practitioners of Dance namely Sucheta Bhide Chapekar, Bharatanayam, Geetanjali Lal, Kathak, Sadanam Krishnan Kutty, Kathakali, Yeleswarapu Nageswara Sarma, Kuchipudi, Ranjana Gauhar, Odissi, Gunakanta Dutta Barbayan, Sattriya, Deepti Omchery Bhalla, Mohiniattam and K. Sivan Nambootiri, Other Major Traditions of Dance/Dance theatre (Kutiyattam) will receive Akademi Award for 2007. In the field of Theatre, eight eminent persons namely Reoti Saran Sharma, Lalthangfala Sailo and Yumnam Rajendra Singh for Playwriting, N. C. Thakur and Harimadhab Mukherjee for Direction, Ramesh Mehta, Acting, Mahendra Kumar, Allied Theatre Arts (Scenic Design) and Kolyur Ramachandra Rao, Major Traditions of Theatre (Yakshagana) have been selected. For their contribution to Traditional/Folk/ Tribal Music/ Dance/ Theatre and Puppetry Th. Brindasabi Devi, Gouranga Leela (Manipur), Prahlad Singh Tipania, Folk Music (Madhya Pradesh), Ram Dayal Munda, Tribal Dance & Music (Jharkhand), Ghulam Mohammad, Dogri Folk Music (Jammu & Kashmir), Subodh Deb Barma, Tribal Dance (Tripura), Amar Pal, Folk Music (West Bengal) and L. Rajappa, Puppetry (Pondicherry) have been selected. Sharafat Abdul Majid Satarmaker of Maharashtra will receive the Award for Making of Musical Instruments. Mukund Lath will be honoured with the Akademi Award 2007 for his contribution to Scholarship in Performing Arts. The Akademi Ratna (Akademi Fellow) and Akademi Puraskar (Akademi Award) which have been conferred since 1952, symbolize the highest standard of excellence and achievements on a national basis and recognize sustained individual work and outstanding contribution to the practice and appreciation of the arts through performance, teaching and scholarship. The Akademi Ratna carries a purse money of Rs. 1,00,000/- and the Akademi Puraskar a purse money of Rs. 50,000/-, besides Tamrapatra and Angavastram.

5184. (20-12-2007) NEW DELHI : The Prime Minister, Dr. Manmohan Singh, has greeted the nation on the auspicious occasion of Id-ul-Zuha. In a message, the Prime Minister said that the festival commemorates the spirit of supreme sacrifice of Hazrat Ibrahim. This selfless sacrifice is an inspiring example of subordinating self-interest to the greater good of humanity. "On this occasion, I call upon the Nation to reaffirm this commitment towards uplift of the poor, the needy and the underprivileged", Dr. Singh added. The Prime Minister expressed hope that Id-ul-Zuha further strengthens the cultural bonds of our country and ushers in joy and prosperity for all.

5185. (20-12-2007) NEW DELHI : The Bharat Heavy Electricals Ltd. would take over M/s Bharat Heavy Plate & Vessels Ltd. (BHPV), Vishakhapatanam as a subsidiary and initially invest Rs. 275 crore as CAPEX apart from investing Rs.

34 crore as equity in the company. The Department of Heavy Industry, had inter alia, proposed that Government may waive/write off loans and interests to BHPV amounting to Rs. 414.95 crore and to settle all outstanding liabilities of BHPV amounting to Rs. 263.97 crore. The Government approved "in principle" the take over of BHPV by BHEL. The Union Cabinet on 26th November, 2007 approved the financial restructuring and strengthening package of BHPV with the direction that the valuation of BHPV be carried out prudently on the basis of established principles. As a follow up to the Government decision, a study has been commissioned by SBI Caps for valuation of BHPV as an on-going concern.

5186. (21-12-2007) NEW DELHI : The Finance Minister, Shri P Chidambaram has stressed the need for strengthening the manufacturing sector to provide large scale employment opportunities for the ever increasing youth population. Speaking at a function in Mumbai to mark the 70th Anniversary of India's leading engineering company, Larsen & Toubro, the Finance Minister observed, that India is set to become the only large country where working population will be higher than the dependent population. He said that since, only 5 per cent of the youth will be vocationally skilled, the services sector, which accounts for 55% of our GDP will not able to absorb them in large numbers. To ensure employment opportunities for the youth, Shri Chidambaram said, the Manufacturing sector, which now accounts for 28 per cent of GDP, will have to grow and expand its activities on a big scale. He said, professionally managed, technology driven companies like L&T, which he placed in a newly coined 'national sector', are needed in more numbers. Shri Chidambaram lamented Indian companies for not thinking big and lacking speed in project implementation, as compared to their Chinese counterparts. He said, the completion of Greenfield airports at Hyderabad and Bangalore, ahead of schedule, is more of an exception than a rule. The Finance Minister revealed a startling figure of Rs 48,961 crores rupees lost in 301 projects due to delays in completion. The Minister said that India was more than a match for China in entrepreneurship, managerial skills and business environment. He called upon the captains of the industry to accept the challenge of taking on China in the manufacturing field as well.. The Civil Aviation Minister, Shri Prafull Patel, informed that the L & T executed Hyderabad and Bangalore International Airports will be opened 12th and 28th of March respectively. Sheri Murli Deora, Minister for Petroleum & Natural Gas, lauded the company's work in nation building, and called upon L & T to take up restoration of dilapidated buildings in Central Mumbai, which mostly house the out of job mill workers. The Governor of Maharashtra, Shri S M Krishna, the Chief Minister, Shri Vilasrao Deshmukh and other leaders of the Indian Industry were also present.

5187. (21-12-2007) NEW DELHI : The first ever Sino-Indian joint military exercise "Hand-in-Hand" started at Kunming Military Academy, China today. The exercise was jointly opened by Brigadier DS Dadwal, Commander of the Indian contingent and Major General Xiong Zuoming of People's Liberation Army,

China. Both the officers expressed their confidence that this exercise would be a prove to be a mile stone in enhancing mutual trust and confidence between two armies and the two Nations. The opening ceremony was followed by a tactics and skills display by the troops of the two sides. Weapon displays were organized by both the armies in which the troops of the two sides showed keen interest.

5188. (21-12-2007) NEW DELHI : The Ministry of Environment and Forests is in process to set up the 4th Regional Museum of Natural History in Rajasthan. Land measuring 7.42 acres has been acquired for this Rajiv Gandhi Regional Museum of Natural History. This has been conceived to be a non-formal centre for Environment Education and creation of public awareness on conservation of nature and natural resources. The Museum proposes to undertake the task of communication and creating public awareness through the potential medium of exhibits and educational activities. It would provide an understanding of the diversity of life on the earth, the factors responsible for their well being, man's dependence upon nature and the necessity to maintain our ecological heritage free from damage and destruction to ensure sustainable development with special emphasis on the Western Arid region of India. It will be the joint responsibility of the Govt. of India and the Govt. of Rajasthan. The museum will develop exhibits depicting flora, fauna and geology of the region and ecological relationship among plants and animals and their evolutionary patterns, including man and to emphasize the importance of conservation through exhibits and educational activities. It will provide special exhibits and activities to enrich the school curriculum in Biology, particularly on environmental aspects. It will develop appropriate educational programmes for children, adults and family groups to create environmental awareness and a state-wide programme for environmental education through activities at the district level. Apart from this, it will publish popular educational material useful for environmental education. The Museum will have foyer hall and four galleries The Foyer Hall will depict Natural History of the region with Aravalli & Satpura ranges and inhabitant flora & fauna. Other galleries will have Pre-historic Gallery depicting Biomes and ecosystem of the region, Desert Ecosystem, Nature's Network and conservation and Forests & Wildlife of Rajasthan. Ministry has established three Regional Museums earlier, one each at Mysore, Karnataka, Bhopal in Madhya Pradesh and Bhubaneswar in Orissa. They are dedicated to Biological Diversity, Introduction to Ecology and Biodiversity respectively.

5189. (21-12-2007) NEW DELHI : The Akash Missile has successfully hit the bull's eye for the fifth time in a row in the last ten days at test range in Balasore. The fifth and last trial successfully took place at 2.15 pm today at Chandipur-on- sea. The missile destroyed an Unmanned Aerial Vehicle (UAV), which was flying simulating the air attack. The target vanished from the radar screen when the missile was guided precisely in close proximity and the warhead blast occurred, much to the delight of users present in the flight campaign. This is the grand finale of the ten days users campaign meticulously planned by the Indian Air Force. Akash is a moblie, mulitiple target handling, medium range Air Defence missile developed under Integrated Guided Missile Development Programme (IGMDP). The missile system has been configured to be part of futuristic network centric operation, most of the operations having been made automated. The entire weapon system has gone through functional evaluation in Kolar near Bangalore followed by operation and mobility trials in Pokharan ranges. The ECCM (Elctronic Counter Counter Measure) evaluation was carried out at Gwalior by Air Force against various types of electronic target and counter measures. The final phase of user evaluation as part of user trials was done in Chandipur. ITR, Balasore provides world's best instrumentation facilities. The flight was conducted under the leadership of Dr. Panyam, Project Director. Dr. Prahlada, who conceptualised Akash and now Chief Controller at DRDO HQ was present during campaign. About 300 strong team was present for ten days campaign. Representatives from public sector BDL, BEL etc. were also present. Indian Air Force officials witnessed users trial. With the conclusion of Akash evaluation, the is now available for indigenous production in the country. The missile system is uniquly configured and customised for Indian Army and Air Force.

5190. (21-12-2007) NEW DELHI : The shocking news of the house arrest of noted writer Taslima Nasreen is a matter of shame for the UPA government, especially in a country that proudly propounds the age old philosophy of "Athithi Devo Bhawa". It is even more shocking that for the sake of their political survival and acting completely under pressure from the CPM, the central government has gone ahead and conveyed to Taslima that she cannot go back to Kolkata, a city that she loves. This has thrown up an extremely relevant and important question as to how a victim of persecution is being treated by a civilized state in which the victim has sought refuge as an assalym. Taslima is a victim of religious persecution in Bangladesh. She is now a refugee in India. To begin with the CPM government forcibly ejected her from Kolkata under the pressure from Islamic fundamentalists. Thereafter, the central government is carrying out further persecution since fellow travelling with the CPM and fundamentalists protects their survival and also wins vote banks. The BJP would like to remind the UPA central government and CPM state government that we are nmo longer living under the emergency rule of 1975 in which the then attorney general had infamously had the audacity to state that "nobody has right to life if government wishes so". The BJP in the strongest possible terms condemns the UPA and CPM for their dismal display of conduct in Taslima episode, which clearly establishes their complete submission to Islamic fundamentalists; a continuation of their known behaviour since the days of the Shahbano case and following the policy of rank opportunism for mere political survival and vote bank politics. The BJP demands that the UPA government should ensure the freedom of movement, provide safety and just treatment to Taslima and allow her to follow her wishes. The CPM's attack on the BJP in their mouthpiece People's democracy is a sign of the growing insecurity amongst its leadership and cadres. They have falsely charged the BJP of going back to basics of aggressive communal poloralisation. This precisely reflects the complete insecurity and frustration of the CPM, in face of the growing popularity of the BJP. What the country has witnessed in Nandigram and in the Taslima case is a clear proof of the CPM going back to its basics of Stalinism. The recent revelation and video footage has clearly unmasked the CPM cadres in masks, in brutal attack on Nandigram. It is not just a clear indication of state complicity but a clear proof of state sponsored terrorism. The use of terms like "Recapture of Nandigram" and "Celebrating the victory in Nandigram" speaks volume of the CPM mindset. The BJP asks what the CPM cadres were celebrating? Were they celebrating the rape of innocent women? Were they celebrating loot and arson? Were they celebrating the murder of protestors and unearthing of skeletons? Were they celebrating continued Stalinist terrorism? It is not surprising that the CPM is not worried about human rights violations and continued terrorism in Nandigram but is instead only worried about how the CBI report got leaked. The BJP is also amused to note the Prime Minister has finally acknowledged the leftwing extremism of Naxals is growing and their base has enlarged. It is the Congress politics, which is responsible for such an enlargement in Naxalism. They allegedly entered into political understanding with these outfits on the eve of election in Andhra and Chhattisgarh. Subsequently the Congress government in Andhra declared ceasefire, which proved a golden opportunity for Naxals to regroup, reinforce and spread its tentacles. The central government discontinued the coordinated action plan and working group arrangement initiated by the NDA to tackle Naxals despite its success. The BJP demands that instead of mere statements, the government must display the resolve and follow it up with a specific action plan to conclusively combat and defeat naxalism across the country.

5191. (21-12-2007) NEW DELHI : The Union Minister of Agriculture, Consumer Affairs, Food and Public Distribution Shri Sharad Pawar has said that the Central Government has taken a number of measures to assist the sugar industry and help sugarcane farmers. He said that almost all the financial assistance to sugar industry is meant for payment of cane dues and therefore, the industry must ensure that farmers are paid their dues without any delay. He stated this while inaugurating the 73rd Annual General Meeting of Indian Sugar Mills Association here today. Enumerating the steps to help the sugar industry, Shri Pawar said that buffer stock of 50 lac tons has been created for a period of one year, for which the Government would pay buffer subsidy of almost Rs. 880 crore from Sugar Development Fund. Besides, he said, the Banks would provide additional credit of about Rs. 970 crore and this amount has already been made available to sugar factories following instructions of RBI and NABARD. He however, reminded the sugar industry that as per the Sugar Development Fund Rules, the buffer subsidy and additional credit are to be used for payment of cane price to sugarcane farmers as the first priority. Thus, he said, about Rs. 1850 crore would be available with the sugar factories to make cane price payment including arrears. He said that another assistance of

300 crore would be available from the Sugar Development Fund on account of defraying of internal transport, handling and marketing charges and ocean freight on sugar exports made on or after 19th April 2007. This assistance is also to be used for payment of cane price including cane price arrears to sugarcane farmers as the first priority, he added. Amongst other measures, Shri Pawar mentioned the NABARD package for restructuring of loans to cooperative sugar mills across the country under which the moratorium on outstanding term loans has been extended from two years to upto five years. He said a special scheme for extending financial assistance to sugar factories has been notified under which scheduled and cooperative banks would give loans to all sugar factories equivalent to the notional central excise duty payable on total production sugar during 2006-07 season and on the estimated production during 2007-08. Though the scheme provides full interest subvention, it would be limited to 12% per annum which would be fully borne by the Central Government, he said and added that this would improve the liquidity position of sugar mills by about Rs. 3800 crore. This amount is also to be used for payment of cane price arrears of 2006-07 and 2007-08, he said. Shri Pawar said that sugar factories would be allowed to convert sugarcane juice or B-Heavy molasses directly into ethanol and a Notification in this regard is likely within a month. He mentioned about the mandatory blending of 5% ethanol with petrol with immediate effect and 10% blending from October 2008 (except in J&K, NE States and Island Territories) which would give an assured market for 600 million litres and 1200 million litres of ethanol respectively.

5192. (22-12-2007) NEW DELHI : Prof. Saifuddin Soz, Union Minister for Water Resources, has expressed his deep shock on the sudden demise of well-known Kashmiri author and writer, Bashir Akhtar, who died in Srinagar last evening. In a condolence message, Prof. Soz described the death of Bashir Akhtar as untimely and a great loss to the Kashmiri literary community. Prof. Soz said, " Bashir had earned a great acclaim for his short stories and made a contribution to the growth of Kashmiri language and literature. Before his superannuation, he held the posts of Publications Officer and Editor of the prestigious "Sheeraza" magazine in the Academy of Art, Culture and Languages, with distinction and ability". Prof. Soz conveyed his deep condolences to the bereaved family.

5193. (22-12-2007) NEW DELHI : The Prime Minister Dr. Manmohan Singh has condoled the demise of Arunachal Pradesh Congress President Smt Omem Moyong Deori. In his message he said, "I am deeply grieved to learn of the sad demise of Smt. Omem Moyong Deori, President of the Arunachal Pradesh Congress Committee. A prominent personality in the public life of Arunachal Pradesh Smt. Omen Moyong Deori was held in high esteem for her important contributions to the progress and development of the State. As a dedicated functionary of the congress-I party she always remained in the forefront to spread its ideals and consolidate its position in the State. Her manifold activities in this direction endeared Smt. Deori to her numerous friends, associates, colleagues and admirers.

A multifaceted personality, she had the distinction of being a Member of Parliament and effectively playing her role as a legislator. Her unfortunate passing away due to illness is a major loss to the people and the State of Arunachal Pradesh. On this sad occasion, I convey my heartfelt condolences to the members of the bereaved family and all those who were close to her. May her soul rest in peace".

5194. (23-12-2007) NEW DELHI : Dr. Hamid Ansari, Vice President of India has said that no textbook in any educational institute teaches about the interaction between humans and animals, humans and the environment or what humans have done with the world's flora and fauna. These textbooks teach us only about the history of what humans did to other humans and what countries did to one another. Laying the foundation stone of the Rajiv Gandhi Regional Museum of Natural History at Jaisinghpura in Sawai Madhopur district of Rajasthan today, Dr. Ansari said that it was time to know what destruction humans have waged on the world's flora and fauna, that the time has come for all of us to learn to preserve, conserve and enhance our forests, trees, animals and biodiversity to preserve our own existence. He said that humans must learn to live harmoniously with all other creatures in this world. Shri Namo Narain Meena, Union Minister of State for Environment and Forests appealed to people to preserve forests and endangered species. Speaking on this occasion as Chief Guest, he said that the government was planning to open another regional center of natural history at Gangtok, Sikkim for the north-eastern region. This regional center was conceived to fill the vacuum of a natural history museum in western India. To be ready in three years, this will be the fourth regional museum under the National Museum of Natural History, New Delhi of the Ministry of Environment and Forests. The museum will be established near the Ranthambhore Sanctuary over an area of 7.42 acres and will be dedicated to desert ecosystems. The state government has contributed land for the project while the centre is financing the building and infrastructure. The Ministry of Environment and Forests earlier established three regional natural history museums at Mysore, Karnataka (for the south zone), Bhopal, Madhya Pradesh (central zone) and Bhubaneshwar, Orissa (eastern zone) with the themes of biological diversity, introduction to ecology and biodiversity respectively. The Rajiv Gandhi Museum of Natural History will be a non-formal center for environmental education and creation of public awareness on conservation of nature and natural resources.

5195. (23-12-2007) NEW DELHI : Air Marshal B N Gokhale PVSM AVSM VM ADC, Vice Chief of the Air Staff, has flown the most powerful fighter aircraft of the Indian Air Force - the Sukhoi 30 MKI in Pune, today. The Air Mshl got commissioned in June 1968 in the fighter stream. He began his flying career on Vampire aircraft at Pune which was then one of the front line fighter aircraft. On the eve of his retirement the Air Marshal was at Pune, today. This sortie in Su 30 MKI marked the end of the most illustrious career as a fighter pilot.

5196. (23-12-2007) NEW DELHI : Today is a historic day for Indian democracy. I sincerely thank the people of Gujarat for reposing their faith, yet again, in the BJP. I also heartily congratulate the state unit of the party, and, in particular, Gujarat's dynamic and highly popular Chief Minister Shri Narendra Modi for scoring a resounding victory. State assembly elections are quite frequent in our country, but rarely does the people's verdict in a particular state become a 'Turning Point' for national politics. The BJP's spectacular victory in Gujarat today is indeed a turning point because it signals the BJP's comeback as the frontrunner in the next parliamentary elections. In my very first press conference after the May 2004 Lok Sabha elections, in which the BJP-led NDA suffered an unexpected defeat, I had said that my party would bounce back. I am confident that the BJP's victory in Gujarat, and our certain victory in Himachal Pradesh (where the results will be known on 28th December), will indeed prove that the BJP is bouncing back. In 2002, our critics attributed the BJP's victory in the state to Godhra-related incidents. It was, of course, not true. By winning a renewed mandate in 2007, my party has conclusively shown that the people of Gujarat have voted for good governance, development and a leadership that delivers. I want to emphasise here that there was not a single communal riot in Gujarat in the last five years; not a single hour of curfew in the last five years; and not a single incident of terrorism in the last five years. People belonging to all castes and religions in Gujarat have been the beneficiaries of Shri Modi's single-minded focus on good governance, development, security and fight against corruption. The Congress campaign in this election was characterized by unprecedented vilification of the BJP. In particular, it was a negative and personalized campaign against Shri Modi. In this sense, the 2007 Gujarat election reminds me of the 1971 general election in which the entire opposition came together on an anti-Indira Gandhi platform (without, of course, the vilification element). Smt. Indira Gandhi made skilful use of this negative campaign to her own advantage by saying, "The Opposition says, 'Indira Hatao'. I say 'Garibi Hatao'." This time the Congress and all the other self-styled secular parties were saying, "Modi Hatao". There is, however, a crucial difference between 1971 and 2007. Smt. Gandhi did very little to implement her 'Garibi Hatao' slogan. In contrast, Shri Modi has won not on the basis of promises made but on the basis of promises fulfilled.

5197. (24-12-2007) NEW DELHI : In exercise of the powers conferred by clause (1) of article 222 of the Constitution of India, the President, after consultation with the Chief Justice of India, is pleased to transfer Shri Justice Bilal Nazki, Judge of the Andhra Pradesh High Court as a Judge of the Bombay High Court. Justice Nazki is to assume charge of his office in the Bombay High Court.

5198. (24-12-2007) NEW DELHI : The Ministry of Tourism today launched a Training Programme under the Scheme titled 'Earn While you Learn' with the primary goal to sensitizing the youth to tourism. The scheme has been envisaged under the direction of Minister of Tourism and Culture Smt. Ambika Soni. The main objective of this programme is to inculcate appropriate tourism traits and knowledge amongst the trainees, which will enable them to act/work as student volunteers. These programmes would be of 21 days duration and the students pursuing graduation/post graduation between 18-25 years of age can apply for the same after obtaining a 'No Objection Certificate' from the concerned college/ university. These programmes would be conducted by the Indian Institute of Tourism & Travel Management, which is a premier institution and has its branches in Gwalior, New Delhi, Bhubneshwar and Goa. The first batch of 62 students have begun their training today at the Indian Institute of Tourism & Travel Management, New Delhi. The Additional Director General (Tourism) Shri Sanjay Kothari interacted with students about the scheme. Applications for this programme were invited through open advertisement in national dailies and the students have been selected through a Written Test. They are presently pursuing their studies in the University of Delhi, Guru Gobind Singh Indraprastha University, Jamia Milia Islamia, Institute of Hotel Management, etc. During the 3 week training programme, the topics which would be covered include Indian Society and Culture, Historical Monuments, Managerial and Behavioural Skills, Etiquettes, Over View of tourism scenario, public speaking/presentation, etc. The Faculty chosen to impart the training are experts in their field and represent renowned universities, institutions and organizations. The theoretical training would be supplemented with study tour to places of tourist interest. After the training programme is over, all successful candidates would undergo a counselling session, wherein representatives of tourism and travel trade industry would be given an opportunity to select these candidates for suitable jobs or assignments.

5199. (24-12-2007) NEW DELHI : Shri Jairam Ramesh, Minister of State for Commerce, Government of India inaugurated the Araku Coffee Processing Unit in Araku Valley, near Vishakapatnam, Andhra Pradesh on Dec 21, 2007. He also launched Araku Emerald, a premium branded coffee grown by small and marginal tribal farmers in the region. Araku Emerald - is Araku's and the country's only coffee grown by a Tribal Cooperative to have got both an international and a Fair Trade certification. Nearly 4000 tribal coffee growers gathered at the venue to celebrate a milestone in the history of tribal development in the valley. The coffee will be ready for export soon to compete with the best organic and Fair Trade certified coffees in the world. And to ensure the produce is processed under strict international processing standards, a central coffee processing unit too has been built which Shri Jairam Ramesh inaugurated. The production of Araku Emerald as a premium organic coffee is part of a unique tribal livelihoods programme facilitated by Naandi Foundation at Araku (presently for 8000 farmers across 8000 acres), in partnership with a host of regional, national and international partners - the ITDA, Paderu, the Coffee Board of India, and international coffee quality control, biodynamic, and organic experts. To ensure Araku Emerald - which is presently being readied for export - is processed under the best international quality standards, a centralized coffee processing plant too has been set up at the village, which was also inaugurated by the Minister. This unit will process 200 metric tonnes of coffee this season and nearly 600 metric tonnes during the next coffee harvest. The idea is to have this unit - and several others that will be set up in phases - provide quality processing of all the coffee grown in the area, in the years to come.

5200. (24-12-2007) NEW DELHI : The Union Government today gave its approval for the amendments in the Air Services Agreement (ASA) between the Government of India and the Government of the Hashemite Kingdom of Jordon signed on 16th October, 1989. During the last round of bilateral air services talks with Jordon held on 15-16th January 2007, both sides agreed to modernize the existing ASA by amending certain provisions thereof. These amendments in the existing Air Services Agreement between Government of India and the Government of Hashemite Kingdom of Jordon have the potential to spur greater trade, investment, tourism and cultural exchanges between the two countries, besides bringing in line with the developments in International Civil Aviation.

5201. (24-12-2007) BANGALORE: Bahujan Samaj Party (BSP) president and Uttar Pradesh Chief Minister Mayawati on Sunday called upon the people of the State to enable the BSP to replicate the Uttar Pradesh model of social change and development here. With the State set to go for the Legislative Assembly elections in a few months, Ms. Mayawati, who was here on a two-day visit to welcome former Minister P.G.R. Sindhia and his followers to BSP, said the party was keen on implementing similar social welfare schemes in the State if it received support from people. Addressing a large convention of party workers, she said, if voted to power at the Centre, the BSP would provide reservation in private sector not only to Dalits, backward classes and minorities but also to the economically weaker among the upper castes. "There is a need to amend the Constitution to provide such a reservation. We will amend the Constitution if we come to power at the Centre," she added. The 10 per cent reservation accorded in the private sector in Uttar Pradesh would be replicated across the country. There was also the need to extend these benefits to Dalits, who had converted to Christianity. Ms. Mayawati said the oppressed sections were losing their reservation rights in government jobs as the Congress, the BJP and other parties were on a spree of privatisation of government undertakings. The main aim of the BSP, she said, was to build a harmonious society, which would be free from caste frictions and also provide equal opportunities to all communities. But this dream could not be realised without convincing the upper castes to accept the BSP ideology, she said and asked the party workers to join hands with members of all the communities in the society. The BSP received a boost with the entry of Mr. P.G.R. Sindhia, who has served as MLA for about 35 years and as a Minister for 16 years.

5202. (24-12-2007) NEW DELHI : The Union Cabinet today gave its ex-post facto approval for signing the Agreement between the Government of India and the Government of Cyprus for cooperation on Combating International Terrorism, Organized Crimes and Illicit Drug Trafficking and also to ratify the Agreement. This Agreement would improve the effectiveness of both countries in the prevention, investigation, prosecution and suppression of crime including crime relating to terrorism and drug trafficking and to establish a framework for enhancing cooperation between the officials of intelligence and law-enforcement agencies of the Parties.

5203. (24-12-2007) NEW DELHI : At around 1115 hrs today 24 Dec 07, a single seater Sea Harrier fighter aircraft crashed at Dabolim, Goa. The aircraft was on a routine sortie flown by Cdr Janak Bevli, who ejected safely. There has been no loss of any other property or person in the accident. A Board of Inquiry has been ordered to investigate the cause.

5204. (24-12-2007) NEW DELHI : The Indian Farmers Fertilizer Cooperative (IFFCO) has signed a Memorandum of Understanding with the Senegal Government for revival of 6.6 lakh tonne capacity Phosphoric acid plant in Senegal. The Industries Chimiques de Senegal (ICS) is a joint venture company with Government of India holding 6.97 per cent, IFFCO 19.1 per cent and Government of Senegal 47 per cent of the equity. Under the MOU, IFFCO will invest 100 million dollars in the next three years for increasing the production to the optimum level of efficiency at approximately 600,000 tonne. IFFCO will also provide a loan of 10 million dollars to the company repayable on priority. Under the MOU, IFFCO will handle the existing debt of the company to ensure its repayment to the Senegalese banks and international financial organizations in 15 years and those to the trade creditors in 2 years. Restructuring of ICS will improve the availability of Phosphoric acid in the country as IFFCO will import bulk of it. It is also expected to have a sobering effect on the international price trend which has been rising for sometime. The MOU was signed by the Minister of Mines and Industry, Government of Senegal and Managing Director of IFFCO Dr. U.S.Awasthi. The MOU will be soon converted into a legal document. The ICS now running at 30 per cent capacity, exports 80 per cent of its produce to IFFCO under an earlier agreement. It has accumulated losses of nearly Rs. 1300 crore over the last few years. Loss of production of ICS has contributed to reduction in supply of Phosphoric Acid whose prices are rising steeply. The IFFCO led consortium had made an offer to inject 80 million dollars in July this year for recapitalisation of ICS but the move suffered a set back after the Senegalese government signed a deal with Gruope Roullier (RG) of France in November this year. The agreement with RG threatened the availability of Phosphoric Acid to India under the long term off take contract but would have also led to management control of ICS in the hands of the French company. Secretary, Department of Fertilisers Dr. J.S.Sarma led the Indian delegation at the detailed negotiations leading to the signing of the MOU.

5205. (24-12-2007) NEW DELHI : The total approximate earnings of Indian Railways on originating basis during the period 1st December - 10th December

2007 were Rs. 1931.02 crore compared to Rs. 1700.57 crore during the same period last year, registering an increase of 13.55 per cent. The total goods earnings have gone up from Rs. 1189.72 crore during 1st December - 10th December 2006 to Rs. 1314.38 crore during 1st December - 10th December 2007, showing an increase of 10.48 per cent. The total passenger revenue earnings during the period 1st to 10th December 2007 were Rs. 553.90 crore compared to Rs. 455.98 crore during the same period last year, reflecting an increase of 21.47 per cent. The revenue earnings from other coaching amounted to Rs. 49.15 crore during this period compared to Rs. 40.88 crore during the same period last year, showing an increase of 20.23 per cent. The total approximate number of passengers booked during the period 1st to 10th December 2007 were 186.96 million compared to 173.92 million during the same period last year, showing an increase of 7.50 per cent. In the suburban and non-suburban sectors, the number of passengers booked during 1-10 December 2007 were 107.13 million and 79.83 million compared to 100.36 million and 73.56 million during the same period last year, registering an increase of 6.75 per cent and 8.52 per cent respectively.

5206. (24-12-2007) NEW DELHI : The President of India, Smt. Pratibha Devisingh Patil today greeted fellow citizens on the auspicious occasion of Christmas, which will be celebrated tomorrow. In a message, the President said, "On the occasion of Christmas, I extend my greetings to all my fellow citizens. Christ's message of love, compassion and forgiveness is a message of universal and timeless relevance. I wish this Christmas fills our heart with joy, happiness and hope."

5207. (24-12-2007) NEW DELHI : The Vice President of India Mohd. Hamid Ansari has greeted the people of our country on the joyous occasion of Christmas. In his greetings, the Vice President said that Jesus Christ showed to mankind the path of compassion, tolerance, love and righteousness. His teachings have the power to save mankind from ignorance, turmoil and moral decay. Together, they could help realize the vision of a peaceful, compassionate and harmonious world. The Vice President said that this festival may bring peace, prosperity, and happiness in our lives.

5208. (24-12-2007) NEW DELHI : The Prime Minister, Dr. Manmohan Singh has greeted the nation on the joyous occasion of Christmas. In a message, Dr. Singh said that Christmas is an occasion to celebrate and imbibe Lord Christ's message of brotherhood, compassion and forgiveness. May the winter festival fill the hearts of people all over the world with warmth, love and goodwill towards fellow beings, the Prime Minister added.

5209. (26-12-2007) NEW DELHI : The Chief of the Air Staff Air Chief Marshal Fali H Major unveiled and installed the Platinum Jubilee Capsule at the Air Force Museum today the 26th of Dec 07. The capsule contains a historical record of major activities conducted during the Platinum Jubilee of the IAF this year such as newspaper bylines, photographs etc. and also a record of activities since the

Diamond Jubilee of the IAF in 1992. The year 2007 was a landmark year for the IAF marking the 75th anniversary of its raising. In the Platinum year, a number of events and activities were planned to commemorate the occasion. The major events included West to East Para Gliding expedition which covered a record distance of 3700 kms from Hindon to Chabua. International Air Power Seminar attended by Chiefs or their representatives from 44 countries, Presidential Fleet Review and a very daunting event, the Round the World Microlite Expedition which completed the task of circumnavigating the world in 80 days. An IAF Hockey team visited UK for exhibition matches and made a clean sweep winning all its matches. In a first of its kind a Military Music festival or Tattoo was organized in which Bands from five countries participated, besides our three Services. A highlight was the performance of the bands at India Gate, which attracted large crowds. The Platinum Jubilee Celebrations came to an end with the Platinum Jubilee Parade on 08 Oct. 07 which was a show to be proud of. In addition to the above, a number of welfare measures were introduced these included creation of new scholarships for various categories of school children, increase in the amounts of existing scholarships, and upgradation of facilities at the special wings of Air Force Schools catering to children with special needs and other welfare activities. As was done after the IAF's Golden and Diamond Jubilee Celebrations, it was decided to place a historical record of the Platinum Jubilee celebrations in a time capsule, to be opened on the centenary of the IAF in 2032. This capsule also includes the historical events of the IAF over the last 15 years since 1992 when the Diamond Jubilee capsule was sealed. The data for the Platinum Jubilee Capsule is stored in digital format as well as in printed copies. They are stored in an inner chamber of the capsule under pressurized nitrogen to prevent deterioration over time. The capsule itself is cast in stainless steel with platinum like finish. The Platinum Jubilee Capsule also includes IAF Commemorative Stamps & Coins released by Hon'ble President of India Smt Pratibha Patil and Hon'ble Prime Minister Shri Man Mohan Singh on AF Day this year alongwith the Book 'Into the Blue Yonder'.

5210. (26-12-2007) NEW DELHI : The North Eastern Region (NER) comprising of Arunachal Pradesh, Assam, Manipur, Meghalaya, Mizoram, Nagaland, Sikkim and Tripura are all special category States and the national planning and resource allocations impart a special emphasis on the economic and social development of NE States. The development plans in the North East are centrally financed on the basis of 90% grant and 10% loan. The NE states have been provided grants under the Non Lapsable Central Pool of Resources (NLCPR) to improve their infrastructure facilities. The Empowered Committee administering the NLCPR has since its inception in 1998-99, approved proposal worth Rs.816.66 crore for the development of educational infrastructure in the NER, out of which, funds amounting to Rs.655.84 crore have been released (as on 30.11.2007). During 2006-07 and 2007-08, an amount of Rs.159.99 crore and Rs.51.87 crore has been released for various educational projects.

5211. (26-12-2007) NEW DELHI : The Sub Committee for Commemoration of Ter-Centenary of Guru-ta-Gaddi of Shri Guru Granth Sahib met here today under the chairpersonship of Tourism & Culture Minister, Smt. Ambika Soni. The meeting discussed development proposals of Anandpur Sahib and Talwandi Sabo as a part of the commemoration. The Chief Minister of Punjab, Shri Prakash Singh Badal, Congress Legislative Party Leader, Punjab, Smt. Rajender Kaur Bhattal, Shri Sukhdev Libra, MP and Shri K.P.Rana, Sant Ajit Singh, MLAs attended the meeting. Secretary, Ministry of Culture, Govt. of India, Shri Abhijit Sengupta and senior officials of the Punjab State Government also attended the meeting. The Tourism & Culture Minister, Smt. Ambika Soni informed the meeting that for Commemoration of Ter-Centenary of Guru-ta-Gaddi of Shri Guru Granth Sahib, State Government of Maharashtra has prepared a developmental plan of Rs. 817 crores. The Ter-Centenary celebrations of Guru-ta-Gaddi are planned for the year 2008 in the month of October in Nanded (Maharashtra) and the event is likely to attract 25-30 lakhs pilgrims from all over the world. After discussions she said the Centre has agreed in principle to the proposals sent by the Punjab Government for the development of Anandpur Sahib and Talwandi Sabo and a Cabinet Note to get the necessary clearances from the Union Government will be moved soon. She said it was decided that out of the works proposed those relating to the development of street lights and fire fight services may be taken up by the State Government for better implementation of these two aspects of the project. The development programmes of Anandpur Sahib and Talwandi Sabo will cost the exchequer about Rs. 183 crores. Smt. Soni said the National Highway from Talwandi Sabo to Nanded is proposed to be named after Guru Gobind Singhji and this project will be developed by the Centre. The Chief Minister of Punjab, Shri Prakash Singh Badal thanked the Minister and the Centre for readily agreeing to the development projects of Anandpur Sahib and Talwandi Sabo. He said that all the Chief Ministers of the concerned States from wherein the proposed Guru Gobind Singh National Highway will pass through have welcomed the move and assured all assistance for upgradation and widening of the route.

5212. (26-12-2007) NEW DELHI : In Nandigram the CPM Cadres under open support and patronage of the State Government unleashed a series of deplorable cycle of murder, mayhem, rape and torture on innocent villagers as also the supporters of TMC and BUPC (Bhumi Uchchhed Pratirodh Committee). The so called recapture of Nandigram was executed with clinical precision by mobilizing CPM goons and cadres from outside who indulged in medieval terror by killing, raping, injuring the villagers and by burning and damaging their houses. It is very significant to note that all the Police Camps in the area were withdrawn by written orders of the S.P. of Purba Medinapur and CPM cadres were given free hands to unleash naked violence and terror with extreme depravity between 8th and 11th Nov. 2007. The media was forcibly prevented from going there. It was not without reason that the Chief Minister of West Bengal Shri Buddhadeb Bhattacharya publicly said that the trouble makers have been paid back in the same coin. He subsequently only regretted having used this expression but never disowned or, criticised his cadres in one of the worst case of State sponsored terror on poor helpless people. About 200 cases have been registered under various sections from January to November 2007. Out of these there are 11 cases of murder (7 under Nandigram P.S. and 4 under Khejuri P.S.). In the police firing on a peaceful rally 14 innocent people were killed which under investigation by C.B.I.. There are 7 cases of rape registered under Nandigram P.S.. Naturally no action much less effective action was taken by the local police in pursuit of these cases. The same situations remains now.

5213. (26-12-2007) NEW DELHI : The Law Commission of India submitted its 203rd Report on Anticipatory Bail to the Government. The Chairman of the Commission Dr. Justice AR. Lakshmanan, former Supreme Court Judge, presented a copy of the said report to the Union Minister of Law & Justice, Dr. H.R. Bhardwaj, today. Section 438 of the Code of Criminal Procedure, dealing with anticipatory bail, was amended by the Code of Criminal Procedure (Amendment) Act, 2005. The enforcement of the amended provision was kept in abeyance and expert opinion of the Law Commission sought to suggest a modified version to make the provision workable with suitable safeguards to protect the rights and liberty of the citizens. The Law Commission examined in details the scope and ambit of the existing as well as the amended section 438 of the Code of Criminal Procedure in the light of various judicial pronouncements on the subject. As regards the Proviso to sub-section (1) of Section 438, as amended, permitting arrest of the applicant by the police without warrant on the basis of the accusation apprehended in the application, the Law Commission has been of the view that the provision is more of explanatory nature and clarifies that there shall be no bar to such arrest if there are otherwise reasonable grounds to make such arrest. Referring to the Supreme Court's decisions in M.C. Abraham and another Vs State of Maharashtra, (2003) 2 SCC 649, the Commission has expressed the view that the mere fact that an anticipatory bail application is rejected is no ground for directing the applicant's immediate arrest. There may be cases where an application may be rejected and yet the applicant is not put up for trial as, after investigation no material is found against him. Power of arrest, therefore, has to be exercised with due caution and circumspection and not in any mechanical manner. The Commission has thus concluded that it is not necessary to have the Proviso inserted in Section 438(1) as the position on this aspect is already very clear. The Commission has, therefore, recommended the omission of Proviso of sub-section (1) of Section 438, as amended. As regards Section 438(1B) relating to the presence of the applicant at the time of final hearing, the Law Commission has critically examined the nitty-gritty of restraint and custody to which the applicant may be subjected to in terms of the court's order under that Section. The Law Commission has come to the conclusion that when the applicant appears in the Court in compliance with the Court's order and is subjected to the Court's directions, he may be viewed as in the Court's custody and this may render the relief of anticipatory bail infructuous. The Commission has, therefore, recommended deletion of sub-section (1B) of Section 438.

5214. (27-12-2007) NEW DELHI : Following is the statement of the Prime Minister Dr. Manmohan Singh on the death of Mrs. Benazir Bhutto. "I was deeply shocked and horrified to hear of the heinous assassination of Mrs. Benazir Bhutto. Mrs. Bhutto was no ordinary political leader, but one who left a deep imprint on her time and age. Her contributions to a previous moment of hope in India Pakistan relations, and her intent to break India Pakistan relations out of the sterile patterns of the past, were exemplary. In her death, the sub continent has lost an outstanding leader who worked for democracy and reconciliation in her country. The manner of her going is a reminder of the common dangers that our region faces from cowardly acts of terrorism and of the need to eradicate this dangerous threat. My heartfelt condolences go to her family and the people of Pakistan who have suffered a grievous blow."

5215. (27-12-2007) NEW DELHI : The Index of Six core-infrastructure industries having a combined weight of 26.7 per cent in the Index of Industrial Production (IIP) with base 1993-94 stood at 237.9 (provisional) in October 2007 and registered a growth of 4.5% (provisional) compared to a growth of 9.9 % in October 2006. During April-October 2007-08, s ix core-infrastructure industries registered a growth of 6.2% (provisional) as against 8.9% during the corresponding period of the previous year.

5216. (27-12-2007) NEW DELHI : The food sector, in 2007, saw acceleration of procurement and movement of foodgrains, which in turn ensured adequate consumption-stocks. A package was introduced to improve liquidity of sugar mills by defraying carry-over costs, offering concessional loans and export assistance to stabilize domestic sugar prices. This was primarily intended to ensure that the dues of sugarcane farmers are paid in time. Effective steps have been taken to strengthen the PDS system and infusing transparency in it. Efforts are on for sprucing up the efficiency in FCI. Enactment of Warehousing (Development and Regulation) Act was another important initiative taken in 2007 with a view to ensure that the farmers are able to keep their goods in certified warehouses and use the warehouses receipts as a negotiable instrument. With the full implementation of this Act, farmers would find it easy to take loans from commercial banks against negotiable warehouse receipts and not resort to distress sales to take care of their urgent cash needs.

5217. (27-12-2007) NEW DELHI : Chitranjan Locomotive Works (CLW) produced 115 electric locomotives against the target of 112 electric locomotives and Diesel Locomotive Works (DLW) produced 154 diesel locomotives against the target of 145 diesel locomotives during first eight months of the fiscal 2007-08 (April-November 2007). Rail Coach Factory (RCF) produced 917 coaches against the target of 911 coaches where as Integral Coach Factory (ICF) produced 788 coaches against the target of 812 coaches during the same period. Rail Wheel Factory (RWF) produced 87105 wheels and 27940 axles against the target of 82177 wheels and 27824 axles during April - November 2007. During the month of November 2007, CLW, DLW, ICF, RCF and RWF have produced 18 electric locomotives, 17 diesel locomotive, 120 coaches, 134 coaches, 13350 wheels and 5604 axles respectively against the target of 18 electric locomotives, 18 diesel locomotive, 130 coaches, 133 coaches, 10830 wheels and 5732 axels. The punctuality percentage of mail/express trains was 92.0 per cent in Broad Gauge and 99.2 per cent in Metre Gauge during the month of November 2007 compared to 91.9 per cent and 99.5 per cent respectively during the same period last year. Railways have realized an amount of Rs. 25 crore approximately during the month of November 2007 through ticket checking.

5218. (27-12-2007) NEW DELHI : The pro-active policies of the Department of Telecommunications have resulted in an unprecedented growth of the Telecom sector during 2007. The Department of Telecommunications has been able to provide state of the art world class infrastructure at globally competitive tariffs and reduce the digital divide by extending connectivity to the unconnected areas. About a quarter million handsets are being sold every day at prices which are within reach of the common man which in turn has made India one of the most sought after telecom manufacturing destinations. The Indian Telecom sector is currently witnessing a resurgent growth and has emerged as the fastest growing telecom market in the world with the addition of over 7 million subscribers per month. With current subscriber base of over 250 million and a monthly addition of about 7 million, the half a billion mark is expected by the year 2010. The growth in this sector is also contributing significantly in the economic growth of the country. As against a target of 250 million telephone connections by December 2007, 264 million telephone connections have already been installed by November 2007. The overall Teledensity is 23.21. The Group of Ministers on 'vacation of spectrum and raising resources for the purpose' has decided to constitute a Committee under the Chairmanship of National Security Advisor with Secretary (Telecom), Defence Secretary and representatives from Department of Space, Ministry of Defence and Department of Telecommunications as members to come up with a workable plan for alternate network to facilitate quick release of spectrum for mobile services without compromising the requirements of Defence and Space Services. To sustain this growth trajectory in the sector, as a major policy initiative, DoT decided to set up seven Telecom Centres of Excellence in collaboration with major Telecom Service Providers and Indian Institutes of Technology, Indian Institute of Science and Indian Institute of Management in Public Private Partnership mode in different parts of country. The main focus of these centres shall be to enhance the talent pool, creating an environment of technology innovation, securing and managing our national information infrastructure during peace/disaster and ensuring general economic upliftment through increased connectivity at an affordable price. Six Memoranda of

Understanding (MOUs) have been signed during the year. "India Telecom 2007", an exhibition-cum-conference was held during 12-15th December 2007 in New Delhi. It was inaugurated by the Prime Minister. 'India Telecom Exhibition 2007' had more than 150 Exhibitors and participation from 30 countries. The exhibitors had put on display latest technology available in the world in the telecom industry which proved to be very useful for the Indian Telecom operators and manufacturers. It also provided opportunities for transfer of technology and setting up of R & D base in collaboration with international firms in the country. The Department of Telecommunications has been actively encouraging the adoption of modern technologies. Pilot projects on the existing and emerging technologies have been undertaken including Wireless Broadband, 3G etc. Emphasis is being given to technologies having potential to improve rural connectivity.

5219. (27-12-2007) NEW DELHI : Textiles Sector has been identified as one of the priority sectors having high growth potential and higher multiplier effects for employment generation. Timely policy intervention can boost the competitiveness of this sector manifold, as the growth impetus prevailing in the sector is vibrant. Textile and Clothing industry plays a dominant role in the country's economy and has a prominent position in the textile world. It has a total market size of US $52 billion and accounts for 26% of the manufacturing sector, 20% of industrial production and 18% of industrial employment. It contributes 15% to gross export earnings and 4% to national GDP. It provides direct employment to about 35 million persons. Besides, another 50 million people are engaged in allied activities. Market size potential for the industry is envisaged at USD 115 bn by FY 2012.

5220. (27-12-2007) NEW DELHI : Led by robust domestic demand the steel sector in the country has been witnessing extraordinary growth, making India the fifth largest crude steel producer in the world as against 8th position held three years back. Production of finished carbon has increased from 35.41 million tonnes in 2002-03 to 49.58 million tonnes in 2006 -07. During the first seven months of the current year from April to October 07, production of finished carbon is estimated to be about 29.37 million tonnes and is expected to be 55.5 million tonnes in FY 08. While exports have remained fairly stable between 2002-03 until last year at around 4.5 million tonnes, imports have increased from 1.51 million tonnes in 2002-03 to 4.10 million tonnes maintaining a rising trend this year, largely to fill the demand supply gap in the domestic market. The demand for steel is expected to remain buoyant, above 10 per cent over the next five years, and in the most likely scenario the steel production capacity in the country is expected to touch 124 million tonnes by 2012. While the brownfield expansion plan over the next five years is expected to add 40.5 million tonnes capacity to the existing capacity of 56.84 million tonnes, the most likely scenario for addition to capacity by setting up of greenfield projects is expected to be 28.72 million tonnes taking the total capacity to 124.06 million tonnes. Furthermore, taking into consideration the intentions expressed by various steel investors including multinationals, domestic steel majors and FDIs, the likely capacity achievable by 2019-20 will be around 275 million tonnes. The Public Sector Undertakings, Steel Authority of India Limited (SAIL) and Rashtriya Ispat Nigam Limited (RINL), are in the midst of ambitious expansion plans. The expansion plan would increase the capacity of SAIL from 14.6 million tonnes of hot metal to 26 million tonnes by 2010 at an estimated cost of around Rs. 53,000 crore. SAIL is also planning to expand its capacity further to 60 million tonnes per annum by 2020. In case of RINL, the expansion would increase its capacity from the present level of 3 million tonnes of hot metal to 6.3 million tonnes by 2009-10 at an estimated cost of around Rs.9,000 crore. RINL also plans to enhance capacity to 16 million tonnes per annum by 2020. An MOU was signed between SAIL, RINL and NMDC this year for setting up a 4 million tonnes steel plant in Chhattisgarh. MECON has been appointed as consultant to prepare the site selection and economic feasibility report by April 2008. In a major move for implementing the project a tripartite MOU was signed between the Railway Ministry, Chhatisgarh Government and SAIL and NMDC for laying a 235 kilometer railway link between Dalli- Rajhara and Rowghat and further to Jagdalpur.

5221. (27-12-2007) NEW DELHI : The President of India, Smt. Pratibha Devisingh Patil, has expressed her deep shock and grief on hearing the tragic news of assassination of Mrs. Benazir Bhutto. The President has further said, "it is a tragedy for the people of Pakistan to lose a leader of her stature in her prime. This tragedy underscores the menace that terrorism poses to us and to the stability of our societies. The assassination of Mrs. Benazir Bhutto is a tragedy not just for Pakistan but for our entire region. We stand with the people of Pakistan in this hour of grief and tragedy".

5222. (27-12-2007) NEW DELHI : The Prime Minister of India said here that I am filled with a deep sense of disbelief, shock and grief at the news of the assassination of Mrs. Benazir Bhutto, the former Prime Minister of Pakistan and president of the Pakistan People's Party, in Rawalpindi a short while ago. Mrs. Bhutto has become a martyr to the cause of defence of democracy and the global war on jehadi terrorism. I strongly condemn this terrorist attack. On behalf of my party, my family and on my own behalf, I send my heartfelt condolences to her husband, Mr. Asif Zardari and their four children. She was a friend of our family and she sincerely desired friendly and peaceful relations between India and Pakistan. I spoke to Mr. Zardari telephonically at Dubai airport before he emplaned for Pakistan. The fact that she fell to the bullet of the assassins in the midst of national elections in Pakistan should leave no one in doubt that Pakistan is not only in the throes of instability but a far more dangerous process of Talibanistion. The enormously sinister implications of this development for India, in our own fight against jehadi terrorism, cannot be overstated. I spoke to Prime Minister Dr. Manmohan Singh, who is in Goa, and expressed my apprehensions on this score. I suggested to him that he should immediately convene a meeting to brief leaders of opposition parties about the deeply worrisome developments in Pakistan and also Nepal. I thanked him for accepting the suggestion. I had first met Benazir Bhutto seventeen years back when she had come to Delhi to participate in Rajiv Gandhi's funeral. Since then, whenever she has come to India, she had invariably met me and discussed with me Indo-Pak relations and the problem of terrorism. The last time I spoke to Mrs. Benazir Bhutto was on 19th October, the day of her arrival in Pakistan, after many years of exile abroad, to resume her battle for her country's democratization. Religious extremists had made their intention known on that day itself, since her courageous return to Pakistan coincided with a terrorist attack in which more than 125 persons were killed. In my telephonic conversation, I said to her: "I am gratified that you have escaped this bid on your life. The people of India are with you in your struggle against both military rule and terrorism." Thanking me for my words of solidarity, she had said: "Advani sahab, I was not in Pakistan when you came here in 2005. Now that I am back, I would like you to come again as our guest." Alas, she is now no more.

5223. (28-12-2007) NEW DELHI : Section 80C of the Income-tax Act provides for a deduction of up to Rs. One lakh to an individual or a Hindu undivided family (HUF) for:- (i) making investments in certain savings instruments; or (ii) incurring expenditure on tuition fee and repayment of housing loan. With a view to encourage small savings, the Government has taken a policy decision to include the investments made in the following two deposit instruments within the ambit of Section 80C:- (i) Five Year Post Office Time Deposit Account; and (ii) Senior Citizens Savings Scheme. Therefore, the investment by an individual or a Hindu undivided family (HUF) in these two instruments during the previous year 2007-08 (relevant to assessment year 2008-09), and subsequent years, shall be eligible for deduction under section 80C of the Income-tax Act, subject to the overall ceiling of Rs. One lakh in that section. It is further clarified that investments made on or after 1.4.2007 (*i.e.* from the beginning of the financial year 2007-08) shall be eligible for this deduction. Drawing and Disbursing Officers (DDOs) may take such investments into consideration while determining the TDS liability of an employee for the previous year 2007-08 (relevant to assessment year 2008-09) and subsequent years.

5224. (28-12-2007) NEW DELHI : As on 31.10.2007, there are about 6.12 crore rural telephones working with rural teledensity of 7.61. This was stated by Shri A. Raja, Minister of Communications and Information Technology at a Consultative Committee attached to his Ministry here today. Shri Raja said that the target of one phone per three rural households in 2007 has already been achieved and hopeful of achieving one phone per two rural households much earlier than targeted date of 2010. Government has decided to introduce a scheme for supporting shared infrastructure to take mobile telephony into the rural areas. An Act has been passed on 29.12.2006 as the Indian Telegraph (Amendment) Act 2006 to amend the Indian Telegraph Act, 1885 in order to enable support for mobile services, broadband connectivity and general infrastructure in rural and remote areas of the country, Shri Raja said. A scheme has recently been launched by USO Fund to erect 7871 number of towers in 500 districts spread over 27 States for providing mobile services in the rural and remote areas, where there is no mobile coverage. Out of these, 1227 towers *i.e.* about 16% of the total are being set up in the border districts while 1912 towers comprising about 24% of the total are being set up in districts having ST population more than 25% members were informed. About 27 Crore population residing in 2,00,000 villages shall be covered under the Scheme. The towers shall be shared by three service providers for provision of mobile services. The first two towers have already been set up in Kangra district of Himachal Pradesh by M/s Reliance Communications. The work for the installation of the other towers is underway. The mobile services in other areas shall be provided in near future and all towers are targeted to be made operational in a phased manner by May 2008. Under this scheme, 24 million rural capacity shall be created. It is proposed to cover the other uncovered areas in the country through mobile services for which about 11,000 additional towers are being identified. These towers will be installed in the second phase of the scheme which is likely to be launched shortly. An estimated 2,40,000 villages with population of about 27 Crore shall be provided mobile services through this scheme. Thereafter, the coverage will be reviewed and uncovered areas, if any, will also be tackled.

5225. (28-12-2007) NEW DELHI : As per data compiled by Agriculture Ministry as on today, sowing is progressing well in the present rabi season. Wheat has been sown in 249.34 lakh ha as compared to 263.31 lakh ha at the end of last year. So far, 4.01 lakh ha area has come under winter rice as against 2.58 lakh ha last year. Coarse cereals have been sown in 64.57 lakh ha as compared to 62.96 lakh ha by this time in 2006. Rabi oilseeds have been sown in 81.94 lakh ha as compared to 90.43 lakh ha in the last rabi. Mustard/rapeseed coverage has reached 59.55. lakh ha (last rabi, up to this time: 65.36 lakh ha). Rabi pulses cover 121.32 lakh ha (last year: 124.32 lakh ha). Gram coverage has reached 75.12 lakh ha (vs. 76.52 lakh ha by this time last year).

5226. (28-12-2007) NEW DELHI : The Prime Minister, Dr. Manmohan Singh visited the Pakistan High Commission to pay his respects to the former Pakistan Prime Minister Benazir Bhutto here today. The Prime Minister conveyed his condolences with a message in the condolence register as below. "It was with the deepest sense of horror and sorrow that I have learnt of the tragic demise of Madam Benazir Bhutto. In her sad and untimely demise, Pakistan and South Asia have lost an outstanding political leader, who was passionately committed to the cause of moderation, democracy and peace and friendship between our two countries. I convey my heartfelt condolences to the members of the bereaved family and the people of Pakistan."

5227. (28-12-2007) NEW DELHI : The President is pleased to appoint Shri D.K. Sarraf to the post of Director (Finance), Oil & Natural Gas Corporation Limited, in Schedule 'B' scale of pay of Rs. 25750-650-30950/-, for a period of five years, with effect from the date of assumption of charge of the post or till the date of his superannuation, or until further orders, whichever event occurs the earliest.

5228. (28-12-2007) NEW DELHI : The Red Ribbon Express, flagged off on December 1, 2007 from Delhi by Ms. Sonia Gandhi, the UPA Chairperson, has chugged through 16 stations crisscrossing Rajasthan, Madhya Pradesh and Maharashtra "This exhibition has been an eye-opener for me, as I knew very little about HIV. Now that I have learnt about it I realize that each one of us must protect ourselves. In my village most people don't know enough, and I will go back and tell them more about HIV," Ram Hari, a coolie from Sawai Madhopur district of Rajasthan, commented. This was a reaction that many people, who visited the exhibition coaches of the Red Ribbon Express, shared with him. The project, which was an idea mooted by Rajiv Gandhi Foundation, is being implemented by National AIDS Control Organisation, in partnership with NYKS, the Ministry of Railways and UNICEF The eight-coach train is a mobile exhibition on HIV/AIDS with a sleek multi-media presentation on all its aspects and Counseling and Training facilities on board. The number of visitors to the exhibition has crossed 75000 and more than 9000, including 2000 women, have benefited from the professional counseling provided on the train. With 102 training sessions having been conducted for a cross-section of citizens keen to get clarity on the issue, the training programme has succeeded in reaching out to over 5400 participants. Government officials, elected representatives from Panchayats, community leaders, educationists, health workers, NGOs and youth groups have attended the training sessions. The cycle troupes travelling on board have performed in over 600 villages disseminating information on HIV/AIDS and adopting healthy life styles by mobilizing about 1.75 lakh people. In addition, an educational bus, which is part of the Project, has covered over 75 block headquarters and villages en-route, reaching out to 35000 people. Exhibition on HIV/AIDS, performances by Song and Drama troupes, condom demonstrations and opening of new condom outlets are the major activities undertaken along the bus route. All this is being supported by additional local level HIV awareness programmes being conducted by the State AIDS Control Societies. The train entered Chhattisgarh today and will stop at Durg and Bilaspur in the State before reaching Katni in Madhya Pradesh in the New Year.

5229. (28-12-2007) NEW DELHI : A 'Commemorative Postage Stamp on Water Year 2007' was released by Thiru A. Raja, the Union Minister of Communications and Information Technology at a function here today. Prof. Saifuddin Soz, the Union Minister for Water Resources presided over the function. With a denomination of Rs. 5.00, this first-ever stamp released for the M/o Water Resources will contribute to the cause of effective water management. Addressing on the occasion, Prof. Saifuddin Soz, said that the Water Resources Ministry was trying its best, with cooperation of various agencies and State Governments to ensure that this scarce natural resource was not only conserved but also reached to all those who need it. He said that the Ministry has been implementing a number of schemes relating to conservation and management of water resources and have initiated steps for communicating directly with masses on the importance of conservation of water. The declaration of Year - 2007 as Water Year, he said, was a step in this direction. He informed that during the year the Ministry took a number of mass awareness initiatives including organization of a National Congress on Ground Water, institution of Annual Award for outstanding Village Community working on Panni Panchayat, training one woman and one man as water master in each Panchayat covering five thousand villages, campaign on conservation of water through radio and television, participation in events like India International Trade Fair (IITF) etc. He expressed his concern that over exploitation of ground water resources has also led to lowering of the ground water level in some pockets. In this connection, the Ministry has circulated a Model Bill to the State Governments for enacting legislation for conservation and recharge of ground water. He said that with judicious use and effective management of water resources, we can overcome the vagaries of nature to a great extent. The participation of the general masses is an essential element of any programme for ensuring judicious use of water. He expressed the hope that the present postage stamp will be used by the general public and will also serve in making them realize the need of proper use of water. Thiru A. Raja in his address said that all great civilizations in the world first developed in river valleys. The history of our country begins with the mention of the Indus Valley Civilization. Our agriculture, trade, customs, traditions, music even religion all grew around rivers and imparted our country a unique multi-dimensional identity. The rain bearing clouds, our lakes and ponds not only inspired poetry and romance but also sustained the livelihood of the people. He expressed his concern that the water conflicts are growing between cities and farmers, between industry and villages, between the farmers and the environment. Such a scenario has created a need for a multi-institutional approach for creating a water balance in the country. He hoped that wherever this stamp goes it carries the message of conserving, harvesting and harmonizing the use of water. Smt. Gauri Chatterjee, Secretary, Ministry of Water Resources in her welcome address informed that a series of events and activities were organized nationwide to celebrate the Water Year - 2007. She said that this stamp will create awareness among masses for the proper use of water resources. Shri S.Manoharan, Addl. Secretary, Ministry of Water Resources proposed the vote of thanks and said that the water resource management system requires immediate attention.

5230. (28-12-2007) NEW DELHI : The Department of Posts tries to bring out special stamps on important occasions, including festivals and seasons. The new year starting on 1st January has now become a big festival in which the people are in tradition of giving their greetings to friends and family members across the globe. Keeping this in mind, the Department of Posts has been bringing Stamps on Greeting every year since the past few years. This year too the Department has brought out five new stamps on greetings, one of which is having inscription "Happy New Year" in English and Hindi. The colourful stamps on Seasons Greetings and Happy New Year represent different elements of nature and their synchronic interplay that sustains life on earth. Apart from this five maxim cards have also been released on this occasion. Delhi Circle has made special arrangements for sale of these stamps and other material through Sansad Marg HO, other Philatelic Counters, important Post Offices. Apart from this, arrangements have also been made for collection and handling of Greeting Cards on this occasion at all the important Post Offices including GPO and Head Post Offices.

5231. (28-12-2007) NEW DELHI : The meeting of the Parliamentary Consultative Committee attached to the Ministry of Youth Affairs and Sports, Panchayati Raj and Development of North Eastern Region was held in New Delhi on 27th of December 2007. It was chaired by Mr. Mani Shankar Aiyar, the Minister for Youth Affairs and Sports, Panchayati Raj and Development of North Eastern Region. A presentation was made on the Comprehensive Sports Policy - 2007(Draft) highlighting the three broad objectives. Sports for All, Excellence in Sports and Contingent Constitutional, Legal and Institutional measures to operationalize the Policy. The presentation laid a special emphasis on the Panchayat Khel and Yuva Krida Abhiyan. The Members cutting across the party lines appreciated the Sports Policy Draft and said that proper financial resources were required to put the Policy into action. They said that strong initiatives need to be taken at the village and panchayat level and primary schools have to be involved in a big way. The Members also emphasized that enough sports opportunities should be given to the youth of the country so that they can consider sports as a career and feel secure there. The Members felt that Panchayat Khel and Yuva Krida Abhiyan is a great initiative and the responsibility for the same should be entrusted with the panchayats. The Members were unanimous in endorsing that sports training should start very early in a child's life.They also said that women should be given special support to choose sports as a career. The Members felt that better budget allocation is required for proper development of sports. Speaking at the meeting the Chairman Shri Mani Shankar Aiyar, Minister for Youth Affairs, Sports, Panchayati Raj and DONER said that the Policy has been made after careful study and the effort would be made to get approval of Parliament and Cabinet for the same. He said that the sports authorities of Cuba and India would have a seminar in the coming year. The purpose of this seminar will be to learn from the Cuba experience in sports. Shri Aiyar said that the original draft of the policy has been modified after holding discussions with various stakeholders like Sports secretaries, eminent sports persons, the general public and sports federations .He said that the Policy would be taken to Cabinet for approval in January 2008. All the Members present expressed their support for the Policy in Parliament. The Members who attended the meeting are: S/Shri Somabhai G. Koli Patel, Ganesh Singh, Kiren Rijiju, D. Venugopal and Moti Lal Vohra. Apart from these, the Sports Secretary Mr. S.K. Arora and other senior officials of the Ministry were also present.

5232. (28-12-2007) NEW DELHI : A commemorative Postage Stamp was released by Shri A. Raja, Minister of Communications and Information Technology on Water Year 2007 here today. In his address the Minister said that while traditional technologies such as Rain Water Harvesting and tanks can play an important local role, a major initiative is needed by the Government and also by the users to bring abstraction from ground water in line with recharge. Global experience shows that a time has come to rationalize the demand to match sustainable supply. This difficult and essential task will require a partnership between the Government and the users, he added. Prof. Saifuddin Soz, the Union Minister of Water Resources in his address emphasized the need for farmers to be made more conscious about the use of water. They have to be told that how to harness the water and then how to use it, he said. Secretaries of the Departments of Posts and Water Resources were present at the function.

5233. (28-12-2007) NEW DELHI : The Union Minister of Culture Smt. Ambika Soni has said that her Ministry will discuss the possibility of organizing a Hindi Sammelan on 10th January, 2009 on the occasion of World Hindi Divas with the Human Resource Development Ministry and External Affairs Ministry. Addressing the meeting of Hindi Salahakar Samiti attached to the Culture Ministry she said Hindi language has a special place in Indian culture and hence Culture Ministry shares more responsibility for its development and promotion. She said through its library network, the Ministry is not only promoting Hindi but regional and other vernacular languages as well. She said for the promotion of Hindi it is necessary that one must use simple and easy words and try to communicate as much as possible in commonly spoken words. Remembering the contribution of Hindi writer late Sh. Kamleshwar in Indian literature, who was a member of the Committee, Smt. Soni said his contribution in Hindi literature and journalism is noteworthy. She assured the Members of the Committee that her Ministry will further promote Hindi language in official work and sufficient training will be provided to the Ministry officials in this regard. The Minister released a special issue of 'Sanskriti' and Hindi glossary for the officials of the Ministry on the occasion. Members of the Committee stressed the need of promotion of Hindi Language in the North Eastern States and wanted filling up of official language vacancies in the Ministry. Some members were of the view that encouragement should be given to women writers so that society gets awakened against the evils like female foeticide. Those who attended the meeting included Sh. H. S. Malik, Sh. K. Chaliha, Sh. R. Kusmaria all MPs, Dr. Ratnakar Pandey, Dr. Parmanand Panchal, Dr. Keshav Phalke, Dr. Rajyalaxmi Shivhare and Union Culture Secretary Dr. Abhijit Sengupta.

5234. (28-12-2007) NEW DELHI : The successful launch of Interceptor Missile (AAD) towards developing a ballistic missile defence system, test flight of Agni-III (A3-02), user trial of Akash Missile by Army and Air Force, Handing over of first batch of land version of BrahMos missile systems to Army and successful conduct of 4th Military World Games were some of the significant events in the

Ministry of Defence during the current year. The issue of Request for Proposal (RFP) for the purchase of 126 Medium Multi-Role Combat Aircraft for Indian Air Force, the arrival of first batch of two Hawk Advanced Jet Trainers from UK, Signing of the Agreement with Russia on the Joint Development of 5th Generation Fighter Aircraft, First meeting of Indo-German High Defence Committee, Meeting of the Indo-French High Committee Meeting and approval of Parliament to the Armed Forces Tribunal Bill were some other major events during the year.

5235. (28-12-2007) NEW DELHI : The Vice President of India Mohd. Hamid Ansari has deeply condoled the sad demise of the famous sculptour, Shri Amarnath Sehgal. Shri Sehgal passed away here yesterday at the age of eighty five.

5236. (28-12-2007) NEW DELHI : The resounding victory of the Bharatiya Janata Party in the elections to the Vidhan Sabha of Himachal Pradesh, coming in the wake of our major triumph in Gujarat a few days ago, shows that 2007 is ending with unmistakable statement about the coming change in the political equation in the country. 2008 will be a PARIVARTAN VARSH (Year of Change) in India. I heartily congratulate the people of Himachal Pradesh for giving a clear mandate to the BJP, under the leadership of Prof. Premkumar Dhumal. The BJP's vote share has been the highest ever in the state. If the BJP's victory in Gujarat was on account of a strong pro-incumbency vote. In Himachal Pradesh, it was because of a strong anti-incumbency vote. In both states, the vote was against the Congress. Of the six assembly elections held in 2007, the BJP won in four states - Punjab, Uttarakhand, Gujarat and Himachal Pradesh. In three of these states, the BJP wrested power from the Congress. Congress had to be satisfied with victory in only one state — Goa. In a few months from now, Karnataka will elect a new legislative assembly. Everybody is aware of how the BJP, which had emerged as the single largest party in 2004, became a victim of betrayal of a venal of political opportunism. I have no doubt that my party will secure a majority on its own whenever the assembly elections are held in Karnataka. The results of Gujarat and Himachal Pradesh should be seen in the context of the rapidly growing unpopularity of the UPA government at the Centre, which has failed on all fronts. The people of India are eagerly looking for liberation from this non-performing government, which is not a coalition but a bundle of contradictions. Soon after the BJP's victory in Gujarat was known, I had stated: "This signals beginning of the BJP's comeback trail." Today's results from Himachal Pradesh have shown that the trail has progressed further. It will reach its ultimate destination whenever the next parliamentary elections are held.

5237. (28-12-2007) NEW DELHI : Tribal welfare and development remained in focus during the year. A number of new initiatives were taken to bring the tribals into mainstream of development by allocating more funds to existing schemes and launching new schemes. These include launching of new scholarship scheme for the higher studies and coaching for the tribal students, more funds for development of tribal villages and Ashram schools and framing of rules to pave the way for legal rights of land to the tribals and forest dwellers. 100% utilization of funds for tribal welfare - As a result of constant monitoring and high priority to the tribal development projects, the Ministry of Tribal Affairs could utilize almost 100% of allocated budget for various programmes. A sum of Rs. 1648.14 crore was utilized till March 2007 against the revised budget allocations of Rs. 1652.68 crore. The Ministry held further review of programmes and schemes in State Ministers meeting in February. A mechanism to monitor implementation of the scheme and utilization of funds for tribal projects at the State level also was finalized in the meeting. The Ministry also had the meeting with CII and other organizations to identify areas in which their expertise could be utilized for improving the delivery of the schemes and programmes being implemented for the tribal peoples. Enactment of Forest Rights Bill: After the enactment of Scheduled Tribes and other traditional forest dwellers Act 2006, to provide legal rights of the land to the tribal and other forest dwellers, the Ministry took up framing of rules for the implementation of the provisions of the Act. A technical support group consisted of reputed experts constituted in March this year held its meetings in Hyderabad, Pune, Ranchi, Shillong and New Delhi to know the views of States and the other concern. After these meetings, draft rules were notified on 19th June inviting comments from all concerns. Very soon the Act will come into the force and rules will be notified to undo the historical injustice done to the tribals by depriving them of their rights. Infrastructure development in tribal areas - The Ministry provided 100% grant-in-aid to the State Governments to support specific schemes being run for the tribal population below the poverty line. Almost 70% of these funds were provided to Self Help Group (SHGs) for community-based employment and income generation in sectors such as agriculture, horticulture, watershed development, animal husbandry and other infrastructure. The Ministry started an exercise to review and modify long-term plans for Primitive Tribal Groups (PTGs) in 17 States. A multi-disciplinary clearance committee's meeting was held on 2nd August for this purpose. The committee decided to prepare conservation-cum-development plans for all the States having PTG population and for Andaman and Nicobar islands. A new scholarship scheme for ST students - The Ministry launched a new Central Sector Scholarship Scheme for higher education, providing upto Rs. 2 lakh, per annum to ST students as tuition fee besides reimbursement of other expenses. Launched in June this year, the scheme will enable meritorious ST students to pursue degree level courses in identified 127 institutes in the area of management, medicine, engineering etc. The student, who falls within the inter-se seniority list of top five meritorious ST students in the institutes, shall be eligible for scholarship covering full tuition fee and other dues up to the ceiling of Rs. 2.00 lakh per annum and Rs. 3.72 lakh per annum in the case of commercial pilot training.

5238. (28-12-2007) NEW DELHI : The Prime Minister Dr. Manmohan Singh attended the convocation of the Goa University. Speaking at the occasion the

Prime Minister asserted that 11th Five Year Plan is India's "Education Plan". The challenge before us is to ensure that every one of our citizens is empowered by access to education and skill building in their chosen fields of activity, the Dr. Singh added.

5239. (29-12-2007) NEW DELHI : In a major new initiative, the Union Government has launched the National Food Security Mission (NFSM). The Mission aims at increasing the production of rice by 10 million tonnes (MT), of wheat by 8 MT, and of pulses by 2 MT during the 11th Five Year Plan with an envisaged outlay of Rs. 4,882.48 crore. NFSM - Rice will be implemented in 133 districts of 12 States, NFSM - Wheat in 138 districts of 9 States, and NFSM - Pulses in 168 districts of 14 States. An amount of Rs. 200 crore has been released to the 14 States so far. Another major intervention in the agriculture sector is the introduction of the Rashtriya Krishi Vikas Yojana (RKVY) envisaging an outlay of Rs. 25,000 crore over the 11th Five Year Plan. This scheme for Additional Central Assistance to the States is designed to boost public investment in a whole range of activities relating to agriculture and allied sectors based on agro-climatic District Agriculture Plans. The approved outlay during 2007-08 is Rs. 1,500 crore. The scheme has elicited good response from the States and the State Level Sanctioning Committees have approved projects worth more than Rs. 700 crore for implementation in 10 States so far. Both the NFSM and the RKVY have been launched in pursuance of the resolution made in the 53rd meeting of the National Development Council on Agriculture and Related Issues held on 29th May, 2007. Based on the recommendations of the National Commission on Farmers, the Government recently approved the "National Policy for Farmers 2007", which was laid on the tables of both Houses of Parliament in November, 2007. The aim of the Policy is to improve the net income of farm families, not only to meet their consumption requirements but also to enhance their capacity to invest in farm related activities. The policy brings out a new definition of 'farmer' covering the gambit of agriculture and allied sectors so that the benefits of the policy are extended to all of them uniformly. The policy provides for asset reforms to empower the farmers in respect of land, water, livestock, fisheries and bio-resources; support services like agricultural bio-security, agro-meteorology; inputs and services; credit and insurance; cooperatives; extension; training and knowledge connectivity; social security; agricultural prices; marketing and trade and curriculum reforms. The policy provides for harnessing science & technology for giving a boost to agriculture and integration with Processing and Value Chain. Credit flow to the agriculture sector recorded a 21.17% increase from 1,67,775 crore in 2005-06 to Rs. 2,03,296 crore in 2006-07. Till October, 2007 credit of Rs. 1,20,062 crore has been made available to farmers. A package for the revival of the short-term Rural Cooperative Credit Structure involving a financial assistance of Rs. 13,596 crore has been approved and Rs. 663.98 crore has been released. A weather based crop insurance scheme (WBCIS) on a pilot basis has been implemented for the Kharif 2007 season in Karnataka. For Rabi 2007-08, a pilot WBCIS is being implemented in selected areas of 12 States. An amount of Rs. 634.37 crore had been released towards insurance in 2006-07 and Rs. 500 crore has been released till date. Under the rehabilitation package of Rs. 16,978.60 crore for 31 suicide prone districts of the four States of Andhra Pradesh, Maharashtra, Karnataka and Kerala, Rs. 9,297.76 crore has been released upto November, 2007. Agricultural Extension has been strengthened and Agricultural Technology Management Agencies (ATMAs) have been set up in 544 districts. By the end of 2007-08 all the rural districts of the country will be covered under the scheme. The programme has been strengthened by promoting Farm Schools and integrating progressive farmers.

5240. (30-12-2007) NEW DELHI : A group of Christian community leaders led by Archbishop Rev. Vincent M. Conscessao called on the Prime Minister, Dr. Manmohan Singh this evening in connection with the recent incidents in Orissa. The Prime Minister expressed his deep concern at the recent incidents and assured them of necessary action in restoring communal peace and harmony in the affected areas. Central paramilitary forces have been sent to the State and the Prime Minister today reviewed the situation while speaking to the Chief Minister of Orissa in the morning. The Prime Minister assured the delegation that any attempts to disturb communal peace and the secular fabric of the country would be sternly dealt with. He said that the Government would take steps to provide full security and protect the religious freedoms guaranteed by the Constitution to all citizens. The Prime Minister assured the delegation that steps would be taken to offer appropriate compensation for damage to property. He also said that a Union minister will visit the State in this regard.

5241. (30-12-2007) NEW DELHI : The Ministry of Railways has decided to run Samjhota Express train as scheduled. Earlier, on Friday (28.12.07) the Ministry of Railways had decided to cancel Samjhota Express and Thar Express trains due to security considerations.

5242. (31-12-2007) NEW DELHI : Congress spokesman Shri Abhishek Singhvi said on the Rama Sethu Project that the Sangh Parivar held a public rally at Delhi on 30.12.2007. It is an irony that the same NDA led by BJP decided to resolve on the present alignment of Rama Sethu Project. The chronological events starting from January 1999 to 2004 are present herein as the BJP had not even mentioned the name of Rama Sethu but just passed on the orders mentioned Adam's Bridge. BJP or the Sangh Parivar which was in deep slumber till UPA Government came to power, reflects the ulterior motive of BJP to remember Lord Rama only when the elections come. The sole objective is to communalize and politicalise the issue and not to preserve the great legacy or heritage or Ram Bhagwan The Project has its origin as early as in 1860 when it was conceived by Commander Taylor of the Indian Marines and thereafter various committees and consultants have examined this issue including a Parliamentary committee of British government in 1862, a survey by the South Indian Rail Company in 1903 the Mudaliyar committee

Report in 1956 and Palavam Transport Consultancy Service Report of 1996. Thereafter, on the basis of inter-ministerial consultation, the National Environmental Engineering Research Institute (NEERI) was asked to prepare an environmental impact assessment (EIA) of the project. After detailed discussions and various rounds of consultation in Government particularly with the Ministry of Environment and Forest and in the light of the fact that the Gulf of Mannar was declared as a Marine National Park in 1986, it was decided to select an alignment (alignment 6) that was at least 20 kms away from the Gulf of Mannar National Park. The decision on alignment was taken in October 2002 during the NDA regime. An application for environmental clearance was made on June 9, 2004. 14 public hearings in 6 districts were held as part of the public consultation process during October 2003 when Dr. Jayalalita was the Chief Minister of Tamil Nadu. No reference to Ram Sethu was made during the process. To summarise, the Project is the culmination of a century old vision which was taken up after protracted and detailed considerations of various alternatives alignments and after careful considerations of economic, ecological, technical and social factors. It is alleged that the Project which will destroy the important element of India's cultural heritage and is the brain child of the UPA government. In fact the project has been pursued by NDA government. In January 1999, Shri George Fernandes, Defence Minister announced that Project will be completed in 3 years. Shri Arun Jaitley, the then Minister (Surface Transport) approved a proposal on 9.3.2001 for techno-economic feasibility studies by NEERI on Sethusamudram Project. Budget 2000-01, the then Finance Minister allocated Rs.4.8 crores for Project preparation. On 29th October 2001, the then Prime Minister, Shri Atal Bihari Vajpayee announced the Project. In a presentation made by the NEERI to the then Minister of Shipping, Shri V.P. Goel, in Tuticorin on 17th June 2002, NEERI made it clear that it would suggest an alignment through Adam's Bridge between Dhanushkodi and the Indo-Srilankan maritime Boundary. A tentative alignment in a pictorial form was also presented. The report of NEERI on 'Environmental Impact Assessment Study' entitled as "Analysis of Alternatives" in Chapter 6.2 recommended "Thus, from all considerations including environmental and ecological, it is proposed that the canal should originate from the Tuticorin New Harbour in the Gulf of Mannar, extend towards east and further northeast up to south of Pamban Island, then cut through the Adam's Bridge, thereafter proceed parallel to the International Medial Line before finally joining the Bay of Bengal Channel. Dr. Jayalalitha, then Chief Minister of Tamil Nadu also wrote to the then Prime Minister, Shri A.B. Vajpayee to expedite the project.

5243. (31-12-2007) NEW DELHI : Lieutenant General Bharat Singh Sisodia, has taken over to day as Director General Ordnance Services at the Army HQ. He was commissioned in the Army Ordnance Corps on December 20, 1970. The General Officer has had an illustrious career spanning nearly four decades. Besides various other courses he has also attended the Long Defence Management Course at College of Defence Management, Secunderabad and the National Defence

Course at National Defence College, Delhi. He has been the Colonel, Military Secretary at Army Headquarters. As a Brigadier, he commanded Central Ordnance Depot, Delhi Cantt and has also been the Brigadier Administration at Army War College, Mhow. For his outstanding contribution he was awarded the "Vishisht Seva Medal" while serving at Army War College, Mhow. As a Major General he has also held the prestigious appointments of Additional Director General Ordnance Services (Technical Stores) and Major General Army Ordnance Corps at Headquarters Western Command before he took over the appointment of Commandant, College of Materials Management, Jabalpur. The General Officer has been a keen sportsman. He has represented the North Zone in Duleep Trophy and has also been a member of the Services Cricket Team in North Zone, Ranji Trophy. He was also the Manager and Coach of the Services Cricket Team from 1985 to 87. He replaces Lt Gen DDS Sandhu, who retired on Monday.

5244. (31-12-2007) NEW DELHI : Shri K. D. Singh today assumed office as Secretary Legal Department in the Ministry of Law & Justice. He succeeds Shri K. N. Chaturvedi who retired on superannuation. Shri K. D. Singh was working as Addl. Secretary in the Department of Legal Affairs, before being elevated to the present post. Born in August 1948, Shri Singh holds a Post Graduate Degree in Law. He served as Assistant Professor of Law in Udaipur University before joining Government of India. During his tenure in the Government, he held several important positions like Member, Central Electricity Authority, Member, Central Coal Tribunal, Member Core Group of Ministry of HRD on World Intellectual Property Organisation (WIPO) and Database for WIPO Treaty.

5245. (31-12-2007) NEW DELHI : The Parliamentary Standing Committee has invited suggestions/views/comments on "Working of Union Public Service Commission" from the general public/organisations/institutions interested in the subject matter. The Department related Committee on Personnel, Public Grievances, Law and Justice, headed by Dr. E. M. Sudarsana Natchiappan, M.P. Rajya Sabha, has decided to take up the "Working of Union Public Service Commission" for detailed examination and report. Those desirous of submitting their memoranda to the Committee may send two copies of their written memoranda (either in English or Hindi) on the above subject to Shri K. P. Singh, Joint Director, Rajya Sabha Secretariat, 212-A, Second Floor, Parliament House Annexe, New Delhi-110001 (Tel: 23034292, Fax: 23016784, E-mail: kpsingh@sansad.nic.in within fifteen days of publication of this advertisement. The memoranda submitted to the Committee would form part of the records of the Committee and would be treated as confidential and would not be circulated to anyone, as such an act would constitute a breach of privilege of the Committee.

5246. (31-12-2007) NEW DELHI : The core or critical tiger habitats as required under section 38-V of the Wild Life (Protection) Act, 1972 have been identified and notified by the states. Out of the 17 states with tiger reserves, eleven states-AP, Arunachal Pradesh, Assam, Karnataka, MP, Maharashtra, Mizoram, Rajasthan,

Tamil Nadu, Uttarakhand, and West Bengal have notified the core tiger habitats. Four tiger states Bihar, Chhattisgarh, Kerala and UP have taken a decision to notify the core tiger habitats. Only two states Jharkhand and Orissa are yet to finalize notification. The notification covers an area of around 31940 sq kms of tiger reserves to support a viable population of wild tigers in the country. These are to be established as per provisions of the Wild Life (Protection) Act.

5247. (31-12-2007) NEW DELHI : The Ministry of Information & Broadcasting is to produce a film on the freedom struggle in partnership with the private producer Firoz Nadiadwala, centering around the character of legendary freedom fighter 'Tatya Tope'. To be named "Tatya", the film will be produced at a cost of Rs. 50 crores with 50:50 contribution from the Government and the private film production house. This was stated by the Minister of Information & Broadcasting and Parliamentary Affairs, Shri P. R. Dasmunsi here today. The film will be directed by Vinay Shukla and is expected to be ready by August 15, 2008. Earlier, the Minister released the official wall calendar as well as desk calendar for the year 2008 brought out by DAVP. The six sheeter wall calendar titled "India @ 60" is a pictorial depiction of the nation's progress in the last 60 years. The desk calendar commemorates 150 years of first war of independence and the country's freedom struggle. The 12-sheeter desk calendar is a tribute to national heroes of India's freedom struggle. The Minister also released the annual reference book "India-2008" and "Bharat-2008" in English and Hindi respectively. In his remarks after the release, the Minister appreciated the efforts of the DAVP as well as Publications Division in bringing out such relevant publications. These are much popular and sought after even by the private sector, the Minister added. This is the 52nd edition of the Reference Annual providing comprehensive and authentic information on varied activities, and achievements of various government departments. It has detailed updated information on Indian polity, economy, art and culture, science and technology and various other aspects of development. To make it more user-friendly, presentable and attractive some new illustrations and line drawings have been included. India-2008 and Bharat-2008 have been uploaded on the Division's official website www.publicationsdivision.nic.in and are available online, free of cost. This is to make the books easily available to the general public. The hard copy is also available at a reasonable price in the market. This Reference Annual would be useful for students, research scholars, academicians, journalists and the general public. Publications Division is among the largest publishing houses in India having published around 8000 titles so far in English, Hindi and other regional languages. The Division has brought out some excellent books on freedom movement of India. Secretary (I&B), Smt. Asha Swarup in her remarks said that the annual wall calendar of DAVP is very much in demand in all quarters. The desk calendar is a new innovation on the part of DAVP for which she appreciated DAVP effort. U. K. Mishra, DG, DAVP delivered the welcome address while ADG, DPD, Smt. Veena Jain proposed a vote of thanks.

5248. (31-12-2007) NEW DELHI : In exercise of the powers conferred by Section 95 of the Constitution of Jammu and Kashmir, the President is pleased to appoint Shri Justice Kalavamkodath Sivasankara Panicker Radhakrishnan, Judge of the Kerala High Court, to be the Chief Justice of the Jammu and Kashmir High Court with effect from the date he assumes charge of his office.

5249. (31-12-2007) NEW DELHI : In exercise of the powers conferred by clause (1) of Article 217 of the Constitution of India, the President is pleased to appoint Shri Justice Anil Ramesh Dave, Judge of the Gujarat High Court, to be the Chief Justice of the Andhra Pradesh High Court with effect from the date he assumes charge of his office.

5250. (31-12-2007) NEW DELHI : In exercise of the powers conferred by clause (1) of article 217 of the Constitution of India, the President is pleased to appoint Shri Justice Rajesh Balia, Judge of the Rajasthan High Court, to be the Chief Justice of the Patna High Court with effect from the date he assumes charge of his office. The President is also pleased to appoint Shri Justice Narayan Roy, Judge of the Patna High Court, to be the Chief Justice of the Rajasthan High Court with effect from the date he assumes charge of his office.

5251. (31-12-2007) NEW DELHI : The Suspension of Operations (SOO) agreement between the security forces and Dima Halam Daogah (DHD), militant outfit operating in the State of Assam, has been extended for a further period of six months *i.e.* up to 30.06.2008. The extension follows a tripartite meeting among the representatives of the Government of India, Government of Assam and DHD on 27th December 2007. The SOO agreement between DHD and the security forces has been in operation since 1.1.2003.

5252. (31-12-2007) NEW DELHI : All India Consumer Price Index Number for Industrial Workers (CPI-IW) on base 2001=100 for the month of November, 2007 remained stationary at 134 (one thirty four). During November, 2007, the index recorded an increase of 4 points each in Chhindwara, Tripura and Rourkela centres, 3 points in 4 centres, 2 points in 8 centres and 1 point in 9 centres. The index decreased 3 points each in Nagpur and Rangapara-Tezpur centres, 2 points in 5 centres, 1 point in 24 centres while in the remaining 23 centres the index remained stationary. The increase of 4 points in Chhindwara centre is mainly on account of increase in the prices of Rice, Wheat, Groundnut Oil, Supari, Firewood, Toilet Soap etc., while in Tripura centre it is due to increase in the prices of Rice, Wheat Atta, Mustard Oil, Poultry, Vegetable & Fruit items, Sugar etc. and in Rourkela centre it is due to increase in prices of Rice, Arhar Dal, Fish Fresh, Vegetable & Fruit items etc. The decrease of 3 points in Nagpur centre is mainly due to decrease in the prices of Groundnut Oil, Onion, Vegetable & Fruit items, while in Rangapara-Tezpur centre it is mainly due to decrease in the prices of Rice, Fish Fresh, Vegetable & Fruit items.

5253. (31-12-2007) NEW DELHI : The process for prequalification of bidders for the development of 22 railway stations as world class stations has been initiated. A global advertisement in this regard has already been issued by the Ministry of Railways. The Request for Qualification (RFQ) document is now available on the Ministry of Railway's website http://indianrailways.gov.in. A calendar for bringing the process to the climax of appointing the concessionaire is also available in the RFQ document. Word class developers have already shown interest and good competition is expected. Ministry of Railways has decided to develop 22 railway stations, located in metropolitan cities and major tourist centres, as world class stations through Public Private Partnership (PPP) route be leveraging a part of the real-estate development potential. Required consultancies are being carried out for architectural, technical, financial and legal activities. Needed coordination with local bodies is being carried out by high level committees specially constituted. To begin with, the development of New Delhi Railway Station has been taken up. M/s Terry Ferrell of Hong Kong has been appointed as the Architect and Technical Consultants for this purpose. They would complete their assignment and submit a Master Plan and Feasibility Report by February 2008. The work will be entrusted to a concessionaire on PPP basis through competitive selection. The selected concessionaire would develop the station and also the entire surrounding areas as an iconic landmark of Delhi. The concessionaire would be allowed specified property development rights for a fixed concession period of 35 years. When completed, the station would provide generous space for departing and arriving passengers with minimum conflict or congestion. Concourses at different levels, elevated first floor and underground, along with generous provision for inter-modal connectivity, vehicle and bus parking have been planned. An empowered Committee under the chairmanship of Cabinet Secretary is coordinating all government agencies to ensure that the Word class project is successfully implemented in time, making a major contribution to the urban landscape of Delhi.

5254. (31-12-2007) NEW DELHI : Consisting of more than 100 settlements spread over 20 square kilometres and of around 1900 residents from some 40 nations live together as one community in Auroville. Auroville was founded by the 'Mother', a disciple of Sri Aurobindo, in February 1968 as an international cultural township on the outskirts of Puducherry where the present community people of different nationalities, from different ethnic, religious and cultural backgrounds, could live and work together in a spirit of mutual respect and collaboration. The true purpose of Auroville is a place for the realization of international understanding, peace and human unity in diversity based upon an inner discovery and transformation of consciousness the way as shown by Sri Aurobindo and The Mother.

5255. (31-12-2007) NEW DELHI : Government has released 41 lakh tonnes of non-levy (free sale) sugar for the quarter January-March 2008. For the month of

January 2008, the non-levy sugar quota released is 13 lakh tonne. In addition, a quantity of 1.98 lakh tonne has been released under levy for distribution in Public Distribution System. Thus, the total availability of sugar in the month of January, 2008 would be 14.98 lakh tonne or say 15 lakh tonne which would be sufficient to meet the internal demand for sugar.

5256. (31-12-2007) NEW DELHI : The term of the Liberhan Ayodhya Commission of Inquiry has been extended by two months up to 29th February, 2008. The Commission is inquiring into the destruction of the Ram Janma Bhoomi-Babri Masjid structure at Ayodhya on 6th December 1992.

5257. (31-12-2007) NEW DELHI : The Appointments Committee of the Cabinet has approved the following appointments:- Shri Pradeep Kumar, IAS (HY:72), presently Secretary, Department of Disinvestment, Ministry of Finance, as Secretary, Department of Defence Production, Ministry of Defence, in the vacancy of Shri K. P. Singh, IAS (KN:71); Shri Siddharth Behura, IAS (UP:73), presently Special Secretary, Ministry of Environment & Forests, as Secretary, Department of Telecommunications (Ministry of Communications and Information Technology), in the vacancy of Shri D. S. Mathur, IAS (MP:71).

5258. (31-12-2007) NEW DELHI : Shri S.S.Khurana took over as the Member Staff, Ministry of Railways, Railway Board, New Delhi with effect from 28th December 2007. Prior to his present assignment, he was General Manager, East Coast Railway from 12th January 2007 to 28th December 2007. Born in the year 1950, Shri Khurana did Electrical Engineering from University of Roorkee (now IIT/Rurkee). An officer of 1971 batch of the Indian Railway Service of Electrical Engineering (IRSEE), Shri Khurana worked in various capacities in Indian Railways. He worked as Additional General Manager, Northeast Frontier Railway from 27th March 2006 to 4th May 2007, Chief Electrical Engineer in the Central Organisation for Railway Electrification (CORE) Allahabad, Divisional Railway Manager Adra (SER), Additional Divisional Railway Manager, Dhanbad, Chief Project Manager, Railway Electrification at Ambala and has also worked in the research and design aspects of electric locomotives in the Research, Design & Standards Organisation (RDSO), Lucknow. He has also received valuable experience in foreign training in Sweden, Japan and USA. He has also attended Advance Leadership Programme at Stern Business School, New York, USA.

5259. (31-12-2007) NEW DELHI : The Culture and Tourism Minister Smt. Ambika Soni has said that the Government is providing alternative commercial hubs to encroachers for necessary livelihood so that the exterior ambience of monuments remains presentable. Addressing the 33rd meeting of the Central Advisory Board of Archaeology here today she said already alternative commercial hubs have been provided at Mahabalipuram, Agra and Bodhgaya. She said encroachment is a major problem the Government is facing in maintaining and improving the ambience of the monuments. Vandalisation against monuments, law

& order situation in the areas where monuments are situated are major concerns for the Government and efforts are needed to be made by the ASI, the state and the local Governments to work together to ensure that cultural heritage of the country is well-preserved and visitor friendly. Smt. Soni said the country is at risk of loosing a number of archaeological sites due to rapid urbanization and developmental work. The Government has therefore decided to create within five years a national register to built heritage and antiquities of India. A National Mission on Monuments and Antiquities has been constituted for this purpose. She said the aim of the mission is to document the monuments and antiquities spread across India and to have a GIS based data based both at the regional as well as national level which can be accessed by the common public and scholars alike. She said her ministry has proposed constitution of National Heritage Site Commission to the Cabinet recently for the identification of heritage structures. She said the Government has also encouraged the participation of the corporate sector in the preservation and conservation of cultural heritage through the National Cultural Fund. Contributions to this fund are 100% tax free, she added. Smt. Ambika Soni said the year 2007 saw an impressive growth of tourism sector in the country and as per estimates the final figure of foreign tourist arrivals in the country is likely to touch 5 million with a foreign exchange earning of over 10 billion US dollars. She said we have to strive hard to keep pace with growing tourism and try to maintain a balance between conservation and development without destruction. The Union Culture Secretary Sh. Abhijit Sengupta in his address said the ASI has recently signed a MoU with the Indian Institute of Technology, Kanpur to collaborate in the application of sciences in archaeology. This MoU has enabled ASI to depute its officers to undergo training in selected fields like, "Plane Surveying and GPS", "Geographical Information System (GIS)" and "Archaeo-materials". He said this venture will built the capacity of ASI Archaeologists as well as facilitate core research in many areas of archaeology. The Director General of ASI Smt. Anshu Vaish said her organization has under its protection 366 monuments and sites which are administered through 24 circles spread throughout India. She said ASI also generates revenue through ticketing of the centrally protected monuments and during the financial year 2006-07 it has contributed a sum of Rs. 63.04 crores to the Government exchequer, which almost a 9% increase over the previous year.

5260. (31-12-2007) NEW DELHI : The Indian agribusiness supply chain is highly fragmented, with independent players engaged in various value-addition activities such as input supplies, cultivation, processing, distribution, storage and retailing. The scale of operations of each entity is limited not only due to the structure of the supply chain, but also on account of Government policies as well as due to demand-related factors. In contrast, internationally, a large number of food companies are integrated across the chain *.e.g.* players such as ADM and Cargill have business interests in agricultural inputs, procurement, transportation and storage of produce processing and value addition. The structural complexion of the Indian supply chain thus translates into limited scale of financing as well as higher risk, given the lack of control of each of the players, on the supply chain. It is important to understand the issues faced in farmer level financing, both from the borrower's as well as the lender's perspective and develop solutions which address these issues comprehensively. Farmer's Perspective - Limited Access to Credit Non-availability of timely credit from organized sources, mainly on account of the processes and procedures of banks/financial institutions. This compels farmers to rely on intermediaries. Inadequacy in credit availability - The scale of finance method, stipulated by RBI, caps total credit availability per farmer. Inability to offer tangible security/collateral cover to access credit from banks. Subsistence farmers, who constitute a large proportion of India's farming community, are unable to benefit from the organized credit system since they cannot offer adequate tangible security. Further, the security offered (land documents) are notional and cannot be enforced by banks. The above factors, thus translate into continued reliance on intermediaries for financing. While intermediary financing is timely, as they do not require the level of documentation as banks, the cost of funds is exorbitant, nearly 4 times that of interest rates charged by banks. The above factors, thus translate into continued reliance on intermediaries for financing. While intermediary financing is timely, as they do not require the level of documentation as banks, the cost of funds is exorbitant, nearly 4 times that of interest rates charged by banks. A more efficient agri-supply chain requires that farmers' financing needs are addressed by banks and linkages of farmers with middlemen are scrapped. Banker's Perspective Lack of credit discipline among borrowers Lack of credit discipline, to some extent is infused by the Government's decision to waive outstanding loans of farmers. Policy-related uncertainties translate into a huge risk for banks. Instead of loan waivers, the Government should seek to impose a short-term moratorium on repayments to enable farmers to overcome the adverse impact of a poor monsoon/crop failure. Lack of tangible security from farmers-as mentioned above, farmers are unable to provide tangible security to financiers. Lack of linkages of farmers with processors - In absence of forward linkages with markets, banks run a huge performance risk, as there is greater potential for farmer default. Inadequate insurance cover the existing crop insurance schemes are inadequate, and this further increases the risk profile of farmers. Norms for priority sector lending - As per the current RBI policy on priority sector lending, Kharif credit is not accounted for in priority sector lending. This results in a lop-sided focus on extending financing to farmers, favouring crops cultivated in the rabi season. Policy-related Issues Cooperatives Act: There are about 95,000 Primary Agriculture Credit Co-operatives (PACS) and about 100,000 marketing co-operatives. As per the Cooperative Act, cooperatives are allowed to borrow from Cooperative Banks, DCCBs and RRBs.

5261. (31-12-2007) NEW DELHI : On the eve of New Year the Chief of Air Staff has wished all the members of IAF and their families his best wishes for year 2008. In his message to all the Air Warriors the Air Chief Marshal Fali H

Major said, the IAF is 76 years old and we have only just celebrated our Platinum Jubilee. We are one of the World's oldest Air Forces and the fourth largest. The reason to celebrate however stems from our continued all-round growth, your acknowledged professionalism and creditable performance in all that you have undertaken. 2007 has been a year of high operational preparedness and one of the safest. All tasks have been successfully executed. The UN missions have done a praiseworthy job and we have done well in international exercises. The modernization plans are proceeding apace. The Hawk AJT has joined the inventory, even as the Canberra and MiG-23 MFs have retired. The serviceability of our fleets has improved. Our training methods are evolving, there have been a number of administrative improvements and welfare measures. I am convinced that the IAF's tasks are set to grow and become more complex. We have to assure the Country of our performance, for which we need the requisite capabilities, the right size, the right people and an efficient organization. Of all these, our people are the most important - they must be our force-multipliers. A lot therefore depends on our professionalism, commitment, character and conviction; which in turn are very dependent upon the leadership at all levels. Fairness, justice, integrity, transparency, probity, service-before-self, accountability and responsibility remain as always, the vital ingredients of leadership. I am confident of our people, our growth and mission-accomplishment. Let us celebrate the New Year and continue to serve, better than we could in the past.

5262. (31-12-2007) NEW DELHI : The total approximate earnings of Indian Railways on originating basis during the period 11th December - 20th December 2007 were Rs. 2020.40 crore compared to Rs. 1714.90 crore during the same period last year, registering an increase of 17.81 per cent. The total goods earnings have gone up from Rs. 1197.01 crore during 11th December - 20th December 2006 to Rs. 1403.88 crore during 11th December - 20th December 2007, showing an increase of 17.28 per cent. The total passenger revenue earnings during the period 11 - 20 December 2007 were Rs. 550.59 crore compared to Rs. 460.59 crore during the same period last year, reflecting an increase of 19.54 per cent. The revenue earnings from other coaching amounted to Rs. 52.29 crore during this period compared to Rs. 42.72 crore during the same period last year, showing an increase of 22.40 per cent. The total approximate number of passengers booked during the period 11 - 20 December 2007 were 186.59 million compared to 185.44 million during the same period last year, showing an increase of 0.62 per cent. In the suburban and non-suburban sectors, the number of passengers booked during 11-20 December 2007 were 108.89 million and 77.70 million compared to 110.79 million and 74.65 million during the same period last year, registering a decrease of -1.71 per cent and an increase of 4.09 per cent respectively.

5263. (31-12-2007) NEW DELHI : The President, Smt. Pratibha Devisingh Patil, has greeted the nation on the eve of New Year 2008. In a message, the President has said, "As the sun rises over 2008, may this New Year bring peace, prosperity and happiness to everyone. In this New Year let us all strive to work for the betterment of the nation and do our little bit in making the world a better place by helping the underprivileged and the needy".

5264. (31-12-2007) NEW DELHI : Following is the text of the Press Statement issued by the Department of Personnel & Training, Ministry of Personnel, Public Grievances and Pensions today, to clarify that there is no proposal before the Government regarding raising the retirement age of Central Government employees from 60 years to 62 years :- "Attention of the Government has been drawn to reports appearing in some sections of the media regarding raising the retirement age of Central Government employees from 60 to 62 years. In order to put at rest all such speculations, it is clarified that there is no such proposal before the Government."

5265. (31-12-2007) NEW DELHI : The Vice President of India Mohd. Hamid Ansari has greeted the people of our country on the New Year. In his greetings, the Vice President said that the dawn of the New Year also ushers in new hopes and expectations. As millions of our citizens face the immense challenges of poverty, illiteracy and ill health, we should resolve to tackle these on a priority basis. This requires the concerted efforts of every one of us. The hopes and expectations of becoming a developed nation free from these problems, where every citizen can fully realize one's potential, can only be fulfilled when we resolve to work in unison with dedication and commitment. The Vice President conveys his greetings and good wishes to the people on the joyous occasion of New Year.

5266. (31-12-2007) NEW DELHI : The Prime Minister, Dr. Manmohan Singh greeted the nation on New Year. In his message, the Prime Minister said that New Year is a time to reflect upon the year gone by, upon our successes, achievements and mistakes. It makes us wise to our strengths and weaknesses and gives us a chance to set new goals. It is a time for stocktaking and making a new start in achieving our individual and collective goals. As a nation, it is a time to rejoice in our democratic traditions and brace ourselves for future challenges, the Prime Minister said. "I wish 2008 brings peace, security and prosperity for the people world over", Dr. Singh added.

5267. (1-1-2008) NEW DELHI : The Union Minister for Information and Broadcasting Shri P.R. Dasmunsi has condoled the demise of the Former Union Minister Shri Pratap Chander Chunder. In his condolence message the Minister said: "I am very sad to learn about the sudden demise of the esteemed leader Shri Pratap Chander Chunder. He was not only a rare politician, dedicated to the gross-roots, but was also a distinguished scholar and had been a Professor at the Law College, Kolkata University. He was the distinguished son of the eminent freedom fighter Shri Nirmal Chander Chunder, and spent his entire life for the socio-economic emancipation and the growth and development of our great country. In his political career, he had been the Chief of the Pradesh Congress Committee of Bengal and Education Minister in the Cabinet of Morarji Bhai Desai. An eminent educationist and scholar, he was actively associated with many social, cultural, educational and other philanthropic organizations, involved in the betterment of the poor, downtrodden and hapless citizens. In his death, Mother India has lost one of the most noble sons. I take this opportunity to extend my homage to the departed leader and pray that his soul may rest in peace in heaven. May God give strength and succour to his family members to bear with this irreparable loss".

5268. (1-1-2008) NEW DELHI : In exercise of the powers conferred by clause (1) of Article 217 of the Constitution of India, the President is pleased to appoint (i) Shri Justice Narayanappa Ananda and (ii) Shri Justice Jawad Rahim, Additional Judges of the Karnataka High Court, to be Judges of the Karnataka High Court, in that order of seniority, with effect from the dates they assume charge of their respective offices.

5269. (1-1-2008) NEW DELHI : Civil Services (Preliminary) Examination, 2008 will be conducted by the Union Public Service Commission on 18th May, 2008 for recruitment to the Indian Administrative Service, Indian Foreign Service, Indian Police Service and certain other Group 'A' and Group 'B' Central Services/ Posts at various centres across the country. For details regarding the Syllabus and Scheme of the Examination, Centres of examination, Guidelines for filling up the application form etc. aspirants must consult the Detailed Notice of the examination published in the Employment News/Rozgar Samachar dated 29th December, 2007. Candidates may note that there are changes in the Syllabi of General Studies Papers and all the Optional Papers of Civil Services (Main) Exam 2008, excepting the Literature Papers of languages.

5270. (1-1-2008) NEW DELHI : The pre dawn dastardly Fidayeen attack on the CRPF camp in Rampur killing eight security personnel including a civilian and injuring several is a heart-rending UPA's New Year's greeting to the Nation. This is possibly the first premeditated Fidayeen attack in the country's hinterland, indicating that Jehadi outfit modules have positioned themselves deep inside the country and are not just confined to borders of Kashmir. This vindicates BJP's repeated assertion that large number of sleeper calls have stealthily positioned themselves in last three years taking advantage of soft policies of the UPA government. This action shows a complete lackadaisical and indifferent approach of the UPA government to fight terrorism and is nothing but an absolute failure. We are aware that today America stands as one of the most sworn and hated enemy for the Jehadis yet after 9/11 not a single terrorist incident has been reported. While in India, terrorist attacks not only remain unabated but there is a marked increase and are even rapidly reaching far flung areas. Not only did the NDA government go hard on prempting terrorist attacks, but also went aggressively detecting and locating ISI and other terrorist modules, bursting and immobilising more than two hundred of them. The UPA government remains unfazed with the spate of terrorist attacks which where done in Uttar Pradesh alone in last two years with the attack on Ayodhya, Varanasi and Jaunpur and recent simultaneous serial blasts in Court complexes of Lucknow, Varanasi and Faizabad where not a single accuse has been apprehended is an obvious outcome of Government soft pedalling on terrorism. It is pertinent to recall that not only the attackers on Parliament were duly thwarted foiling their murderous attempt and in less then a year and half the perpetrators were tracked and punished, despite that Afzal Guru remains unexecuted even after six years where the conviction has been even upheld by the highest Court. It is the attitude and intent of the UPA government not only to go soft and slow on terrorism but also deliberately display such actions emboldening Jehadi outfits and terrorist organisation to have a free play on the Indian soil. The UPA government has neither the will nor the desire or strength to fight terrorism and instead it continues to indulge in the flip-flop blame game.

5271. (1-1-2008) NEW DELHI : Industry is a major contributor to the fast growing Indian economy. Heavy Industry and Public Sector Enterprises played a pivotal role in almost all the sectors of the economy, including those of infrastructure, such as power, rail and road transport during 2007. They catered to the requirements of equipment for basic industries like steel, non-ferrous metals, fertilizers, refineries, petrochemicals, shipping, textiles and a host of industrial machineries including paper, cement, sugar, etc. The Ministry of Heavy Industries and Public Enterprises continued to play an important role for the development of a wide range of intermediate engineering products like castings, forgings, diesel engines, industrial gears and gear boxes during 2007.

5272. (1-8-2007) NEW DELHI : BJP National Spokesperson Shri Rajiv Pratap Rudy today said that the BJP holds the President of the Congress Party Mrs. Sonia Gandhi solely responsible for the unconstitutional and illegal action orchestrated in the Goa Assembly that resulted in the butchering of democracy. Shri Rudy said that the Speaker of the Goa Assembly Mr. Pratap Singh Rane, a staunch Congressman who has been the Chief Minister of the state for 18 years, by acting on direct instructions from the Congress High Command, completely denigrated Constitutional propriety by fraudulently conducting the proceedings of the House to save the Digambar Kamat Government which had lost its majority. Shri Rudy demanded answers from the Congress party on the following relevant issues: a. Why the three elected members were restrained from voting and debarred from the proceedings of the House while a no Confidence Motion was pending against the Speaker himself? b. Why did the Speaker defy the directive of the Governor issued under Article 175 Clause 2 where the first business listed was Vote of Confidence? (Copy enclosed.) c. Why did the Speaker take up the disqualification notice as the first item which was not listed without serving a copy of the complaint or a notice or even giving the concerned MLAs an opportunity of being heard? d. On what grounds did the Speaker give the ex-parte order, when the Members purported to be disqualified were present in the House? e. Why was the resignation offer by one of the members not considered prior to the Speaker issuing an order of restrainment? f. ON what grounds did the Speaker debar a whole political party from participating in the proceedings of the House?

5273. (1-1-2008) NEW DELHI : India's exports during November 2007 were valued at US $ 12425.11 million, which was 26.82% higher than the level of US $ 9797.67 million during November 2006. In rupee terms, exports touched Rs. 49000.16 crore, which was 11.51 % higher than the value of exports during November 2006. Cumulative value of exports for the period April-November, 2007 was US$ 98386.06 million (Rs. 398385.78 Crore) as against US$ 80590.19 million (Rs. 368807.15 Crore) registering a growth of 22.08% in Dollar terms and 8.02% in Rupee terms during the same period last year. Imports during November 2007 were valued at US $ 19831.79 million representing an increase of 29.26 % over the level of imports valued at US $ 15342.36 million in November 2006. In Rupee terms, imports increased by 13.66%. Cumulative value of imports for the period April-November, 2007 was US$ 151190.37 million (Rs. 612356.61 Crore) as against US$ 119078.24 million (Rs. 544674.11 Crore) registering a growth of 26.97% in Dollar terms and 12.43% in Rupee terms during the same period last year. Oil imports during November, 2007 were valued at US $ 5823.49 million which was 16.72% higher than oil imports valued at US $ 4989.14 million in the corresponding period last year. Oil imports during April-November, 2007 were valued at US$ 43348.93 million, which was 10.19% higher than the oil imports of US$ 39338.91 million in the corresponding period last year. Non-oil imports during November 2007 were estimated at US $ 14008.30 million, which was 35.30% higher than growth of non-oil imports of US$ 10353.22 million in November 2006. Non-oil imports during April-November, 2007 were valued at US$ 107841.44 million which was 35.24% higher than the level of such imports valued at US$ 79739.33 million in April-November, 2006.

5274. (1-1-2008) NEW DELHI : Central Board of Excise and Customs (CBEC), Department of Revenue issued Notification No. 1/2008-Customs (N.T.) dated 1st January, 2008 notifying tariff values of edible oils and brass scrap (all grades) and Poppy seeds as shown in the Table below. The tariff values of six palm group oils, crude soyabean oil and Poppy seeds remain unchanged. However, tariff value of brass scrap (all grades) has been revised.

5275. (1-1-2008) NEW DELHI : Air Marshal PK Barbora, Vayu Sena Medal, has taken over as Air Officer Commanding-in-Chief, Western Air Command of IAF in New Delhi, today. The Air Marshal was born in December 1950 in Shillong and commissioned as a fighter pilot in June 1970. He is a very experienced flier and has flown over 3500 hours. He took part in the 1971 war. He is a Qualified Flying Instructor and a Fighter Combat Leader and has been on the Staff of Tactics and Air Combat Development Establishment. He has also served two tenures in the Directorate of Air Staff Inspection at Air Headquarters. He is a graduate of College of Combat, Mhow (Higher Command). During his service career he has had the distinction of being part of the team during formation of the first Jaguar Squadron of the IAF and also inducting the Air Combat Simulator into the IAF, the first of its kind in Asia. He has held many operational assignments, such as Commanding Officer of a MiG-21 Squadron and Air combat Simulator Unit, Chief Operations Officer of a fighter Wing. He has served as Air Officer Commanding of a premier fighter Station. He has held the appointment of Air Attache at the Embassy of India, Moscow and Assistant Chief of Integrated Defence Staff (Perspective Plans and Force Structure) in HQ Integrated Defence Staff and Assistant Chief of Air Staff (Inspection) at Air Headquarters (RK Puram). The Air Officer was promoted to the rank of Air Marshal on 07 Sep 05 and assigned the appointment of Senior Air Staff Officer at Eastern Air Command, IAF. With effect from 02 Apr 07 the Air Marshal, who is the first personality from the Defence Services hailing from the North East, was promoted and posted to the prestigious appointment of Air Officer Commanding-in-Chief Eastern Air Command.

5276. (1-1-2008) NEW DELHI : Air Marshal PV Naik VSM ADC has taken over as the Vice Chief of the Air Staff at Air Headquarters in New Delhi, today. The Air Marshal was born on 22 Jul. 1949 at Nagpur. He is a graduate of Sainik School Satara, National Defence Academy, Defence Services Staff College and National Defence College. He was commissioned in the fighter stream on 21 Jun. 1969. During his distinguished career of 38 years in Air Force, he has flown all MiG-21 variants and MiG-23-BNs. He is a Qualified Flying Instructor, a Fighter Combat Leader, Graduate of the Defence Services Staff College and the National Defence College. He has held many important command and staff appointments. These include the command of a MiG-21 Bis Squadron at Pathankot, Chief Operations Officer at Bareilly, Directing Staff at TACDE and Defence Services Staff College, Battalion Commander at the National Defence Academy, Air-I of Western Air Command, Air Defence Commander of South Western Air Command and Director General of the Air Force Naval Housing Board. He has commanded two bases, AF Station Srinagar, an operational base in the Kashmir Valley and AF Station Bidar. He has functioned as Senior Air Staff Officer at Western Air Command and Air Officer Commanding-in-Chief of Central Air Command prior to taking over as the Vice Chief of Air Staff at Air Headquarters. For distinguished service he was awarded the Vishisht Seva Medal on 26 Jan 03 and appointed Honorary ADC to the Hon'ble President of India wef 25 Jul. 07.

5277. (1-1-2008) NEW DELHI : The Union Home Minister, Shri Shivraj Patil has condemned the attack on the CRPF Group Centre at Rampur in Uttar Pradesh. The following is the text of his statement. " I condemn today's attack on the CRPF Group Centre at Rampur in Uttar Pradesh. The Home Ministry is in touch with the Uttar Pradesh Government and CRPF authorities following the incident. A detailed report has been sought about the facts and circumstances of the incident and concerned authorities have been asked to take immediate and effective measures to identify and trace the culprits and bring them to book. I convey my sympathies to the kin of those killed in the attack and pray for speedy recovery of the injured."

5278. (1-1-2008) NEW DELHI : Prime Minister, Dr. Manmohan Singh has condoled the death of Dr. Pratap Chandra Chunder here today. Following is the text of the Prime Minister's condolence message: "I was deeply saddened to learn of the passing away of Dr. Pratap Chandra Chunder, an eminent educationist, legislator, lawyer and author earlier today. He was a distinguished member of the Union Cabinet in charge of Education and Social Welfare in the late 1970s, and served the State of West Bengal as a legislator and minister in the 1960s. Dr. Chunder was a multi-faceted personality with wide-ranging intellectual interests. He will be remembered both for his contribution as a legal luminary and as an educationist. I convey my sincere condolences to members of his family and his numerous friends and admirers."

5279. (2-1-2008) NEW DELHI : The Board of Approval of the Special Economic Zones (SEZs) met on 2nd January 2008 to consider proposals for setting up of Special Economic Zones and also approve other miscellaneous requests pertaining to SEZs. Addressing the Board of Approval members, the Chairman informed that so far formal approvals have been granted for setting up of 404 SEZs out of which 187 have been notified as on date. He informed that over Rs.52193 crores have been invested in these notified SEZs and that these SEZs are providing direct employment to over 59356 persons. Employment to over 35477 persons have also been provided by the new generation private sector/State Government SEZs which came up prior to the SEZ Act. This is in addition to the employment provided by the 7 Central Government established SEZs which is over 1.75 lakh persons.

5280. (2-1-2008) THRISSUR: Chief Minister V. S. Achuthanandan on Tuesday did not attend a public meeting at the finale of the district conference of the Communist Party of India (Marxist) that he was scheduled to inaugurate. The public meeting was inaugurated by CPI(M) leader T. Sivadasa Menon. Mr. Achuthanandan, however, took part in a function here on Tuesday to inaugurate the Road Safety Authority. It is alleged that party members close to Mr. Achuthanandan did not get adequate representation in the district committee. In the 40-member committee, those reportedly close to Mr. Achuthanandan were A. Padmanabhan, C.K. Kumaran, K.V. Peethambaran, V. R. Karappan, K.F. Davis, P.K. Davis and Varghese Kandamkulathi. All of them, except Mr. Peethambaran, were included in the 38-member panel to represent the district in the upcoming State conference. Sources close to the Chief Minister were also reportedly irked by the fact that T. Sasidharan was not allowed to participate in the district conference. There were also reports that Mr. Achuthanandan's manner of functioning was criticised by some of the delegates. Two CPI(M) State committee members reportedly played a major role in forging a consensus between activists close to

Mr. Achuthanandan and party secretary Pinarayi Vijayan. An election of the district panel was thus averted. Inaugurating the delegate session on Sunday, Mr. Vijayan had said that factionalism in the party would end with the State conference in Kottayam.

5281. (2-1-2008) NEW DELHI : Shri Pradeep Kumar has taken over as Secretary (Defence Production) in the Ministry of Defence. He belongs to 1972 batch of Indian Administrative Service. Shri Kumar who is a Haryana Cadre officer, is a graduate in Electrical Engineering from Indian Institute of Technology, Delhi and Masters in Economic and Social Studies from the University of Wales, UK. He has a rich and wide experience in the field of public administration and has held many senior positions in the Government of Haryana and Government of India. He has worked as Director of Industries, Principal Secretary, Power Irrigation, Science and Technology, Town and Country Planning and Urban Estates departments in the Government of Haryana. He has also worked as Joint Secretary in the Department of Heavy Industry, Additional Secretary in the Ministry of Coal, Chairman, National Highways Authority of India and Secretary (Disinvestment) in the Ministry of Finance, Government of India. Shri Pradeep Kumar has served on the Boards of a number of leading companies including Bharat Heavy Electricals Ltd., Maruti Udyog Ltd., Andrew Yule Ltd., Hindustan Paper Corporation Ltd., Coal India Ltd. and Nyvelli Lignite Corporation Ltd.

5282. (2-1-2008) NEW DELHI : Employment generation is one of the major priorities drawing the attention of the governments and economic planners all over the world. India is no exception. The approach to tackling unemployment problem have varied from time to time. In the initial years of planning no attempt was made to define an independent employment strategy. The focus on economic growth was viewed as essential for improving the employment situation. Thus, in the Five Year Plans, the generation of employment was viewed as part of the process of development. It was, however, observed that the rate of growth of employment was generally much lower than the GDP rate of growth of the economy. Seasons of severe drought and failure of monsoons exposed large sections of population to extensive deprivations and compounded the situation. Successive plan strategies, policies and programmes were, therefore, re-designed to bring about a special focus on employment generation as a specific objective. The seventies and eighties saw the emergence of special schemes like NREP, RLEGP to provide wage employment through public works programmes and schemes to promote self-employment and entrepreneurship to the unemployed and the poor. Employment levels expanded steadily during the seventies and eighties but the rate of growth of employment continued to lag behind that of the labour force. Unemployment among the educated showed a rising trend. In 1998-99, various poverty alleviation and employment generation programmes were re-grouped under two broad categories of self-employment schemes and wage employment schemes. Funding and organizational patterns were also rationalized for better results.

5283. (2-1-2008) NEW DELHI : The Ministry of New and Renewable Energy launches a new scheme for installation of Megawatt Capacity Grid Interactive Solar Power Plants. During interaction with media today, Minister of State for New & Renewable Energy, Shri Vilas Muttemwar said the Ministry will provide financial assistance amounting to Rs.12 per KW hour in case of solar photovoltaic and Rs.10/KW hour in case of solar thermal power fed to the electricity grid. 50MW solar power plants have been considered for the 11th Five Year Plan period. A maximum of 10MW capacity in State will be considered under this scheme. It will be implemented through Indian Renewable Energy Development Agency (IREDA). The Private sectors will invest about Rs.1,000 crore as developers. The Ministry has decided to provide generation based incentive for grid interactive solar power generation for the first time. Under this project the Ministry will provide a generation based incentive of a maximum of Rs.12 per KWh for the electricity generated from Solar Photovoltaic and the maximum of Rs.10 per KWh for the electricity generated through Solar Thermal Power Plants and fed to the grid from a grid interactive solar power plant of a capacity of 1 MWp and above. Shri Muttemwar explained that this incentive will be provided to the project developers at a fix rate for a period of ten years. Mr. Muttemwar clarified that this incentive will be worked out taking into account the tariff provided by the utility to the solar power producer. The utilities are expected to purchase solar power at the rate provided by the utilities for medium term power purchase of the highest rate fixed by the State Electricity Regulatory Commission for purchase of power for any other renewable energy source. Mr. Muttemwar said this programme will be limited to an aggregate installed capacity of 50MWp of Solar Power during the 11th Plan period. He also informed that each State will be allowed to set up upto 10MWp aggregate capacity under this programme. Additional investments of about Rs. 1000 crores is expected through this initiative from this private sector. The developers are expected to get land allotted from the State and will have to enter into PPA for seeking generation based incentive from IREDA who will approve the proposals on first come first serve basis. This scheme is also expected to increase the direct and indirect employment opportunities. On average each MW of solar manufacturing capacity is likely to produce 25 to 40 direct jobs and solar power plants are expected to create another 400 indirect jobs.

5284. (2-1-2008) THIRUVANANTHAURAM: The CPI(M) State leadership has decided to organise evening dharnas all over the State on Wednesday to protest against the attacks on Christians in Orissa. In a statement here, the CPI(M) State secretariat called upon all secular and democratic sections of the people to join the dharna programme. It accused the BJP-Janata Dal government in Orissa of having failed to put down the violence and the Central government of gross failure to react adequately to the situation. Although the State government claimed that only two persons died in the violence, Archbishop Raphael Cheenath had put the death toll at eight. The series of attacks had even hit the Orissa capital BHUBANESHWAR. Around 75 Christian institutions were attacked and priests and nuns were forced to remain in hiding for several days. Around 500 houses were destroyed in the violence planned and executed meticulously by the Sangh Parivar forces under the leadership of the Viswa Hindu Parishad (VHP)-Bajrang Dal combine. It was left to parties such as the CPI(M) to wake up to the situation and an all-party meeting to bring the violence under control was called at the CPI(M) State committee office.

5285. (2-8-2007) NEW DELHI : BJP National Vice-President Shri Mukhtar Abbas Naqvi said that the "Victory celebration" of the Congress – Communist Party on the acquittal of India's Osama-Bin-Laden Abdul Rashid Madani is a brazen Climax of Hypocrisy-Secularism. Shri Naqvi strongly condemned the "Victory Celebration" by the Congress and Communist Party on the acquittal of Abdul Rashid Madni – the hard-core fanatic and a mastermind of terrorist acts. He termed this celebration an act of terror glorification" by hypocrisy secular forces of the State. Shri Naqvi further stated that the competition between the Congress Party and the Communist Party to save Madani who was accused of Coimbatore blasts and other terrorist acts, clearly shows that the State Government, the Congress Party and the Communist Party were using their full might not to punish the culprits but to get Madani released from the jail. Shri Naqvi added that few months back, when the Congress and Communist parties were tied in competition to paste posters with the photo of Abdul Rashid Madani during bye-elections in Kerala and when these parties were equating the terrorist Madani with Gandhi, Nehru, Marx, Lenin etc. the people of the country had then realized that the Congress men and the Communists shamelessly feel themselves proud in capitulating for vote bank politics. Shri Naqvi added that passing resolutions in Kerala Assembly by the Congress and Communist party to release Madani, meeting Madani in Jail by so-called secular parties and their leaders, getting photographed with Madani to be shown in hoardings and posters on the roads of Kerala and launching campaign to secure Madani's release are proof of the fact that the UPA Government and the State Government have betrayed the country on this issue and have surrendered before the terrorism. Shri Naqvi said that from the very beginning the brazen surrender of the Congress and Communist Parties before the terrorism – be it the repeal of the POTA, be it the hanging of Afzal Guru on gallows or be it the release of Madani from jail, all these moves go to boost the moral of the terrorist and separatist elements. These anti-national forces have started to feel that a terror friendly era has began in the country in the name of secularism. Shri Naqvi warned the Congress and Communist parties and cautioned them to draw lesson from pro-terror policies of Pravez Musharraf. The terrorism which was nursed by Pakistan so far is proving to be the greatest danger to the existence of Pakistan. Crores of Patriotic Indians would give befitting reply to the victory celebrations by the Congress and Communist Parties in support of Madani.

5286. (2-1-2008) NEW DELHI : The Union Minister of Shipping, Road Transport and Highways, Thiru T.R. Baalu reviewed here today the progress of projects being implemented by National Highways Authority of India (NHAI) in the state of Tamil Nadu. There are 31 projects costing Rs. 9650 crore presently in progress covering a length of 1788 km. The projects are in the Hosur-Kaniakumari section of North South corridors, between Tindivanam and Trichy, Trichy and Didigul, Trichy and Madurai, Karur and Coimbatore, Coimbator and Mettupalayam, Salem and Kerala border. In addition other four laning projects between Madurai and Tuticorin, Pondichery and Tindivanam, Thanjavur and Trichy, Trichy and Karur, and Salem and Ulundurpet have also been undertaken. In and around Chennai city two projects, *viz.* Chennai bypass and improvement of access to Golden Quadrilateral by providing free flow facilities are also under construction. Of the 31 projects, 16 projects are expected to be completed during the calendar year 2008. Two of these 16 projects are expected to be completed by July 2008 (Thumipadi-Salem and Lalapet ROB), 3 (on North South corridor) by November 2008 and 11 (6 on North South corridor, 4 between Trichy and Madurai and 1 in Chennai city) by December 2008. The remaining 15 projects are likely to spill over to calendar year 2009, of which 6 will be completed during the first quarter itself. The remaining 9 projects will spill beyond March 2009. The Minister impressed upon NHAI officials and the Consultants supervising the projects to monitor the projects very closely and ensure that not only the projects are completed as per the targets fixed in the review, but sincere efforts are made by the contractors to complete the projects ahead of schedule. The Minister noted that the projects suffered some setbacks on account of heavy rains causing the quarries becoming inaccessible and the efforts being concentrated on restoration work rather than the main work. The works in Chennai city projects which were in critical stage suffered badly due to rains as well as certain unforeseen circumstances like emergence of certain leaking pipelines. Now that the rains are over, he urged all concerned to take up the work in the right earnest.

5287. (2-1-2008) NEW DELHI : The Indian National Congress strongly condemns the cowardly terror attack on the Rampur CRPF Camp. This is another attempt by terrorists to destabilize peace in the region. The blame game being indulged in by the State Government will not facilitate the joint efforts to tackle effectively the terrorist attacks. The fact is that the terrorists are finding U.P. as a soft target as also a vulnerable region for their attacks. The State Government has the basic and fundamental responsibility to handle law and order situation. We do not have a federal law to deal with such crimes. At the same time, the Union Government has a role to play to provide necessary intelligence inputs collected by them and also to provide logistic and para military forces or any other necessary support to the State Government. Unless, the State Government tightens and firms up measures for security, the situation cannot be brought under control. Basic intelligence information will have to be collected and acted upon by the State Government. If there is any gap, they should always seek backup from the Central agencies. When the terrorist outfits are active outside J&K, the State Government should all the more take steps for building their capacity to effectively tackle terrorism. The feeling of helplessness will not help a State Government to discharge its basic responsibilities. Unless precautions are taken, the Central Government agencies alone cannot tackle effectively such situations in the national security domain. It is better that the blame game being indulged in is stopped and the authorities concerned take security measures seriously. Ms. Mayawati appears to be preoccupied with travelling around the country in order to build up her party. In the process, she should not lose her focus on the primary and pressing importance of governance of a large and sensitive state like Uttar Pradesh. The Indian National Congress expresses heartfelt condolences to the bereaved families of the victims. To a question that you are putting the onus on the state government regarding the CRPF camp attack whereas Smt. Mayawati is squarely blaming the Centre, Smt Jayanthi Natarajan said, we are saying that the blame game is of least importance of priority at this time and it is the responsibility of all concerned, particularly the state government. Naturally the Central government has the responsibility to provide the intelligence information, which was done and also to provide back up logistic support on the request of the state government thereafter the state government should also effectively play its role. At this point of time the blame game, as being indulged in by the chief minister, is not advisable in a situation like this. To a question that the point remains that those security personnel whose job is to protect the lives of citizens were caught napping and came under attack, how can they protect citizens, Smt Natarajan said, I think we should be very sensitive to the challenges being faced by those who are given the task of protecting the lives of citizens, particularly important and sensitive forces like the CRPF which performs a very admirable task as a whole. It would be very unfair and unjust to say that they failed. It is a collective failure and it is very important that all concerned should come together to see that such events are never again repeated. To a question whether the Congress Party favours law to tackle the terrorist activities, Smt Jayanti said, I feel that the existing laws, if all concerned take their responsibility seriously and function effectively, the existing laws are enough. To a question that the BJP has demanded a white paper on terrorist attacks, what is your view, Smt. Natarajan said, whenever the questions are asked and details are requested for, all information will be provided by the Central government to every leader and parties who ask for it. I am sure they will come out and explain as to what happened during the NDA government when all the attacks, including the attack on Parliament and escorting a dreaded terrorist by then foreign minister to Kandahar, will all be part of it. To a question that do you think that the present UPA government can get away with all sorts of terrorist attacks that are taking place and because what happened during NDA regime was more serious, Smt Natarajan said, I would not like to categorise things that were done. The UPA government is not getting away with anything.

5288. (2-1-2008) NEW DELHI : Rules notified for the implementation of the Scheduled Tribes and other Traditional Forest Dwellers (recognition of forest rights) Act on 1 st Jan 2008, has finally paved the way to undo the injustice to tribals and other forest dwellers. After the enactment of the Act now tribals and other forest dwellers will have the right to cultivate forest land to the extent under occupation, the right to own, collect, use and dispose of minor forest produce, rights inside forests which are traditional and customary like grazing. Tribals who have been living in and depending on forests, for their livelihood prior to 13 December, 2005, and other traditional forest dwellers who have been living in and depending on forests for their livelihood, for three generations prior to 13th December, 2005 will have these rights. Gram Panchayats will call for claims, which will be examined by Forest Rights Committee consisting of 10-15 members of Gram Panchayats. At least one third of these members will be schedule tribe and one third women. The committee will visit the site and physically verify the nature and extent of the claims. After satisfying itself, it shall forward its recommendations to Sub Divisional level Committee, which will further send the proposal to the district level committee for final consideration. District level committee will also have three members from district panchayats of whom at least two shall be the Scheduled Tribes, preferably those who are forest dwellers or who belong to the primitive tribal groups.

5289. (2-1-2008) NEW DELHI : It appears that the UPA government is all poised to illegally and clandestinely impose President's rule in Nagaland, which will be absolutely unconstitutional and sans all political ethics & norms. It would possibly be a record and for the first time where a duly elected government is being placed under President's rule a fortnight ahead of the announcement of the State Assembly elections. The decision of the Union Cabinet to sack the NPF led DAN government where BJP is a major constituent partner headed by Dr. Neiphiu Rio is with an obvious design too manipulate and influence the forthcoming elections where the Congress party is in disarray and out of power since five years. Pertinently if the ruling of the speaker disqualifying Members under the anti defection law is the premise for imposing President's rule in Nagaland then the Union Government will have to immediately dismiss the Congress Government in Goa as the Speaker Sh. Pratap Singh Rane had acted similarly using the same provisions disqualifying three members from voting in the crucial vote on the floor of the Assembly on 30th July, 2007 claiming to have mustered a majority enabling the continuation of the Digambar Kamat Government. Interestingly the Governor of Goa, Mr. S.C. Jamir, who has active interests in Nagaland had refused to take the appeal of the BJP led opposition in Goa and had obviously colluded with the UPA leadership at the centre. The Bharitya Janata Party would like to question how could there be two divergent laws and rules under the same Constitution and how such a glaring impropriety can go unquestioned in a Democratic State? While the Left and other partners of the UPA have been usually giving moralistic sound bites, their deafening silence to the political sleaze in Nagaland truly depicts their double standards and blatant political dishonesty. The people of Nagaland have been watching the actions of the beleaguered UPA Government at the centre and they are all set to give a befitting reply to the unconstitutional action being thrust on them by the Congress leadership at centre in the dawn of the New Year.

5290. (2-1-2008) NEW DELHI : Public Diplomacy Division of the Ministry of External Affairs, in association with Utkal University, Bhubaneshwar, is organizing a seminar on Indian Foreign Policy and Strategic Issues at Bhubaneshwar on 5-6 January 2008. The Chief Minister of Orissa, Shri Naveen Patnaik will be the Chief Guest and preside over the inaugural session of the seminar on 5 January 2008. The seminar will see the participation of a large number of academicians, think tanks, representatives of industry, intelligentsia, journalists, civil society and senior officials.

5291. (2-8-2007) NEW DELHI : The Congress Party's lack of commitment and conviction was main reason for the plight of Dalits and other weaker sections in the country, former president of Bharatiya Janata Party Mr. M. Venkaiah Naidu said. He was inaugurating two-day national executive of the Party's Dalit Morcha here today. While addressing the gathering Mr. Naidu criticized that the Congress Party has always approached these weaker sections and Dalits with faulty policies, short-term, narrow-minded and partition mindset. The Congress has craze for sloganeering but never care to implement them, he said. Economic disparities, social inequalities, regional imbalances, communal disharmony are all offshoots of congress misrule of around 50 years out of 60 years of our Independence, Mr. Naidu said. The congress always talked about the poor and walked about rich. 'Words for the poor and deeds for the rich' and 'Only talking no walking' are the hallmarks of the congress, Mr. Naidu charged. The UPA Government is totally insensible to the sufferings of poor in general and Dalits and weaker sections in particular, he said. These sections are vulnerable to the price raise, rising of interest rates on housing and other sectors. The centre has no clue how to control the prices of even essential commodities, he said. The congress and its allies in various states are trying to suppress the agitations of Dalits and weaker sections. Take instances of Dalits burnt alive in Maharashtra or police firings with AK-47 weapons on weaker sections, resulting loss of seven unarmed poor people, who were demonstrating peacefully for house sites and government land for their livelihood in Andhra Pradesh. We have witnessed how the CPM government in West Bengal, a main ally of UPA at the centre, dealt with the poor peasants in Nandigram. These are live examples of the congress's and communists attitude towards the poor. He suggested that the reforms should continue in the larger interest of the country. But, fruits of development should reach to all sections of the country. Common man should feel that he is an integral part of the developmental process. He said that equitable growth is the need of the hour. He said that the land is a national asset and the people are the owners. The surplus land and vacant land after earmarking for public purposes should be distributed among eligible poor people. The BJP is not in favour of forceful occupation of land but supports the poor people agitating for the land. Mr. Naidu called upon the BJP governments in various states to expedite the programme, which they have already taken up the distribution of land to poor, in a time bound basis. Mr. Naidu said that the BJP strongly opposes the move of Communal Reservations as it is aimed at dividing the people on communal lines. This move is not only anti-secular but also anti-nation. It will hurt mostly the interests of the backward classes and SC and ST communities. Quoting the congress ruled AP government's decision in this regard, he apprehended that it is bound to be emulated by other state governments that are locked in competitive pseudo-secularism today, thus expanding the geographical spread of the poisonous seed. It is also certain to cause a cascading effect in the form of the louder articulation of demands for reservation for Muslims in police and security forces, administration and the judiciary, and sub reservation for Muslims within the proposed 33% reservation for women in Parliament and State legislatures. Does the Congress party know the implications and consequences of what it is doing? Mr. Naidu questioned. Has the party become so ideologically bankrupt and so politically pervert today that it is willing to mortgage the nation's unity and integrity for its own narrow and short-term political interests. This is a retrograde move which, if not immediately reversed, will sow the poisonous seed for the growth of a new communal movement. This proposal was considered more thoroughly by the Constituent Assembly's Advisory Committee on Fundamental Rights. Minorities and Tribal and Excluded Areas headed by Sardar Vallabhai Patel. This Advisory committee had a galaxy of great leaders of the Freedom Movement including Dr. B.R. Ambedkar, Dr. S.P Mookerjee, Maulana Azad, Dr. K.M Munshi, Shri Purushottamdas Tandon, Pandit Govind Vallabh Pant and Shri Gopinath Bardoloi. Pandit Nehru was a special invitee to the meeting of the committee which finally expressed that " the committee are satisfied that the minorities themselves feel that in their own interests, no less than in the interests of the country as a whole, the statutory reservation of seats for religious minorities should be abolished.", Mr. Naidu emphasized. The Nehru government kept Muslims and Christians outside the purview of reservation for SC's in education and government jobs. This was done through a Presidential order amending Article 341 of the constitution, which enables the President of India to notify a particular caste as a Schedule Caste. Mr. Naidu called upon Morcha cadres to fight it out tooth and nail both inside and outside the legislature and to challenge this move in both the judicial court and people's court. The Party SC Morcha President Dr. Satya Narayan Jatiya presided over the two-day national executive meeting.

5292. (3-1-2008) NEW DELHI : The Union Cabinet today gave its approval for adoption of the Model Concession Agreement for private sector participation projects in Major Ports which will thereafter replace the Model License Agreement of March 2000 (MLA 2000), which had been in use in the Major Ports since March 2000. This decision will benefit as under : i) Enhanced bankability of private sector projects in the Major Ports on account of improvements effected in the model viz-a-viz the MLA 2000. ii) Standarisation of financial and commercial terms for award of concessions for port projects. iii) Speedy decision making. iv) Equitable and efficient allocation of risks between the contracting parties. v) Protection of user interests through adherence to Performance Standards.

5293. (3-1-2008) NEW DELHI : The Union Cabinet today gave its approval for extension the term of the E-Committee up to February, 2009 or till its work is completed whichever is earlier. The Cabinet also gave its approval for making the following modifications in the manner of selection and appointment of the Chairman and Members on the E-Committee: a) The Chairman shall be a retired Chief Justice or a retired Judge of any High Court to be appoint by Chief justice of India; b) The Members shall be appointed either on deputation or on contract basis by the CJI on emoluments not exceeding the total emoluments as per the scale of pay provided for deputations subject to the condition that terms and conditions of appointment will be finalized in consultation with the Deptt. of Expenditure. The extended term will enable the E-Committee in monitoring the implementation of the ongoing E-Courts Project for the Indian Judiciary. The modifications in manner of appointment of Chairman and Members on the E-Committee will give the Hon'ble Chief Justice of India a free hand in selection and appointment of Chairman and Members on the E-Committee.

5294. (3-1-2008) NEW DELHI : The Union Cabinet today gave its approval for continuation of helicopter services for inter-island communication in Lakshadweep Islands for a further period of 5 years with effect from 01.04.2007 to 31.03.2012 and also approval for meeting the cost of hiring /chartering helicopter from PHHL by provision of subsidy of the order of Rs. 1310.31 lakhs annually by Administration of the Union Territory of Lakshadweep / Ministry of Home Affairs for this purpose. The helicopter service provided by Pawan Hans Helicopters Limited during the last 20 years has proved very useful to Union Territory Administration of Lakshadweep in interconnecting chain of its Islands scattered in Arabian Sea. The helicopter is functioning as an ambulance service in evacuating emergent cases requiring medical attendance at Government Hospital, Kavaratti to hospitals in mainland and the service is also catering as a feeder service for connecting passengers from Kavaratti to Agatti and vice versa.

5295. (3-1-2008) NEW DELHI : The Union Cabinet today gave its approval for waiving of the outstanding Central loans of Ministry of Finance pertaining to the period of ex-UT of Goa, Daman & Diu amounting to Rs. 239.22 crore along with interest accrued thereon the date of write off. This is a long pending matter awaiting decision since 1998-99 in pursuance of the Goa, Daman & Diu Reorganization Act which is devoid of any enabling provision for making the State of Goa to pay up pre-1987 loans. A decision on this issue would set right the records of the State of Goa and Ministry of Finance.

5296. (3-1-2008) NEW DELHI : The Union Cabinet today gave its ex-post facto approval for modifying the payment & Settlement Systems Bill, 2006 (Bill No. 50 of 2006). The Bill has since been passed by Lok Sabha on 26th November, 2007 and by Rajya Sabha on 3rd December, 2007. An official amendment in Clause 4 of the Bill is as under : "After line 9, in Clause 4 : (2) 'The Reserve bank may, under sub-section (1) of this section, authorize a company or corporation to operate or regulate the existing clearing houses or new clearing houses of banks in order to have a common retail clearing house system for the banks throughout the country; Provided, however, that not less than fifty one percent of the equity of such company or corporation shall be held by public sector banks. Explanation: For the purposes of this clause, "public sector banks' shall include a 'corresponding new bank", "State Bank of India" and "subsidiary bank" as defined in Section 5 of the Banking Regulation Act, 1949 (10 of 1949).'

5297. (3-1-2008) NEW DELHI : The Union Cabinet today gave its approval to the Memorandum of Understanding on Indo-Iceland Renewable Energy Cooperation. The MoU was signed on 9th October, 2007 in New Delhi and became effective from that date. The objectives of the MoU are as under :-Identifying areas of mutual interest and cooperation for the development of new and renewable energy technologies, systems, sub-systems, devices, components, etc. and-Monitoring and evaluating cooperation activities.

5298. (3-1-2008) NEW DELHI : The Parliamentary Standing Committee on Rural Development has invited suggestions on "The Land Acquisition (Amendment) Bill, 2007 and 'The Rehabilitation & Resettlement Bill, 2007' from the public in general and experts/professionals/organisations/associations/stakeholders interested in the subject in particular. 'The Land Acquisition (Amendment) Bill, 2007' and 'The Rehabilitation & Resettlement Bill, 2007' as introduced in Lok Sabha have been referred to Hon'ble Speaker, Lok Sabha in December, 2007 to Parliamentary Standing Committee on Rural Development headed by Shri Kalyan Singh, Member of Parliament, Lok Sabha for examination and report to the Parliament. The text of the Bill as introduced in Lok Sabha is available at website 'http://loksabha.nic.in' under the icon 'New Events' on internt. The Land Acquisition (Amendment) Bill, 2007 seeks to amend the various provisions of The Land Acquisition Act, 1894 with a view to strike a balance between the need for land for development and other purposes and protecting the interests of the persons whose lands are statutorily acquired. Besides, The Rehabilitation and Resettlement Bill, 2007 is an attempt to give a statutory backing to the provisions of The National Rehabilitation and Resettlement Policy, 2007. The said legislation propose to provide for the basic minimum that all projects, leading to involuntary displacement, must do to address the grievances of the affected persons. The Bill also contains a saving clause to enable the State Governments, Public Section Undertakings or agencies, or other requiring bodies to continue to provide or put in place greater benefit levels than those prescribed under the Bill. Interested persons may send five copies of the memoranda (in English or Hindi versions only) containing their opinion/views on the subject to Shrimati Sudesh Luthra, Director, Lok Sabha Secretariat, Room No. 151, Parliament House Annexe, New Delhi-110001, in a sealed cover so as to reach her on or before 15 January, 2008. The memoranda can also be faxed. (Fax No. 011-23010756). Those who are desirous of giving oral evidence before the Committee, besides sending memoranda, are requested to intimate at the aforesaid address for the consideration of the Committee. The memoranda, which might be submitted to the Committee would form part of the records of the Committee and would be treated as strictly confidential and would not be circulated by anyone, as such an act would constitute a breach of privilege of the Committee.

5299. (3-1-2008) NEW DELHI : The kharif rice procurement by government agencies today out-stepped the procurement as on the corresponding date last year. After a slow start, the pace of procurement picked up in the last fortnight and crossed the last year's procurement. The procurement as of today includes 26.63 lakh tonne levy rice and 162.18 lakh tonne paddy as against 23.8 lakh tonne levy rice and 166.34 lakh tonne paddy procured by 3rd January last year. Though the daily procurement figures of this year may go up and down vis-a-vis last year's in the coming days, depending upon variation in daily arrival of paddy in mandis, the total procurement this year is likely to reach or cross last year's total procurement of 250.75 lakh tonnes [in terms of rice]. Out of the total procurement of paddy so far[162.18 lakh tonnes], FCI has been able to procure 14.4 lakh tonnes, state agencies 36.46 lakh tonnes, Civil Supply Corporations 33.26 lakh tonnes, cooperatives 47.46 lakh tonnes, agro-industries 14.37 lakh tonnes and CONFED 2.06 lakh tonnes. In the coming days, procurement is likely to further pick up, especially in the eastern rice-growing states such as Orissa and Chhattisgarh. Procurement of foodgrains is done under a decentralised procurement scheme since 1997-98. Under this scheme, the State Government itself undertakes procurement of paddy/rice and wheat on behalf of Government of India, and also stores and distributes these foodgrains under PDS and other welfare schemes. The Central Government reimburses the entire expenditure incurred by the State Governments on the procurement operations.

5300. (3-1-2008) NEW DELHI : The Prime Minister, Dr. Manmohan Singh today inaugurated the 95th Indian Science Congress at Visakhapatnam today. Speaking at the occasion, Dr. Manmohan Singh reiterated the Government's commitment to invest more in science education. The Eleventh Five Year Plan is in fact a National Education Plan, the Prime Minister said. He stressed on the need for a global response, a national response and a local response to meet the challenge of climate change. Dr. Singh also urged the scientific community to tap into our traditional knowledge base, to develop environment-friendly and efficient technologies. (Full text of Prime Minister's inaugural address available in the PIB release issued earlier today on the same topic.) The Theme of the Science Congress this year is " Knowledge Based Society using Environmentally Sustainable Science and Technology" Addressing the gathering the Union Minister for Science and Technology and Earth Sciences Shri Kapil Sibal said a Centre for Climate Change, initially to be located within the campus of Indian Institute of Tropical Meteorology (IITM), Pune is being established to address the scientific issues related to Global

Warming and Climate Change. Terming it a global problem requiring global solutions, the Minister said that these solutions should be inclusive benefiting and encompassing one and all. Stating that technology efficiency could eliminate the power shortages in the country, Shri Kapil Sibal urged upon the scientific community to increasingly assist and partner industry to develop and deploy more and more of alternate and renewable energy sources. He said the earlier we join the low carbon development trajectories, the greater the chances of sustainability. The Minister suggested that the development patterns in India could opt for innovations away from the energy-intensive "new world" pattern exemplified by the United States, Canada, Australia, and New Zealand. In doing so, he said, we could become an important actor in energy-related research and development, as the markets for their applications have enormous potential. Shri Sibal shared with the audience his observation that the Clean Development Mechanism (CDM), one of the flexibility mechanisms incorporated into the Kyoto Protocol, offers great possibilities to India in helping mobilize foreign direct investment, by providing commercial incentives for the private sector to invest in mitigation projects and providing opportunities for the scientific community to team up with Indian industry for affordable and sustainable domestic solutions. Prof. R. Ramamurthi, General President of the Indian Science Congress said that in spite of major efforts in farming sector, National Environment policy, National Biodiversity Authority, enhancing space technology applications in disaster mitigation, telemedicine, upgrading efforts in water security, energy options and knowledge transfer systems unable to bring more people above the poverty line. He said the present conference is aimed to address several thrust areas through plenary, symposia, panels and round table deliberations to make the world in general and India in particular a knowledge empowered society. In his welcome address Prof.L.Venugopal Reddy,Vice-Chancellor of Andhra University said that the university has been continuously striving to keep pace with the advances in science and Technology and maintaining standards in teaching and research. Besides a galaxy of Scientists from across the country and abroad, the Chief minister of Andhra Pradesh Dr.Y.S.Rajasekhar Reddy, the Union Minister of state for Mines Dr. T. Subbarami Reddy and Union Minister of State for Defence Shri M.M. Pallam Raju were also present on the occasion. The Prime Minister launched 'Outreach Campaign' logo and released its booklet. He also presented ISCA awards for 2007-2008 to the scientists. An Exhibition showcasing the achievements in Science and Technology was also organized to mark the event.

5301. (3-8-2007) NEW DELHI : Bharatiya Janata Party will launch a massive farmer's nation wide agitation and will March to Parliament on 20th August (Monday) to protest against anti-farmer policies of UPA government. More than 1 lakh farmers from neighbouring states will hold a massive rally at Ramlila Maidan and will March to Parliament on the first day of agitation. The rally will focus on six major demands of farmers viz CBI inquiry in wheat import scam, immediate increase in MSP so as to ensure farmers remunerative prices, agriculture loans at 4% interest, ensure minimum income guarantee by implementing income guarantee insurance scheme, immediate availability of seeds and fertilisers and immediate payment to sugarcane growers. Sh. Atal Bihari Vajpayee, Sh. L.K. Advani and Party President Sh. Rajnath Singh will address the rally. Party Gen. Secretary Sh. Gopinath Munde has been put incharge of the rally. Wheat import scam is not only an error of judgment as is made out by the government. Only CBI inquiry can reveal why the government cancelled the first tenders in May, 2007 @ of $263 per MT and accepted the July, 2007 tenders with much higher prices of $320-360 per MT. In the month of June the prices rose on Chicago board of trade and only detailed enquiry can unravel the forces behind such a dramatic rise in the prices. It is pertinent to know why government did not wait until September, when international prices are expected to fall. It is also important to know why government persisted with import plan even after realising that the indigenous production has increased by 5 million tonnes over last year. What has hurt Indian farmers most is the fact that the government, which is paying Rs. 1400 per quintal to foreign farmers is paying only Rs. 850 per quintal to Indian farmers. The MSP declared last week by the UPA government is an insult added to the injuries of the farmers. BJP demands immediate upward review of prices of all the food grains, so as to ensure real remunerative prices. BJP demands increase of at least Rs. 100 per quintal in the MSP across the board. The UP farmers have not received their dues of sugarcane and are suffering because of non-payment. Immediate disbursal of funds will at least relieve them temporarily. The seeds and fertilisers have disappeared from the market and are not available to farmers at nominative prices. He has to shell more money for the same. Government is absent and is not taking any remedial measures to help the farmers. The agrarian crisis in India is much deeper and needs courageous action plan, which will ensure inputs at reasonable prices, new research in productivity, comprehensive insurance, total institutional credit and assured remunerative prices. The UPA government has failed to live to the expectations of farmers. The BJP agitation will bring to fore the abject failure and inept handling by UPA government.

5302. (3-1-2008) NEW DELHI : Air Marshal PS Bhangu AVSM VM took over as Senior Air Staff Officer of the prestigious Western Air Command of Indian Air Force. He brings with him a wealth of experience in Strategic, Tactical, Flight Safety and staff matters. The Air Marshal is an alumni of Defence Services Staff College, Wellington. During his illustrious services he has served in a number of fighter squadrons and achieved A2 category Flying Instructor and Fighter Combat Leader. He has commanded a front line fighter squadron and the prestigious Tactics and Air Combat Development Establishment (TACDE). He has over 4500 hours of combat flying experience. He has also held the appointments as Joint Director Air Defence and Director Flight Safety, Flying Instructor in one of the friendly countries and Air Attache in Embassy of India at Moscow, Russia. In addition to, he also held the appointment of Director General, Air Force Naval Housing Board, Assistant Chief of Air Staff (Personnel Officers) and Assistant

Chief of Air Staff (Personnel Airmen & Civilians) at Air Headquarters (Vayu Bhavan). The Air Marshal was decorated with Ati Vishist Seva Medal in 1966 for his exceptional devotion to duty.

5303. (3-1-2008) NEW DELHI : Union Minister of Information & Broadcasting and Parliamentary Affairs, Shri P. R. Dasmunsi presented awards to the winners of the National Photo Contest today. To mark the 60 years of Independence, Photo Division organised its 20th National Photo Contest on an unique theme "Spirit of Independent India". Shri Vivek Desai of Ahmedabad bagged the first prize for both the sections (black & white and colour). Shri Anirudha Pal and Shri Supriya Biswas of Kolkata got the second prize in black & white and colour section respectively, where as Shri Girish J. Kingar and Shri Upendra Upadhyay of Indore got third prizes in the Contest. The first prize consists of Rs. 20,000/- the second prize Rs. 15,000/- and the third prize of Rs. 10,000/-. In addition, a citation and a plaque is distributed to the winners. 10 commendation prizes in both the section were also awarded. In his remarks, Shri Dasmunsi said that photography preserves history and carries forward a message for the future. Appreciating the creativity of a photography artist the Minister said that a photographer captures images, which can be enjoyed for generations to come. Referring to the nuances of good photography, the Minister said it is an art as well as science. Secretary (I&B), Smt. Asha Swarup in her address said that despite new technologies, still photography has retained its relevance and has continued to fascinate the viewers. Photo images are more lasting and leave an imprint on the viewer's mind. Our endeavour is to reach the photo exhibition to the other parts of the country as well as at various places within the capital so that maximum number of people can see it and appreciate this art, she added. A high level jury comprising of Shri Sondeep Shankar, National Editor of 'The Hindustan Times' Delhi, Shri Hoshi Jal, Photo Editor of 'Times of India' group, Mumbai, Padmashree Virender Prabhakar, former Chief Photographer of 'Hindustan', Smt. Stuti Kacker, Joint Secretary (P) from Ministry of I&B and Debatosh Sengupta, Director, Photo Division screened all the entries and selected the award winning as well as photographs to be put up for Exhibition. 294 photographers from 17 States sent 1157 photographs for the competition, which is in two sections black & white and colour. Shri Dasmunsi also inaugurated the Exhibition of the award winning and selected photographs at National Bal Bhavan, New Delhi, where it will be on till January 05, 2008. The next phase of the Exhibition will be held from 15-21 January 2008 at AIFACS Gallery, New Delhi.

5304. (3-1-2008) NEW DELHI : 6th Battalion of the Sikh Regiment has departed from Delhi for UN Peace Keeping Mission in Congo today. 6 SIKH was raised in 1962 and has been nominated based on their outstanding performance in 1971 war and thereafter in Counter Insurgency Operations in the North East and Jammu & Kashmir. This gallant battalion has the honour of being awarded the Battle Honour for Defence of Poonch, Theatre Honour of J & K, COAS unit citation and a long tally of gallantry awards to include 01 UYSM, 01 PVSM, 01 AVSM, 01 MVC, 05 VrC, 05 SC, 13 SM and 02 mention-in-despatches. Maj Gen Vinay Bhatnagar, Additional Directorate General (Staff Duties) addressed the troops of this battalion. He reminded the troops of the challenging task ahead of them, which requires utmost dedication, devotion and humanitarian approach for ensuring peace in Democratic Republic of Congo.

5305. (3-1-2008) NEW DELHI : The Union Minister for Shipping Road Transport & Highways Thiru T.R. Baalu has said that the Government intends to set up a suitably designed Inspection and Maintenance system throughout the country for rigorous inspection of motor vehicles and to remove the defects before they are allowed to ply on road. Speaking at the National Convention of the All India Motor Transport Congress here today, the Minister said that presently, the Government is in the process of designing a model of Inspection and Maintenance centres and this has been included in the Plan scheme of the Department during the Eleventh Five Year Plan. The Minister said that a Working Group has been set up to formulate the Rules for the Carriage by Road Act, 2007 which has been notified in October last. The Minister hoped that once the new Act comes into effect, it would cater to the need of the modern day trade and transport by road and would help make the transport system transparent. It would also modernise the systems and procedures of the transportation trade through registration of common carrier and would provide scope for apportionment of liability between the common carrier and the consignor, the Minister hoped. Thiru Baalu also disclosed that the already notified rules for setting up of Accreditation Boards for giving accreditation to bus body builders would come into effect on 23rd March this year. Once the accreditation system for bus body builders is established, this would be extended to truck body builders also. He hoped that it would bring uniformity in body building as the Code of Practice for bus body design lays down dimension for floor height, gangway and footsteps for different categories of buses; minimum specifications for seats, seating lay out and illumination, minimum requirements for driver's workplace and special provisions for persons with disabilities etc. The Minister also informed that the Government is in the process of creation of a National Road Safety and Traffic Management Board through a separate Act of Parliament. The Board shall have powers to set safety standards for design, construction and operation of National Highways and to set standard for safety features of motor vehicles. Regarding the menace of overloading the Minister said that it is being proposed in the Motor Vehicles (Amendments) Bill, 2007 that the consignor and the common carrier shall also be responsible, besides driver or owner of the vehicle, as overloading is mostly done with the knowledge of consignor/common carrier. Now, the officials of the Motor Vehicles Department in the States would necessarily have to weigh the vehicles suspected to be overloaded, off-load the excess load, and not allow the overloaded vehicle to move further without payment of fine, he added. Thiru Baalu also informed that the Government has recently approved the proposal for establishment of an integrated network of

Trauma Centres along the Golden Quadrilateral, North-South and East-West Corridors of the National Highways by upgrading the trauma care facilities in 140 identified State Government Hospitals at a total cost of Rs.732.75 crores during the Eleventh Five Year Plan period. This will ensure that each accident victim on these corridors is able to get competent medical assistance within the shortest possible time thereby saving precious lives, he said.

5306. (3-1-2008) NEW DELHI : India has assumed the Chair of the Kimberley Process Certification Scheme (KPCS) for the period 1/1/2008 to 31/12/2008. India as KP Chair will continue to build on the traditions and conventions of the previous KP Chairs and ensure effective implementation of the KPCS, thereby ensuring growth of legitimate diamond trade and protection of livelihoods of millions of people across the globe. Moreover, India will extend all possible assistance to participants to build effective internal controls and work in close cooperation with UN, KP participants, industry and civil society in order to continue the remarkable progress achieved by this scheme in the past few years. India will be sixth in succession to hold the Chair after South Africa, Canada, Russian Federation, Botswana and European Commission. India is one of the founding members of KPCS. In November 2006, India was unanimously selected to hold the Vice Chair of the KPCS for 2007. Namibia has been selected as the Vice Chair for 2008. The KPCS requires each participant to impose internal controls over production and trade of rough diamonds. Trading in rough diamonds with a non-participant is not allowed. All exports of rough diamonds have to be accompanied by a valid KP Certificate stating that diamonds are conflict free. KPCS currently has 48 member states including the European Community representing 27 member states. Thus, it has a membership of 74 countries. All major diamond producing, trading and polishing centres are members of KP. Civil Society and industry groups also actively participate in the KP. The UN General Assembly adopted Resolution 55/56 in December 2000 endorsing and legitimizing the Kimberley Process.

5307. (3-1-2008) NEW DELHI : The Prime Minister, Dr. Manmohan Singh inaugurated the 95th Indian Science Congress at Visakhapatnam today. Speaking at the occasion, Dr. Manmohan Singh reiterated the Government's commitment to invest more in science education. The Eleventh Five Year Plan is in fact a National Education Plan, the Prime Minister said. He stressed on the need for a global response, a national response and a local response to meet the challenge of climate change. Dr. Singh also urged the scientific community to tap into our traditional knowledge base, to develop environment-friendly and efficient technologies. Following is the Text of the Prime Minister's address on the occasion: "I should begin by wishing you all a very happy new year. I am also very happy that this year the theme for the 95th Indian Science Congress is "Knowledge Based Society Using Environmentally Sustainable Science And Technology." It is appropriate that such a theme should be discussed at this venue, along this beautiful scenic coastline. The beauty of the Coromandel Coast, of the Eastern Ghats and of the Andhra University campus, is a reminder of the richness of our natural heritage. It is incumbent upon us, therefore, to protect, preserve and rejuvenate this heritage even as we seek accelerated social and economic development. Let me begin by paying tribute to the contribution of the Andhra people and, in particular, the Andhra University to modern science in India. The greatest scientist of the 20th Century, Dr. C V Raman, was closely associated with this great University. Andhra University had also had the distinction of being home to Dr. Sarvepalli Radhakrishnan, the great philosopher, Statesman and our former President. I take this opportunity to also pay tribute to one of the Andhra University's more distinguished alumni, Professor C R Rao, a great mathematician and statistician. Professor Rao has inspired several generations of students at Andhra University to study statistics, and many of them have earned international recognition for their work. Your theme at this Congress, of a "knowledge-based" approach to the pursuit of environmentally sustainable development, draws attention to the role of applied research based on observed facts. The recent global concern about climate change and global warming is in fact based on painstaking statistical work. When this concern was first flagged nearly two decades ago it did not elicit as much global public attention because it's statistical basis was still weak. At that time much of the ground, much of the argument was based on theoretical models. That, of course, is how science moves forward. Let me, therefore, take this opportunity on this campus to emphasise the importance of collecting relevant data, especially with regard to climate change. For example we need data on what is happening to the Himalayan glaciers and not just on what is happening on our side of the border but to the system as a whole. I believe we must improve the quality of data we collect and also improve the quality of analysis of the available data. We have adopted a pro-active and pragmatic approach to the problems of environmental degradation. Our approach is based on our understanding that as our economy grows and modernizes, we must pay increasing attention to the environmental impact of the technological choices we make, the investment choices we make and the consumption choices we make as individuals and as a nation.

5308. (3-1-2008) NEW DELHI : The Minister for Civil Aviation, Shri Praful Patel will lay the foundation stone for the construction of new Integrated Terminal Building at the Chandigarh Airport tomorrow. He will also be present at the signing of a MoU for the development of International Civil Air Terminal Complex at Mohali. Airports Authority of India (AAI) has major plans to develop a civil enclave at Chandigarh to international standards. The State Government of Punjab has been requested to give approximately 300 acres of land, identified on the other side of runway with independent access from the city side.

5309. (3-1-2008) NEW DELHI : The Prime Minister, Dr. Manmohan Singh has said that the government is closely monitoring the situation in Kenya regarding the problems faced by the Gujarati community and that it had already been in touch with the Kenyan authorities and the Indian origin community in Kenya. Replying to the Gujarat Chief Minister's letter Dr. Manmohan Singh reassured him that the External Affairs Ministry has been asked to take immediate action.

5310. (4-1-2008) NEW DELHI : Oil India Limited (OIL), a Premier National Oil Company, declared an interim dividend of 125% for the financial year 2007-2008. The Company had last year paid a total Dividend of 260% for the year 2006-07. The Company handed-over a Cheque for Rs.262.50 Crore to Government of India, as first interim dividend @ 125% for the financial year 2007-2008. The Cheque for the said amount was presented to Shri M.S.Srinivasan, Secretary, Ministry of Petroleum and Natural Gas, Govt. of India by Shri M.R.Pasrija, Chairman and Managing Director of Oil India Limited. Total Dividend paid to the Government of India for the year 2006-2007 was to Rs.546.00 Crore being 260% of the paid up capital of Rs.210 Crore held by the President of India, out of which the first interim dividend was @ 110%. OIL's proposed IPO, and issuance of shares to employees have already been approved by the Government. The Company is targeting the IPO during the 1st Quarter of 2008, subject to SEBI's clearance. The issue comprises a net issue to the public of upto 2,40,45,438 equity shares and a reservation of upto 24,04,554 equity shares for subscription by eligible employees as defined in the Draft Red Herring prospectus.

5311. (4-1-2008) NEW DELHI : Government of India have announced the sale (re-issue) of "7.99 per cent Government Stock, 2017 for a notified amount of Rs. 6,000 crore (nominal) through a priced based auction using multiple price method. Government of India have also announced the sale (re-issue) of "8.33 per cent Government Stock, 2036" for a notified amount of Rs. 4,000 crore (nominal) through a price based auction using multiple price method. The auctions will be conducted by the Reserve Bank of India, Mumbai Office, Fort, Mumbai on January 11, 2008 (Friday). Up to 5% of the notified amount of the sale of both the stocks will be allotted to eligible individuals and Institutions as per the Scheme for Non-Competitive Bidding Facility in the Auction of Government Securities. Bids in the prescribed form obtainable from the Regional Director, Reserve Bank of India, Mumbai Office (Public Debt Office), Fort, Mumbai-400 001 and RBI website www.rbi.org.in should be submitted to that Office on January 11, 2008. The NDS members should submit competitive as well as non-competitive bids in electronic format using Primary Market Operation (PMO) module of NDS. All bids should be submitted by 12.30 P.M. The result of the auctions will be announced on January 11, 2008 and payment by successful bidders will be during banking hours on January 14, 2008 (Monday). The Stocks will be eligible for "When Issued" trading in accordance with the guidelines on 'When Issued transactions in Central Government Securities' issued by the Reserve Bank of India.

5312. (4-1-2008) NEW DELHI : Following consideration of reports received from the Governor of Nagaland, it has been decided to invoke Article 356(1) of the Constitution and impose President's rule in the State, while keeping the Legislative Assembly in suspended animation. The President issued the Presidential Proclamation in this regard yesterday. The reports of the Governor indicated that for the past few months, the political situation in Nagaland has been in a state of flux, which climaxed in the developments in the State Assembly on 13th December, 2007 when a motion of no confidence was taken up for consideration. The voting pattern clearly demonstrated that the Government of the day had lost the majority support. Votes cast by nine members of the Legislative Assembly were not counted and three members were not allowed to vote by the Speaker. The decision not to count or allow the votes was against the Constitutional provisions. These facts amounted to Constitutional break-down of the State machinery, and the Government of the day was not in a position to be run in accordance with the provisions of the Constitution. In these circumstances, there was no option except to invoke the provisions of Article 356(1) and recommend imposition of President's rule in the State. The Governor and the State Administration have been asked to take all measures so that a fair and impartial administration and governance as per the Constitution and provisions of law are provided to the people of the State. Necessary steps for the appointment of Advisers to assist the Governor are also being taken.

5313. (4-1-2008) NEW DELHI : Finance Minister, Shri P. Chidambaram met his Japanese counterpart Mr. Fukushiro Nukaga, here today. Both the leaders noted with satisfaction that relations between India and Japan have steadily progressed in the last few years. The visits of the Indian Prime Minister to Japan in 2006 and the visit of the Japanese Prime Minister to India in 2007 have further strengthened the India-Japan Global Partnership. The two sides expressed the hope that this partnership would further deepen. Both sides called for increasing bilateral collaboration in infrastructure sector, including the Dedicated Freight Corridor Project and the Delhi Mumbai Industrial Corridor Project. Increasing collaboration in the Financial sector was also discussed, during the meeting.

5314. (4-8-2007) NEW DELHI : Preliminary comments of the BJP on the Agreement between the Government of India and the Government of the USA concerning peaceful uses of nuclear energy. 1. The BJP has been expressing its reservations regarding the Indo-US nuclear deal from the very beginning. When the Joint Statement was issued at the end of the visit of Prime Minister Manmohan Singh to Washington in July 2005, Shri Vajpayee issued a statement in which he expressed his reservations about the deal, specially with regard to its impact on our strategic nuclear programme. He had expressed his apprehension at the proposed separation plan of our nuclear facilities between civilian and military. Later, when the separation plan was presented to Parliament, we expressed our opposition to it. We warned the Government of India when the Senate Foreign Relations Committee and the House International Relations Committee of the US Congress adopted the draft bills for enabling this cooperation between the two countries.

We protested strongly when the Hyde Act was passed by the US Congress. We have consistently opposed the deal in Parliament whenever discussions on this deal have taken place. None of our fears and apprehensions was ever given serious consideration by the Government of India. No effort was ever made by it to evolve a national consensus on this vital issue of national concern before making commitments to the US.

5315. (4-1-2008) NEW DELHI : Speaking at the Launch of the Pilot Phase of the National Programme for Prevention and Control of Diabetes, Cardio-vascular Diseases and Stroke (NPCDS), here today, the Union Minister for Health & Family Welfare, Dr. Anbumani Ramadoss said that due to an ageing population and environmentally driven changes in behaviour, the Non-Communicable Diseases (NCDs), especially Cardiovascular Diseases (CVD's), Diabetes Mellitus, Cancer, Stroke and Chronic Lung Diseases have emerged as major public health problems. To take care of these issues, the Ministry has been planning a National Programme for quite sometime and today I am happy that we have succeeded in this mission. The Deputy Chairman of the Planning Commission, Shri Montek Singh Ahluwalia formally launched the Programme wherein Smt. Panabaka Lakshmi, Minister of State (HFW), Shri Naresh Dayal, Secretary (HFW), Dr. R.K. Srivastava, DGHS, Dr. K. Srinath Reddy, Director (PHFI) and other senior officials from the Ministry were also present.

5316. (4-1-2008) NEW DELHI : The ASI, with a view to introduce various scientific applications in archaeology, has entered into a MoU with the IIT (Kanpur) recently. The collaboration is basically aimed at capacity building of ASI officers in various scientific methodologies that can be of use in archaeology and also to have joint projects in various application areas. Two of the projects that are under process are "Terrain Mapping and Archaeo-Scientific Investigations of Ahichchhatra, district Bareilly, U.P." in which various scientific applications like GPS, Total Station, GPR, GIS will be put into use. The other project is that of "Seismic Retrofitting of Ancient Monuments" with the Civil Engineering Department of IIT. The Rumi Gate, Lucknow has been identified for formulating a Pilot Project in this regard. Several other areas have also been identified in which ASI will have active collaboration with IIT, like (i) database management using various applications and custom-made software, (ii) laser scanning of ancient structures, (iii) antiquity identification system, (iv) analysis of various antiquities using non-destructive methodologies to know about ancient technology, provenance studies, interaction networks, etc., (v) dating of archaeological samples through various dating methods, and (vi) statistical applications in archaeology. A promising step that has been initiated by IIT (Kanpur) in this regard is that of setting up a "National Centre for the Archaeological Sciences and Technology" in its campus which will have various components like dating labs, sophisticated equipment to carry out various studies in archaeology, training centres for capacity building of archaeologists, undertake various kinds of research in scientific applications of archaeology.

5317. (4-1-2008) NEW DELHI : The conduct of the MP government and the ruling party in that state in respect of the Sabbharwal case is reprehensible. It is devious, it is opportunistic, it is collusive and it is designed to exculpate the accused. When Prof. Sabbharwal was brutally assaulted and killed, the direct involvement of the ABVP, RSS and BJP cadres was captured on candid cameras. The accused are well-known members of the party or associated organizations. They were neither arrested nor prosecuted. After a hue and cry and court proceedings, cases were filed but the stand of the prosecution was clearly in favour of the accused. The Chief Minister has never made any bones regarding the innocence of the accused. This is a case of the state directly supporting the accused. Now the Chief Minister takes the unprecedented step of visiting the accused in hospital. The "inspection" story is a fig leaf and a pretence. Who will guard the state and its ordinary citizens from the guardians itself? What happens when the fence starts eating the crop? Can this farce of a prosecution succeed? Witnesses have already been bought over and threatened by both the state and the accused. Who will now give evidence? We demand transfer of the case outside MP. This is a blatant and active collusion between the state and the accused. It is a prosecution by the accused, for the accused, of the accused. IMPOSITION OF PRESIDENT RULE IN NAGALAND Statement of Senior Nationalist Congress Party (NCP) Shri Purno A. Sangma criticizing the UPA Government imposing President's Rule in Nagaland is self incriminatory. He forgets that his party is also a partner in the Government. Assembly has been put under suspended animation. Government of India has adhered to the strict provisions of the Constitution and SR Bommai case of Supreme Court of India. No motive can be attributed. The Union Government has taken a decision for imposition of President's Rule as the Government led by Shrl Nephieo Rio has been reduced to minority. It was Congress which was the single largest party in Nagaland and the outgoing Chief Minister formed the minority Government with the support of others. The statement of Shri P.A. Sangma that it is designed to destabilize the region is against perspective of national security. North Eastern region is quite sensitive and it is the Congress Party which has provided space for democratic aspiration by entering into accords even at the cost of the prospects of the Congress Party. The word used by Shri Sangma about destabilization is quite unfortunate and smacks of impropriety and is contrary to the interest of the region which is very precious to the country. When Assembly met in December, 2007, 31 members voted in favour of the no confidence motion and Nephieo Rio Government has come to a minority. The Speaker refused to consider the verdict of no confidence motion. Head count was taken and 31 MLAs walked out of the House and met Governor. Governor deputed the observer and it was found that the Chief Minister had lost majority. It is only on the basis of the Report of the Governor that the Union Government recommended imposition of President's rule in Goa. CONTROVERSY ON THE STATEMENT OF KASHMIR FINANCE MINISTER The proposal for separate currency is preposterous and unviable and defies economic logic apart from national interests involved. It is totally contrary to all constitutional principles, norms and conventions. We strongly refute it. Such statements create uncertainty and confusion and should never be repeated. SEZ GOA Shri Digambar Kamat, Chief Minister, Goa, sought cancellation of all 15 SEZs in the state including the three notified by the Government following protests. He also met Shri Kamal Nath, Union Minister for Commerce & Industry. The issue centred around three SEZs which have already been notified. Other 12 are at various stages of approval of the Central and State Government. Congress President raised the issue of agricultural land at the Chief Minister's Conference at Nainital in the year 2006 and this was followed by a letter from the Congress President to the Union Government. It was at the instance of the Congress President GOM was formed to examine the issue relating to SEZ. After deliberations with all political parties and stake holders, the policy for resettlement and rehabilitation, the Government policy of acquiring land for SEZs, payment of compensation, etc. were thoroughly revised and a new policy was formulated as a result of initiative taken by the Congress President. SEZs are meant to provide employment to the local people taking advantage of the boom in the economy in a focused manner. It may be significant to note that SEZs were practically a non-starter during the NDA regime and consequently there was steep dip in the employment potential. The employment graph has now picked up and we may have to keep up the tempo by focusing on creation of employment in industry and also in agriculture. Each State may have its own local issues and it is for the respective States to evolve its own policy on SEZs in the context of the National policy. To a question on the Cabinet Committee on Political Affairs clearing the Delimitation Commission's report and recommendation, does your Party support it, Shri Singhvi said, the matter is presently under serious consideration of the government. It is for the government to decide but we believe that it is not only long over due but will also give appropriate, proper representation to, in particular, the SC/ST categories which has not happened in the existing set –up because of the long gap in the Census.

5318. (4-1-2008) NEW DELHI : The Union Home Minister, Shri Shivraj Patil will be leaving for Egypt tomorrow on a five-day official visit. During the visit, he will hold discussions with Egyptian leaders including Egyptian Interior Minister, General Habib Ibrahim Habib El Adly on issues of bilateral interest. Shri Patil will also meet with the Egyptian President, Mohammed Hosni Mubarak. During the visit, both the countries will be signing two bilateral agreements, *viz.*, Agreement on Mutual Legal Assistance Treaty on Criminal Matters and the Agreement on Transfer of Sentenced Persons.

5319. (4-8-2007) NEW DELHI : Sh Rajnath Singh, National President BJP, while addressing a Press Conference at Dimapur welcomed the Peace process and extension of the ceasefire and said that Central government should seize this initiative and give impetus to the peace process as it happened during the NDA government led by Sh Atal Behari Vajpayee. It is important that the Central

Government takes all sections of Naga society into confidence, at the same time all factions of underground should also be involved in the wider arena of peace process. Sh Rajnath Singh said that Nagaland has a special place and status for BJP as Nagaland has given BJP its first government in North East. BJP has cherished this support from the people of Nagaland and wishes to receive the same love and support in the coming 2008 assembly election. BJP is credited of providing a stable Government in Nagaland after a long gap. BJP's slogan in 2003 elections was 3Ps – Peace, Progress and Prosperity. We are happy that because of BJP's constructive support Peace and Progress has happened and therefore we seek from people of Nagaland a better positive mandate so that we can also deliver Prosperity. He further added that BJP in Nagaland will be a major party in the coming elections and will play an important role in the government formation. Sh Rajnath Singh said that BJP is confident of forming the government at Centre in 2009 and therefore will be in a position to provide large packages of development funds for Nagaland in areas such as roads, electricity, education, health and agriculture. Sh Rajnath Singh said that he being a farmer has a special attention for the farmers of Nagaland and would ensure that better quality and timely delivery of certified seeds, creation of cold storage facilities and warehousing is brought in the next 5 years once voted to power. He criticized the Congress led Central Government of not pushing Kissan credit cards for Nagaland farmers, a scheme he had introduced as Agriculture Minister during NDA government. Congress has a policy of misleading citizens for their own political benefits by making empty promises. BJP as a party has a policy to fulfil what they promise. When Sh Atal Behari Vajpayee was the Prime Minister of India and visited Nagaland in 2003 he announced a package of Rs 1052 crores for development in the area of roads, employment of 25000 youths and so forth apart from Rs 365 crores to wipe out once for all State's deficit. Unfortunately when the Congress led government came in 2004 they purposely forgot to fulfil and delivered the package given by Sh Vajpayee. Sh Rajnath Singh questioned the Prime Minister and Planning Commission's move to select backward 90 districts on the basis of religion and provide development funds. Selection of districts should be on the basis of their backwardness and not religion. However the Congress led Central government has gone ahead against the spirit of the Constitution of India and selected Muslim populated districts and once again proved their Muslim appeasement policy.. Sh Ranjath Singh made an appeal to the citizens of Nagaland to be careful of Congress divide and rule policy and not be disillusioned by their campaign of secularism versus communalism. BJP believes in equality for all and appeasement of none. Sh Rajnath Singh cautioned the people of Nagaland to be alert against the influx of Bangladeshi infiltrators a subject which Congress Party has mastered in Assam, so as to change the demographic nature of the state for their own narrow political gains.

5320. (4-1-2008) NEW DELHI : Taking the country's Look East Policy a step further, the Defence Minister Shri AK Antony, who went to Vietnam last month, will now be leaving for Malaysia for a three-day official visit, on Sunday. He will be accompanied by a high-level delegation including the Defence Secretary Shri Vijay Singh, Advisor to Raksha Mantri Shri Sundaram Krishna, Deputy Chief of Army Staff Lt Gen ZU Shah, Deputy Chief of Air Staff Air Marshal NAK Browne, Vice Admiral KN Sushil and Joint Secretary (South), Ministry of External Affair Shri Biren Nanda. During his stay in capital Kuala Lumpur, Shri Antony will hold detailed discussions with his Malaysian counterpart and the Deputy Prime Minister Mohd Najib Bin Tun Hajiabdul Razak and the Foreign Minister Ahmed Syed Hamid Albar. He will also call on the Prime Minister Abdullah bin Haji Ahmad Badawi. Shri Antony will also visit Penang, where he would meet Governor Haji Abdul Rahman bin Haji Abbas. Malaysia is celebrating the 50th Anniversary of its Independence and the current year also marks the 50th Anniversary of the establishment of diplomatic relations between the two countries. Over the years, India and Malaysia have developed strong bilateral relationship encompassing political, economic, education, cultural and defence fields. The Defence Cooperation between the two countries was formalized by signing a MoU in 1993 and it has been expanding steadily since then. The primary area of cooperation has been in training to Malaysian Defence personnel at various levels including at the National Defence College and Staff College. The Defence Cooperation between the two countries is also characterized by high-level exchange of visits, visit of ships of the two navies, India's regular participation in Langkawi International Maritime and Aerospace (LIMA) exhibition including the one which was held from 04-08 December 2007. Both the countries have participated in bilateral exercises such as PASSEX and MILAN. Last month the Sixth Malaysia-India Defence Cooperation Meeting (MIDCOM) was held in New Delhi when both sides had meaningful discussions on strengthening defence cooperation as well as to explore new areas of cooperation. The two countries last month signed a Protocol on training of Royal Malaysian Air Force (RMAF) Pilots by Indian Air Force on SU-30 MKM aircraft. Earlier in May 2007, a MoU was signed by Hindustan Aeronautics Limited with the Malaysian Ministry of Defence for the technical training of RMAF personnel on SU-30 MKM aircraft.

5321. (4-1-2008) NEW DELHI : The Ministry of Environment and Forests has prepared a draft of the National Biodiversity Action Plan (NBAP) to identify threats and constraints in bio-diversity conservation. The draft NBAP has been circulated to various Central Government Ministries and Departments and will be placed for approval before the Cabinet soon. Addressing the thirteenth meeting of the Consultative Committee of the Ministry today, Minister of State for Environment & Forests, Shri Namo Narayan Meena said the bio-diversity is fundamental to the fulfilment of human need and vital for the survival of this planet. Shri Meena explained that the environment reach in biological diversities offers a broad array of options for sustainable economic activity, for sustaining human welfare and for adopting to change. Shri Meena added that this makes sustainable development possible, protecting life from the potential consequences of change, including sudden changes of eco system. Human activities place severe pressure on biological resources and increasingly leading to fragmentation and degradation of habitats. This results in loss of bio-diversity he added. Another significant threat to bio-diversity he said is greenhouse gases in the atmosphere. The Minister said that biodiversity and global warming are closely linked and each impacts upon the other. Presentation was made on National Biodiversity Action Plan which explained the values of bio-diversity, convention on biological diversity, measures for bio-diversity conservation in India and Draft NBAP. It is in consonance of National Environment Policy (NEP). NEP's centre of concern is for sustainable development of human beings and to secure basis to obtain better livelihood from conservation than degradation. It was informed that seventeen countries, which are rich in bio-diversity and are associated with traditional knowledge, have formed a group of Like Minded Megadiverse Countries (LMMCs). Measures and strategies for conservation and sustainable use of biodiversity and use of bio-resources are ingrained in Indian ethos and are way of life. India has long history of conservation and sustainable use of natural resources. Thus Convention on Biological Diversity (CBD) in India did not start recently but it is part of our culture from ancient times. Members of the Parliamentary Consultative Committee expressed concern about degradation of bio-diversity. They suggested to create awareness through media and to start a campaign involving masses. Members also suggested to work at global level, because saving of environment of only our nation cannot solve this problem. They also agreed that to reverse the speed of our industrial progress is not possible though industrialization is one of the factors affecting our bio-diversity. Terming increased population and consumerism as another two factors affecting bio-diversity, members suggested to concentrate on conservation and preservation of forests and natural resources. Members also appreciated the working of joint forests management committees at village level. The Member who attended the Consultative Committee Meeting are: S/Shri Ananta Nayak, Mahaveer Bhogora, Basudeb Barman, Ramji Lal Suman, R. Shunmuga Sundaram, Satyavrat Chatruvedi, Ramdas Aggarwal, Dr. M. Baburao and Smt. Karuna Shukla.

5322. (4-1-2008) NEW DELHI : The Union Tourism Ministry has sanctioned Central Finance Assistance for Integrated Development of Hoshiarpur, Punjab as a Tourist Destination under Integrated Development of Tourist Circuit Scheme at a total cost of Rs. 397.89 lakh. The proposal for this project was received from the Punjab State Government and approved by the Minister of Tourism and Culture Smt. Ambika Soni. Eighty percent amount (318.31 lakh) of the central finance assistance of Rs. 397.89 lakh has been released to the State Government as the first instalment as an advance for starting the work.

5323. (4-1-2008) NEW DELHI : National Pharmaceutical Pricing Authority (NPPA) has sought cost data from the Pharma manufacturing units, companies and formulators to revise and fix the norms for Conversion Cost (CC), Packing

Charges (PC), Process Loss (PL) and Packing Material (PM) for the year 2008 as per the provisions of DPCO' 1995. Two detailed questionnaire in printed form have already been sent to pharma units and Industry Associations. Soft copies of both the questionnaires are available on the official website of NPPA *i.e.* www.nppaindia.nic.in These norms for CC, PC, PL & PM are to be worked out based on actual cost data/information received from various manufacturers & formulators.

5324. (4-1-2008) NEW DELHI : The mandate of the Ministry of Culture is to preserve and promote all forms of art and culture. Along with programmes for the preservation of India's ancient heritage, the activities of the Ministry encourage and disseminate a variety of contemporary creative arts as well. During the year 2007, the Ministry with its two attached offices (ASI and NAI), six subordinate offices, 33 autonomous organizations and two missions (National Mission for Manuscripts and National Mission on Monuments and Antiquities) have worked ceaselessly to generate cultural awareness at the grassroot level and to promote cultural exchanges at the national and international level.

5325. (4-1-2008) NEW DELHI : Shri. Vayalar Ravi, Minister for Overseas Indian Affairs said that we want to engage the diaspora at every level through the Pravasi Bharatiya Divas. He was addressing a curtain-raiser press conference for the 6th Pravasi Bharatiya Divas to be held New Delhi from 7-9 January 2008. The theme of the convention is 'engaging the Diaspora: the way forward'. He said that Education and healthcare are major issues to be focused in the PBD-2008. The PBD will project these social issues and enable overseas Indians to express their ideas and ways of possible participation. A single window system will allow concrete participation from persons of Indian origin and non-resident Indians with the block level as the basic unit for philanthropy and investment. While thousands of NRIs are working today in the social space, more organized efforts are needed and the single window system will provide this, said Mr. Ravi. Other issues that will be addressed during the conference are women empowerment through microfinance and child welfare. Investments and business engagement sessions are also part of the programme, briefed the Minister. As the issues of overseas Indians differ from region to region, working sessions for Gulf, Asia-Pacific, Africa, Europe, and Americas will be held. Mr. Ravi also stressed that the problems of women's marriages to NRIs will be addressed. 12 Union Ministers and six Ministers from overseas will take part in the proceedings. The state governments will be fully involved in the sessions so that participants can directly interact with government representatives and address their concerns and have exposure to the government' programmes for the common man and how they could be involved in these. Chief Ministers from Delhi, Gujarat, Haryana, Maharashtra, Jharkhand have confirmed their participation in the PBD.. The Pravasi Bharatiya Divas is the annual flagship event of the Ministry of Overseas Indian Affairs. The 6th PBD will focus on development of the common man and rural women. The Prime

Minister of India, Dr. Manmohan Singh, will inaugurate the convention, and it will culminate with valedictory address and conferment of Pravasi Bharatiya Samman Award by President of India. The Chief Guest is Dr. Navinchandra Ramgoolam, Prime Minister of Mauritius.

5326. (5-1-2008) NEW DELHI : Smt. Renuka Chowdhury, Union Minister of State (Independent Charge) for Women and Child Development has said that Information Technology has helped bridge the gap between urban and rural areas. Speaking at the inaugural of the First National Virtual Congress of "MAHILA KISAN" at the ongoing Indian Science Congress here today, she said that women farmers who are attending to the dual chores of farming and cattle rearing besides looking after the household duties need to be provided with the Pattas for the land on which they depend. The first virtual conference brought together women farmers in arid, semi-arid, coastal, hill and irrigated areas for a discussion on both the opportunities and constraints facing women in agriculture. The Minister said that due to lack of joint pattas, women farmers are not able to get institutional credit and Kisan credit cards as the lending agencies are yet to become adequately gender sensitive. She acknowledged the demand for a policy favouring the women folk in the villages. The virtual conference was organized with women farmers coordinated through the local Village Resource Centres spread across seven places from Andhra Pradesh, Tamil Nadu, Orissa, Maharashtra and Rajasthan. It has highlighted to the scientific community the urgent need for attending to the technological and sociological needs of women farmers which are mostly male-centric till now. During the interaction the women farmers put forth various demands including medical and risk allowances, post harvest technology, community godowns, threshing floors and water harvesting facilities. Smt. Renuka Chowdhury also inaugurated the Children's Science Congress. The Exhibition has been organized as a part of the event showcasing the projects of winners from state and national level competitions. Later Dr. M.S. Swaminathan gave away cash awards and certificates of merit to fourteen ISCA Young Scientist Awardees and released Prof. B.P. Pal Commemoratory Stamp on the occasion.

5327. (5-1-2008) NEW DELHI : Following is the text of the keynote address delivered by Shri Kapil Sibal, Union Minister for Science and Technology and Earth Sciences, at the inauguration of the 95th Indian Science Congress, Andhra University, Visakhapatnam on the 3rd of January 2008. "Dr. Manmohan Singh ji, Hon'ble Prime Minister of India; Dr. Rajasekhara Reddy, Hon'ble Chief Minister of Andhra Pradesh; Shri Subbrami Reddy, Hon'ble Minister of State for Mines; Shri Pallam Raju, Hon'ble Minister of State for Defence; Dr. Dasari Narayana Rao, Hon'ble Minister of State for Coal; Prof. Ramamurthi Rallapali, President of the 95th Indian Science Congress, Dr. Harsh Gupta, Immediate Past President of the Indian Science Congress, Dr. T. Ramasami, Secretary of the Department of Science & Technology and the President-elect of the 96th Indian Science Congress, distinguished members of the scientific community, delegates, media personnel, invitees, ladies and gentlemen. Sir, I have had the privilege of addressing the Indian Science Congress three times. This, at Visakhapatnam is my fourth. To be with India's best and brightest scientific minds is a great honour and kindles the hope of India keeping its tryst with destiny. Sir, every generation considers that its times are unparalleled, its achievements unsurpassed and the problems/ challenges it confronts insurmountable. So do we. Science & Technology has enhanced human welfare to enviable and unprecedented levels. New materials, new technologies, new production/distribution systems are continuously made and refined to render our lives more leisurely and less burdensome. S & T becomes part and parcel of our lives much the same way as a shell is to the snail or a web to the spider-as the famous physicist Heisenberg so beautifully put it. Technology enslaves us even while it empowers us. Prodigious consumption, unbridled monetization, untrammeled energy profligacy are threatening the sustainability of our civilization. Today, human civilization is faced with the challenge of global warming. Global and local climate may change faster than our ability to adapt. Climate change is thus an assault on all evolutionary forms of life. For years the world's leading atmospheric scientists have been cautioning us that a gradual warming of global climate was underway, but we paid no heed. As most of you know, the 1990s were the hottest decade of the entire century; perhaps even the millennium, and 1998, 2001, and 2002 were three of the hottest years ever recorded. The growing scientific consensus is that this warming is largely the result of emissions of carbon dioxide and other greenhouse gases from human activities including industrial processes, fossil fuel combustion, and changes in land use, such as deforestation. The scientific community has adduced evidence requiring us to decrease green house gases emissions, mainly CO2 and methane, by 60-70% from the present, for several decades. This will revolutionize the supply and demand of energy. We must do our utmost to develop technologies for energy production which are not, or are to a much lower degree, linked with the emission of greenhouse gases. Unluckily, in the past, de-carbonization of the energy supply was obstructed by the fact that CO2 could be emitted at zero price. The energy price of the fossil fuel economy was and is until today being heavily subsidized by nature, by the capacity of the atmosphere to assimilate. The Fourth Report of the IPCC has unequivocally reiterated this. As a result the international debate has now moved beyond the reality of climate change to what must be done to mitigate it and to prepare proactively for its consequences. It is a global problem requiring global solutions based on the principle of common but differentiated responsibilities. The solution should be inclusive benefiting and encompassing all. Low carbon economies alone can ensure global sustainability. What we do to achieve this globally should be discussed, planned and acted upon. In India, there is little doubt that climate will become more unstable in the years ahead. We will witness more unpredictable and extreme weather patterns.

5328. (6-1-2008) NEW DELHI : In a rare case of organ donation, the organs from war veteran brigadier from the Indian Army were retrieved late last night and transplanted till the early hours today. Brigadier YP Bakshi was shot in head at his residence in Shastri Nagar in Meerut on Friday, 4 January by unknown assailants. Commissioned into 5th Battalion of the 1st Gorkha Rifles, he raised 5th Battalion and commanded 4th Battalion of the same regiment. For his services, he was mentioned in dispatches. Brig Bakshi was brought to Army Hospital (R&R), Delhi Cantt, after the shooting incident in Meerut. However he was declared brain dead late last evening. Mrs. Kamini Mehta the daughter of the slain brigadier and her husband, Maj Gen PK Mehta, who has retired recently from the Army readily agreed to donate the organs of Brig Bakshi so that other in need of various organs could get a lease of life. Being a medico legal case, the procedure of organ retrieval required the requisite legal clearances from the police departments of Uttar Pradesh and Delhi. According to Maj Gen OP Mathew, Commandant of Army Hospital (R & R), the entire operation was coordinated by the Armed Forces Organ Retrieval & Transplantation Authority (AORTA) with active cooperation from Dr. Jagdish Prasad, Medical Superintendent of Safdarjang Hospital and Dept of Forensic Medicine along with police officials from New Delhi and Meerut. Surgical teams at Army Hospital worked in tandem to transplant the liver into a serving soldier with cirrhosis and one kidney into a 14 year old. The second kidney has been sent to AIIMS transplantation. One cornea and heart valves have been stored for use on needy recipients. The Armed Forces have been promoting organ donation and over 1000 serving personnel, veterans and their families have already pledged to donate their organs. This was the third medico-legal case and the seventh multi-organ donation organized by Army Organ Retrieval and Transplant Authority. The mortal remains of the slain brigadier were consigned to flames at noon today.

5329. (6-8-2007) NEW DELHI : A Parliamentary delegation consisting of three BJP MPs had a meeting with the Rajyapal and the Chief Minister of J&K to apprise them of the atrocities, misbehaviour being committed on them and a plot to eject them out of the state. The delegation was headed by Sh. Syed Shahnawaz Hussain, the President of the BJP Minority Morcha and consisted of two other MPs – Sh. Sukhdev Paswan and Sh. Brijbhushan Sharan Singh. The delegation informed the Rajyapal and the Chief Minister that non-Kashmiris, majority of whom is from UP and Bihar are being subjected to unprecedented tyranny in J&K, which the BJP would never tolerate. The state govt. and the UPA govt. at the centre are totally insensitive to this human tragedy and constant atrocious onslaught on non-Kashmiris have forced them to flee from the state. Non-Kashmiris were not only contributing towards the development of the state but also were giving solid support to all big-small developmental projects being carried out in the valley. Such happenings with them will hinder the developmental process in the state. The delegation impressed upon that Kashmiris are known world over for their communal harmony and hospitability and such acts of terrorism and separatism will tarnish the image of J&K. When the country was scorching under the impact of division, it was J&K state alone that remained unscathed from the brunt of division. The constitution of the country has bestowed right upon every citizen to reside at the place of his choice. Then, why the state govt. and the central govt. are not intervening in the matter. As per state govt.'s record and data, only 7,000 persons have fled from the state but it is devoid of truth. Virtually, 35,000 persons have fled from the state so far. The evil designs with which the anti-national forces are trying to spoil communal and social harmony will create hatred towards persons, who have come from other parts of the country to contribute to the progress of the J&K state and ultimately put hurdles in economic progress of the state. Earlier, Kashmiri Pandits were also subjected to such attacks and such events tarnished the image of J&K internationally. The reduction of armed forces in J&K during such grim conditions has become a cause for great alarm. The BJP is immensely concerned over this development in J&K. The apathetic attitude of the central govt. and the Congress-PDP govt. of the state so far makes it clear that these governments believe in vote-bank politics. These governments have completely renounced human values and human sensitivities. The BJP demands that the central government and the state government should inculcate the sense of security in the minds of non-Kashmiri labourers and provide them adequate protection as well as should make genuine and serous efforts to stop fleeing of non-Kashmiri labourers from the state.

5330. (7-1-2008) NEW DELHI : The ISRO Chairman, Dr. Madhavan Nair has been elected to preside over the 97th Indian Science Congress in 2010. This was announced by the General President of the 95th ISCA, Prof. R. Ramamurthi after the General Body Meeting held on the concluding day of the 5-day 95th Science Congress in Visakhapatnam. Dr. T. Ramasami, Secretary, Department of Science and Technology is the president-elect for the 96th Indian Science Congress. Winding up the 95th Session of the Congress this evening here, Prof. Ramamurthi was all praised the efforts by the Andhra University who helped host the event. He said, the participation of three Noble laureates and participation of 2500 scientific delegates were the highlights of the Congress. Other innovative activities included innovative a special session on 'Vedic Sciences' conducted by Rashtriya Sanskrit Vidya Peeth of Tirupathi, Mahila Kisan Congress-an interactive national virtual congress with the women farmers of remote areas from rural India for the first time as a Public-Private Participation. Dr. Ramamurthi also announced that 5 national universities namely Punjab University, Nagpur University, Magadh University, North Eastern Hill University and NIT Surathkal are in the fray for hosting the 96th ISCA. The Best Poster Presentation Awards for 2007-08 were given to 24 faculty members, researchers and students. Another 10 ISCA-INFOSYS travel awards to school students were also distributed.

5331. (7-1-2008) NEW DELHI : The President of India, Smt Pratibha Devisingh Patil has condoled the passing away of the inventor of the Jaipur Foot, Dr. Pramod Karan Sethi. In her condolence message, the President said, "Dr. Sethi was a renowned orthopaedic surgeon whose invention of the Jaipur Foot brought smiles to lakhs of amputees across the world. His invention helped amputees to continue their lives without the feeling of inadequacy for which he shall always be remembered".

5332. (7-1-2008) NEW DELHI : At a ceremony held today at 1145 hrs in the Ashok Hall, Rashtrapati Bhavan, Shri Vinod Rai was sworn in as the Comptroller and Auditor-General of India. He made and subscribed the oath of office before the President, Shrimati Pratibha Devisingh Patil.

5333. (7-1-2008) NEW DELHI : The demand of the Jammu and Kashmir Finance Minister Tariq Hameed Karra asking for a separate currency for the state is fraught with a separatist insinuation and deserves an outright condemnation. In the garb of autonomy the statement spews separatism and such a demand by senior Minister does not absolve the Congress leadership in the state or the Chief Minister Ghulam Nabi Azad who is heading a coalition government in Kashmir. The failure to sack the Minister so far amply proves this point. The deafening silence maintained by the top brass leadership of the Congress party in general and Prime Minister and Sonia Gandhi in particular on an issue which has major ramification on country's sovereignty is appalling. The indifference exhibited by them amply confirms misplaced priorities on issues of National concern. It is shocking that with an eye on the impending elections in the state and the greed to hold power even at the cost of country's sovereignty, the Congress has chosen to ignore the bizarre and divisive statement. While states and Nations across the globe are working towards integration and adopting a common currency as witnessed in the European Union, here is a state of the Federal India which is asking for a separate currency. The demand is the total negation of the Constitution and such a preposterous proposal never ever has been mooted in the past. It would be pertinent to recall that Late Dr. Shyama Prasad Mukherjee the founder president of BJP (erstwhile Jansangh) had sacrificed himself attaining martyrdom while opposing the permit system for Indian's visiting Kashmir. The party had positioned the foundation and fundamentals of Nationalism by categorically stating "two Constitutions, two Flags and two PMs " are completely unacceptable. The Prime Minister and the Congress party must come out categorical on such a fundamentalist and divisive remark especially in a border sensitive state of Kashmir. The errant Minister is unfit to be in the government and should be sacked.

5334. (7-1-2008) NEW DELHI : Shri Murli Deora, the Minister of Petroleum & Natural Gas held extensive talks with Shri Vilasrao Deshmukh, Chief Minister of Maharashtra for ensuring successful implementation of the National Programme for supply of Ethanol Blended Petrol (EBP) which has been implemented in several States and Union Territories of the Country. In a meeting held at Mumbai today, Shri Deora requested the Chief Minister to completely remove the export duty on ethanol so that excess production in Maharashtra could be supplied to other States which will ultimately benefit sugarcane farmers of Maharashtra. Later, briefing media persons, Shri Vilasrao Deshmukh stated that his government will withdraw the export fee of Rs.1500 per kilo litre (Rs.1.5 per litre), presently being imposed on ethanol supplies to other States. The Petroleum Minister stressed that the EBP Programme at 5% blending of ethanol with petrol was launched commencing 1st November, 2006 through out the country (except North eastern States, Jammu & Kashmir, Andaman & Nicobar Islands & Lakshadweep Islands). This programme is aimed at contributing to energy security through use of alternative fuel sources and also help sugarcane farmers to earn additional income. This initiative is environment friendly as oxygenate nature of ethanol ensures greater petrol combustion leading to lesser emission of pollutants. So far, EBP is being supplied in 11 States and 3 Union Territories covering about 70% of the identified States. Out of total requirement of 180 crore litres ethanol for 3 years, Oil Marketing Companies (OMCs) have already contracted a quantity of 140 crore litres. They have so far procured 19.35 crore litres under the programme as on 31st December, 2007. The programme in few States like West Bengal, Tamil Nadu, Chhattisgarh, Kerala could not be implemented for various reasons. In case of Kerala, OMCs have finalized tenders but the State excise department is required to issue necessary import permits. The Government of West Bengal is required to issue notification permitting import of ethanol and indicating taxes/levies applicable. Government of Tamil Nadu has stopped ethanol supplies due to reported shortage, while in Orissa & Chhattisgarh procurement could not be finalized due to high duties/levies. There are certain procedural impediments which have affected the free movement of ethanol across States. These are in the nature of multiple clearances to be obtained for issue of permits for export of ethanol from one State to another. For ensuring successful implementation of EBP programme, the Minister of Petroleum & Natural Gas Shri Murli Deora has held regional level meetings with representatives of various States to sort out these issues. A meeting was held in Srinagar on 16th June, 2007 covering the hill states of Jammu & Kashmir, Himachal Pradesh and Uttarakhand. Another meeting was convened in Kochi on 23rd June, 2007 to discuss and resolve issues pertaining to southern States of Kerala, Karnataka and Tamil Nadu. The matter has also been taken up with Chief Ministers of concerned States from time to time. Recently, Prime Minister has also written to the Chief Ministers. Shri Murli Deora also reiterated his earlier demand for rationalization octroi levied by Brihan-Mumbai Municipal Corporation (BMC) on crude oil procured by Mumbai refineries of BPCL & HPCL. This levy has been putting additional burden on these two OMCs, who are already facing heavy under recoveries in their effort to insulate consumers against high volatility in global crude oil prices. In addition they expressed satisfaction on the progress made by Mahanagar Gas Limited (MGL) in expanding compressed natural gas (CNG) & piped natural gas (PNG) infrastructure/ supplies in Mumbai and surrounding areas.

5335. (7-8-2007) NEW DELHI : The BJP deeply appreciates the judgment of Madras High Court rejecting the challenge by the Switzerland Multinational Drug Company Novartis AG against the constitutional validity of section 3d of the Indian Patents Act. It is the victory of developing countries over monopolies of multi-nationals. It is victory of health for the poor against the pure commerce. It would help the availability of anti cancer drug at affordable price..

5336. (7-1-2008) NEW DELHI : Waghadi, a small village in Dahanu taluka of Thane district attained the Status of a Nirmal Gram through its efforts for public cleanliness. Each and every house in Waghadi today has its own latrine. The village has practically utilized every village development scheme of the government and become an ideal village. The village consists of five padas (hamlets) spread over two kilometres. The padas are connected by concrete roads built under village road scheme. The village roads are maintained clean through the voluntary efforts of youth in the village. Gram Panchayat has built 10 public latrines under the National Rural Employment Guarantee Scheme in 2005-06. Under the Sarva Shiksha Abhiyan the school in the village has built clean drinking water facility for students and toilets. The village consists of 256 households and has about 700 students from Anganwadi onwards. The village also has a small tribal student's hostel run by an NGO Thane Zilla Adivasi Samajonati Sangh. The village is mainly of rice cultivators. Thane Zilla Parishad has built a check dam on the Surya river near the village. A village tank has been built as a water resource for the drinking water needs of the village connected through a canal to the check dam. During the high summer days even this dries and the village depends on 11 bore wells as on alternative. The typical topography of Dahanu taluka has two main features. On the one side sea beaches and fisherfolk villages the other is a hilly terrain and populated by tribal and other farmers. Waghadi is at the Western foothills of Sahyadri. Jay Bajrang Bachat Gat (Self Help Group of men) has dug a big wormiculture pit. After providing wormiculture products like natural manure to the villagers they are engaged in selling it too. They are able to sell their product to the tune of Rs. 1 lakh per annum.

5337. (7-1-2008) NEW DELHI : The Vice-President of India Mohd. Hamid Ansari inaugurated the NCC Republic Day Camp-2008 here today. Addressing on the occasion he called upon the NCC Cadets to aim high and have great dreams of a strong, prosperous and fully developed India. Applauding the cadets the Vice President said that these cadets have gathered here representing the varied values of our society through their sense of discipline, unity and social service. The Vice President visited the various plaques put up the State NCC units. Later he got himself photographed with the cadets of all State units and signed in the Visitors book. A Memento was also presented to him. He congratulated DG, NCC, his officers and the cadets for the impressive parade and the display of NCC activities.

5338. (7-1-2008) NEW DELHI : The 9th Meeting of the Maritime States' Development Council (MSDC), the apex consultation mechanism between the Centre and Maritime States/UT Administrations on development of Port and Shipping Sector was held under the Chairmanship of the Union Minister for Shipping Road Transport & Highways Thiru T.R. Baalu at Goa today. The meeting assumed significance in the backdrop of continued boom period in the international shipping dovetailed with an unprecedented economic growth of the country at 8% to 9 % per annum during the last three years, necessitating an urgent need for strengthening and up-gradation of Indian Ports infrastructure from the current total handling capacity of 733 million tones to 1.5 billion tones by the year 2011-2012 and providing enabling environment for the growth of Shipping and ship building activities. While focusing on the need for comprehensive capacity augmentation plans by the respective Maritime States for the 11th Five Year Plan period, Thiru Baalu advised them to adopt the Public Private Partnership mode of implementation utilizing the recently approved central Model Concession Agreement (MCA) as a standard for Port sector projects and assured them the needed support in their endeavours from the Government of India. Thiru Baalu expressed satisfaction on the resolve of the Maritime States to enhance their non-major Ports handling capacity to 1086 million tones and the commitments by the Andhra Pradesh, Kerala, Orissa and Goa for setting up of their respective State Maritime Boards by April 2008. The Minister also called upon the Maritime State to expedite submission of concrete proposals for setting up of International standard shipyards to enable the Central government to finalise further course of action. The Maritime States requested Thiru Baalu to continue the Centrally Sponsored Scheme for the development of Inland Waterways Transport during the 11th Plan period also. The Coastal Shipping Policy was also discussed and a Committee under Chairman, National Shipping Board was requested to prepare an Action Plan for its growth and development. In order to ensure harmonized training and certification for Inland Vessel operators, the Minister directed the Director General, Shipping to prepare guidelines for "model training and certification" in consultation with Maritime States. This would not only meet the burgeoning demand for trained manpower but also provide an impetus for up-gradation of candidates holding fishing and Inland Vessel qualifications to operate sea-going vessels. The Council Meeting was attended by Shri M. Venkata Ramana Rao, Minister for Infrastructure and Investments, Ports, Airports, Natural Gas, Government of Andhra Pradesh, Shri Francisco X. Pacheco, Minister for Tourism and Ports, Government of Goa, Shri M.P. Saminathan, Minister for Highways and Ports, Government of Tamil Nadu and Shri Pritamkumar Sheagaonkar, Minister of State for Ports, Government of Maharashtra besides senior officials of the Central and Maritime and State Governments, Major and Non-Major Ports and State Maritime Boards. Earlier in the day the Chief Minister of Goa Shri Digamber Kamat, along with his cabinet colleagues Shri Francisco Pacheco, Minister for Tourism & Ports and Shri Churchill Alemao, Minister for PWD called on Thiru T.R. Baalu to discuss important issues on the Central Road sector projects.

5339. (7-1-2008) NEW DELHI : In arguably the first effort of its kind, the Department of Economic Affairs (DEA) went on an off-site Retreat to Surajkund outside of Delhi last weekend. Led by Finance Secretary Dr. D. Subbarao, about 50 officers of DEA of the rank of Deputy Secretary and above, spent an entire day and indeed a good part of the night, intensively brainstorming on their vision of the emerging role of DEA in the fast changing economic situation and how best they might contribute to that vision. Reflecting the theme of the Retreat which was "Improving the Way We Work", each Division of the Department made a presentation on the 'best practices' they are evolving and identified one or two tasks where they will bring about a 'paradigm shift' in quality of output. The highlight of the Retreat was a two hour session with the Finance Minister, Shri P. Chidambaram. Shorn of the hierarchical barriers that inhibit communication in the Government, and in a remarkably frank and honest exchange of views with the senior officers of DEA, the Finance Minister said that maintaining and accelerating economic growth should be central to all the work of DEA. He admitted that Ministry of Finance does not have policy control of the entire economic agenda because of democratic structures and coalition politics, but officers must capitalize on that part of the agenda on which they do have control, such as for example, driving the FRBM targets. He agreed that all policies must have a pro-poor bias, but was quick to add that economic growth was at the heart of poverty reduction. There cannot be any sustainable poverty reduction without economic growth. The strength of DEA, in the Finance Minister's view is a sense of pride that the officers had in working in this premier Department of the Government. Their high academic qualifications made them specially suited to give their best to their department. Pressed by the participants to let them know of their weaknesses or shortcomings, the FM said that the weakness, if any, was the quality of written communications. Written communication needs to be precise, brief in content and with sharply delineated positions for getting decisions from him. He also said officers must be on top of the subjects that they deal with. When asked to give his view on whether and what kind of changes he has observed in the civil service over the last 20 years, the Finance Minister said that while the civil service attracted the best talent in the country over 20 years ago, today a lot of talented youngsters seek careers outside the Government, notably in the financial sector. He also thought that the life style of civil servants has become more ostentatious over the years. This he thought was not a positive development. Responding to a concern that even as the majority of the civil servants are competent and clean, the stereotype view of the entire civil service is shaped by a few corrupt officers, the Finance Minister said that while our civil service is not entirely meritocratic, and there may be a few exceptions, but in the long run competent and clean officers do rise to the top.

5340. (7-1-2008) NEW DELHI : The Vice President Mohd. Hamid Ansari inaugurated the National Cadet Corps Republic Day Camp-2008, here today. A contingent of smartly turned out NCC cadets drawn from all the three wings namely Army, Navy and Air Force, presented a Guard of Honour to the Vice President on his arrival at the NCC camp. 1900 cadets, both boys and girls drawn from 17 NCC Directorates covering all the States and Union Territories of the country are participating in this RD camp. The cadets will take part in a number of activities like Cultural, National Integration Awareness and Institutional Training

Competitions. The nearly one-month long camp will conclude with the Prime Minister's Rally on Jan 28. In his brief address, the Vice President said that the cadets hailing from different parts of the country, with different linguistic and religious background, represented a 'Mini India'. He added that the rigorous discipline the NCC cadets are put through is a very useful training of both the body and the mind. Dr. Hamid Ansari expressed the hope that the NCC cadets would rise above parochialism and regionalism and develop a broad national outlook to make a united and prosperous India. Later, addressing the cadets Lt Gen Prakash Chaudhary, Director General NCC said the NCC has signed an MoU with the UNICEF under which the NCC Girl Cadets would participate in a pilot project on the literacy mission. To the applause of the cadets, Gen Chaudhary said that the NCC Boys lifted the Subroto Cup last year, probably for the first time.

5341. (7-1-2008) NEW DELHI : Consequent to policy changes and procedural simplifications, FDI equity inflows have registered a phenomenal upswing. FDI inflows have gone up from US $ 2.2 billion in 2003-04 to US $ 15.7 billion in 2006-07; a five-fold increase in FDI inflows during the last 3 years. Accordingly, a target of US$ 30 billion has been fixed for 2007-08. FDI has increased just from 0.77% of GDP in 2003-04 to 2.31% in 2006-07. Similarly as a percentage of total investment this has gone up from 2.55% in 2003-04 to 6.42% in 2006-07. Due to progressive delicensing, only a handful of five sectors remain within the ambit of compulsory licensing, and that on account of safety, security and environmental concerns. These are distillation and brewing of alcoholic drinks; cigars and cigarettes of tobacco and manufactured tobacco substitutes; electronics aerospace and defence equipment: all types; industrial explosive including detonating fuses, safety fuses, gun powder, nitrocellulose and matches; specified hazardous chemicals *viz.* : (i) hydrocyanic acid & derivatives (ii) phosgene derivatives and (iii) isocyanates & disocyanates of hydrocarbon. In 1991, 839 items were under reservation for SSI sector. After progressive liberalization now only 114 items are left reserved for SSI sector. In the last three years, 561 items have been de-reserved from SSI sector. Consequent to the policy undertaken the share of the Industrial Sector to the GDP (at constant prices) has grown from 25.6% in 2003-04 to 26.6% in 2006-07. This has been possible due to growth of the Industrial sector from 7.4% in 2003-04 to 10.9% in 2006-07 and along with a double digit growth of the manufacturing sector from 6.6% in 2003-04 to 12.3% in 2006-07. The capital goods sector recorded a growth of 13.9% in 2004-05, 15.8% in 2005-06 and 18.2% in 2006-07. This indicates a robust capacity addition in the industrial sector.

5342. (7-8-2007) NEW DELHI : The BJP demands that the government of India take all requisite diplomatic steps and all other available leverages to secure the extradition of Dawood Ibrahim and his very close associate Tiger Menon to India to face the consequences of all their crimes including terrorism and waging a war against the nation. We need to remind ourselves that Dawood Ibrahim is a proclaimed terrorist who masterminded the 1993 Mumbai blast alongwith Tiger Menon. These two deliberately and persistently refused to submit to the process of law in spite of a red corner Interpole notice and found a safe sanctuary in Pakistan. Let us not forget that more than ten accused have been given capital punishment in the trial, which is a very conclusive evidence to demonstrate the severity of the crime. We take note of the reported arrest of Dawood in Pakistan though we seriously apprehend that Pakistan, as usual; would deny his very presence there. The government must ensure that the occasion is properly used to expose the patent falsehood of Pakistan. It needs to be reminded that it was during the NDA regime that the issue of deporting Dawood Ibrahim was taken in the most focused manner. Shri L.K. Advani as the then Home Minister raised it with President Musharraf immediately before the Agra Summit. It was the persistence of the then Prime Minister Shri A. B. Vajpayee wherein by the agreement dated January 6, 2004, Pakistan for the first time acknowledged and agreed that it shall not permit its territory to be used for the spread of terror related activities. It is our charge that the UPA government has for all practical purposes forgotten this agreement. Terror and terrorism is a politically dirty word for them. The close links of Dawood Ibrahim with Al-Qaida elements are increasingly coming into focus. Only last week the US said Dawood's smuggling route converge with that used by Al-Qaida to move arms. This is also the occasion for the USA to demonstrate its bonafides and earnest commitment to the global war on terror. It must prevail upon Pakistan to extradite Dawood to India. In a way the declared commitment of USA against terrorism is on test. The threat of Al-Qaida terror including its affiliates continues to loom large. The latest threat video needs to be taken seriously and the comical theatre being indulged into by some Ministers needs to be controlled. India must use all diplomatic pressure to get Jamat-Ud-Dawa, which is the new name for the banned Lashkar-e-Taiba; banned under Security Council resolution no. 1373. It is reported that China is opposing this move in concert with Pakistan for their own obvious interest.

5343. (7-1-2008) NEW DELHI : Shri Kamal Nath, Union Minister of Commerce and Industry, has stated that the developments in the real estate sector symbolize the changing face of India and it is a reflection of the growth in the Indian economy brought about by high rates of GDP and also by India's integration with the global economy. He was speaking at the " National Convention 'NATCON 2008': Real Estate for All" organised by the Confederation of Real Estate Developer's Association of India (CREDAI), here today. He also stated that in the recent years, services sector has been the main driving engine of Indian economy's growth. "With the economy on an upswing, the emphasis and requirement today is on creating international standard infrastructure and housing facility to sustain the growth rate projected in the 11th Five Year Plan. The Real Estate Development sector has the capacity to pay for itself without straining the limited resources of the State Government", Shri Kamal Nath said. The Minister further stated that we have already opened construction development sector for FDI and the policy permits wholly owned subsidiary in this sector in India by a foreign company.

"Of course, there are conditions regarding minimum area for development and minimum capitalization to be brought in by the foreign investor. A number of global players have entered the Indian market and many more have shown interest. Growth and investment have also created opportunities for investment in real estate sector, he said. "While the role of the Government is expected to be primarily as a facilitator to the development process, the private sector participation is aimed at bringing technical and managerial expertise in delivering good quality mass housing projects. It is a good sign that many State governments are joining hands with private entrepreneurs in resolving the acute housing problem in urban areas. The private sector and Government has to work in tandem towards a common goal. It is equally important to address the institutional and regulatory aspects as well as strengthen and expand the capacity of financing institutions for further growth of the sector", Shri Kamal Nath said.

5344. (7-8-2007) NEW DELHI : The National Democratic Alliance strongly denounces the highly unconstitutional unethical and patently partisan way in which attempts were made to save the minority Congress government in Goa headed by Chief Minister Mr. Digamber Kamath, in spite of the fact that Goa Democratic Alliance headed by the former Chief Minister Shri Manohar Parikkar had a clear majority in the Vidhan Sabha. It is too well known to recall that on 25-07-2007, as many as 21 MLAs in a House of 40, conveyed a joint request in writing to the Governor to dismiss the Kamath Ministry which was in minority and allow Shri Manohar Parikkar to form the government. These MLAs also presented themselves before the President of India to ensure that constitutional propriety be followed. In view of the public outcry the Governor of Goa directed that on 30th July 2007 before transacting any business the Goa Vidhan Sabha must take up the motion of confidence in the ministry headed by Mr. Kamath. On the said day, in the most blatant subversion of constitutional propriety, before taking the motion of confidence as directed, by an ex-parte interim order two members of Maharashtravadi Gomantak Party (MGP) were restrained from participating in the proceeding of the House or, even voting. There was no notice or hearing. It is relevant to recall that the President of the MGP has already conveyed in writing to the Governor about the decision of the Party to withdraw support from the Digamber Kamath government. Similarly its two MLAs who formed the Legislature Party had conveyed to the Governor their decision to withdraw support and further provide unconditional support to the coalition headed by Shri Manohar Parikkar. The NDA is constrained to observe that this blatant partisan and highly unconstitutional conspiracy to force a rank minority government in Goa would not have been possible but for the active patronage support and shelter of the top leadership of the Congress Party including its President and the Prime Minister of the UPA government. The Congress Party has not learnt any lesson from the past. The UPA government had to suffer serious reprimand from the Hon'ble Supreme Court in the case of Jharkhand and Bihar when its Assembly was arbitrarily dissolved. We are sure this brazen decision would invite equally strong judicial reversal. The NDA pledges itself towards the upholding of democratic and constitutional norms and demands that the minority illegitimate government headed by Mr. Digamber Kamath be dismissed forthwith and Mr. Manohar Parikkar be given the opportunity to form the government. The NDA would raise this gross case of constitutional impropriety on the floor of the Parliament very vigorously in the coming session.

5345. (7-1-2008) NEW DELHI : The Indian National Congress strongly condemns the shocking statement made by the SGPC that the assassins of former Prime Minister of India, Smt. Indira Gandhi, as martyrs of the Sikh nation. This is a disturbing, dangerous and divisive statement. This is a statement that attempts to eulogies the assassins of a prime minister of this country thereby not only condoning but also calling upon people to take to violence and terror. This statement is totally violative of the Constitution of India and borders upon treason. It is all the more shocking because the statement has emanated from office bearers of a statutory body *i.e.*, the SGPC. We therefore, strongly condemn and reject the statement in the most vehement term. To a question whether you will press for registration of treason charges against the SGPC office bearers, Smt. Jayanthi Natrajan said, I said that it borders on treason and the issue is that the statement is unconstitutional and incites and supports violence and terror and to that extent we condemn the statement with all the emphasis at our command. To a question about the statement made by Smt. Mayawati accusing the Congress Party of trying to kill her and threatening to withdraw support Smt. Natrajan said, the two are different issues. Smt. Mayawati, the chief minister of Uttar Pradesh, has said that somebody in the Congress Party was plotting to kill her and I would like to categorically state that the allegation is completely baseless and contrary to facts. If Smt. Mayawati fears any threat to her life, certainly her security should be appropriately extended to protect her life and on our part, in the Indian National Congress, we to would appeal, as we are all aware, security is something that is jointly decided upon by the state and Central government in as much as the state government is concerned, she herself is the chief minister, and in so far as the government at the Centre is concerned, the Indian National Congress will appeal to the government, to the Prime Minister, to extend to Smt. Mayawati whatever security is required to keep her safe and secure against threats to her life. And as far as withdrawing support, this is a democracy and it is her prerogative to take whatever political decisions that she feels obliged to take that are in the best interests of her party. To a question that can we safely assume that the honeymoon between the BSP and the Congress Party is finally over, Smt. Natrajan said, we can safely say that we appeal to the government to keep her life safe and secure. I understand that she is going to announce her decision and whatever decision she announces we will only comment at that time. To a question that Atiq Ahmed who is absconding and has been expelled by the Samajwadi Party and is being allegedly sheltered by the Congress Party and who is suspected to behind the plot, Smt. Natrajan said, I would like to categorically state that nobody in the Congress Party nor the Party itself will be a party to any illegal or unlawful act. To a question on the support price to paddy farmers what are the Congress Party's views, Smt. Natrajan said, as you are aware the Indian National Congress and the UPA alliance has placed the farmers at the centre of all our economic development and we will take all steps to ensure that the best interests of the farmers is protected including the minimum support price which the government has been considering and revising from time to time. As far as the UNPA is concerned, we have no problem with any democratic activity that they take up. It's their right to demonstrate on whatever issues they feel important. To a question that the Centre is planning to turn Delhi into a police state, do you have any view on the Lt.-Governor's abortive move to make it mandatory on the ID card issue, Smt. Natrajan said, certainly we are not in agreement with that view. But the matter is now academic from newspapers reports, the Lt.-Governor will withdraw his proposal. The Chief Minister, Smt Shiela Dikshit, has also said that she was not consulted, DPCC president has already condemned it and we were hour and hour against the move.

5346. (7-1-2008) NEW DELHI : The Department of Public Enterprises (DPE) under the Ministry of Heavy Industries & Public Enterprises received a number of references from different Ministries, Public Sector Enterprises and other agencies seeking clarification in regard to the definition of a Public Sector Mutual Fund. DPE has examined the matter and has clarified that "Public Sector Mutual Fund means the Mutual Fund registered with and regulated by SEBI where the Government of India, its financial institutions and public sector banks holds/hold individually or collectively more than 50 per cent of equity/shares in the Asset Management Company of that Mutual Fund." The Department of Public Enterprises has also requested the Administrative Ministries/Departments to suitably advise the Navratna/ Miniratna Public Enterprises under their administrative control accordingly.

5347. (7-1-2008) NEW DELHI : The Minister of Corporate Affairs Shri Prem Chand Gupta will inaugurate the "Global Summit on Management Accounting" on 10th January 2008. This three-day Mega event of Management Accounting bodies across the globe is being organized by the Institute of Cost and Works Accountants of India (ICWAI) at Vigyan Bhawan New Delhi from 10th-12th January 2008. The summit is first of its kind and is expected to create a historical turn in the evolution of the management accounting profession globally. The Minister of External Affairs Shri Pranab Mukherjee will deliver the Valedictory Address on 12th January 2008. Deliberations during the Summit would focus on Management Accounting in its new manifestation including the territories of accounting, strategy and management of enterprises. As the management accounting bodies of the Western world has already been witnessing and turning them to such a paradigm, some beginning has to be made to complete the process across the globe among similar bodies. It is with this objective that the Summit is being organised by the ICWAI. The ICWAI will play the key role as the main host for this Global Summit. Co-hosts include Institute of Cost and Management Accountants of Bangladesh (ICMAB), Institute of Cost and Management Accountants of Pakistan (ICMAP) and the Society of Certified Management Accountants of Sri Lanka (SCMASL). Besides these SAARC bodies, the Summit will have technical partnership with other counterparts from the Western world such as Certified Management Accountants (CMA), Canada, Certified Institute of Management Accountants (CIMA), UK and the Institute of Management Accountants (IMA), USA. Around 1200 delegates are expected to participate in the programme out of which about 200 would be foreign delegates. A special feature of the Summit is a roundtable conference of the heads of all these Accounting bodies on the sidelines of the Summit to evolve a global strategy for repositioning the management accounting profession. The Institute of Cost and Works Accountants of India (ICWAI) was set up by an Act of Parliament *i.e.*, the Cost and Works Accountants Act, 1959. ICWAI is now bracing itself to a new leadership role in the global scenario. The event holds a special significance to the Indian economy as it is surging forward at a high growth rate with many business enterprises and institutions spreading their wings and taking on a global role encouraged by the environment and the motivation provided by the present Government.

5348. (7-1-2008) NEW DELHI : The Union Government has notified the Armed Forces Tribunal Act, 2007 which will pave the way for the setting up of a tribunal dealing with disputes relating to the personnel of the three Services. The Armed Forces Tribunal Bill 2007, passed by the Parliament, received the assent of the President on December 25, 2007. The Act provides for the setting up of the Tribunal's Principal Bench in New Delhi and branches at other places as the Government may deem necessary. Only a former Judge of the Supreme Court or a former Chief Justice of a High Court can be its chairperson and will hold office for a four year term. The Tribunal and its benches, having powers of a High Court, will consist of such number of judicial and administrative members as required. While judicial members will be retired high court judges, the administrative members will be drawn from the forces, who have served as Judge Advocate General for atleast one year. Once the Tribunal is constituted, all pending trials before civil courts including the High Courts covered under the Army Act 1950, Navy Act 1957 and the Air Force Act 1950 will stand transferred before the Tribunal. Appeals against the verdicts of court martial can thereafter be made only before the tribunal.

5349. (7-1-2008) NEW DELHI : Against Central Budget support of Rs. 10671 crore provided in the Budget Estimates 2007-08 for implementation of SSA programme, an amount of Rs. 9359 crore stand released to States/UTs (Annexure). To further speed up the SSA programme in 2007-08, a supplementary grant of Rs. 2300 crore has been obtained. In the XI plan, SSA has a funding pattern between Centre and States in the ratio of 65:25 for the first two years of the XI plan *i.e.* 2007-08 and 2008-09; 60:40 for the third year *i.e.* 2009-10; 55:45 for the fourth year *i.e.* 2010-11 and 50:50 thereafter *i.e.* from 2011-12 onwards. For the North Eastern States the fund sharing pattern between Centre and States shall be 90:10 under the programme with the Centre's share resource from the 10% earmarked funds for the NE Region in the SSA Central Budget. The outlay approved for Sarva Shiksha Abhiyan for the XI plan is Rs. 71,000 crores.

5350. (7-1-2008) NEW DELHI : The year 2008 marks the 50th year of the Defence Research and Development Organisation's (DRDO) service to the nation. Since its inception in 1958, DRDO has grown multi-dimensionally from a humble beginning and is today a major technology generator for the nation effectively meeting the requirement of developing and fielding defence systems to the Services and paramilitary forces. DRDO, today has a proven competence to produce a wide range of highly strategic defence equipment and technologies for our armed forces. DRDO has not only attained self-reliance in strategic defence weapons and delivery systems which no country is willing to part with, but has also provide the country with an array of tactical battlefield systems like Light Combat Aircraft (Tejas), Main Battle Tank (Arjun), family of missile such as Agni, Prithvi, Akash, Nag and BrahMos with capability of delivery of different payloads to varying ranges. The recent successful launch of Agni III and Interceptor missile technologies developed by DRDO has taken India to an elite club of developed nations having similar capability. DRDO's other success story has been the development of a series of radars, electronic warfare systems, secured communication, sonars, torpedoes and armaments. Most of them have been inducted into the Armed Forces. Specialized materials relevant to defence applications have also been indigenously developed including composites, armor for battle tanks, titanium sponge and special steel for naval weapon platforms. The life support technologies developed by DRDO have helped to improve the operational efficiency of our troops in extremes of environmental and operational conditions. In the current global political scenario, Nuclear Biological Chemical defence also has assumed a great significance. DRDO has achieved a significant level of self-reliance in this area. The defence spin-offs in civil sector and the DRDO societal missions have immensely benefited the society at large. After 50 years of commitment towards self-reliance in defence, the DRDO community feels that it should consolidate all that have been achieved and also present how it will organize itself for the coming decades by organizing a Year-long Golden Jubilee Programme. This endeavour will provide a unique opportunity to showcase its achievements and core competencies. It will create greater awareness of DRDOs tangible and intangible contributions to nation building among the scientific and technological organizations, academia, industry, foreign partners, as well as educate the general public and media and attract talent into DRDO fraternity.

5351. (8-1-2008) NEW DELHI : In arguably the first effort of its kind, the Department of Economic Affairs (DEA) went on an off-site Retreat to Surajkund outside of Delhi last weekend. Led by Finance Secretary Dr. D. Subbarao, about 50 officers of DEA of the rank of Deputy Secretary and above, spent an entire day and indeed a good part of the night, intensively brainstorming on their vision of the emerging role of DEA in the fast changing economic situation and how best they might contribute to that vision. Reflecting the theme of the Retreat which was "Improving the Way We Work", each Division of the Department made a presentation on the 'best practices' they are evolving and identified one or two tasks where they will bring about a 'paradigm shift' in quality of output. The highlight of the Retreat was a two hour session with the Finance Minister, Shri P. Chidambaram. Shorn of the hierarchical barriers that inhibit communication in the Government, and in a remarkably frank and honest exchange of views with the senior officers of DEA, the Finance Minister said that maintaining and accelerating economic growth should be central to all the work of DEA. He admitted that Ministry of Finance does not have policy control of the entire economic agenda because of democratic structures and coalition politics, but officers must capitalize on that part of the agenda on which they do have control, such as for example, driving the FRBM targets. He agreed that all policies must have a pro-poor bias, but was quick to add that economic growth was at the heart of poverty reduction. There cannot be any sustainable poverty reduction without economic growth. The strength of DEA, in the Finance Minister's view is a sense of pride that the officers had in working in this premier Department of the Government. Their high academic qualifications made them specially suited to give their best to their department. Pressed by the participants to let them know of their weaknesses or shortcomings, the FM said that the weakness, if any, was the quality of written communications. Written communication needs to be precise, brief in content and with sharply delineated positions for getting decisions from him. He also said officers must be on top of the subjects that they deal with. When asked to give his view on whether and what kind of changes he has observed in the civil service over the last 20 years, the Finance Minister said that while the civil service attracted the best talent in the country over 20 years ago, today a lot of talented youngsters seek careers outside the Government, notably in the financial sector. He also thought that the life style of civil servants has become more ostentatious over the years. This he thought was not a positive development. Responding to a concern that even as the majority of the civil servants are competent and clean, the stereotype view of the entire civil service is shaped by a few corrupt officers, the Finance Minister said that while our civil service is not entirely meritocratic, and there may be a few exceptions, but in the long run competent and clean officers do rise to the top.

5352. (8-1-2008) HYDERABAD: Congress MP from Narsapur Chegondi Harirama Jogaiah has been summoned by AICC general secretary in-charge of State Veerappa Moily to New Delhi on January 10 in the wake of his controversial remarks that people would support film star Chiranjeevi for the Chief Minister's post. Mr. Moily called up Mr. Jogaiah over phone on Monday and asked him to meet him in Delhi. The Congress MP said that he would call on the AICC leader in tune with his request. He said Mr. Moily sounded sympathetic towards him and did not sound negative about his statement. Mr. Moily issued the summons after receiving a report submitted to him by APCC in-charge president G. S. Rao about Mr. Jogaiah's remarks and his subsequent statement darlng the party to initiate disciplinary action against him. The AICC general secretary will be in the city on Wednesday to attend a training camp of Youth Congress and address a party meeting at Gandhi Bhavan. But sources said he was unlikely to go into the issue at these fora. K. Mrityunjaya Ram writes from Nellore: After the unsuccessful efforts of Bahujan Samaj Party (BSP), it might be the turn of the Bharatiya Janata Party (BJP) to woo film star Chiranjeevi. A top BJP leader from Andhra Pradesh, who has cordial relations with Chiranjeevi, is likely to hold talks with the film star any day after Sankranti on the latter's likely entry into politics and his yet-to-take shape outfit. Meanwhile, BJP senior leader M. Venkaiah Naidu, refused to comment on Chiranjeevi's political plans but gave enough hints that the latter might make his debut soon than later. He claimed that significant political developments would take place in Andhra Pradesh in the coming months. "The ruling Congress has clearly been losing its support in the State, but things have not been that bright for the Telugu Desam Party (TDP) either despite its tall claims. At the same time, people had lost faith in the Left parties while the Bahujan Samaj Party (BSP) had little political space and could only damage the Congress party's prospects by grabbing a certain percentage of votes from its traditional vote bank. Against this backdrop, the BJP, which had been riding high after spectacular electoral victories in Gujarat and Himachal Pradesh Assembly elections, would take the centre-stage in the State, he said on Monday.

5353. (8-1-2008) NEW DELHI : Shri Digambar Kamat, Chief Minister of Goa, along with Members of Parliament from Goa and senior officials of the State Government called on the Union Minister of Shipping, Road Transport & Highways, Thiru T.R. Baalu here today to discuss the status of implementation of Central Sector Road projects including the two prestigious four-laning projects on NH-4A and NH-17 in Goa. Thiru T.R. Baalu told the Chief Minister of Goa that the Feasibility Study is already in progress for the four-laning of the 137-km stretch of NH-17 in Goa (from the Maharashtra border to the Karnataka border) and is likely to be completed by June 2008 after which it would be referred to the Public-Private Participation Appraisal Committee (PPPAC) for obtaining the requisite approval for implementation. He informed the Chief Minister that for the four-laning of NH-4A, the Detailed Project Report has already been prepared and the Ministry is in the process of referring it to the PPPAC for obtaining its approval for its implementation under Phase-III of the National Highways Development Project (NHDP). Thiru Baalu also agreed for consideration a small modification in the alignment of NH-17 from Chauri to Maxem region to reduce the four-laning length by about 10 kms by providing two new bridges at Talpona and Galgibaga. Shri Digambar Kamat requested Thiru Baalu for the support of the Ministry for upgradation of the Major District Roads and other District Roads in Goa on priority basis for which the Government of Goa is formulating a comprehensive proposal for consideration of the Planning Commission and the Union Finance Ministry for sanction at an estimated cost of Rs.615.00 crore. Thiru Baalu assured Shri Kamat that considering the importance of the State as a major tourist destination, the Ministry would extend all support and cooperation in its development initiatives.

5354. (8-1-2008) THRISSUR: The CPI will strongly oppose the LDF government's reported move to go ahead with the 163 MW Athirappilly hydel project, CPI district secretary C.N. Jayadevan has said. Mr. Jayadevan was unanimously selected for the post at the party district conference in Guruvayur on Sunday. "I do not think the LDF government will construct the dam considering the protests against the project," he said, addressing a press conference here on Monday. He said the CPI district conference had discussed possible reunification of Communist parties. In resolutions adopted at the conference, the party demanded approval of new railway lines, availability of water for paddy cultivation, a medical university in Thrissur, better cancer treatment facilities in Thrissur Medical College, measures to check price rise and steps to make clay available under strict conditions to tile factories. Asked to comment on veteran Marxist leader Jyoti Basu's reported statement that capitalism had its own role in the development process, Mr. Jayadevan said that the former West Bengal Chief Minister's remarks were misinterpreted. "What he said was that there were limitations in implementing Marxist-Leninist principles in a capitalist development programme the country pursued," Mr. Jayadevan said. A 51-member district committee was also formed at the district conference on Sunday. Fifty-two members were selected to represent the district at the State conference in March. In all, 305 delegates attended the conference. As many as 10,000 party workers took part in the meetings.

5355. (8-1-2008) NEW DELHI : Shri Murli Deora, Hon'ble Minister of Petroleum and Natural Gas inaugurated the first Road Show of seventh round of New Exploration Licensing Policy (NELP-VII) at Mumbai on 8th January, 2008. He invited exploration and production companies and prospective investors to avail of the highly attractive investment opportunities being offered under NELP-VII. Shri Deora delivered a key note address at the first ever Road Show held in Mumbai under NELP regime, to promote the highly prospective 57 exploration blocks offered for global competitive bidding. Shri Deora stated that NELP-VII is being offered in the backdrop of 49 oil & gas discoveries which have already been made in 15 exploration blocks by accretion of in place hydrocarbon reserves of more than 600 Million Metric Tonne of oil equivalent. Under NELP regime, natural gas production in KG basin is likely to commence from July, 2008 at the rate of 40 MMSCMD with peak production of 80 MMSCMD. Other discoveries of ONGC and GSPC are also likely to come into production establishing the deepwater expertise of Indian companies. It was also highlighted that every fifth block under first three rounds of NELP has proven to be oil & gas bearing, as against world average of one out of 10 blocks. As exploration work is progressing, results of later round of NELP blocks in terms of more oil & gas discoveries will be available. Shri Deora informed that to leverage the recent huge discoveries, which have significantly changed perceptions about the geological prospectivity of India's sedimentary basins, Government of India would undertake an effective promotional programme to highlight the attractive investment opportunities available under NELP-VII to prospective investors and to bring home to global investors the advantages that India offers under NELP as well as information on the exciting new development in E&P Sector.

5356. (8-1-2008) NEW DELHI : Shri Vishwanathan Anand and Ms. Dola Banerjee have made the country proud by winning World Championship titles in 2007. Shri Vishwanathan Anand won the World Chess Championship, 2007 held in Mexico City in September, 2007 and Ms. Dola Banerjee won the World Cup Final title in the Recurve Women's Division held in Dubai in November, 2007. In appreciation of their outstanding achievements, Shri Mani Shankar Aiyar, Minister of Youth Affairs & Sports presented them with a cheque of Rs. 10.00 Lakh each at a brief function held in the Ministry. While Ms. Dola Banerjee personally received the cash award from Shri Aiyar, a cheque of Rs. 10.0 Lakh was collected by Shri Sunder, Honorary Secretary, Indian Chess Federation on behalf of Shri Vishwanathan Anand, who, at present, is abroad. Speaking on the occasion Shri Sunder said that the efforts of the Sports Ministry was the only reason for India to be doing so well in chess. Also present on the occasion was Shri S.K.Arora, Secretary, Youth Affairs & Sports.

5357. (8-1-2008) MADURAI: Communist Party of India (Marxist) will discuss the possibilities of evolving a third front without Congress or Bharatiya Janata Party (BJP) at its State and national conferences, its State secretary N. Varadharajan said here on Sunday. Briefing presspersons, he said that the BJP victories in Gujarat and Himachal Pradesh assembly elections had provided a strong platform for the communal forces to grow faster. "Despite our differences of opinion with the Congress relating to foreign policies, steep rise in essential commodities, failure to protect public sector enterprises and non-implementation of the common minimum programme, we still support the Congress-led United Progressive Alliance Government just because of its secular character," he said.

5358. (8-1-2008) NEW DELHI : The Union Minister of Social Justice and Empowerment, Smt. Meira Kumar has called for overall development of women. Chairing the session on 'Challenges in Women's Empowerment and Leadership' on the occasion of 6th Pravasi Bharatiya Divas (PBD) here today. The Minister said that gender equality is a necessary pre-requisite for achieving social justice. UPA Government is fully committed to empower women politically, economically, educationally and legally. She said that the Government is taking special efforts to earmark at least 1/3 of all funds flowing to panchayats for the development of women and children is also ensuring creation of facilities for schooling and extending special care to the girl child. With a threat to the very survival and basic health of the girl child, the Minister observed that there is a long way to go for developing the spirit and capability for leadership of women at the macro-level. Smt. Meira Kumar underlined the importance to reframe the policies for access to employment and quality of employment in the light of new challenges posed by globalization in the process of women's empowerment. 'Attention must be given to monitoring, mitigating and combating global trends that have the potential to undermine the global targets with regard to women's empowerment. Strategies must be designed to enhance the capacity of women and empower them to meet the negative social and economic impacts, which may flow from the globalization process.' The Minister said that initiatives for women's empowerment and gender equality has to be 'inclusive' covering the men as well. Noting that it is essential to develop a consciousness amongst both men and women as being partners in national development, the Minister called for joint effort on the part of national Government's and trans-national organizations which will help in refining strategies fuel creativity and innovation. The session was also addressed by Dr. Girija Vyas, Chairperson, National Commission for Women and Brinda Karat, MP, Rajya Sabha.

5359. (8-1-2008) NEW DELHI : The Prime Minister has constituted a High Powered Group under the Chairmanship of Dr. V. Krishnamurthy, Chairman, National Manufacturing Competitiveness Council (NMCC) for suggesting various measures to ensure the continuing growth of the manufacturing sector in the country which of late is showing signs of deceleration. The Secretaries to the Government Finance, Revenue, Commerce, Textiles and Industrial Policy & Promotion as well as the Member Secretary of the NMCC are the other Members of the Committee.

5360. (8-1-2008) LUCKNOW: Chief Minister Mayawati on Sunday derided attempts to drive away the Brahmins from her party in the aftermath of the Bahujan Samaj Party's defeat in the Ballia Lok Sabha by-election. She dismissed reports that the moves were afoot to sideline the Brahmins after the party's performance in the by-poll. Addressing a late night press conference on her return from Hyderabad, the Chief Minister denied reports attributed to her that following the Ballia poll debacle she had dissolved the Brahmin "bhaichara samiti" (Brahmin brotherhood committee). "When no such committee had been formed, where was the question of its dissolution?" she asked.

5361. (8-1-2008) NEW DELHI : The Appointments Committee of Cabinet has approved the appointment of Shri Arun Ramanathan, IAS (TN:73) presently Secretary, Department of Chemicals & Petrochemicals, Ministry of Chemicals & Fertilizers, as Secretary, Department of Financial Services, Ministry of Finance, in the vacancy of Shri Vinod Rai IAS (KL:72) with immediate effect.

5362. (8-1-2008) NEW DELHI : The Prime Minister, Dr. Manmohan Singh inaugurated the 6th Pravasi Bharatiya Divas (PBD) meet here today and reiterated Government's commitment to promote interests of Pravasi Bharatiyas across the world. He announced setting up of a Primem Minister's Global Advisory Council of people of Indian Origin to serve as a high level platform to draw upon the experience and knowledge of the best Indian minds wherever they may be based. The Prime Minister also announced launching of an Overseas Workers Resource Centre (OWRC) which will provide relevant information and assistance to potential migrant workers, and will also operate a multi-lingual help line for grievance redressal and interventions for overseas workers in distress. Highlighting the initiatives taken by the Government to sustain a mutually rewarding relationship between India and its Diaspora, Minister of Overseas Indian Affairs, Sri Vayalar Ravi said that the Government had issued over two hundred thousand Overseas Citizenship of India (OCI) cards during last two years and a much larger number of overseas Indians would be provided these cards in the ensuing year. The Government is also working on extending a wider range of benefits to OCI cardholders, he added. The Minister said that efforts were being made to provide the opportunity to the overseas Indian professionals for working in the country, the inter-ministerial consultations for this purpose have been completed and implementation process will start very soon. In a bid to provide secured working opportunities abroad and to safeguard interests of persons of Indian origin, the Minister said that the Government is working on bilateral agreements with number of European countries. Beside this Memorandum of Understanding were being stressed with the countries where protection of the labour laws is not available to safeguard the interests of the persons working in informal sectors, the Minister informed. Underlining the importance of the role of the Pravasi Bharatiyas in the development of the country, Sri Vayalar Ravi said that our objective is to raise the level of engagement to go, beyond mere investment related issues, and address a broader agenda. He expressed the hope that the conference would provide the opportunity to NRIs to contribute to the development of the country in their own way. Inaugural session was also addressed by Dr. Navin Ramagoolam, Prime Minister of Mauritius and Smt. Shiela Dixit, Chief Minister of Delhi. It was followed by the plenary sessions focused on the issue of social development, role of Diaspora Philanthropy, specially the potential of micro-credit in empowerment of rural women. The themes of the two-day conference reflect the national priorities, set out in the 11th Five Year Plan.

5363. (8-1-2008) RAJAHMUNDRY: Congress MP from Amalapuram G.V. Harsha Kumar said on Monday that Bahujan Samaj Party, which has no roots in the State, would hardly make any impact. He said that BSP's leader Mayawati was forgetting the fact that she was the Chief Minister of Utter Pradesh only. Addressing a press conference here, he said that Mayawati in her speech in Hyderabad made long promises to the people which were nothing but old wine in a new bottle. He said the Congress from the beginning was against classification of SCs. He said that no forum in Congress had discussed classification of SCs and UPA partners like Lalu Prasad, Ram Vilas Paswan and many other leaders were expressed their support for united SC community. "So, BSP's statement on classification, free education to Dalits and separate Telangana are not new," he added. He said that barring BJP and TDP all parties were against classification. About Dalit Christians demand, Harsha Kumar said Justice Bhagavati Commission had made recommendations on this and Parliament had to make Bill on this. He showered praises on Chief Minister Y.S. Rajasekhara Reddy for implementing several good programmes like Indiramma, Pavala Vaddi, Arogya Sri and others.

5364. (8-1-2008) NEW DELHI : RITES Ltd, Government of India Enterprise under the Ministry of Railways has announced issue of bonus shares of Rs.36 crore to its existing shareholders, in the ratio of 9 shares for one share held in the Company. The paid-up capital of the Company with this bonus issue will stand increased to Rs.40 crore from Rs.4 crore. Entire paid-up capital of the Company is held by the Government of India. The Company has also decided to split Face Value of its share from Rs.100/- to Rs.10/- each. The Shareholders have also approved increasing the authorized capital of the Company to Rs.100 crore. The Company has accumulated Reserves of Rs.521 crore as on September 30,2007. RITES has been upgraded as a Schedule 'A' Company in July 2007.The Company was the first PSU under the Ministry of Railways established in 1974 as Schedule 'C' Company with initial capital of Rs.10 lakh. In the face of extremely competitive business scenario, RITES has an operational experience in over 60 countries and is the leading multi-disciplinary organization of consultant, project managers and engineers in transport and infrastructure sector such as railways, highways, urban transport, ports and harbours, airports, inland waterways, ropeways, concessioning and export packages of rolling stock etc.

5365. (8-1-2008) NEW DELHI : The National Programme of Mid-Day Meals in Schools, the largest school feeding programme in the world, covers nearly 9.70 crore children studying at the primary stage of education in classes I-V in 9.50 lakh Government (including local body) and Government aided schools, and the Centres run under Education Guarantee Scheme (EGS) and Alternative & Innovative Education (AIE). The programme was extended, with effect from 1.10.2007, to children in the upper primary stage of education (classes VI-VIII) in 3,479 Educationally Backward Blocks (EBBs). Approximately 1.7 crore additional children in classes VI-VIII in EBBs are expected to be included.

5366. (8-1-2008) VIJAYAWADA: The Communist Party of India (CPI) has demanded that the provisions of GO 1567 be extended to other poor people who settled down by encroaching on various Government lands on the slopes of hills in the city and other places. The party made this demand in a representation submitted to Minister for Revenue Dharmana Prasada Rao in Hyderabad on Sunday. CPI city secretary and former MLA K. Subba Raju, MLC Jalli Wilson and Vijayawada West MLA Sk. Nasar Vali were among those who met the Minister. The copy of the memorandum released by the party here on Monday said though several families had been relocated from different places in the city, house sites had not been registered in their name. The owners, who settled down in various colonies, were unable to raise any loan from banks by mortgaging their properties when they needed it during an emergency or for family functions like weddings. The memorandum said nearly 30,000 poor families were in a state of unrest because of the Government's reluctance to register these properties to them for a nominal price. House sites were registered at nominal rates in the past to families relocated at Ajit Singh Nagar, Payakapuram, Urmilanagar and a few other places because of an agitation launched by the CPI, they said. Similarly, the Government had, as a result of an agitation launched by the CPI and other political parties, issued GO 1567, fixing a nominal registration fee of Rs. 30 a square yard for those who encroached on a house site and Rs. 100 a square yard for those who purchased it from the first encroachers. But, it was unfair to restrict this benefit only to the dwellers of Ranigari Thota and it must be extended to all other areas.

5367. (8-1-2008) NEW DELHI : The Prime Minister, Dr. Manmohan Singh, inaugurated the Sixth Pravasi Bharatiya Divas, here today. Speaking at the occasion, Dr. Singh said that the idea of India transcends the narrow barriers of religion, language, caste or class, both within and outside the Indian nation. The Prime Minister announced the launch of an 'Overseas Workers Resource Centre' (OWRC) which will provide all relevant information and assistance to potential migrant workers. He also announced the establishment of Prime Minister's Global Advisory Council of People of Indian Origin. The security and welfare of Indian residents living abroad is a top priority of our diplomatic missions, the Prime Minister said.

5368. (8-1-2008) NEW DELHI : The Culture and Tourism Minister Smt. Ambika Soni has said India is expanding incredibly on the global cultural canvas and people all over the world have started noticing India. Addressing Pravasi Bhartiya Divas here today she said there are several factors of this new cultural emergence-Indian films, music, dance, cuisines and fashion. She said her ministry for promoting and strengthening cultural heritage of the country is taking several steps. On one hand it is taking exhibitions of artifacts to countries such as America, France, Belgium and China and holding programmes such as Incredible India@60 abroad and on the other hand building tourism around cultural destinations, upgrading museums, creating book banks through its network of libraries so that not only the non-resident Indians but young generation also see and feel about their rich cultural heritage and traditions. Smt. Soni said the Government by commemorating 150th Anniversary of 1857, Bhagat Singh Birth Centenary and 60th Year of India's Independence, is promoting bonding with the past for the internet generation. The Minister said the hallmark of Indian culture is its diversity which promotes love, peace and harmony among various sections of society. She said our adaptability and tolerance to various cultural and social milieus is the secret of doing well in various parts of the world. She called upon the NRIs to showcase new India that is forward looking and flooded with opportunities, creative charm of our heritage and scientific foundations of our traditions. In this context, the field of Yoga, medical and spiritual tourism, export of cultural products etc. are few to name that we should explore, Smt. Soni added. On the part of the Pravasi Bhartiya, the Minister said, there are ways in which they can help in strengthening the cultural bonds between them and India. Firstly, those who are motivated by the ideals of philanthropy can contribute immensely by helping in setting up new cultural institutions such as museums, academic and training centres for music, dance, drama etc. Government would be happy to join hands in some of these areas through public private partnership. Secondly, Pravasi Bhartiya may help a large number of artists and artisans in India particularly in the rural areas by way of promoting their traditional arts and crafts abroad.

5369. (8-1-2008) NEW DELHI : Shri Kamal Nath, Union Minister of Commerce & Industry, has invited the overseas Indians to reach out to global SME's (small and medium enterprises) for catalysing their economic engagement with India, while speaking at the Pravasi Bharatiya Divas Plenary Session on "Trade and Business Opportunities", here today. He said: "I invite you to form meaningful partnerships with Indian firms looking to set up beach heads overseas by providing technology, logistical marketing and financial support. I also invite you to invest in Indian markets as financial investors. Overseas Indian investors would also find it lucrative to invest in India's skill based industries. The achievements of the IT and automobile industries have been well showcased. I invite you to put your money into the other emerging centres of excellence". Shri Vayalar Ravi, Minister for Overseas Indian Affairs; Shri T.K. A. Nair, Principal Secretary to the Prime Minister and Shri Sunil Bharti Mittal, CMD of Bharti Group were present on the occasion. Shri Kamal Nath stated that to secure the growth story, there are four levels of collaboration currently taking place *viz.*, Private-public partnerships for infrastructure projects; Private companies partnering with universities to work around the skilled labour constraint; Private companies partnering with each other to build efficient supply chains; and, Private companies partnering with foreign investors. As regards healthcare industry, the Minister said that India has the capabilities to develop world-class healthcare innovations for global use, from product development such as drug discovery, clinical trials and manufacturing, to services like diagnostics and drug delivery. He further emphasised that India has huge investment potential in the sectors like entertainment industry, tourism industry, chemicals industry and education. The Minister said that as a trading nation, India is now firmly established at the top of the table of the World Trade Organisation (WTO), irrespective of the outcome of the Doha Development Round, and bilateral trade agreements are currently in the pipeline with at least ten potential partners ranging from ASEAN via the EU to the US and Canada.

5370. (9-1-2008) NEW DELHI : Annual Plan size for Kerala for the year 2008-2009 was finalized, here today at a meeting between the Deputy Chairman, Planning Commission, Shri Montek Singh Ahluwalia and Chief Minister of Kerala,

Shri V.S Achutanandan. The Plan outlay has been agreed at Rs.7700 crores. This includes additional Central assistance of Rs.100 crores for projects of special importance to the State. Deputy Chairman, Planning Commission, Mr. Ahluwalia said that the commission was keen on improving utilization of funds under centrally sponsored schemes and would like to work in coordination with the State government for removing rigidity in the guidelines for these schemes. He said the Planning Commission was in support of maximizing flexibility and would welcome suggestions in this regard from States. For effective deployment of resources States need more flexibility, he added. Mr. Ahluwalia said the State government should work for providing better infrastructure for higher education, skill development and tourism. He appreciated State government's efforts in maintaining fiscal discipline while improving plan performance. The State has remarkable performance in empowering Panchayats and District Planning Board. Planning Commission complemented the State for continued emphasis on social sector development. Achievements universalizing elementary education, life expectancy and male to female ratio were appreciated. Innovative schemes in health and education sectors like revision of text books, diversification of secondary education and free health care to bottom 30 per cent of population were in line with the national priorities. Efforts to revive agriculture and allied activities with significant increases for crop husbandry, coconut development, animal husbandry, dairy development and fisheries were steps in the right direction. The Chief Minister said that the fiscal squeeze imposed during Tenth Plan had detrimental effects on all development sectors. This had particularly adverse impact on the social sectors, including education and health. The fiscal crisis had crippled the ability of the State to cope with the impact of the agrarian crisis, and more generally of the crisis of petty production. He said efforts are on to put the planning process back on the right track. More funds are being earmarked to the crisis-ridden sectors. Support to agriculture, education, health, social welfare and security, traditional and small scale industries are being maximized without compromising promotion of sun-rise sectors like I.T., modern industries and tourism, he said.

5371. (9-1-2008) NEW DELHI : The Union Minister for Overseas Indian Affairs, Sri Vayalar Ravi has said that the 6th edition of the Pravasi Bharatiya Divas (PBD) marks a watershed in its relationship between India and its Diaspora, as the theme of this year's meet has gone beyond the narrow confines of inward investment and business. Speaking at the valedictory session of Pravasi meet here today, the Minister said the focus of PBD-2008 has been the potential role of Indian Diaspora in the social development of the country. With its emphasis on the role of Diaspora in the empowerment of rural women through innovative means like micro-credit and self-help groups, the Minister said that three important modes of engagement *viz.* knowledge, philanthropy and social entrepreneurship has been discussed to build strong partnerships. Observing that the vast majority of overseas Indians have both the ability and willingness to partner in India's progress, Sri Ravi said that they represent a reservoir of knowledge and skill to productively engage with

India. The two-day Pravasi meet was inaugurated by the Prime Minister, Dr. Manmohan Singh yesterday. Inaugural session was followed by detailed interactive sessions on the social development, knowledge economy, investment and infrastructure, trade and business opportunities, empowerment of women and leadership and cultural issues. Apart from this, state specific development challenges, working session on Gulf and Asia Pacific, Africa America and Europe were held. A special session on Diaspora philanthropy with its thrust on empowerment of rural women was the hallmark of the two-day event. Outlining the four key initiatives of this year's meet, Sri Vayalar Ravi expressed his resolve for establishment of an 'India Development Foundation' to channel overseas Indian philanthropic capital into social development causes in India. Setting up of the Global advisory council of PIOs to serve as 'think tank', establishment of a PIO University, implementing a mutually beneficial knowledge transfer programme encompassing a variety of disciplines are the other three initiatives highlighted in the 2-day meet. Noting that the mini-Pravasi conclave organized in September last year was a huge success, the Minister said that India proposes to hold such mini-PBDs in other parts of the world in partnership with overseas Indian associations.

5372. (9-1-2008) NEW DELHI : Following is the text of the address delivered by Shri M Natarajan, Scientific Advisor to Defence Minister and DRDO Chief, at the launch of the Golden Jubilee Celebrations of the Defence Research and Development Organisation (DRDO) here today:-The year 2008 is a special year for all of us, being the DRDO Golden Jubilee Year. We are today entering into 50th year of DRDO's dedicated service towards nation building. Since its inception in 1958, DRDO has grown multi-dimensionally and is today a major technology generator for the nation effectively meeting its mandate of developing and fielding defence systems for the Services and paramilitary forces. Having established a sound ecosystem and supported by a large pool of committed manpower, we have today a proven competence to produce strategic and state-of-the-art tactical military hardware and related technologies, in diverse disciplines covering Aeronautics, Missiles, Naval Systems, Armament & Combat Engineering, Electronics, Materials and Life Sciences. Some recent successes have added a feather in the cap of this organization. The missile launch test of the LCA was the first step in the weaponisation of this state-of-art combat aircraft. This was quickly followed up by flights with drop tanks including transfer and litening pad. The development programme has involved the maximum number of national agencies and is truly a national endeavour. The second was the successful test launch of Agni-3, our Intermediate Range Ballistic missile. The third major success was the successful test launch of the Interceptor missile-the first step towards setting up a missile shield for the country. These achievements have propelled India into an elite club of technologically advanced countries of the world. DRDO has also a number of other achievements to its credit. In the field of Aeronautics, apart from the successful LCA programme is the development of Unmanned Aerial Vehicles

Lakshya and Nishant, the modular avionics suites for imported combat aircrafts. Secondly the Indian missile showcase consists of almost every conceivable missile viz, the strategic Agni and Prithvi, the surface to air missile-Akash, the anti-tank missile, Nag and the supersonic Cruise missile, Brahmos. The Electronics systems category has seen the successful development of a variety of radars for every platform and service, the critical Electronic warfare programmes of Samyukta and Sangraha, in addition to development in Communications, networking and information security. Land warfare systems like the MBT Arjun, armament systems like Pinaka-the rocket launching system have been some of the other notable achievements. While on the naval side the development of sonars and torpedoes for the services have been the major highlights. Material science development has seen the indigenous development of armours, naval steel and titanium sponge. Life sciences labs have produced critical systems for defence like NBC systems and protection systems for the man behind the machine.

5373. (9-1-2008) NEW DELHI : The President of India, Smt. Pratibha Devisingh Patil met the members of the Jalgaon Zila Mahila Association at Rashtrapati Bhavan on January 9, 2008. During the meeting, the President urged the members to relentlessly work for the welfare of women. The President said that a number of laws and programmes for the benefit of women are in existence at present or are in the process of implementation. The members of social welfare organisations should work with commitment so that the benefits are received by every single woman in the country. Smt. Patil asked the members to be facilitators in this process. Referring to female foeticide practised in many parts of the country, the President asked the women to establish a dialogue with expectant mothers so that they would resist such negative practices. The President once again emphasised the grave danger that a dis-balance in male-female ratio due to female foeticide would create in society. The members of the Mahila Association presented a memorandum to the President seeking corrective actions in implementation of Acts for the benefit of women and prevention of crime against women.

5374. (9-1-2008) NEW DELHI : The Government has today approved the names of three medical centres for conducting initial Class I Medical Examinations for Flight Crew. The medical centres approved include Max Health Care Institute in Panchsheel Park, New Delhi, Dr. Balabhai Nanavati Hospital in Bombay and Apollo Hospital in Chennai. These are in addition to the existing three Air Force Medical Centres at AFCME, Delhi; IAM, Bangalore; and MEC Jorhat. The Government feels that this move will help in considerably reducing the waiting time for medical examination of aspirant pilots.

5375. (9-1-2008) NEW DELHI : Dr. Ashwani Kumar, Minister of State for Industry, has observed that there is a strong case for the Indian diaspora to step up their level of engagement with India. The global experience that the effects of overseas networks as sources and facilitators of trade and investment, purveyors of remittances and as 'brain banks' can be substantial, he added. The Minister was addressing a session on "America's" during Pravasi Bharatiya Divas 2008, here today. The Minister further stated that education and skills are among India's most important challenges and Indian corporates are waiting to participate in primary and higher education and skill development in India and this remains the best possible area of partnership for overseas Indians. "An institutional framework for private sector initiatives is needed on the lines of the Indian American Council. The need for work is in the districts, and not just in cities. I would like to use this forum to call upon diaspora members to go back to their villages and small towns, and contribute in local development in any area they can", the Minister added. Dr. Kumar further stated that the second generation Indian origin kids are sure to have ingrained Indian values but perhaps have a world-view completely at odds with their parents and we need to find mechanisms to attract them to come and spend some time in India.

5376. (9-1-2008) NEW DELHI : Smt. D. Purandeswari, Minister of State for Human Resource Development has said that the challenge before us is to provide adequate infrastructure in every school irrespective of its location and backwardness, have every teacher trained in the enabling environment of ICT and make every school a hub for its community in exchanging information. Smt. Purandeswari was speaking today at the World Seminar of Education Ministers at London, UK. This is a world Ministerial Seminar on information and communication technologies in education organized by "Moving Young Minds" which has established itself, the premier world ministerial seminar on the development and implementation of ICT and e-learning in education. The MOS has also said that keeping in view of its critical role in ensuring education of good quality, Government of India plans to augment the allocation for the programme by about four times higher than the current year's budget provision of about 62.50 million dollars for the next fiscal. Here is the full text of the speech: "India is a land of diversity. This diversity spans across culture, tradition, language, geography and the economic condition of the people. It is a nation that has a significant number of people who are below the minimal socio-economic benchmarks. This includes rural and urban poor, women in rural areas, street children, people belonging to historically disadvantaged castes and people living in less developed areas. The vulnerability of these sections of society has increased with globalization and this section is prone to become even more marginalized-economically and socially. Successive governments have committed themselves to addressing these divides, but effective implementation of various economic development programmes aimed at individuals belonging to these sections of society has proved an elusive goal. We however, are firmly committed to wipe out the wide discrepancy between the 'haves and have nots' a problem which we have bequeathed as a result of exploitation and depravation for centuries. The traditional notion that land, labour, capital and entrepreneurship are the indispensable ingredients of the production process has outlived its relevance. In the context of growing importance of I.T, Bio-technology, Nano Technology etc. the component in the productive system, Education today is no longer considered a mere transfer of knowledge, but is recognized as the most important facilitator of social and economic development of any country. Combined with sound macroeconomic policies, education is fundamental for the construction of globally competitive economies and democratic societies. It augments cognitive and other skills and in the process leads to higher productivity and development. Education builds what the Noble Laureate Amartya Sen rightfully calls "human capabilities' and it is one of the most powerful instruments known for reducing proverty and inequality and for laying the basis for sustained economic growth and sound governance. Hence it is very important that when we talk of development, we should discuss it in the context of excellence on education. The 21st Century is acknowledged by all as the "Knowledge Century" which means that Knowledge or brain power should be reflected in a country's competitiveness, advancement and human capabilities Human capabilities are a function of the well-being of a people and the investment we make in human capital formation. The ability of a nation to make best use of its knowledge or brain power will ultimately determine its place in the global development scenario in the present century. Lifelong learning education should therefore be a high priority for all.

5377. (9-1-2008) NEW DELHI : One hundred and forty-five years ago, on 12th January, Swami Vivekananda was born. He has been described as 'Yogi of the highest spiritual level in direct communion with Truth, who had consecrated his whole life to the moral and spiritual uplift of his nation and humanity', and as a bridge between the East and the West. A firebrand nationalist, Swamiji had a strong vision for India. He was a social reform activist, an educationist and above all a humanist who believed in the innate greatness of man. Swamiji was the earliest nationalist thinkers to claim the Indo-Islamic past as part of the Indian heritage. After all, the first great Indian exponent of tolerance and liberalism in religion was Vivekananda's Master Sri Ramakrishna Paramahansa whose 'Yata Mat Tata Path' (All beliefs are ways to God) became the final word of religious harmony in the modern world. English historian Arnold Joseph Toynbee mentioned that Ramakrishna, "Practised successively almost every form of Indian religion and philosophy and went on to practice Islam and Christianity as well." On June 10, 1898, at Almora, Swamiji spoke "for our own motherland a junction of the two great systems, Hinduism and Islam-Vedanta brain and Islamic body-is the only hope." Swamiji was of the view that "without the help of practical Islam, theories of Vedantism, however fine and wonderful they may be, are entirely valueless to the vast mass of mankind." The life and message of Swami Vivekananda are still an infinite source of great inspiration to youth. The nation celebrates his birth day as National Youth Day on January 12 a befitting tribute to one who personifies the fiery youth. This year the 13th National Youth Festival will be held at Chennai, Tamil Nadu. The theme is "Youth For Progress and Excellence". The National Youth Festival is a mega National Integration Camp where about 4000 youth from all over India will participate in the five-day Festival. Variety of cultural programmes (both competitive and non-competitive), Youth Convention, Suvichar and Exhibition etc. are organized to show the talent and creative energy of youth.

5378. (9-1-2008) NEW DELHI : Central Water Commission (CWC) under Ministry of Water Resources is monitoring storage position of 81 important reservoirs spread all over the country, of which as many as 36 reservoirs have significant hydro-power benefits with installed capacity of more than 60 MW each. The combined live storage in these 81 reservoirs at the beginning of monsoon *i.e.* 1st June, 2007was 25 per cent of their designed capacity and stood at 63 per cent of the designed capacity as on 27th December 2007. The present storage is 94 per cent of the last year's storage and 119 per cent of last 10 years average storage during the same period. Out of these 81 reservoirs there are presently 10 reservoirs where this year's storage is 80 per cent or less than the average of previous 10 years and in the remaining 73 reservoirs the storage is more than 80 per cent of the average of previous 10 years. In order to derive the best possible benefits from the available water, Central Water Commission is keeping in touch with the Department of Agriculture and Cooperation and providing information of the weekly storage position to the Crop Weather Watch Group for evolving suitable crop strategies and also apprising the situation to various Departments and Ministries involved in Water Resources Planning.

5379. (9-1-2008) NEW DELHI : Congress spokesman Dr. Shakeel Ahmed said that a few days ago a news item appeared which said that workers of Indian origin working in Malaysia were being banned from working there and because of which the people in India and the Congress Party were rather worried. But a positive development has taken place in this direction as Malaysian Minister of Works, Shri Samy Vellu, who has come to attend the Parvasi Bharatiya Divas, has assured our NRI Minister, Shri Vayalar Ravi that no such steps have been taken by the Malaysian government. We welcome the step and hope that people of Indian origin will continue to work there peacefully in the future. On the Global Advisory Council issue, the Prime Minister, Dr. Manmohan Singh, has asked the Non-resident Indians in various countries to come together and participate in this council for better understanding of our relations and exchange of ideas. We also appreciate this step of the Prime Minister and hope that this will strengthen their relations with the Motherland. To a question that Shri L.K. Advani has demanded that Shri Atal Behari Vajpayee be honoured with Bharat Ratna award, do you support this demand and what is the Congress Party's stand in this regard, Dr. Ahmed said, there is a Committee which decides as to who is the person who should be awarded the Bharat Ratna and in this no party's suggestion is taken or sought for and the Committee is the only deciding factor. It is not for us to decide as to who is fit or who is not. It is for the Committee to decide. The Congress Party' stand is that whoever is worthy of this award should be given this distinction. The person who has done exceptionally good in the interest of the country is the deserving person for this award. To a question that does the Congress Party believe that Shri Vajpayee has done outstanding work, Dr. Ahmed said, we have appreciated and at times criticized and in some cases supported his works which were done at the time his government was in power. Hence it is not a matter of party as such and it is for that particular Committee to decide who is the deserving person for that coveted award. To a question whether your Party endorses Shri Advani's suggestion or not, Dr. Ahmed said, I have nothing to add or delete. What I have said a while ago I stand by it. Let the Committee decide. To a question that as per you there is a committee which decides, so in your opinion who should Shri Advani write to, the Committee or the Prime Minister, Dr. Ahmed said, in this regard I would only like to say that this question should be addressed to Shri L. K. Advani and not me. To a question that Shri Vajpayee was given the best Parliamentarian award during the Narasimha Rao regime, what would you like to say, Dr. Ahmed said, there are four persons who have been bestowed with this award such as Shri Somnath Chatterjee, Shri Chandra Shekhar, former prime minister, Shri Pranab Mukherjee and Shri Mani Shankar Iyer. They were all worthy of this award and were bestowed with it. There are few others who have been given this award which includes names such as Smt. Sushma Swaraj and Shri P. Chidambram. They have done excellent work in their fields and hence were awarded the best parliamentarian award. To a question that whether the Committee is above the prime minister and the government, Dr. Ahmed said, that the Committee is independent. It is under the Ministry of Home no doubt but it functions independently without any political influence. To a question whether Shri Advani's demand is politically motivated, Dr. Ahmed said, I do not think anybody should mix politics with such an award. The Bharat Ratna is the highest award and if anybody brings in politics it should be condemned at the highest level. To a question that last week one of your spokespersons had said that if Shri Narendra Modi wants a national role, he has to have a profile like Shri Vajpayee. So in this context do you think that Shri Vajpayee qualifies for the Bharat Ratna, Dr. Ahmed said, what is the link between national role and Bharat Ratna. Let me tell you that Bharat Ratna is the rarest of rare awards and a secretary of any national political party, at national level, whosoever he may be, is playing a national role and after considering anybody for that award ever aspect of his role is judged by the Committee and only then is he awarded this prestigious award. To a question that the Samajwadi Party is demonstrating in UP against the misbehaviour of the law enforcing agencies and that one of their leaders was slapped, what do you have to say, Dr. Ahmed said, we are not aware of the happenings in UP right now. Once we get the details of the report we will respond. To a question that there are reports that the second SRC is going to be set up by the Central government and do you think that there is a need for a second SRC, Dr. Ahmed said, I am not aware of the actual facts but the PMO has contradicted the newspaper reports and denied that there is going to be a second sitting of the SRC.

5380. (9-1-2008) NEW DELHI : Following is the text of the address delivered by the Defence Minister Shri AK Antony at the launch of the Golden Jubilee

Celebrations of the Defence Research and Development Organisation (DRDO) here today:-I am indeed delighted to be amidst the Scientists and other members of DRDO family on this happy occasion of launching of Golden Jubilee activities of DRDO. My greetings to the whole DRDO fraternity and best wishes for a great future for all of you and the organisation for greater accomplishments in the years to come. It is gratifying to note that DRDO has emerged as a strong Science and Technology force to reckon with, having a strength of about 30,000 knowledge workers serving in 50 laboratories located along the length and breadth of our country. An organisation which had a modest beginning with a mission to advise the services in Defence Technologies, today has evolved to ensure the strategic defence as well as provide state-of-the art Tactical Weapon Systems. No nation will be willing to part with strategic defence technologies. DRDO has, therefore, played the crucial role in providing the strategic defence to our country with suitable delivery systems. Tactical systems such as Main Battle Tank (Arjun), Light Combat Aircraft (Tejas), a family of Radars, Electronic Warfare systems, sonars, torpedoes, armaments and Missiles have also been successfully developed and many of them are being delivered to our armed forces. The recent success of DRDO in launch of Interceptor Missile and Agni-III has taken our country to elite club of a few developed nations with similar capability. I am glad to know that DRDO has achieved appreciable level of self reliance in NBC defence technologies and a large quantity of these products are already delivered to the defence forces. Life support technologies and products developed by DRDO have significantly enhanced the health and operational efficiency of our soldiers operating in extremes of environmental and operational conditions. These include high altitudes over the Himalayas, deserts of Western borders, underwater, aerospace and Low Intensity Conflict environments. Some of the specialized materials such as Composites, armour, Titanium, sponge and AB Steel have now been indigenously developed for various military applications.

5381. (9-1-2008) NEW DELHI : 176 candidates have been recommended for appointment to the medical posts in the Railways, Indian Ordnance Factories Health Service, Central Government Health Service and Municipal Corporation of Delhi on the result of the Combined Medical Services Examination, 2007 held by the Union Public Service Commission on 21.01.2007, for recruitment to medical posts under the Central Government and the Municipal Corporation of Delhi. Candidates recommended for appointment include 85 General Candidates (including 05 Physically Handicapped candidates), 59 candidates belonging to Other Backward Classes (including 02 Physically Handicapped candidates), 19 Scheduled Caste and 13 Scheduled Tribe candidates.

5382. (9-1-2008) NEW DELHI : Dr. Navinchandra Ramgoolam, the Prime Minister of Mauritius called on the President of India, Smt. Pratibha Devisingh Patil today. Dr. Ramgoolam is visiting India and is the Chief Guest at the Pravasi Bharatiya Divas, 2008 at which he is also being conferred the Pravasi Bharatiya

Samman Award. The President congratulated the Prime Minister of Mauritius. Bilateral, regional and international issues of mutual interest were discussed at the meeting.

5383. (9-1-2008) NEW DELHI : Shri Arun Ramanathan assumed the office of Secretary, Department of Financial Services, Ministry of Finance; here this morning. He was Secretary, Department of Chemicals and Petrochemicals before taking up this new assignment. Shri Ramanathan belongs to 1973 batch of IAS of Tamil Nadu Cadre. He joins in place of Shri Vinod Rai who took over as Comptroller and Auditor General of India on 7th of this month.

5384. (9-1-2008) NEW DELHI : In pursuance of the recommendation of the National Statistical Commission, the Central Statistical Organization, Ministry of Statistics and PI, Government of India has constituted a High Level Committee on Estimation of Savings and Investments under Dr. C. Rangarajan, Chairman of the Economic Advisory Council to the Prime Minister. Members of the Committee are Dr. Kirit Parikh, Member, Planning Commission; Prof. Ravindra Dholakia, IIM, Ahmedabad; Dr. S. L. Shetty, EPW Research Foundation; Dr. Saumitra Chaudhuri, Member of the Economic Advisory Council to Prime Minister; Shri Ramesh Kolli, Additional Director General, Central Statistical Organisation: Dr. R.B. Barman, Executive Director, Reserve Bank of India (Member Secretary).

5385. (9-1-2008) NEW DELHI : The first phase of Eco-City programme is in advance stage of completion at the close of 10th five year plan. It covered six towns namely Kottayam, Tirupati, Ujjain, Puri, Thanjavur and Vrindavan. It aimed at improving the existing environment and at changing those aspects that are causing environment damage. In Kottayam, rejuvenation of Mudar river and renovation of Kacherikadavu Boat Jetty Canal were taken up. The canal had severe situation and pollution problem. In Ujjain, improvement of the area around Mahakal Temple and the cleaning by excavation and embankment of Rudra Sagar has been taken up. The Rudra Sagar Lake was highly silted and polluted with sewage. In addition, traffic and transportation, road improvement, drainage, laying of the water supply line for Rudra Sagar, underground electric cabling and plantation as well as landscaping activities are still on. The Eco-city Programme in Vrindavan aimed at improvement of the core-zone of the city, improvement of 2 kms. stretch from Kaliadaha Ghat to Kesi Ghat on 'Parikrama Path' and Banke Bihari Temple surroundings. This also includes the improvement around Rangnath Temple. For implementation of the above activities, the Vrindavan Municipality has identified funding agencies to meet these financial contribution. The core area of the town around Govinda Raja Swami Temple have been improved in Tirupati. The activities carried out are covering storm water drains in the Northern, Southern and Western sides of the temple, connecting water pipeline from Konneru to Narshimha Tirtha and cleaning and de-silting of drains in the core area. Similarly development in Puri has been carried out the Jagannath Temple for improvement of drinking water in Lion's gate, improvement of public toilet near 'Narendra tank' and construction of cement concrete drains with cover slabs along the roads around the Lord Jagannath Temple, renovation of three of the religious ponds. Besides this garages and automobile workshops will be shifted and existing solid waste disposal facility will be modernised. In Thanjavur town renovation of old tanks have been taken up. Various measures have been taken to protect usable aquifers from further degradation. The Central Pollution Control Board (CPCB) undertook the Programme to bring visible change in the environmental improvement schemes in these towns on 50:50 sharing basis.

5386. (9-1-2008) NEW DELHI : The National Institute of Food Technology Entrepreneurship & Management (NIFTEM) & the College of Agriculture and Life Sciences at Cornell University (CALS) have signed a MoU to collaborate in the promotion of areas of human resource development, applied research and industry oriented innovation in the food processing sector. It was signed in the presence of Shri P. I. Suvrathan, Secretary, Ministry of Food Processing Industries. The Memorandum was signed by Shri Goutam Sanyal, Director, NIFTEM and OSD, NIFTEM Shri S.S. Chahal and Dr. W. Ronnie Coffman, Director, International Programmes, College of Agriculture and Life Sciences, Cornell University, USA & Shri K. Vijayaraghavan, Vice Chairman, Cornell-Sathguru Foundation. The public-private venture would be carried out through Cornell-Sathguru foundation. The Cornell-Sathguru Foundation is Hyderabad based and will provide guidance and knowledge linkages to NIFTEM through its "NIFTEM support offices' both at Cornell, USA and in India. The foundation, which focuses on the development of agriculture and food chain India through public-private participation is to foster education and joint research. It will also provide basic and strategic guidance for the design facilities to carry out food science research, conducting education programmes in the areas of food science and above all creating enterprise development. It will also provide guidance for NIFTEM faculty in design and developing comprehensive contemporary course modules, relevant to food and allied industries. It will also facilitate deputation of faculty members in key disciplines. The National Institute of Food Technology Entrepreneurship & Management (NIFTEM) would be developed as a world class Institute. It is being set up by the Ministry of Food Processing Industries on 100 acres of land at Kundli, Sonepat (Haryana) at a cost of 245 crore rupees. The Institute is to cater to the needs of booming Food Processing sector and various stake holders including entrepreneurs, industrialists, exporters, policy makers, government agencies and other research institutions. The Ministry of Food Processing Industries aims to develop NIFTEM into a world class Institute. The NIFTEM will also develop priority areas of research and development in various areas of food science. The Cornell-Sathguru Foundation is to development Intellectual Property and Technology Transfer Policy and development of a strategic plan for technology transfer and enterprise development. The foundation will back up NIFTEM in training needs for continuing education. The foundation will provide support to NIFTEM for designing food enterprise incubator centre and also design Undergraduate and Graduate courses in areas of food science.

5387. (9-1-2008) NEW DELHI : The Corps of Army Air Defence (AAD) the youngest arm of Indian Army celebrates its raising day tomorrow. Army Air Defence has dedicated itself to the service of the nation with it's motto of "Akashe Shatrun Jahi", a firm resolve to keep our skies free from enemy intrusions. A vibrant and effective air defence environment backed up with low and medium level surveillance and automated control and reporting system, is essential to protect the key strategic installations as well as the combat potential and freedom of manoeuvre of our fighting force. With ever changing face of technology, it is imperative that the Corps remains modern and well equipped in its equipment profile and in operational preparedness. Army Air Defence has stood steadfast to the needs of the Army.

5388. (9-1-2008) NEW DELHI : It has been reported in a section of the media today that "Integrated Guided Missile Development Programme (IGMDP) as a Strategic Programme stands Scrapped". It is hereby clarified that except for Agni demonstrator, which was successfully completed in 1989, all other projects under IGMDP are related to Tactical Missiles such as anti-tank Nag, short range Trishul, medium range Akash and Prithvi for artillery role with conventional warheads. All these missiles have since been developed. All are entering Service in one form or other. With this, objectives of IGMDP originally envisaged stand completed. Strategic Missile Program is entirely indigenous and is being pursued through a number of separate projects. All of them are progressing as per schedule and no Strategic System has been scrapped.

5389. (9-1-2008) NEW DELHI : The Tourism and Culture Minister Smt. Ambika Soni has said that infrastructure and skilled man power have to be in right place in the next five years in the wake of boom in tourism sector and economic growth of the country. Addressing a group of budding air hostesses here today, she said it is projected that by 2010 about 10 million foreign tourists will arrive in the country and the out bound tourism will also grow manifolds which currently stands at 8 million tourists. She said modernisation/ upgradation of international airports at Mumbai and Delhi, creation of about one lakh fifty thousand additonal rooms in budget and star category hotels are the main challenges before all the stakeholders in civil aviation and tourism sector. The phenomenal growth in these two sectors has far reaching implications. The country will witness tremendous employment generation in the skilled and semi-skilled sector *viz.* pilots, aviation engineers, air hostesses, stewards, ground handling staff, guides, travel agents, tour operators and freight agencies. The Minister said the tourism sector is likely to generate two lakh plus jobs by 2010 in the wake of commonwealth games. She said tourism and civil aviation are inextircably linked; these two sectors feed upon each other and support each other. A strategy to develop manpower resource should take into account the demands and the growth trajectories of both aviation and tourism. Smt. Soni said Government is ready to have public private partnership both in tourism infrastructure development and training and upgradation of skills through specilized institutions.

5390. (9-1-2008) NEW DELHI : Shri Kamal Nath, Union Minister of Commerce & Industry, has invited the overseas Indians to reach out to global SME's (small and medium enterprises) for catalysing their economic engagement with India, while speaking at the Pravasi Bharatiya Divas Plenary Session on "Trade and Business Opportunities", here today. He said: "I invite you to form meaningful partnerships with Indian firms looking to set up beach heads overseas by providing technology, logistical marketing and financial support. I also invite you to invest in Indian markets as financial investors. Overseas Indian investors would also find it lucrative to invest in India's skill based industries. The achievements of the IT and automobile industries have been well showcased. I invite you to put your money into the other emerging centres of excellence". Shri Vayalar Ravi, Minister for Overseas Indian Affairs; Shri T.K. A. Nair, Principal Secretary to the Prime Minister and Shri Sunil Bharti Mittal, CMD of Bharti Group were present on the occasion. Shri Kamal Nath stated that to secure the growth story, there are four levels of collaboration currently taking place *viz.*, Private-public partnerships for infrastructure projects; Private companies partnering with universities to work around the skilled labour constraint; Private companies partnering with each other to build efficient supply chains; and, Private companies partnering with foreign investors. As regards healthcare industry, the Minister said that India has the capabilities to develop world-class healthcare innovations for global use, from product development such as drug discovery, clinical trials and manufacturing, to services like diagnostics and drug delivery. He further emphasised that India has huge investment potential in the sectors like entertainment industry, tourism industry, chemicals industry and education. The Minister said that as a trading nation, India is now firmly established at the top of the table of the World Trade Organisation (WTO), irrespective of the outcome of the Doha Development Round, and bilateral trade agreements are currently in the pipeline with at least ten potential partners ranging from ASEAN via the EU to the US and Canada.

5391. (9-1-2008) NEW DELHI : The National Youth Awards for the year 2006-07 have been announced. These awards are conferred on youth who have demonstrably excelled in different fields of developmental activities and social service. The Award to individual comprises a medal, a scroll and Rs 20,000/-. The award of one Voluntary organisation comprises a trophy, a scroll and Rs. 1,00,000/-. The list of this year youth Awards is attached. The awards will be given away at the 13th National Youth Festival to be held at Chennai, Tamil Nadu from 12-16th January, 2008. The theme for the 13th National Youth Festival is "YOUTH

FOR PROGRESS AND EXCELLENCE." The National Youth Festival is a mega National Integration Camp. About 4000 youth from all over India will participate in the Festival. Each State/UT administration is expected to send a contingent of participants for competing in designated events and also participating in other activities. Variety of cultural programmes (both competitive and non-competitive), Youth Convention, Suvichar and Exhibition etc. will be organized to show the talent and creative energy of our youth. The Festival will conclude on 16th January, 2008. His excellency the Governor of Tamil Nadu will be the Chief Guest on this occasion and he will also give away Indira Gandhi National Service Scheme Awards. The National Youth Festival is held annually from 12th to 16th January in one of the States willing to host the Festival to commemorate the birth anniversary of Swami Vivekanand. The 12th January, being the birth anniversary of Swami Vivekanand is also observed as National Youth Day.

5392. (9-1-2008) NEW DELHI : Thiru. Mons Joseph, PWD Minister of Kerala, called on Thiru. T.R. Baalu, Union Minister of Shipping, Road Transport & Highways, yesterday evening and discussed the status of implementation of Central Sector Road projects in Kerala. The PWD Minister of Kerala requested for four-laning of NH-213 in view of the increased traffic on this Highway. Considering this request, Thiru. Baalu directed the officials of the Ministry to undertake the Feasibility Study and preparation of the Detailed Project Report for this Highway. Shri Mons Joseph also requested Thiru. Baalu to include NH-49, NH-220 and NH-212 under Phase-IV of the National Highways Development Project (NHDP). Thiru. Baalu agreed to consider inclusion of NH-49 and NH-220 for development to 2-lanes with paved shoulders under Phase-IV of NHDP, and NH-212 would be developed under the National Highways (Original Works) programme of the Ministry in a phased manner. The Kerala Minister also requested for construction of flyover to decongest Cochin City and for construction of the Coastal Highway linking Cochin withNH-17 under Phase-VII of NHDP to which Thiru Baalu advised him to forward the requisite proposals for consideration of the Union Government.

5393. (9-1-2008) NEW DELHI : The Government of India, Ministry of Health & Family Welfare, Department of Health has issued a draft notification proposing amendment to standards of olive oil under Prevention of Food Adulteration Rules, 1955. This notification has been published in Part II, section 3, sub-section (i) of the Gazette of India (Extraordinary) vide GSR No. 726(E) dated 20.11.2007. By this amendment, the standards of olive oil are being amended to harmonize them with those of Codex. A time period of sixty days have been given for sending objections/suggestions. The notification is available on the website of Ministry of Health & Family Welfare *i.e.* http://www.mohfw.nic.in/pfa.htm. Objections/suggestions, if any on the draft rules, may be sent to the Secretary, Department of Health, Ministry of Health and Family Welfare, Government of India, Nirman Bhawan, New Delhi within the stipulated period.

5394. (9-1-2008) NEW DELHI : The President of India, Smt. Pratibha Devisingh Patil, called upon the overseas Indian community to proactively engage in the growth of the country. Urging the community to come up with innovative ideas that can help build a critical mass of development, she observed that the overseas Indian community is impressive in terms of its size, spread and growing influence, estimated at about 25 million in 130 countries and has emerged as a significant economic social and cultural force in the world today. Speaking at the valedictory session of the 6th edition of Pravasi Bharatiya Divas here today, Smt. Devisingh Patil urged the overseas Indians to explore ways in which they can be partners in the growth of the country. On the occasion, the President conferred Pravasi Bharatiya Samman awards to fifteen outstanding Pravasi Bharatiyas for stellar achievements in different fields. Dr. Navinchandra Ramgoolam, Prime Minister of Mauritius was awarded for his leadership with genuine concern for the underprivileged and disadvantaged sections of the community. As a popular leader, he has also endeavoured to nurture and strengthen the bonds between Mauritius and India in all dimensions and has provided exemplary leadership to the Indian Diaspora. Dr. Ravi Pillai was awarded for his outstanding services in the area of employment generation. He has provided gainful employment to over 25,000 NRIs in his business establishments in the Gulf. Mr. A. P. S. Mani was awarded for running an effective forum for networking and also cultural and professional interaction amongst members of the Indian community in Japan. He is also recognized for his pioneering work on community welfare in Japan. Judge Ajit Swarn Singh of New Zealand was recognized for his yeomen services in inspiring the younger generation to strive and scale higher levels of excellence in their professions. While Mr. Rafiudin S. Fazulbhoy was awarded for his signification work in the field of education of children of Indian origin and the services to Haj pilgrims, Mr. Bicky Chakraborty of Sweden made the mark for his sterling contribution in education and health sectors. The National Council of Indian Culture based in Trinidad & Tobago was recognized for creating awareness in the present generation of people of Indian origin of their heritage and the cultural values. Mr. Krishnamurthy Kumar was awarded for his work towards expanding India's interests and extending understanding on issues pertaining to Indian diversity and religious harmony in the UAE. Lord Karan Bilimoria, Chairman of the Indo-British Partnership, has bagged the Samman for aggressively pitching closer and deeper business relations between the U.K. and India. While Dr. Thomas Abraham won the acclaimed for his immense contribution to the NRI movement in the USA in the last three decades and for organizing the first convention of people of Indian origin in New York in 1989, Dr. Joy Cherian of the US has been awarded for his profound services for the Indian community in the US. He has also guided a number of exploratory business missions to India for several major North American insurance companies.

5395. (9-1-2008) NEW DELHI: With roughly 15 months left for the next general election and 9 assembly elections due from now to the Lok Sabha election, the

Bharatiya Janata Party has signalled it is in election mode. A 19-member central election management committee has been set up with BJP president Rajnath Singh in the chair. The decision was apparently firmed up at a meeting between Mr. Rajnath Singh and Leader of the Opposition L.K. Advani on Monday. The "informal group" of Mr. Advani's camp followers in the party that had met 11 days ago, on December 29, at Mr. Advani's residence to discuss the next Lok Sabha election and other State Assembly elections has been replaced by the 19-member committee that party leaders see as being more "balanced." Senior party leaders such as Yashwant Sinha, Gopinath Munde, Bal Apte and others who had been left out by Mr. Advani have been included in the management committee. Sudheendra Kulkarni, who had resigned as office-bearer of the BJP and from the party membership following the 2005 "Jinnah is secular' episode and whose presence at the December 29 meeting had party leaders raise eyebrows, has been left out. Senior leaders said on Tuesday that the effort was to ensure that the party moved into election year as one entity, not as a divided house. "If in 1998 and 1999, Mr. Advani was heading the election management committee and Mr. Atal Bihari Vajpayee was the prime ministerial candidate, in 2008 when Mr. Advani has been declared as the party's prime ministerial candidate, Mr. Singh is chairing the committee," a leader said. The committee includes leaders such as Murli Manohar Joshi, Yashwant Sinha, Bal Apte, Ramlal, Gopinath Munde, Mukhtar Abbas Naqvi and Vinay Katiyar, who are not favoured by Mr. Advani, and others such as Jaswant Singh, Sushma Swaraj, Venkaiah Naidu, Vijay Kumar Malhotra and Arun Shourie, who are seen as close to Mr. Advani. All six general secretaries, including Arun Jaitley and Thawarchand Gehlot, are on the committee. The seventh position of general secretary is vacant with Om Mathur recently appointed Rajasthan state president. Ms. Sushma Swaraj has been asked to coordinate the party's efforts to get new allies ahead of the Lok Sabha election. To this end, the party would hold state-wise meetings to ask senior state unit leaders what alliances were possible. "Of course, the central party here can always overrule the State unit," Ms. Swaraj said. She also disclosed that George Fernandes, the Janata Dal (United) leader, will continue to function as the NDA convenor. When it was pointed out to her that Mr. Fernandes no longer enjoyed the trust and confidence of even his own party, not to speak of other NDA partners, Ms. Swaraj said that nobody from the JD (U) had objected to Mr. Fernandes continuing as convener. On the Trinamool Congress Party remaining within the NDA, Ms. Swaraj said party president Mamta Banerjee had not conveyed to the BJP that she wanted her party to drop out of the NDA. A meeting of NDA Chief Ministers and party presidents is expected to be called between January 22 and 25 to discuss cooperation between the BJP and its alliance partners, Ms. Swaraj said.

5396. (10-1-2008) NEW DELHI : The Prime Minister, Dr. Manmohan Singh has released the first edition of Journal, "India & Global Affairs" edited by Shri Dileep Padgaonkar, here today. Following is the text of the Prime Minister's speech on the occasion:-"I compliment Abhijit Pawar and Dileep Padgaonkar for taking this important initiative to launch a new journal on "India and Global Affairs". I do hope this journal becomes an important and informed window to the outside world for thinking citizens of our country. I also hope it will help students and scholars in international affairs, diplomats and policymakers to get a better appreciation of the world around us. We live in interesting times, indeed in challenging times, in this fast-changing world. There are great opportunities awaiting us but also profound challenges facing us. As India re-engages the world, as a more self-confident nation, we must be better informed about the world to be able to deal with it. Understanding the processes of change is the first step in trying to change these processes. An honest, factually informed and analytically rigorous discussion is, therefore, necessary for us to be able to deal with reality, as it exists, and shape it in a manner that serves our national interest and global peace and stability. I therefore hope that this journal will contribute to a better informed discourse on global change and the tasks before us as a nation. How will they impact on our country? How can we influence them so that we can ensure a neighbourhood of peace, prosperity and stability? I find that the first issue of this journal is devoted to a discussion of political and social developments in Pakistan. It seems events have already over-taken the contents of the journal. The questions raised on the cover of this issue have acquired even greater importance. We must look for informed and convincing answers. I have referred to some of these issues on more than one occasion in the past three years, including in the essay that has been published in this inaugural volume. I do feel that policy making at home is often more reactive than pro-active. Governments are driven by the force of events. One does not always have the luxury of time to plan. But, it is important and necessary to try to do so. Creating a body of informed opinion is part of that process of preparing oneself and our country to deal with unexpected events. Pro-active planning is the goal of strategic thinkers worldwide. This is where scholars and analysts must step in and identify problems, highlight trends, develop scenarios, and suggest policy options, before events and crises overtake us. I have often felt that there is a dearth of long term planning on strategic policy issues in our country. Of course, there is the problem that purely academic work can appear impractical to policy makers and, on the other hand, the policy options Governments deal with are sometimes bereft of long term vision. There is a certain "chicken-and-egg" sort of problem with the relationship between the academia and government in these matters. Some in government feel purely academic analysis is ivory tower stuff and bereft of practical relevance. Some in academia feel governments are insular and knowledge-proof! A healthy interaction is useful for both. There is, therefore, a need to foster mutual interaction and respect between the world of policy making and the world of analysis.

5397. (10-1-2008) NEW DELHI : Prof. Saifuddin Soz, the Union Minister for Water Resources presided over the 28th Annual General Meeting (AGM) of National Institute of Hydrology (NIH), Roorkee here today. Addressing on the occasion, the Minister said that the NIH was doing commendable job in studying the problems of Hydrology, particularly improving the system of irrigation and flood management in the country. A number of scientists attended today's meeting and made several suggestions for bringing in efficiency in the system of irrigation and flood management in the country. Prof. Soz, particularly expressed satisfaction that the NIH had responded positively to his suggestions during the last Annual General Meeting that the Institute should take up a comprehensive study in examining the snow melt at the glaciers and accordingly the National Institute of Hydrology had instituted studies regarding snow melt at Gangotri (in Uttarakhand) and Zanskar (in Ladakh region). The Minister was told that the first phase of the study would be completed in June this year. Prof. Soz said that it would be interesting to understand from these studies as to whether climate change had impacted adversely on the glaciers or not. Smt. Gauri Chatterjee, Secretary and Shri S. Manoharan, Additional Secretary, senior officers of the Ministry of Water Resources, the Chairman, Central Ground Water Board and many scientists participated in the meeting. Dr. K. D. Sharma, Director, NIH gave a presentation on the working and achievements of the Institute and said that the scientists of the Institute had contributed 44 research papers that were published in prestigious journals at the international level. The Minister congratulated the scientists working at the Institute.

5398. (10-1-2008) NEW DELHI : First working session on MoU between India and Mauritius for cooperation in the field of social defence and disability was held in New Delhi today. The Indian delegation was led by the Minister of Social Justice and Empowerment, Smt. Meira Kumar and the Mauritius delegation was led by Smt. Sheilbai Bapoo, the Minister of Social Security and National Solidarity. Addressing the session, Smt. Meira Kumar said that this the first kind of MoU in the social sector for long term cooperation in the areas of age care, drug demand reduction, community development and empowerment of person with disability. She further said that India and Mauritius have a common agenda to address the social sector issues. With the signing of the MoU, the two countries have agreed to exchange expertise and capabilities for training, research and documentation as well as preparation of database in the field of age care, substance and alcohol abuse prevention, empowerment of persons with disabilities and other areas of social welfare and community development. The MoU will certainly enhance the scope of cooperation between the Governments and Civil Societies of the two countries and facilitates closer interaction at people to people level. She expressed her hope that the MoU will open new vistas of cooperation between the two countries. Elaborating the various welfare schemes of the Ministry of Social Justice and Empowerment, Smt. Kumar said that that the Ministry has launched National Policy on Older Persons (NPOP) to ensure active and productive ageing by evolving a framework of providing financial, medical, social and emotional support. She said that Government has been taking a number of steps for treatment, care and rehabilitation of the victims of drugs. Treatment and Rehabilitation services are being provided through four hundred centres. These Centres are run by NGOs and are financially supported by the Ministry. For reducing the demand for drugs and alcohol, we have mounted a national campaign, 'I decide, I don't take drugs'. Highlighting the achievements in disability sector, the Minister said that the Ministry has made taken pioneering initiatives for empowerment of persons with disability. The Persons with Disabilities Act is a very pro-active socially beneficial legislation. This deals with various aspects including education, employment, social security etc. of persons with disabilities. She said that the seven National Institutes in disability sector as listed out in the MoU have together scripted an inspiring story of providing help, support and rehabilitation to scores of disabled people across the length and breadth of the country. On the Occasion, Smt. Sheilabai Bappoo said that this is a comprehensive MoU between the two countries. Both the countries will be benefited by sharing their experience in social sector. She expressed her hope that it will address the issues like welfare of elderly, persons with disabilities, children in difficult circumstances and prevention of substance and alcohol abuse.

5399. (10-1-2008) NEW DELHI : Shri Kamal Nath, Union Minister of Commerce and Industry, has stressed that innovative fuels, environmental engineering, and greater fuel efficiency are some of the issues that would need greater attention from auto companies. Speaking at the inaugural session of the Auto Expo 2008, here today, the Minister said that India is fortunate to have a high engineering skill level, and it must become a leader in innovation for environmental protection within the tenets of development. Shri Sontsh Mohan Dev, Minister of Heavy Industry & public Enterprises; Mr. Sunil Bharti Mittal, President, Confederation of Indian Industry (CII); Mr. Sanjay Labroo, President, Automotive component Manufacturers Association (ACMA); Mr. Ravi Kant, President, Society of Indian Automobile Manufacturers (SIAM); Mr. Carlo Sinceri, President, International Organisation of Motor Vehicle Manufacturers; and Mr. Rajive Kaul, Chairman, CII Apex Council for Trade Affairs, were spoke on the occasion. Earlier, India's Own People's Car by Tatas was unveiled in the presence of Shri Kamal Nath. Shri Kamal Nath has informed the participants that in consultation with the industry associations and experts, Government has already developed the blueprint for the industry through Automotive Mission Plan, which lays down some of the policies that need to be strategised and put into play for promotion of the industry. The Minister further said: "Increasing integration of the global economy will offer greater opportunities for India in coming years. Already, India's overseas engagement as represented by the export and import of goods and services has crossed the level of half of GDP, reaching an aggregate of $450 billion. In the last four years, the growth of merchandise exports has been over 20%, while services exports have been expanding even faster". In 2006-07, India crossed the milestone of 10 million vehicles sold. Passenger cars alone vaulted over the one million mark, and commercial vehicles sales grew by over 33%. Exports are also going up by rates of about 20%. "I believe that auto component exports themselves are slated to double from close to $3 billion this year to $6 billion within the coming financial year. Deriving from sophisticated engineering skills, formidable cost advantage and end-to-end production capabilities, India is becoming a destination of choice for sourcing of auto parts", Shri Kamal Nath said. India's auto industry has been rapidly attaining a name for itself as a global player. The auto component industry has similarly exhibited tremendous innovation and competitiveness and is able to match global standards of production. The scale of the industry is expected to expand exponentially as more and more auto majors from other countries enter the market.

5400. (10-1-2008) NEW DELHI : The Prime Minister, Dr. Manmohan Singh, called on the President, Smt. Pratibha Devisingh Patil at Rashtrapati Bhavan today. The meeting lasted for about 30 minutes. They discussed issues related with the Prime Minister's forthcoming visit to the People's Republic of China as well as reviewed recent national developments, including the follow-up action on the Report of the Delimitation Commission.

5401. (10-1-2008) NEW DELHI : Government has notified Industrial Park Scheme, 2008. According to a notification issued by the Central Board of Direct Taxes, Ministry of Finance, the Scheme is applicable to undertakings which begin to develop, develop and operate or maintain and operate an Industrial Park during the period from 1st April, 2006 to 31st March, 2009. The notification is available on the website incometaxindia.gov.in.

5402. (10-1-2008) NEW DELHI : The Appointments Committee of the Cabinet has approved the appointment of Shri Pulok Chatterji, IAS (UP:74) as Secretary in the Prime Ministers Office w.e.f. January 2, 2008 (AN). The competent authority has also approved the assignment of additional charge of the post of Secretary, Department of Chemicals and Petrochemicals, Ministry of Chemicals and Fertilizers to Dr. J.S.Sarma, IAS (AP:71), Secretary, Department of Fertilizers, Ministry of Chemicals and Fertilizers, with immediate effect, for a period of three months or till regular appointment is made to the post, or until further orders, whichever is the earliest.

5403. (10-1-2008) NEW DELHI : The Government will provide appropriate incentives relating to large investment both in automobile and auto component sectors. The joint effort between the industry and the government will succeed in giving a major boost to the auto sector. This was stated by Shri Sontosh Mohan Dev, Minister for Heavy Industries & Public Enterprises at the inauguration of the "9th Auto Expo 2008" here today. Shri Dev said that the Indian auto sector has emerged as a "Sunrise Sector" in our economy. It is a focal point sector for the Government. On 29th January 2007, Prime Minister Dr. Manmohan Singh launched the "Automotive Mission Plan" (AMP) for the country. This Plan, which is a joint document prepared by Industry and the Government, envisages to make auto sector a 145 billion US dollar industry creating additional employment for 25 million people by 2016. It also envisages additional investment of about

40 billion dollars apart from huge investment downstream. AMP encompasses pro-active action in attracting investment, affirmative action with regard to expansion of infrastructure and development of human resources. The Government is fully focused in achieving the targets, which have been agreed upon in the Automotive Mission Plan, the Minister added. Shri Dev announced that the National Automotive Testing and R&D Infrastructure Project (NATRIP) would be providing state-of-the-art facilities for testing and homologation by 2009. One of the biggest tracks in the world is being built at Indore for the auto sector. This half-a-billion dollar project will ensure that the auto sector is fully complemented with facilities and we are not dependent on outside world. NATRIP will also have several centres of excellence in component design, engine and vehicle dynamics by 2011-12. This will facilitate technology flow to the SMEs in the auto sector. Shri Dev cautioned that "we must ensure that the Free Trade Agreements and bilateral trade negotiations should not stand on the growth path of this new emerging sector. Every country has given protection to the Auto Sector during its initial growth stage. Unless we do so, we might end up as net importer of automobile and auto components. We have to be globally competitive. If we were to be globally competitive, we need to achieve economy of scale. I would like the industry to bear this aspect in mind so that while investment are made, global competitiveness should be the first priority. There is enough scope to improve the productivity of labour in Auto Sector. We are certainly much more economic in terms of infrastructure costs compared to Europe and North America, but we need to be more competitive with regard to the emerging economies by achieving higher productivity."

5404. (10-1-2008) NEW DELHI : Taking note of the sustained efforts and continued contributions by Non-Resident Indians (NRIs) in the country's economic development, India once again renewed its plea for more inflow of investments with an assurance to provide profitable opportunities to the overseas Indians. For millions of Indian Diaspora spread over 130 countries, the message from the Sixth Pravasi Bharatiya Divas, which concluded in New Delhi yesterday, is loud and clear-"Come and be a part of the exciting growth. Rediscover the New India and Profit from the Experience." The President, Smt. Prathiba Patil and the Prime Minister, Dr. Manmohan Singh and others, presented a detailed account of the measures taken by UPA government in creating a congenial atmosphere for investments in the country. The President, who gave away the Pravasi Bharatiya Samman awards to several NRIs from various fields, called for more contributions for the development of their motherland while stressing the need for an inclusive development aimed at reducing the widening gap between the rich and the poor. Several delegates echoed their focus on giving back to the country must shift from multi-million investments to the micro-level saying this is necessary to ensure a feeling of participation in the Diaspora. In his inaugural address to the three-day conclave, the Prime Minister, Dr. Manmohan Singh, made a number of announcements including a proposal to create a framework to provide profitable opportunities to the overseas Indians while reiterating the government's commitment to promote the interests of the overseas Indian communities. Dr. Singh made it clear that security and the welfare of the Indian residents living abroad is a top priority for his government. Last year, the Prime Minister had asked the overseas Indian communities to invest in a new India…not just financially but intellectually, socially, culturally and above all, emotionally. But, this time, Dr. Singh was confident when he said that conditions are favourable to sustain 9 to 10 per cent growth in the country and this growth process will transform the economy to emerge India as a major powerhouse of the world. He observed that the emphasis was to see India emerge as a leading knowledge-based economy and major education hub. His announcement for the setting up of a Prime Minister's Global Advisory Council of People of Indian Origin (PIO) is a welcome measure as it will serve as a high level platform to draw upon the experience and the knowledge of the best Overseas Indian minds. He said there is also a proposal to set up an Indian Development Foundation to seek greater participation of NRIs in philanthropic activities. This will serve as a credible institutional mechanism to direct overseas Indian Philanthropic efforts in human development in India, he remarked. Other announcements included the launching of an Overseas Workers Resource Centre to provide relevant information and assistance to potential migrant workers. Dr. Singh said that the work on the University for People of Indian Origin in a Private-Public-Partnership, commencing this year, was well received at the conclave. He particularly, expressed his gratitude to the Indian community in USA for mobilizing support of the political leadership for Indo-US cooperation in civilian nuclear energy. The Prime Minister also acknowledged that India is the largest recipient of remittance from its overseas community, which was estimated at 26 billion US dollars in 2006. He said that India took great pride in the achievements of the people of Indian origin in diverse fields of human endeavour in different parts of the world. In this context, he made a special reference to four women of Indian origin, who had scaled the heights in their respective professions.

5405. (10-1-2008) NEW DELHI : Minister of Corporate Affairs, Shri Prem Chand Gupta inaugurated the Global Summit on "Repositioning the Management Accountant" here today. This three-day Mega event of Management Accounting bodies across the globe is being organized by the Institute of Cost and Works Accountants of India (ICWAI) at Vigyan Bhawan, New Delhi on January 10-12, 2008. The ICWAI is the main host for this Global Summit. Co-hosts include Institute of Cost and Management Accountants of Bangladesh (ICMAB), Institute of Cost and Management Accountants of Pakistan (ICMAP) and the Society of Certified Management Accountants of Sri Lanka (SCMASL). Besides these SAARC bodies, the Summit has technical partnership with other counterparts from the Western world such as Certified Management Accountants (CMA), Canada, Certified Institute of Management Accountants (CIMA), UK and the Institute of Management Accountants (IMA), USA. Speaking on the occasion, Shri Gupta urged the management accountants to constantly re-equip themselves to keep pace with the developments all over the world and ensure that needs of their clients are met with requisite skill set, knowledge and experience. The Minister emphasised that the philosophy of the UPA Government is to provide more freedom to corporate and professionals under a self-regulatory regime with minimum interference from the Government.

5406. (10-1-2008) NEW DELHI : Dr. Satyanarayana Dash has taken over as the Secretary of the Department of Ex-Servicemen Welfare. This is the first time the department created in the Defence Ministry for the rehabilitation of a large ex-servicemen workforce is being headed by separate Secretary-level officer. The move will give a boost to ex-Servicemen's Welfare, thus fulfilling an agenda in the United Progressive Front (UPA) government's National Common Minimum Programme (NCMP). Dr. Dash will be responsible for issues related to ex-servicemen welfare, Directorate General of Resettlement & Kendriya & Rajya Sainik Boards. The 1973 Kerala Cadre IAS officer served as Principal Adviser in the Planning Commission till last month. In his chequered career spanning over three decades, Dr. Dash, 57, has a rich and varied administrative experience, serving in capacities such as MD, Travancore Titanium Products Ltd, Director of Scheduled Castes Development Board and Member (Finance), NHAI.

5407. (10-1-2008) NEW DELHI : Union Minister for Rural Development Dr. Raghuvansh Prasad Singh has called for promoting Roof top Water Harvesting (RWH) in rural areas of the country. In a letter addressed to all Chief Ministers of States the Minister said that his Ministry propose to introduce and promote individual roof top RWH structures in all rural households similar to individual household toilets and will provide all necessary technical and financial support for the same. We must bring sustainability to our Drinking Water Supply programme and this can be achieved in quantitative and qualitative terms by reducing/eliminating dependence on depleting ground water or poor quality ground water and increasing the Availability and Quality of water through Surface Water, Rain Water Harvesting, Roof Top Collection of Rain Water, Dr. Singh added. This will be to ensure RWH for rooftop collection and storage of drinking water, both for individual and community purposes, becomes a part of all new Drinking Water Supply projects along with in situ recharge of all existing drinking water sources and borewells, The Minister has further instructed the ministry officials to also ensure that not less than 2-3 ponds/surface water collection systems are developed in each habitation under the NREGA programme. These may be rejuvenation of existing ponds/lakes or even construction of new ones. He also stressed on the need to integrate Water Conservation and structures augmenting Drinking Water Supply under NREGA with the drinking water supply system in each and every habitation. He said hydro-geological maps have also been supplied to some States for facilitating construction of recharge structures and it will be towards Governments commitment to cover all habitations with safe drinking water by 2009 under the Bharat Nirman Programme by successfully addressing the challenge of "slipped back habitations" and ensuring that this phenomena does not recur again, calls for serious changes in strategies so far adopted. Referring to the Dilution and Improvement of Ground Water by Recharge methods Dr. Singh said a Decentralized; appropriate Purification and Treatment systems at Panchayat/habitation levels can ensure potability of the water at the consumption point. He has expressed the hope that States active cooperation of in this regard will lead in bringing sustainability to rural drinking water and sanitation and ensuring that potable water is within the reach of every citizen in the villages.

5408. (10-1-2008) NEW DELHI : In exercise of the powers conferred by clause (1) of Article 224 of the Constitution of India, the President is pleased to appoint Shri Tankeshwar Prasad Sharma, to be an Additional Judge of the Chhattisgarh High Court for a period of two years with effect from the date he assumes charge of his office.

5409. (10-1-2008) NEW DELHI : The Centre has decided to review the safety and security of the tourists particularly women tourist with the State Governments on 24th January, 2008. A communication in this regard has been sent to all Chief Secretaries of the State/ UT Governments by the Secretary (Tourism) Shri S. Banerjee today. State Tourism Secretaries are meeting the Union Tourism Ministry on that day to review the tourism projects and related issues in New Delhi. It has now been decided that safety and security of the tourists would be one of the main topics on the agenda. In his letter to the Chief Secretaries, Shri Shilabhadra Banerjee has referred to recent media reports of harassment of women tourists and reminded to State Governments about the concerns of the Centre on the safety and security of the foreign as well as domestic tourists. It said that the Centre had advised in the past about the need for deployment of Tourist Police at the places of tourist importance.

5410. (10-1-2008) NEW DELHI : The Cabinet Committee on Economic Affairs today gave its approval for doubling of Udhna-Jalgaon with Electrification (306.93 kms) at a total cost of Rs.714.60 crore. The doubling of this section will: (i) provide additional capacity on this section for catering to the projected traffic to meet with the requirement of Thermal Power Plants particularly of Wanakbhori, Gandhinagar and Ukai-Sonagadh. The projected traffic by 2010-11 is 35 trains each way as against 23 to 26 being handled at present. (ii) Reduce the lead involved in movement of coal from Korba area to Gujarat Power Plant by about 200 kms as compared to movement via Itarsi-Bhopal-Ratlam. The work is likely to be completed within 5 years.

5411. (10-1-2008) NEW DELHI : The Government today approved the Capacity Building Scheme for taking National e-Governance Plan (NeGP) forward across the country in all the States & UTs. The scheme is mainly for providing technical & professional support to State level policy & decision-making bodies and to develop specialized skills for e-governance. The scheme has an outlay of Rs.313 crore for a period of three years and will be implemented by the Department of

Information Technology. The scheme envisions: (i) Establishment of Institutional Framework for State Level Strategic decision-making including setting-up of State e-Governance Mission Team (SeMT). (ii) Imparting of specialized training, Orientation programme for SeMTs and decision makers (state legislature and senior bureaucrats), knowledge sharing and bringing in international best practices. (iii) Strengthening of Training Institutions in States. The approval would help in setting up of a central Capacity Building Management Cell for coordination and implementation of the scheme, which will be working under the Empowered Committee for CB under the chairmanship of Secretary (IT) especially set-up for the scheme.

5412. (10-1-2008) NEW DELHI : In order the safeguard the interest of coconut growers in the country, the Government approved, on the recommendations of CACP, the MSP of Copra for 2008 season. The MSP for Fair Average Quality (FAQ) of Milling Copra has been fixed at Rs.3660/- per quintal and for Fair Average Quality of Ball Copra, the MSP has been fixed at Rs.3910/- per quintal. This represents an increase of Rs.40/- per quintal for both "Milling" and "Ball" Copra over the MSP announced for last season. The increase in the MSP of Copra is expected to encourage the farmers to step up investment in coconut cultivation and increase production and productivity of coconut in the country.

5413. (10-1-2008) NEW DELHI : The Government today gave its approval for raising fresh equity through IPO of 1 crore shares (face value of Rs.10 each). After the IPO, paid up equity of RITES Ltd. will rise from Rs.4 crore to Rs. 5 crore and the Government's holding in the company will be reduced to 72%. RITES Ltd. has entered in newly emerging business of concession of existing railway lines, BOT of rail and infrastructure project, leasing of rail equipment etc. IPO will facilitate raising funds for investment for these projects.

5414. (10-1-2008) NEW DELHI : The Cabinet Committee on Economic Affairs today gave its approval for supporting the ITPO under MAI Scheme for organizing India's participation in the Expo 2010 World Exhibition, Shanghai, China (May 1-October 31, 2010) for meeting expenditure between the period 2007-2010. It is expected that India's participation in Expo 2010, Shanghai, China would provide a forum to project the progress made by India in a variety of fields such as rural development, education, telecommunication, science and technology and showcase India's technological advance and contribution to synthesis nature and technology for the benefit of mankind. World Expos are held once in five years in different cities with specific themes. The next World Expo will be held in Shanghai (China). The theme of the Expo is "Better City, Better Life".

5415. (10-1-2008) ARIYALUR: The Communist Party of India (CPI) has urged the State Government to initiate steps to modernise the 'Arasu Cement' factory, run by the Tamil Nadu Cements Corporation, near here for stepping up its productivity and profitability. A resolution adapted to this effect at its meeting held here recently, said that the factory should be modernised through the use of latest technological developments in the production sector. The scope for expansion was also bright, as the limestone in a vast area of lands owned by it, was yet to be mined out. The expansion and modernisation, the resolution added, would avoid the need for importing cement and also result in improving the productivity and profitability of the factory. Another resolution urged the State Government to announce a compensation of Rs.5,000 an acre to the farmers whose crop had been badly damaged by last month's torrential rain. Maize-growers, chilly cultivators, groundnut farmers and paddy cultivators had been hard hit by the flood-like situation in parts of the district, the resolution pointed out. The meeting, through a resolution, 'urged the district administration to initiate steps for starting an additional kerosene pump to cater to the needs of the ration-cardholders in the town. There was only one pump in the town and the presence of a huge crowd often caused more inconvenience in the distribution of the commodity. Resolutions pleading for the introduction of share-autorickshaws in the town; clearing of encroachments on the Marudaiyar River to protect the cultivable lands during floods in future; merger of the Madurakudikadu and Periyammapalayam village panchayats were also adopted on the occasion. The District secretary of the party A. Venugopal inaugurated the meeting. The Ariyalur unit secretary T. Dhandapani and the State Executive member V. Duraimanickam were among those who spoke.

5416. (10-1-2008) NEW DELHI : The Union Cabinet today gave its approval for promulgating an ordinance to amend the Railways Act, 1989 for carrying out the amendments for expeditious land acquisition for Special Railway Projects and to replace the Ordinance by a Bill by introducing a Bill in the ensuing session of Parliament. The proposed amendments would facilitate expeditious land acquisition for Special Railway Projects.

5417. (10-1-2008) NEW DELHI : The Union Cabinet today gave its approval for signing of a MoU between India and Italy on cooperation in the agro-food sector. The MoU will promote bilateral cooperation between the two Parties for promotion of agro-food products facilitating creation of a 'Joint Foundation" and exchange of know-how, technologies between Indian and Italian agro-food enterprises. The MoU shall remain valid for a period of 5 years.

5418. (10-1-2008) NEW DELHI : The Union Cabinet today gave its approval for signing of a MoU between India and Italy in the field of agriculture and phytosanitary issues. The MoU will be signed during the Prime Minister's forthcoming visit to China in 2008. The MoU will promote further bilateral cooperation joint activities and exchanges in the areas of agriculture and phytosanitary issues through exchange of scientific delegations and experts between the two counties. The MoU shall remain valid for a period of 5 years.

5419. (10-1-2008) NEW DELHI : The Union Cabinet today gave its approval for signing of an Agreement between India and Hungary on cooperation in the field of agriculture and allied sectors. The Agreement will promote further cooperation through joint activities and exchanges in the areas of agriculture through exchange of scientific delegations and experts between the two countries. This Agreement shall remain valid for a period of 5 years.

5420. (10-1-2008) NEW DELHI : The Union Cabinet today gave its approval for signing of a MoU between India and China for cooperation in the Rail sector. The MoU will be signed during the Prime Minister's forthcoming visit to China in 2008. The MoU will help promote cooperation in the Rail sector between Chinese Railways and Indian Railways. The MoU will be valid for 3 years.

5421. (10-1-2008) NEW DELHI : The Union Cabinet today gave its approval for signing of a MoU between India and China for cooperation in land resource management, land administration, resettlement and rehabilitation. The MoU will be signed during the Prime Minister's forthcoming visit to China in 2008. The MoU shall facilitate cooperation between the two countries for mutual cooperation based on the principles of equality, mutual benefit and reciprocity on matters related to land resource management, land administration, and resettlement and rehabilitation.

5422. (10-1-2008) NEW DELHI : The Union Cabinet today gave its approval for signing of a MoU between India and China for cooperation in housing sector. It will be signed during the forthcoming visit of PM to China in January 2008. The MoU will provide a basic framework for cooperation in the area of housing between the two counties.

5423. (10-1-2008) NEW DELHI : The Union Cabinet today gave its approval for signing of a MoU between India and China for cooperation in the field of geosciences. The MoU will provide an institutional mechanism between India and China for cooperation in the field of geosciences.

5424. (10-1-2008) NEW DELHI : The Union Cabinet today gave its approval for signing of MoU between India and China for the development of their respective Traditional Medicine. This will provide a legal framework to the cooperation among the two countries for the development of their respective traditional medicine systems and adoption of common strategies for global positioning of these systems.

5425. (10-1-2008) NEW DELHI : The Union Cabinet today gave its ex-post facto approval to the signed trilateral MoU in the field of Health and Medicine among India, Brazil and South Africa. It was signed on 17th October, 2007 during the 2nd IBSA Summit held in South Africa. The trilateral Memorandum of Understanding shall facilitate cooperation among the three countries in the field of Health and Medicine on the basis of equality, reciprocity and mutual benefit.

5426. (10-1-2008) NEW DELHI : In the light of Unified Access Services Licence (UASL) guidelines issued on 14th December 2005 by the department regarding number of Licences in a Service Area, a reference was made to TRAI on 13-4.2007. The TRAI on 28-8-2007 recommended that no cap be placed on the number of access service providers in any service area. The Government accepted this recommendation of TRAI. Accordingly, DOT has decided to issue LOI to all the eligible applicants on the date of application who applied upto 25-9-2007. UAS licence authorizes licencee to rollout telecom access services using any digital technology which includes wire-line and/or wireless (GSM and/or CDMA) services. They can also provide Internet Telephony, Internet Services and Broadband services. UAS licence in broader terms is an umbrella licence and does not automatically authorize UAS licencees usage of spectrum to rollout Mobile (GSM and/or CDMA) services. For this, UAS licencee has to obtain another licence, *i.e.* Wireless Operating Licence which is granted on first-come-first served basis subject to availability of spectrum in particular service area. DOT has been implementing a policy of First-cum-First Served for grant of UAS licences under which initially an application which is received front will be processed first and thereafter if found eligible will be granted LOI and then whosoever complies with the conditions of LOI first will be granted UAS licence.

5427. (10-1-2008) NEW DELHI : The Ministry of Youth Affairs and Sports has announced the Indira Gandhi National Service Scheme Awards (IGNSS Awards) for the year 2006-07 to the following NSS Volunteers, Programme Officers and Programme Coordinators in recognition of their exemplary service to the community. The awards will be presented by His Excellency the Governor of Tamil Nadu on 16th January 2008 in the closing ceremony of the 13th National Youth Festival being held at Chennai. Shri Krishna Dutta Rao Shinde, Programme Coordinator Directorate of Vocational Education and Training, Mumbai has been conferred the highest award of Rs. one lakh cash award, shield & scroll.

5428. (10-1-2008) NEW DELHI : Shri Kamal Nath, Minister for Commerce and Industry, has stated that the EOU/SEZ Sector is playing a very important role in encouraging manufacturing activity, providing substantial employment opportunities, thereby accelerating the pace of economic growth. The units set up under these schemes are already providing direct employment to over 6.5 lakh people. He was speaking at the Export Awards function, organised by the Export Promotion Council for EOUs and SEZ Units (EPCES), here last evening. Shri R. Gopalan, Additional Secretary, Department of Commerce; Shri R.S. Gujral, Director General of Foreign Trade (DGFT); Shri T. Vasu, Chairman, EPCES and Shri L.B. Singhal, Director General of EPCES, apart from Development Commissioners of various EPZs and SEZs were present on the occasion. As regards Sunset Clause, the Minister said: "I am aware of the need of the removal of the Sunset Clause under Section 10B of the Income Tax Act, so that EOUs continue to avail the exemption from income tax, especially at this juncture when all the exporters have been hit badly on account of rupee appreciation. I have taken up the issue with Prime Minister as well as Finance Minister". The Minister observed that SEZ units and developers are facing certain problems in the context of Service Tax, benefit of DEPB/Duty Drawback on supplies to SEZ Developers, interpretation of Section 10AA of the Income Tax Act etc. "We are working on these issues and hopefully will be able to resolve these suitably. There are certain issues related to State Governments as well like implementation of Single Window Mechanism, Exemption from Stamp Duty etc. I have asked Commerce Secretary to take a meeting with various State Governments this month for an early resolution of these issues", he added. Shri Kamal Nath stated that the exports from SEZs in the year 2006-07 was Rs.34,787 crore, which was 52% higher than the previous year's exports. "This year, I am expecting a growth of 100% and the exports from SEZs are likely to touch Rs.67,000 crore. Exports from SEZs is like to cross Rs.1,00,000 crore in the year 2008-09. At present, over 42 SEZs have already started operations and many more new SEZs are in the advance stage of operation. Many of these SEZs are recruiting people from rural areas and providing them training for operations in the SEZs, as we have seen from Gem & Jewellery SEZ in Hyderabad, Textiles units in Mahindra SEZ in Chennai and other new SEZs like Nokia, Flextronics in Chennai, Apache SEZ, Brandix Apparel SEZ, Divy's Laboratories in Andhra Pradesh and Rajiv Gandhi Technology Park in Chandigarh", he said. While congratulating the award winners, the Minister said that "I am sure, all of you will strive towards achieving the full export potential of your establishments, thereby contributing to the country's economy as well as creation of further employment". Speaking on the occasion, Shri Vasu, Chairman, EPCES, informed that EOUs and SEZs encourage manufacturing, exports, and employment generation and accelerate the process of inclusive growth. He further added that EOUs and SEZs provide direct employment to over 6.5 lakh people and indirect employment nearly 5 times. Most of the employment is generated in rural and semi-rural areas. EOUs are operating in 27 states and new SEZs have been approved in 22 states. 420 SEZs have already started operations and have already started exporting. The total number of awards presented were 47 and are in the fields of gem & jewellery, engineering, plastic products, electronic, computer hardware, services, readymade garments, handicrafts, chemical & allied products, textile products, food products etc.

5429. (11-1-2008) NEW DELHI : The Ministry of Information and Broadcasting has deferred the dates for submission of financial bids for 97 FM Radio Stations in 48 cities. The next dates shall be notified in due course. This follows the dismissal of review petition filed by the government in this regard in Delhi High Court, today. The bidding was scheduled for, January 14 & 24, 2008. The Government invited bids for 97 vacant FM Channels on 08.06.2007 in 48 cities including Dehradun, Imphal, Kohima, Port Blair and Sagar which do not have any FM channel at present. Minimum networth requirements have been prescribed under the terms and conditions of the tender for the companies to make them eligible to bid for various categories of cities. The method of calculation of networth as prescribed in the tender conditions requires the applicants to deduct intangible assets amongst others from the book value of assets. On deduction of intangible assets, certain parties were not found eligible for submission of financial bids. One such party, viz M/s Radio Today Broadcasting Limited filed a writ petition No. 9266/2007 in Hon'ble High Court of Delhi on 11.12.2007 and challenged the deduction of one time entry fee already paid by them to the Government during the last phase of bidding from their networth. The Hon'ble High Court in its order dated 20.12.2007 while upholding the method of calculation of networth adopted by the Government has, however, allowed the petitioner to make another bid after increasing the net worth and directed the Government to consider the same appropriately. The Central Government filed a review petition as in the opinion of the Government, the opportunity for increasing networth could have been given till the last date of submission of the pre-qualification bids *i.e.* up to 23.07.2007 and not thereafter as per the terms and conditions of tender. In this regard, the Government is exploring further legal options.

5430. (11-1-2008) NEW DELHI : The Annual Plan for Mizoram for the year 2008-09 was finalized here today at a meeting between Deputy Chairman, Planning Commission Shri Montek Singh Ahluwalia and Chief Minister of Mizoram Shri Zoramthanga. The Annual Plan was finalized at Rs.1,000 crore. This includes Additional Central Assistance of Rs 70 crore for projects of special interest to the State. Mr. Ahluwalia appreciated the efforts being made for accelerating infrastructure development and said that significant progress has been achieved in the sectors of Road Transport, Power, Education and Health. While 94.4 per cent of the villages have been connected with approach roads, 98.6 per cent villages have been electrified. Some sectors like transport, education and health have expanded rapidly contributing to the tertiary sector income. He said the State needs to explore horticulture and floriculture potential. He said all districts of the State would be covered under NREG from next year. Appreciating efforts at establishing health infrastructure, it was pointed out that efforts should be intensified to fill gap in trained teachers and doctors. Attention was also drawn to decrease in dense forests. The Chief Minister said that the priorities of XIth Plan as well as holistic development have been kept in mind while formulating the annual plan 2008-09. He said that agriculture and allied sector and rural development with emphasis on self sufficiency in food production, employment generation and poverty eradication will be priority of the Annual Plan 2008-09. He said the State was facing food crisis as no harvesting could be taken up because of Bamboo Flowering. To cope up with the famine like situation arising as a result of bamboo flowering the state government is expecting additional help under National Rural Employment Guaranteed Scheme (NREGS) in increasing agriculture production and developing rural infrastructure.

5431. (11-1-2008) NEW DELHI : In exercise of the powers conferred by clause (1) of article 217 of the Constitution of India, the President is pleased to appoint (i) Shri Justice Vishwa Diwakar Chaturvedi, (ii) Shri Justice Ravindra Nath Misra and (iii) Shri Justice Ran Vijai Singh, Additional judges of the Allahabad High Court, to be judges of the Allahabad High Court, in that order of seniority, with effect from the dates they assume charge of their respective offices.

5432. (11-1-2008) NEW DELHI : The Congress Party whole-heartedly welcomes the implementation of the delimitation proposals by the Government of India. The Congress Party has always stood for meaningful electoral reforms. In particular the Congress Party is enthused about the delimitation proposals because they seek to rectify historical imbalances affecting the aam aadmi in general and especially the Scheduled Castes and Scheduled Tribes, the two most vulnerable sections of society. The Congress Party believes that any measure, be it constitutional, economic, social, electoral which benefits the Scheduled Castes and the Scheduled Tribes and restores to them their true place in society, should be promoted and propagated. The new delimitation proposals will not only give a far larger electoral role to these historically depressed classes, at both the national level but very importantly, and in large measure, at the State Assembly level. Conversely, redistributing constituencies or redefining constituencies will allow those classes whose numerical strength justifies their participation in democracy to be more fully involved in electoral politics, although for many years, on account of lack of redefinition, they have remained excluded. We have no doubt that this will inaugurate a more representative body politic which will not only correctly reflect our diverse democracy but will reflect more correctly our inclusive democracy, will reflect more clearly social justice which the Congress Party stands for first and foremost. Finally the Congress Party has always been a rainbow of coalitions and the new delimitation boundaries are bound to reflect the true depth and the true picture of the Congress Party as a truly pan-Indian Party. To a question that the Congress Party favours 1/3rd reservation for women but the Congress President, Smt. Sonia Gandhi says that there are others who oppose the 1/3rd reservation and even though I am in favour of the reservation I just cannot get it implemented, Shri Singhvi said, the Congress Party was the first to favour the reservation at the governmental level, or when it was in opposition or when it was at the Centre. We all know that there are some reasons, there are some parties and there are some sections of society who, unless they are not made a party, and till 2/3rds majority is not achieved, getting the reservation implemented is not possible and the Congress Party is all for it but it is a matter of getting that 2/3rds majority first. To a question as to how the delimitation proposals will help the SCs/STs, Shri Singhvi said, it is going to benefit the SCs/STs obviously in many ways. At the national level, it's not only a question of the 8, 9, 10, 11 additional seats but it's a more important question of accurately defining the boundaries where the true numerical numbers have not been reflected or rather have not been translated into electoral participation. Second, and more importantly, at the Assembly level, the numbers are far more. The exact figures will have to be calculated but they may be upwards of 40, 50 or 60. So that is a significant feature and these are sections whose numerical strength justifies, indeed obliges them to participate in elections in reserved constituencies. That was the intention of our constitutional framers, that was the whole spirit of promoting their well-being by giving them a feeling of ownership in our democracy. Democracy is all about ownership, that by the people, of the people, for the people. That of the people is ownership of democracy by every section and the historically depressed classes have a right to be more representatively owning that democracy. To a question as per analytic recommendations that there are many SC seats which have an overwhelming Muslim presence, which tops the state of Muslim leadership at the top, don't you think that would have been taken care of separately, Shri Singhvi said, it would not be correct to say so. Point number one, delimitation is a constitutional exercise which has to be done according to constitutional provisions and it has to be done periodically and it was already underway even before or around the time the Sachar Committee was set up. Much of the work had already gone underway when the Sachar Committee report came. Point two although, in future, each and every aspect of the Sachar Committee report will be looked into and wherever possible, by consensus, changes can and will be made and to expect that in the 2007 report of the delimitation commission you can incorporate those changes would be far-fetched and not correct because that will retard and set back the entire delimitation clock. That does not mean that the Sachar Committee suggestions will not be looked into. They are being processed and in periodic intervals, whenever possible, they will be very carefully looked into but not for the 2007-2008 exercise which is already substantially over. To a question whether you would like Karnataka Assembly elections to be held under the redrawn constituencies, Shri Singhvi said, absolutely. We are confident. We are looking forward to it and yesterday there was an official statement by Shri Pranab Mukherjee which makes it clear that future elections, barring those three, four states where there has been Supreme Court stay, where Justice Kuldip Singh's Commission has made no recommendations, approximately 23 or 24 states will go to elections on the basis of the delimited boundaries. Anybody else may be apprehensive of those delimited boundaries, the Congress Party is not only confident but looking forward to it. To a question that your Party has supported the move in toto but whether the numerous important leaders in the Party are serious about the entire exercise and has the Party been able to convince those leaders, Shri Singhvi said, let me emphasise the point you are making.

5433. (11-1-2008) NEW DELHI : The Prime Minister, Dr. Manmohan Singh has condoled the passing away of Sir Edmund Hillary describing him as one who drew our attention to the grandeur of Mother Earth. In his condolence message Dr. Singh said we must seek inspiration from Sir Edmund Hillary's sense of adventure, enterprise and his love of nature.

5434. (11-1-2008) NEW DELHI : A 3-member delegation led by the Union Health Minister, Dr. Anbumani Ramadoss, currently on an official visit to France met the France Minister for Health, Youth Affairs and Sports, Ms. Roselyne

Bachelot on 9th January at Paris. During the meeting, besides bilateral issues relating to the health sector, the following areas of cooperation were identified for focused attention; Medical Research, Biotechnology, Development of vaccine, Promotion of Indian Systems of medicines and cooperation between ICMR and INSERM of France. The Indian Ambassador for France Mr. Ranjan Mathai and officials of both the countries also participated in the meeting. The Health Minister also visited the French National Institute of Health and Medical Research (INSERM) and Robert Debre Hospital, Paris. The Director General of INSERM, Prof. Andre Syrota and the Director of the Hospital Dr. (Ms.). Christine were also present with him. The INSERM is the only French public research body entirely dedicated to human health. Its researchers are committed to studying all diseases, whether common or rare, through their research in the fields of biology, medicine and public health.

5435. (11-1-2008) NEW DELHI : The Union Minister for Rural Development Dr. Raghuvansh Prasad Singh has stressed upon paying extra attention towards rural masses living below the Poverty Line, *i.e.* the BPL families for the effective Implementation of Sampoorna Grameen Swarojgar Yojana (SGRY) and Swarna Jayanti Gram Swarozgar Yojana (SGSY) so as to benefit the rural masses in the country. Presiding over a review meeting. of the two programmes held recently here the Minister said that the proposal to recast the SGSY programme during the 11th Five year plan is under active consideration. It was observed that during the current financial year (2007-08) a total of Rs. 1654.48 crore was allocated under SGRY for the 264 districts in the country of which the first instalment of Rs. 1025.13 crore was released to 256 districts. For the release of 2nd instalment proposals from 239 districts have been received. Of them funds as 2nd instalment amounting to Rs. 1340.93 crore have been released to 57 DRDAs. Proposals from 25 DRDAs are under process and proposals from 54 DRDAs are pending with the IFD whereas clarification have been sought from 103 DRDAs. The total amount during the year thus is to the tune of Rs. 1159.23 crores. This include budget allocation of Rs.2600 crore as cash and Rs. 200 crore as foodgrains under the programme. Of the total allocation of Rs.3031.02 crore, Rs. 2535.02 crore was released till January 09, 2008. The allocations under SGRY as on January 09, 2008 was Rs.1654.48 crore as cash of which Rs.1159.23 crore was released, as foodgrains/ FCI payment it was Rs. 1376.54 crore of the entire amount was released for the allocation of 9.60 lakh Metric Tonnes of foodgrains during the year so far. Under SGSY a total of 588 DRDAs were considered for budgetary allocations during the fiscal year 2007-08. From the earmarked Central Allocation of Rs.1702.24 crore, Rs. 1126.02 crore have been released to 33 States/UTs. This include release of Rs.740.59 crore to 530 DRDAs as 1st instalment and Rs.385.44 crore to 322 DRDAs as 2nd instalment till January 10, 2008. The amount released under SGSY is supposed to be spent on self-employment programme to assist the BPL families by organizing them into Self-Help Groups (SHGs) through the process of social mobilization. Since marketing of the rural products made by these self-help groups is the prime concerns of the Ministry of Rural Development efforts should be made for setting up of permanent infrastructure in all the major locations of the country. The minister was also apprised of the progress of work done so far in New Delhi and other State Capitals and big cities and towns. Dr. Singh also expressed the need to have a better coordination between the financial institutions and the DRDAs and agencies like CAPART and other NGOs in this regard.

5436. (11-1-2008) NEW DELHI : Government of India have announced the sale (re-issue) of "11.30 percent Government Stock, 2010" under Market Stabilization Scheme for a notified amount of Rs. 4,000 crore (nominal). The Government Stock will be sold through price based auction using multiple price method. The auctions will be conducted by the Reserve Bank of India, Mumbai Office, Fort, Mumbai on January 17, 2008 (Thursday). Up to 5 per cent of the amount notified for the sale of stock is reserved for allotment to eligible individuals and Institutions on non-competitive basis as per the Scheme for Non-Competitive Bidding Facility in the Auction of Government Securities. Bids in the prescribed form obtainable from the Regional Director, Reserve Bank of India.

5437. (11-1-2008) NEW DELHI : The Advisory Board of the Centre for Joint Warfare Studies (CENJOWS) meets for the first time here tomorrow. The Defence Minister Shri AK Antony will be delivering the inaugural address and also launch the centre's website. The CENJOWS was set up last year following a recommendation of the Group of Ministers who went into the need for reforms after the Kargil conflict (Op Vijay) that emphasized on the need to create integrative synergy in our procedures and executive Institutions. Their report recommended the urgent need to move away from our historical fixations and circumvent the inertia of the status quo. The Ministry of Defence approved the establishment of the Centre and it has also been registered under the 'Societies Registration Act 1860'. The Centre was inaugurated by the then Chairman, Chiefs of Staff Committee General JJ Singh on 27 Aug 07 at the Kashmir House, Rajaji Marg, New Delhi. The CENJOWS seeks to be an enabler of Jointness and Integration at all levels and throughout the National Power Matrix. Military is just the baseline on which the superstructure has to be built. The unipolar orientation of the world allows India to be in a unique position of a State with choices and opportunities. As an important part of the Asian continent towards which the centricity of global interests is shifting, India needs to move out of her historical fixations. As a nation with a capability to swing power equations, India not only needs to define her friends and foes but also has to reorient herself towards global leadership and in the process graduate from the existing Third World focus. Technology and globalisation are delivering their advantages but are also accompanied by increased level of uncertainties. This demands additional security assurances based on capabilities and not merely threat defrayment. The India National Power, therefore, needs to seek greater impact and reach. The quest for increased relevance can succeed only if there is Jointness and Integration amongst the constituents of National Power. While all elements of National Power and decision matrix exist in the country, there is a lack of synergy amongst the components. We need to reassess the processes of connecting the dots to create a synergistic whole. This is more so, when, increased unit cost of capabilities demands partnership in development as well as exploitation. Procedures and structures are mere tools of change. Transformation has to be empowered through changed attitudes. Mental pre-dispositions towards the comfort zone of the status quo can be corrected only if change is brought about through National Will. For this graduation to current realties there is a need for debate at multiple platforms. Creative research needs to support the change and the demystification process has to leveraged with the assistance of all formats of Indian media.

5438. (11-1-2008) NEW DELHI : The telecom revolution has contributed enormously to the increased efficiency in the economy. It has reduced transaction costs and has increased connectivity across the length and breadth of our vast subcontinent. It has brought us closer to each other. Today, India has emerged as a major base for the telecom industry worldwide and it is the endeavour of the Government to facilitate further growth of this vital industry as it is not just the growth of a sector but it has a 'multiplier effect' on the entire economy. The Indian telecommunications network with over 250 million connections today is third largest in the world and the second largest among the emerging economies of Asia. The telecommunication sector continues to register significant growth during the year and has emerged as one of the key sectors responsible for India's resurgent economic growth. The targeted growth of 250 million by the end of 2007 was achieved in the month of October 2007 itself, when the total number of telephones touched 256.55 million. The current addition of about eight million lines per month puts the telecommunication sector on a strong footing to achieve the target of 500 million connections by 2010. This could be possible due to supportive government policies that, inter-alia, focus on network expansion, rural telephony, broadband coverage and R&D and also provide enabling regulatory environment for the growth of the sector coupled with private sector participation.

5439. (11-1-2008) NEW DELHI : The Prime Minister, Dr. Manmohan Singh has written to the Chief Ministers of all the states seeking their cooperation and commitment to ensure effective implementation of the Scheduled Tribes and Traditional Forest Dwellers (Recognition of Forest Rights) Act, 2006. The act requires State governments to constitute committees that will process the cases and ensure distribution of land rights. The Prime Minister has urged the state governments to set up, at the earliest, the State and District Level Monitoring Committees and the local-below district level committees so that the work can be commenced promptly. Dr. Singh also stressed on the need to ensure wide publicity of the provisions of the act at the local level. He pointed out that while implementing the act it should be ensured that adequate protection is provided to critical wildlife habitats as provided for in the act.

5440. (11-1-2008) NEW DELHI : Milan is a biennial conglomeration of Asia-Pacific Maritime Navies at Port Blair to foster bonds of 'Friendship Across the Seas' and share views on common maritime issues. Milan 08 is scheduled at Port Blair from 18-23 January this year, wherein ships and delegations from Australia, New Zealand, Myanmar, Thailand, Indonesia, Sri Lanka, Singapore, Malaysia, Bangaladesh, Vietnam and Brunei have expressed willingness to take part. The event assumed significance in view of the increasing maritime trade in the areas of common interest and need to safeguard the sea lanes of communications from poaching and terrorist activities. Besides, the event will showcase the beautiful Andman and Nicobar Islands and its rich heritage to the visitors from these countries. The five-day event will comprise professional interaction in the form of seminar and social interaction during cultural presentations. Milan 08 will culminate with a grand city parade off Marina on 22 January 08 consisting of colourful march past by the Navies, local school children, NCC and police contingents, daredevil motor cycle display by Army, spectacular aerobatic show by the IAF front line supersonic fighters, Sukhoi-30's, breath taking demonstration and water Para jumps by the Indian Navy's Marine Commandos, impressive illumination of Indian Naval Ships and dazzling firework display. The visiting ships and delegates will have a ceremonial see off on 23 January 08 from the Naval Wharf.

5441. (11-1-2008) NEW DELHI : Shri Kamal Nath, Union Minister of Commerce and Industry, has stated that bilateral trade in the services sector holds great promise, as India is emerging as a global services provider especially in the information technology and software sector. While addressing at the Luncheon Meeting with the Prime Minister of Greece, Mr. Kostas Karamanlis, here today, the Minister stated that bilateral investment flows have seen an uptrend and major Indian IT companies like Infosys, TCS already have a presence in Greece. Similarly, Greek companies such as Eurodyn, Pisani Group MJ Mailis, have invested in India, he added. The Foreign Affairs Minister of Greece, senior officials from both the sides besides a business delegation was present on the occasion. The Minister mentioned about the agreement on Cooperation in Science & Technology signed during the visit of the President of India to Greece in April 2007 and hoped that it will provide a basis for greater engagement in innovative areas and lay the foundation for enhanced cooperation. During the meeting, the Prime Minister of Greece, stated that, "our bilateral trade volume keeps up a steady growth. Nevertheless, we firmly believe that it remains beneath the two countries potential and can be further developed and diversified. The target to double the volume of our bilateral trade by 2010, seems attainable and viable". He added that Greek economy is being transformed into a more dynamic, more open and more competitive economy....And as a result, FDI in Greece has reached 4.3 billion in 2006, nine times higher than in 2005.... Greece is a safe market with modern infrastructure in the fields of combined transportation, telecommunications and a complete legal framework which offers incentives, such as tax or grant exemptions for attracting foreign investors. He drew the attention of the gathering and said that Greek products with good export potential to the Indian market are machinery, lubricants, tobacco, pharmaceuticals, cosmetics, packaging and construction materials, processed food and beverages, clothing, informatics and services. Shri Kamal Nath observed that both governments have a crucial role to play in bringing together businesses. "Our commitment is to provide a positive business environment to foster the bilateral trading relationship. The effort made by the industry associations on both sides to enhance the levels of contacts among businesses is heartening and they deserve to be congratulated for their efforts", he further stated. The Commerce Minister stated that the current visit of the Greek Prime Minister with a strong business delegation could help both sides in building upon the strong bilateral relationship that exits. He said that during the visit of the Indian President to Greece, a commitment was made by both sides to double trade between the two countries to reach and exceed 1 billion Euros by 2010. "A large potential exists and both sides have to actively undertake measures to realise this potential. Bilateral trade between the two countries has shown a robust growth during the last two years", he added.

5442. (11-1-2008) NEW DELHI : Minister of State for Mines Dr. T. Subbarami Reddy met Canadian delegation to discuss about mining related bilateral issues, here today. The delegation was headed by Ms. Sandra Pupatello, Minister of Economic Development and Trade. The other members of the delegation include Mr. Harinder Taklhar, Ontario Minister of Small Business and Entrepreneurship, Mr. Fareed Amin, Deputy Minister of Economic Development and Trade, Mr. Bill Forward, Assistant Deputy Minister of Economic Development and Trade and Ms. Shirley Townsend, Counsellor-(Commercial-Ontario), Canadian High Commission. Canada is known for its rich mineral resources of Nickel, Coal, Copper, Iron Ore and Gold. Canadian Mineral Metal Industry is contributing 3.7% of its GDP employing over 6% of its work force. The minerals and metals constitute 17% of total Canada's export. Union Government of India is committed for self-sufficiency in exploration and mining of gold and diamonds, which is accounting for an annual import bill for Rs. 1.4 lakh crores. Dr. Reddy, Minister of State for Mines has requested Canadian Government for transfer of technology for exploration and mining of gold and diamonds for which the delegation responded favourably. Minister is confident to achieve unearthing of huge resources of gold and diamonds in next five years in which Canada also agreed to extend their technology. At the request of Dr. Reddy, the Canadian delegation assured to expedite the supply of Helicopter with modern state of air-borne technology to Geological Survey of India for exploration of mineral wealth of the nation. Dr. Reddy also requested the delegation for training Indian Geo-Scientists in Canada and also deputing a team of Canadian experts of mining technology to train experts of Indian mining in India. Dr. Reddy also enquired about the progress of monitoring and mitigating landslide at selected sites in India under Indo-Canadian Collaborative Projects as follow-up of the MoU.

5443. (11-1-2008) NEW DELHI : As per data compiled by Agriculture Ministry as on today, sowing is progressing well in the present rabi season. Wheat has been sown in 270.40 lakh ha as compared to 277.45 lakh ha on the same date last year. 8.54 lakh ha area has come under winter rice as against 9.05 lakh ha last year. Coarse cereals have been sown in 65.36 lakh ha as compared to 64.22 lakh ha by this time in 2007. Barley and maize have been grown in more area than last year's {barley 7.25 lakh ha, maize 8.96 lakh ha}. Rabi oilseeds have been sown in 84.55 lakh ha as compared to 93.93 lakh ha in the last rabi. Mustard/rapeseed coverage has reached 58.72 lakh ha (last rabi, up to this time: 66.41 lakh ha). Rabi pulses cover 127.80 lakh ha (last year: 132.67 lakh ha). Gram coverage has reached 78.44 lakh ha (vs. 81.20 lakh ha by this time last year).

5444. (11-1-2008) NEW DELHI : The Minister for Civil Aviation, Shri Praful Patel today launched the International Exhibition and Conference on Civil Aviation "India Aviation 2008", here today. Speaking on the occasion the Minister said that it is for the first time that a sector specific focused show was being organized for Indian Civil Aviation which being in nascent stage needed more space to grow. India Aviation 2008 will be the first international exhibition of its kind in India on the Indian civil aviation sector. The exhibition is being organized by the Ministry of Civil Aviation, Government of India jointly with the Federation of Indian Chambers of Commerce and Industry from 15-18 October 2008 at Hyderabad. The show will be supported by Airports Authority of India (AAI), Air India, the Directorate General of Civil Aviation and Pawan Hans Helicopters Ltd. The international promotion of the event will be undertaken by the Farnborough International Ltd., the organizations of the Farnborough Air Show. It will be the only event on the Civil Aviation sector in India that will be hosted at an airport- the show will be organized at the present Hyderabad Airport. The civil aviation operation would have shifted to the new Begumpet Airport in Hyderabad. While it will showcase the tremendous business opportunities for aviation companies to do business in India. It will have conferences and other meets during the show. On the occasion The Minister also added that a few areas of focus had not yet got due attention in the aviation sector. Though India had about 80 operational airports and about 20 more Greenfield airports lined up, there are at least 300 odd airstrips which are lying unused and must be brought into the mainstream of activity. For this purpose the States have to be involved and have to bring the infrastructure and the PPP model into play. The Central Government and the AAI alone cannot drive the growth of the aviation sector. Speaking about vexed issue of taxation he said that the States have to be more reasonable with their taxes- the increase in volumes would compensate if the taxes were lowered. The States have a significant role to play in ensuring a greater growth in the aviation sector. He added that the Hyderabad and Bangalore airports were ready and would get operational by March this year,-but the related infrastructure like multi-modal activities and connectivity with the city were still not in place properly. The Minister announced that the year 2008 would be the 'Year for the Helicopters' and the next focus area for the Ministry would be the helicopters and the seaplanes. He stressed upon the need of building Heliport especially in crowed cities like Mumbai and Delhi. Seaplanes, he said, had immense possibilities with India's large coastline. They have a huge potential for added connectivity, which is required in this country.

5445. (11-1-2008) NEW DELHI : The World Bank conducted a Detailed Implementation Review (DIR) in 2006-07 of five Bank-funded Health Sector projects in India, of which four were central-sector projects and one state-sector project. The Review pertained to the implementation of these projects during the period 1997-2006. The review was agreed upon and facilitated by Government of India. World Bank has shared the findings of the Review with Government of India. The Review is in the nature of a fact-finding report and does not extend to detailed investigation. It is an exercise to identify indicators of systemic weaknesses and areas for follow-up intervention. The DIR has found indications of systemic deficiencies and probable fraud and corruption in procurement and implementation and insufficient oversight in the projects reviewed. It has recommended improvements in project design, supervision and evaluation as well as in procurement processes. Government of India values its relationship with the World Bank and is fully committed to continuous systemic improvement in the implementation of all health sector projects, including those funded by the Bank and other development partners. It welcomes reviews, evaluations, inputs and suggestions from all quarters to better inform and assist the efforts at progressive improvement. Systemic deficiencies that plague all development programmes are to be addressed and loopholes plugged. Government of India is sensitive to the issues raised in the DIR and has taken the findings of the review seriously. It has been decided that the lessons flowing out of the DIR would be reflected through additional measures in the procurement and implementation arrangements of the ongoing as well as pipeline health sector projects. The action plan for health sector projects, finalized with the Bank in 2006, would be revised in the light of the lessons emanating from the DIR and in consultation with the Bank. The revised action plan would be in place and would apply both to on-going as well as future health sector projects. In addition to the above, based on the inputs of the DIR and other information that may be furnished by the Bank, necessary action under the relevant laws, rules and regulations would be taken against those suspected of wrong-doing and, if found guilty, they will be visited with exemplary punishment.

5446. (11-1-2008) NEW DELHI : On the basis of the result of the written part of the Engineering Services Examination, 2007 held by UPSC in June, 2007, the candidates with the under mentioned roll numbers have qualified for interview for Personality Test. The candidature of these candidates is provisional subject to their being found eligible in all respects. The candidates would be required to produce the original certificates in support of their claims relating to age, educational qualifications, community, physically disability etc. at the time of the Personality Test. They are, therefore, advised to keep the said certificates ready. Detailed Application Forms (DAF) would be issued to all the qualified candidates shortly and the candidates are required to submit the same duly filled in within 10 days from the date of issue of the same. In case the candidates don't receive the DAF by January 18, 2008, they should contact the Commission on Telephone No.23387402 or on Fax No.011-23387310. Interview of candidates who have qualified for the Personality Test are scheduled to be held from March 17, 2008 onwards. The exact date of interview will, however, be intimated to the candidates through Interview Letter. No request for change in the date and time of the Personality Test intimated to the candidates will be entertained under any circumstances. The marks-sheets of candidates who have not qualified will be available on the Commission's website within one month from the date of publication of the result and would be available for a period of 60 days. The candidates can access the marks-sheets after keying in their Roll Numbers and date of birth. The printed/hard copies of the marks-sheet would, however, be issued by UPSC to candidates based on specific request accompanied by a self-addressed stamped envelope. Candidates desirous of obtaining printed/hard copies of the marks sheets should make the request within thirty days of the display of the marks on the Commission's website, beyond which such requests would not be entertained. Candidates are advised to intimate change in their addresses, if any, to the UPSC immediately to facilitate dispatch of Interview Letters to them promptly.

5447. (11-1-2008) NEW DELHI : A report has appeared in a section of the media that avian flu was suspected in death of 11 peacocks at Ladhowal forest area near Ludhiana. It is clarified that the death of birds as reported was not due to avian influenza (bird flu). Details are as follows:-The samples from peacocks were sent to the High Security Animal Disease Laboratory (HSADL), Bhopal. The laboratory has indicated that the samples collected from peacocks are negative for avian influenza. However, another set of samples submitted for toxicological examination reveal presence of pesticides. No outbreak of the disease is reported in the country after the last outbreak in village Chingmeirong, East Imphal district, Manipur on 25th July 2007. The disease was restricted to a small unit in East Imphal district without further evidence of spread based on clinical and virological investigations. India achieved freedom from disease on 7th November 2007. This has been notified to OIE in accordance with international obligations.

5448. (11-1-2008) NEW DELHI : The President of India, Smt. Pratibha Devisingh Patil has condoled the passing away of the Everest pioneer, Sir Edmund Hillary. In her condolence message, the President has said, "Sir Edmund Hillary represented the positive approach to life, which was described by him after his conquest of Mount Everest. Sir Edmund Hillary had described his conquest of Mount Everest as his ability to overcome challenges and problems to reach the summit. Apart from being a keen mountaineer, he was also sensitive to the needs of the people of the Himalayan region by devoting his time and energy to their welfare. A humble person, he helped fund, the building of hospitals and health clinics for the Sherpas. He was also a conservationist who was acutely aware of the need to keep the environment around the Himalayan region clean. In his passing away the world has lost one of the 20th Century's greatest adventurers".

5449. (11-1-2008) NEW DELHI : The Prime Minister said here, Shri Kamal Nath, Union Minister of Commerce and Industry, has stated that India is very conscious of the critical importance of quality and conformity to safety norms, particularly for food and drugs consumed by people. This was stated by the Minister when Mr. Michael O. Leavitt, U.S. Department of Health and Human Services Secretary along with a delegation called on him here last evening. Both the sides discussed the progress of ongoing cooperation in many US-India health and life sciences activities and the safety of consumer products, particularly in the fields of research, vaccine and vaccine production. During the discussions, Shri Kamal Nath referred to the setting up of a Working Group by the Planning Commission to focus on quality and food safety issues and recommendations for the implementation of good hygiene and good management practices, in a phased manner. He further stated that India and US have bilateral institutional frameworks to further trade *i.e.*, India-US Trade Policy Forum and the India-US Commercial Dialogue. As far as safety of drugs and medical devices exported from India to the US is concerned, Shri Kamal Nath explained that US FDA conducts thorough examination before certifying Indian facilities for production of goods destined for the US and inspects them regularly. Indian companies have always been very cooperative in verification of requisite standards. Prior to his current service, Mr. Leavit was head of the U.S. Environmental Protection Agency and served three terms as Governor of Utah. He organised a nationwide campaign to transform the Nation's healthcare sector into a value-driven healthcare system. This is his first official visit to India.

5450. (12-1-2008) NEW DELHI : The Prime Minister of India said here that "I will be paying an official visit to China at the invitation of Premier Wen Jiabao from January 13 to 15, 2008. During my visit, I look forward to calling on His Excellency Mr. Hu Jintao, President of the People's Republic of China, and meeting with His Excellency Mr. Wu Bangguo, Chairman of the National People's Congress. I will hold bilateral discussions with Premier Wen Jiabao on matters of mutual interest. China is our largest neighbour and also a focal point of our "Look East" policy. We attach high priority to strengthening our relations with China. We established a Strategic and Cooperative Partnership for Peace and Prosperity when Premier Wen Jiabao visited India in April 2005. During President Hu Jintao's visit in November 2006 we laid down a ten-pronged strategy to qualitatively upgrade our bilateral ties. Our bilateral relations are now poised to enter a vibrant and dynamic phase, based on a common recognition that the growth and development of both India and China will make positive and long term contributions to regional and global peace, security and stability. We share a desire to enhance our relationship both bilaterally and at the global level. I look forward to my discussions with the Chinese leadership on the entire gamut of our relationship. We are engaged in the process of giving substantive content to our partnership through comprehensive economic engagement and developing mutually beneficial cooperation in the areas of science and technology, culture, education, defence and security, and increasing people-to-people contacts. Issues relating to the boundary and cooperation with regard to trans-boundary rivers will be discussed. I will be discussing how we can work more closely with China on regional, multilateral and global issues. I look forward to my visit. It is my belief that regular Summit level interaction with China contributes to strengthening our cooperative engagement and enhancing mutual trust and understanding."

5451. (12-1-2008) NEW DELHI : The Annual Plan for Jammu & Kashmir for the year2008-09 was finalized here today at a meeting between Deputy Chairman, Planning Commission Shri Montek Singh Ahluwalia and Chief Minister of J & K Mr. Ghulam Nabi Azad. The Annual Plan was finalized at Rs.4,500 crores. Deputy Chairman, Planning Commission complemented the State Government for turning around the economy. Hesaid growth rate was showing positive trend and States' own resources are positive for two years. Plan expenditure has grown by 150 per cent as compared to 2001-02. During the same period development expenditure has shown a growth of 276 per cent while plan salaries have come down by 31 per cent. He said the State was progressing satisfactorily in power sector reforms. Revision of tariff after two decades and introduction of metering system were steps in the right direction. The State was also complemented for performance in Prime Minister's reconstruction plan. He said tourism which was badly affected due to militancy is also showing definite signs of revival. Tourists' arrival which was only 0.73 lakhs in 2001 had gone up to 6.05 lakhs in 2005. The State was advised to give more emphasis on agriculture, conservation of Dal Lake and catchment area programme. Attention was drawn to shortage of human resources in health sector and gender gap in literacy. Improvement in processing facilities in Leh and Kargil was also suggested. Mr. Ghulam Nabi Azad in his remarks on the performance of the State pointed out that the State needs to carry forward growth performance and to meet the target of 8% growth rate during Eleventh Plan period a large plan needs to be implemented. To further accelerate development process, he suggested a system of proportionate allocation form SPA & ACA to ensure that there was no liquidity mismatch. He said during 11th Plan the State Government would give priority to allocating public expenditure in sectors having high employment elasticity. Restructuring of cooperative banks and downsizing of PSUs would be initiated shortly. Mr. Azad said the State had registered an employment growth of 6.8 per cent in economic enterprises which was highest in the country. In line with the national priorities among the State Government would have emphasis on flagship programmes including Sarva Shiksha Abhiyan, ARWSP, NRHM and JNNURM.

5452. (12-1-2008) NEW DELHI : The Minister of External Affairs, Shri Pranab Mukherjee Delivered the valedictory address at the Global Summit on "Repositioning the Management Accountant" here today. The three-day Mega event of Management Accounting bodies across the globe was organized by the Institute of Cost and Works Accountants of India (ICWAI) at New Delhi on January 10-12, 2008 with the objective to showcase the management accountant as a strategist and performance management specialists. The ICWAI was the main host for this Global Summit. Co-hosts were Institute of Cost and Management Accountants of Bangladesh (ICMAB), Institute of Cost and Management Accountants of Pakistan (ICMAP) and the Society of Certified Management Accountants of Sri Lanka (SCMASL). Besides these SAARC bodies, the Summit had technical partnership with other counterparts from the Western world such as Certified Management Accountants (CMA), Canada, Certified Institute of Management Accountants (CIMA), UK and the Institute of Management Accountants (IMA), USA. Speaking on the occasion Shri Mukherjee urged the management accountants to ethically drive enterprises in the emerging global context and take lead in helping the government in policy making to ensure good governance.

5453. (12-1-2008) NEW DELHI : Following is the text of the address delivered by the Defence Minister Shri AK Antony at the First Advisory Board Meeting of the Centre for Joint Warfare Studies (CENJOWS) here today:-'I am happy to be present at the inauguration of the First Advisory Board Meeting of Centre for Joint Warfare Studies. In today's world when physical distances have practically ceased to exist, cooperation through jointness is the need of the hour. The concepts of jointness and integration are not new by any means. With a fast growing economy, our military might also increase in proportionate terms. India is being increasingly seen and respected as a peace loving and a responsible force in a multi-polar world. If we are to enhance our status in the comity of nations further, it will require an integrated and a unified approach at all levels. As far as the Armed Forces are concerned, 'jointness' implies jointness in operation, as well as command. Today, economy and technology are expanding in tandem. However, unrestrained growth in both these sectors also has its pitfalls-like increasing the divide between the rich and poor, environmental degradation, increase in incidents of terrorism-both nationally as well as internationally, proliferation of weapons of mass destruction and the risk of their falling into wrong hands, energy security and climate change. Each of these issues is not merely an academic concern, but ones which pose a real challenge. We must think and act together-as a nation in overcoming these challenges. Jointness thus has to be followed-both individually, as well as collectively. On a wider scale, nations of the world today face similar challenges. As the means of communication and connectivity become faster, nations will have to think and act collectively. India has since times immemorial, espoused the concept of 'Vasudhaiv Kutumbukam' (the whole universe is one family). This ideal has to be translated into reality at the international level. The chances of the outbreak of a traditional conflict are bleak. The latest challenges necessarily need not be of a military nature outbreak of man-made and natural disasters, diseases like HIV / AIDS. Terrorism continues to be the most crucial challenge facing the international community. Common challenges require common solutions, keeping in view a region's and nation's diversities. Jointness therefore, should not be confined merely to military tactics, but seen in the widest possible context.

5454. (12-1-2008) NEW DELHI : In view of the Railways having been identified as a soft target by extremists, terrorists and anti social elements, the overall security system in Railways was reviewed at a high level meeting between Union Railway Minister Shri Lalu Prasad and Union Home Minister Shri Shivraj Patil, here today. The meeting was attended by the senior officials of Ministries of Railways and Home. The Railway Ministry officials included Shri V.N. Mathur, Member Traffic, Shri S.K. Vij, Member Engineering, Shri S.S. Khurana, Member Staff, Mrs. Sudha Chaubey, Financial Commissioner and Shri M.K. Sinha, DG, RPF. The Home Ministry officials included Shri Pradyot Chandra Haldar, Director, Intelligence Bureau, Shri Syed Iftikar Sultan Ahmed, Director General, CRPF, Shri Mahendra Lal Kumawat, Special Secretary, (Internal Security) and Shri Ranjit Kumar Bhatia, Addl. Director General, CISF. It was decided to ensure better cooperation between Railway Protection Force (RPF) and Government Railway Police (GRP) of respective State Governments. For this purpose state-wise Nodal Officers will be nominated by the Ministry of Railways. A mechanism for intelligence sharing and dissemination for action among the stakeholders will be set up. It was accepted that there is a need to increase the strength of RPF on account of threefold increase in its charter of responsibilities after amendment in the RPF Act and decided to initiate suitable action for increasing the strength of the Force. The Railway Minister emphasized that passenger security will be accorded top most priority by RPF among its charter of duties and adequate funds will be made available for modernization of the Force. Shri Lalu Prasad also requested the Home Minister to provide information about latest technology and equipment suitable for Railway security.

5455. (12-1-2008) NEW DELHI : The Vice President, Mohd. Hamid Ansari has greeted the people of our country and extended his good wishes on the auspicious occasion of Makara Sankranti and Pongal. In a message, he said that these festivals, mark the beginning of the auspicious period of 'Uttarayana' and harvest season. These festivals are celebrated in diverse ways with traditional gaiety and enthusiasm in various parts of the country, these festivals reflect our glorious cultural traditions and promote the values of sharing, generosity and goodwill among people. The Vice President said that this auspicious occasion would bring amity, prosperity and happiness in the lives of all.

5456. (12-8-2007) NEW DELHI : BJP National President Shri Rajnath Singh and Janata Dal (U) President Shri Sharad Yadav today appointed a six member

High Level Committee of MPs and senior leaders to visit Assam and take stock of the violence affected areas and ground level situation there. The Committee will be led by Shri Kalraj Mishra and the other members are Shri Vikram Verma, Shri Kharvel Swain, Shri Kiren Rijiju, Shri Mahendra Sahani (JDU) and Shri Janardan Sigriwal, Minister from Bihar. After visiting the areas, the Committee will present its report to BJP President Shri Rajnath Singh and Janata Dal (U) President Shri Sharad Yadav.

5457. (12-1-2008) NEW DELHI : 15 Corps celebrated its 93rd raising day at Srinagar today with traditional enthusiasm at a solemn and austere ceremony at Badami Bagh Cantonment. GOC, 15 Corps Lt Gen Mukesh Sabharwal laid floral wreath at the Corps War Memorial on behalf of all ranks of 15 Corps as a mark of respect to all martyrs who laid down their lives in the call of duty. A special philatelic cancellation ceremony and photo exhibition organised at Badami Bagh Cantt, was attended by large number of senior civil and military dignitaries as part of day long celebrations. His Excellency Lt Gen S K Sinha (Retd), the Governor of J&K released the special cover on the occasion. 15 Corps was first raised pre-independence on 12 Jan 1916 at Port Said in Egypt. After independence, the Corps was re-raised in 1955 at Udhampur and made responsible for security of complete state of J&K. Subsequently on raising of HQ Northern Command the Corps shifted to its present location at Badami Bagh, Cantt Srinagar in 1972. 15 Corps also known as "Chinar Corps", derives its name from the formation sign of a Chinar leaf with a battle axe on it. Since independence 15 Corps has kept vigil over the Line of Control in J&K and has been instrumental in saving Kashmir from evil designs of our enemy. Gallant soldiers of Chinar Corps bravely fought all the wars post-independence in 1965, 1971 and 1999 and have been fighting the menance of terrorism since late 1980's. Return of peace and prosperity in Kashmir valley has been achieved due to the dedication, courage and hard work of the troops under command of 15 Corps. The Corps has excelled in all operations it has undertaken and has an enviable record of gallantry. Gallant actions of brave soldiers of Chinar Corps continue to be recorded in the annals of military history in gold. Pre-independence, Corps was awarded 06 Victoria Cross, 03 Military Cross and 01 Distinguished Service Order. After independence, 15 Corps has won 13 Param Vir Chakras, 83 Maha Vir Chakras, 281 Shaurya Chakras, 13 Ashok Chakras, 61 Kirti Chakras, 473 Vir Chakras, 05 Param Vishist Seva Medal, 13 Uttam Yudh Seva Medal, 28 Ati Vishist Seva Medal, 47 Yudh Seva Medal, 1694 Sena Medal, and 95 Vishist Seva Medal till date. Troops of Chinar Corps have always worked tirelessly for the welfare of the Awaam in valley. Some of the recent notable achievements have been the relief and rehabilitation provided to the victims of earthquake and snow tsunami, empowerment of youth and women through imparting of quality education, opening of community development centres and organisation of tours and sports activities. It has also cared for the children who have been the hardest hit due to terrorism by opening and assisting orphanages.

The list of activities undertaken by troops of Chinar Corps in the service of Awaam is endless.

5458. (13-1-2008) NEW DELHI : The Vice President Shri M. Hamid Ansari dedicated the Centenary Faculty Block in the Campus of National Institute of Advanced Study in Bangalore today. Following is the text of his speech: "It is a privilege to be amidst this distinguished gathering today, in an institution reflective of the vision of J.R.D Tata. His critical role in synthesizing India's scientific, medical and artistic genius is under-appreciated. I believe the concept of an institute for advanced study, dedicated to theoretical research and intellectual inquiry, emanated in 1930 with the one at Princeton made famous, amongst others, by Albert Einstein. Its purpose, 'to encourage the original, often speculative, thinking that produces advances in knowledge' has been fulfilled in good measure. In India we made the first effort in 1964 with the Indian Institute of Advanced Study, Shimla. Its mentor was none other than President Sarvepalli Radhakrishnan. The aim was to facilitate free and creative inquiry into the themes and problems of life and thought. JRD Tata's approach, in 1988, was somewhat more focused. He recognized that in the Indian context a multidisciplinary approach and bringing together of civil servants and managers from industry, leaders in public affairs, eminent personalities and academic scholars from the natural and social sciences was important for public policy formulation and implementation. We live in an age where the only constant is change. The physical, mental and virtual landscape around us is being rapidly transformed, imposing constant demands on individuals and institutions to adapt and reinvent themselves. In its wake one tends to lose sight of the inherent unity in nature and the impulse for harmony. It is this underlying harmony that binds the strands of human enquiry across various disciplines. This was understood, even practised, in an earlier age when inter-disciplinary studies facilitated cross-pollination of ideas. Overtime, however, what commenced as a functional division of work tended to crystallize into rigid boundaries. The problem has been accentuated by the structure of our higher education system and of our research institutions. Increasingly universities have parted ways with research and development activities; even within the universities, academic pursuits are rigidly delineated within specific departments. As a result, the intellectual output of our universities leaves much to be desired. Against such a bleak backdrop, the National Institute of Advanced Studies is an oasis. The books, reports, working papers published by it bear testimony to the scope of work being done and are perhaps unique for an Indian academic institution. The study under the same roof of archaeometallurgy with primatology, sociology and anthropology with nuclear and strategic issues, philosophy with astrophysics and aeronautics, rural development and gender issues, philosophy and number theory makes for new and fascinating outcomes.

5459. (13-1-2008) BEIJING : Shortly after his arrival in Beijing, Prime Minister Dr. Manmohan Singh met representatives of Indian business accompanying the Prime Minister on his visit to China. Led by the two business associates, CII and FICCI, the delegation of business leaders appraised the Prime Minister on recent trends in bilateral trade and investment flows. They drew attention both to the opportunities and to challenges faced by Indian business in China. After listening to their statements and observations, the Prime Minister called for increased economic engagement between India and China. He urged Indian business leaders to study China and to identify opportunities for business and greater engagement. Dr. Singh observed that a large part of the thinking in India about China is shaped by western views of China, and that there is need for greater investment in India in a better understanding of the processes of change in China. The Prime Minister said, "The rise of China and India should be viewed as an 'international public good' by the global community, since it offers new opportunities to sustain global growth. At a time when there are concerns about a global economic slowdown, China and India can sustain global growth through their own development." Dr. Singh added, "It is a historic necessity for the two great neighbours to work together. There will be areas of competition, and there will be areas for cooperation. There is enough space in the world for both countries to continue to grow and address the developmental aspirations of their peoples." Urging Indian business to "think big", the Prime Minister said, "Indian business is ready to face the brave new world of globalization. China is an important part of that brave new world. We must engage China and learn to both compete and cooperate."

5460. (13-1-2008) LUCKNOW: Uttar Pradesh Chief Minister Mayawati on Saturday demanded that the nation's highest civilian honour, Bharat Ratna, be conferred posthumously on her political mentor and founder of the Bahujan Samaj Party, Kanshi Ram, for his contribution towards creating social and political awareness among the crores of Dalits. Addressing a press conference here, she said she had placed the demand in a letter to Prime Minister Manmohan Singh. Ms. Mayawati said Kanshi Ram deserved the honour as he had devoted his entire life for the uplift of the downtrodden sections. She said he had instilled self-confidence in the Dalits, deprived and backward sections, who had been divided into several castes. Referring to media reports that the names of the former Prime Minister, Atal Bihari Vajpayee and the former West Bengal Chief Minister, Jyoti Basu, were under consideration, the Chief Minister said her government and the ruling party welcomed the move. However, conferring the Bharat Ratna on the BSP founder would be an honour for the people of the country.

5461. (13-1-2008) NEW DELHI : The Prime Minister, Dr. Manmohan Singh, has greeted the nation on Lohri, Makar Sankranti and Pongal. Dr. Manmohan Singh, in his message, said that the festivals are a strong symbol of our shared ethos and culture. These harvest festivals, celebrated across the country, bring the promise of growth and prosperity. May this year's Lohri, Makar Sankranti and Pongal bring good luck and happiness in all our lives.

5462. (13-1-2008) BEIJING : The Prime Minister, Dr. Manmohan Singh visited the Beijing Olympic site here today. Following is the text of the Prime Minister's Inscription for the Visitors' book. : "On Behalf of the Government and the people of India, I extend my best wishes for the success of the Olympic games in Beijing. I hope that the Olympic spirit and the traditional hospitality and warmth of the great city of Beijing will promote friendship, peace and understanding among all the Participants, and the countries they represent"

5463. (14-1-2008) NEW DELHI : The Union Minister for Rural Development Dr. Raghuvansh Prasad Singh has termed the Implementation Performance of National Rural Employment Guarantee Act (NREGA) as steady going. Addressing Media persons here today the minister said that it was his ministry that requested the Comptroller and Auditor General (CAG) office to have a thorough scanning of the implementation part of NREGA and other Rural Development schemes currently being implemented across the country. Giving details he said during the current financial year (2007-08) upto Nov., 2007, 2.59 crore household demanded employment of which 2.54 crore household were given employment. A total of 84.49 crore person-days of employment have been generated. The average person-days per household while 33 person till November, 07 (going as high as 46 in Madhya Pradesh, 54 in Rajasthan and 62 in Tamil Nadu). Nearly 9.47 lakh households availed of 100 days of employment during the same period. A total of 12.07 works were taken up of which 3.64 lakhs have been completed and 8.43 lakhs works are in progress. In the Ist phase of implementation of NREGA during 2006-07, 2.10 crore people got employed. An average 44 person-days work was generated and 22 lakh people got 100 days employment during the period. This includes water conservation and water harvesting (3.40 lakh), renovation of traditional water bodies (96 thousand), provision of irrigation facility (1.58 lakh), micro-irrigation works (53 thousands), drought proofing (1.13 lakhs), flood control and protection (20 thousands), rural connectivity (2.03 lakh) and land development (1.17 lakh). The second phase of implementation is under progress and the IIIrd phase beginning April 1st 2008, NREGA will be implemented in all districts of the country, Dr. Singh added. Referring to the Swarna Jayanti Gram Swarojgar Yojana (SGSY) he said a budget allocation of Rs.1800 crore for the current financial year has been earmarked and this is likely to go up to Rs.3000 crore during 2008-09. Thrust will be on the provision of productive self employment, skill development and adequate placement of persons from rural BPL families in infrastructure development activities like construction and textile industries. He also referred to the recently launched the Indira Gandhi National Old Age Pension Scheme (IGNOAPS) and said an allocation of Rs.2391.91 crores were allocated for the current financial year which is likely to go up to Rs.3200 crores, Rs.2169.62 crores has been released of which a total expenditure of Rs.106.97 crore has been reported. The total number of beneficiaries so far reported have been 1.10 crore which is likely to go up to 1.60 crore. The Minister also greeted the countrymen specially the farmer community on the occasion of Makar Sakranti, Maghi Beehu and Pongal on this occasion.

5464. (14-1-2008) NEW DELHI : The second phase of the Exhibition 'Spirit of Independent India' gets underway at the AIFACS Art Gallery, Rafi Marg, New Delhi tomorrow. Organised as part of the celebration of the 60 years of independence, the Exhibition has award-winning photographs of the 20th National Photo Contest, besides other select photos from the Contest. A total number of 111 photographs have been displayed in the Exhibition showing the unique moments of the spirit of the people of independent India. Shri Vivek Desai of Ahmedabad who is the winner of the first prize for both the black and white as well as colour section has presented the Spirit of Independent India with his fantastic idea of bringing the computer science among the women worker simultaneously attached to the spinning of the thread. His other picture (colour) is a moment of happiness and joy from a festival and capture a unique spirit of the feeling of the people. The award winning photographs by Shri Aniruddha Pal of Kolkata, Shri Girish J. Kinger from Indore, Shri Supriya Biswas from Kolkata and Upendra Upadhyay from Indore, besides other selected photographs from the Contest are on display.

5465. (14-1-2008) BEIJING : Following is the text of the Prime Minister, Dr. Manmohan Singh's statement to the press at Beijing today: "It is a pleasure and honour for me to be in Beijing. I have always looked forward to my meetings with Premier Wen, and to benefit from his great wisdom knowledge and experience. I would like to express my heartfelt thanks to the Government and people of China and Premier Wen Jiabao, for the courtesy and warmth of their hospitality. Our talks were held in an atmosphere of sincerity, warmth and friendship. They were constructive and forward looking. This gives me cause for optimism for the future of our ties. India-China relations are of regional and global significance. The profound changes taking place in the world today present both our countries with a historic opportunity to work together towards a 21st century that is conducive to peace and development. The Shared Vision of the 21st Century that Premier Wen and I have just signed is an important milestone in the evolution of our relations. It reflects not only our common perceptions but also our desire to purposefully cooperate in the future. We have agreed to continue deepening the mutual understanding and trust between our armed forces. We welcomed the successful conclusion off our first joint military training exercise, and agreed to have a second exercise in India this year. We recognized that our strategic and cooperative partnership should be based on strong, diversified and mutually beneficial economic ties. We have decided to increase our bilateral trade target from 40 billion US dollars by the year 2010 to 60 billion US dollars. We have mandated our Ministers of commerce to examine the Feasibility Study on the Benefits of a Regional Trading Arrangement and make suitable recommendations at an early date. We have decided to establish a high level Business Leaders Forum to advise us on the future of our economic ties. We had useful discussions on the outstanding issue of the Boundary Question. We welcomed the progress made by our Special Representatives in seeking a framework for settlement of the boundary question that is fair, reasonable, mutually acceptable, and based on the Agreement on Guiding Principles and Political Parameters signed in April 2005.

5466. (14-1-2008) NEW DELHI : The Minister of Petroleum & Natural Gas Shri Murli Deora inaugurated the LPG Cavern Storage of South Asia LPG Company Private Limited which is a Joint Venture of the Oil majors HPCL and Total, France at Visakhapatanam today. The minister also graced the Golden Jubilee Celebrations of HPCL's Visakh Refinery. During his speech, Shri Deora applauded the pioneering efforts of HPCL and Total in shaping the first Indian Cavern storage into reality. The minister indicated that, in fact, the Cavern is the first of its kind in South and Southeast Asia. The facility has helped the Country join the select group of advanced nations. The Cavern storage is a unique achievement and engineering marvel. In his speech the minister hailed Larsen & Toubro, who are the Engineering, Procurement, Construction, and Commissioning (EPCC) contractors for the project. The bottom most point in LPG Cavern is 182 M below mean seal level (MSL) and ranks among the deepest Caverns in the world. The Cavern has a storage capacity of 60,000 MT LPG and is the largest single point storage in the country. The large Cavern storage will help in ensuring uninterrupted availability of LPG in the east coast and will bring-in freight economics through Very Large Gas Carriers (VLGC). Underground Caverns are the safest mode of storage and environment friendly. They are isolated from external hazards like Fire, War, Sabotage, Explosions, and Natural calamities. The Cavern-Marine Terminal, located at Lovagarden, near Dolphins Hill Nose, is provided with the world class State of art Instrumentation, Control, and Safety systems. Speaking on the Golden Jubilee Celebrations, the Minister complemented HPCL Visakh Refinery on completing 50 marvellous performance years. Visakh Refinery has been the first refinery on the east coast set up as Caltex Oil Refining India Ltd. (CORIL) in the city of destiny, Visakhapatnam. Started with the modest installed capacity of 0.65 MMTPA in 1957, Visakh Refinery was expanded in phases to its current capacity of 7.5 MMTPA. The Refinery is now consistently operating at more than 9 MMTPA from 2006-07 onwards. Several dignitaries comprising Ministers from Central & State Government, Officials from Central & State Government, MOP&NG, Vizag Port Trust, Indian Navy, other various Industries and Statutory Authorities etc. also graced the occasion.

5467. (14-1-2008) NEW DELHI : 850 students from Delhi will participate in this year's Republic Day parade. The boys and girls drawn from 25 government, government-aided and private schools will present lively musical and cultural items. The cultural pageant will be headed by Band contingent playing the musical tune of Surya. They will be followed by girls and boys marchers having National Flags in their hand. Tiranga Sakshi Hai, a musical presentation by Kamal Model Senior Secondary School, Mohan Garden and Vandana International Senior

Secondary School, Dwarka will show how India's National Flag witnessed each and every moment of hardship and sacrifice made by our freedom fighters during the freedom struggle. It will portray the Nation's golden past and present through a journey of progress and development during the last sixty years. Another significant aspect will be the role of Indian women in the Freedom movement. Today, women have not only become a power on earth but have explored space also. In the presentation an endeavour has been made to show that Woman force will become instrumental in making India a Super Power. While Gaurav by Zone-2 schools portrays the contribution of Indian women in national unity, harmony and zest for victory, Jai Bharat by Government Senior Secondary School, Padam Nagar will present how martyrs sacrificed their lives to unshackle their motherland from the slavery of a foreign power.

5468. (14-1-2008) NEW DELHI : The terms of the Legislative Assemblies of Meghalaya, Nagaland and Tripura are normally due to expire on 10.03.2008, 13.03.2008 and 19.03.2008 respectively. By virtue of its powers, duties and functions under Article 324 read with Article 172(1) of the Constitution of India, Section 15 of Representation of the People Act, 1951, the Commission is under a constitutional mandate to hold general elections to constitute the new Legislative Assemblies in these States at any time within a period of six months before the expiry of the present term.

5469. (14-1-2008) NEW DELHI : The Ministry of Labour & Employment had completed the General Verification of registered Trade Unions affiliated to various Central Trade Union Organizations with 31st December, 2002 as the date of reckoning for the purpose of determining the strength of the Central Trade Union Organizations in order to give them representation in international and National Conferences, Committees and Councils. This verification was conducted by the Chief Labour Commissioner (Central) and his field officers in pursuance of the orders of the High Court of Delhi dated 25th July, 2003 and subsequent orders of the Ministry of Labour & Employment. The Central Trade Union Organisations having verified membership of at least 5,00,000 and spread over a minimum of four States and four industries including agriculture and rural sectors were to be recognized by the Government as Central Trade Union Organizations. The report of the Chief Labour Commissioner (Central) was considered by the Ministry of Labour & Employment and thereafter a Notification of strength of various Central Trade Unions has been declared and sent to various Trade Unions.

5470. (14-1-2008) NEW DELHI : Rivers Ganga and Yamuna will get back their original quality of water with the help of Action Plans initiated by the Government. More than 500 million litres of industrial waste is being discharged every day in the rivers Ganga and Yamuna. The river Ganga is suffering with more burden of 365 million litres of industrial waste whereas the river Yamuna gets 149 million litres of industrial waste every day. The Government has taken various measures to check the industrial pollution in these rivers. The Charter on Corporate

Responsibility for Environmental Protection (CREP) for 17 categories of polluting industries and its implementation through various task forces have been adopted. Notifications have been issued to the industries for specific standards. Industries have also been asked to set up Effluent Treatment Plants (ETPs). They have been also asked to adopt clean technology to minimize their waste output. Central Pollution Control Board (CPCB) State Pollution Control Boards (SPCBs) and Pollution Control Boards (PCBs) will conduct regular environmental monitoring and surveillance. Action also has been taken against grossly polluting industries as per the provisions of Water (Prevention and Control of Pollution) Act, 1974 and the Environment (Protection) Act, 1986. The Small Scale Industries (SSIs) have been given special incentives. They can set up new Common Effluent Treatment Plant (CETP) for their wastes and upgrade the existing ones with financial assistance from the Centre. The Ministry of Environment and Forests has taken up the Ganga Action Plan (GAP), for sewage treatment capacity of 865 MLD under Phase I at an expenditure of Rs.452 crores. Additional works are being taken up in 60 cities at an approved cost of Rs.652.89 crores. The water quality of river Ganga is being monitored at 27 locations from Rishikesh in Uttarakhand to Uluberia in West Bengal by various institutions. The Yamuna Action Plan (YAP) is a bilateral project of Governments of India and Japan. Japan Bank of International Cooperation has given 13.33 billion Yen for YAP Phase II. Under this Project abatement of pollution of the river in Delhi, Uttar Pradesh (9 towns) and Haryana (8 towns) is being taken up. Replacement of Trunk Sewers and improvements in efficiency of existing Sewage Treatment Plants (STPs) are main works under YAP II.

5471. (14-1-2008) NEW DELHI : The Minister of Petroleum & Natural Gas Shri Murli Deora has emphasized at Hyderabad today that the Government of India and Oil Companies have taken several steps to enhance energy security for the country. These inter-alia include: (a) increasing exploration and production activities in the country (b) acquiring oil and gas assets abroad (c) development of alternate sources of oil and gas (d) strategic storage of crude oil (e) conservation and implementation of environment friendly policies. He was speaking after inaugurating 7th International Conference & Exposition of Society of Petroleum Geophysicists. The Minister underlined that economic growth rate of 8% to 10% in the country calls for rapid development of the energy market. Shri Deora added that the development of E&P sector has been significantly boosted through New Exploration Licensing Policy (NELP), which brought major liberalization in the sector and opened it up for private and foreign investment allowing 100% Foreign Direct Investment (FDI). With exploration and development efforts made under NELP, natural gas production in the country is likely to double by the end of 11th Five Year Plan (2007-12) from the present level of about 87 million standard cubic metres per day (MMSCMD). Besides, Indian PSUs and other private companies have presence in more than 20 countries with ONGC Videsh Limited maintaining a leading role by producing about 8 Million tonnes of oil and oil equivalent of gas. He also said that apart from intensifying exploratory efforts for oil and gas in the Indian sedimentary basins and abroad, steps are being taken to harness other alternate sources of energy like Coal Bed Methane, Gas Hyderates, Coal Liquefaction, Ethanol and bio-diesel, etc. Stating that first CBM gas production from Raniganj CBM block in West Bengal has started in July 2007, Shri Deora called upon global scientific community to spare no effort to find solutions which should be environment-sensitive and socially acceptable. "We should not forget the fact that the environment we are enjoying today belongs to future generations and we are merely custodians of these environs", he said.

5472. (14-1-2008) NEW DELHI : The Ministry of Rural Development is to organize a series of programmes during the year 2008 as declared the International year of Sanitation. Accordingly a calendar of events have been worked out by the Department of Drinking Water Supply on Rural Sanitation, Rural Solid and Liquid Waste Management and a Clean Rural India programme which will take place in the National Capital and in all the States. The department has already marked the commencement of the International Year of Sanitation by releasing an advertisement in 185 newspapers across the country on 2.1.2008. To make the events success, Union Minister for Rural Development Dr. Raghuvansh Prasad Singh has urged the Chief Ministers of all States/ Administrators of Union Territories to cooperate actively for the advocacy and promotional activities of programmes as under: Raising awareness of the importance of sanitation and its impact on achieving other Millennium Development Goals (MDGs), from three perspectives: hygiene, household sanitation and wastewater. Encouraging state Governments and districts to promote and implement policies and actions for meeting the sanitation target. Mobilizing communities, particularly women's groups, towards changing sanitation and hygiene practices through sanitation-health-education campaigns. Highliting the SACOSAN International Conference on Sanitation for the South Asian countries is also to be hosted this year here, Dr. Singh said that his ministry propose to utilize the opportunity in bringing extra vigour and add momentum to the Total Sanitation Campaign of the Government of India. Under the Total Sanitation Campaign to achieve the goal of "Total Sanitation" in Rural India by 2012 work is actively being propelled against "open defecation" and, and motivation for toilet construction in the rural areas. Reffering to the presentation of Nirmal Gram Puraskar (NGP) last year, to 5000 rural Panchayats he has expected the numbers getting doubled this year and also to have School Sanitation completed throughout the country by March, 2008. The first major event will be the symbolic participation of NGP Winners as State Guests in the Republic Day Celebrations on 26.1.2008. One Gram Panchayat representative who has won NGP award and one representative from each Block Panchayat who have won the NGP award so far have been invited to witness the Republic Day Parade, 2008 as State Guests. States have already been communicated for arranging a similar participation of all NGP winners in the Republic Day Celebrations at State capital and District headquarters on 26.1.2008. The detailed Calendar of Events to celebrate the International Year of Sanitation will be sent to the State Governments separately. The minister has also urged the Chief Ministers for the following awareness generation activities in their respective State: Advertisement in vernacular newspapers/ magazines about importance of the International Year of Sanitation 2008 and its aim, activities, etc.; Participation of NGP awardees at district and State level Republic Day parade ceremony; State level competition for best toilet, best teacher, best Rural Sanitary Mart, best NGO, etc.; District-wise exhibition showcasing the achievements made in TSC; Developing films for State's achievements and success in TSC; Honouring of NGP awardees in the State function by the Chief Minister and other VIPs and introduce them to His/ Her Excellency the Governor of the State; State-wise calendar on International Year of Sanitation 2008 to be prepared with intensive TSC campaign; Regional workshop on solid & liquid waste management; Pledge on Sanitation on Gandhi Jayanti; Conduct sanitation rallies which will culmination in National rally in Delhi; Message on International Year of Sanitation by you in the State and Spots, messages about sanitation on newspapers, radio / TV and cables, cinema halls, etc.

5473. (14-1-2008) NEW DELHI : The Ministry of Rural Development has convened a two day long meeting for reviewing the performance of the Department of Rural Development and the Department of Land Resources on the 17th of this month. The programmes of the Department of Rural Development and the Department of Land Resources will be reviewed during the meeting. The focus will be on, (a) Financial and physical review of all schemes releases upto December, 2007 and requirement of funds for rural development schemesduring 2007-08; (b) Status of finalization of BPL List and Indira Awaas Yojana (IAY) waitlist, in view of the revised pension scheme of Indira Gandhi National Old age Pension Scheme (IGNOAPS) and new scheme of Rashtriya Swasthya Bima Yojana for Unorganised Sector Workers; (c) Utility of DRDAs and alternative arrangements for effective implementation of various rural development schemes;and (d) specific shortcomings and inadequacy in the implementation of the programmes by individual States and to get an indication of the strategies proposed by them to further improve their performance in the next financial year, *i.e.* 2008-09. The meeting is expected to generate adequate inputs for streamlining processes as well as appropriate revision of guidelines, procedures instructions for implementation of individual programmes and also to help remove bottlenecks, if any in the smooth operation of the programmes.

5474. (14-1-2008) NEW DELHI : The Congress Party whole-heartedly and strongly welcomes the inauguration of a new era in Indo-Chinese relationship. The Congress Party reminds you of the historic initiative taken in this regard, many years ago, by then Prime Minister Shri Rajiv Gandhi. The Congress Party harkens back to the recent continuing initiatives by the Congress President, Smt. Sonia Gandhi, who also visited China, accompanied by Shri Rahul Gandhi, in the recent past. The visit of the Hon' ble Prime Minister, the first to China, has taken a historic step forward in these initiatives. The warmth and the comprehensiveness on all issues with which the Prime Minister and his delegation have been received by their Chinese hosts, the ambience of candid exchanges and detailed discussion on a diverse range of issues and the tremendous respect and dignity and status accorded to the Indian delegation, led by the Prime Minister, are all indicative of significant movement in the right direction in continuation of the historic initiative of Shri Rajiv Gandhi. We also welcome it because this is the consistent outlook of the 'Look East Policy' of India which the Congress Party fully supports, the policy of inaugurating an era of exchanges and peace, not only with our immediate neighbours but within the wider neighbourhood of Asia. These are significant confidence-building measures (CBMs) and these CBMs are part of a continuous and continuing process. And we have no doubt, no shadow of doubt, that they will continue to propel Indo-Chinese relations on the right path. To a question that is the Congress Party going to support the moves against the rise in oil prices, Shri Singhvi said, the Congress Party would wish to put on record that it hopes and trusts and that it has no manner of doubt that the government will take all steps to minimize and to soften to the maximum degree possible any impact of a global rise in oil prices. The Congress Party hopes and trusts that all reasonable steps, within the larger macro-economic policy perspective, approaches, which do not only base themselves on spot prices, which are very high, approaches which see that the entire international spot price movement is not passed through and particularly focused approaches on diesel, kerosene and on other items of mass and common consumption, that these factors will be deeply and carefully considered and only then in an overall all-India perspective will a final decision be taken. To a question whether you agree to the perception that the West stress on Chinese relations is more to obstruct the views that India was too much on the side of America, Shri Singhvi said, I absolutely deny any such perception, I absolutely deny any such connection or inclination or sentiment. First, as you know, and it is a relevant important question and it is the right time to restate that old known principle. You know that India's relations and India's foreign policy with a particular country is always based on our relationships, our historic contemporary relationship with that country. It is never dependent upon or conditioned by relationships with other countries. These are individual, separate autonomous links and to mix them up with different countries is not right. Second, as I said it's a historic continuing step because there is a huge benefit to both countries of increased interaction and it is to exploit that huge common area of benefit and interest that such initiatives have a vital significance. We have to engage, we have to interact and we have to become more and more intertwined because from that not only flows common benefit but also frequently other unrelated issues between the two countries also get solved by that deeper engagement.

5475. (14-1-2008) NEW DELHI : The President of India, Smt. Pratibha Devisingh Patil has greeted her fellow countrymen on the occasion of the festivals of Makara Sankranti and Pongal, which fall on January 14th and 15th respectively. In her message the President has said, "On the occasion of Makara Sankranti and Pongal, I extend my greetings and felicitations to all my fellow citizens and wish them happiness and prosperity. Makara Sankranti and Pongal are days of great festivity and rejoicing. May these festivals bind each one of us in fraternal love and affection and inspire us to work for the unity, progress and well being of our nation".

5476. (14-1-2008) NEW DELHI : Agriculture in India is at crossroads today: on one hand there has been deceleration of growth in recent years, and on the other hand many new opportunities and possibilities are emerging. Percentage of the population depending on agriculture has not declined significantly even though the share of agriculture in the country's gross domestic product (GDP) has substantially gone down. The green revolution transformed the agriculture sector and there was tremendous growth till the 1980s and early 1990s. Then there was stagnation in agricultural growth for about a decade. However there are signs of accelerated growth during the last two years. Furthermore, there are indications of structural changes with immense possibilities of a demand driven agriculture. The interest shown by corporate sector and the new focus on agriculture as a part of public policy and government efforts could bring about radical transformation in the agriculture sector. Yet, the predominance of small farms, rainfed agriculture on more than half of the arable land and lack of rural infrastructure are some of the aspects which need to be addressed in order to rejuvenate the agriculture sector and bring about faster, sustainable and inclusive growth. Agriculture, particularly traditional farming, is risky-riskier than other types of business because of the nature of the crop cycle. Various factors such as the time taken by the crops to mature, energy used for crop cultivation, resource availability and their production response, dependence on weather, proneness to natural calamities and markets are either too demanding or fraught with uncertainty. Owing to various factors the growth rate in the agriculture sector decelerated during the last decade. The production of food grains stagnated, the issue of food security re-emerged. Farmers' distress and cases of suicides were reported form some parts of the country. The accentuation of debt burden on farmers was attributed to the declining production efficiency, lack of access to institutional credit, high cost of inputs and unfavourable market conditions. Yield and price risks, and reduction in farm size have made agriculture less remunerative. The GDP from agriculture and allied sectors grew at a paltry 2.1 per cent during the Ninth Plan and 2.3 per cent during the Tenth Plan. Of course, the growth rate was much higher in the areas such as flower exports, organic food production, food processing and dairy, where new opportunities arose because of the rising urban demand and globalization.

5477. (14-1-2008) NEW DELHI : Death of poultry birds has been reported from parts of Birbhum and South Dinajpur districts of West Bengal. Samples of dead birds have been sent to High Security Animal Disease Laboratory (HSADL), Bhopal. Report from the lab is likely to be received by late night today or tomorrow. The State and Central governments are in constant touch and teams have been dispatched to the affected areas to take necessary steps to contain the disease. As a precautionary measure, trade in poultry bird in Birbhum and South Dinajpur districts and movement of birds in an out of these districts has been restricted. Till the report from HSADL, Bhopal is received, it cannot be said whether mortality of poultry birds has been due to Avian Influenza or some other disease. In case it is found to be due to the bird flu virus, immediate steps as per the standard action plan will be carried out. In the meantime, necessary logistics are being put in place to be in readiness for any eventuality.

5478. (14-1-2008) NEW DELHI : The Year 2007 has witnessed a remarkable growth in the tourism sector especially in terms of Foreign Tourist Arrivals (FTA) and Foreign Exchange Earnings (FEE). The estimated number of FTA in 2007 touched 5 million as compared to 4.45 million in 2006 registering a growth rate of over 12% in 2007 over 2006. The estimated FEE during 2007 was US$ 11.96 billion as compared to US$ 8.93 billion in 2006. The growth rate in FEE in 2007 over 2006 is 33.8% as compared to the growth rate of 19.2% in 2006 over 2005. In Rupee terms, the FEE in 2007 was Rs. 49413 crore as compared to Rs. 40375 crore in 2006 with a growth rate of 22.4 % as compared to the growth rate of 21.9% in 2006 over 2005. The impressive performance of the tourism sector is a result of the positive image created about the country through successful branding of "Incredible India". The promotional campaigns run by the Union Ministry of Tourism have led to immense interest in India as a tourist destination. India has been awarded 'Favourite Country of the Year' in the 'Conde Nast Traveller Readers' Travel Awards-2007-a renowned magazine in the travel trade and has also won WTA's 'Asia's Best Destination Award' for the year 2007.

5479. (14-1-2008) BEIJING : The Prime Minister, Dr. Manmohan Singh, attended the India-China Economic, Trade and Investment Summit in Beijing today. Following is the text of the Prime Minister's address on the occasion: "I am delighted to have this opportunity to meet you all, a unique gathering of businessmen and businesswomen from the two of the fastest growing economies of the world, today. Businessmen throughout history have been promters and protectors of human civilization. The India-China Economic Trade and Investment Summit is a unique gathering of businesspersons representing as I said two most populous countries of the world. You have grown competitive by starting from continent-sized markets and graduating to world markets. Businesmen of India and China are the symbols of the growth stories of both our countries. Businessmen are the creators of wealth. I therefore, salute your dynamism and entrepreneurship. Your meeting today is an expression of your confidence in the potential for economic cooperation between our two great countries. It is equally a testimony to the progress that business communities from our two countries have made in working with each other. Much has been done, much has been achieved but I honestly believe the best is yet to come. India and China are today the fastest growing large economies in the world. We should remember that China, India and Europe had almost equal shares of world income in the early 18th century. As the 21st century unfolds, both India and China stand poised to regain their weight in the evolving global economy. Our two countries will need to work together to ensure that we contribute to, even as we benefit from, the economic resurgence and integration of Asia. Our two economies are becoming engines of economic growth and must use our natural and human resources, technology and capital for the common benefit of our region and indeed the world as a whole. The Indian economy has witnessed growth rates of close to 9% per year in the last three years. Our macro-economic fundamentals are strong. We have undertaken a series of economic reform measures to facilitate investment and growth. Our savings and investment rates have increased to 35% of our GDP and are rising. With a predominantly young population, there is potential for further increase in these rates. Although India is more integrated with the global economy than ever before, our growth has been largely fuelled by an expanding domestic market. All these factors give us confidence that we will be able to step up our annual growth rate to 10% within the next five years.

5480. (15-1-2008) NEW DELHI : The Union Cabinet Minister for Steel, Chemicals and Fertiliser, Shri Ram Vilas Paswan today formally launched the "Grameen Pushti Yojna" to be implemented in the district of Dantewada. Noting the critical partnership of the National Mineral Development Corporation {NMDC} and the United Nations World Food Programme {WFP} in this social development project, the Minister hoped that other organizations will follow such partnerships to improve lives of the needy people. The Grameen Pushti Yojna launched today in about 35 villages will make available fortified blended food (Indiamix) to children, pregnant and lactating mothers. Indiamix contains wheat, soya, vitamins and minerals which are very important for the vulnerable population. These products are already part of government's ICDS programme and are distributed through Anganwadi centres in other states. This scheme will become fully operational in Dantewada. While the United Nations World Food Programme will implement this project, the entire financing will be ensured by the NMDC with the assistance of the State. Over 50,000 children and lactating mothers are expected to benefit from this project. The Chairman and Managing Director of NMDC, and the Country-Director of WFP India, have also discussed other aspects of working together on integrated social development projects beginning the next 3 months in about 25-50 villages in Dantewada. This project will cover food and nutrition, health, sanitation, income generation activities, horticulture and grain banks. The vision of the NMDC is to see visible improvement in the life of every individual in Dantewada. NMDC is committed to provide all the financial assistance necessary for the above project. NMDC is a premier mining organization in the country, currently operating 3 major mechanized iron ore mines in Chattisgarh and Karnataka, with expansion and diversification plans in other states. Around 90% of NMDC production is supplied to domestic market. The NMDC committed to corporate social responsibility has earmarked Rs.90 crore for such activities in the current year. WFP is the world's largest humanitarian agency providing food aid to an average of 100 million people in more than 80 countries of the world every year.

5481. (15-1-2008) NEW DELHI : Dr. Ashwani Kumar, Minister of State for Industry, has stressed the need for enhanced FDI from the UK as a component of the private sector funding in infrastructure in India. With an estimated investment of approximately US D 500 billion in infrastructure during the 11th Five Year Plan, the Minister called for greater bilateral cooperation in project management skills from UK to sustain 8.5 to 9% annual GDP growth in India. He observed that the investment from Britain in India was far below its potential. Lord Digby Jones, Britain's Minister of Trade and Investment, called on Dr. Ashwani Kumar here this evening and held extensive discussions on ways and means to expand the Indo-UK economic engagement in furtherance of the strategic partnership between the two countries. Earlier, both Lord Digby Jones and Dr. Kumar co-chaired a CII-Department of Trade (UK) sponsored meet on economic cooperation in the infrastructure sector and released a KPMG Report on the Transport sector in India. The UK Minister also supported seat for India in UNSC and a greater role in G-8. Lord Jones informed Dr. Kumar that for various reasons including a shared history, cultural and personal bonds, similar legal systems and UK's known expertise in the conceptualization, executing and managements of infrastructure projects, UK and India could have a mutually reinforcing relationship which could enhance the level of economic engagement between the two countries. He further informed that Prime Minister Gordon Brown's visit to India later this month would give a further boost to ties between the two countries. He also suggested the opening of India's professional services including legal, banking, insurance and shipping to foreign investments in response to the challenges of globalisation.

5482. (15-1-2008) NEW DELHI : Annual Plan size for Rajasthan for the year 2008-09 was today finalized at a meeting between Deputy Chairman, Planning Commission, Shri Montek Singh Ahluwalia and the Chief Minister of Rajasthan, Smt. Vasundhara Raje Scindia. The Plan outlay was agreed at Rs.14000 crores. This includes additional Central assistance of Rs.100 crores provided for projects of special interest to the State. Deputy Chairman, Planning Commission appreciated the State Government for efforts aimed at improving fiscal health. He noticed that the State has not only achieved the targets laid down in the FRBM act but also achieved additional improvements in the revenue deficit and fiscal deficit. The State is expected to generate revenue surplus next year. Interest payment liability has been contained and substantial increase registered in capital outlay. Debt-GSDP ratio was much higher than the national average. On human development the State has succeeded in marginally reducing the decadal growth rate of population. Literacy rate is lower than the national average and both birth rate and infant mortality rate are also higher than the national average. Growth rate of 5.58 per cent was achieved during tenth plan against the target of 8.28 per cent. However it is better than the growth rate reached during ninth plan. Attention was drawn to problems in the agriculture, drinking water and power sectors. Reforms initiated in the health and urban sectors were also appreciated. New initiatives have been taken to improve child health services and ensuring safe delivery. Urban Land Ceiling and Regulation act has been repealed and stamp and registration duty reduced to 8 per cent. Briefing the Commission on Plan performance and future strategies, the Chief Minister said that the State was improving emphasis on social sector while maintaining fiscal discipline. Private sector participation in social sector including health and education was being encouraged. She said viability gap funding was being provided for public private partnership in social sector projects. Investment climate has improved substantially. The State was fast moving out of Bimaru status. Efforts are on to further reduce debt burden. Gender budgeting has been introduced in 14 departments and Rajasthan Knowledge Corporation was being set up to improve employability.

5483. (15-1-2008) NEW DELHI : Hydro Power Development in the country got a major boost today when the loan agreement for USD 400 million for 412 MW Rampur Hydro Electric Project located in the State of Himachal Pradesh was signed by Shri H.K. Sharma, CMD, Satluj Jal Vidyut Nigam Ltd., the Central Public Sector Undertaking established as a joint venture of Govt. of India and Govt. of Himachal Pradesh, implementing the project, Ms. Isabella Guerrio, Country Director (India Operation) World Bank, Shri Madhusudan Prasad, Joint Secretary, Deptt. of Economic Affairs, Ministry of Finance, Govt. of India and Smt. Rashima Gupta, Resident Commissioner, Govt. of Himachal Pradesh at New Delhi today. Rampur Hydro Electric Project (412 MW) is the immediate downstream of existing Nathpa Jhakri Hydro Electric Power Station (1500 MW), the country's largest hydro electric plant in operation. RHEP is slated to be commissioned by January 2012 within the 11th plan period and shall generate 1770 million units of electricity each year. Govt. of H.P. having an equity partnership of 30% in the project shall be allocated 30% of generated power on bus bar rates apart from 12% free power and also shall have additional power allocation as its entitlement under the Gadgil formula as a part of northern grid state. The balance power shall be allocated to all the constituents of the northern grid namely UP, Uttarakhand, Delhi, Punjab, Haryana, Chandigarh, Rajasthan & J&K. The local populace shall be immensely benefited with overall development of the area as well as the project affected persons shall be entitled to medical, educational, income generation and other ambitious schemes undertaken by SJVN for fulfilment of its social commitments and its responsibility as a Corporate Citizen.

5484. (15-1-2008) NEW DELHI : In exercise of the powers conferred by clause (1) of Article 224 of the Constitution of India, the President is pleased to appoint (i) Shri Lalit Kumar Mishra, and (ii) Shri Bijaya Krishna Patel, to be Additional Judges of the Orissa High Court, in that order of seniority, for a period of two years, with effect from the dates they assume charge of their respective offices.

5485. (15-1-2008) NEW DELHI : Unusual mortality of poultry was reported from Birbhum and Dakshin Dinajpur districts of West Bengal by Director, Department of Animal Resources and Animal Health, Government of West Bengal on 11th January, 2008 (A.N.). The samples were collected and forwarded to High Security Animal Disease Laboratory, Bhopal by Government of West Bengal as per specified regime of tests on 12.1.2008. One sample from each district of Birbhum and South Dinajpur have been found positive for Highly Pathogenic Avian Influenza H5 Virus by the laboratory. Based on the initial assessment of the State Government, death of approximately 35,525 poultry in 102 villages of six blocks of Birbhum district and death of 288 poultry in one state poultry farm in Dakshim Dinajpur district has taken place during last seven days. The outbreak of the disease appears to be localized only to few blocks in Birbhum and only one farm in Dakshin Dinajpupr districts of West Bengal. There is no report of unusual mortality or sickness in the neighbouring areas, in the State of West Bengal. On getting the report of unusual mortality of poultry from Birbhum and Dakshin Dinajpur districts of West Bengal, the Govt. of India had immediately deputed officers from the Department of Animal Husbandry, Dairying & Fisheries to reach the site. These officers have been present on the site since 12th January, 2008 to advice and guide the officers of State Govt. The State Govt. of West Bengal was also advised to seal the border with neighbouring countries and also the affected areas so that there is no movement of animals across these borders. The disease has been confined to only two districts of Birbhum and Dakshin Dinajpur of West Bengal. Government of West Bengal has set up 60 rapid response teams for implementation of action plan in the affected areas in Birbhum district. These teams are equipped with necessary protective equipments like masks, gloves etc. 5,000 more personal protective equipment and masks are being made available to Government of West Bengal today as per their request. Government of India has impressed upon Government of West Bengal to provide compensation to the affected farmers whose birds are being culled simultaneously when the culling takes place. Necessary funds have been provided by Government of India under its scheme for the purpose.

5486. (15-1-2008) NEW DELHI : The 14th annual meeting of the National Magnetic Resonance Society (NMRS-2008) is being organized by DRDO's Institute of Nuclear Medicine & Allied Sciences (INMAS) at Dr. S Bhagwantam Auditorium, Metcalfe House, Civil Lines, Delhi from 16th to 19th January 2008. During this meeting a special international symposium on "Advanced MR Applications" is being held during the first two days. The symposium will deal with the developments and advancements in the frontier areas of biomedical magnetic resonance imaging and spectroscopy with special emphasis on functional, metabolic and neuro-imaging. The meeting is being attended by about 250 Indian and 25 international delegates from national and international academic and research institutes with several of them legends in their area of work. The event will be inaugurated on 16th January 2008 at 0930 hrs by Dr. T Ramasami, Secretary, Department of

Science and Technology, Govt. of India and Lt. Gen. Yogendra Singh Director General Armed Forces Medical Service (DGAFMS) will be the guest of honour. Prof. Seiji Ogawa of Japan, the inventor of the Blood Oxygenation Level Dependent (BOLD) signal based MR contrast which forms the basis of functional MRI, one of the most upcoming and promising application of MRI will also be present in the inauguration. The other eminent scientists include Dr. W Selvamurthy, distinguished scientist and Chief Controller (LS&HR) DRDO, Prof. K V Ramanathan, President NMR Society and Dr. R P Tripathi, Director, INMAS. During the inauguration session Maj Gen (Retd) Dr. N Lakshmipathi, VSM, Former Director of INMAS will be felicitated by the Society for bringing in the first MRI in the country. The international delegates include Prof. David G Gadian from University College London, Prof. Elaine Holmes Imperial College London, Prof. Uwe Klose and Dr. Michael Erb from University of Tuebingen Germany, Dr. Stefan Posse, University of New Mexico, Prof. Veena Kumari from Kings College London, Dr. Kohkan Shamsi, Acunova life sciences USA, Dr. Tony Stocker from Research centre Juelich Germany. The meeting would be a great opportunity for the entire scientist community in the country to meet the experts and learn about the advanced techniques and applications of MR. The event has a special significance for INMAS and DRDO as it coincides with Golden Jubilee celebrations of the DRDO. The National Magnetic Resonance Society (NMRS) of India was established in the year 1995, with the aim of bringing together scientists working in the different areas of magnetic resonance on one platform. The major participating institutes include Indian Institute of Science, Bangalore, Tata Institute of Fundamental research (TIFR) Mumbai, Centre of Cellular and Molecular Biology (CCMB), Hyderabad, Indian Institute of Chemical Technology (IICT) Hyderabad, National Chemical Laboratory (NCL) Pune, IIT Chennai, All India Institute of Medical Sciences (AIIMS), New Delhi, Centre for Biomedical Magnetic Resonance (CBMR), SGPGI Lucknow, besides INMAS, Delhi.

5487. (15-1-2008) NEW DELHI : Dr. Shubhashis Gangopadhyay joined as Adviser to the Finance Minister in the Ministry of Finance, Government of India, here today. He fills-up this post which fell vacant after the resignation of Dr. Parthasarthi Some. He assumed the charge of his office from today after his appointment was approved by the Appointments Committee of Cabinet. His appointment will be in the rank and pay of the Secretary to the Government of India. Dr. Gangopadhyay was currently working as Director, India Development Foundation. He is Bertil Danielsson Guest Professor, Universities of Gothenburg and Stockhom. He is the Chief Editor, Journal of Emerging Market Finance and Associate Editor of Journal of Financial stability. He is the President, Society for the Promotion of Game Theory and its Applications. Dr. Gangopadhyay is the Member of internationally renowned professional bodies like CAF Board of Advisors, Indian School of Business, Hyderabad, Bankruptcy Task Force, IPD, Columbia University, International Advisory Board, LEFIC, Copenhagen Business School, Denmark, SAsia Chief Economists' Advisory Council, World Bank.

Dr. Gangopadhyay is Ph.D in Economics from Cornell University, USA. He was earlier Professor at Indian Statistical Institute and has distinguished teaching career including at the University of Gothenburg, Sweden, Rutgers University, USA and University of Southern California, USA. Dr. Gangopadhyay has a number of important publications to his credit and has handled very prestigious projects at the national and international organisations including at the World Bank.

5488. (15-1-2008) NEW DELHI : Indian Railways have exported four numbers of 2300 HP metre gauge diesel electric locomotives, one to Senegal and three to Mali, through RITES recently. In a stiff bidding, Diesel Locomotive Works (DLW), a production unit of Indian Railways, had grabbed an export order for four numbers of locomotives for these countries. DLW has executed this order within the stipulated time. These locomotives having 12 cylinders V-engine are provided with dual cabs, air brake system, parking brake and electric AC-DC transmission. It is worth mentioning here that due to high level of performance and warranty support, the demand of DLW's locomotives has been surged in the world market. By manufacturing the state-of-the-art locomotives, suitable to the geographical background and climatic conditions of the purchaser countries, DLW has been receiving export order from various countries

5489. (15-1-2008) BEIJING : The Prime Minister, Dr. Manmohan Singh, addressed the Chinese Academy Of Social Sciences in beijing, today. Following is the text of the Prime Minister's address on the occasion: "I am greatly honoured to address this distinguished gathering at the prestigious Chinese Academy of Social Sciences. Yours is a premier institution, which has been at China's intellectual vanguard over the last three decades and has contributed immensely to China's reform and development. I am delighted to be in this great country. We in India admire the remarkable economic progress that China has made. The rise of China is among the most important developments of our times. As China's largest neighbour, and a friend, we cannot remain untouched by this momentous process. The great Chinese scholar and one of the foremost Indologists of our times, Professor Ji Xianlin, has rightly said and I quote : The two great cultural circles-China and India-have always learned from and influenced each other, and this process greatly speeded the development of the two cultures, which is both history and reality, unquote. Today, both India and China are in the midst of rapid transformation. The development agenda has taken centre-stage in both our countries. Our systems are different, but people in both countries are united in their aspiration for a better future. When countries of the size of China and India, together accounting for 2.5 billion people begin to unshackle their creative energies, it is bound to impact the whole world. The world knows it and is watching with great interest. I therefore would like to use this opportunity to speak to you on India's development experience and on what I see as a special opportunity for India and China to work together in the twenty-first century. Premier Wen Jiabao recently spoke in Singapore about how it was only with openness and inclusiveness that a country can become strong and prosperous. In the past few decades, China has benefited enormously from opening its economy to the rest of the world, and so has India. India is changing and I would like to acknowledge that the success of China has been a stimulus to change. This process began in the 1980s and was intensified in 1991. In our system change can only be brought about through public debate and it takes time to build a political consensus. However, I am happy to say that in the 16 years that have elapsed since 1991, successive governments in India have carried forward the reform process, with the result that today India is on a high growth path. Our economic growth during the last five years has averaged about 8.5% per year. This is unprecedented, and has created confidence that we can do even better. We are aiming to raise our growth rate to 10% per year in the near future. There is a palpable sense of confidence in the country and there is optimism about the future. The Indian economy has demonstrated resilience in meeting the challenges posed by globalization. In the last two decades, our industry-especially large and medium industry-has restructured to become globally competitive. This process is continuing.

5490. (16-1-2008) NEW DELHI : Human Resource Development Minister, Shri Arjun Singh has said that there is near unanimity in reforms in Madarasa Education. As there are some differences on some issues including issues related to Sarva Shiksha Abhiyan (SSA), a Committee has been appointed under the chairmanship of Minister of State for HRD, Shri M.A.A Fatimi. This Committee will submit its report within two months. Shri Arjun Singh was addressing media after the conclusion of the meeting of National Monitoring Committee for Minorities Education (NMCME), here today. The 3rd Meeting of the National Monitoring Committee for Minorities Education was held under the Chairmanship of Shri Arjun Singh. The two Ministers of State Shri M.A.A. Fatimi and Smt. Purandeshwari were also present. After inaugurating the meeting Shri Arjun Singh briefly outlined the major activities taken up by the Ministry for the educational development of minorities. Presentations were made by the Chairman UGC, Acting Chairman, AICTE, Chairman NIOS, Joint Secretary SSA and Joint Secretary, School Education. Prof. Prithipal Singh Kapur gave the report of the work done by the Standing Committee of the NMCME. For encouraging minority education, AICTE gives a 20% relaxation in the processing fees from applications for setting up institutions as well as in the amount required to be kept in a joint Fixed Deposit. The Council informed the Committee that in its different Boards/Committees of AICTE the representation of the Minority Community has been ensured with as many as 18 such members, including two Chairpersons belonging to Minority Community on the bodies of the Council. There are about 118 Experts from the minorities who are in the Directory of Experts of the AICTE nominated by the Council on the Expert Committees which go for inspection of institutions seeking affiliation to AICTE. The UGC has directed all universities and institutions to associate a member from the Minority Community in the various Selection Committees. Out of 370 proposed degree colleges to be set up in Eleventh Plan, 88 Muslim concentration districts will be covered. A new centrally sponsored scheme is proposed for assistance to polytechnics which ensures that each Muslim Minority Concentration District has a polytechnic for which non recurring expenditure is proposed to be made available. Out of 4707 degree level technical institutions, 377 are minority institutions out of which 51 were sanctioned by AICTE in 2007-08. Total intake of minority institutions is 88259 at present. UGC has appointed a committee to suggest a comprehensive policy for fair share in various schemes for minorities and new guidelines are being developed for the implementation of its schemes during the 11th Plan.

5491. (16-1-2008) NEW DELHI : Shri Kamal Nath, Union Minister of Commerce and Industry, has underlined the need to empower the poor of India by providing basic necessities such as shelter, education, health and jobs. "We have made a start. The 2007 Budget has provided a 31% rise in rural infrastructure expenditure and broadened the availability of farm credit. But we have still miles to go", the Minister said while addressing the Special Plenary Session of Partnership Summit titled "Accelerating Inclusive & Sustainable Growth, Integrating with the Globe", here today. He further stated that the time has come to make our reform process interactive and collaborative to include all parts of society, including business, politics and civil society. Mr. Ferenc Gyurcsany, Prime Minister of Hungary; Shri Bhupinder Singh Hooda, Chief Minister of Haryana; and Shri Sunil Bharti Mittal, President, Confederation of Indian Industry (CII) besides representatives from various countries such as Sri Lanka, Singapore, UK, Ethiopia, Australia, Syria, South Africa, Japan, UAE, El Salvador and Ontario participated and spoke on the occasion. Shri Kamal Nath said: "our Prime Minister has repeatedly reminded the private sector of the need for inclusive growth across the country. I would like to add to this. By partnering us in the development process, you will be unlocking a market that has been estimated at over $ 170 billion by international agencies. You should capitalize on this opportunity to provide productive and constructive direction to the reform process". While quoting the recent McKinsey study, the Minister observed that people in rural India have a per capita income, which is almost 30% lower than the national average. This probably explains why we know so little about rural India. It also explains why most of our businesses, jobs, products and processes are urban-centric. "To ensure inclusive growth, we need to see rural India through new eyes. As companies, you will need to develop new price points and set up alternative supply chains to address rural needs. You will need to develop durable relationships with NGOs, self help groups and micro finance institutions to penetrate rural India. To unearth the wealth in rural India, you must innovate. Today, Indian companies are rethinking the way they manage assets, distribute products and use technologies to create new services. I believe many of these can help rural India. For example, I know that a leading private sector Indian bank is expanding its rural network by setting up automated teller machines in villages and providing credit and deposit facilities to millions of

Indians who had limited access to financial institutions. Then again, the e-chaupal experience has been well documented", Shri Kamal Nath said. The Minister added that "Inclusive Growth" is also about the successful management of demographics. With half the population under the age of twenty-five, India already has the youngest labour force in the world and will have more young workers aged 20 to 24 by 2013. "I have no doubt that if these workers are adequately trained and skilled, they will give the country a huge competitive advantage in terms of raising per capita incomes and reducing dependency ratios. I call upon Indian industry to play its part in skill-building.

5492. (16-1-2008) NEW DELHI : Shri Kamal Nath, Union Minister of Commerce and Industry, has said that India's pace of globalisation has picked up dramatically in the past five years, particularly the trade in goods and services. He was addressing at a session on "How can Trade Negotiations Ensure Inclusive Growth" at the Partnership Summit, here today. The Minister mentioned that trade in goods and services amounts to $450 billion, more than half of India's GDP. Both exports and imports benefited from the strengthening of world trade and grew in double digits. Exports crossed $126 billion in 2006-07, growing by over 25% each year from 2004, while imports stood at $191 billion. The exports to GDP ratio have dramatically gone up to 13.9%, and imports now form 21.1% of GDP. In 2000-01, exports of services were $16.2 billion-by 2006-07, the figure went up to $81.3 billion, almost five-fold increase. Foreign direct investment of almost $13 billion has come into the country between January and August 2007. Ministers from South Africa, Indonesia and Ethiopia also addressed the session. As regards FTAs, Shri Kamal Nath stated that Free Trade Agreements (FTAs) have been put in place with Singapore and Thailand. FTAs are in the negotiations stage with many other regions and countries. These include the European Union, ASEAN, South Korea and Japan, MERCOSUR of South America, Gulf Cooperation Council, etc. More than half of the world trade is currently being carried out under trading agreements. South-South Trade-the India-Brazil-South Africa (IBSA) initiative is expected to diversify India's export basket even further. Not only has the number of FTAs involving India have increased but their scope widened to include services and investment. The Minister further stated that: "While foreign investments have flowed into sectors such as IT, telecom, and manufacturing, they have primarily entered the large corporate sector in the form of equity. Angel investing, venture capital, and private equity placements have only recently begun to see an upward trend. India's huge base of small and medium enterprises produces about half of aggregate output of the country, and contribute directly and indirectly to over 50% of exports. They also employ about 28 million people and exhibit excellent flexibility to rapidly changing global environments".

5493. (16-1-2008) NEW DELHI : Shri Kamal Nath, Union Minister of Commerce and Industry, has stressed on the need to take concrete action to translate political friendship into economic partnership and work on sectors where India and Hungary can cooperate. "I urge businesses of both sides to establish sectoral platforms for trade and investment that can identify the existing roadblocks and devise solutions for dismantling them. Hungary has high skills in engineering, machinery, food processing, electricity, metallurgy and other value added sectors. India currently requires equipment and machinery for its infrastructure development, and should be a market of interest for Hungarian businesses", the Minister said. He was addressing the luncheon session on "Hungary-Regional Integration: The EU Experience for Inclusive Growth", in honour of the Prime Minister of Hungary, Mr. Ferenc Gyurcsany, here today. As far as the regional integration is concerned, Shri Kamal Nath stated that it is increasingly being recognized as an important element of economic growth strategy. In this environment, the European Union presents a paradigm of integration. It has succeeded in bringing together diverse ideologies as well as economies in varying stages of development. The common market and single currency are one of the most significant developments in the global trade arena. "The benefits of this integration are visible in the faster rates of growth in both GDP and trade in the region. The EU is no longer at the bottom of global growth ladders, but has revitalized into a dynamic and vibrant economic region. Robust economic fundamentals are helping the region's interaction with the rest of the world. Hungary joined the EU in 2004 and since then has experienced the economic benefits of regional integration", he emphasised. India's trade with the EU has been going up correspondingly. EU is India's largest regional trade partner, with exports from India at $27 billion in 2006-07 and a percentage share of 23%. The investment flows have similarly seen a surge. The EU including Hungary are witnessing increased interest from Indian companies. Earlier during his one-to-one meeting with the Prime Minister of Hungary, Shri Kamal Nath stated that India is a vibrant economy with huge opportunities for doing business. He further informed that development of relations between the two countries provide a valuable base to enhance bilateral relations in all spheres and the goodwill that exists between the two countries and its people should lead to enhanced interaction between the two sides in all fields of mutual concern. He also outlined the potential area for collaboration between the two countries in Auto Components, IT and e-Governance, Health Care, Pharmaceuticals, Ayurveda, Energy, Environment Protection and Water Management, Investments, Finance and Banking, R&D/ S&T Cooperation, Bio-Technology, Innovation, Transport & Tourism and Agriculture. FDI approvals during the period 1991 to October, 2007 stood at US $ 3.05 Million and the actual inflow is US $ 0.33 Million.

5494. (16-1-2008) NEW DELHI : To a question as to what is the government doing on the Ramsethu issue, Congress spokesman Shri Abhishek Singhvi said, the government has appeared in the Court today and sought time and the Court has granted it time. This will all be decided only after appropriate affidavits and pleadings are filed and the Court takes up the matter. Today the matter was adjourned because the government asked for time and the Court granted it. To a question that today the Goa Government is faced with a crisis. What are your

Party's views, Shri Singhvi said, we have heard so. We do not have the facts but we would like to assure you that there is no crisis and whatever the matter it will be settled. To a question whether the government has made up its mind as to who will be honoured with the Bharat Ratna, Shri Singhvi said, let me repeat what I said a few days ago that the Bharat Ratna is an award of the highest significance, of the highest stature in this country. Bharat is proud of its Ratnas and for that reason this is not an award which we can or should discuss through the press. It is not an award which where names can be lightly floated or thrown up. There are institutional mechanisms, established mechanisms, historical mechanisms which will take care of it. To a question that is it the view point of the Congress Party and the UPA government that there is nobody fit for the Bharat Ratna, Shri Singhvi said, it is the government's view point that in the years in which the award is not given to any one is obvious that no one is found deserving for the award. Since 2004 the government has not thought it fit to award it to anyone and that is fully within the government's right. Perhaps you would want to file a mandamus petition in the court to say that every year there should be an award of the Bharat Ratna. To a question on the oil price rise what is your party's stand in this regard and whether there should be an increase in the prices or not, Shri Singhvi said, first, it is the GOM tomorrow which is going to decide the issue. Second, the Congress Party's stand was spelt out by me two days ago and I repeat it, we have no doubt, we are confident that every possible step will be taken to minimize the impact of oil price increase globally. Third, we are also confident and we hope and trust that wild fluctuations or movements in the spot price on the international market will not be allowed to be automatically transmitted to the Indian market and all other possible steps will be taken to minimize the impact of an increase, if any, especially in regard to fuels like diesel, kerosene etc. To a question whether the Congress Party has any explanation as to why Mahatma Gandhi was not considered for such an award, Shri Singhvi said, there are some personages who are beyond awards and Mahatma Gandhi was one such person. The fact that Mahatma Gandhi had not been posthumously awarded do you think any of us or anybody is suggesting that he is not the utmost jewel of India. There are some people who are outside of the boundaries of awards. So let us not try to diminish that stature by encapsulating their personalities in terms of awards. To a question that Smt. Mayawati has demanded that UP should be divided into more smaller states, do you support her demand, Shri Singhvi said, please don't forget that it is Smt. Mayawati who has supported our demand. Let us get the record clear, it is we who initiated the demand and we started with Bundelkhand.

5495. (16-1-2008) NEW DELHI : The Union Minister for Science and Technology and Earth Sciences Shri Kapil Sibal today launched a portal www.piousnetwork.com for information on the groups of professionals of Indian origin based in the USA. Speaking at a press conference in New Delhi today the Minister said that there was a crying need to systematize, diversify and scale up the disparate information available on the groups of professionals of Indian origin based in the USA. He said the idea of developing and continuously maintaining a dynamic, interactive portal giving accurate and up-to-date information of professionals of Indian origin was conceived by him while interacting with the Indian diaspora during his visit to the USA in October, 2006. Majority of the Indian diaspora is based in the United States of America. Their dominant position in the US knowledge sector is legendary. In the Silicon Valley alone, nearly 5 lakh Indian professionals are now working. They are well represented in all walks of life-be they Professors, Scientists, Technologists, Doctors or Lawyers. Their median income is higher than that of the average Americans. It is also estimated that around 50,000 Scientists, Engineers and Technologists of Indian origin working in the USA hold senior and key positions in various Universities and R&D Laboratories there. The forces of globalization based on connectivity, mobility and interdependence offer unprecedented opportunity to the diaspora for playing key roles in the development of the countries of their origin. In today's world, no firm, no organization and even no nation can go ahead of its own-there is need for businesses and organizations to be embedded in and be part of complex system of networks. Some forms of networking do exist among the Indian diaspora based in the USA. PanIIT, TiE, Silicon Valley Indian Professionals Association, Worldwide Indian Network, International Associations of Scientific and Engineering and Technologists of Bharatiya Origin are some examples. Admittedly these associations have narrow focus and are of limited utility. The portal developed by M/s Phoenix Rose LLC, Columbia, Maryland under a project sponsored by the Department of Science and Technology, Ministry of Science and Technology, Government of India through the Indian Embassy in Washington DC entitled www.piousnetwork.com is a dynamic and interactive portal. The details of more than 200 groups of professionals have already been collected. Information has also been collected on more than 20,000 records of innovations and patents in last few years that include large number of professionals of Indian origin. This data will be useful to identify innovators and their technologies to build partnerships. The members joining this initiative on voluntary basis will have the benefit of interacting with the professionals in their areas. Each user would be provided an exclusive password so that they could update their data as and when they feel so. The portal incorporates the search facility using predefined key words. Thus, it is possible to get information on professionals as desired-field wise, city wise or as per the specialized areas of their profession. The members are to provide information on their expertise, patents generated, technologies and other know-how developed. The information so made available can be accessed not only by the Indian professionals in USA but also by professionals working in various fields in India so that the expertise and services of PIOUS could be used for the development and growth of S&T and other fields in India.

5496. (16-1-2008) NEW DELHI : Maize is the third major food crop in India. It is a rich source of calories and proteins for the disadvantaged sections of the society. The Indian variety of maize is deficient in essential amino acids *i.e.* lysine and tryptophan. Under a project sponsored by the Department of Biotechnology (DBT) a high quality protein maize has been developed which has 40% more of the essential amino acids than the normal variety. The Union Minister for Science and Technology and Earth Sciences, Shri Kapil Sibal revealed this at a press conference in New Delhi today. Vivek Hybrid 9 is one of the best maize hybrids developed by Vivekananda Parvathiya Krishi Anusandhan Sansthan (VPKAS) and is being cultivated in the states of Uttarakhand, Himahcal Pradesh, J&K, Andhra Pradesh, Karnataka, Tamil Nadu and Maharashtra. Its disadvantage is that it is late maturing. Thus it does not normally fit into the cropping pattern of the cultivators in the hilly States. Accordingly DBT sought to rectify the disadvantages of Vivek and improve upon its quality protein content. It sponsored a project at VPKAS with the twin objectives. Success has been achieved on both these counts. The new early maturing Hybrid variety (FQH 4567) has been developed with 40% more lysine and tryptophan content and a 10% higher yield. Field trials in several States have given excellent results in cultivation of FQH 4567. Accordingly, it has been accepted for release for commercial cultivation. It is envisaged that with the release of the new variety for commercial cultivation nutritional food security of the disadvantaged sections of the society would be better ensured.

5497. (16-1-2008) NEW DELHI : The report from the High Security Animal Disease Laboratory, Bhopal that one sample each from districts of Birbhum and South Dinajpur has tested positive for H5 A1 virus was received in the afternoon of 15th January 2008 around 1.30 p.m. The laboratory tests to establish N-typing of the virus take 5 or 6 days. Immediately after getting the report from the HSADL, Bhopal, the Government of West Bengal was notified and they were requested to take immediate necessary action as per the Action Plan communicated to all the State Governments in November, 2006. Senior officers of DADF are already available on the spot in both Birbhum and South Dinajpur districts to advise and guide the State Government officers. As per the report received from the State of West Bengal, 55 Rapid Response Teams (RRTs) have started operation of culling the birds in the affected area of Birbhum district from this morning. Two teams have started operations of culling in the South Dinajpur district. Training and health checkup of the RRTs to be deployed for culling operations was completed on 15th January, 2008. All the members of the team have been provided personal protective equipment like gloves, masks etc. For digging of pits of dispose off the culled birds, 10 JCBs have been mobilized in Birbhum and one in South Dinajpur. Arrangements for payment of compensation on the spot have been made by the State Revenue Department. As per the available information, the mortality has taken place in three areas *viz.* five blocks and one municipality in Birbhum, State Poultry Farm, Balurghat, Dakshin Dinajpur and three villages of adjoining Murshidabad district. The problem is, therefore, localized. However, Government of West Bengal and another neighbouring States like Jharkhand and Bihar have already been alerted for maintaining high level of surveillance.

5498. (16-1-2008) NEW DELHI : Union Home Minister Shri Shivraj Patil has said that Government is taking steps to implement the provisions of Sachar Committee report and also the Prime Ministers 15-point programme for minorities in right spirit. Inaugurating the Annual Conference of the State Minorities Commissions organized by the National Commission for Minorities here today he said it is the duty of Government to provide full opportunities of development to minorities and protect their life, property and culture. In the present scenario of liberalization, the minorities should also explore avenues of self-employment like setting up of industrial units and opt for professions for which financial assistance should be provided to them on easy term and long term basis. He laid emphasis on the opening of more educational institutions, either by the government or by private bodies so as to make education accessible to everybody. Earlier, Welcoming the Home Minister, Shri Mohamed Shafi Qureshi, Chairperson, National Commission for Minorities in his address urged that if the Commission has to play a more pro active role for the benefit of the minority communities, its finances and man power base have to be augmented and strengthened. To this end, the Government should expedite the process of conferring the Constitutional Status on the National Commission for Minorities. Chairperson observed that the recommendation of the Commission for creation of a Minority Sub-Plan did not find a place in the Eleventh Plan Document. However, he welcomed the step taken by the Government for creation of a National Data Bank through comprehensive surveys on quantitative aspects of socio-religious communities and commission qualitative studies to understand patterns of discrimination and to identify bottlenecks in the various programmes, for course correction. Chairperson, NCM stressed the need for concerted efforts required to implement recommendations of the Sachhar Committee Report. Dr. Bhalchandra Mungekar, Member, Planning Commission was the guest speaker in the first working session of the Conference in which the Eleventh Plan Document with reference to Minorities and Prime Minister's 15 Point Programme for the Welfare of Minorities was discussed. In the second working session the status and role of the State Minorities Commissions were deliberated upon with a view to strengthening the State Commissions and empowering them to play a more pro-active role in the development of the minorities in the country.

5499. (16-1-2008) NEW DELHI : Leopard has been accorded highest degree of protection by including them in the Schedule I of the Wild Life (Protection) Act, 1972. The Government took this action noticing leopards deaths during last year. It is reported that more than 150 leopards died during last year at various places. There are more than 11,000 leopards in the country today. Madhya Pradesh, Chhattisgarh, Uttar Pradesh and Uttaranchal states have maximum number of leopards followed by Gujarat. There are also cases of poaching/seizure incidents, including skins, involving major species, namely, tiger, leopard, elephant, rhino, star tortoise, bear, musk deer and otter during three years from 2003. The measures taken by Government of India to ensure protection of leopards, inter alia, include a network of National Parks and Wildlife Sanctuaries has been set up across the country to protect wildlife including leopards.

5500. (16-1-2008) NEW DELHI : The Press Council of India has been reconstituted in its tenth term. The Council stands constituted with a strength of 28 members other than the Chairman for a three year terms w.e.f. January 7, 2008. 20 members represent the Press, five are members of Parliament and one nominee each of University Grants Commission, Sahitya Academy and Bar Council of India.

5501. (16-1-2008) NEW DELHI : India and Iran today held a wide ranging discussion to enhance cooperation in the oil and gas sector including LNG import contract signed in June, 2005. At a meeting between Shri Murli Deora, Minister for Petroleum & Natural Gas and Dr. Davood Danesh Jafari, Minister for Economic Affairs & Finance of the Islamic Republic pf Iran here today, Shri Deora emphasized that a solution to implement the LNG deal should be arrived at by the two countries. He also expressed keen interest in finalizing the Iran-Pakistan-India gas pipeline project. On his part the visiting Minister said that Iran is open to hold discussions on the LNG contract. In addition, he invited investments by both private and public sector companies in developing gas fields in Iran with a possibility to set up LNG facilities and an arrangement to export LNG to India. He also emphasized the need for finalizing agreements in respect of IPI gas pipeline project.

5502. (16-1-2008) NEW DELHI : The Union Finance Minister, Shri P. Chidambaram complemented the Chief Commissioners of Income Tax for the remarkable performance of the department, particularly on the revenue side. Addressing them on a live video conference here today, the Finance Minister stated that the department had done well in collecting higher revenues in 2006-07 and was performing even better in 2007-08. Total direct tax collections were up 42.8 percent as in December 2007, while collection of personal income tax was even higher. Outlining the factors responsible for the unprecedented growth in revenue collection such as moderate tax rates, change in taxpayer behaviour towards better compliance with tax laws and a technology driven tax department which had become more taxpayer friendly, the Finance Minister observed that while the tax collection mechanism has become more technology driven, nondiscrimination and transparent, the department needed to become more friendly towards the bulk of taxpayers who were voluntarily complying with the tax laws and tough on the miniscule minority of recalcitrant taxpayers. Shri Chidambaram said that he had sanctioned an incentive of Rs.195 crore to enable the department to improve infrastructure for increasing its operational efficiency by providing more vehicles and telephones but the department needed to further improve basic facilities for taxpayers such as potable water and clean toilets. The Finance Minister said that the department would need to find still better ways and means to utilize these amounts for a lasting impact on its functioning.

5503. (16-1-2008) NEW DELHI : The Memorandum of Understanding (MoU)k has been signed by Shri Subodh Kant Sahai, Minister of State (Independent Charge) for Food Processing Industries, and Mr. Paolo De Castro, Italian Minister for Agricultural Food and Forestry Policies in the presence of Shri Sharad Pawar, Minister of Agriculture, Consumer Affairs, Food and Public Distribution. The memorandum aims at establishing a Knowledge Based Partnership between the two countries and create an enabling environment for a long term partnership between the industries of the two countries. The Minister said that the Memorandum proposes to facilitate creation of a "Joint Foundation" for exchange of know-how and technology between Indian and Italian Agro Food enterprises for the promotion of the Agro Food Sector. It will also aim at creation of business joint ventures, support to research and development activities, setting up of Agro-Food Parks etc. in India. The Memorandum also provides creation of an Agro Food Park in India within a period of 18 months from the date of signing the memorandum, the Minister informed. Further, both parties agree to identify and facilitate creation of demand driven projects/food parks keeping in view raw materials availability, peripheral infrastructure like air, rail, road linkages, power, skilled manpower etc. to attract investments. Such projects will be eligible for financial assistance from Ministry of Food Processing Industries and other agencies of Government of India as per scheme and guidelines.

5504. (16-1-2008) NEW DELHI : The Ministry of Food Processing Industries, Government of India and the Italian Ministry of Agricultural Food and Forestry Policies have signed today a Memorandum of Understanding (MoU), on "Cooperation in the Agri Food Sector", committing themselves to the promotion of Agro Food Sector. The Memorandum of Understanding (MoU) has been signed by Shri Subodh Kant Sahai, Minister of State (Independent Charge for Food Processing Industries, Government of India and Mr. Paolo De Castro, Italian Minister for Agricultural Food and Forestry Policies in the presence of Shri Sharad Pawar, Minister of Agriculture, Consumer Affairs, Food and Public Distribution.

5505. (16-1-2008) NEW DELHI : The President of India, Smt. Pratibha Devisingh Patil met participants of the 8th Know India Programme at Rashtrapati Bhavan today. The Ministry of Overseas Indian Affairs, Government of India has been organising this programme with the objective of familiarising the younger generation of the Indian Diaspora with India. The programme involves a three-week stay in India by the participants in the age group of 20 to 28 years. The Government of Tamil Nadu and the Confederation of Indian Industry (CII) are partners with the Government of India. The President had a very lively interaction with the more than 30 participants who came from Canada, Fiji, Guyana, Israel, Malaysia, the Netherlands, New Zealand, the Reunion Islands, South Africa, Trinidad and Tobago, the United Kingdom and the United States of America. During the interaction Smt. Patil said, on return to their countries the participants would become ambassadors for India and was happy that the programme allows youth of Indian origin to meet with Indian youth to create long lasting contacts. The President was keen to know about the impressions of the participants about India before and after participating in the programme. The President was also very keen to know about social work being done by some of the participants. The participants said after visiting both rural and urban areas, they were struck by the India's rising economic power, high level of motivation of the people, the intelligence of its people, the country's globalised nature, its vibrancy, love and hospitality of the people despite progress, advances in urban infrastructure and the progress of its women. The President told the group that India was indeed on the path of fast economic growth, with GDP growth at more than 9 percent for the past three years and a projection of 10 percent per annum GDP growth in the latter part of the 11th Five Year Plan. 55 percent of the economy was made up of the service sector, with IT and IT enabled services doing well, industrial growth on the pick-up and foreign investment being attracted to the country because of its growth, she added. She also spoke about the higher education system and measures taken by the Late Prime Minister, Shri Rajiv Gandhi to amend the Constitution to reserve one-third of the seats in local elected bodies for women, so that women could be empowered. Smt. Patil also mentioned the problem areas and challenges faced by India, such as poverty and illiteracy, reduction of which is being focused on by the Sarva Shiksha Abhiyan Programme of the Government of India.

5506. (16-1-2008) NEW DELHI : A meeting was held today between the Indian delegation led by Union Agriculture Minister Shri Sharad Pawar and the Italian delegation led by Agriculture Minister of Italy, Mr. Paolo de Castro. Shri Subodh Kant Sahai, Minister of State (Independent Charge), Ministry of Food Processing Industries also participated along with senior officers. Discussions were held on wide ranging issues to enhance cooperation between the two countries in the fields of agriculture and allied activities including food processing, agricultural research, phytosanitary issues relating to trade and engagement of private sector of both countries in the areas of mutual interest. The Memorandum of Understanding (MoUs) were also signed between Ministry of Agriculture, India and Italian Ministry of Agriculture, food and forestry policies and between Ministry of Food Processing Industries and Italian Ministry of Agriculture, food and forestry policies. The MoUs will provide institutional arrangements for enhancing bilateral cooperation between the two countries in the fields of agriculture and allied sector and food processing.

5507. (16-1-2008) NEW DELHI : Today, The Minister of Civil Aviation, Shri Praful Patel held a meeting with Shri Iqbal Ahmed Saradgi, Member of Parliament and Chairman, Haj Committee of India and other senior officials to review the on-going Haj-2007 operations. The Secretary, Ministry of Civil Aviation, Shri Ashok Chawla, CMD, Air India, Shri V.Thulasidas, CEO, Haj Committee of India Shri Mohd. Owais and other senior officials from Air India and Ministry of Civil Aviation participated in the discussions. The meeting took stock of the on-going second phase of Haj operations and noted with concern that there have been some delays in the arrival of flights carrying the Hajis on their return journey from Saudi Arabia by Saudi Arabian Airlines and Air India. It was also noted that for almost all stations, there have been delays in the delivery of baggage. There have also been constraints in carrying the Zam Zam water leading to some backlog on this count also. After a detailed review of the operations, it was decided that Air India would, within 24 hours, notify a detailed schedule indicating the plan for delivery of the baggage and Zam Zam water including the backlog. A date-wise and destination-wise plan will be drawn up indicating thereof the details of delivery of baggage and Zam Zam water including the backlog till date. This plan will be furnished to the Ministry of Civil Aviation, the Haj Committee of India and will be displayed at all the disembarkation points for widest possible dissemination to the Haj pilgrims so that the inconvenience on this account is minimized. It was also decided that the Ministry of Civil Aviation will coordinate with the Saudi Arabian Airlines to facilitate the drawing up of a similar plan for delivery of baggage and Zam Zam water. Likewise, CGI, Jeddah would also be requested to facilitate the transportation of the remaining Haj pilgrims along with their baggage and Zam Zam water. The Minister, Civil Aviation also suggested that certain remedial measures should be taken to ensure that future Haj operations are smooth and orderly. One such measure decided upon was that Air India should go in for a long-term lease of wide-bodied aircraft with a view to ensuring timely availability of the suitable aircraft as well as to bring down the cost of operations. Air India renewed its commitment to undertake the Haj operations, which are carried out in larger national interest and urged all concerned for their cooperation and understanding in ensuring the success of the operations. Air India also expressed regret for delays and inconveniences which may have been caused to some of the pilgrims and assured that with the finalization of the above plan, the baggage and Zam Zam water would be delivered within the shortest possible time.

5508. (16-1-2008) NEW DELHI : The Data received from various States/UTs reveals an encouraging trend in the number of beneficiaries getting financial as well as technical help during the current financial year (2007-08) under the Swarna Jayanti Gram Swarojgar Yojana (SGSY). A recent review of the programme says that till November, 2007 a total of 1,99,120 Self-Help Groups (SHGs) were formed. In all 1,67,715 SHGs have passed Grade-I, 67,756 SHGs Grade-II and 90,903 SHGs have taken up economic activities with a total membership of 5,85,290. The percentage of SHGs, which have taken up economic activities, to those have passed Grade-II since inception is 65.63 %. The number of SHGs that have taken up economic activities varies widely from one in Lakshdweep to 18,088 in West Bengal. A total of 6,92,635 Swrozgaries were assisted during the current year till November, 2007. Out of this 1,07,345 were individual Swarozgaries. This include an assistance to 3,41,900 SC/ST Swarozgaries (*i.e.* 49.25%). The coverage of Minority Swarozgaries was 50,766 (7.33%) during the year. Women Swarozgaries accounted to 4,22,297 which was 60.97% of the total coverage.

Most of the States except Gujarat, Jharkhand, Meghalaya, Uttar Pradesh and UT of Lakshdweep faired well above the national level (40%). The coverage of physically challenged persons was comparatively better in Andhra Pradesh, Jharkhand, Kerala, Meghalaya, Sikkim and Tamil Nadu with a national level of only 1.77%. During 2007-08, the Central share of allocation to the States/UTs is Rs.1702.24 crore. Against this, 1st instalment amounting to Rs.740.58 crore to 530 District Rural Development Agencies (DRDAs) and 2nd instalment amounting to Rs.373.97 crore to 315 DRDAs has been released. The Total available funds under SGSY (including Opening balance+Central Releases+State Releases+Misc. receipts) during this period upto November, 2007 was Rs. 1720.25 crore. The utilization of funds up to November, 2007 was Rs. 914.27 crore (53.15%). However, due to technical reasons State Governments of Andhra Pradesh, Arunachal Pradesh, Bihar, Gujarat, Haryana, Himachal Pradesh, J & K, Jharkhand, Karnataka, Kerala, Madhya Pradesh, Manipur,, Meghalaya, Mizoram, Nagaland, Orissa, Rajasthan, Uttarakhand and all UTs except Pondicherry have utilized less than the national level upto the reporting date. The report received from the states suggest that the subsidy amounting to Rs.489.71 crores to SHGs and Rs. 95.69 crore to individual swarozgaries have been distributed. The total subsidy disbursed up to November, 2007 was RRs.585.41 crore. The amount spent on infrastructure development and training/capacity building was Rs.119.37 crores and Rs.78.49 crore respectively. The amount spent on revolving fund was Rs.104.41 crore. The credit target during 2007-08 was Rs.3743.55 crores. The mobilized credit upto November, 2007 was Rs.1278.85 crore. The credit disbursed for the self-Help Groups (SHGs) and Individual Swarozgaries was Rs.1035.19 crore and Rs. 243.66 crores, respectively. All the state Government except Andhra Pradesh, Chattisgarh, Goa, Gujarat, Haryana, Himachal Pradesh, Karnataka, Kerala, Madhya Pradesh, Punjab, Rajasthan, Tamil Nadu, Uttar Pradesh, Uttarakhand and UT of Pondicherry have achieved more than national average of credit disbursed upto the reporting date.

5509. (16-1-2008) NEW DELHI : A 22 member delegation headed by Mrs. Belinda Scott from Natal Province of the Republic of South Africa yesterday called on Union Minister for Rural Development Dr. Raghuvansh Prasad Singh here today. Welcoming the delegation the minister called for a better understanding of different kind of schemes and programmes related with rural development currently being implemented in India as well as in South Africa. A composite pack of the organizational set up of Rural Development Ministry and its programmes on providing employment to rural folks like NREGP (under the NREGA), the self-employment programmes under SGSY, construction of rural roads under PMGSY, the IAY highlighting the rural housing activities, rural drinking water supply under the ARWSP and the activities of technology mission, the rural sanitation, ground water recharge under the watershed development programme, the desert and drought prone area development programme as well as the resettlement and rehabilitation aspects and the digital, satellite borne upkeep of land records were detailed out during the deleberations. The African delegation took interest specifically in the water conservation and land records management. It was agreed during the deliberations that there is ample scope for mutual collaboration between the two nations in the field of rural development programmes. The delegation is on a 18 days visit to India and will study the mechanism of rural development during their stay

5510. (16-1-2008) NEW DELHI : The Minister for Micro, Small & Medium Enterprises, Shri Mahabir Prasad has set 31st March 2008 as the deadline for implementing various schemes under the Khadi & Village Industries Commission (KVIC). Presiding over the Second Meeting of National Khadi & Village Industries Board (NKVIB) here today, Shri Prasad said that the Government was making special attempts for the development of khadi sector in the 11th Plan as compared to the 10th Plan. He said, "Workshed for Spinners, Enhancing the Productivity and Marketing in a holistic and planned manner for selected 200 institutions in which we are including 50 institutions that are managed by persons belonging to Scheduled Castes and Scheduled Tribes, to institute a nursing fund to support around 200 institutions which have become financially weak and modernisation of around 30 Sales Outlets are some examples." He said, he had instructed the Ministry and KVIC to ensure that these schemes get implemented positively by 31.03.2008. The Minister said he expected full cooperation from the Ministry of Finance, Banks and Planning Commission continuously in these efforts. The principle issues identified for special discussion in the Second Meeting of NKVIB were Scheme of Fund for Regeneration of Traditional Industries (SFURTI) and Rural Employment Generation Programme (REGP). SFURTI was launched to develop around 100 clusters in khadi, village industries and coir sectors with a total plan allocation of Rs. 97.25 crore. Release of funds under this scheme is cluster specific. The Government of India releases funds to the Nodal Agencies *i.e.* KVIC and Coir Board who are responsible for holding and disbursement of funds to the approved Implementing Agencies and monitoring of the scheme. These funds are released by them to the Implementing Agencies as per their requirement. Khadi, village and coir industries including leather and pottery are covered under SFURTI. 122 traditional industry clusters from khadi, village and coir sectors covering all the States/UTs have been approved for their development under SFURTI. Earlier, the Chairperson of KVIC, Smt. Kumud Joshi said KVIC could not sustain by merely selling ideas and ideals and that it was high time to take a hard look at the marketing strategy. She also informed that there was a tremendous demand for e-charkhas, which had caught on the imagination of the teeming millions of our country. Some of the members suggested that the banks should be more forthcoming in giving collateral free loans to the micro & small entrepreneurs. Members from across the country attended the day-long deliberation. The first meeting of NKVIB held in New Delhi on 8 June 2007 deliberated on various subjects like new schemes approved by the Government, ensuring remunerating wages, convergence with like minded originations, rebate system, opening of SC/STs new institution and clusters and export of Khadi through various exhibitions and outlets abroad etc.

5511. (16-1-2008) NEW DELHI : The "National Conclave on Promoting North-East as a Destination for LTC Travellers" was held today in Vigyan Bhavan, New Delhi. Minister, DoNER, Shri Mani Shankar Aiyar in his inaugural address allayed the misplaced perceptions about the entire North-East Region being unsafe and ridden with insurgency. He said that the fact is that a vast swathe of the Region is not merely free from any extremist related activity but is among the most peaceful place in the country and this fact has to be highlighted not just by the governments but also by the travel industry and the media. The Minister added that recent years have seen, as a result of the efforts of the Central Government, coordinated by the Ministry of DoNER, a significant improvement in road, rail and air connectivity to the region. This process is being intensified to make travel to the region fast and hassle free. The ministry is also exploring ways to incentivize LTC tourists to visit the region in consultations with the other Central Ministries concerned. Mr. Aiyar said the Conclave is a simple but significant attempt by the Ministry of DoNER to motivate the vast number of government employees, who are entitled to LTC facility, to include the North-East States in their itinerary. The Conclave has been organized as a sequel to the Special Summit of the North Eastern Council on Tourism Sector which was held at Gangtok in April 2007. During the Conclave, presentations were made by the North-East States as well as by Ministry of Tourism, IL&FS and WWF-India. Indian Railways Catering and Travel Corporation (IRCTC) and Air India explained the various packages and schemes being run by them for visiting the region. A number of new measures and incentives are also being planned in coordination with the States and the hospitality industry. The Region is also seeing a great deal activity for the construction of new hotels and other tourist facilities. The North East Industrial and Investment Promotion Policy, 2007 provides a host of concessions to industry which have, for the first time, been extended to tourism sector. These should encourage more and more private entrepreneurs to invest in the development of tourist facilities so that the region can get its due share in this one of the fast growing sector which will benefit the people of the region by creating employment opportunities. The participants included a large number of central government officials, public sector employees and tour operators. The Conclave was a major attempt to provide information and sensitize the LTC travellers about the fascinating and beautiful North-East Region and its potential for nature, heritage, adventure and religious tourism. A befitting culmination to the daylong event was provided by an exhibition put up by the States and Central Ministries/Organisations covering all aspects of tourism in the region.

5512. (16-1-2008) NEW DELHI : The Government is taking up Bus Rapid Transit System (BRTS) under the Jawaharlal Nehru National Urban Renewal Mission (JNNURM) as a cost effective solution for providing high quality public transport service in urban areas. At present, BRTS is being taken up in eight cities, namely, Pune/Pimpri Chinchwad, Ahemdabad, Indore, Bhopal, Vijayawada, Vishakhapatnam, Jaipur and Rajkot involving a length of 310 Kms at a total cost of Rs. 2740 crore. Delhi is also implementing BRTS as a State Government funded project. Announcing this at the National Consultation on Urban Bus Based Transportation Solutions in New Delhi, Secretary Urban Develcpment Shri. Ramachndran, pointed out the need to introduce a modern city bus service in all the 0.5 million plus cities and State Capitals to start with. These modern buses will be sleek and have wider doors and windows with level boarding and alighting and advance fare collection and vehicle tracking system. The aim would be to exhort the public to shift from personal modes to public transport. Shri Ramachandran said that this has to be done on a PPP model like the system in Indore in Madhya Pradesh. He said that the Government in consultation with SIAM, IIT. Delhi, ARAI, Pune, M/s Urban Mass Transit Company have developed urban bus Specifications which has been sent to the States in October, 2007 for their comments. Today's seminar is being organized in the context of the draft bus specifications already circulated. The specifications finalized after today's deliberations would be the minimum specifications for the urban buses and the State Governments would be at liberty to adopt higher specifications. The draft specifications would also be only recommendatory in nature. Today's deliberations would also focus on implementation and efficiency issues of BRTS which because of lack of appropriate care during implementation had become an issue in Delhi, the Secretary said.